Austrian Foreign Policy *in* Historical Context

Contemporary Austrian Studies

Sponsored by the University of New Orleans and Universität Innsbruck

Publication of this volume has been made possible through a generous grant from the Austrian Ministry of Foreign Affairs through the Austrian Cultural Forum in New York and the Austrian Marshall Plan Anniversary Foundation in Vienna. The University of Innsbruck and Metropolitan College of the University of New Orleans have also provided financial support.

Contemporary Austrian Studies,
Volume 14

Austrian Foreign Policy *in* Historical Context

Günter Bischof
Anton Pelinka
Michael Gehler
editors

LONDON AND NEW YORK

First published 2006 by Transaction Publishers

Published 2017 by Routledge
2 Park Square, Milton Park, Abingdon, Oxon OX14 4RN
711 Third Avenue, New York, NY 10017, USA

Routledge is an imprint of the Taylor & Francis Group, an informa business

Library of Congress Catalog Number: 2005055906

Library of Congress Cataloging-in-Publication Data

Austrian foreign policy in historical context / edited by Günter Bischof, Anton Pelinka, Michael Gehler.
p. cm.—(Contemporary Austrian studies ; v. 14)
Includes bibliographical references.
ISBN 1-4128-0521-X (alk. paper)
1. Austria—Foreign relations—20th century. I. Bischof, Günter, 1953- II. Pelinka, Anton, 1941- III. Gehler, Michael. IV. Series.

DB96.A87 2005
327.436009'04—dc22

2005055906

ISBN 13: 978-1-4128-0521-6 (pbk)

Table of Contents

III. Second Republic Foreign Policy: Turning Points and Coontinuities

NON-TOPICAL ESSAY

ROUNDTABLE
The Historiography and Memory of the Austrian Occupation (1945-1955)

REVIEW ESSAYS

BOOK REVIEWS

ANNUAL REVIEW

INTRODUCTION

Austrian Foreign Policy after World War II

Michael Gehler and Günter Bischof

The Second Austrian Republic (1945/55 to present) has been a much more successful democratic regime than the first one (1918-1933/38). Sixty years is a long period in history, and it is time to take stock. In this introduction, we are suggesting a framework of periods for the entire postwar foreign policy era. Austrian foreign policy saw its ups and downs over the past sixty years, but experienced even more difficult choices between the two World Wars. The "primacy of foreign policy"[1] for the elites in the Austrian center of power on Vienna's Ballhausplatz may be the defining subtext of these essays.

Austria is a small country and experienced an unusual amount of interference in its foreign policy choices from the international arena. Austria-Hungary's defeat in World War I led to the breakup of the Habsburg Empire. The German speakers in the Alps and along the Danube, "left over" from the dissolution of the "dual monarchy" and not appropriated by the succession states, began to build an untested and unstable new state. Stuck between unfriendly neighbors to the south and east and torn between Italy and Germany, Austria tried to negotiate an independent and quasi-neutral course during the interwar period. Abandoned by Benito Mussolini after 1936/37, Austria was absorbed by Adolph Hitler's Nazi Germany in 1938 and wiped off the map for the next seven years.

The experience of the Nazi occupation, more than anything, stirred both the desire among many Austrians and the will among the Allies fighting Hitler to reestablish a viable Austrian state and to build a "nation." Liberated by Allied armies in April/May 1945, Austria suffered under an interminable four-power occupation for the next ten years, but also managed to stabilize its democratic system and its economy under the tutelage of the Western powers. From 1955 to 1989/90, neutral Austria sailed an "independent" course between the power blocks in the

East and the West. The great Austrian historian Friedrich Heer said many years ago that no country in Europe has been shaped more dramatically by outside forces and factors than Austria.[2]

Austria's location in the center of Europe determines its difficult geopolitical environment. During the Cold War, a quasi-Iron Curtain divided the country for ten years (1945-1955). With the advent of neutrality in 1955, the Iron Curtain dividing Europe overshadowed Austria's freedom to act in the international arena. Austrian statesmen took an active role in overcoming this East-West divide to ease Austrian foreign policy choices. When the Cold War ended, Austria again found itself in a position to mediate and broker between East and West. It has availed itself of this opportunity more in the business and financial realm than in the political arena.

Austrian accession into the European Union in 1995 was as radical a turning point for Austrian foreign policy as the end of the four-power occupation and the arrival of neutrality in 1955. The Ballhausplatz henceforth ceded much of its foreign policy sovereignty to the joint EU institutions in Brussels. This tacit "loss of sovereignty" and space for maneuvering within foreign policy is one of the foci of this volume. At no point in time over the past sixty years, then, was Austria an agent entirely free to maneuver in the international arena as it saw fit. Yet Austrian statesmen were frequently hindered by domestic constrictions as well—political, economic, personal, and others. Such domestic policy factors in a democratic polity can never be ignored. These essays show that Austrian diplomacy and Austrian statesmanship found ways both to mitigate the domestic pressures and the constrictions of the respective international regimes before and after World War II. Like any government, Austria pursued its own distinct foreign policy goals circumscribed by its geopolitical position. The main story of the following essays in many ways concentrates on the "leverage of the weak"—the maneuvering space Austrian foreign policy elites created *vis-á-vis* the overpowering embraces of these defining international regimes, but also the foreign policy maneuvering space lost by the Ballhausplatz in the wake of EU integration in 1995.[3]

The "Long Fifties": Independence and Emancipation (1945-1961)

The "long fifties" (so designated by Werner Abelshauser and Ernst Hanisch[4]) were characterized by Grand Coalition's (the conservative ÖVP and the socialist SPÖ) intentions to get rid of the occupation regime and its desire to establish and to stabilize an independent and sovereign state. Closely tied to these goals was the ability to negotiate a path from a condition free from alliances to a policy of neutrality, while simultaneously being predominantly oriented to the West both economically and politically. This first phase is subdivided into two different parts: first, the four-power Allied occupation and the withdrawal of their troops (1945-1955) followed by the attainment and exercise of sovereignty and a careful Western orientation (1956-1961). The occupation powers were symbolized by the "four in the jeep." The Austrian intention was not to see them driving around Vienna any more, but driving home. Of course, they were welcomed back as paying tourists, as Karl Gruber, Austria's maverick first foreign minister after the war, demanded defiantly and self-confidently in public. At the center stood the principle of reestablishing Austria's complete independence as provided by the Moscow Declaration. Parallel to it ran the desire to prevent the country from continuing to be an "occupied Ally" (as Josef Rupieper[5] had once called the Federal Republic of Germany) and, thus, an active party in the Cold War. Austria was always reluctant to participate in the Cold War.[6]

In their position of extreme weakness and powerlessness, the Austrians had to practice an unconventional diplomacy. In any case, both Austrian foreign policy and diplomacy were primarily geared towards the goal of building a bearable relationship with *all* four occupation powers. The four separate military governments of the occupation powers and the Allied Council—the quadripartite governing body of the occupiers—in Vienna's Schwarzenbergplatz (during the occupation, "Stalinplatz"), were the starting points. Full diplomatic relations were established only in the course of the 1950s when appointments on the ambassadorial level were finally made.[7] With the attainment of Austria's sovereignty, the year 1955 played a special role in this expansion of Austria's diplomatic role.

After the safeguarding of the entity of the Austrian state and the final attainment of its freedom, the first independent positioning took place both within the global framework of politics with United Nations membership in 1955,[8] as well as with membership in the Council of Europe in 1946 within the context of a fledgling integrated Europe. The complex diplomacy of the state treaty has found a master historian with Gerald Stourzh's comprehensive and expansive *Um Einheit und Freiheit.*[9] Both the United Nations and Council of Europe memberships were in clear contrast to the Swiss model of a cautiously defined and practiced neutrality. The crises in Hungary (October-November 1956)[10] and Lebanon (July 1958)[11] were perceived by the Ballhausplatz as opportunities for positioning Austrian foreign policy more firmly and self-confidently in the conflicted Cold War environment. At the time, the East-West conflict vacillated between the first signs of a relaxation of tensions in light of the Geneva Summit Conference (July 1955)[12] and the new confrontations during the second Berlin and the Cuban crises (1958-1962). Austria's foreign policy and neutrality policy were groping towards a tolerable stance within this crisis-ridden Cold War context.

Austria had to back out of memberships in the European Coal and Steel Community (ECSE) already announced (October 1956) and keep out of the European Economic Community (EEC) and European Atomic Energy Community (EURATOM) (1957-1958). This left the fledgling and export-dependent republic with very little maneuvering space in terms of foreign trade policy. As a result of the door being shut on full economic integration into Western Europe and the "Common Market," various options were considered. In 1958, the concept of a large free trade zone encompassing all of the Organization for European Economic Cooperation (OEEC) states failed. The "non-six" states excluded by the EEC "community of six" (Germany, France, Italy, and the Benelux nations) proceeded with the establishment of the European Free Trade Association (EFTA) in 1959/1960. EFTA initially was only conceived of as an interim solution. Soon after EFTA was launched, Austria, along with the other EFTA neutrals—Sweden and Switzerland—attempted to jump ship and to form a separate association with the EEC in 1961-1962.[13] The domestic politics of the decade after 1955 and their impact on foreign policy maneuvers is covered in detail by Manfried Rauchensteiner's standard work, *Die Zwei*.[14]

Rauchensteiner, and after him Helmut Kramer, saw the period of the late 1950s and 1960s as the trajectory of Austria's "emancipation" from the former occupation powers.[15] The conservative and socialist coalition relationship was transformed during this decade. Using a metaphor of matrimony, Rauchensteiner viewed the trajectory of their growing estrangement as one of initial "engagement" (1945-1952), progressing to "wedding" (1953-1957), and then "divorce" (1958-1966). More dramatically, in the field of foreign affairs a natural process of alienation and detachment from the previous occupiers, who were still acting as tutors, slowly transpired. The former occupation powers continued to exert some control over Austria resulting from their "responsibility" as signatories to the state treaty. This especially held true for France and the USSR, but also for the United States and, to a lesser extent, Great Britain. What was uncontested on the Ballhausplatz was Austria's growing Western orientation. In crucial Cold War crises on Austria's borders sounding alarm bells in Vienna, this basic orientation was never in question, as the Cold War crises on Austria's border in 1956, 1968, and 1989 would prove.

Beginning with the Gruber-De Gasperi Agreement of September 1946, Austria dared to raise this controversial issue with Italy before the world forum. Austria managed to get two UN resolutions passed on the South Tyrol issue (1960-1961). This maneuver on the grand international stage injected renewed self-confidence in the Ballhausplatz's foreign policy elites. Given this preoccupation with the protection of the German-speaking minority in the South Tyrol,[16] South Tyrol became a high priority of Vienna's foreign policy and a proving ground for Austrian diplomacy. The South Tyrol issue was later superseded and overshadowed by the European integration issue, the second predominant topic of Austrian 1960s diplomacy. Autonomy for South Tyrol and European integration were the defining issues of Austrian foreign policy in this "emancipation" phase.

The "Short Sixties" (1961-1969): Groping towards Western Europe and *Ostpolitik*

First, during the "short sixties," in domestic politics the Grand Coalition system showed significant signs of erosion as a result of both the domestic "Habsburg crisis" of 1963 and the "Fußach affair" of 1964; second, the single party government by the Austrian People's Party, ÖVP, (1966-1970) was a unique one-time experiment in governing during the Second Republic and apparently not a successful one, if one takes the 1970 election results as an indicator; third, the *Alleingang* ("lone march") towards Brussels without the other EFTA neutrals, and opposed by incessant Soviet vetoes, failed to materialize and to achieve a bilateral agreement with the EEC (1963-1967 and 1969), but it quickened the pace of Austria's Western integration.[17] Vienna only emancipated itself gradually both from the tutelage of the signatory powers of the State Treaty and the "Swiss model" of neutrality. This occurred in spite of the Ballhausplatz's initial inclination to "Helveticize" Austrian neutrality in the wake of both the Hungarian and Lebanon crises.

As a result of the radical political changes in the neighboring countries in 1956—the massive exodus of Hungarians amounted to a veritable human catastrophe—Austria provided various forms of humanitarian aid (for example, food and housing) to the refugees (see also the Granville essay in this volume). Later Chancellor Julius Raab's efforts to stop American military flights over Austrian air space during the Lebanon crisis of 1958 once again indicated a course in Austrian neutrality orientation akin to a quasi-"Swissification." Yet on other issues, Austrian neutrality[18] distanced itself from the cautious Swiss model. Austria's foreign policy towards a rapid EEC rapprochement and, to a lesser degree, its diplomacy towards the neighboring states of Central and Eastern Europe, is testimony to that. Austria's "active" neutrality policy did not even shy away from open partisanship in the Cold War and began to parrot the passive Swiss model even less.

During this phase of a quickening emancipation of Austrian foreign policy, it is necessary to point to the *Ostpolitik* (Eastern policy) of Foreign Minister Bruno Kreisky (1959-1966) and Chancellor Josef Klaus (1964-1970). The entire scope of the actions of these two Austrian foreign policy innovators and the potential "model effect" that their bold *Ostpolitik* might have had on the Federal Republic of Germany[19] of the late 1960s and 1970s (the Brandt-Scheel era) still demands further archival research. It does constitute a departure towards a more global orientation of Austrian foreign policy. Moreover, the dramatic 1969 breakthrough in the controversial South Tyrol question—with both the "package deal" and the "operations calendar"—represents a major diplomatic achievement in the annals of postwar Ballhausplatz diplomacy. This was a historic compromise in the lasting bilateral postwar conflict with Italy. The German population in the South Tyrol received an improved second autonomy statute that initiated even further future advances.

"Long Seventies" (1970-1986): A New Kind of Neutrality

The "long seventies" experienced the culmination of the much vaunted Austrian welfare state. The Socialist governments of Bruno Kreisky (and to a lesser degree his successor, Fred Sinowatz) put their stamp on this durable phase. This period was also characterized by a strengthening of Austrian identity and nationhood. At the same time, Austria's "eternal neutrality" became both dogma and myth, which in turn fed into Austrians' comfort with and growing prosperity of the Second Republic.

The formation of a nation's foreign policy is also a reaction to perceptions of a country abroad, even more so in an age where policies are increasingly media driven. During the 1970s, Austria's perception abroad was remarkably positive. The topoi and myths of Austria as a "bridge between East and West" as well as Austria as an "island of the blessed," were frequently bandied about. Foreigners' praise fed into a self-deceptive Austrian pride and a somewhat hyperbolic view of Austrians' own accomplishments. If Austria was no longer a great power, it became a darling of the world.

The "long seventies" above all were characterized by a transformation of domestic and social policies as a result of comprehensive reforms in the judicial sphere and the welfare state. Foreign affairs went through an increasingly international and global turn, particularly as a result of Kreisky's departures in "active neutrality" policy and "bridge-building" efforts in the East-West conflict. Just like his friend Willy Brandt's courageous *Ostpolitik*, Kreisky's maverick policy of reducing tensions within the framework of the Conference of Security and Cooperation in Europe (the "Helsinki process") helped shape and strengthen East-West détente in Europe. Austrian "peace keeping forces" played a very active role in the United Nations' peace efforts from the 1960s to the 1990s.[20]

Chancellor Kreisky[21] also went out on a limb as a champion of the Palestinian people and a forceful mediator in the Middle Eastern conflict. Here he was way ahead of his time and predated the "Oslo peace process" by two decades. The conservative ÖVP opposition detested the socialists' stance of "equidistance" in the East-West conflict and their active neutrality policies. Kreisky also joined in the growing Western appreciation of the problems of the North-South conflict and Third World problems, often in conjunction with his friend Olof Palme, the socialist prime minister of Sweden. But Kreisky's foreign aid budgets spoke to the fact that he did not put his money where his mouth was.

The myth of Austria's "manifest destiny" as a "bridge-builder" between East and West has never been seriously deconstructed and investigated by scholars. Neither has the opposing thesis that Austria allegedly was a "secret ally of the West" from 1955 onwards and an early "promoter" of the neutrals' Western integration policy.

Bruno Kreisky's at times feverish foreign policy activism went far beyond the real political significance of his country in Europe and the world. Since Austria never developed an adequate equivalent in military strength to buttress its security policy, this injection into world politics came to an end in the 1980s. While ignoring Austria's armed forces set off conditions of frustration and depression within the military, it also signified major relief for Kreisky's debt-ridden national budgets. Kreisky's distinct "Austro-Keynesianism" worried about full employment more than it was aggrieved by massive budget deficits. These were generated by the hypertrophic welfare state, along with the frequent injections of state-provided relief for the bloated nationalized industrial sector.

Kurt Waldheim's election as President and Jörg Haider's crowning as the leader of the Freedom Party in 1986 rang in the end of these generous Socialist policies of the "long seventies." The diplomat Waldheim was a two-time general secretary of the United Nations (1971-1982). He also sympathized and even partnered with Kreisky's foreign policy initiatives, especially in the Middle East. But his election as president in 1986 was a turning point. While Pope Paul VI designated Austria as an "island of the fortunate" ("*Insel der Glücklichen*") during a visit by President Franz Jonas in Rome (1971), the passionate and divisive debates about Lieutenant Waldheim's—and by extension Austria's—role in World War II hardly betrayed such a state of bliss. Bitter battles in Austrians' post-World War II "memory regimes" shaped much of the late twentieth century. Legacies and memories of Austrians' as "victims and perpetrators" have been an obsession in the national discourse for much of the two past decades.[22]

The Waldheim debate, along with Austria and Austrians facing their difficult World War II past, unleashed a serious crisis domestically and a grave loss of prestige abroad.[23] The Vienna government tried to engage in damage control abroad and rolled out World War II Austrian resistance fighters against the Nazis to reinforce the old topos of Austrians' opposition to the Hitler regime. Elder statesmen and former diplomats Hans Reichmann, Karl Gruber, and Fritz Molden were activated as "special emissaries" to battle Austria's negative image abroad, spawned by the "Waldheim affair."[24] The emissaries' alternate picture of Austrians' World War II heroism and humanity painted in state visits in Western Europe and the United States may have been credible from a personal perspective, but ignored the complexity of Austrians' World War II experience that was increasingly stressed by historians. The emissaries' ill-fated tour represented the last hurrah of the defunct post-war victim's doctrine.

"Short Eighties" (1986-1992): Isolation and Liberation from the Past

The election of Waldheim as president of Austria was fateful for Austria's image abroad. During his six years in office, Waldheim only received invitations for state visits from Jordan, Pakistan, and the Holy See. This distancing from and cocooning of the highest elected state official was unprecedented in the annals of Austrian diplomacy. High state visitors from abroad frequented the provincial capitals in order to avoid making contact with the internationally ostracized Waldheim, or saw Chancellor Franz Vranitzky abroad. Thus shunned, Waldheim pouted in his imperial offices in Vienna's Ballhausplatz. He was like a man in a golden cage. Statesmen refused to be seen shaking hands with Waldheim in Vienna photo ops.

Austria's image in the world was in the dumps during this era. The country's unsavory World War II past had caught up with it. Historians revealed a growing parade of Austrian Holocaust perpetrators and involvement in Hitlerite war crimes.[25] Austrians had contributed to Hitler's war of aggression and annihilation. Waldheim's stubborn insistence of simply "having done his duty" during the war came to stand for Austrians' refusal to face their past. Former Chancellor Kreisky was angry with the Sinowatz government and his own party for having unleashed the "Waldheim affair." He saw his life's work threatened by the divisive politics of history (1986-1988) and Austria's international reputation seriously impugned. Waldheim's refusal to acknowledge the *Wehrmacht*'s lethal role in the Balkans theater, where he had served, angered Kreisky. Waldheim's waffling led him to terminate their friendship. Both of them had been young men of "the first hour" in 1945/46, rebuilding the Austrian foreign service and helping to build the country's viability after the war (see the Bischof essay in this volume). It was a defining and very painful moment for both of them.

In the 1980s, Austria's positive image not only suffered abroad, but at home as well. The myth of the "island of the blessed" was replaced by the perceptions of the "corruptible republic" and the "scandal republic." A wine scandal, the Lucona affair, and the Noricum arms smuggling scandal rocked the nation. Again, this image was hyperbolic, for such insider deal scandals and business deals rock other nations as well. Moreover, comparable mega-scandals had occurred in Austria before the 1980s. But now growing hordes of self-important and aggressive "investigative journalists" and "peeping toms" in the proliferating media dramatized the scandals and made them "state business."[26]

What was new after 1986, however, was the antics of young upstart Jörg Haider's populist politics of assaulting the entrenched grand coalition and their traditional back-room deal making and dividing up of the spoils of public service. He wanted a piece of the action for his Freedom Party. Haider's confrontational leadership style and right-wing populism—and an at times, seemingly radical FPÖ—shook the well-entrenched consensual politics of the Second Republic. His hidebound infatuation with and verbal rescue of Nazi policies exacerbated Austrians' incapacity to acknowledge the full depravity of Hitler's regime. Haider practically lived with his foot in his mouth. His antics and verbal gaffes hardly helped the recovery of Austria's image abroad.[27]

It took an entire decade for Austria's image to recover from Waldheim's election and from Haider's assaults on the powers that be. In the first half of the 1990s, Chancellor Franz Vranitzky and President Thomas Klestil delivered notable speeches in Jerusalem acknowledging Austrians' responsibility for World War II war crimes.

In 1986, the SPÖ returned to the old consociational "grand coalition" arrangements with the People's Party. This revival of the corporatist consensus politics of yesteryear was the last hurrah of the two dominant parties of postwar Austrian domestic politics. Under Socialist Chancellors Vranitzky and Victor Klima, these grand coalitions survived 1999. But political scandals and Haider's permanent attacks sped up the demise of this consensual system in the late 1980s and early 1990s. After the highpoint of the social partnership and the oversized nationalized economy during Kreisky's "long seventies," these arrangements finally collapsed.[28]

In the coalition deal worked out by Chancellor Vranitzky in 1986—and to the lasting chagrin of Kreisky in his retirement—Alois Mock of the People's Party took over the Foreign Ministry in 1987. Mock's new foreign policy priorities concentrated on the strengthening of Austria's orientation towards Western Europe and the launching of its formal membership in the European Communities (EC). Chancellor Vranitzky (1986-1997) willy-nilly became a top foreign policy player and balancer of ÖVP predominance. The experienced banker and former Finance Minister performed ably as a "Waldheim substitute" in representing Austria abroad and *vis-à-vis* foreign dignitaries at home. Mock's "Western Europeanization" of Austrian foreign policy culminated in the "letter to Brussels" in 1989, the first step in the EEC membership application process. The EC's regulatory Internal Market Project ("*Binnenmarktprojekt*") of 1992 also forced changes in Austrian foreign trade policy. Austria's path towards Brussels was designed to lead the country out of its increasingly marginalized position as a result of Waldheim's election.[29]

The renaissance of the Grand Coalition in 1987 also needs to be seen as a move towards patching up the domestic political cleavages growing out of the Waldheim debates, the rise of Haider, the advent of the growing strength of the irreverent Green Party, and the "Western Europeanization" of Austrian politics into a multi-party regime. In addition, a papering over of these domestic differences and a consensus-oriented show of strength was needed to launch the historic step towards membership in the European Community. In the years 1987 to 1989, public opinion in the domestic and foreign policy arenas had to be prepared for Austria's EEC accession and its second "solo run" towards Brussels (after 1963). Acceptance into the coveted EC took time. During the long accession process, Austria was pacified in 1992 with an interim solution of membership in the European Economic Area, a multilateral, associational relationship with the EEC.

Austria had to cast off the historical ballast of the interminable South Tyrol conflict with Italy (an European Economic Community founding member) as a crucial preliminary step for acceptance into the EC. This issue was still pending before the United Nations in spite of the 1969 bilateral "package deal." But the dispute before the UN was finally settled in 1992, ending this long-standing Austro-Italian conflict and pushing wide open the gate to the European Community for Austria. In the end, Ballhausplatz diplomacy focused on safeguarding the survival of the South Tyrolese as a national minority, maximizing the openness of the vital trade link over the Brenner Pass border, and creating conflict-free coexistence between the German and Italian, as well as the minute Ladin, minorities in the South Tyrol. Once Austria entered the European Union in 1995 and the Schengen Agreement of unrestricted crossing of borders within the European Union came into the force, border controls also ceased on the Brenner Pass. Schengen's opening of borders within the European Union on 1 April 1998, more than anything, ended the interminable South Tyrol conflict.[30]

All of this happened against a dramatic international backdrop of the Iron Curtain collapsing, the Soviet empire in Eastern Europe and the Soviet Union itself disintegrating, Germany unifying, Yugoslavia imploding, and the Cold War ending. Scholars have not yet explored the full extent of these massive transformations on Austria's borders and their impact on the Ballhausplatz's foreign policy maneuvering space. It is safe to say, however, that they were profound and certainly paved the way for Austrian EEC/EU membership. With NATO enlargement all along Austria's Eastern borders, the repercussions of these post-Cold War transformations on Austria's new security situation are still being fully gauged and probed.[31]

EU Entry and EU Membership (1993-2000): Losing Maneuvering Space in the New Europe

In 1993, Austria entered into the accession negotiations with the European Union along with the Scandinavian countries Finland, Sweden, and Norway. In the Second Republic, two plebiscites marked the fundamental direction of Austrian foreign policy. In the first postwar parliamentary elections of 25 November 1945, Austrians forcefully rejected communism. In the historic "EU referendum" of 12 June 1994, a remarkable two-thirds of the Austrian voting population ratified Austria's EU membership. This latter plebiscite had been preceded by Foreign Minister Mock's negotiating marathon with Brussels and an intensive advertising campaign by the Vranitzky government on behalf of EU membership.[32]

Austria finally entered the European Union in 1995.[33] It was a "net contributor" from the beginning (namely, its transfers to Brussels exceeded payments received from the EU). Austria also worked hard to fulfill the tough EU budgetary "convergence" criteria towards joining the new "Euro" currency from its inception in 1999. The Grand Coalitions of Chancellors Vranitzky (1986-1997) and Klima (1997-2000) worked diligently to arrive at and adhere to the convergence criteria. FPÖ opposition leader and populist tribune Haider tried to stop Austria's membership in the "Euro zone" with a referendum that failed miserably.

In the second half of 1998, Austria executed the revolving presidency of the EU admirably and demonstrated its rapid maturation as a young EU member.

Austria also learned from being a responsible EU member. As a result of EU membership, two core elements of the Second Republic's political bargains and Austria's identity began to wobble and crumble. The controversy over Waldheim effectively ended the postwar "doctrine" of Austria's as an exclusive victim of Nazi policies as explained above. After the Cold War came to an end (1989-1991) and the East-West conflict abated, Austria's international position as a neutral became increasingly scrutinized. "Permanent neutrality" seemed an obsolete policy at a time when Austria's formerly communist neighbors flocked into NATO with reckless abandon. Austria's "Western Europeanization" replaced neutrality and the "island of the blessed" mentality as a major new element in reshaping Austrian identity.

The Schüssel coalition government formed in early February 2000 quickly dissipated this "EU high" of the late 1990s. Austria's cozy position as an EU member proved to be deceptive. From one day to the next, the EU darling Austria became the Community's pariah. On 31 January 2000, the fourteen EU countries threatened "sanctions" against Austria in the event that the ÖVP embraced Haider's FPÖ for a coalition government after the November election of 1999. When an icy President Thomas Klestil swore in the new coalition of Wolfgang Schüssel (ÖVP) and Susanne Riess-Passer (FPÖ) on 4 February, the EU fourteen launched their sanctions. The EU fourteen wanted to demonstrate their displeasure against Haider's "right-wing" FPÖ being heaved into a position of power, which broke the dam thrown up against such parties on the right all over democratic Europe (Haider, the governor of the marginal southern Austrian state of Carinthia, was not a member of the new cabinet). Such EU sanctions against a member state with a democratically elected government were unique in the history of the European Community.[34] The major effect was that the fourteen EU countries (led by Belgium and France) froze bilateral relations with Austria to a minimum of diplomatic contacts in Vienna and Brussels. For some observers, this seemed like an eerie relapse into "ancient" prewar history.[35]

Ironically, it was the controversial ÖVP coalition with the FPÖ, formed in February 2000, that faced these skeletons in the closet and worked out restitution settlements with World War II victim's groups. The government of Wolfgang Schüssel, under enormous EU and international pressure, concluded restitution agreements with forced laborers and with the Austrian Jewish community for their property losses.[36] Such comprehensive restitution settlements had been negotiated by the Federal

Republic of Germany, but had been rejected by the Ballhausplatz as a result of the "victim's doctrine" before and after 1955.[37]

As noted above, Austrian foreign policy had experienced an unusual degree of control by the international community. During the financial crisis of the early 1920s, Austria had been placed under the control of the League of Nations when a Dutch commissioner was imposed on the country to supervise finances and state budgets. Austria twice received loans from the League of Nations (Geneva in 1922 and Lausanne in 1932) with such controls and a general "Anschluß Prohibition" attached. After the Nazi period (1938-1945), the country was under four-power Allied tutelage (1945-1955).[38] It was extended beyond the conclusion of the State Treaty in 1955, as the four signatory powers still supervised the country neutrality policy in a fashion. During the one-term Waldheim presidency (1986-1992), the world had treated Austria as a pariah. Moreover, an International Commission of Historians was appointed in 1986 to investigate Waldheim's personal—and by extension Austria's—culpability during World War II. The international community signaled that if Austria would not make an honest accounting of its past, it would be led to do so by the outside world. Such a post-Holocaust politics of history had become increasingly dominant in the EU.

More than anything, this brusque action by the EU fourteen served to make Austria painfully aware of its loss of national sovereignty as a result of EU membership. The rest of the EU members were even prepared to interfere directly in Austrian domestic politics. While Austrians may have become insensitive to Haider's right-wing populism and habitual breaking of taboos, politicians in countries such as Belgium and France were less tolerant of such in-your-face right-wing populism. They feared that "Haiderism" might spill over into their own polities and encourage fringe groups on the right.

Should Austrian diplomacy have been more alert in warning Vienna of this somber mood in the EU? Should Foreign Minister Wolfgang Schüssel's representatives abroad (he was the foreign minister and vice-chancellor in the Klima government) have warned their "boss" about these perceptions in EU capitals about the threat of "Haiderism"?

The ÖVP/FPÖ Coalition (2000-2004): EU Constrictions

After the short honeymoon when it joined the union in 1995, Austria turned into a somewhat controversial new EU member. During the 2000 crisis over the controversial Schüssel coalition government, Austrians reinforced the impression that they could be a difficult EU partner. Austria turned out to be particularly uppity when it came to transit problems with the huge flow of traffic over the great Alpine transverses between Germany and Italy—some of the busiest and most commercially active freeways in the world. Austria also behaved in an ornery fashion over the issue of EU Eastern enlargement.

In the modern age of growing prosperity and mobility, traffic has become a no-win issue in the political arena. The settling of the transit treaty due to expire in 2003 demanded much patience on the part of the negotiators on both sides. Quantitative restrictions on truck traffic through the Alpine valleys of western Austria and across the passes was unpopular everywhere in the EU, but especially so in Austria. For residents of the Tyrolese Alpine valleys along the major European freeways, plagued by traffic fumes, emissions, and the growing environmental degradation of picturesque tourist landscapes, the exploding traffic was more than a "quality of life" issue. It amounted to an existential question and fuelled "green" politics in a deeply conservative state.

Success or failure of these negotiations also affected the sensitive climate *vis-à-vis* EU Eastern enlargement. The new EU members on Austria's borders to the east would generate additional massive traffic burdens on eastern and southern Austrian throughways. An extension of the EU traffic treaty with Austria seemed out of the question since all EU countries opposed the quantitative restrictions demanded by Vienna. Instead, new EU guidelines permitted levying higher freeway tolls in the sensitive Alpine regions. It was hard to forecast whether these EU guidelines coming into effect in 2003 would alleviate these heavy traffic burdens in the long run. EU summit meetings in Laeken (Belgium) and Copenhagen (Denmark) went back and forth on the traffic issue. Vienna wanted the EU Commission to prolong the system of "ecopoints" designed to cap traffic across the Alpine passes. There was also an issue of whether the transit treaty applied to the entire Austrian territory or only to the north-south axis.

In the complex EU bargaining process, Austria found itself in a position of painful isolation as a result of the EU fourteen sanctions (January to September 2000). Austria was not a member of any of the regional networks pulling considerable weight within EU decision making, namely informal "friendship groups" such as the Benelux, the Northern European, or the Southern European country groupings. In the selective alliances and package deals gelling around issues, Austria was not a member of any alliances and was devoid of reliable partners (so much for the old Soviet fear during the Cold War that Austrian EU membership would inevitably lead to a new Anschluß to Germany).

These painful experiences led the Ballhausplatz to engage in a foreign policy offensive, trying to reassert its traditional role as "bridge builder" in East Central Europe. In the drawn out process of EU Eastern enlargement, Vienna offered the Central and Eastern European accession candidates (the so-called "CEE countries") a "strategic partnership." The charming Foreign Minister Benita Ferrero-Waldner suggested a renewal of her party colleague Erhard Buseks 1980s "*Mitteleuropa-Politik*"[39]—an old Viennese dream built on nostalgic visions of a glorious past.[40] This concept might have succeeded were it not for the reemergence of skeletons from the past. Haider and the populist Freedom Party, Ferrero-Waldner's uncooperative coalition partner, raised the issue of the "Beneš Decrees" and the Czechoslovak expulsion of the Sudeten Germans in 1945/46. The FPÖ insisted that the EU force the Czechs and Slovaks to repeal these laws as a condition to their accession.[41]

Ferrero-Waldner's "strategic partnership" among the Central European accession candidates quickly foundered on the rock of Haider's politics of pestering the coalition partners and maligning neighbors. It was downgraded to a less ambitious "regional partnership." The FPÖ and the Austrian Green Party also strained Austro-Czech relations with their demands for closing down the controversial nuclear power plant in Temelín, close to Austria's borders. It became more doubtful by the day whether Prague (and Bratislava) might view Vienna as an avid "advocate" of their EU accession interests.

In the EU Eastern enlargement effort, a conspicuous chasm opened between the decision makers and the public at large. Apart from Haider's FPÖ, the political elite was mostly supportive of Eastern enlargement. But large segments of the public held opinions ranging from highly skeptical to outright disapproving. While government officials in charge of enlargement matters such as Busek (2000-2002) and Ferrero-Waldner, along with most of her top foreign ministry staff, were extremely supportive of the complex Eastern enlargement diplomacy, they were counteracted regularly by FPÖ shenanigans. Haider and his minions aimed at preventing membership of the Czech Republic by veto and/or referendum threats.

These contrary noises from hidebound Austrians all but wrecked the vision of Central European partnership envisioned by Ferrero-Waldner. Brussels increasingly came to see Austria as a leading brakeman in slowing down its Eastern enlargement train. Worse, Austrian skepticism spilled over into other EU member states. The EU Commission noticed a worrisome trend that a growing number of member states were bargaining with the enlargement issue to gain concessions on other demands they had on the national level. The former pariah, Austria, now lived up to its name; it seemed to be "setting precedents" by providing other EU members with methods and strategies to undermine common EU policies.

Once the EU lifted its sanctions against Austria in September 2000, large and small EU members shifted their focus towards the Nice Summit, which turned out to be one of the most controversial EU summits in recent memory. Austria continues to share its lot with the rest of the small EU states, while the course of the EU's core integration policy is being set by the large member states France and Germany. These large members played the decisive role in setting the "precedent" of ostracizing Austria in 2000. As a result of these EU fourteen sanctions,[42] Austria has been carrying even less weight than before. In the important transit issue, Austria has stood alone as noted above. During the Danish Council presidency in the second half of 2002, no progress was made on this issue. During the EU Eastern enlargement process, Austria—rather than being the bridge builder the Foreign Ministry hoped to be—unleashed untoward dissonances.[43] This also had repercussions among the enlargement-hostile forces in the ambitious debates in the EU "*Konvent*" writing a constitution for Europe.[44]

As earlier in the twentieth century, Austria's Central European geopolitical location posits it in a unique position and in a potentially powerful role. Its geographical location gives it a capacity to be in the driver's seat when it comes to improving opportunities for EU Eastern enlargement, similar to its role in Cold War summitry. Yet Austria paid a heavy price in its foreign policy clout as a result of its isolation in 2000, when its leverage within Europe was significantly curtailed. On top of this, its quaint neutrality status is limiting its maneuvering space in the international arena. Austrians no longer plead being a "*Sonderfall*" (special case), as they often did during the Cold War. "*Alleingänge*" and "isolationist impulses" are no longer viable foreign policy instruments for Vienna's Ballhausplatz. The Cold War era is over, and Austria's cherished unique status between the military blocs is defunct. The European Union is a community of nations shaping foreign policies along lines of solidarity and common interest. Austria had better get used to it.

The topical essays in this volume expound on and enlarge upon the themes outlined in this introduction. In the introductory portion, *Eva Nowotny*, the current ambassador in Washington, analyzes the transformations in the job descriptions of professional diplomats during her service on the Ballhausplatz since 1973. When she entered the Austrian Ministry of Foreign Affairs more than thirty years ago, it was still a rigidly hierarchical place not far removed from the practices of Metternich's system. In today's world of diplomacy, instant communication techniques in an integrating and interlocking global arena have greatly changed the job of the professional diplomat and have "flattened" hierarchies and transformed traditional bureaucracies. The core diplomatic tasks for a small state like Austria, integrated in the European Union, have become less bilateral and increasingly multilateral. *Rudolf Agstner*, Austria's diplomatic representative in Bonn, presents an institutional history of the Austrian foreign office after World War I. *Michael Gehler* provides an expansive overview of the state of research on Austrian foreign policy and the archival situation expediting such scholarship. This constitutes a valuable introduction to students of postwar Austrian foreign policy and diplomacy regarding where to begin their research.

Two historical case studies establish the context for pre-post World War II Austrian foreign policy. The German scholar *Günter Kronenbitter* demonstrates how Austrian foreign policy was increasingly "militarized" on the eve of World War I as a result of a weakening Habsburg Monarchy and a grim perception of foreign threats. The often "pacifist" and "neutralist" Ballhausplatz foreign policies of the First (1918-1938) and Second (1945 to present) Austrian Republics may have drawn lessons from this inordinate influence and aggressive pre-World War I policies by the powerful Viennese military establishment contributing so much to the outbreak of the "Great War," which ultimately destroyed the 600 year-old Habsburg dynastic rule over the Austrian lands. The revisionist young American historian *Alexander Lassner* traces the increasingly difficult international environment in which authoritarian Chancellors Engelbert Dollfuss and Kurt Schuschnigg tried to salvage Austrian independence. Caught between the Scylla of Mussolini's fascist Italy and the Charybdis of Hitler's Nazi Germany, they abandoned democratic government and maneuvered for Western guarantees of Austrian independence. Abandoned by the Western powers and appeasement, the Third Reich fully absorbed Austria in March 1938. Lassner, based on his vast archival research, shows much more empathy for Dollfuss' and Schuschnigg's high-wire diplomacy in a deteriorating international arena than the frequently partisan Austrian scholars traditionally have done. His is international history in the best sense of the word.

The core of the essays in this volume deals with the foreign policy of the Second Republic. *Günter Bischof* traces the difficult beginnings of the institution of the Foreign Office in Vienna in the final days of World War II and during 1945/46. The provisional government of Karl Renner found itself totally isolated and struggled long and hard to break out of this international isolation. Leopold Figl's government established the first foreign missions working towards economic viability and eventual political independence, ending the four-power occupation. *Johanna Granville* picks up the thread once that full independence materialized in the fall of 1955. Within a year, the government of Julius

Raab found itself embroiled in a dangerous Cold War crisis in Hungary. When the Red Army intervened to squash the rebellion in Budapest, tens of thousands of Hungarian refugees poured across Austria's borders. Similar to the Sudenten German refugees from Czechoslovakia in 1945, Austria was unprepared and tried to get rid of these refugees as quickly as possible. Granville's revisionist essay maintains that Raab's government floundered in furthering the cause of Hungarian freedom and experienced worsening relations with Hungary and the Soviet Union. The smug assessment of earlier scholarship that Austrian neutrality passed the "test" of the 1956 Hungarian crisis with flying colors needs to be revised in Granville's view.

Two further historical case studies round out the picture of struggling Austrian postwar diplomacy. *Martin Kofler*'s essay focuses on a fascinating window of Ballhausplatz efforts to mediate the Cold War. In 1961, President John F. Kennedy and Soviet CP Chairman Nikita Khrushchev met in Vienna for an important Cold War summit. The Berlin crisis was at the heart of East-West tensions. After the summit, well-informed Austrian Foreign Minister Bruno Kreisky was utilized by Kennedy as a back-channel mediator with West Berlin's mayor, Willi Brandt, and Khrushchev, but without much progress on the Berlin issue. For the young Austrian foreign minister, this was heady stuff; it further strengthened Kreisky's already considerable self-confidence allowing him to stake out a claim for Ballhausplatz diplomacy in the East-West conflict and beyond that to seize power within his own country.

Ambassador *Wolfgang Petritsch* found himself in a similarly heady role (as had his former boss, Kreisky) in 1990s Balkans diplomacy, when Yugoslavia imploded after the end of the Cold War. As the experienced former Austrian ambassador to Belgrade, he knew the region well and became one of the international community's principal negotiators and then administrators in both the Bosnian and Kosovo crises. In his essay, he reflects back upon the failures of post-Cold War European diplomacy in quickly pacifying this region when it blew up in ancient ethnic hostilities. It is a cautionary tale of an international community acting too cautiously, waiting too long, and in the end being forced to confront a descent into Serbian genocidal practices.

After these historical case studies, three political scientists survey more recent trends in Austrian foreign policy and its options. *Stefan Mayer*, who himself works in the "foreign relations" office of the Austrian federal state of Salzburg, analyzes the foreign policies of the nine Austrian federal states. He looks back on their modest attempts after World War II to form good relations with neighboring provinces across national borders. This eventually led to a flowering of regional groupings, particularly after the collapse of the Iron Curtain and the opening of borders to the east and southeast. In the encouraging environment of cross-border regional cooperation within the EU, such foreign policy activities by the individual states have further prospered.

Viennese defense expert *Gunther Hauser* analyzes the increasingly complex security options the Ballhausplatz and the defense establishment in Vienna face between holding onto Austria's anemic neutrality within the larger context of common European and Western security. The strengthening of a central EU Common Foreign and Security Policy (CFSP) and NATO expansion far into Eastern Europe leaves Vienna neutralists increasingly isolated. In a strengthening security community of solidarity, Austrian security "free riding" will become increasingly less tolerable. Luxembourg diplomat *Romain Kirt* demonstrates how globalization trends and a centralizing European Union foreign policy and security regime diminish and severely circumscribe an independent foreign policy for small states such as Austria. Within a larger federal community, the foreign policy sovereignty and leverage of member states are slowly absorbed by the center of power.

The "non-topical" essay in this volume falls within the larger realm of "cultural diplomacy" and the efficacy of "soft power" (J. Nye) in the Cold War. The young Innsbruck American Studies specialist *Susanne Mettauer* highlights the emergence of the American Studies community in postwar Austria as a result of massive help by American cultural diplomats and the Austrian Fulbright organization. A case study of the establishment of the American Studies Department in Innsbruck demonstrates the archetypical politics of professorial appointments and institutional infighting both at the University of Innsbruck and in postwar Austria. The American Embassy and the Fulbright organization had to be patient and generous, keeping the pressure on in order to finally appoint a chair in Innsbruck seventeen years after the establishment of an American Studies department. This seems to be the archetypical story of the emerging field of American Studies in Austria.

The "Roundtable" on the postwar Austrian Occupation is *Contemporary Austrian Studies'* (*CAS*) contribution to the big Austrian "anniversary year" in 2005 (celebrating sixty years of Austria's liberation in 1945, fifty years of signing the Austrian State Treaty in 1955, and ten years of EU membership), when the Schüssel government's politics of history, with its curious tinge of nostalgia, is flowering in numerous historical exhibits and symposia. *Günter Bischof* recounts the generational cycles of historical scholarship on the Austrian occupation. *Oliver Rathkolb* critically deconstructs the trajectories of political discourses and Austrian collective memories of both the occupation/s and the state treaty signing. *Michael Gehler* analyzes Austrians' difficult postwar relationship with (West) Germany in Austria's struggle for independence and towards nationhood in the shadow of the German colossus. Based on the rich archival record of newly opened Russian sources, the young Viennese historian *Wolfgang Mueller* presents a "traditionalist" view of Soviet intentions in postwar Austria. Contrary to older "revisionist" views, Stalin did try to establish a "people's republic" in Austria, yet given Austrian and Western resistance, he failed. Stanford's *Norman Naimark*, a doyen of historians of Eastern Europe in the United States, completes the picture of Stalin's intentions *vis-à-vis* Austria. By the late 1940s, Stalin recognized the failure of Moscow's policies in Vienna and was ready to abandon Austria. The short essays in this "Roundtable" demonstrate that occupation scholarship still has to go along way to resolve all the complex historiographical issues of this complex decade when the four powers interacted amongst themselves and with the Austrian government, taking a long time to resolve issues. The postwar, four-power occupation remains one of the most exciting and challenging research fields of Austrian contemporary history.

Review essays and book reviews and the annual review of Austrian politics complete this volume.

The production of this volume met the usual challenges of commissioning essays, reminding contributors of deadlines, and meeting production schedules. We are most grateful to our contributors for their highly professional cooperation, unusual punctuality in delivering their essays, and good cheer. Three papers (Lassner, Bischof, Gehler) were delivered and engagingly discussed at the annual meeting of the German Studies Association (GSA) in early October 2004 in Arlington, Virginia. Ambassador Nowotny chaired this panel and Thomas Nowotny commented on the papers and helped to improve them. The GSA has become a mainstay for the discourses on "Austrian Studies" in the United States. Professor Gerald Kleinfeld, the outgoing executive director of the GSA and founder of this important national and international scholarly organization, has made sure that the GSA provided an annual venue for sophisticated debates on Austrian history, politics, and literature. "Gerry" Kleinfeld deserves our sincere gratitude for his continuous embrace and support of Austrian studies at the GSA over many years. In the United States, it is fair to say now, Austrian studies has emerged as a recognizably separate field within the larger purview of German Studies.

At UNO, our production team worked hard and long hours to put this volume together. Josef Köstelbauer, a dissertation fellow financed through the Austrian Ministry of Education, the Arts and Research, very ably shepherded the two dozen manuscripts through the process of copy-editing and proof-reading with the authors. He went well beyond the call of duty by getting involved in reading and correcting the texts and streamlining many an endnote. He was an absolute joy to work with. So was the gracious Jennifer Shimek, our outstanding copy-editor at Loyola University of New Orleans. Jennifer hammered out too many "Germanisms" to count, ironed out numerous stylistic infelicities, and applied herself in her exquisitely painstaking fashion in formatting the endnotes into our in-house style. By now she knows more about complex German syntax and endless "sausages" of relative clauses and how to break them up than many a sturdy grammarian. Gertraud Griessner helped along when her support was needed, and Dean and Vice-Chancellor Robert Dupont gave us his customary blessings and good cheer. We have come to expect the best of this team, and they deliver year after year.

On the University of Innsbruck side, Ellen and Wolfgang Palli typeset the texts, producing photo-ready copy. Their attention to endless details with texts, tables, and pictures is admirable. Franz Mathis, the UNO coordinator at the university, shepherded *CAS* matters cheerfully around all obstacles, and Matthias Schennach from the *Auslandsamt* provided financial support.

At our publisher, Transaction, our editor, Anne Schneider, has kept the manuscript moving and acted as a kind "in-house" advocate of all *CAS* business. To her and her colleagues in production and marketing, we are most grateful. Irving Louis Horowitz, the founder, and Mary Curtis, the publisher, deserve our gratitude for having made Transaction one of the premier publishers of Austrian studies in America.

The Austrian Marshall Plan Anniversary Foundation has been generously supporting CenterAustria and its activities with a major grant. Ambassador Emil Brix at the Foreign Ministry in Vienna and Ernst Aichinger at the Austrian Cultural Forum in New York have stalwartly supported *CAS* in their usual fashion by arranging for the buying of a contingent of volumes for the Austrian libraries around the world. Ultimately, our thanks then also go to the Austrian taxpayers for their generous support! We hope the reader can appreciate all these people's efforts to produce such a volume.

Louvain (Belgium)/Innsbruck and Larose, Louisiana, April 2005

Notes

1. *For this periodization scheme see* Michael Gehler, *Öster-reichs Außenpolitik in der Zweiten Republik. Von der alliierten Besatzung bis zum Europa des 21. Jahrhunderts* (Innsbruck: Studienverlag, 2005) *und wird dort vorgestellt und zusammenfassend analysiert*: 3-19, 993-1026.

2. *Es gebe "kein historisch-politisches Gebilde in Europa, das so sehr aussengesteuert ist wie Österreich."* See Friedrich Heer, *Der Kampf um Österreichs Identität* (Vienna: Böhlau 1996), 17f. On this vital theme of postwar Austrian foreign policy, see also Thomas Angerer, "Der 'bevormundete Vormund': Die französische Besatzungsmacht in Österreich," in *Österreich unter Alliierter Besatzung 1945-1955*, ed. Alfred Ableitinger, Siegfried Beer, and Eduard G. Staudinger (Vienna: Böhlau 1998), 159-204.

3. For a case study of Austria's maneuvering space *vis-à-vis* the occupation power during the first postwar decade, see Günter Bischof, *Austria in the First Cold War, 1945-55: The Leverage of the Weak* (Bastingstoke: Macmillan, 1999).

4. Ernst Hanisch, *Der lange Schatten des Staates. Österreichische Gesellschaftsgeschichte im 20. Jahrhundert 1890-1990*, 2nd ed. (Vienna: Ueberreuter, 1995).

5. Hermann-Josef Rupieper, *Der besetzte Verbündete. Die amerikanische Deutschlandpolitik 1949–1955*, Studien zur Sozialwissenschaft 95 (Opladen: Leske & Budrich, 1991).

6. Bischof, *Austria in the First Cold War.*

7. For the beginning of postwar Austrian diplomacy, see the Bischof essay in this volume.

8. Wolfgang Strasser, *Österreich und die Vereinten Nationen. Eine Bestandsaufnahme von 10 Jahren Mitgliedschaft*, Schriftenreihe der Österreichischen Gesellschaft für Außenpolitik und Internationale Beziehungen 1 (Vienna: Braumüller, 1967).

9. Gerald Storuzh, *Um Einheit und Freiheit. Staatsvertrag, Neutralität und das Ende der Ost-West-Besetzung Österreichs 1945-1955* (Vienna: Böhlau, 1998).

10. Reiner Eger, *Krisen an Österreichs Grenzen. Das Verhalten Österreichs während des Ungarnaufstandes 1956 und der tschechoslowakischen Krise 1968. Ein Vergleich* (Vienna: Herold, 1981).

11. Walter Blasi, "Die Libanonkrise 1958 und die US-Überflüge," in *Österreich. Im frühen Kalten Krieg 1945-1958. Spione, Partisanen, Kriegspläne*, ed. Erwin A. Schmidl (Vienna: Böhlau, 2000), 239-59.

12. Günter Bischof and Saki Dockrill, eds., *Cold War Respite: The Geneva Summit of 1955*, Eisenhower Center Studies on War and Peace (Baton Rouge: Louisiana State Univ. Press, 2000).

13. Gehler, *Langer Weg*, 211-14.

14. Manfried Rauchensteiner, *Die Zwei. Die Große Koalition in Österreich 1945-1966* (Vienna: Oesterreichischer Bundesverlag, 1987).

15. Helmut Kramer, "Strukturentwicklung der Außenpolitik (1945-1990)," in *Handbuch des politischen Systems Österreichs*, ed. Herbert Dachs et al. (Vienna: Manz, 1991), 637-57, here 637.

16. Rolf Steininger, ed., *Südtirol im 20. Jahrhundert. Dokumente* (Innsbruck: Studienverlag, 1999); Rolf Steininger, *Südtirol zwischen Diplomatie und Terror 1947-1969*, 3 vols., Veröffentlichungen des Südtiroler Landesarchivs 6 (Bozen: Athesia, 1999).

17. Gehler, *Der lange Weg*, 215-18, 226-31.

18. Günter Bischof, Anton Pelinka, and Ruth Wodak, eds., *Neutrality in Austria, vol. 9, Contemporary Austrian Studies* (New Brunswick: Transaction, 2001).

19. André Biever, *L'Autriche et les Origines de l'Ostpolitik de la République Fédérale d'Allemagne 1958-1969*, Mémoire de Maîtrise (Paris: Université Paris IV Sorbonne, 2001); idem, "L'Autriche et les origines de l'Ostpolitik de la République fédérale d'Alle-

magne, 1958-1969," *Relations Internationales* (Summer 2003): 213-30.

20. Erwin A. Schmidl, *Blaue Helme—Rotes Kreuz. Das österreichische Sanitätskontingent im Kongo 1960 bis 1963*, Innsbrucker Forschungen zur Zeitgeschichte 13 (Innsbruck: Studienverlag, 1995); idem, "In the Service of Peace...." 35 Jahre österreichische Teilnahme an UN-Friedensoperationen," *Österreichische Militärische Zeitschrift* 33 (March/April 1995): 125-34; idem, "Friedensoperationen nach 1945," in *Österreichisches Jahrbuch für internationale Sicherheitspolitik 1997*, ed. Erich Reiter (Graz: Styria, 1997), 451-75, here 451-53; Helmut Freudenschuß, "Drei Generationen von Friedensoperationen der Vereinten Nationen: Stand und Ausblick," in *Österreichisches Jahrbuch für internationale Politik* 10 (Vienna: Braumüller, 1993), 44-72, here 44f.

21. Günter Bischof and Anton Pelinka, eds., *The Kreisky Era in Austria, vol. 2,Contemporary Austrian Studies* (New Brunswick, NJ: Transaction, 1994); Oliver Rathkolb, "The Kreisky Era: 1970-2983," in *Austria in the Twentieth Century*, ed. Rolf Steininger, Michael Gehler, and Günter Bischof, Studies in Austrian and Central European History and Culture (New Brunswick, NJ: Transaction, 2002), 263-93.

22. Günter Bischof, "Victims? Perpetrators? 'Punching Bags' of European Historical Memory? The Austrians and Their World War II Legacies," *German Studies Review* 27 (February 2004): 17-32.

23. Richard Mitten, *The Politics of Anti-Semitic Prejudice: The Waldheim Phenomenon in Austria* (Boulder, CO: Westview, 1992).

24. Kurt Waldheim, "'. . . für Völkerverständigung und internationale Zusammenarbeit,'" in *Demokratie und Geschichte*, ed. Helmuth Wohnout, Jahrbuch des Karl von Vogelsang-Instituts zur Erforschung der Geschichte der christlichen Demokratie in Österreich 4 (Vienna: Böhlau, 2000), 13-57.

25. Represetnative of this trend are the essays in Anton Pelinka and Erika Weinzierl, eds., *Das Grosse Tabu: Österreichs Umgang mit seiner Vergangenheit* (Vienna: Edition S, 1987).

26. Michael Gehler and Hubert Sickinger, eds., *Politische Skandale und Affären in Österreich. Von Mayerling bis Waldheim*, 2nd ed. (Vienna, 1996).

27. Highly critical accounts of Haider's populist politics are the essays in Ruth Wodak and Anton Pelinka, eds., *The Haider Phenomenon in Austria* (New Brunswick, NJ: Transaction, 2002; a sympathetic perspective is provided by Lothar Höbelt, *Defiant Populist: Jörg Haider and the Politics of Austria* (West Lafayette, IN: Purdue Univ. Press, 2003).

28. Anton Pelinka, *Austria: Out of the Shadow of the Past* (Boulder, CO: Westview, 1998).

29. Günter Bischof and Anton Pelinka, eds., *The Vranitzky Era in Austria, vol. 7, Contemporary Austrian Studies* (New Brunswick, NJ: Transaction, 1999).

30. Rolf Steininger, *South Tyrol: A Minority Conflict of the Twentieth Century*, Studies in Austrian and Central European History and Culture (New Brunswick, NJ: Transaction, 2003).

31. For a beginning assessment of Austria's post-Cold War international position and security options, see Erich Reiter, *Neutralität oder NATO. Die sicherheitspolitischen Konsequenzen aus der europäischen Aufgabe Österreichs*, Forschungen zur Sicherheitspolitik 1 (Graz: Styria, 1996); and idem, ed., *Österreich und die NATO. Die sicherheitspolitische Situation Österreichs nach der NATO-Erweiterung*, Forschungen zur Sicherheitspolitik 2 (Graz: Styria, 1998); see also the essay by Gunther Hauser in this volume.

32. Gehler, *Der lange Weg* I, 273-357.

33. Günter Bischof, Anton Pelinka, and Michael Gehler, eds., *Austria in the New Europe, vol. 10, Contemporary Austrian Studies* (New Brunswick, NJ: Transaction, 2002).

34. Michael Gehler, "Kontraproduktive Intervention: Die 'EU 14' und der Fall Österreich oder vom Triumph des 'Primats der Innenpolitik' 2000-2003," in Gehler, Pelinka, Bischof, eds., *Österreich in der Europäischen Union*, 121-81.

35. Thomas Angerer, "'Österreich ist Europa.' Identifikationen Österreichs mit Europa seit dem 18. Jahrhundert," *Wiener Zeitschrift zur Geschichte der Neuzeit* 1.1 (2001): 55-72; idem, "Welches Österreich für welches Europa? Die Krise von 2000 im Lichte europäischer Österreichprobleme und österreichischer Europaprobleme seit dem 19. Jahrhundert," in Gehler, Pelinka, and Bischof, eds., *Österreich in der Europäischen Union*, 85-120.

36. Günter Bischof, "'Watschenmann der österreichischen Erinnerung'? Internationales Image und Vergangenheitspolitik der Schüssel/Riess-Passer-ÖVP/FPÖ-Koalitionsregierung," in *Österreich in der Europäischen Union. Bilanz seiner Mitgliedschaf (Austria in the European Union. Assessment of her Membership)*, ed. Michael Gehler, Anton Pelinka, and Günter Bischof, Schriften des DDr.-Herbert-Batliner-Europainstitutes 7 (Vienna: Böhlau, 2003), 445-78.

37. Brigitte Bailer, *Wiedergutmachung kein Thema. Österreich und der Nationalsozialismus* (Vienna: Löcker, 1993).

38. Günter Bischof and Josef Leidenfrost, eds., *Die bevormundete Nation. Österreich und die Alliierten 1945-1949*, Innsbrucker Forschungen zur Zeitgeschichte 4 (Innsbruck: Haymon-Verlag, 1988); Thomas Albrich, Klaus Eisterer, Michael Gehler, and Rolf Steininger, eds., *Österreich in den Fünfzigern. Zwischen Bevormundung und Emanzipation*, Innsbrucker Forschungen zur Zeitgeschichte 3 (Innsbruck: Studienverlag, 1995); Angerer, "Der 'bevormundete Vormund,'" 159-204.

39. Vladislav Marjanovic, *Die Mitteleuropa-Idee und die Mitteleuropa-Politik Österreichs 1945-1995*, Europäische Hochschulschriften, XXXI, Politikwissenschaft 360 (Frankfurt: Peter Lang Verlag, 1998); Wolfgang Baumann and Gunther Hauser, *Mitteleuropa—Im geopolitischen Interesse Österreichs* (Vienna: Militärwissenschaftliches Büro, 2001).

40. For a critique of Austrian visions of *Mitteleuropa*, see Charles S. Maier, "Whose *Mitteleuropa*? Central Europe between Memory and Obsolescence," in Günter Bischof and Anton Pelinka, eds., *Austria in the New Europe, vol. 1, Contemporary Austrian Studies* (New Brunswick, NJ: Transaction, 1993), 8-19. As Maier put it acerbically, Austria's *Mitteleuropa* in religious terms was a "community of Catholic humanists and dead Jews" (p. 12).

41. Barbara Coudenhove-Kalergi and Oliver Rathkolb, eds., *Die Beneš Dekrete* (Vienna: Czernin, 2002).

42. Waldemar Hummer and Anton Pelinka, *Österreich unter "EU-Quarantäne." Die "Maßnahmen der 14" gegen die österreichische Bundesregierung aus politikwissenschaftlicher und juristischer Sicht. Chronologie, Kommentar, Dokumentation* (Vienna: Linde Verlag, 2002).

43. Martin Lugmayr, *Österreich und die EU-Osterweiterung. Maximale Chancen—Maximale Risiken*, Europäische Hochschulschriften XXXI, Politikwissenschaft 447 (Frankfurt: Peter Lang, 2002).

44. Michael Gehler, Günter Bischof, Ludger Kühnhardt, and Rolf Steininger, eds., *Towards a European Constitution: A Historical and Political Comparison with the United States*, Europäische Reihe des Herbert-Batliner-Europainstitutes 4 (Vienna: Böhlau, 2005).

TOPICAL ESSAYS

I. Introduction

Diplomats: Symbols of Sovereignty become Managers of Interdependence: The Transformation of the Austrian Diplomatic Service

Eva Nowotny

Introduction

One hundred years ago, Sir Ernest Satow—the author of the much used guide to diplomatic practice—defined the task of diplomats as "the application of intelligence and tact to the conduct of official relations between the governments of independent states." This definition seems rather quaint or even dysfunctional today. An informed public would hardly support and legitimize the arrogance inherent in the claim that only professional diplomats would be endowed with the "tact and intelligence" required for this task.

Nor can the claim be supported that diplomats should have a kind of monopoly of being active in this field. Indeed, it seems presumptuous to raise such a claim, given the fact that today politicians do not find it difficult to contact one another directly without the intercession of their respective ambassadors. In doing so, they could—it seems—avoid misunderstandings and ambiguities that would be bound to arise so easily from the interposition of a third and fourth person. Indeed, these direct contacts between rulers proliferate.

The insistence on "official relations" seems outmoded, too, for in today's world, the distinction between "official" and "not official" has lost much of its meaning. Prime ministers lobby potent transnational firms for selecting their country as the site for their new investments. Criticism by non-governmental bodies like Amnesty International, Greenpeace, or Transparency International usually carries greater weight, consequence, and relevance than some critical remarks made by Ambassador A to Ambassador B at a cocktail reception of Ambassador C.

Additionally, funding this diplomatic apparatus is expensive. In the case of Austria, several hundred of diplomats have to be maintained abroad, with official residences, chauffeurs, cooks, and other support staff in a lifestyle that seems a leftover from feudal times and is not in accord with the egalitarian ethos of the democratic republic they represent.

So, if all of this is true, why, then, are diplomats still around a hundred years after their demise had been predicted? Why have they become even more numerous instead of quietly becoming extinct as a species no longer adapted to the new habitat of a modern, democratic, information- and knowledge-based society?

It is true, of course, that all bureaucracies tend to perpetuate themselves and that they tend to do so beyond the time of their functionality. This pertains, in particular, to the bureaucracies of the state. The diplomatic service should be no exception. Motivated by the narrow interest of preserving its privileges and shielded by a fog of nationalist myth about its unique symbolic value, the diplomatic corps of the world would, thus, have been able to survive even after having lost all practical usefulness.

But it seems doubtful that these are the true reasons for the survival and even expansion of the diplomatic services of the world. For one should doubt that over decades ministers of finance and critical members of parliaments would have been willing to budget for institutions which might be charming, but useless.

Using the Austrian diplomatic service as an example and drawing on my personal experience as a diplomat, political advisor, and historian, I will argue that the diplomatic service flourishes because, while preserving and honing some of its core skills, it has changed, adapting to the radically changed environment of a deeply interdependent world and developing new tools and modes of action to tackle the new tasks presented by this new environment.

Changes in the Terrain of Diplomacy

When I entered the Austrian Ministry for Foreign Affairs on 1 March 1973, my first boss installed me in an empty office and handed me a thick file which he advised me to study diligently and carefully. It was entitled "*Runderlass über die Formen der schriftlichen Aktenerledigung*" ("Circular Instruction *ad omnia* on the Appropriate Forms of Written Communications"). Having come to diplomacy with a doctorate in history and having gone through years of archival research in preparation for my dissertation on Klemens von Metternich, I discovered very quickly that there was nothing in this "*Runderlass*" which was in any way new or surprising. On the contrary, all the various elements contained therein, from the proper way of drafting the "*Aktenvermerk*", giving the reader of a file a brief synopsis of the case at hand and explaining the reasoning of the author for a proposed course of action, to the political report, the political instruction or the correct filing, were deeply familiar to me. They were the same used by Metternich and his staff as he drafted and negotiated his European-wide diplomatic network. These first hours on my first day into a new career gave me insight into the astounding degree of continuity, which through all the vagaries of history has marked and still marks Austrian diplomacy—a degree of continuity and a sense of tradition combined, as it is, with openness for change and the capacity to adapt very quickly to changed circumstances.

When I entered the diplomatic service, faxes and xerox machines were not yet in use. Making a long distance call (even within Austria) required prior approval by the head of the department. Diplomats were still supposed to travel to new overseas assignments by boat. Hierarchies were steep and strict. The "*Du*" among colleagues, a leftover from the feudal era of the empire, was strictly reserved for the A-level officers. In matters relating to official business, communication other than via the official hierarchic channels was not only frowned upon, but it was also punished. Truly relevant were only the things that happened within the confines of this monastic entity. Other state bureaucracies were automatically assumed to be of a lesser kind and of negligible relevance. The role model was the elegant, slightly cynical ambassador writing, every two months or so, witty, highly readable, and quotable reports based on his periodic encounters with the political director of the Foreign Ministry of his receiving state.

It was at that time, too, that Austria—a young state in many respects—had just managed to gain a firmer sense of its own identity and place in the world. But this identity being young and that place still being uncertain, much unease persisted. It influenced some activities and claims that today may seem quixotic (such as the claim that Austria should politically use its weight as a "cultural super-power," with the Vienna Philharmonic orchestra being equivalent to the armament of bigger states). But the same unease and uncertainty also fueled the desire to gain acceptance and respectability by being useful to others by:

- lowering the risks inherent in the East-West confrontation,
- broadening contacts with its neighbors in Central and Eastern Europe in the hope of preserving their European identity,

- strengthening European fora of cooperation like the Council of Europe, and
- promoting on a global level the rule of law and widening and deepening the reach of cooperation in and through international organizations.

The new Austrian Federal Chancellor Bruno Kreisky was about to broaden this agenda further by claiming for Austria a role in the viciously explosive conflict between Israelis and Palestinians, and—more generally—in efforts to narrow the gap between the rich and the poor nations of the world.

Thus, in terms of the tasks set for Austrian diplomats, this was a time of transition and significant change. The prior, obvious, and somehow externally imposed tasks had been completed. Independence and sovereignty were secured. Austria had adhered to stipulations by the United Nations and the Council of Europe. With neutrality, a viable security policy had been defined. To the extent possible, the rights of the Austrian population living in South Tyrol had been safeguarded. With Germany, claims and counter claims arising from the Second World War had been settled. Last but not least, Austria had managed to participate in the economic integration of Western Europe through its membership in the European Free Trade Association (EFTA).

These immediate tasks completed, Austria now sought its place and function in a wider regional and global setting. The concept of a "national interest" was broadened and was subsumed under the notion of "*Aktive Neutralitätspolitik*," a policy of pro-active neutrality. Austrian diplomats, their mode of work and the tools they used, had to adapt. But this need to adapt did not just reflect the new priorities in Austria's own foreign and security policy; it also reflected the changes in the wider world.

There is a tendency to regard the period between 1950 and 1990 as a period of great stability, in which all the main parameters of the global order remained unchanged, with the two structural cleavages being the one between the Communist "East" and the democratic "West" and the one between a poor, post-colonial "South" and the wealthy "North." This era of tranquility would have come to an end just at the end of the last century with the downfall of the Communist empire and with terrorists smashing the twin towers of New York's World Trade Center ten years later.

But this image of an uneventful forty years is misleading. Actually, the time between 1950 and 1990 was one of massive transformation in the very structure of the global system. The relative power of the United States became somewhat lesser, and the power of its Soviet counterpart had been in irreversible decline since the early 1960s. Japan and Germany regained their former economic status, yet renounced their historic geo-political ambitions. The number of states doubled, and next to these numerous new states, other actors became active as players on the global scene: transnational corporations and transnational groups pursuing a political agenda became both more numerous and relevant. So did the official international organizations whose number also doubled in that period.

But that was not all, and this increase in the numbers of international actors and the shifts in their relative power were not changes of a truly revolutionary kind. What had truly transformed the global order was the growing interconnectedness of all of these players. As the world's population doubled and as the world's wealth grew even faster, each one came to depend on the other in a very direct way, with lower transportation costs and the general lowering of the "transaction costs" merging the world into a single economic space and making increasingly porous the international borders that once had so clearly divided the realm of one sovereign from the territory of another.

Many profited. Quite a number of persons and states did not. While the world as such became wealthy as it has never been before, the chasm that divides wealth and poverty also became deeper than it had ever been before.

Complex systems such as a highly interconnected and interdependent world are accident-prone and vulnerable. They are in need of steerage and protection, and this is what the actors in the international system have to provide. A good part of that task falls to the agents of states, who remain, after all, the dominant players on the global scene. In fulfilling these tasks, states may, of course, use different agents. Heads of governments themselves have become more directly involved in this task. They congregate at the ever more frequent summit meetings of various sorts. In between, they have adopted the habit of calling one another on the phone, or as in the European Union, they have at their disposal a special e-mail system for instant communication. Within the public administration, many different branches of government have installed special offices to administer their international agenda. Indeed, there are only few not touched by global interdependence and, thus, not obliged to interact with their counterparts in other countries of the world. Even provinces and towns have an international agenda and their own strategies and instruments for achieving it. Nevertheless, diplomats remain active, and looking at Austria, I would maintain that their assignments have multiplied. Far from receding into the irrelevance that had been predicted for them, they are multi-tasking professionals and now till fields they had not touched before.

Certainly, this could not be the case had the Austrian diplomatic service remained as it was at the time when I was initiated into its ranks. Had it remained unchanged, it would have been reduced to a reliquary of merely symbolic value, surviving in reduced scope, out of bureaucratic inertia and not because of services rendered to the public. Instead, it has been transformed. An old ambassador who retired in 1970 would feel lost after passing through the gates of Ballhausplatz 2. He would no longer recognize as his the ministry now in place.

Three forces are behind this wholesale makeover:

- the need to adapt to changes in the international environment and in the global order;
- the unprecedented ease of communication both within and outside of the country, together with the ease of providing and accessing information on a global scale; and
- finally, socio-cultural changes, which affected most nations and had their impact also on Austria.

Changes in the Austrian Diplomatic Service

Let me point to a few of the most prominent and visible of these changes in the Austrian diplomatic service and in its mode of operation.

The Flattening of Hierarchies

When I entered the service, all written communication leaving the house (and much of information that merely circulated within the house) had been drafted and re-drafted several times over and had been approved by at least three levels of the hierarchy. In part, this reflected the hierarchical inclinations common to all bureaucracies. But in a way it also was functional. Papers—and with them information—just came together at the top. Only the highest diplomats, the secretary general and the political director, were in possession of all relevant information emanating from various sources, all of which were isolated from one another. Nowadays, however, someone wishing to affect an impending decision is well advised not to call those at the top of the hierarchy, but those who actually do the drafting. The heightened workload and the greater speed of transactions has put a natural curb on repeated re-drafting as well as on too much interference or changes from higher levels. More importantly, the one doing the drafting now has access to a vast amount of information, while his superior, being less specialized and targeted, has the capacity to access a smaller amount of such information as it pertains to the specific issue under consideration. *De facto*, the power of decision making has shifted downwards. Other factors, too, contributed to the ensuing flattening of hierarchies. The number of positions that need to be filled has expanded; thus they are no longer reserved for the most senior staff only. The tougher working conditions also favor the young over the old. In addition, the younger colleagues are also better adapted to networking across national borders and diverse disciplines, while their more status conscious seniors have difficulty embracing such skills.

Information Collection and Distribution

This flattening of hierarchies would not have been possible in the absence of changes in the distribution and retrieval of information. Xerox copying alone had a vast impact. Before these machines became accessible to the staff, there was neither the desire to nor the physical possibility of distributing to a wider group the information contained in a written document. Information was to go to and to serve the superior. Xeroxing changed that, and desk officers were quick to discover that information is a commodity that can be exchanged and traded. The better the information, the wider the list of those benefiting from its distribution, the more secure the position of the distributor in the network of his or her peers. Also, it is no longer the case that mere seniority guarantees access to more complete or more relevant information. Foreign ambassadors might call on the political director at periodic intervals as they have done since diplomatic services became established. But according to my reckoning, there is a good chance that some junior officer adept at surfing the Internet and with personal contacts to other junior foreign diplomats will come up with information more complete and less slanted by political intent than the information conveyed to the political director by the foreign ambassador he has received.

E-Communications

Email and the Internet have continued and dramatically accelerated the evolutionary process started by the use of xerox copying and faxed messages. The consequences were revolutionary. Not just the mode of transaction was transformed, so, too, was the structure of the whole diplomatic apparatus, even the content of diplomatic transactions.

Central Office and Embassy Relations

In the diplomatic services, there used to be a stark division between the work at the central office and the service at some embassy abroad.

The latter was regarded as more desirable, not just because of the perks and privileges associated with diplomatic postings, but also because working abroad was considered to be the true core of diplomacy. Now thanks to effortless, cheap, broad, and instant communication, the line between work at the central office and the work abroad has become very much blurred. Each week, approximately 20 percent of the staff of the central office is away on some mission or another. "Roving ambassadors" working on specific issues or on a specific group of countries travel about the world and are received with as much honor as their colleagues residing in the country they just are visiting. The embassies, on the other hand, have come to be led on a much shorter leash. Whereas before they were given quite some leeway in deciding their priorities and in framing the political messages they tried to convey, they now are more closely integrated into the work of the central office. In some aspects, they have come to resemble extended desks of the central office, replacing or at least supplementing the "country desks" in the headquarters. Via e-mail, they have their direct input into position papers, drafts for speeches, periodic reports to parliament, and so forth. Generally, though, it is clear that in the relationship between the Foreign Ministry and its embassies abroad the weight has shifted to the detriment of the latter.

Multilateral Diplomacy

Contrary to what their name might imply, international relations are no longer mainly about what one nation does to another. Increasingly, they reflect the need of the community of states to address problems they are well advised to tackle together. Because these problems are very distinct from another, finding solutions calls for specialists with a very specific knowledge of the issues involved and the tools that might be used in resolving problems. The work shifts from bilateral diplomacy to work in and with various multilateral agencies, each of which is addressing one specific set of problems. In the diplomatic service, bilateral diplomacy and generalists are being pushed into second rank behind multilateral diplomacy and specialists. The role model is no longer the skilled and powerful bilateral ambassador, but the colleague who has contributed most to an advance in global governance and the development of international law, or, specifically within the European Union, one who works for very direct and concrete Austrian interests on a daily basis.

Diplomatic Reporting

John K. Galbraith was not just a prominent economist; he also served for a few years as U.S. Ambassador to India. Reflecting on this period of his life, he once stated that "diplomatic reporting was one of the most undervalued forms of literary art." Characteristic for Galbraith, that was tongue in cheek, with an intended ambivalence on whether diplomatic reporting was essential and, thus, wrongly neglected, or whether it was void of real substance and existed merely as a piece of an art created for its own sake. The verdict of the present is clear. In Austria at least, the old form of diplomatic reports no longer exists. These were five or more page essays, frequently betraying otherwise unfulfilled literary ambitions. They were mimeographed to be forwarded to others more as a proof of the author's writing skills than in order to convey information to be acted upon. This form of reporting was formally abolished several years ago. While it may be that this is the end of a precious (if little known) genre of literature, the decision was justified and even inevitable if seen from the perspective of a bureaucracy that has to maintain its practical usefulness in shaping international relations.

Reporting is now targeted on issues that have to be acted upon, that are actually on the agenda in Austria's bilateral or multilateral relations. Such reports are artless and to the point, the shorter the better. As a source of more general information on the country of residence, embassies have ceded their function to competitors in journalism, academia, databases, and high finance. Someone searching for general information is well advised to first search the databases of the Economist Intelligence Unit, of the Institute of International Finance, of Keesing, of Reuters, and so forth. Embassies then supplement background information or add greater details on this or that point. Of course, new modes of communication have sped up not only the transmission of information, but also the rate of decision making, and have made the wide distribution of information much easier.

Distributing Information

The easier supply of decentralized information dovetails with a greater need for such wider distribution. It used to be that the Ministry for Foreign Affairs was an island unto itself. It was captive to its own mechanisms, fascinated by its own internal power plays, absorbed by its own internal administration. Such tendencies towards insularity are, of course, not peculiar to Ministries for Foreign Affairs. They are endemic in all bigger bureaucracies. In the case of Austrian diplomacy, extraneous developments and entry into the European Union forced the recognition that others also had entered the realm of external relations, rightfully or at least in a way that could not be reversed. If Austrian diplomats were to retain some role in the coordination of the country's overall external relations and to retain their claim of shaping its overall direction, they had to accept the direct communication between these other players and the international realm. They were well advised to facilitate it, for, by facilitating it, they conserve some function and control. From being a self sufficient and self enclosed institution, the Austrian Ministry for Foreign Affairs has, thus, morphed into one providing services not just directly to citizens, but to other Austrian ministries, as well as to state and local government and to the various non governmental organizations active in the international arena.

Sharing Power and Information

Some claim that the European Union presents the image of things to come in relations among all states of the world. I hope that this is true and that nations will indeed move ever closer to a more peaceful, more institutionalized, more law based and democratically legitimized form of interaction. The patterns that have emerged since 1995 in managing our membership in the Union might then become applicable in managing an ever greater number of relations to other countries. But for the time being, EU membership alone has radically transformed the Austrian diplomatic services and its mode of operation. It has accelerated and reinforced the trends that have been described above. Since the Union might be seen as a federal state in the process of being born, the lines between internal and external policy have become blurred to the extent of no longer being discernible. In the pecking order of the various European councils, the Ministers of Foreign Affairs have managed to preserve in the General Affairs Council a special and privileged role as overall coordinators. Frequently, however, it was not the General Affairs Council that had the last say in important matters, but the council of the Ministers of Finance, because it has control over the purse strings. The Austrian embassy in Brussels consists of delegates from practically all Austrian ministries, from Austrian *Länder*, and from all major official organizations. Most of them report directly to the organizations in Austria that had sent them to Brussels. Yet even when reporting directly to their home base, they might be bypassed by the European Commission itself, which also distributes its documents electronically to all institutions in Austria that are affected by a decision about to be taken. Reports on the outcome of a meeting have to be expedited the very same day, even if that implies a deadline close to or after midnight. The list of the addressees of such reports is very long, and the Ministry for Foreign Affairs is just one of them. Politically sensitive instructions based upon such reports must be cleared—in the short interval of just two or three days—in a complex intergovernmental procedure.

Responding to Increased Pressures

Pressure emanating from internal political coordination, managing a vast network of interdependent organizations, the quantity of work, the number of decision makers involved, and accomplishing much in a short period of time, all that adds up to a workload widely removed from the image of diplomatic work as it is assiduously preserved in the public: of neatly dressed, overprivileged and underemployed champagne drinkers, bestowing upon each other the gift of redundant phrases and cultivated irrelevancies.

The Evolution of Diplomatic Tasks

The Austrian diplomatic service has quite successfully adjusted to new tasks and to a changed global order. But that opens yet another question. Why should it be that diplomats alone may rise to this challenge? What is it that should so eminently qualify them for being better at that job than others?

One part of the answer has already been provided. Many persons from very different backgrounds and very different organizational cultures have now become involved in a field that once was the exclusive domain of diplomats. Nevertheless, and more often than not, diplomats still lead the pack. If issues become controversial, others tend to defer to them, accepting them in a role as negotiators and mediators. But if the diplomatic service has changed as radically as I claim, why insist that it is still the old diplomatic service? Where, in such a deep overhaul, is the element of continuity that evidences a link to the past, to past codes of conduct and to a very special professional ethos?

My tentative answer would be that—then as now—diplomats are facilitators of consensus, that they have internalized the need to think with the other's head, and that unlike other professionals, they base their craft not on the unchangeable certainty of fixed rules, but on the rule of uncertainty and the art of navigating in fog.

It is exactly these skills that are responsible for the continuing ambivalence of the public and their enduring distrust of everything "diplomatic." In a world hungry for predictability, security, and certainty, diplomats stand for the open-ended and the non-committal. With borders having become porous and societies multicultural, there is a yearning for stable, secure, and unchallenged identities and symbols like flags and anthems to confirm them. While formerly diplomats had been such symbols, affirming the presence of their own state on the world stage, they have now and by their actual work become the symbol of things that are difficult to internalize and to accommodate. They recall that, in most cases, there are two sides to a coin, that things are not simply black or white. They remind the public that besides the "us" there also is the "other" with equal claim for respect. In the public's perception, diplomats have come to stand for a world order in which no one is truly independent and where every actor, thus, has to make concessions. This perception, much more than the trappings of a privileged life, made diplomats suspect. The remark that someone has been "too diplomatic" is pejorative and implies a lack of resolve and conviction and the failure to be blunt, direct, and final.

But these negative perceptions in the public provide proof of the functionality of diplomatic ethos and culture. Globalization has not been a steamroller, squeezing everything and everybody into a flat sameness. On the contrary, it has made for a closer confrontation of values, lifestyles, and ideologies, which often are at variance and irreconcilable by their very nature. Neither have things become more predictable and certain. With so many international actors in place, the need for coordinated action has become more pressing and also more difficult. The desired more stable, more humane, and just world order cannot be built by representatives who stand unyieldingly on the base of supposedly unchangeable "national interest." On the contrary, the task calls for the capacity to listen, to keep an open mind, to understand. It calls for skills in networking, for the resolve of never completely closing the channels of communication, for persistence in working for a positive outcome, and last but not least, for the preparedness to accept an unsatisfactory outcome in preference to an even worse one.

These are the old, traditional, and sound operating principles of diplomacy. In today's world, they have lost nothing of their relevance. In fact, they have even become more useful and precious. The tasks of diplomacy have changed. The operating field and the tools of trade have undergone change. However, the ethos and the culture that have sustained diplomacy over the centuries have remained the same.

Conclusion

If in the definition of Satow at the beginning of this article diplomats are credited with having tact and intelligence—not in a sense of superiority, but as an indicator of the enduring relevance of the traditional diplomatic culture—then I can accept it also as a definition of today's diplomacy. I would, however, change the application of these virtues from Satow's words, "to the task of facilitating, for the national and for the general benefit, cooperation among all who impact upon the world order."

Despite its successes at responding to a changing environment, I see Austria's diplomacy as still deficient and its apparatus in need of repair in four areas.

First, it is under-funded and too small. For example, only two of the present EU members have embassies in Washington smaller than the Austrian embassy: Cyprus and Malta. The number of international actors has expanded and so have the tasks of diplomacy. The Austrian Foreign Service, however, has over the last several years shrunk to a point no longer commensurate with the expansion of its tasks.

Second, the opening of the service is still incomplete, both to the outside world as well as to the Austrian public and other Austrian institutions. I certainly do not mean that the career should be open to everyone regardless of aptitude and training. On the contrary, I hold it as absolutely essential that the service preserves its integrity through the barrier of an objective and demanding entrance exam. But this should not impede closer cooperation and even some form of integration with other ministries dealing in international affairs. Greater openness and interchange of personnel could and should also be sought with other EU member countries, the EU Commission, and international organizations. Closer cooperation with the Austrian and the international academic community would be advantageous to both sides, as well.

Third, the internal structure of the Ministry for Foreign Affairs no longer corresponds to its present tasks, and in some respects has become dysfunctional. The traditional separation of the multilateral and the bilateral from European integration no longer makes sense because European politics permeate almost every area of our involvement abroad.

Fourth, it was not by accident or chance that the Austrian Ministry for Foreign Affairs was the first to change to a paperless office and to work fully on electronic files. Its website is up to international standards; all of the staff is computer literate. All this confirms my claim that the diplomatic service was under great pressure to respond to changes in global affairs and in global governance. What remains to be accomplished is a tighter and more complete insertion into the overall electronic flow of information.

Things are evolving fast. Austria's specific function in the East-West conflict has disappeared together with that conflict. Others now are better placed to provide the services Austria once rendered. Many chances resulting from the new membership in the European Union have been wasted, and Austria still has to find a steady pace and solid place in the formulation of EU policies. There is still uncertainty about its own future security strategy. The cleavage between Austria's public opinion and its actual foreign policy has become wider, as has the distance between rhetoric and actual commitment. In the realm of international politics, nothing is ever securely achieved and permanent. Standing still implies falling behind. Austria's diplomatic service and Austria's diplomacy have changed and adapted over time. But the process must continue and even accelerate.

An Institutional History of the Austrian Foreign Office in the Twentieth Century

Rudolf Agstner

The Imperial & Royal Austro-Hungarian Foreign Ministry from 1900 to 1918

The Austro-Hungarian Foreign Office in the beautiful palais known as "Ballhausplatz"[1], was, as a result of the "*Ausgleich*" with Hungary of 1867, a "common affair" of both Austria and Hungary. It was financed by both parts of the dual monarchy according to the formula Austria 70: Hungary 30. In 1908, the formula was modified to 63,6 : 36,4, reflecting the growing strength of the Hungarian economy and Hungarian political aspirations.

The "*Ballhausplatz*" traditionally consisted of three branches: diplomatic, consular and ministerial. The "Imperial and Royal Ministry of the Imperial and Royal House and of Foreign Affairs" in 1900 was made up of the cabinet of the minister, a political division of 4, and an administrative division of 11 departments. In 1900, Austria-Hungary maintained the following diplomatic and consular presence abroad:

Embassies: Berlin, Constantinople, London, Madrid, Paris, Rome, Rome-Holy See, St. Petersburg (8)

Legations: Athens, Belgrade, Bern, Brussels, Bucarest, Buenos Aires, Dresden, Kopenhagen, Lisbon, Munich, Peking, Rio de Janeiro, Stockholm, Stuttgart, Teheran, The Hague, Tokio, Washington (18)

Minister Residents: Cetinje (1)

Diplomatic Agencies: Cairo, Sofia, Tanger (3)

The consular organisation in 1900 consisted of 414, mostly honorary, offices:

consulates general 38, including 14 honorary
consulates 146, including 106 honorary
vice-consulates 114, including 103 honorary
consular agencies 113, including 111 honorary

As legations in the US and in Japan were upgraded to embassies in 1903 and 1908, and new legations established in Mexico City (1901), Santiago de Chile (1902), Bangkok (1912) and Durazzo/Durres, Albania (1914), as well as existing missions upgraded to legations (Cetinje 1908, Sofia 1909), the number of embassies by the outbreak of World War I had risen to 10, and the number of legations to 23, with only one diplomatic agency in Cairo left.

By July of 1914, the consular network had reached the figure of 468, as emigration to Argentina, Australia, Brazil, Canada and the US required a larger consular presence. 34 were consulates general, 58 consulates, 10 vice-consulates and 2 consular agencies, and 364 honorary offices of all categories.

World War I resulted in a considerable reduction of diplomatic and consular missions. In November of 1918, embassies had dwindled to 4 (Berlin, Constantinople, Madrid and Vatican embassy in exile in Switzerland[2]), and legations to 12, including a new one in Christiania (Oslo[3]). The consular network was down to 134 (consulates-general: 13 and 5 honorary, consulates 21 and 54 honorary, vice-consulates 3 and 36 honorary, consular agencies 1 and 59 honorary), almost all honorary offices of the two latter categories in neutral Spain and allied Turkey.

1918-1920: End and New Beginning

Based on the manifesto of Emperor Charles I. of 16 October 1918, the "provisional national aysembly" had constituted itself in the Lower Austrian diet on 30 October. It established a "State Council", composed of "*Staatsämter*", among them a "*Staatsamt des Äußern.*"

On 2 November 1918 Emperor Charles I. appointed Ludwig Baron Flotow Austro-Hungarian Foreign Minister; he was to be the last one. Dr. Victor Adler[4], the new "state secretary for foreign affairs" set up his office at the Ballhausplatz too. Adler was assisted by Otto Bauer as under-secretary. After Adler's death, Bauer succeeded him on 21 November 1918 at the helm of diplomacy of the new Republic of Austria.

On 12 November 1918 the "Republic of Deutschösterreich" was proclaimed; the Provisional National Assembly decreed in Legal Gazette 5/1918 Article 4 that *"The Imperial & Royal (= Austro-Hungarian) and the I.R. (=Austrian) ministries are dissolved. Their tasks and powers are transferred to the German-Austrian 'Staatsämter'"*. The new foreign office acted as trustee of the other successor states in the process of liquidating the former I.&R. foreign service and its assets, consisting of palaces abroad like Hôtel Matignon in Paris, Palais Polovtsov in St. Petersburg or the "palazzi di Venezia" in Rome[5] and Constantinople. At

Mio Schilling in 1931 to 6 Mio in 1932[11]) required downgrading the consulate general in Trieste to honorary consulate, and closing consulates in Montreal, Cairo and Buenos Aires, while the legation in The Hague was run by chargés d' affaires from 1932 to 1936.

In 1933, the international situation changed again—Hitler's ascension to power in Germany made it all the more necessary for Austria to increase her presence in the international arena. The matter became urgent, as many Austrian colonies abroad had succumbed to the propaganda of local Nazi organisations. In 1934, leader of the Heimwehr Dr. Richard Steidle was appointed consul general in Trieste. Other Heimwehr-leaders too were disposed of by making them diplomats: Odo Neustädter-Stürmer[12] became Austrian minister in Budapest (February to November 1936), where he was succeeded by former vice-chancellor Eduard Baar-Baarenfels. The Austrian steel industry in 1936 urged opening a legation in Tokio—to no avail. The legation in Cairo was re-established 1937; a few months later, plans for a consulate general in Shanghai fell victim to the Sino-Japanese war, a consulate in Addis Abeba to the Anschluss. A 1935 project for an Austrian "cultural institute" in Chicago, which was to have a patriotic effect on the local Burgenländer colony, was shelved.

In March of 1938, the "Federal State of Austria" maintained 20 legations abroad (Ankara, Athens, Belgrade, Berlin, Bern, Bucarest, Cairo, Holy See, London, Moscow, Paris, Prague, Rio de Janeiro, Rome, Sofia, Stockholm, The Hague, Warsaw, Washington), a mission at the League of Nations, six consulates general (Cologne, Jerusalem, Milan, Munich, New York, Trieste) and two consulates (Bratislava, Ljubljana). The staff of the Austrian Foreign Service comprised 379 civil servants, 115 of whom worked in the Federal Chancellery-Foreign Affairs (34 diplomats), while 203 were posted to 21 diplomatic missions (54 of them diplomats, 28 administrative officers) and 61 (10 diplomats, 14 administrative staff) in consulates and honorary consulates.

From 11 to 13 March Dr. Wilhelm Wolf[13] was foreign minister of the nationalsocialist government Arthur Seyss-Inquart. Following the Anschluß, the Federal Chancellery-Foreign Affairs became the "*Dienststelle des Auswärtigen Amtes Wien*", which was to liquidate Austrian missions abroad by 30 June. Former Austrian missions were instructed on 14 March to notify the Anschluß to the authorities of the host country, and to hand over buildings, archives, seals, accounts etc. to the local German mission. From 13 to 20 March 1938 former Austrian missions were to fly the flags of the former "Federal State of Austria" and the swastika of Germany.

As far as the buildings of former Austrian missions that were Austrian property were concerned, the German Foreign Office soon proceeded to have the property registerd in the name of the German Reich.[14] Buildings were either used by German diplomacy (e.g. London, Moscow, Sofia), sold (e.g. Paris), or rented to other states (e.g. Washington to Denmark, Rome-Vatican to Slovakia). The branch office of the German Foreign Office in Vienna was closed on 31 August 1938. In July 1940 the Ballhausplatz was chosen by the new Viennese Gauleiter Baldur von Schirach as seat of his "*Statthalterei*".

Finis Austriae—the flags of the "Federal State of Austria" (left) and the swastika flying in unison at the former Austrian legation in Warsaw/Poland, 13-20 March 1938

1938-1945: Ex-Austrian Diplomats— Victims or Perpetrators ?

In the entrance of the Federal Ministry for Foreign Affairs in Vienna a marble plaque commemorates in golden letters those Austrian diplomats "*who in loyalty to their fatherland became victims of Nazi persecution...*", raising the question of the role of former Austrian diplomats in the years from 1938 to 1945. Some Austrian diplomats had indeed been arrested and taken to concentration camps.

Dr. Erich Bielka (* Vienna 12 May 1908 + Bad Aussee 1 September 1992), vice-consul at the Munich consulate general, was arrested by the Gestapo from 17 March to 19 April 1938, and then incarcerated in the KZ Dachau until 8 August 1938.

Theodor Hornbostel (* Vienna 9 January 1889 + Gmunden 8 June 1973) was head of the political department in the Federal Chancellery-Foreign Affairs from 1933 to 1938; arrested 12 March 1938, taken to the KZ Dachau on 1 April 1938, to the KZ Buchenwald on 26 September 1939.

Dr. Ludwig Jordan (* Radmannsdorf, Krain / Radovljice, Slovenia 15 April 1895 + Frankfurt/Oder, Germany 10 November 1945). Consul general in Munich, arrested by the Gestapo on 16 March and taken to the KZ Dachau; he was released in December 1938.

Dr. Ludwig Kleinwächter (* Czernowitz, Bukowina/Cernovci, Ukraine 9 October 1882 + Vienna 12 March 1973), in the Federal Press Service in 1938, arrested on 12 March 1938 on racial grounds, taken to the KZ Dachau and Buchenwald from 1 April 1938 to 3 May 1939.

Odo Neustädter-Stürmer (* Laibach, Krain/Ljubljana, Slovenia 3 November 1885 + Mödling/Hinterbrühl 19 March 1938), Austrian minister to Hungary in 1936, committed suicide.

Dr. Richard Steidle (* Untermais/Meran, South Tyrol 20 September 1881 + KZ Buchenwald 30 August 1940), prominent leader of the Heimwehr, consul general in Trieste 1934-1938. He was incarcerated in the KZ Buchenwald from September 1938 onwards.

Several Austrian diplomats, some of who even had signed the oath of allegiance to Hitler in March 1938, sooner or later refused to follow orders from Vienna to return home, and preferred to stay in their host country.

Georg Alexich (* Vienna 14 September 1893 + Washington, D.C. 15 July 1949) was Austrian minister in the Netherlands. Having signed the oath of allegiance on 31 March 1938, he was dismissed without pension, emigrated to France, obtained Netherlands nationality in 1939, and escaped to the US via Portugal. He studied at Georgetown University, where he taught international comparative law and diplomacy after 1943.

Egon Berger-Waldenegg (* Vienna 14 February 1880 + Graz 12 September 1960), minister to Italy since 1936, stayed in Rome.

Dr. Aurelio Faccioli-Grimani (* Stockerau 7 April 1885 + Rio de Janeiro 23 December 1946), since 1934 counsellor at the legation in Rio de Janeiro, was dismissed from service in early 1939.

Georg Franckenstein (* Dresden 18 March 1878 + Kelsterbach/ Frankfurt 1 October 1953), Austrian minister to the Court of St. James, stayed in London, obtained British citizenship in July 1938 and was made Sir by King George VI.

Adolf Karl Kunz (*Vienna 23 May 1885 + Vienna 26 November 1969), counsellor at the legation in London, continued his career in the German Foreign Service. Following his marriage with Esther Waldegrave (daughter of Lord Radstock) he served with the German Academic Exchange Program. Refusing to return home after the outbreak of World War II, he was dismissed and in 1942 deprived of German nationality.

Ferdinand Marek (* Karolinenthal/Böhmen 25 January 1881 + Lefertowskaja prison camp /USSR 4 May 1947), Austrian minister in Prague since 1922; he stayed on in Prague, Austrian representative in the CSR from 7 May until arrested 24 May 1945.

Edith Popper (* Vienna 6 June 1897 d. London 20 August 1981), chancellor of the legation in London; dismissed as "non-Aryan", she refused to return to Vienna.

Edgar Prochnik (* Amboina, Neth. India 21 January 1879 + Vienna 12 April 1964), Austrian minister to the US since 1921/1925, stayed in the US, lectured at the Foreign Service School of George Washington University until 1960.

Anton Retschek (Unin, Nyitra/Hungary 8 April 1885 + Vienna 18 July 1950) was Austrian minister-resident in Rio de Janeiro since 1925, minister since 1928. Dismissed from service, he stayed in Rio de Janeiro. Retschek was officially recognized by the Government of Brazil as Austrian representative in 1943.

Other Austrian diplomats for a variety of reasons chose to continue their career in the Nazi German Foreign Service. 17 career diplomats and 12 officials in low-ranking positions were admitted to the German Foreign Service. Most of them did not make a career, not even those who had joined the NSDAP before the Anschluß.[15]

Franz Adamovic von Waagstätten (*Cracow 27 May 1893 + Innsbruck 26 February 1946). Joined NSDAP 1 October 1940.

Dr. Karl Dreihann-Holenia (Moradel/Moravec near Brno, Moravia 15 July 1906 + Aschach, Upper Austria 2 July 1978). Joined NSDAP 1 March 1939.

Josef Hans Lazar (* Constantinople 5 October 1895 + Vienna 9 May 1961), a former correspondent of the "Neue Freie Presse"" for the Balkans, was press attaché at the legation in Berlin. In the night of 12 to 13 March 1938 he was recalled to Vienna, made head of the Press Service, his only task being to read on 13 March, at 8 p.m., the text of the law of reunification to the correspondents of the foreign press in Vienna. Having settled in Spain in 1938, he joined the German Foreign Office after the outbreak of WW II and was made head of the press department of the German legation in Madrid, where he was considered its *eminence grise*.

Eduard Lurtz (* Reichenberg, Bohemia / Liberec, Czech Rep. 8 October 1894 + ?), counsellor in Belgrade in 1938, continued to serve there until April 1941. 1941-1944 consul in Großwardein (Oradea, Romania).

Siegmar Lurtz (* Reichenberg, Böhmen / Liberec, Czech Rep. 22 September 1897 + Vienna 22 August 1958), secretary in the Federal Chancellery in 1938. Transferred to Asuncion in 1938, and to New York in 1939 (responsible for movies, radio, press and counter intelligence). Deported in June 1941 with German and Italian consular officers to Lisbon. Served in Berlin until March 1945.

Dr. Heinrich Meran (* Szekesfehervar, Hungary 26 April 1908) was secretary of legation in London in 1938. German Foreign Office 1938-1940, vice-consul in Gothenburg / Sweden 1940, transferred to German legation Bucarest 1943. Interned by Soviet forces after the occupation of Bucarest, Meran managed to escape.

Dr. Oskar (von) Mitis (* Vienna 8 December 1909 + Vienna 3 July 1981). Attaché at the Prague legation in 1938, he remained in Prague with the German legation, as of March 1939 "*Amt des Reichsprotektors*", being responsible for liquidating the former CSR foreign ministry. From 1940 to 1942 with the representative of the Foreign Office in Copenhagen. On leave since 1943, he was dismissed in 1944.

Paul August Navé (* Vienna 15 January 1891 + Vienna 3 July 1949), counsellor in the Federal Chancellery in 1938, worked in the German Foreign Office until 1940, when he became German consul in Vinkovci (Croatia). Joined NSDAP 1 February 1940.

Dr. Heinrich Pacher (von Theinburg) (* Vienna 12 July 1889 + Salzburg 28 October 1960), Austrian minister in Moscow since since 1933, served in the German Foreign Office until 1943. Joined NSDAP 1 July 1939 (No. 7.101.439).

Dr. Otto Peter Pirkham (Pola 27 July 1905 +?) served in the Federal Chancellery in 1938. Remained in the Vienna branch of the German Foreign Office, and was attached to the German embassy with Franco in San Sebastian from September 1938 to January 1939. In the protocol department from 1939 to 1944, he became consul general in Madrid in March of 1944, where he remained after 1945. Joined NSDAP 1 July 1940 (No. 8.159.833), honorary rank of "NSKK-Obersturmführer" (1st Lieutenant).

Dr. Erhard Schiffner (* Pola 8 January 1887 + Vienna 30 July 1964), counsellor in the Federal Chancellery in 1938 and consular judge in Cairo, joined the German Foreign service on 27 March 1938. Joined NSDAP 1 January 1940 (No. 7.383.982).

Dr. Karl Schwagula (* Graz 6 February 1886 + Feldkirch 4 February 1968), consul general in the Federal Chancellery, served in the legal department of the German Foreign office in Berlin as of 22 March 1938. Joined NSDAP 1 January 1941 (No. 8.289.721).

Alfred Schwinner (* Vienna 19 February 1891 + Bodensdorf 5 February 1970), counsellor at the legation in Moscow in 1938, remained in Moscow at the German embassy. Consul in San Remo 1941-1942 and consul in Lausanne 1942, he was recalled to Berlin in October 1942.

Felix (von) Strautz (* Jerusalem 14.5.1884 + ?) was counsellor at the legation in Rome (Quirinal), later at the German embassy until October of 1940. Dismissed 1942 after lengthy illness. Joined NSDAP 1 July 1940 (No. 7.685.761), dismissed 5 April 1945.

Heinrich Graf Thun (* Tolna/Hungary 9 November 1900 + Salzburg 26 July 1971) was counsellor at the legation in Paris, where he remained with the German embassy until the outbreak of World War II. Luxemburg 1939 to 1940, Paris 1940 to 1941. Consul at the consulate general in Marseille 1942 to 1944. Interned in Dijon and later in Taormina 1944/45. Joined NSDAP 1 April 1938 (No. 6.321.111).

Hanns Winter (NSDAP-alias Walter Hengauf) (* Adrianopel/Edirne 18 July 1897 + Vienna 22 September 1961) was head of the consular office in Istanbul, where he remained until November 1938. Head of consular department of the German legation Prague until June 1939, he was chargé d' affaires in Panama from August 1939 to December 1941, when he was interned in White Sulphur Springs (USA) until his deportation to Germany. Served in Berlin until 1945. Joined NSDAP 3 March 1932 (No. 896.020); NSDAP-*Zellenleiter* Istanbul.

Peter (Freiherr von) Woinovich (* Vienna 17 October 1898 + Vienna 9 January 1955) was secretary of legation in Ankara. In Berlin from 1938 to 1940, he served as German consul in Presov (Eperjes) in Eastern Slovakia from 1940 to 1944. Joined NSDAP in March 1940 (No. 7.550.833).

Not all of the Austrian—turned—German diplomats were refused readmittance to the Austrian Foreign Service after World War II, as can be seen from the following curricula.

Maximilian (Graf von) Attems-Gilleis (*Laibach, Krain / Ljubljana, Slovenia 9 October 1892 + Vienna 1 February 1977). Joined NSDAP 1 April 1940 (No. 7.617.176); left NSDAP 1942. Re-admitted to Austrian Foreign Service 8 September 1947.

Dr. rer. pol. Karl Braunias (* Vienna 16 June 1899 + Vienna 19 August 1965) Readmitted 30 April1945.

Dr. Heinrich Calice (* Stuttgart 9 October 1909 + Vienna 26 February 1946). Joined NSDAP 1 July 1940 (No. 7.685.757) Re-admitted 5 January 1950.

Dr. Arno Halusa (* Lans/Tyrol 13 August 1911 + Vienna 26 June 1979). Re-admitted 16 December 1946.

Dr. Wolfgang Hoeller (*Rodenkirchen, Cologne 14 February 1909 + Vienna 21 December 1994) Joined NSDAP 1 August 1942. Re-admitted 17 November 1947.

Dr. Karl Hudeczek (* Josefstadt, Böhmen 15 September 1889 + Vienna 23 October 1971). Re-admitted 29 March 1949.

Dr. Wilfried Platzer (* Hafslund/Norway 5 April 1909 + Laxenburg 12 November 1981) was secretary of legation in the Federal Chancellery in 1938; he moved to Berlin, where he remained in the German Foreign until April 1945. Joined NSDAP 1 October 1940 (No. 8.185.644). Re-admitted 28 August 1947, Platzer was Secretary-General for Foreign Affairs from 1967 to 1970.

Nikolaus Schleinitz-Prokesch (* Innsbruck 25 February 1895 + Bern 5 August 1955), at the legation in Prague in 1938, where he remained until 1939. 1939-1941 counsellor at the legation in Reval (Tallinn/Estonia), 1942-1945 consul general in Madrid. Re-admitted 2 January 1950.

Karl Zeileissen (von Hergetenstein) (* Vienna 9 November 1895 + Schruns/Vlbg. 13 October 1955), counsellor in the cabinet of Guido Schmidt in 1938. Foreign Office Berlin 1938-1941, German consul in Canea (Crete) 1941-1942, in Calamata (Peloponnes) 1942-1943, head of consular department in Athens 1943-1944, German legation Agram 1944 – 1945. Re-admitted 15 July 1947.

1945-1959: The Federal Chancellery—Foreign Affairs[16]

While figthing between Soviet and German troops was still raging in some parts of Vienna, former Austrian diplomats met on 16 April 1945 at the severly damaged Ballhausplatz. Heinrich Wildner, the first secretary-general, recalls the event:

> *"... I was directed to the Red Saloon, where 30 to 40 civil servants were present. Dr. Sobek[17] made a calm, conciliatory, yet solemn statement, identified himself as illegal member of the association "Free Austria 05" and called on the civil servants to get together to prepare the readmission of civil servants. He would not know, when and how there would be a new government, however, it might arrive very shortly. Co-operation concerned only those civil servants, who had not been active Nazis. As far as 'March violets'[18] were concerned, a special order will follow. Whoever has been an ardent Nazi at the beginning, and had striven for reconciliation and compensation of damage inflicted, was invited to participate in the work.[19] Only Austrians would be taken into consideration. Whoever had been an 'illegal' was kindly asked to leave, and Sobek turned around. Nobody left however... the times required peace and reconciliation... Minister Ludwig[20] from the Federal Chancellery and Counsellor Bischoff[21] for the Foreign Affairs were charged to supervise repair work..."*[22]

By 18 April, a few diplomats were busy already to clean the former office of the minister and the antechambre. *"Apart from 8 typewriters, we organised vast amounts of paper, lexica, office material etc..."*[23].

On 27 April 1945 the Second Republic was proclaimed; in the new provisional government State Chancellor Karl Renner was responsible for the "Staatskanzlei—Amt für die Auswärtigen Angelegenheiten", until Karl Gruber was appointed "Undersecretary for Foreign Affairs" on 26 September 1945.

In the new federal government constituted on 20 December 1945, Gruber kept the foreign affairs portfolio as "Federal Minister for the Foreign Affairs". His "ministry" was nothing but the division IV "foreign affairs" in the federal chancellery. In July of 1946, division IV-foreign affairs consisted of the minister's cabinet, protocol, dept. 5 with sub-departments policy and economic policy, dept. 6 with sub-departments 6 VR (international law), 6 RS (legal protection), 6 H (displaced persons), dept. 7 (service) with two sub-departments and dept. 8 (cipher and translation), and chancery D. Altogether, six ministers plenipotentiary, an aulic councillor, a ministerial councillor, a consul general and a secretary of legation was all it took to guide Austria's foreign affairs in this starting phase after the war.

Under Gruber the Austrian foreign service was rapidly re-established; he reported to a meeting of the parliamentary finance and budget-committee on 11 November 1947:

> *"60 % of all diplomatic personnel admitted since 1945 belong to the age-group 20 to 45, reducing the average age of the diplomatic staff to 41 years. It is totally incorrect, that any kind of preference was given to certain groupings in the admission process. We could certainly have sent abroad people at random, without training, whose qualifications are unknown at present after a ten-year mess... I believe that we were right in selecting, for the time being, experienced people, in so far as they have no political record, have declared themselves as Austrians and dispose of a certain experience. In the end, it was pioneering work. All governments, which have accredited Austrian diplomats, have expressed their satisfaction that we did not send politicians... The overwhelming majority of the 60 newly admitted civil servants in the foreign service has already held positions in industry, trade unions etc. There has been no preference whatsoever in admitting these civil servants..."*[24]

Gruber forgot to mention that on 28 August 1947 Dr. Wilfried Platzer had been readmitted to the "Ballhausplatz", a former Austrian diplomat, who had served the Third Reich and had been a member of the NSDAP.

He might also have informed members of parliament of a new and more pleasant phenomenon – the first women having joined the Austrian diplomatic service. On 1 October 1947 Johanna Nestor became Austria's first woman diplomat, followed by Johanna Monschein and Sigillindis Lentner, who completed the trio by December 1947.[25]

In 1948 three diplomats started drafting a "Manual for the Austrian Foreign Service". When it was published in May 1949, Austrian diplomats for the first time since the two-volume, 2033 page manual of the Austro-Hungarian consular service of 1904 had a complete collection of all relevant ordnances and instructions.

In 1950, Austria's foreign service registered its first diplomat killed abroad in service—secretary of legation Dr. Karl Pereira, chargé d'affaires in New Delhi, was killed in a plane crash near Srinagar on 17 July.

1946-1959: Establishing Diplomatic and Consular Missions Abroad

One of the most important tasks of the government Figl I was to gain international recognition, and subsequently to establish Austrian missions abroad. In its 4th session on 22 January 1946, Chancellor Figl informed the Council of Ministers:

> *"That, as is already known from the press, the governments of the USA, Great Britain and the French government have granted the exequaturs requested for Dr. Ludwig Kleinwächter, Heinrich Schmid*[26] *and Norbert Bischoff. The agreement from Russia will be granted in the very near future... Austria already has a plenipotentiary representative in Czechoslovakia, and in view of recognition by Norway, the Netherlands and Poland it will soon be possible to send official representatives there in the near future. By establishing a direct contact with those states a giant leap forward has been made."*[27]

The Second Republic did not repeat the mistake of the First Republic and decided to establish a dense network of missions abroad as soon as circumstances would permit. This was made possible by Art. 7 of the 2nd *Kontrollabkommen* of 28 June 1946, granting the right to the Austrian Government to enter to diplomatic and consular relations with the governments of the United Nations, making establishment of diplomatic and consular relations with other governments subject to previous authorization by the Allied Council.

The first missions abroad had started operating without any involvement of the Ballhausplatz, as in many capitals "Austrian support committees" took over protection of Austrians; these were often recognized de facto by the host country, sometimes as early as in 1943 by

Brazil. *"The first operational Austrian mission seems to have been in Prague, which under former minister Marek and later Vollgruber*[28] *has rendered great service to the protection of Austrians in those turbulent times..."*[29]

Under the tenure of Karl Gruber (1945-1953) a total of 46 diplomatic and consular as well as observer missions to international organisations were established. Already in 1948, the number of missions exceeded 29, the figure of missions maintained by the First Republic in March 1938.

Diplomatic missions were established in the capitals of the Allied Powers (1946: London, Moscow, Paris, Washington) and neighbouring states (1945 Prague, 1946 – Bern, Rome, Holy See, 1947 – Belgrade, Bratislava, Budapest, Bucarest) as well as other European and overseas states and with the military governors in the Western zones of occuptation of Germany (1946 – Brussels, Warsaw, The Hague, Ankara, Rio de Janeiro, Sofia; 1947 – Buenos Aires, Cairo, New York, Stockholm; 1948 – Milan, Trieste, Zurich, Baden-Baden (closed 1952), Düsseldorf, Frankfurt (closed 1956), Santiago, Nanking/Shanghai (closed 1949); 1949 – Munich, Mexico City, New Delhi, Ottawa; 1950 – Athens, Bonn, Tel Aviv, UN Geneva, Johannesburg; 1952 – Zagreb, Berlin-West, Canberra, Istanbul; 1953 – Strasbourg / Council of Europe, Luxemburg/ECCS, New York/UN). In addition, numerous honorary consulates were opened worldwide. Although the budget for foreign affairs was always rather limited, the Ballhausplatz saw to it to acquire appropriate buildings in good neighbourhoods as offices and residences, as in Paris 1949, New York 1952 or Bonn 1954. Beginning in the 1970s, prominent Austrian architects were chosen to design office buildings and residences.[30]

The end of 1951 saw the first appointments of Austrian ambassadors since 1916. Heinrich Schmid presented his credentials as ambassador in Paris on 18 December 1951, followed by Ludwig Kleinwächter in Washington on 19 December, and Lothar Wimmer in London on 30 January 1952. Norbert Bischoff in Moscow had to wait until 27 July 1953 to present his credentials as ambassador.

Leopold Figl, who on 26 November 1953 had taken over at the helm of Austrian diplomacy, continued to expand the network of Austrian missions, particularly in Northern and Southern Europe and overseas. The task was made easier by Austria having recovered her full sovereignty in 1955. New posts included Bangkok, Pretoria, Karachi, Lisbon, Copenhagen, Oslo (1954), Beirut, Bogota, Chicago, Teheran, Tokio (1955), as well as Hamburg and Helsinki (1956).

1959- 2005: The Federal Ministry for Foreign Affairs

The elections to the Austrian parliament of 10 May 1959 brought a majority of votes for the Socialist Party (SPÖ), which however did not translate into a majority of seats in parliament, where the People's Party (ÖVP) obtained 79 (1955: 82) seats, while the SPÖ increased her seats from 74 to 78; the FPÖ (Freedom Party) obtained 8 (previously 6), the Communist Party (1955:3) was no longer represented. The result of the elections had to be reflected in the composition of the ÖVP-SPÖ coalition government, where a federal ministry held by the ÖVP had to be allotted to the SPÖ. Bruno Kreisky, a career diplomat, state secretary in the Federal Chancellery-Foreign Affairs since 1953, was offered the Finance Ministry. He was not interested—and so, *"much to the uneasiness of many, the Austrian Foreign Ministry was created in 1959 out of a division of the Federal Chancellery."*[31]

The government Raab (III), in office from 16 July 1959 to 3 November 1961, was the first since 1923 to include a "Federal Ministry for Foreign Affairs". In its first meeting on 16 July 1959, the council of ministers considered and approved a draft law on the establishment of a foreign ministry, which made no mention of the underlying political "deal". The establishment of the new ministry was considered necessary,

> *"as the tasks of Austria in the field of foreign affairs have reached such a scope and become so diverse in recent years, that it is deemed necessary to establish in Austria, as is the case in all other countries, a separate ministry to take care of foreign affairs. This measure is justified also in view of the particular problems arising from the permanent neutrality of Austria, and the need to develop, in this context, a coherent and constructive foreign policy concept..."*[32].

The law, which defined the responsibilities of the new ministry, was approved by parliament on 22 July 1959.[33] Bruno Kreisky, the new foreign minister, took office on 31 July 1959.

The youngest – and from a historical perspective oldest – Austrian ministry was made up of 4 divisions (I – Administration, II – Policy, III – Economic Policy, IV – Consular Matters) and various departments. Its civil servants consisted of the secretary-general for foreign affairs with the title ambassador, 11 ministers plenipotentiary, 15 counsellors, 15 secretaries of legation and 11 attachés. Austria in 1959 maintained 24 embassies, 16 legations, 8 consulates general, a "delegation" in West-Berlin, and missions to the UN in New York and Geneva, the Council of Europe in Strasbourg and the High Authority of the ECCS in Luxemburg. During Kreisky's tenure as foreign minister from 1959 to 1966 12 new missions, mostly in Third World countries, which had recently gained their independence, were established: 1960 – EEC-Brussels,

EFTA-Geneva, Rabat; 1961 – Jakarta, consulate Strasbourg; 1962 – Lagos; 1964 – Dakar, Addis Ababa, Caracas, Hongkong; 1965 – Nairobi; 1966 – Tunis).

In 1964, the Diplomatic Academy, successor to the Consular Academy, was established in Vienna as a post-graduate training center for Austrian and foreign diplomats and international civil servants.

In the years 1966 to 1970, the ÖVP led government decided to establish new missions in Djeddah (transferred to Riyadh in 1985), Bagdad and Dublin (1966, Bagdad being closed since 1991), Algiers (1967) and Lima (1968) as well as a consulate-general in Los Angeles, which became the political springboard for the late Austrian president Thomas Klestil.

When Kreisky became Federal Chancellor in 1970, he saw to it that responsibility for cultural matters was transferred from the ministry of education, deemed a conservative stronghold, to the foreign ministry[34], adding one division to the Ballhausplatz later numbered V.

Foreign ministers Kirchschläger, Bielka and Pahr of the SPÖ government continued expanding the network of diplomatic representatives abroad particularly in Asia and the Arab world: 1971 Peking; 1972 Kinshasa (closed 1993); 1973 East-Berlin/GDR (closed 1990), Kuala Lumpur; 1974 Tripoli, Abidjan (closed 2005), upgrading the last remaining legation in Prague to embassy; 1975 Lusaka (closed 1989); 1978 Damascus; Havana; 1980 Manila; 1982 Amman, Harare; 1983 Kuwait. The SPÖ-FPÖ–coalition established only one embassy in Seoul (1985).

In 1985, responsibility for "economic co-operation" moved from the federal chancellery to the foreign ministry, the new division being numbered VII. Competence and civil servants returned to the chancellery in 1991, reflecting changes in the distribution of political power between SPÖ and ÖVP. In 1995, economic co-operation was again transferred to the foreign ministry.

Under foreign minister Alois Mock (ÖVP) an embassy was established in Muscat (Oman) in 1989. The political changes at the end of 1989, the re-unification of Germany and the dismemberment of the Soviet Union, Jugoslavia and Czechoslovakia resulted in numerous changes in the network of Austrian diplomatic and consular missions: 1991 – consulate general Cracow, embassy in Tirana; 1992 – embassies in Lubljana, Zagreb and Kiew; 1993 – embassy in Bratislava; 1994 embassy in Guatemala City. Consulates general were established in Cape Town and Frankfurt (closed in 1997). During the tenure of Wolfgang Schüssel as Foreign Minister the following embassies were established: Sarajevo in 1996, Skopje, Tallinn, Riga, Vilnius in 1997, Saigon as well as an office in Ramallah/West Bank in 1998. In 1999 the embassy in

Germany moved to Berlin, an office remaining in Bonn. The consulate general in Düsseldorf, a consulate since 1998, was closed in 2000. In 2002 Austria opened a branch office of the Belgrade embassy in Pristina/Kosovo, and in 2003 an embassy in Abu Dhabi.

The establishment of the "Austrian Development Agency" (ADA)[35] on 1 January 2004 was the latest change in the responsibilities of the foreign ministry, as operative matters of development co-operation were transferred to ADA. Another branch office of the Belgrade embassy in Podgorica/Montenegro, run by ADA and operated jointly with Hungary is the latest addition to the Austrian diplomatic network abroad.

In February 2005 the Austrian Foreign Ministry moved from ist venerable address Ballhausplatz 2, headquarters of Austrian diplomacy[36] since 1719, and other palaces in the inner city government district, which had housed various of its divisions, to Minoritenplatz 8, a palais built in 1846/47 as Governorate of Lower Austria. From its new headquarters with its state of the art technology Austrian diplomacy seems well equipped for the challenges of the 21st century.

Notes

1. Revised version of Rudolf Agstner, "Abschied vom Ballhausplatz", *Wiener Geschichtsblätter*, vol 1/2005, 58-81.

2. Rudolf Agstner/Agathon Aerni, "Die k.u.k. Botschaft beim Heiligen Stuhl im Exil - Vom Palazzo di Venezia in die Schweiz – Eine Chronik Mai 1915-Februar 1920", in *Römische Historische Mitteilungen*, vol. 43 (Vienna: Austrian Academy of Sciences, 2001), 681-708.

3. Rudolf Agstner, "Die Leute sind sehr demokratisch"—Notizen zu 130 Jahren österreichischer Präsenz in Norwegen, *Wiener Zeitung*, Vienna, 31 July 1997, 3

4. * Prague 24 June 1852 + Vienna 11 November 1918.

5. Rudolf Agstner, "Palazzo di Venezia und Palazzo Chigi als k.u.k. Botschaften beim Heiligen Stuhl und am Königlich Italienischen Hofe 1871—1915. Samt Anhang über die Österreichischen Gesandtschaften und Botschaften in Rom 1921-1997". *Römische Historische Mitteilungen* (Vienna: Austrian Academy of Sciences, 1998), vol. 40, 489-571.

6. Agathon Aerni/Rudolf Agstner, Von k.k. Gesandtschaft zur Österreichischen Botschaft – Festschrift 150 Jahre Österreichische Botschaft Bern—Österreich(—Ungarn) und seine diplomatischen und konsularischen Vertretungsbehörden in der Schweiz und Liechtenstein, (Vienna: Occasional Paper Diplomatic Academy, 2000).

7. * Gaaden near Vienna 10 May 1876 + Vienna 27 March 1950.

8. * Karlsbad, Böhmen / Karlovy Vary, Czech Rep. 15 October 1875 + Paris 25 April 1935.

9. *St.Margarethen/Styria 31 July 1859 + Vienna 9 April 1945.

10. * Bludenz 15. January 1901 + Vienna 5 December 1957.

11. 1 Schilling corresponding to 2.80 € in 2005.

12. * Laibach, Krain /Ljubljana, Slovenia 3 November 1885 + Hinterbrühl/Mödling 19 March 1938 (suicide).

13. * Bludenz 17 January 1897 + Vienna 27 July 1939 (car accident).

14. The property of the ex-Austrian legation 2343 Massachusetts Avenue, NW, Washington, D.C., was registered on 20 April 1938, Hitler's 49th birthday, in the name of the German Reich.

15. For details to the respective careers in the German Foreign Office see *Biographisches Handbuch des deutschen Auswärtigen Dienstes 1871-1945, vols. A-F and G-K;* (Paderborn-Munich-Vienna-Zurich: Schönigh, 2000 and 2005).

16. For the beginnings of Austria diplomacy see also the essay by Günter Bischof in this volume.

17. Dr. Franz Sobek, * Brünn/Brno 29 May 1903 + Vienna 10 December 1975, Federal Chancellery-Federal Press Office, 1955-1968 Director General of Austrian State Printing Office.

18. Members who had joined the NSDAP immediately after the Anschluß in March 1938.

19. As has been outlined in the preceding chapter, this originally rather generous attitude towards former Nazis did not prevail and only few members of the NSDAP were re-admitted.

20. Eduard Ludwig * Persenbeug 9 January 1883 + Brunn bei Pitten, Erlach, Lower Austria 26 December 1967; Austrian observer, later representative to the Council of Europe, Strasbourg 1953-1958.

21. Norbert Bischoff (Edler von Klammstein) * Vienna 26 November 1894 + Schruns / Vlbg. 30 June 1960; pol. representative to France 1946, pol. repr./minister/ambassador to USSR 1947-1960.

22. Austria State Archive, KA, E/1791, estate Heinrich Wildner.

23. Josef Schöner, *Wiener Tagebuch 1944/1945* (Vienna: Böhlau 1992), 163-164.

24. During the First Republic Heimwehr politicians Baar-Baarenfels and Neustädter-Stürmer had been ministers to Hungary, Steidle had served as consul general in Trieste, MPs Frank and Tauschitz had been ministers to Berlin, ex-governor Rintelen of Styria minister to Rome. In the Second Republic, diplomats turned politicians, like Bruno Kreisky (Foreign Minister 1959-1966, Federal Chancellor 1970-1973), Kurt Waldheim (Foreign Minister 1968-1970, Federal President 1986-1992, Rudolf Kirchschläger (Foreign Minister 1970-1974, Federal President 1974-1986) or Thomas Klestil (Federal President 1992-2004), Peter Jankowitsch (Foreign Minister 1986-1987) and Alois Mock (Foreign Minister 1987-1995).

25. Johanna Nestor (* Munkacs/Slovakia 24 December 1917) was ambassador to India (1966-1970), Israel (1972-1976) and Ireland (1979-1982), Johanna Monschein (* Vienna 16 December 1907 + Vienna 14 May 1997) was minister/ambassador to Norway (1957-1965) and ambassador to Belgium ((1965-1968), Dr. Lentner (* Braunau/Upper Austria 15 September 1924) left the service in 1961 after having married in 1952 her colleague Dr. Franz Haromy (* Graz 7 April 1920 + Las Vegas, Nevada 2 February 2004), consul general in Chicago 1959-1963.

26. * Vienna 17 March 1888 + Vienna 27 November 1968; minister to France 1932-1933, to Switzerland 1933-1935, to Jugoslavia 1935-1937, to Poland 1937-1938, pol. repr./minister to the UK 1946-1950, minister/ambassador to France 1950-1953, pol. repr. in Bonn 1953-1954.

27. *Protokolle des Ministerrates der Zweiten Republik, Kabinett Leopold Figl I*, vol. I (Vienna, 2004), 67-68.

28. Alois Vollgruber, * Josefstadt, Bohemia 17 August 1890 + Vienna 29 November 1976; minister to Romania 1933-1934, Italy 1934-1936, CSR 1945-1947, France 1947-1950 and 1953-1958.

29. Josef Schöner, "Der Österreichische Diplomat", in: Karl Braunias/Gerald Stourzh, eds., *Diplomatie unserer Zeit* (Vienna, 1959), 259.

30. Karl Schwanzer (Brasilia, 1975); Leopold Boeckl (Washington, 1991), Hannes Lintl (Riyadh, 1998); Hans Hollein (Berlin, 2000); Raimund Abraham (New York cultural forum, 2002). In the First Republic, Clemens Holzmeister had designed the legation in Ankara (1934) and Karl Holey the cultural institute in Rome (1935).

31. *Bruno Kreisky, Im Strom der Politik—Der Memoiren zweiter Teil* (Berlin: Siedler, 1988), 63.

32. Protocol Nr. 1 of the session of the council of ministers, 16 July 1959, item 45 (item 29c of agenda).

33. Legal Gazette (BGBl.) Nr. 172/1959.

34. Federal Law of 9 September 1970, Legal Gazette (BGBl.) 205/70.

35. EZA-Gesetz-Novelle 2003, Legal Gazette (BGBl.) I Nr. 65/2003

36. Austrian Foreign Service based at headquarters 585, serving abroad 749.

Sources on the Diplomacy of the Ballhausplatz

Michael Gehler

The Ballhausplatz, which is located in Vienna at the eastern corner of the Volksgarten between the Hofburg and the *Bundeskanzleramt*, has for centuries been the stage for significant historical events. Just like the Quai d'Orsay, Number 10 Downing Street, or the Wilhelmstraße, it is a standing term in European diplomacy and policy. Important decisions have been made in the secret *Hof- und Staatskanzlei*, later the Ministry of the Imperial and Royal House and Foreign Affairs, today the *Bundeskanzleramt*. One is reminded of the reversal of the alliances ("*renversement des alliances*") of 1756, the reorganization of Europe ("*Konzert der Mächte*") through the Vienna Congress of 1814-1815, or the decisive ultimatum issued to Serbia in the summer of 1914 that unleashed the First World War.[1]

The Austrian foreign service was first under the authority of the *Hof- und Staatskanzlei* from 1720 to 1742, then under the secret *(Haus-,) Hof- und Staatskanzlei* from 1742 to 1848, and later, from 1848 to 1918, under the Ministry of the Imperial and Royal House and Foreign Affairs, whose formal dissolution took place in 1920.[2]

Even before the proclamation of the *Republik* "*Deutsch-Österreich*" on 12 November 1918, the "*Deutschösterreichische Staatsamt des Äußern,*" which was part of the government formed by the provisional *Nationalversammlung für Deutsch-Österreich*, had moved into the former office of Count Wenzel Anton von Kaunitz-Rietberg and Prince Klemens Lothar Wenzel von Metternich-Winneburg, which it occupied from 30 October 1918 to 14 March 1919. From then until 20 November 1920, it was known as the "*Österreichische Staatsamt für Äußeres.*" The *Bundesministerium für Äußeres* (20 November 1920 to 17 April 1923), which was created by the constitution of 1920, then fell victim to the government's austerity program,[3] which was closely linked to the Geneva loan from the League of Nations taken out by the First Republic in 1922. From then until the end of Austria as a sovereign state on 11 March 1938, the Section IV "*Auswärtige Angelegenheiten des Bundeskanzleramtes*" was in existence.[4]

Tradition and pragmatism were good reasons for this incorporation into the *Bundeskanzleramt* (BKA). The *Auswärtige Dienste* had been separated in 1848. The repeated practice of a single person serving both in the chancellor's office and as foreign minister with Rudolf Ramek (1926), Ignaz Seipel (1926-1929), Ernst Streeruwitz (1929-1930), Vice-Chancellor Johann Schober (1930-1932), Karl Buresch (1932), Engelbert Dollfuss (1932-1934), and Kurt Schuschnigg (1936) shows that in spite of the fact that the nominal title of the leading figures of the *Auswärtige Amt* was "*Bundesminister*"—with the exception of Undersecretary of State Stephan Tauschitz (1934) and Guido Schmidt (1936-1938)—foreign policy lay in the boss' domain.[5]

This method was maintained after 1945 at the beginning of the Second Republic. The *Außenamt* remained an integral part of the BKA,[6] and Karl Gruber (1945-1953) and Leopold Figl (1954-1958) were ministers in name only. Only under Bruno Kreisky in 1959 was a freestanding department, the Foreign Ministry (*Außenministerium*), created, which is still in existence today. This process is to be understood as a conscious enhancing of the status of the foreign service.

Up to the 1980s, foreign policy in Austria was a matter reserved for a small class of elites (officials, diplomats, experts from academe, party functionaries, and party politicians). After 1918, the foreign service and diplomatic corps were recruited from the old imperial bureaucracy, the new republican administration, special interest groups, and more and more from the spectrum of political parties (Christian Social and gradually also Social Democratic). At this point, it must be emphasized that it is impossible to conceive of or to understand Ballhausplatz diplomacy of the twentieth century without taking into consideration the modern Austrian multiparty federated state.[7] This state managed to structure the Foreign Ministry proportionally according to party affiliation (Austrian People's Party, ÖVP; or Social Democrats, SPÖ).[8] Members of the so-called "*Blutgruppe Null*" ("blood type zero") that is, not belonging to a party, were in the minority. Therefore, research in Austrian foreign policy must also consult party archives.

The diplomacy of the Ballhausplatz was for a long time the monopoly of the government and the officials of the Foreign Ministry. In Austrian history after 1918, foreign policy themes and decision processes were hardly a matter of parliamentary debate. Spectacular exceptions were the controversies over the question of the Anschluß with Germany, the extremely controversial ratification of the loans from the League of Nations in Geneva in 1922 and Lausanne in 1932, the hotly debated South Tyrol "package" and its Operation Calendar in 1969,[9] and the process for EU membership in 1994-1995. Austrian foreign policy was traditionally so much the prerogative of the executive[10] that for a long time it was, to a large extent, beyond the scope of parliamentary action and control.[11] From the beginning of the 1990s, a sea change took place. The question of participation in UN sanctions in the second Gulf War in 1991, the Yugoslavia crisis of the same year, the declaration settling the South Tyrol issue in 1992 (*Streitbeilegungserklärung*), and the EU membership negotiations of 1993-1994 placed foreign policy questions, earlier a fringe issue in the Alpine republic, right at the center of activity in Austrian legislative bodies.[12]

Archival Sources

Official Sources

Only in January 1999 did the safeguarding, storage, and use of the archival materials of the federal government come to be governed by law (the *Bundesarchivgesetz*), which also regulated access to the archives. Among the clauses under "Decontrol of the Archival Materials for Use, Period of Confidentiality" ("*Freigabe von Archivgut zur Nutzung, Schutzfristen*") in §8 is one ensuring that archival materials are only released after a period of thirty years from the beginning of the confidentiality period. If this release will endanger "public safety, national security, or foreign relations" or institutions of the national government, then the archival materials "are released for use only if such grounds no longer exist, at the latest, however, after a period of fifty years from the beginning of the confidentiality period."[13] Thus, for the first time in the republic, the thirty year or fifty year lack of access to archival materials has been regulated by law and has essentially been aligned with international standards.

Among the archives to which public access is granted are first and foremost the collections of the *Österreichische Staatsarchiv* in Vienna, that is, its subsidiaries, above all the *Archiv der Republik* (AdR), *Bundeskanzleramt/Auswärtige Angelegenheiten* (BKA/AA), and the *Bundesministerium für Äußeres* (BMfAA). The AdR stores foreign policy files under the "*Gruppe 01.*" Especially relevant for the period between the wars are the materials from the "*Staatsamt des Äußern*" (1918-1919), the "*Staatsamt für Äußeres*" (1919-1920), the "*Bundesministerium für Äußeres*" (1920-1923), the peace delegation to St. Germain 1918-1919, files from the "*Neue Politische Archiv*" (NPA) 1918-1938, and departments thirteen "*Personal*" ("Personnel"), fourteen "*Handelspolitik*" (HP) ("Trade Policy"), and fifteen "*Völkerrecht*" (VR) ("International Law"). For the "*Gruppe 01*" collection "*Auswärtige Angelegenheiten,*" the documents of "*Sektion II-pol*" are of particular interest. These are currently accessible in the following manner: *II-pol* covering 1945-1966 and *II-pol 2* covering 1967-1980. They are organized according to a key as follows: 1 *Staatsoberhaupt/Regierungschef* (Head of State/Head of Government), 2 *Außenpolitik (Missionen, Diplomatische Beziehungen)* (Foreign Policy [Missions, Diplomatic Relations]), 3 *Innenpolitik* (Domestic Policy), 4 *Kirche* (Church), 5 *Militaria* (Military Affairs), 6 *Medien* (Media), 7 *Personalia* (Vital Statistics), 8 *Finanzen* (Finance), 9 *Grenzen* (Borders), 10 *Minderheiten* (Minorities), 11 *Flüchtlinge* (Refugees), 12 *Kongresse* (Conferences), 13 *Restitutionen* (Restitution), 14 *Gesellschaften und Vereine* (Societies and Associations), 15 *Truppenrückzug* (Troop Withdrawal), 16 *Friedensverträge* (Peace Treaties), 17 *Vermögensfragen* (Matters Regarding Assets), 18 *Auslandsdeutsche und deutsches Eigentum* (Germans Living Abroad and German Property), 21 *österreichische Vertretungen* (Austrian Foreign Representation), and so on. The collections "*Kabinett des Ministers*" (KdM) of Minister Karl Gruber and "*Südtirol*" should also be mentioned. In addition, there is access to materials on culture policy abroad (KULT) with regard to the period 1945-1963 and the Department of Economic Policy (Wpol) for 1946-1954. The latter has restricted access only for the period 1955-1960, and from 1962 onward, it is not accessible.

A further reference is the collection of files in *Sektion V* in the *Bundeskanzleramt "ERP-Angelegenheiten"* which is accessible for the period up to 1973. Not all embassy archives are open for research yet. Among the Austrian foreign offices abroad, at least some are accessible, namely, the collections in Ankara (legation), Bucharest (legation), London (embassy), Shanghai (consulate), New York (United Nations mission), Paris (cultural institute), Sofia (legation), Madrid (Austrian-Spanish Institute), Geneva (EFTA mission), and Bratislava (legation). In particular, with regard to State Treaty questions, the vast collection of files at the Austrian Embassy in London should be mentioned here.

Since Austria was under military occupation from 1945 to 1955, the files from the former Allied Occupation Forces should be pointed out as valuable resources, especially materials from the National Archives in Washington, D.C., and College Park, Maryland, the Public Record Office in London/Kew, and the Quai d'Orsay (*Ministère des Affaires Étrangères*) in Paris as well as the *Archives de l'Occupation française en Allemagne et en Autriche* in Colmar.[14] In the ÖStA/AdR are a collection of files regarding the liaison office of the *Bundeskanzleramt* and the Allied Council in Vienna. It contains material on the individual occupied zones in Austria and touches upon questions about the relationship between the Austrian federal government and the Allied military administrations.

The situation of the material left to the *Staatsarchiv* is complicated and, thus, far from clear. In the ÖStA, it is not uniformly grouped into a single collection; rather, it is divided into different subsidiary archives. In the AdR, "*Sammlungen/Nachlässe*" is to be found under Group 09. Above all, it is worthy to mention here the material left by Eduard Ludwig, the publicist and ÖVP representative and Austrian representative to the Council of Europe. In the *Allgemeinen Verwaltungsarchiv* (AVA) are to be found materials (such as that of the imperial diplomat Johann Andreas Baron v. Eichhoff) which partially cover the period up to 1918 and partially the period after. The "*Nachlässe und Sammlungen*" were administered by the *Kriegsarchiv* are also worthy of mention. Counselor Dr. Peter Broucek was a diligent collector and meticulously stored collections of high-ranking Austrian foreign policy figures and diplomats, such as the diplomats Norbert Bischoff, Ludo Moritz Hartmann, Theodor von Hornbostel, Ferdinand Marek, and Richard Schüller; the ministers Alfred Grünberger (1923) and Heinrich Mataja (1923-1924); the ambassadors Josef Schöner and Walter Wodak; the General Secretary of the Foreign Ministry Heinrich Wildner, and others. However, these collections are still partly unavailable and partly available only with (special) permission. Those responsible for providing permission are family members or experts in the particular field, such as Professor Emeritus Gerald Stourzh (Vienna) for the Bischoff Collection, or Professor Emeritus Franz Matscher (Salzburg) for the Schöner Collection.

Specific problems with sources were and are partially responsible for the lack of foreign policy publication projects for the period after 1945. There are no concrete instructions on how to navigate through the file collection *II-pol* which has been available for some time. Files on the Council of Ministers and the corresponding passages relevant to foreign policy contained therein have only been accessible for a few years and then only with special permission. The files of the *Völkerrechtsbüro* (Office of International Law, Department I/2) (1955-1987) have only recently arrived in the *Staatsarchiv* (although, again, only in part). They were, however, for a long time generally inaccessible; in recent times, they are partially accessible. Numerous diplomats and ministers had "*Handakten,*" that is, they maintained these files at home and kept them there even after leaving office. This circumstance demonstrates the significance of papers and collections of Austrian foreign policy observers and decision makers that remain in private hands.

Files on the committees of the provisional and constitutional National Assembly dealing with foreign policy questions are held in the *Parlamentsarchiv* in Vienna. In those legislative sessions in which there was no foreign policy committee, the executive committee (plenum) of the National Assembly dealt with foreign policy matters as a rule. Very many bilateral and also multilateral international treaties were referred to the competent specialized committees for consultation. The executive committee, which had already been in charge of negotiations with the European Economic Community (EEC), has, since Austria's membership in the European Union, been responsible for exercising the rights of the National Assembly with regard to EU matters, and, with the beginning of the twenty-first Legislative Session, has installed for the first time a standing subcommittee for EU matters.

From 1924 to 1934, there was a Committee for Foreign Policy Matters (*Ausschuß für auswärtige Angelegenheiten*) in the Council of Ministers. It was reestablished in 1946, and in 1967 it absorbed the Committee for Economic Integration (*Ausschuß für wirtschaftliche Integration*), which had been established in 1960. Since 1973, it has existed as the Foreign Policy Committee (*Außenpolitischer Ausschuß*). In 1994, a committee for the EEC came into existence in the Council of Ministers, and in 1995 the Council of Ministers established an EU committee which, since 1997, has been responsible for exercising the rights of the Council of Ministers with regard to EU matters.

The official minutes of the aforementioned committees make up a part of the "*Politische Akten*" collection of the *Parlamentsarchiv*. With regard to how meaningful they are, it should be mentioned that they deal primarily with procedural material, above all applications, voting results, minutes of resolutions, lists of participants, and so on. With regard to the discussions of the executive committee of the National Assembly in EU matters, accounts are excerpted which are then being published as appendices to the stenographic minutes of the National Assembly. Like all other parliamentary material, these are available from the beginning of the Twentieth Legislative Session as complete texts on the parliament administration's website.

Private Sources

Among the most important non-national and private archives that are accessible in Austria may be counted the *Verein für Geschichte der Arbeiterbewegung* (VGA), the *Institut für Zeitgeschichte der Universität Wien* (IfZ Wien), the *Stiftung Bruno Kreisky Archiv* (StBKA), and the *Karl-von-Vogelsang-Institut* (KvVI), all of which are located in Vienna.

The VGA stores a number of significant (partial) collections of prominent personalities from the Austrian social democratic movement. The VGA has developed into a documentation center which is significant not only for the Austrian labor movement, but for European social history, as well. From the period of the party ban (1934-1945), the files that should be emphasized most are those which document activities in exile, such as the collection of the London bureau (correspondence of those who emigrated to Britain with the British Labour Party, as well as exiles in France, Sweden, Switzerland, and South America). With regard to the time period, this correspondence continued well after 1945 and originates primarily from the collection of the renowned exile and later editor-in-chief of the *Arbeiter-Zeitung* (1945-1963), Oscar Pollak. Collections of important statesmen of the Second Republic that should be mentioned include: Theodor Körner, president from 1951-1957 and Adolf Schärf, chairman of the SPÖ and vice-chancellor from 1945-1957 and president from 1957-1963. Because Schärf had a great interest in foreign policy questions and actively participated in negotiations for the State Treaty, his collection contains valuable documents for our topic.[15]

The written legacy available in the StBKA is made up of approximately 2,000 archive boxes. That corresponds to approximately two million documents, which are organized according to the following criteria: materials produced after Kreisky's resignation (1983), correspondence of the chancellor (1970-1983) (which is relevant insofar as Kreisky considered foreign policy to be his personal domain and was extremely active in its formulation), travels and state visits (1970-1983), Middle East questions, discussions on nuclear power, correspondence as Undersecretary of State for Foreign Affairs (1953-1959) and Foreign Minister (1959-1966), and materials from the Foreign Ministry (1953-1966). In addition to these collections, the StBKA, following the example of U.S. presidential libraries, holds notes and private documents of Kreisky's former ministers and close collaborators: Josef Staribacher, Hans Thalberg, Ferdinand Lacina, Wolfgang Petritsch, Ernst Lemberger, Sr., and others. In addition, the archive also stores the collections of the International Office of the SPÖ. This collection, though, is subject to special rules of use including permission, especially to view the more recent collections. A video department is being created with about 400 videos available with an emphasis on the 1960s and 1970s. An index on all films existing in Austria that are related to Kreisky is available, but it is found at a different location in the *Bruno Kreisky-Forum für den Internationalen Dialog* in Armbrustergasse. In addition, the StBKA also stores copied material from foreign archives related to Kreisky and Austria (matters regarding reduction of tension, the Middle East, and developed vs. developing nations, among others) from the former Soviet Union, the USA (National Archives, Washington, D.C.), Germany (*Bundesarchiv*, Koblenz), and Switzerland (*Bundesarchiv*, Bern). Archive material of former minister Johanna Dohnal on the International Women's Movement should also be noted. The *Bruno Kreisky-Forum für den Internationalen Dialog* stores no files, but it contains a research library on matters of international relations and the Middle East conflict which is unique, at least for Vienna.

The KvVI is a scholarly institution that deals with the reappraisal of more recent Austrian history. It represents the central archive of Christian Democratic, middle-class party politics in Austria. It collects and archives the materials of the *Christlichsozialen*, the *Österreichischen Volkspartei* (ÖVP), which has been in existence since 1945, and their leading representatives, bodies, and organizations. In the KvVI archives may be found, among other things, collections on foreign policy, European integration, economy, and foreign trade. In addition, the alignment of European Christian Democratic parties is documented, such as materials on the *Nouvelles Equipes Internationales* (NEI). Of special interest are the private paper collections and official documents of Chancellors Julius Raab (1953-1961), Alfons Gorbach (1961-1964), and Josef Klaus (1964-1970); Fritz Bock, who served as trade minister (1956-1968) (and thus was responsible for integration policy starting in 1962) and vice-chancellor (1966-1968); Karl Schleinzer, who served as minister for defense (1961-1964) and agriculture (1964-1970); Erhard Busek, who was a Central Europe policy maker, deputy mayor of Vienna (1978-1987) and vice-chancellor (1991-1995); and Ludwig Steiner, the South Tyrolean expert who also served as ambassador.

With the FPÖ, diplomatic sources are hardly to be found. The party archives have been removed from the party headquarters and are not accessible at the time of this writing. An archive collection is supposed to be assembled from the private papers of former ambassador Willfried Gredler which will include, among other information, materials on foreign policy.[16]

At the *Institut für Zeitgeschichte* (Department of Contemporary History) at the University of Vienna, there are occasional relevant collections, such as fragments of excerpts from the diaries of Ferdinand Marek, the Austrian representative in Prague, and partly unpublished, though not especially helpful, memoirs of Egon Berger-Waldenegg, who served as foreign minister (1934-1936) and envoy to Rome (1936-1938).[17] In any case, especially worthy of mention are the valuable collections covering the period from 1947 to 1969 of the ÖVP General Secretary Felix Hurdes (especially regarding NEI material), and diaries, private papers as well as official documents from Martin Fuchs, ambassador and general secretary of the Foreign Ministry (covering the period from 1947 to 1969).

The handwritten collection of the *Österreichischen Nationalbibliothek* (ÖNB) contains hardly any diplomatic or political archives. The only private papers collection known to this author is that of Kurt Waldheim, who was foreign minister (1968-1970) and federal president of Austria (1986-1992), a collection which may be viewed but not copied. It deals primarily with personal materials from Waldheim's tenure as general secretary of the United Nations (1972-1981).[18] Political and partial collections have also occasionally been placed in university institutions for research projects, such as the *Karl Gruber Archiv* (KGA) in the Department of Contemporary History (*Institut für Zeitgeschichte*) at the University of Innsbruck.[19] Private papers of national politicians are also sometimes stored in provincial archives, such as the collection of Leopold Figl, who served as chancellor (1945-1953) and foreign minister (1954-1958), which is located in the *Niederösterreichischen Landesarchiv* in St. Pölten.

Published Sources

Official Sources

It is taken for granted that Western states reappraise, document, and publish the history of their foreign policies. In Austria, foreign policy garnered the interest of the print media and entered the public consciousness more fully during the debate on EU membership in the late 1980s. With membership in the European Union in 1995, Austria underwent an increased process of Europeanization. Against this background, it is even more astonishing that, in contrast to the period between the two World Wars,[20] there is no *series* of editions on Austrian foreign policy after 1945! Such an endeavor—a multi-volume series with each volume providing an overview of an individual theme—was jointly suggested in 1996 by the General Administration of the *Österreichisches Staatsarchiv* and the *Institut für Zeitgeschichte* of the University of Innsbruck, but up until now, the project is still on ice. Restricted access to sources, limited resources, budgetary restraints, and a lack of interest have been primarily responsible for this unfortunate state of affairs.

The research of and writing on Austrian contemporary history still remains a historiography of the first half of the twentieth century. Studies with an international or comparative European dimension are lacking. Works in the area published thus far come to the same conclusion. Evidence of this is the pioneering work of the *Dokumentationsarchivs des österreichischen Widerstandes* (DÖW) on the topics of "Resistance and Persecution" ("*Widerstand und Verfolgung*") and "Exile" ("*Exil*") (1933/34-1945).[21]

Definitely important are the activities of the *Österreichischen Gesellschaft für Historische Quellenstudien* (ÖGHQ), whose staff members are primarily based at the ÖStA and have already made a name for themselves through the publication of the minutes of the Council of

Ministers of the First Republic. They have already begun the publication of the minutes of the cabinet of Renner's provisional government of 1945.[22] Further volumes on the minutes of the Council of Ministers of the Figl governments I and II (1945-1949, 1949-1953) are in progress and will also provide important evaluations and assessments of questions regarding Austrian foreign policy.

Since there is still a great lack of publications on topics of foreign policy history in Austria, within this context it is also very advisable to refer to the published volumes of *Foreign Relations of the United States* (FRUS)[23] and the *Documents Diplomatiques Français* (DDF),[24] which consist not only of informative direct information on the Allies' Austrian policy during the occupation, but also of indirect information on Austria's foreign policy. Files of the former Soviet occupation authorities are still restricted or are accessible only through informal channels. Collections from Soviet Russia on Austrian policy have so far only been opened up in a piecemeal fashion.[25] With regard to the South Tyrol question, the series of files from the Italian Foreign Ministry should also be consulted.[26]

Private Sources

While the war eras and the period between the wars have been documented at a level that ranges from good to impressive, the period after 1945 represents an editorial no man's land. A few individual initiatives are to be named, above all those publications initiated and collaborated on by the Professors Emeritus Gerald Stourzh (Vienna) and Fritz Fellner (Salzburg).[27]

There is older, but still useful, documentation originating from experts on national and international law.[28] The *Institut für Zeitgeschichte* at the University of Innsbruck has recently published editions on the policies of the first foreign minister, Karl Gruber (1945-1953), and on the South Tyrol question and has prepared an edition on Austria's relationship with the European integration process.[29] However, the department's existence was being threatened by an internal and crippling university debate on structural reform (1998-2005); thus its financial resources for the continuation of current projects and the initiation of further works have become very uncertain.

Apart from these past and humble present initiatives, there are no coordinated research projects on the foreign policy of the Second Republic. This is one expression of the fixation of Austrian contemporary history research on the interwar and Nazi periods. More recent periods, let alone the most recent history, have hardly been dealt with up to now. Critics in the field have already implied that the contemporary historians of this country have not done their "homework."[30] The foreign policy dimension of the country and Austria's perception from abroad have up to now not been documented in large-scale form, nor portrayed in the form of a monographic overview.[31]

Even though the history of the State Treaty has already been very well documented,[32] documentation based upon the relevant archival materials and government files covering the relationships to the four signatory powers of the Austrian State Treaty (the USSR, the USA, France, and Great Britain) before and after 1955 is still missing, not to mention documentation of neutrality and European policies after 1955. A cooperative project for the publication of Allied and Austrian files on the history of the State Treaty has been repeatedly proposed and discussed on the occasion of several anniversaries of and symposia on the "*annus mirabilis.*" Gerald Stourzh in particular has made efforts to achieve this end.[33] Unfortunately, this is yet to materialize, and it is to be feared that it never will. One exception is represented by the project on the history of Austrian political parties in the Second Republic (1945-1953) under the direction of Maria Mesner and Helmut Wohnout within the framework of the Jubilee Fund of the *Österreichischen Nationalbank* (OeNB) in which the relationship of the political parties (ÖVP and SPÖ) to foreign policy will be documented.[34]

There are two ongoing projects currently in progress at the *Institut für Zeitgeschichte* at the University of Innsbruck on Austria's South Tyrol policy 1945-1969.[35] One very big edition project on Austro-Israeli Relations covering thirteen volumes, financed by the Federal Ministry of Science and Culture, recently appeared, which was finished by Rolf Steininger.[36]

The editing of the collections on foreign trade policy and economic policy (Compensation Treaties 1945-1948, Organization for European Economic Cooperation [OEEC], EEC, Coordinating Committee for Multilateral Export Controls [COCOM], East Embargo, on European and integration policy, Council of Europe, European Coal and Steel Community [ECSC], Free Trade Zone, European Free Trade Association [EFTA], and European Communities{EC]), and on many other important thematic areas has continued to be left fallow until the last years. An absence of resources and a lack of interest may be held responsible for a long time.[37]

Scholarly periodicals which contain relevant articles on foreign policy history are the *Österreichische Zeitschrift für Außenpolitik* (ÖZA, edited by the *Österreichische Gesellschaft für Außenpolitik und Internationale Beziehungen*), which was initiated in 1960 and, unfortunately, ceased publication in 1980; also the *Österreichisches Jahrbuch für Internationale Politik*[38] and the *Österreichische Zeitschrift für Politik-*

wissenschaft (ÖZP), in existence since 1971; the journal *Zeitgeschichte*, in existence since 1973; and the *Österreichische Jahrbücher für Politik*, published by the *Politische Akademie*, edited by Andreas Khol, Günther Ofner, and Alfred Stirnemann. Further materials worthy of mention include the publications of the *Bundesministerium für Landesverteidigung* (BMfLV) and the *Militärwissenschaftlichen Büros* in Vienna, the *Österreichische Jahrbücher für Internationale Sicherheitspolitik*,[39] edited by Erich Reiter (representative for Strategic Studies, director of the Department of Military Sciences in the BMLV); the *Informationen zur Sicherheitspolitik*, edited by Erich Reiter and Ernest König; and the *Österreichisches Handbuch des Völkerrechts*, edited by Hanspeter Neuhold, Waldemar Hummer, and Christoph Schreurer,[40] as well as the numerous publications in scholarly journals and periodicals by the envoy Rudolf Agstner of the BMfAA in German, English, French, Arabic, and Bulgarian on the history of the Austrian foreign service, its embassies, and consulates. Together with Counselor Gertrude Enderle-Burcel and Michaela Follner of the ÖStA, Agstner is preparing a history, with biographies, of the Austrian foreign service from 1918 to 1959 that will contain a complete list of the country's representation during that period and which will appear soon.

Relevant Official Publications

Some of the official public sources are the *Jahrbuch der österreichischen Außenpolitik*, published yearly since 1979, and the annual *Außenpolitische Bericht*, which is published by the *Bundesministerium für Auswärtige Angelegenheiten* (BMfAA). The latter consists of a detailed documentation which is drawn up by the BMfAA and is confirmed by the Council of Ministers of the national government, thereby fulfilling two purposes. First, it is a report on the activities of the BMfAA to the parliamentary organs; second, it serves to inform the public about Austrian foreign policy. It makes an effort to provide a differentiated and understandable portrayal to give both the parliament and the public a broad basis for the discussion of foreign policy questions. It is the most comprehensive source of information and has the character of a reference work. Since 1988, the journal has also appeared in a parallel English version, *Austrian Foreign Policy Yearbook*.

As an example, the foreign policy report from 1993 is divided into the following sections: A) Europe, B) Vienna: Meeting Point for the Further Development of Human Rights, C) The Extra-European Area, D) International Cooperation, E) Austria and the World Economy, F) Cooperation with the Developing World, G) International Disarmament and Arms Control, H) Ecology and Energy, I) Foreign Culture Policy, J) The Humanitarian Dimension in International Relations, K) The Legal Dimension in Austrian Foreign Policy, L) Media and Information, M) The Parliament, N) The *Rat für Auswärtige Angelegenheiten*, and O) The Austrian Foreign Service. One appendix consists of information on provinces, on Austria's relationships to foreign countries, and on the diplomatic and consular corps in Austria; of a chronicle of all accredited foreign ambassadors in Vienna, of Austria's role in international organizations, of an overview of concluded treaties (bilateral and multilateral) and state visits (of Austrian statesmen to foreign countries and vice-versa), and of the category Austria in Numbers and in International Comparison (*Österreich in Zahlen und im internationalen Vergleich*). The ordering of the sections mentioned of the foreign policy report may vary according to the focus of interest in a given year. It is important also to mention the different *Außenpolitische Dokumentationen* edited by the Federal Ministry for Foreign Affairs in Vienna.[41]

Also to be pointed out is the *Jahrbuch der Diplomatischen Akademie*, which has been in existence since 1964 and which refers to diplomats trained in Vienna in the corresponding year. Yearbook number thirty-one covers the academic year 1995-1996. Yearbook number twenty-six is different in size and content from those of previous years. The political changes in Central and Eastern Europe in 1989-1990 forced the national government to make means available for the training of young diplomats from the reform states at the *Diplomatische Akademie*. In October 1990, the first two semester course of study began.[42]

Memoirs and Diaries

While there is a lack of scholarly works and editions of files on Austrian foreign policy after 1945, there are a number of memoirs from the pens of former foreign policy figures and diplomats;[43] unfortunately, diaries, which are much more authentic, are to be found only occasionally.[44] The first "memoirs" of a foreign minister written while in office brought about his ouster.[45] As a consequence, his successors have had a certain reticence and perhaps have even gone so far as to consciously leave out inopportune aspects of their biographies,[46] a phenomenon that is in no way specifically Austrian. For most of the ministers who served in the postwar period, there are memoirs and portrayals of their activities,[47] commemorative publications,[48] and non-scholarly or authorized biographies.[49] A strictly scholarly biography of an Austrian foreign minister for the period after 1945 in published form is still anticipated.[50]

Oral History Collections

Until now, oral history research in the historiography of Austrian contemporary history contains little reference to "upper-level history," that is, history centered on diplomats or the political elite, but has been more of a "lower-level history," that is, history of family, daily life, or mentality. Oral history collections on Austrian diplomacy and foreign policy with public access do not exist. Individual experts in the field have begun private collections of interviews (Günter Bischof, Oliver Rathkolb, myself). The StBKA occasionally stores taped interviews with contemporary witnesses and transcripts of them, as does the *Institut für Zeitgeschichte* at the University of Vienna. Since its first issue in 1997, the KvVI yearbook *Demokratie und Geschichte* edited by Helmut Wohnout has dedicated itself to the documentation of interviews with contemporary witnesses who were former ÖVP politicians and diplomats.[51]

Material on CD-ROM

No relevant collections are known to the author at the time of this writing in 2005.

Internet Resources

There are a number of new channels of access to be named under this category of sources. The stenographic minutes of sessions of the Council of Ministers starting from 1995 (http://www.parlinkom.gv.at/pd/pm/BR/BRSP/BRSP_gm.html) and sessions of the Parliament starting from 1996 (http://www.parlinkom.gv.at/pd/pm/XX/NRSP/NRSP_gm.html) may be accessed online, as can official documents of the BMfAA, above all speeches and press declarations (http://www.bmaa.gv.at/index.html.en). This information contains, among other things, "Press Releases/Statements from 1 January 1997 to present," "The Austrian Development Cooperation: One World for All," "*Österreich in der EU/Bilanz der österreichischen EU-Präsidentschaft (1. Juli-31. Dezember 1998)*,"[52] "Austria's European Presidency in the United States," "*aktuelle EU-Themen*," "*Österreich und die GASP*," and so on.

The *Institut für Zeitgeschichte* at the University of Innsbruck has prepared over 100 digitized sources on Austrian history in the twentieth century (http://zis.uibk.ac.at). Of interest are "Austria and European Integration 1947-1995," "The Moscow Declaration of 1943 and Allied Postwar Planning," "Allied Planning and Policies towards Austria 1940-1954," "Austria under Allied Occupation 1945-1955," "The Way to the

Austrian State Treaty," "The Waldheim Affair: A Case Study in dealing with Austria's Nazi-Past during the late 1980s," and "The Question of South Tyrol 1945-1992."

Contacts

Militärwissenschaftliches Büro des Bundesministeriums für Landesverteidigung (BMLV), Stiftgasse 2a, A-1070 Wien; phone: +43/1/520027022 or 520027021; fax: +43/1/520017112

Niederösterreichisches Landesarchiv, Landhausplatz 1, A-3109 St. Pölten; phone: +43/1/2742/2006252; fax: +43/1/2742/2006550

Österreichische Gesellschaft für Außenpolitik und Internationale Beziehungen, Hofburg, Schweizerhof/Brunnenstiege, A-1010 Wien; email: oeag@start.at

Österreichisches Staatsarchiv, Nottendorfer Gasse 2, A-1030 Wien; phone: +43/1/79540505 (reading room); fax: +43/1/79540109; e-mail: adrpost@oesta.gv.at; web address: http://www.oesta.gv.at/bestand/adr/best1.htm

Österreichischer Nationalrat, Parlamentsdirektion, Abteilung Parl./Dok./Archiv, Dr Günther Schefbeck, fax: +43/1/40110/2537; web address: http://www.parlament.gv.at or http://www.parlinkom.gv.at (Menu selection "Parlamentarische Materialien").

Verein für Geschichte der Arbeiterbewegung, Rechte Wienzeile 97, A-1050 Wien; phone: +43/1/4315457870; fax: +43/1/4315440734; e-mail: lai@m08.magwien.gv.at; web address: http://www.magwien.gv.at/ma08/vga.htm

Stiftung Bruno Kreisky Archiv, Rechte Wienzeile 97, A-1050 Wien; phone: +43/1/545753532; fax: +43/1/5453097; e-mail: archive@kreisky.vienna.at; web address: http://members.vienna.at/kreisky/

Karl von Vogelsang-Institut, Tivoligasse 73, A-1120 Wien; phone: +43/1/8142034; fax: +43/1/8154481; e-mail: kvvi@modernpoliticsor.at; web address: http://www.modernpolitics.or.at/vogelsang.htm

Österreichisches Institut für Internationale Politik (ÖIIP), Operngasse 20B, A-1040 Wien; phone: +43/1/5811106; fax: +43/1/581110610; web address: http://www.oiip.at

Institut für Zeitgeschichte der Universität Innsbruck, Innrain 52, A-6020 Innsbruck; phone: +43/512/507/4401; web address: http://www.uibk.ac.at and the "Zeitgeschichtliches Informationssystem" organized by Mag. Ingrid Böhler, web address: http://www.zis.uibk.ac.at

Institut für Zeitgeschichte der Universität Wien, Spitalgasse 2-4 (Hof 1), A-1090 Wien; phone: +43/1/427741201; fax: +43/1/42779412; e-mail: zeitgeschichte@univie.ac.at; web address: http://www.univie.ac.at zeitgeschichte

Dr Rudolf Agstner, Gesandter BMfAA- II.11 a, Ballhausplatz 2, A-1014 Wien; e-mail: rudolf.agstner@bmaa.gv.at

Österreichische Nationalbibliothek, Handschriften-, Autographen- und Nachlaßsammlung, Josefsplatz 1, Postfach 308, A-1015 Wien; e-mail: onb@email.omb.ac.at; web address: http://www.onb.ac.at

Österreichisches Außenministerium/Federal Ministry for Foreign Affairs, A-1014 Wien, Ballhausplatz 1; phone: +43/1/53115; fax: +43/1/53185-0; web address: http://www.bmaa.gv.at

Notes

1. With twenty-five illustrations and fifteen diagrams, see the volume by Adam Wandruszka and Mariella Reininghaus, *Der Ballhausplatz*, vol. 33 of Wiener Geschichtsbücher (Vienna: Paul Zsolnay, 1984); Manfried Rauchensteiner, *Der Tod des Doppeladlers: Österreich-Ungarn und der Erste Weltkrieg*, 2nd ed. (Graz: Styria, 1994).

2. Erwin Matsch, "Die Auflösung des österreichisch-ungarischen Auswärtigen Dienstes 1918/20," *Mitteilungen des Österreichischen Staatsarchivs* 30 (1977): 288-316; idem, *Der Auswärtige Dienst von Österreich (-Ungarn) 1720-1920* (Vienna: Böhlau, 1986). For a social history of the Ballhausplatz, see William D. Godsey, Jr, *Aristocratic Redoubt: The Austro-Hungarian Foreign Office on the Eve of the First World War* (West Lafayette, IN: Purdue Univ. Press, 1999).

3. Rudolf Agstner, "Vom Hausherrn zum Untermieter - Sparpaket vor 75 Jahren war das Aus 'für Bundesministerium für Äußeres,'" *Wiener Zeitung*, 11 April 1998, p. 3. Rudolf Agstner from the Federal Ministry of Foreign Affairs has worked on a large collection of data concerning Austrian diplomats and the history of Austrians embassies. He intends to publish his materials as an encyclopedia. See also his essay in this volume.

4. See the comprehensive work by Martha Maria Giefing, *Die Organisation des österreichischen Auswärtigen Dienstes in den Jahren 1918 bis 1938*, Ph.D. diss, University of Vienna, 1990, 43-66, here 63. Another comprehensive work is that of Arnold Suppan, *Jugoslawien und Österreich 1918-1938: Bilaterale Außenpolitik im europäischen Umfeld* (Vienna: Verlag für Geschichte und Politik/Oldenbourg, 1996), which can be designated as a history of Austrian foreign policy for this period.

5. The author is grateful to Thomas Angerer, University of Vienna, for some helpful information (24 August 1999); Giefing, *Die Organisation des österreichischen Auswärtigen Dienstes in den Jahren 1918 bis 1938*, 62-63.

6. Klaus Fiesinger, *Ballhausplatz-Diplomatie 1945-1949. Reetablierung der Nachbarschaftsbeziehungen und Reorganisation des Auswärtigen Dienstes als Formen außenpolitischer Reemanzipation Österreichs* (Munich: tuduv, 1993), 65-94.

7. Ernst Hanisch, *Der lange Schatten des Staates. Österreichische Gesellschaftsgeschichte im 20. Jahrhundert*, 2nd ed., Österreichische Geschichte 1890-1990, ed. Herwig Wolfram (Vienna: Ueberreuther, 1995).

8. Günter Bischof, "Spielball der Mächtigen? Österreichs außenpolitischer Spielraum im beginnenden Kalten Krieg," in *Inventur 45/55. Österreich im ersten Jahrzehnt der Zweiten Republik*, ed. Wolfgang Kos and Georg Rigele (Vienna: Sonderzahl, 1996), 126-56.

9. See also Reinhard Meier-Walser, *Die Außenpolitik der monocoloren Regierung Klaus in Österreich 1966-1970* (Munich: tuduv, 1988).

10. Heribert F. Köck, "Die Rolle des Parlaments in der Außenpolitik," in *Parlamentarismus und öffentliches Recht in Österreich. Entwicklung und Gegenwartsprobleme*, 2nd partial volume, ed. Herbert Schambeck (Berlin: Duncker & Humblot, 1993), vol. 1, 297-396, here 297.

11. See also Renate Kicker, Andreas Khol, and Hanspeter Neuhold, eds., *Außenpolitik und Demokratie in Österreich: Strukturen, Strategien, Stellungnahmen, Ein Handbuch* (Salzburg: Neugebauer, 1983); Hanspeter Neuhold and Paul Luif, eds., *Das Außenpolitische Bewußtsein der Österreicher. Aktuelle internationale Probleme im Spiegel der Meinungsforschung* (Laxenburger Internationale Studien 4) (Vienna: Braumüller, 1992).

12. Helmut Wohnout, "Die Mitwirkungsrechte des österreichischen Parlaments an der Willensbildung in der EU," *Die Union. Vierteljahreszeitschrift für Integrationsfragen* 1 (1999): 69-80, here 69.

13. Federal Law: Bundesarchivgesetz, National Assembly, XX. Legislative Session, government submission (1897 of the Supplement to the Stenographic Minutes of the National Assembly), 4; Report of the Constitutional Committee (2030 of the Supplement to the Stenographic Minutes of the National Assembly, XX. Legislative Session), 8.

14. See the articles by Robert Wolfe, "Records of U.S. Occupation Forces in Austria, 1945-1955"; Robert Knight, "The Main Records of the Public Record Office for Post-War Austria"; Klaus Eisterer, "Die französischen Archivalien zur Nachkriegsgeschichte Österreichs (1945-1955)," in *Die bevormundete Nation. Österreich und die Alliierten 1945-1949*, ed. Günter Bischof and Josef Leidenfrost (Innsbrucker Forschungen zur Zeitgeschichte 4) (Innsbruck: Haymon, 1988), 415-32, 427-32, 433-45; updated, refined, and much expanded for France: Jürgen Klöckler, "Quellen zu Österreichs Nachkriegsgeschichte in französischen Archiven. Tirol, Vorarlberg und Wien nach dem Zweiten Weltkrieg," *Montfort. Vierteljahresschrift für Geschichte und Gegenwart Vorarlbergs* 48.1 (1996): 7-82. Eisterer's and Klöckler's contributions are limited because the archival file numbers have been changed! See the most recently appearing monograph by Günter Bischof, *Austria in the First Cold War, 1945-1955: The Leverage of the Weak* (London: St. Martin's, 1999) with the latest literature and research on the topic on Austria and the Cold War.

15. Archiv der österreichischen Arbeiterbewegung. Verein zur Geschichte der Arbeiterbewegung (VGA), Documentation 3/97.

16. Information from Lothar Höbelt, University of Vienna, 27 September 1999.

17. Now published as Egon Berger von Waldenegg and Heinrich Berger-Waldenegg, *Biographie im Spiegel: Die Memoiren zweier Generationen*, ed. Georg Christoph Berger-Waldenegg (Vienna: Böhlau, 1998).

18. Information from ÖNB/ Handwritten, Autograph, and Private Collection, Counselor Dr Eva Irblich, 22 September 1999; See also: Das Dr. Kurt Waldheim-Archiv. Die Archivbestände des Generalsekretärs der Vereinten Nationen in der Österreichischen Nationalbibliothek, Wien 1998.

19. See the generally helpful reference work by Gerhard Renner, *Die Nachlässe in den Bibliotheken und Museen der Republik Österreich. Ausgenommen die österreichische Nationalbibliothek und das österreichische Theatermuseum* (Vienna: Böhlau, 1993), with more details on the Gruber collection, 142-3. The availability of these private papers are connected with a ongoing research project at the Institute of Contemporary History. When this project is finished, the files will all be accessible.

20. See Klaus Koch, Walter Rauscher, and Arnold Suppan, eds., *Die Außenpolitischen Dokumente der Republik Österreich 1918-1938 (ADÖ)*, Vol. 1, Selbstbestimmung der Republik 21. Okt. 1918 - 14. März 1919; Vol. 2, Im Schatten von Saint-Germain 15. März 1919 - 10. September 1919; Vol. 3, Österreich im System der Nachfolgestaaten 11. September 1919 - 10. Juni 1921; Vol. 4, Zwischen Staatsbankrott und Genfer Sanierung 11. Juni 1921 - 6. November 1922; Vol. 5, Unter der Finanzkontrolle des Völkerbundes 7. November 1922 bis 15. Juni 1926; Jahre der Souveränität 16. Juni 1926 bis 11.

Februar 1930 (in press) (Vienna: Verlag für Geschichte und Politik/Oldenbourg, 1993-2002). For the period before 1918, see Österreich-Ungarns Außenpolitik von der Bosnischen Krise 1908 bis zum Kriegsausbruch 1914. Diplomatische Aktenstücke des Österreichisch-Ungarischen Ministeriums des Äußeren, selected and edited by Ludwig Bittner and Hans Uebersberger Band 1-9, (Wien/Leipzig 1930) (Veröffentlichungen der Kommission für Neuere Geschichte Österreichs 19-27), Vol. 1-9, (Vienna – Leipzig 1930 ff.)

21. New publications of the Dokumentationsarchivs des österreichischen Widerstandes are to be found regularly in the *Mitteilungen of the DöW*/Vienna.

22. Österreichischen Gesellschaft für historische Quellenstudien, ed., *Protokolle des Kabinettsrates der Provisorischen Regierung Karl Renner 1945*; Vol. 1, "[. . .] im eigenen Haus Ordnung schaffen." Gertrude Enderle-Burcel, Rudolf Jerábek, and Leopold Kammerhofer, eds., *Protokolle des Kabinettsrates 29. April bis 10. Juli 1945*; Vol. 2: Protokolle des Kabinettsrates 17. Juli 1945 bis 5. September 1945; Vol 3: Protokolle des Kabinettsrates 12. September 1945 bis 17. Dezember 1945, ed. Peter Mähner (Vienna: Verlag Berger, 1995-2003). The edition of the Reports of the Austrian Ministers Council after 1945 is prepared by the Österreichische Gesellschaft für historische Quellenkunde (ÖGfHK) under direction of Gertrude Enderle-Burcel from the Austrian State Archive. The first volume just appeared: Protokolle des Ministerrates der Zweiten Republik, Kabinett Figl I, 20. Dezember 1945 bis 8. November 1949, Vol. 1: 20. Dezember 1945 bis 9. April 1946, ed. Gertrude Enderle-Burcel and Rudolf Jerábek, selected by Peter Mähner und Walter Mentzel (Vienna 2004).

23. For references to Austria, see, for example, *Foreign Relations of the United States 1949*, Vol. III, Council of Foreign Ministers, Germany and Austria, Washington DC, 1974.

24. For a major reference to Austria, see, for example, *Documents Diplomatiques Français* 1955, Vol. I (1 janvier-30 juin), Paris, 1987.

25. Gerald Stourzh was able to view the Soviet-Russian files in the Foreign Policy Archives of the Russian Federation (Archiv Vnesney Politiki Rossiyskoy Federacii [AVPRF]) and make use of them for his reference work, *Um Einheit und Freiheit. Staatsvertrag, Neutralität und das Ende der Ost-West-Besetzung Österreichs 1945-1955*, 4th ed. (Vienna: Böhlau, 1998).

26. For many references to South Tyrol, see for example: *I documenti diplomatici italiani (DDI)*, Tenth Series: 1943-1948, Volume IV (1946-1947), Rome, 1996.

27. Eva-Marie Csáky, ed., *Der Weg zu Freiheit und Neutralität. Dokumentation zur österreichischen Außenpolitik 1945-1955* (series from the Österreichischen Gesellschaft für Außenpolitik und Internationale Beziehungen 10) (Vienna: Braumüller, 1980); Reinhold Wagnleitner, ed., *Diplomatie zwischen Parteiproporz und Weltpolitik. Briefe, Dokumente und Memoranden aus dem Nachlaß Walter Wodaks 1945-1950* (bibliography for 19th and 20th Century History, edited by Fritz Fellner, 3) (Salzburg: Verlag Wolfgang Neugebauer, 1980); idem., ed., *Understanding Austria: The Political Reports and Analyses of Martin F. Herz, Political Officer of the U.S. Legation in Vienna, 1945-1948* (bibliography for 19th and 20th Century History, edited by Fritz Fellner, 4) (Salzburg: Verlag Wolfgang Neugebauer, 1984); in addition, the individual initiatives of Alfons Schilcher, ed., *Österreich und die Großmächte. Dokumente zur österreichischen Außenpolitik, 1945-1955* (*Materialien zur Zeitgeschichte* 2), (Vienna, Salzburg: Edition Geyer, 1980) [and the critical review of Schilcher by Gerald Stourzh, in: *Mitteilungen des Österreichischen Staatsarchivs* 36 (1983), 434-440]; Oliver Rathkolb, ed., *Gesellschaft und Politik am Beginn der Zweiten Republik. Vertrauliche Berichte der US-Militäradministration aus Österreich 1945 in englischer Originalfassung* (Vienna:

Böhlau, 1985); as well as the partial edition published by Robert Knight, *"Ich bin dafür die Sache in die Länge zu ziehen." Die Wortprotokolle der österreichischen Bundesregierung von 1945 bis 1952 über die Entschädigung der Juden* (Frankfurt: Äthenaum, 1988), which was broadly covered in the media and, thus, widely diffused to the public, although in academic circles it was not without controversy. For this, see Thomas Albrich, "Heiligt der Zweck die Mittel? Anmerkungen zu Robert Knights Auswahledition der Wortprotokolle der österreichischen Bundesregierung von 1945 bis 1952 über die Entschädigung der Juden," *Innsbrucker Historische Studien* 10/11 (1988): 407-11.

28. For Austria's international role and its integration policy, see Stephan Verosta, *Die internationale Stellung Österreichs 1938 bis 1947: Eine Sammlung von Erklärungen und Verträgen aus den Jahren 1938 bis 1947* (Vienna: Manz, 1947); Heinrich Siegler, *Austria: Problems and Achievements, 1945-1963* (Bonn: Verlag für Zeitarchive, n.d.); Heinrich Siegler, *Austria: Problems and Achievements since 1945* (Bonn: Verlag für Zeitarchive, 1969); Heinrich Siegler, *Dokumentation der Europäischen Integration 1946-1961, unter besonderer Beachtung des Verhältnisses EWG - EFTA* (Bonn: Verlag für Zeitarchive, 1961); Heinrich Siegler, *Österreichs Souveränität, Neutralität, Prosperität* (Bonn: Verlag für Zeitarchive, 1967); Hans Mayrzedt and Waldemar Hummer, eds., *20 Jahre österreichische Neutralitäts- und Europapolitik (1955-1975): Dokumentation*, 2 vols., Österreichische Gesellschaft für Außenpolitik und Internationale Beziehungen 9 (Vienna: Braumueller, 1976); Gerhard Kunnert, *Spurensicherung auf dem österreichischen Weg nach Brüssel* (Europa series from the Bundeskanzleramt, special volume) (Vienna: Österreichische Staatsdruckerei, 1992); Michael Gehler and Rolf Steininger, eds., *Österreich und die europäische Integration 1945-1993. Aspekte einer wechselvollen Entwicklung*, Institut für Zeitgeschichte, University of Innsbruck, European Integration Working group, Historical Research 1 (Vienna: Böhlau, 1993); Michael Gehler and Rolf Steininger, eds., *Die Neutralen und die europäische Integration 1945-1995/The Neutrals and the European Integration 1945-1995*, Institut für Zeitgeschichte, University of Innsbruck, European Integration Working group, Historical Research 3 (Vienna: Böhlau, 2000); Michael Gehler, Wolfram Kaiser, and Helmut Wohnout, eds., *Christian Democracy in Twentieth Century Europe*, Institut für Zeitgeschichte, University of Innsbruck, European Integration Working group, Historical Research 4 (Vienna: Böhlau, 2001); Michael Gehler, *Finis Neutralität? Historische und politische Aspekte im europäischen Vergleich: Irland, Finnland, Schweden, Schweiz und Österreich*, Center for European Integration Studies, Rheinische Friedrich-Wilhelms-Universität Bonn C 92 (Bonn, 2001).

29. Michael Gehler, ed., *Karl Gruber: Reden und Dokumente, 1945-1953, Eine Auswahl*, Institut für Zeitgeschichte, University of Innsbruck, European Integration Working group, Historical Research 2 (Vienna: Böhlau 1994); Michael Gehler, ed., *Verspielte Selbstbestimmung? Die Südtirolfrage 1945/46 in US-Geheimdienstberichten und österreichischen Akten. Eine Dokumentation*, Schlern-Schriften 302 (Innsbruck: Universitaetsverlag Wagner, 1996); and Rolf Steininger, ed., *Südtirol im 20. Jahrhundert. Dokumente* (Innsbruck: Studienverlag, 1999); and the three large volumes by Rolf Steininger, ed., *Südtirol zwischen Diplomatie und Terror 1947-1969*, Südtiroler Landesarchiv Vol. 6/1-3 (Bolzano: Athesia, 1999); Günter Bischof, Anton Pelinka, Michael Gehler, eds., *Austria in the European Union, vol. 10, Contemporary Austrian Studies* (New Brunswick, NJ: Transaction, 2002); Michael Gehler, *Der lange Weg nach Europa. Österreich vom Ende der Monarchie bis zur EU* (Vol. 1: Monograph); Michael Gehler, *Der lange Weg nach Europa. Österreich von Paneuropa bis zum EU-Beitritt* (Vol. 2: Documents) (Innsbruck: Studienverlag, 2002).

30. Thomas Angerer, "An Incomplete Discipline: Austrian *Zeitgeschichte* and Recent History," in *Austria in the Nineteen Fifties, vol. 3, Contemporary Austrian Studies*, ed. Günter Bischof and Anton Pelinka (New Brunswick, NJ: Transaction, 1994), 207-51; for the situation of Austrian contemporary history see, Michael Gehler, *Zeitgeschichte im dynamischen Mehrebenensystem. Zwischen Regionalisierung, Nationalstaat, Europäisierung, internationaler Arena und Globalisierung* (Bochum: Winkler, 2001), 37-71.

31. See the modern overview by Ernst Hanisch, *Der lange Schatten des Staates. Österreichische Gesellschaftsgeschichte im 20. Jahrhundert*, 2nd ed., Österreichische Geschichte 1890-1990, ed. Herwig Wolfram (Vienna: Ueberreuther, 1995). In this work, the foreign policy dimension is almost completely missing.

32. See the work by Stourzh, *Um Einheit und Freiheit*, with the detailed, revised, and refined appendix of documents, 607-779, especially the new edited diaries of Josef Schöner during the State Treaty negotiations in Moscow should be mentioned here 615-666.

33. The author is grateful to Thomas Angerer, University of Vienna for helpful information, 7 September 1999.

34. Contact address: Projekt Quellenedition zur österreichischen Parteiengeschichte der Zweiten Republik, Renner-Institut, Khleslplatz 12, A- 1120 Wien, Phone: ++43/1/804650139.

35. Under the direction of Michael Gehler: "Österreichische Südtirolpolitik vom Gruber-De Gasperi-Abkommen und seiner Vorgeschichte bis zum 'Los von Trient' 1945/46-1957/58," and under the direction of Rolf Steininger: "Vom österreichischen Gang vor die UNO bis zur Paketlösung 1959-1969." Project assistants were Evi-Rosa Unterthiner, Eva Pfanzelter, Sabine Falch and are now Harald Dunajtschik and Sabine Pitscheider.

36. Rolf Steininger, ed., *Berichte aus Israel*, 13 vols. (Munich: Olzog, 2004).

37. In the meantime, Herbert Matis and Dieter Stiefel (University of Vienna) have started a comparative European research project on embargo policies *vis-à-vis* the Middle and Eastern European countries in the first Cold War. Information by Andreas Resch, 10 September 2003.

38. See, for example, the since 1983 existing *Österreichisches Jahrbuch für Internationale Politik* 19 (2002) (Vienna: Braumueller, 2002), edited by the Österreichische Gesellschaft für Außenpolitik und Internationale Beziehungen, Hofburg, Schweizerhof/Brunnenstiege, 1010 Wien and the Österreichisches Institut für Internationale Politik, Operngasse 20 B, 1040 Wien. See also oeag@start.at.

39. Erich Reiter, ed., *Jahrbuch für internationale Sicherheitspolitik 2001* (Hamburg: Verlag E.S. Mitter & Sohn, 2002).

40. Hanspeter Neuhold, Waldemar Hummer, and Christoph Schreuer, eds., *Österreichisches Handbuch des Völkerrechts*, , Vol. 1: Textteil; Vol. 2: Materialienteil, 3rd.ed. (Vienna: Manz, 1997).

41. Österreichische außenpolitische Dokumentation. Texte und Dokumente, edited by the Bundesministerium für Auswärtige Angelegenheiten (1990-1997) and then *Außenpolitische Dokumentation. Texte und Dokumente*, edited by the Bundesministerium für Auswärtige Angelegenheiten (1998-). These documents focus on special subjects like the Yugoslavian crisis in 1991 or Austria's EU presidency in 1998. See also Kurt Richard Luther and Iain Ogilvie, eds., *Austria and the European Union Presidency: Background and Perspectives* (The Royal Institute of International Affairs: Keele European Research Center, 1998). See also the Working Papers of the Österreichisches Institut für Internationale Politik, recently "Ungleiche Brüder." Österreich und Deutsch-

land 1945 bis 1965 (Arbeitspapier 38/Dezember 2001).

42. See also the impressive "Festschrift" by Oliver Rathkolb, ed., *250 Jahre Von der Orientalischen zur Diplomatischen Akadmie in Wien/250 Years From the Oriental to the Diplomatic Academy in Vienna* (Innsbruck: Studienverlag, 2004).

43. Clemens Wildner, *Von Wien nach Wien* (Vienna: Herold, 1961); Walter Wodak, *Diplomatie zwischen Ost und West* (Graz: Styria, 1976); Karl Czernetz, *Europäer und Sozialist. Reden und Aufsätze* (Vienna: Verlag der Wiener Volksbuchhandlung, 1980); Colienne Meran-Schwarzenberg, ed., *Johannes Prinz zu Schwarzenberg. Gedanken und Erinnerungen. Niedergeschrieben für meine Kinder und Enkel* (Klagenfurt: Eigenverlag, 1981); Fritz Kolb, *Es kam ganz anders. Betrachtungen eines alt gewordenen Sozialisten* (Vienna: Oesterreichischer Bundesverlag, 1981); Hans J. Thalberg, *Von der Kunst Österreicher zu sein: Erinnerungen und Tagebuchnotizen* (Vienna: Böhlau, 1984); Otto Pleinert, *Diplomat und Civil Servant. Erinnerungen eines österreichischen Staatsdieners 1958 bis 1993* (Vienna: Böhlau, 1994); Otto Eiselsberg, *Erlebte Geschichte 1919-1997* (Vienna: Böhlau, 1997); Heinrich Pfusterschmid-Hardtenstein, *Kleinstaat – Kleinstaat?* (Vienna: Böhlau, 2001); Albert Rohan, *Diplomat am Rande der Weltpolitik. Begegnungen, Beobachtungen, Erkenntnisse* (Vienna: Molden, 2002).

44. Partly excerpts from diaries in: Lothar Wimmer, *Zwischen Ballhausplatz und Downing Street* (Vienna: Verlag Georg Fromme, 1958); Josef Schöner, *Wiener Tagebuch 1944/45*, ed. Eva-Marie Csáky, Franz Matscher, and Gerald Stourzh (Vienna: Böhlau, 1992).

45. Karl Gruber, *Zwischen Befreiung und Freiheit. Der Sonderfall Österreich* (Berlin: Ullstein, 1953).

46. Kurt Waldheim, *Im Glaspalast der Weltpolitik*, 2nd ed. (Düsseldorf: Econ, 1985); Kurt Waldheim, *Die Antwort* (Vienna: Amalthea, 1996).

47. Kurt Waldheim, *Der österreichische Weg. Aus der Isolation zur Neutralität* (Vienna: Molden, 1971); Bruno Kreisky, *Zwischen den Zeiten. Erinnerungen aus fünf Jahrzehnten* (Berlin: Siedler/Kremayr & Scheriau, 1986); Idem, *Im Strom der Politik. Der Memoiren zweiter Teil* (Berlin: Siedler/Kremayr & Scheriau, 1988); Matthew Paul Berg, ed., with Jill Lewis and Oliver Rathkolb, *The Struggle for a Democratic Austria: Bruno Kreisky on Peace and Social Justice*, trans. Helen Atkins and Matthew Paul Berg (New York: Berghahn Books, 1999); Lujo Tonćić-Sorinj, *Erfüllte Träume. Kroatien – Österreich – Europa* (Vienna: Amalthea, 1982); Karl Gruber, *Meine Partei ist Österreich. Privates und Diplomatisches* (Vienna: Amalthea, 1988); Alois Mock, *Heimat Europa. Der Countdown von Wien nach Brüssel* (Vienna: Edition S, Verlag Österreich, Oesterreichische Staatsdruckerei, 1994); Rudolf Martins, *Von der Souveränität zur Globalisierung im Erlebnis eines Diplomaten. Wien – Zürich – Genf – Zagreb* (Vienna: Böhlau, 1998).

48. As an example, see Erhard Busek, Andreas Khol, and Heinrich Neisser, eds., *Politik für das dritte Jahrtausend. Festschrift für Alois Mock zum 60. Geburtstag* (Graz: styria medienservice, 1994).

49. Susanne Seltenreich, *Leopold Figl – Ein Österreicher* (Vienna: Erwin Metten Betriebsgesellschaft, 1962); Ernst Trost, *Figl von Österreich* (Vienna: Molden, 1972).

50. This was true even while I was in the process of working for publication of my successfully defended postdoctoral dissertation 'Habilitation': Vom Telegraphenamt zum Ballhausplatz: Karl Gruber und die österreichische Außenpolitik bis zum Scheitern der Staatsvertragsverhandlungen 1927-1949," Habil., University of Innsbruck, 1999. This work still needs to be expanded, though, to include the years 1950-1953. An overview of Austrian foreign policy from 1945 to the present which should provide a compre-

hensive illustration of the state of research is offered by Michael Gehler, *Österreichs Außenpolitik der Zweiten Republik. Von der alliierten Besatzung bis zum Europa des 21. Jahrhunderts* (Innsbruck: Studienverlag, 2005).

51. Helmut Wohnout, ed., *Demokratie und Geschichte. Jahrbuch des Karl von Vogelsang-Instituts zur Erforschung der Geschichte der christlichen Demokratie in Österreich 1-6 (1997-2002)* (Vienna: Böhlau, 1997-2003). I had the opportunity to prepare and organize the eye witness talks together with Wohnout for the first five volumes.

52. Alexander Schallenberg and Christoph Thun-Hohenstein, *Die EU-Präsidentschaft Österreichs. Eine umfassende Analyse und Dokumentation des zweiten Halbjahres 1998*, Dr. Herbert Batliner Europainstitute 1 (Vienna: Manz, 1999).

II: Late Habsburg and First Republic Foreign Policy

The Militarization of Austrian Foreign Policy on the Eve of World War I

Günter Kronenbitter

It was Austria-Hungary, the least of the traditional Great Powers in terms of economic and military might, that triggered the third Balkan war and thereby provoked the outbreak of World War I. Explanations vary, with some historians blaming domestic reasons and others focusing more on the international context.[1] When it comes to analyzing this fateful decision, the military leadership tends to be among the usual suspects. Little wonder: relentlessly lobbying for preventive war against unruly neighbors like Italy and Serbia, the chief of the General Staff, Franz Conrad von Hötzendorf, provides historians with an outstanding example of a warmongering social Darwinist, even according to pre-1914 top brass' standards. But as a closer look at the social position and the self-image of the military elite and its strictly limited influence on the political process within the Dual Monarchy reveals, the way to hell wasn't paved with the military's good or bad intentions. Austria-Hungary's stand in the July Crisis was shaped by structural shifts in professional military risk assessment and by the rise of "militant diplomacy" in 1912 and 1913.[2] The latter was not the result of Conrad and his colleagues' machinations, but the politicians' preferred method of dealing with a changed situation in a system of international relations increasingly dominated by arms races and political instability. It took this shift in the Foreign Office's notion of security and the dilemma of military professionalism to make diplomats and soldiers opt for war in July 1914. In order to understand the decisions made in 1914, the emergence, the constraints, and the results of this militarization of foreign policy have to be taken into account.

The Habsburgs had not shied away from waging war whenever it was deemed necessary to defend or to expand their realm. In the eighteenth century, the dynasty's hereditary holdings saw sweeping changes in the recruitment of soldiers, the organizational structure of the army, and the training of officers. All in all, Austria emulated the example of other European powers and combined modernization and militarization.[3] The close ties between the armed forces and the dynasty were reinforced in the nineteenth century. Archduke Carl and Archduke Albrecht were successful field commanders in 1809 and 1866 respectively, and male Habsburgs were supposed to become officers. The army saved the Habsburgs from invasion by Piedmont, revolutionary uprisings in Bohemia and Vienna, and the Hungarian forces fighting for independence in 1848-1849. After the military debacles at Solferino and Königgrätz, the military did not lose its special relationship with the Habsburgs. As the *Ausgleich*, the Compromise of 1867, changed the constitutional foundations of the Habsburg Empire, the common army and navy became the backbone of centripetal forces in the Dual Monarchy. Loyalty to Franz Joseph, the emperor/king, and the popularity of military ceremonies and apparel quite often went hand in hand. Universal conscription and the establishment of a reserve officer corps made sure that Austria-Hungary would see the same kind of widespread adoption of military norms and practices in society as elsewhere in Europe. To blend militarism and nationalism as in France or Germany was anathema to the elites running the foreign and military affairs of the Habsburg Monarchy. But this did not preclude new forms of preparations for modern warfare, affecting society as a whole, such as economic emergency plans. The militarization of state and society in Austria-Hungary, incomplete yet on the rise, followed a European trend, and to some extent, the same holds true for militarism.[4]

Franz Joseph had a keen interest in the army, and as an untiring reader of files, he kept track of many details concerning the armed forces, from minor changes of the shapes or colors of uniforms to the War Ministry's budget. But he was also well aware of diplomacy and international relations. By tradition, foreign affairs were the most prestigious and arcane part of politics. It is not surprising that, in the absence of the monarch, the minister of foreign affairs, as a *primus inter pares*, conducted the meeting of the Common Ministerial Council. Foreign affairs and the command of the armed forces were the sole prerogative of the monarch. The Compromise of 1867 didn't challenge the monarch's central position in the decision-making process in these areas of policy. In questions of war and peace, neither the parliaments in Budapest and Vienna nor their delegations had a say. To be sure, the Common Ministerial Council, consisting of the prime ministers of

Austria and Hungary (sometimes their finance ministers, too) and the three common ministers for foreign affairs, war, and common finances, advised the monarch. But most of all, the Emperor would give those who where in charge of any military or civilian top position leeway to run their branch of the state apparatus. If Franz Joseph disagreed with one of them or if he wanted to try a different tack, he would replace the office holder. Staff policy and changes of direction went hand in hand. In the meantime, Franz Joseph took care that each of his ministers and high-ranking officials would keep within his proper sphere of competence.[5]

Archduke Franz Ferdinand, Austria-Hungary's heir apparent to the throne, favored a completely different approach to leadership. In foreign or domestic affairs, he did not have much clout, but in the military forces, he held official posts and was appointed General Inspector of the armed forces in 1913. His military chancellery offered to him an institutional platform to launch political campaigns. He and his staff watched over domestic politics and tried to make and break careers in government, civil administration, and the military according to Franz Ferdinand's judgement regarding the loyalty and reliability of office-holders and seekers. The Belvedere circle, as the Archduke and his faithful followers came to be known, often publicly attacked ministers appointed by Franz Joseph or privately conspired against them. Franz Ferdinand was deeply convinced that the Habsburg Monarchy would go down the drain if the centrifugal forces of nationalist strife and constitutional quarrelling were not reined in as soon as possible. In Franz Ferdinand's mind, the Hungarian political elite posed the biggest threat to the Monarchy's existence, followed by nationalism in the hereditary lands and by socialism. It is wrong to think of Franz Ferdinand as a protector of the Slavs and an ardent federalist who would have rescued Austria-Hungary by implementing a wide-ranging constitutional reform if he had not been killed at Sarajevo in 1914. He desperately tried to reduce the influence of the Hungarian political elite, the liberals, the Protestants, and the Jews. Resentment, not reform, shaped Franz Ferdinand's political mind-set. But at the same time, his reactionary leanings induced him to oppose an armed clash with Russia—a farsighted view of foreign policy, inspired by a nostalgic longing for solidarity among the conservative monarchies in Europe.[6]

Franz Ferdinand was glad when in 1906 younger and more energetic office holders were promoted to leading positions in the foreign policy and military apparatus. Franz von Schönaich, the new minister of war, was expected to push through an army reform; Franz Conrad von Hötzendorf would modernize the General Staff and update Austria-Hungary's war preparations; and the foreign minister, Alois Lexa von

Aehrenthal, committed himself to the revival of the prestige and the fortunes of the Habsburg Monarchy by a more assertive diplomacy. From the Belvedere's point of view, Schönaich and Aehrenthal soon turned out to be failures. In the case of Conrad, alienation took a little longer to set in, but in late 1913, Franz Ferdinand began to look for a more amenable replacement. The heir apparent proved to be a disruptive element in Austria-Hungary's political process because his intra-dynastic opposition could not be quelled by the Emperor and caused a lot of trouble for ambitious civil servants and officers. But Conrad could be almost as much of a troublemaker as Franz Ferdinand.[7] Whenever he deemed it necessary, the chief of the General Staff, a prolific writer of memoranda and letters, tried to harangue his superiors into radical solutions to the Habsburg Monarchy's security problems. Conrad's recipe for Austria-Hungary's self-assertion as a Great Power was simple: in order to avoid a multi-front war which would overtax the military forces, the probable future foes of the Dual Monarchy had to be dealt with one after another.

Up to 1911, the army leadership considered Italy its enemy of choice. Fighting against the Italian army looked like a golden opportunity to achieve a glorious victory—and revenge for 1859 and 1866. The creation of the Italian nation-state had come at the expense of Austria, but there were still strategically important Habsburg territories with an Italian-speaking population. Nineteenth-century experiences and the enduring problems with competing nationalisms in Austria-Hungary and Europe as a whole lend plausibility to the expectation that the *Risorgimento* was not over yet. As Conrad put it, the Italian government might be willing to cooperate with Austria-Hungary, but in the long run, the decisive factors of international politics, nationalism, and the struggle for survival would make an armed clash between the Habsburg Monarchy and its southern ally inevitable. A farsighted Austro-Hungarian foreign policy would have to keep this in mind. Whatever was deemed necessary to prepare for the inevitable "settling of accounts" had to have priority. The alliance with Italy, due in 1912 to be prolonged for another five years, might be a instrument to win time or a free hand to deal with Serbia, but it should never hinder Austria-Hungary from waging war on the Italians whenever there was an opportunity to do so.[8]

This pattern of perception shaped Conrad's memoranda with regard to Italy from 1906 onward. He found a receptive audience for his views among the general staff officers imbued with the heritage of Austria's Italian armies in the nineteenth century. Franz Ferdinand, a staunch Catholic and unforgiving heir to the Habsburg's Italian domains, hated everything that smacked of Italian nationalism. With many high-ranking officers and the Belvedere firmly on his side, Conrad challenged Aehrenthal's policy of détente and limited cooperation with Italy. The divergent views of the chief of the General Staff and the foreign minister on Italy came to a head in 1907 when Conrad called for what he considered a preventive war. Aehrenthal and Franz Joseph refused to accept Conrad's advice, but this could not discourage the chief of the General Staff. Even during the Annexation crisis of 1908-1909, Conrad was optimistic that in case of a war against Serbia Italy might side with the Serbs; in such a case, the first offensive should be launched in the southwest. As soon as the crisis subsided without leading to a war, the chief of the General Staff once again focused on Italy. To overcome Aehrenthal's resistance, Conrad presented information from the intelligence section of the General Staff and military attachés to support his claim that Italy was preparing for war against Austria-Hungary. Little wonder that the cooperation between the Foreign Office and the General Staff suffered severely. Aehrenthal kept the lid on the funds available for military espionage, opposed the establishment of new posts for military attachés, and restricted the flow of information between diplomats and the military. Instead of winning the monarch's approval for an anti-Italian policy, Conrad's attacks on the foreign minister strengthened the position of Aehrenthal. The Emperor finally sacked the chief of the General Staff in late 1911 because he disliked Conrad's political proposals and could not stand his systematic encroachment on foreign affairs.[9]

The foreign minister's victory frustrated the Belvedere since Aehrenthal—like Schönaich—was seen as too soft on the Hungarians. But Franz Ferdinand's chancellery would pick Conrad's successor, Blasius Schemua. As a kind of compensation, the Archduke got the Emperor's approval to replace Schönaich with Moritz von Auffenberg, a protégé of the Belvedere.[10] Nevertheless, for the moment, neither the General Staff nor the Belvedere could challenge the foreign policy of Aehrenthal. From an institutional point of view, there was militarization of international policy in Vienna until Aehrenthal's death from leukemia in February 1912. In the Hietzing memorandum, written in summer 1909, Aehrenthal quoted Carl von Clausewitz to support his claim that the foreign minister, not the military, should be the Emperor's advisor on questions of war and peace. In 1911, the foreign minister prevailed. But it was Aehrenthal who had employed the armed forces as a tool of diplomacy before and thereby had invited the General Staff's incursions into foreign affairs.

With regard to the Sanjak of Novibazar, he used Conrad's evaluation of the strategic irrelevance of the area to justify his plan to trade the occupation of the Sanjak for the annexation of Bosnia-Herzegovina.

Military reports on increasing instability in the region and Conrad's reassuring assessment of Russia's ability to intervene helped Aehrenthal to get the approval of the Common Ministerial Council for the annexation. During the crisis, the foreign minister encouraged Conrad to reach an agreement with the General Staff in Berlin on a European war, and used military measures to put pressure on Serbia and, indirectly, on Russia, too. The German commitment to Austria-Hungary's cause forced the Russians to back down, and an isolated Serbia could not risk a war against the Habsburg Monarchy. Much to the army's chagrin, Aehrenthal did not heed the calls for war against Serbia, but only sought a diplomatic victory. He managed to keep control of military measures and geared the troop increases in Bosnia-Herzegovina and the steps to partial mobilization to his diplomacy and not the other way round.[11]

Aehrenthal left a mixed heritage to his successor, Count Leopold Berchtold. Not only had he damaged the relationship with Russia almost beyond repair, but at the same time, his assertive foreign policy was admired by most of the younger diplomats and officials in Vienna's Foreign Ministry. Berchtold, conservative and cautious, and an advocate of a rapprochement with Russia, was able to win Franz Ferdinand's favor, but his own staff called for a more vigorous foreign policy.[12] This became evident as Austria-Hungary's international position deteriorated in 1912-1913. The Hietzing memorandum was based on the assumption that Bulgaria and Serbia were perennial rivals and would never cooperate, and military intelligence did not question this assessment.

The Foreign Ministry and the General Staff were, thus, taken by surprise when early in the summer of 1912 Vienna finally got wind that a Balkan league had been formed, directed against the Habsburg Monarchy's influence on the peninsula and Ottoman rule in Macedonia. Berchtold resorted to Great Power diplomacy as the best way to avoid war and to defend Austria-Hungary's vital interests in the region. First of all, he had to define Austria-Hungary's essential interests in case of a Turkish defeat. The Foreign Ministry came up with two major points: Albania should be an independent state, and Serbia shouldn't be allowed to gain direct access to the Adriatic. It would be possible to get Italian support for Albanian independence as a way to strengthen the Triple alliance and to avoid isolation. Berchtold went even further in his efforts to use Concert of Europe politics in order to stabilize the situation on the Balkan Peninsula. It proved to be impossible to prevent the outbreak of the first Balkan war, but the peace settlement would not be left to the warring states alone; it was also shaped by the Great Powers. The creation of an independent Albanian state, at least on paper, seemed to vindicate Berchtold's crisis management.

Unfortunately for Austria-Hungary, the second Balkan war strained the Habsburg Monarchy's relations with Romania, strengthened Serbia, and worst of all, demonstrated Vienna's isolated stand on most Balkan issues. Berchtold's prestige suffered as he was seen as too dovish by his own staff, the military, and many journalists. This was not a fair judgement of Berchtold because he had not shied away from using the armed forces in a campaign of intimidation against Montenegro and Serbia. But militant diplomacy could not conceal Austria-Hungary's relative decline as a Great Power.[13]

This was partly due to shifts in the international system and the problems of a multi-ethnic state in an age of nationalism.[14] But it also reflected the contradiction between the claim to Great Power status and the lack of military muscle: Austria-Hungary's militant diplomacy suffered from a "credibility gap." It was well-known throughout Europe that the k.u.k. Army was lagging behind in extremely important fields of armaments.[15] In relation to its population and economy, the Habsburg Monarchy spent less money on military expenditures than France, Germany, or Russia.[16] In an age of relatively modest changes in weapons technology and of mass armies relying on millions of trained reservists, troop numbers were still by far the clearest yardstick to measure military strength. Among the Great Powers on the European continent, only Italy had fewer soldiers than the forces of the Habsburg Monarchy on a peacetime footing.[17] Austria-Hungary had not seen any increase in the number of recruits—and therefore of trained reservists, too—for more than two decades when a new army bill passed the Hungarian Diet in 1912. Because of the incessant quarrelling about Hungary's place in the Habsburg Monarchy, the k.u.k. Army sometimes had trouble ensuring that the new conscripts could be drawn at all. It took the rather robust political management of István Tisza to force an army bill that provided for a remarkable improvement.[18] Meanwhile, as the Austro-Hungarian forces suffered from lack of funds to keep up with friend and foe, Tisza promised to support another spending spree. For so much high-level attention to be paid to the needs of the army was unambiguously welcome. So, too, was the spirit of assertiveness with which diplomats, politicians, public opinion leaders, and the monarch judged Austria-Hungary's international position.

The navy managed to get an increasing share of military expenses in the years prior to 1912. The build-up of a modern battle fleet swallowed a remarkable share of what little money was available for discretionary spending on armaments.[19] Archduke Franz Ferdinand, like Wilhelm II an ardent follower of navalism, supported the program wholeheartedly. But there was enthusiasm for a strong navy from different quarters of Austria's and Hungary's elites, stirred by a propaganda campaign and skillfully exploited by the navy's rather efficient lobbying. Battleships were all the rage for several reasons. First, they were symbols of technological progress, and second, their construction would boost industrial growth; they were the best way to project power globally, protecting Austria-Hungary's commercial interests and defending the Habsburg Monarchy's prestige in an era of imperialism. Finally, they could be used to put pressure on Italy, Austria-Hungary's rival in the competition for influence on the eastern shores of the Adriatic Sea. In a remarkable fit of self-restraint, the army leadership did not question the priority of naval armaments until 1911. The absence of inter-service rivalry can be explained as the result of three factors. Up to a point, army leaders like Conrad followed the fashion of navalism; additionally, Franz Ferdinand's soft spot for the battle fleet made it hard to challenge the budgetary priorities. Third, as long as there was no chance to push an increase of the number of recruits through parliaments, the naval build-up offered at least one possibility for strengthening Austria-Hungary's military might.

At least as striking as the navy's spending spree is the allocation of funds available to the army. One of the most expensive armaments projects was the construction of new fortifications along the Italian border. A sizeable amount of money and a lot of effort was put into new heavy guns and mountain artillery. The modernization of the k.u.k.'s field artillery, extremely important in case of a Great Power war, was pursued at a more leisurely pace. When war broke out in 1914, the k.u.k. Army was still out-gunned by the Russians on the Eastern front and didn't have a reserve army to make up for the casualties of the first weeks of fighting. But the 30.5 cm mortars, the pride of the k.u.k. artillery, designed to crush fortifications, would have lain idle had the Germans not asked for their support on the Western front. To put it bluntly, the k.u.k. Army was well prepared to wage war on Austria-Hungary's unreliable ally, Italy, but not for fighting against the Russians. To shield the southernmost parts of the Dual Monarchy against Serbia and Montenegro, some fortifications were built prior to World War I, and mountain artillery was useful on the Balkan Peninsula as in the Alps. But given the most likely war scenario in 1913/14, a two-front war against Russia and Serbia, the allocation of funds in the prewar period looks foolish. In order to explain this focus, one has to keep in mind that Italy was ranking high on the General Staff's strategic agenda until 1911. As a result, the k.u.k. Army wasn't capable of effectively deterring Russia in 1912-1913.[20]

The lack of striking power shaped the military's stand on Berchtold's militant diplomacy in 1912. Initially, army leadership called for some precautionary measures in Bosnia-Herzegovina and Dalmatia, but not for a military intervention that might bring about war against Russia. War minister Auffenberg even advised the Common Ministerial Council to avoid a European war as long as the k.u.k.'s field artillery was still inadequate. In early October 1912, Vienna learned of a massive increase in the number of soldiers in Russian units along the border. Now Auffenberg asked for the General Staff's assessment of the strategic situation. Schemua deliberately minimized the shortcomings in Austria-Hungary's war preparations and argued that the k.u.k. Army might even go it alone against Russia. This is amazing, to say the least, but it was meant to encourage a more aggressive Balkan policy. Only an overtly optimistic picture of the Habsburg Monarchy's strategic options would stiffen Berchtold's back. But as the Balkan league's armies defeated the Turks within a couple of weeks, as Serbian troops seized Albanian territory, and as the Russian military build-up along the Galician border went on, the situation changed dramatically. Measures to counter the growing discrepancies in troop numbers in the northeast were taken at the behest of the General Staff and the War Ministry. To a certain degree, escalation was part of Berchtold's diplomatic strategy; otherwise, the Habsburg Monarchy would have been left alone with its troubles on the Balkan. But in December, as Concert of Europe politics seemed to work, Berchtold had to face a major challenge to his crisis management. For a couple of days, Franz Ferdinand followed the advice of his chancellery and called for a more assertive policy and a settling of accounts with Serbia and Montenegro. Conrad took over from Schemua, and the hawkish Alexander von Krobatin replaced Auffenberg at the War Ministry. Europe had come close to a major war. Finally, Berchtold prevailed in the debate with the heir apparent because German backing against Russia seemed doubtful and diplomacy had started to work. Franz Ferdinand gave way as the Emperor sided with Berchtold. As Russia and Austria-Hungary reduced their troops along the border, the Winter Crisis of 1912-13 was over.[21]

Two other war or peace crises were to follow in 1913, one in May when Montenegrin troops were evicted from Scutari, and one in October when Serbia had to withdraw from Albanian territory. In the case of Scutari, Berchtold wanted to rely mostly on multilateral coercion within the framework of the Concert of Europe. Due to the stubborn reaction of Montenegro's King Nikita, the Habsburg Monarchy changed tack and decided to put the troops in Bosnia-Herzegovina and Dalmatia at the status of war readiness and delivered an ultimatum to Montenegro. Berchtold was in firm control of the decision-making process and made sure that the confrontation with Nikita would not lead to a general conflagration. In October 1913, as Serbia defied Austro-Hungarian warnings to evacuate Albanian territory, the Habsburg Monarchy again used an ultimatum to force its opponent to capitulate. This time, Berchtold was pushed to action by Conrad and Tisza. Therefore, the lesson learned from this successful bullying of Serbia proved to be important in 1914: aggressive diplomacy would pay off.

Yet while the results of Austria-Hungary's militant diplomacy in 1912-1913 were inspiring in the short run, they did nothing to improve the Habsburg Monarchy's security in terms of military power. During the sequence of war or peace crises that began in 1904, politicians in all European capitals became increasingly better acquainted with a notion of security defined by military capabilities. According to this restricted concept of security, Berchtold had not achieved that much. Moreover, with the repercussions of mobilization measures on finances and the troops' morale perceived as disastrous, militant diplomacy increasingly looked like a dead-end.[22] To the political, diplomatic, and military elites, to back down and accept the deteriorating strategic situation would have implied the Habsburg Monarchy's abdication as a Great Power. Only war seemed to offer a way out of this impasse.

Notes

1. For the focus on the domestic background, see Solomon Wank, "Desperate Counsel in Vienna in July 1914: Berthold Molden's Unpublished Memorandum," *Central European History* 26 (1993): 281-310; for an analysis focusing on the international system, see Paul W. Schroeder, "World War I as Galloping Gertie: A Reply to Joachim Remak," *Journal of Modern History* 44 (1972): 319-45.

2. Samuel R. Williamson, Jr, *Austria-Hungary and the Origins of the First World War* (London: Macmillan, 1991), 121.

3. Michael Hochedlinger, *Austria's Wars of Emergence: War, State, and Society in the Habsburg Monarchy, 1683-1797* (London: Longman, 2003), 267-329.

4. Günther Kronenbitter, *"Krieg im Frieden". Die Führung der k. u. k. Armee und die Großmachtpolitik Öaterreich-Ungarns 1906-1914* (München: Oldenbourg, 2003), 197-232.

5. For the decision making circles in foreign and military affairs, see Williamson, *Austria-Hungary*, 13-57.

6. For Franz Ferdinand's role in Austro-Hungarian domestic, military, and foreign policy, see Robert A. Kann, *Franz Ferdinand Studien* (Vienna: Böhlau, 1976); Samuel R. Williamson, "Influence, Power, and the Policy Process: The Case of Franz Ferdinand, 1906-1914," *Historical Journal* 17 (1974): 417-34.

7. Kronenbitter, *"Krieg im Frieden,"* 58-77.

8. Hans Jürgen Pantenius, *Der Angriffsgedanke gegen Italien bei Conrad von Hötzendorf. Ein Beitrag zur Koalitionskriegsführung im Ersten Weltkrieg*, vol. 1 (Cologne: Böhlau, 1984), 288-309.

9. Ibid., 309-46; Kronenbitter, *"Krieg im Frieden,"* 243-46, 261-63, 318-25, 359-66; Berthold Molden, *Alois Graf Aehrenthal. Sechs Jahre äußere Politik Österreich-Ungarns* (Stuttgart: Deutsche Verlags-Anstalt, 1917), 154-92.

10. Solomon Wank, "The Archduke and Aehrenthal: The Origins of a Hatred," *Austrian History Yearbook* 33 (2002): 77-104.

11. Kronenbitter, *"Krieg im Frieden,"* 332-59.

12. Hugo Hantsch, *Leopold Graf Berchtold. Grandseigneur und Staatsmann*, vol. 1 (Graz: Styria, 1963), 239-52; Williamson, *Austria-Hungary*, 80-81.

13. Williamson, *Austria-Hungary*, 121-63.

14. F[rancis] R. Bridge, *The Habsburg Monarchy Among the Great Powers, 1815-1918* (New York: Berg, 1990), 288-334; Paul W. Schroeder, "Embedded Counterfactuals and World War I as an Unavoidable War," in Paul W. Schroeder, *Systems, Stability, and Statecraft: Essays on the International History of Modern Europe*, ed. David Wetzel, Robert Jervis, and Jack S. Levy (New York: Palgrave Macmillan, 2004), 157-91.

15. For land armaments, see David G. Herrmann, *The Arming of Europe and the Making of the First World War* (Princeton, NJ: Princeton Univ. Press, 1996); David Stevenson, *Armaments and the Coming of War: Europe, 1904-1914* (Oxford: Clarendon, 1996).

16. Stevenson, *Armaments*, 6.

17. Herrmann, *Arming of Europe*, 233-35.

18. Kronenbitter, *"Krieg im Frieden,"* 145-96.

19. For Austria-Hungary's naval build-up, see Lawrence Sondhaus, *The Naval Policy of Austria-Hungary, 1867-1918: Navalism, Industrial Development, and the Politics of Dualism* (West Lafayette, IN: Purdue Univ. Press, 1994), 170-232; Milan N. Vego, *Austro-Hungarian Naval Policy, 1904-14* (London: Frank Cass, 1996), 35-86.

20. Kronenbitter, *"Krieg im Frieden,"* 179-96.

21. Ibid., 376-402, 412-13; Williamson, *Austria-Hungary*, 130-32.

22. Williamson, *Austria-Hungary*, 136-39, 150-56; Kronenbitter, *"Krieg im Frieden,"* 414-28.

Austria between Mussolini and Hitler: War by Other Means

Alexander N. Lassner

At the end of World War I, the Austrian state was vulnerable and unstable. By the treaty of St. Germain, Austria suffered geographic, demographic, and economic retribution, most egregiously the loss of almost one-third of Imperial Austria-Hungary's German speaking subjects and essential coal supplies from Silesia and Bohemia. The newly created Republic endured ruinous postwar inflation until 1923, a short economic recovery 1925-1929, and then the consequences of the world depression and the collapse of the largest Austrian bank (the *Creditanstalt*) 1930-1933. Throughout the period 1918-1933, the "Successor States" of Czechoslovakia, Romania, and Yugoslavia largely avoided commerce with Austria in order to protect their own fragile economies. Thus, with the exception of the period from 1925 to 1929, Austria endured high unemployment, stagnant trade, and industrial atrophy.[1]

From an internal political perspective, Austria experienced greater disarray. Members of the two largest political parties, the *Sozialdemokratische Partei* (Social Democratic Party of Austria, or SDP) and the *Christlichsoziale Partei* (Christian Social Party of Austria, or CSP), were actively suspicious and hostile towards one another.[2] The former party embraced Marxist rhetoric and anti-clericalism, even if it remained more moderate in its actions. The CSP, by contrast, was both clerical and anti-Marxist. In the Austrian parliament, distrust and mutual antagonism was the result. More dangerously, the SDP and CSP maintained or received support from paramilitary groups: the *Schutzbund* and *Heimwehr/Heimatschutz*, whose leadership played an active role in Austrian politics, including participation in the parliament and cabinet (the *Schutzbund* was the left-wing paramilitary force of the SDP while the *Heimwehr* was a collection of right-wing paramilitary forces associated with the CSP). Political distrust in the new state was thus combined from the outset with the potential for armed violence in support of political parties.

The failure of either party to win an absolute majority in parliament and the refusal of the Socialists to participate in a national government after November 1920 led to a series of unstable coalition governments between the CSP and other smaller parties like the *Großdeustsche Volkspartei* (GVP, a largely bourgeois pan-German party in favor of the Anschluß). It also created parliamentary deadlock.

Exacerbating matters was the persistent desire of many Austrians to achieve the goal of an Anschluß with Germany.[3] This idea was first articulated in the nineteenth century, forbidden by the allied powers after World War I, and officially espoused by the SDP, the GVP, and the *Landbund* until the Nazi *Machtergreifung* (seizure of power) in 1933. Indeed, the Anschluß question was favored by CSP Chancellor Ignaz Seipel and by other prominent CSP members like Karl Gottfried Hugelman and Anton Rintelen. Combined with Austria's real economic problems and political instability, the Anschluß movement helped to keep in doubt the issue of Austria's long term viability from 1918 to 1933.[4]

The Austrian state was similarly vulnerable. By 1921, the small Danubian state had already been attacked by Yugoslavia in 1919 and Hungary in 1921, both countries seeking to conquer additional territory at Austria's expense. The various formal and informal armed forces of the Austrian government failed to repel the Yugoslavian attack on Klagenfurt, and only international involvement returned the disputed region to Austria. By 1925, the continued threat posed by Czechoslovakia, Hungary, Italy, and Yugoslavia to Austria's territorial integrity (above all as the result of a war waged by Hungary and Italy through Austria and against Yugoslavia) led to the development of Austrian operational plans to prevent any territorial breach of the Austrian border. Despite these plans, until 1933 the Austrian *Bundesheer* (Federal Army) remained underfunded, undertrained, underequipped, and ill-prepared for national defense. It served primarily to support the government and to undertake domestic emergency relief efforts. Furthermore, the SDP and, subsequently, the CSP, GVP, and Austrian Nazis carried their political battles into the ranks of the army by creating unions for soldiers and officers and by competing for their loyalty.[5]

At the level of international security, Austria maintained *de facto* neutrality until 1929, when Austrian Chancellor Johannes Schober officially espoused neutrality and friendship towards all neighboring countries as official Austrian policy, a stance that harmonized with the restrictions placed on Austria by the Treaty of St. Germain, but also by the subsequent October 1922 Geneva Protocol, and the Kellogg-Briand Anti-War Pact. Nevertheless, this did not prevent the Schober government from flirting with Italian dictator Benito Mussolini in order to acquire weapons for the *Bundesheer* and to address the issue of the repressed former Austrian population of Italian South Tyrol.

Nor did Austrian neutrality prevent Schober from proposing an Austro-German customs union in February 1930 and following up on that proposal in March 1931 as foreign minister in the Otto Ender government. Although Austrian statesmen did indeed attempt to preserve their country's independence within the framework of the customs union, the attempt ended in failure; not without reason, Italy, France, and the Little Entente feared a customs union as a first step towards an Anschluß. Badly undermined, the Ender government collapsed and was replaced by that of Chancellor Karl Buresch. In his cabinet two men came to the fore: Engelbert Dollfuss and Kurt Schuschnigg. In May 1932 Dollfuss succeeded Buresch as chancellor by seeking support from Heimwehr deputies in the parliament and promising to appoint two of their members to the cabinet.[6]

Dollfuss acceded to a fragile political, economic, and international situation, and domestically, his government rested on a one-vote majority in the *Nationalrat* (Federal Diet). Dollfuss also faced a terror campaign conducted by Austrian Nazis throughout 1932 led by Theo Habicht, a German national. By 1933, after the Nazi *Machtergreifung* in Germany, this terror campaign in Austria received support from Adolf Hitler. Habicht and his associates prepared and employed much the same tactics perfected by Hitler and his followers over the last decade in Bavaria. These included the organization of Nazi spectacles, the use of printed propaganda, and, most significantly, violence and terror. Their purpose, as articulated by Habicht, was to enlarge the Nazi party, to overthrow the Austrian government, and to bring about an Anschluß. Habicht was equally clear in his own mind as to what such an event would mean internationally, noting that "[w]hoever controls Austria, controls central Europe."[7] Hitler, for his part, privately noted on 26 May that

> [t]he contest [between the Nazis and the Austrian government] will be decided before the end of the summer. The sacrifices which Germany must make now are nothing compared to the sacrifices which would have to be borne if the development in Austria continued in its present course.

Hitler's 26 May statement provides an important example of Nazi euphemisms *vis-à-vis* the goal of conquering Austria, and within the Nazi's broader use of linguistic perversion, the term "development" meant nothing less than subversion directed at the overthrow of a foreign government through the use of terrorism, propaganda, and seduction.

Hitler went on to aid and abet Habicht by imposing a 1000 DM penalty on all Germans traveling to Austria in order to destabilize Dollfuss' position by eliminating tourist traffic, which accounted for 30 percent of Austria's annual tourism income. On 10 June 1933, Dollfuss countered intensifying Nazi belligerence by prohibiting the sale of the official Nazi paper the *Völkischer Beobachter*, and closing all Nazi offices in Austria. The following day, he made membership in the Nazi party illegal for members of the army and government, while ordering the expulsion from Austria of known Nazi party members and sympathizers. Habicht and more than one thousand of his supporters found shelter and sympathy in Germany while continuing their subversive activities from Bavaria with Berlin's sanction. Slightly more than one week later, the Nazi party in Austria was made illegal.[8] None of these actions deterred the Nazis, who intensified their brutal proceedings while invoking typical linguistic distortions: the communists were really to blame for the terror; murder and bombings were only "harmless shows of strength."[9]

Dollfuss remained desirous of, as he put the matter, avoiding "all anti-German positions," but he nonetheless requested that Britain, France, and Italy protest against Germany's sponsorship of and participation in sedition against Austria, in violation of Article 11 of the League of Nations charter and Article 80 of the Treaty of Versailles.[10] At the *Wilhelmstraße* (German Foreign Office), debate began as to how the Austrian accusations could be defused. German officials considered several approaches. The overall problem, as the German Foreign Office noted, was that "the battle with Austria, which already had lasted much longer than we had expected, costs us exceptionally."

Germany was losing the sympathy of small countries and making enemies of larger ones. Most significantly, the battle in Austria was stripping away illusions as to what kind of men ran the Third Reich and what their aims were: "[I]f a weak Germany proceeds in this manner against a weak country," an unnamed foreign ambassador had recently indicated to the *Wilhelmstraße*, "will it not proceed similarly against its larger neighbors after it has strengthened itself?"[11] Although the Austrian accusations did lead Hitler to stop the most easily detectable and visually spectacular offenses, namely the violations of Austrian airspace, it produced no overall effect. Hitler would not rein in the Nazis operating from Germany, and Habicht continued his campaign from Munich in collusion with leaders in Berlin. When London and Paris made a joint *démarche* on 7 August in protest of Berlin's complicity, the *Wilhelmstraße* asserted its innocence and insisted that it did not intend to threaten Austria.[12]

Throughout the rest of 1933, the Nazi campaign of terror in Austria continued virtually unabated, provoking Vienna to issue a proclamation of martial law in November 1933 and other strong counter-measures. The intensity of the campaign reached new heights in February 1934 when the frequency of bombings climbed as high as forty per day. This was done in order to convince Austrians that the government could not protect them and was bound to lose in the end, as well as to destroy the tourist industry.[13] On 17 January 1934, the Austrian ambassador to Germany, Stefan Tauschitz, protested in Berlin by issuing an *aide-mémoire* that amounted to an indictment of the German government.[14]

The Austrian document concluded by emphasizing that "[t]he German Government cannot well disclaim responsibility or power to control the responsible circles of the National Socialist party [in Germany], for the fact that it was found possible not long ago to stop the propagandist air raids on Austria shows that if desired the other methods of attacking the Austrian Government could also be called off." Tauschitz further indicated that "unless the German Government took prompt and complete measures to stop these machinations, Austria would seriously consider making an appeal to the League of Nations." A few days later, the Austrian ambassadors in London, Paris, and Rome informed the three governments of Austria's protest and provided the governments with *résumés* containing further details regarding the Nazi subversion. Parallel to these steps, the *Ballhausplatz* requested that Mussolini use his influence in Berlin to stop the attacks.[15]

The official German refutation—which also set forth an anti-Austria argument from which Berlin would never deviate—was published on 2 February. It was notable for its counterfeit history, brazen lies and half-truths, and perversion of language. At the same time, the response depended on either the sympathy, apathy, weak-mindedness, or at least the willful gullibility of its readers in order to be effective. The Vienna government, Berlin claimed, was only giving a "one-sided picture of events" and showing things in a "false light." In order to correct this "false point of view" it was necessary to see that

> [i]t is a question not of a conflict between two German States of a kind covered by the formal conceptions of international law as laid down by the Austrian Government, but of the dispute between the Austrian Government and a historical movement of the whole German people. . . . [and thus] [i]t is only natural that the feeling of national and spiritual unity between Germany and Austria cannot be broken by a political frontier and that ideas which can rouse a people cannot be prevented from spreading across the frontier.

The German foreign office twisted the issue away from matter of illegal Nazi subversion, violence, and propaganda—supported by Germany and directed against another sovereign nation —and presented a palatable conceptual framework that was readily understandable, morally convenient, and "natural": nationalism, spiritualism, and biology were the only issues involved; Nazis in Austria were simply a naturally occurring phenomenon and *only* part of the historical pan-German movement. Political borders and international laws, therefore, were irrelevant and inadmissible.

Of course the Nazis were far more than the benign representatives of pan-Germanism. But in co-opting the pan-German movement, they obtained cover—on the international diplomatic stage—for their insidious machinations. Such cover could not, and indeed did not, hold up to scrutiny. But for those European statesmen and diplomats (some of whom were philo-Nazis themselves) who sought to excuse Nazi behavior, the Nazis' self-proclaimed pan-German mission provided a convenient delusion.

The German Foreign Office went on to deny, excuse, and/or pervert specific charges while registering indignation and fabricating counter-accusations. It "rejected as untrue" that the Austrian Legion was to be used against the Austrian government. Although Berlin admitted that explosives used by the Nazis against the Austrian government came from Germany and that the German press had attacked the Austrian government, this was of no import. In the former case, it "appear[ed] impossible that consignments of explosive material could . . . have been sent to any large extent from Germany to Austria" while in the latter circumstance "it must be remarked that . . . attacks . . . on the Austrian Government . . . only represent the answer to a number of particularly offensive statements in the Austrian press regarding the new Germany." Supposed wireless propaganda against Vienna was an Austrian lie. Such "lectures on the wireless" were "intended for the listeners in Germany and [kept them] informed of developments in Austria." Indeed it was Germany that had been provoked and made a victim given that "the wireless has been misused in Austria for intensive propaganda against the new Germany, and . . . the official news-service itself is not ashamed of the worst slander."

Overall, the *Wilhelmstraße* feigned disappointment, noting its "great astonishment that the Austrian Government on several occasions had suspected the German Government of threatening the independence of Austria." The situation in the small Danubian state was unfortunate but "a purely internal conflict" and should not be permitted to come before the League of Nations. More ominously, Berlin noted that "[t]he Austrian Government cannot expect that Germany should remain indifferent to a system of Government which outlaws and suppresses everything which is filling German people with new courage and new confidence."[16]

In other words, a "system of Government" which recognized Nazi tactics and sought to counter them would be punished.

Upset but unintimidated, Dollfuss publicly condemned Nazi terrorism the next day. It was the twelfth such condemnation of his chancellorship.[17] Within the week, the *Ballhausplatz* submitted a 168 page dossier to London, Paris, and Rome further detailing German interference in Austria. The Dollfuss cabinet now leaned towards bringing the matter before the League of Nations in Geneva. However, Mussolini preferred a different course of action. In order not to provoke him, Dollfuss consented to the Duce's wish for the Great Powers "to consult amongst themselves in regard to the policy to be adopted." Vienna waited for news.[18]

While negotiations abroad proceeded, on his own initiative Dollfuss suppressed the SDP between 12 and 15 February 1934 after the socialist paramilitary *Schutzbund* fired on police attempting to confiscate weapons caches. The consequent outlawing of the socialists reflected the increasing pressure from Rome for such measures and the precepts of a corporate state without parties, which Dollfuss came to espouse as a more effective way of governing.[19] The socialists, taken largely by surprise and lacking any coherent strategy, collapsed after a revolt lasting several days, while then-Minister of Justice Schuschnigg helped to direct the arrest of socialist leaders; others fled into exile.

The suppression of the SDP somewhat cooled public support for Austria in Britain and France and, combined with Italian obstinacy, influenced Dollfuss to delay an appeal to the League.[20] But it did not end Vienna's international appeal against Berlin. On 16 and 17 February, the *Ballhausplatz* inquired in London, Paris, and Rome "as to their attitude with regard to the dossier which [Austria] has prepared with a view to establishing German interference in the internal affairs of Austria. . . ."[21] Czechoslovak, British, French, Italian, and Romanian statesmen accepted the veracity of Austrian accusations *vis-à-vis* Germany. But differing calculations, aims, and perceived interests between London, Paris, Rome, Budapest, and the governments of the Little Entente—some reasonable and honest, others excusive and deceitful—undermined potential agreement as to what steps to take for Austria. All that could be agreed upon was to issue a vaguely worded 17 February communiqué that indicated a "common view as to the necessity of maintaining Austria's independence and integrity in accordance with the relevant treaties."

In March, Austria signed the Roman Protocols Agreement with Italy and Hungary. The agreement represented a political and economic grouping that provided Austria and Hungary needed economic preferences from Italy, as well as strengthening politico-diplomatic ties, thereby affording Austria protection from German intimidation. At the same time, of course, the Roman Protocols increased Austria's reliance on Hungary and Fascist Italy.[22] Although it was not yet clear in Vienna, association with these two countries was dangerous since, despite the bloc's common authoritarian orientation, there existed a crucial and potentially divisive issue. Rome and Budapest were fervent territorial revisionists and ultimately willing to resort to war, while Vienna was resolutely in favor of the European *status quo* and desperately wished to avoid conflict.

Notwithstanding this potential rift, the Dollfuss government's position briefly was made better from March to April 1934. The Roman Protocols provided a measure of security and economic relief, Germany had been chastised internationally, and, in March, Hitler temporarily stopped highly visible Nazi terrorism and radio/press attacks against Austria in order to remove the most visible causes for protests by Austria, France, Great Britain, and Italy.[23] Though Hitler considered a change in method, he did not commit himself to differing tactics. Rather, violence directed against Austria by the Nazis, illegal Nazi propaganda, and economic warfare soon recommenced producing greater tension.

Increased tension and violence led, on 25 July 1934, to an attempted Austrian Nazi putsch in which Dollfuss was murdered. The action was planned and directed by Habicht from Munich and was undertaken with Hitler's knowledge and approval. Hitler's well known aphorism that "nothing happens in the Movement without my wish" was on the mark; until the murder of Dollfuss, the Führer hoped that direct and obvious brutality would be successful.[24]

During the course of 1932-1933, the Nazis worked persistently to subvert the Austrian state by all means, and Dollfuss had taken steps in order to counter Nazi activities. He appealed to so-called "moderate" Nazis in order to take advantage of splits in the Party, while attempting to move the battle for control of Austria into the political arena; he helped to create the *Vaterländische Front* in order to develop Austrian nationalism, to augment the armed forces, and to control subversive political activities; and he made appeals to France, Great Britain, and Italy in order to obtain financial assistance and to stop Nazi terrorism and subversion sponsored by Berlin. Dollfuss took these steps despite his assertions to the Reich's emissaries that he wished to avoid any "anti-German" stance.[25] In fact, this utterance served a useful dual purpose: it suggested pan-Germanic sentiments and Austro-German cooperation in order not to provoke the Reich and its sympathizers, but it left ample room for interpretation and real resistance to the Nazis.

Nevertheless, under Dollfuss, Austrian defense policy continued to stagnate. The armed forces received insufficient funding; such military planning as existed was inadequate; and among Austria's diplomatic corps and newly deployed military attachés, far- reaching confusion existed with respect to Austrian national security policy. Indeed, Austria's uncertain fifteen year history, lack of a unified civil-military leadership (from 1919 to 1934 Austria only periodically possessed a foreign minister and had no chief of the general staff), and the chancellor's constant resorts to domestic and foreign maneuvering served to undermine the coherent articulation of national defense priorities and goals both among some civilian officials in Vienna but especially among Austria's diplomatic representatives abroad. In July 1934, the situation was disturbing enough that the Austrian military attaché to Budapest and Bucharest, Colonel Oskar Regele, wrote an extensive critique entitled "On the Direction of National Defense in Austria." It was immediately made top secret by the *Bundesministerium für Landesverteidigung* (Federal Defense Ministry or BMfLV) and attracted the attention of leading men such as newly appointed State Secretary of Defense General Wilhelm Zehner, Army Inspector General Sigismund Schilhausky, and Chief of Department II (Materiel) General Eugen Luschinsky. Regele observed that amongst an "[a]larmingly large number of [Austrian diplomats and officers abroad]" there existed a "far reaching confusion in the judgement of the most elementary basic questions of [Austrian] state policy and the foreign policy side of national defense." In short, there was an "atomization" (*Atomisierung*) of opinion. Regele noted that he was "astounded" to hear in these circles such questions as "[W]hat will become of Austria tomorrow?" "[I]s this a transitional phase?" and "[Can] this state [Austria] live in the long-run?"

Equally worrisome was that many of Austria's civil leaders in Vienna and abroad still labored under the pre-Great War misapprehension that national defense was the duty of the BMfLV alone and not a joint, and indeed primarily governmental, obligation. In order to correct this view, Regele wrote, the *Bundesheer*'s leadership had to "draw the attention of the responsible civilian administration to the pressing responsibilities at hand [for national defense]" and, in particular, to the exigencies of the moment, for Austria was no longer at the head of an Empire but only a "*small state that [found] itself in a national defense situation of extreme danger.*" To this end, Regele believed that the Dollfuss government had to define clearly a number of pressing national security issues including:

1. *"The Question of Austria's Permanency."* Vienna should create propaganda that reaffirmed the notion of the Austrian state and its long term viability, especially by means of comparative analysis with other small nations.
2. *"Can Austria Remain Neutral in a European War?"* Was such a stance really possible in case of war? The Ballhausplatz had to take a clear stand here since so many in the diplomatic community held neutrality as their "*Lieblingsidee*" (most treasured idea).
3. "How should [Austria's representatives] think about the *Treaty of St. Germain*? . . . How should [they] think about the *League of Nations*?" Did the restrictions of St. Germain remain the basis for Austrian national defense? Were Germany, Hungary and Bulgaria, adhering to their respective treaties? How might the League of Nations function *vis-à-vis* disarmament and upholding the peace of Europe? Would it function? Of greatest significance, what was the League of Nations' mechanism for aid to Austria in the case of danger?
4. *"What Type of [Military] Preparations are Necessary if the Government Recognizes the Possibility of a War?"* Did the government accept that Austria could become involved in a war despite a policy of neutrality? What were the means required for a defense of Austria? In a modern war, Regele added, a small state like Austria had particular strategic vulnerabilities: small military forces, little geo-strategic depth and the need to give ground on the defensive, the possibility of having to fight after being forced out of Austria, and an easily exhausted military-industrial potential.
5. *"Examination of Coalition Warfare."* Assuming Austria recognized the potential to have to fight a war despite its neutrality, it was urgent for Vienna to define possible coalitions (Austria-Germany, Austria-Italy, or Austria-Hungary), revise operational war-planning (war against Germany-Italy-Hungary, or war against the Little Entente), and to build up existing treaties from a military perspective.

Regele concluded his critique with the plea for the creation of the post chief of the general staff (banned by the Treaty of St. Germain) in order to work with the civilian administration and to help correct what he termed the "the backwardness in our national defense which is so frightening that the strongest [critique] appears too weak."[26] These deficiencies needed to be corrected. In the wake of the assassination of Dollfuss, responsibility for the defense of Austria would fall to Schuschnigg.

The Schuschnigg Years

Mussolini, as he had promised Dollfuss, responded to the attempted Nazi overthrow in the small Danubian state by moving already mobilized Italian divisions, which were on maneuvers at the time, to the Brenner—a move that prompted the Yugoslav government to threaten an invasion of Austria should Italian troops cross the Austro-Italian border.[27] Within Austria, Schuschnigg became chancellor and minister of defense. Thereafter, the *Bundesheer* and *Heimwehr* organizations quickly crushed the Nazi insurrection which had spread, as part of a coordinated uprising, to Carinthia, Styria, Upper Austria, and Salzburg. The number of killed amounted to slightly over 100 government and *Heimwehr* troops and 140 Austrian Nazis.

Hitler, for his part, issued denials of German complicity and, for the moment, took measures to separate the Nazi party in Germany from that in Austria. These included further promises to dissolve the Austrian Legion, "liquidating all connections between the Reich leadership of the N.S.D.A.P. in Germany and of the N.S.D.A.P. in Austria," and severing connections between Nazi party organizations in both countries. The Führer also relieved Rieth for having agreed to mediate a settlement between the Nazi putschists and the Austrian government and disavowed Rieth's statements. Temporarily cut off from the Reich, fleeing Nazis found refuge in Yugoslavia. Nazi Germany's goals remained unchanged: the eventual takeover of Austria.[28]

Schuschnigg was aware of the danger in which Austria found itself in the wake of the Nazi uprising. Furthermore, he was greatly concerned about the inaction of France and Great Britain and the unilateral Italian deployment of already mobilized troops to the Austro-Italian border.[29] The new chancellor realized that an effective protection of Austria was necessary, in addition to existing guarantees as provided in Article 88 of the Treaty of St. Germain, Articles 10 and 16 of the Covenant of the League of Nations, and the 1922 Geneva Agreement.[30] This was necessary, he understood, above and beyond the Nazi Reich forswearing interference in Austria and recognizing its independence. The *Ballhausplatz* recommenced collecting evidence of the Reich's support of terrorism in August and September, and this evidence was not just limited to such documents as the well-known *Kollerschlager Dokument*.

Thus, on 28 August 1934, Schuschnigg let London, Paris, and Rome know of his intention to pursue an "Austrian Pact" at Geneva that September, and on 12 September Schuschnigg, then-Foreign Minister Egon Berger-Waldenegg, and Political Director Theodor Hornbostel arrived in Geneva at the head of the Austrian delegation in order to craft the politico-military guarantee. The Austrian Pact, as presented by Hornbostel that same day, contained three articles. First, any threat to Austria was contrary to the interests of the contracting parties; second, "in the case that the independence of Austria is threatened by acts of interference coming from outside and directed against the internal order or stability of its government, the signatories promise to give Austria their aid in order to make the external cause of the threat disappear[;]" and third, the pact would subsequently be open to membership by countries beyond the original contracting signatories.[31] Schuschnigg rejected Mussolini's September proposals for a bilateral pact of joint military assistance between Italy and Austria, which, only at some later date, could have been opened to British, French, and German participation.[32]

Yet the result of Austria's effort at Geneva was failure. A British refusal to take part in guarantees of any sort (including, at the time, to Belgium), the national security concerns and obstructionism of Czechoslovakia and Yugoslavia, France's desire to defend its allies' interests, and the suspicion of Italian intentions towards the Little Entente together created insurmountable obstacles. Nor were Italian leaders even willing to consider the interests of the Little Entente.[33] All that could be agreed upon by British, French, and Italian officials was to reiterate, on 27 September, a slightly elaborated version of the 17 February 1934 declaration, which stressed the "necessity of maintaining Austria's independence and integrity in accordance with the relevant treaties."[34]

Throughout the rest of 1934 and the spring of 1935, the Schuschnigg government made repeated attempts to procure some kind of effective defense of Austria from France and Italy. In this undertaking, the Austrian government was aided by the recognition in Paris and Rome that Austria did indeed require some practical form of defense against Germany. In addition, in August 1935, operational planning began within the BMfLV, which envisioned an attack on Austria by the Third Reich. These plans were formulated between General Alfred Jansa (soon-to-be chief of the general staff), the operations department of Section III of the BMfLV, and the commanders of the 4th and 6th Infantry Divisions.[35] All the while, German representatives (most especially the philo-Nazi German ambassador to Austria, Franz Papen) made regular attacks against the Viennese government for its alleged "anti-German" actions at home and abroad.

Although during the Stresa Conference in April 1935 British Prime Minister Ramsay MacDonald and Foreign Secretary John Simon explicitly refused to take measures to defend Austria (agreeing only to what they understood was a meaningless "consultation" on Austria in the case of a threat to its independence), the Austro-French-Italian discussions on a guarantee of Austrian defense made real progress in May and June. This was especially due to the improved relations between Rome and Belgrade. As Schuschnigg noted during talks in Venice with Mussolini in May, "the big concern for Austria up to now has been that of having to face not only an attack from Bavaria but also from Yugoslavia. If Italian troops would have had to come to the aid [*soccorso*] of Austria, they could have faced a Yugoslavian penetration in Carinthia. So the Italian-Yugoslav agreement avoids this." At the same time Schuschnigg prudently rejected Mussolini's offer—made during the same meeting—of unilateral Italian aid to Austria in the case of German aggression, correctly understanding that

> . . . in this case [of a German attack] there are only two choices: to submit or to rely on European aid. The first choice is out of the question, so in this scenario we are compelled to put forward a claim for help. Thus we are of the view that, with respect to the current foreign political situation, [Austria] cannot rely on unilateral Italian assistance. The other powers also [would] have to stand up for the territorial status quo in central Europe directly and immediately.

On 2 July 1935, the Austrian government received good news. Schuschnigg's efforts to obtain a guarantee of Austria, as envisaged in the August/September 1934 Austrian Pact, had been realized in a different form. Thus, Italian Undersecretary for Foreign Affairs Fulvio Suvich informed the Austrian chancellor that, in agreement with the Roman Accords of 7 January 1935, a Franco-Italian engagement had been concluded at last, namely the Franco-Italian Military Accords of 27 June 1935.

The Military Accords dealt exclusively with mutual Franco-Italian military assistance in case of a German attack on either country and with the defense of Austria by French and Italian troops (the accords even contemplated forces from Yugoslavia and Czechoslovakia participating in the defense of Austria, though this remained problematic). Although the Military Accords were never officially ratified, both French Foreign Minister Pierre Laval (later Pierre-Etienne Flandin and, briefly, Léon Blum) and Mussolini considered them operational. But Austrian civil and military authorities refused French requests that troops be permitted to transit Austria in order to reinforce the states of the Little Entente, while reiterating that they would not take part in offensive operations against Germany. Short of a direct attack on Austria, which the Danubian state would resist, officials at the *Ballhausplatz* still hoped to avoid being dragged into war.[36]

Despite this Austrian success, however, clouds were on the horizon. Throughout the summer of 1935, Mussolini directed the buildup of Italian forces in Africa as part of his policy of building an Italian empire in the Mediterranean and Africa. Unsurprisingly, this led to a growing tension between Rome and London that threatened European peace. By summer, the foremost question at the *Ballhausplatz* was what would happen if Italian prestige became bound up in Abyssinia, especially if military operations commenced. In September, British leaders took the lead in advocating sanctions against Italy should it commence hostilities against Abyssinia, which posed a threat to British imperial lines of communication. Consequently, an Anglo-Italian war threatened.

For the *Ballhausplatz*, this posed a significant and multifaceted hazard. First, sanctions against Rome could encourage an Italo-German rapprochement, thereby calling into question Italy's commitment to Austrian independence. Second, the commencement of sanctions would jeopardize three more immediate issues: the admittedly weak Stresa front; the 27 June 1935 Franco-Italian Military Accords; and Italian membership in the League altogether. In light of the deteriorating situation, Berger-Waldenegg, before leaving for Geneva in mid-September, informed U.S. Ambassador to Vienna George Messersmith that one of the principle objectives of his trip was to see how far Laval and the newly appointed British Foreign Secretary, Samuel Hoare, were prepared to go in supporting Austria if it came to a confrontation in Europe over the Abyssinian crisis.

Unfortunately, the British refused to offer effective aid to the Austrian government should it alienate Italy, even as Hoare unequivocally insisted that Austria support the sanctions. By the end of September 1935, the members of the Schuschnigg government correctly understood that Anglo-Italian antagonism had led to the *de facto* collapse of the Stresa front and endangered the Franco-Italian Military Accords. Thus, throughout October and November, the Schuschnigg government engaged in a diplomatic balancing act aimed at preserving Italian support, avoiding British hostility, and maintaining recourse to aid from the League against German aggression. While this maneuver proved to be successful for the moment, Austria's international position continued to degenerate. A plan to settle the Abyssinian conflict at the cost of Ethiopia (the Hoare-Laval Plan) collapsed in mid-December, and Anglo-Italian animosity surged. Vienna was thrust into a constricting international position in which Italy stood defiantly against the League, and a furiously rearming Nazi Reich loomed ominously. Officials at the *Ballhausplatz* viewed this circumstance with great trepidation and hoped, along with leaders at the *Quai d'Orsay*, for an early end to the Italo-Abyssinian conflict. But war in Africa continued into the spring of 1936, and on 7 March 1936, Germany remilitarized the Rhineland in contravention of the Versailles and Locarno Treaties.

On 8 March, a deeply troubled Schuschnigg told the French Ambassador to Austria, Gabriel Puaux, "[N]ow that the treaty of Versailles is abolished the Führer will execute his pan-German program." The chancellor indicated to numerous statesmen and diplomats who would be the next victim: Austria.

Thus, in March, with Austrian security at stake, leaders at the *Ballhausplatz* decided to accept Mussolini's offer to strengthen the Roman Protocols. This, they believed, would help stabilize the situation in the short term. More significantly, leaders at the *Ballhausplatz* worked to promote Franco-Italian reconciliation, since relations between Paris and Rome had continued to degenerate after Laval's fall from power in January. They further attempted to forge anew security for Austria with France, Italy, and, if possible, Britain; poor relations between the French and Italians necessarily threatened the 27 June 1935 Franco-Italian Military Accords.

But, as is frequently the case, the Austrian cabinet records omit much, and they do not tell the story of Vienna's proposal for a reworked politico-military guarantee. In fact, Schuschnigg, Berger-Waldenegg, and Hornbostel, among others, believed that Italy represented a necessary but insufficient ally for Austria against potential German aggression. Consequently, on 20 March, the Austrian government contacted the French government to solicit, in strictest secrecy, the creation of a system of collective security through a pact with Britain, France, and Italy. This would be built upon the already existing and still functional, if endangered, 27 June 1935 Franco-Italian Military Accords. Given the gravity of the situation and in order to promote the pact, the *Ballhausplatz* asked—even begged—the *Quai d'Orsay* at the end of March and repeatedly throughout April to begin a rapprochement with Italy.

Unfortunately, no response from Paris was forthcoming. For complex domestic and foreign politico-military reasons, the transitory government of Albert Sarraut permitted the matter to languish. Moreover, in April the Italians began hinting to Vienna that they desired a settlement of the Austro-German conflict, while, at the same time, they repeatedly assured the Austrians that this would in no way change Italian support for Austria. Italian civil and military authorities followed up these assurances by collaborating with the Austrians militarily.

Thus, by the end of April 1936, Schuschnigg began to consider the necessity of reaching a *modus vivendi* with Germany in consideration of a confluence of factors: the immediate threat of a German attack, as suggested by Austrian intelligence reports; the risks implied by potential League oil sanctions against Italy and the ongoing Italo-German conversations; no response from Paris to Vienna's proposal for "a pact with the western Powers"; the lack of Franco-Italian rapprochement; massive German rearmament; and the categorical British unwillingness to participate in any guarantee of Austria. The Austrian chancellor, therefore, asked Guido Schmidt, who was a longtime friend and the liaison between the office of the president and the chancellery, to select names of supposedly moderate Nationals that might be brought into the government. Among the names were those of Arthur Seyss-Inquart and Edmund Glaise-Horstenau. On 4 May 1936, Schuschnigg suggested to Papen that they discuss "the possibility of a German-Austrian reconciliation" and that he, Schuschnigg, was prepared to consider representatives of the Nationals for a position in the government. Over the next two months, Austrian and German statesmen debated the contents of an Austro-German settlement.

Unsurprisingly, given Papen's frequent and inept duplicity in Vienna from 1934 to 1936, Schuschnigg well understood the Nazis' *modus operandi* and goal of conquering Austria. Schuschnigg and his colleagues were not honest and forthright in their talks with Papen and his collaborators but, rather, wily and deceitful—downplaying issues, omitting key proceedings, feigning goodwill, playing linguistic games, and often mixing truth and falsehood in order to misdirect the Nazis.

In their negotiations for an Austro-German settlement, Schuschnigg and his colleagues acted with cold calculation and with the knowledge that the Nazis and their agents were pathological liars. The 11 July 1936 Austro-German *Abkommen* (hereafter referred to as *Abkommen*) was a carefully constructed piece of writing in which clarity deliberately alternated with vagueness and which represented the centerpiece of Schuschnigg's second strategy of resistance to Nazi Germany from May 1936 to September 1937, that of feigned friendship. Making full use of the wording that he, Berger-Waldenegg, and Hornbostel had helped to draft (wrangling with Papen), Schuschnigg waged battle with Hitler by means of the spoken and written word. In this way, Schuschnigg tried to buy time for a reconstitution of the Franco-Italian front with whatever British support could be garnered, or, at least, to avoid the armed German expansion that he believed would undoubtedly come. In the ensuing battle of wits, the Austrians repeatedly proved themselves superior to the Nazis and their agents.

The conclusion of the *Abkommen* did not stop Schuschnigg's appeals for a guarantee, which he again undertook in July 1936 and April/May 1937. At the same time as the Austrian chancellor made his penultimate appeal for guarantee in April/May 1937, Schuschnigg acknowledged to the French that he could no longer depend upon Mussolini to oppose Germany with force; the best that could be hoped for was to keep Hitler and his cronies guessing as to Italy's attitude.

In what was by now an established pattern, neither of Schuschnigg's appeals to London and Paris produced results. The French Popular Front government of Léon Blum became suspicious of Vienna after seeing portions of the *Abkommen* communiqué, especially in light of Austria's membership in the Roman Protocols. In addition, they hoped to revitalize the League and procure the cooperation of Britain, Italy, and the USSR in establishing collective security. Finally, Blum and Delbos were still not convinced that they could not strike a deal with Germany.

But in April 1937, Blum and French Foreign Minister Yvon Delbos' views underwent a drastic revision in favor of Schuschnigg and in comprehending German intentions of aggression. Thereafter, until the destruction of the Austrian state, Delbos in particular did all that he could to aid Schuschnigg, while showing great admiration and understanding for Austria's resistance. Unfortunately, by April 1937 it had also become apparent to French civil and military leaders that they could only take forceful action on behalf of Austria—or indeed Czechoslovakia—if they had the absolute support of Britain. This the British had no intention of providing, believing that central Europe was not a vital interest for the British Empire and could, therefore, be given to Germany irrespective of any obligations or the will of its inhabitants. This forward the end of February 1938, Austria was explicitly abandoned by Great Britain, France and Italy.

By 1 March 1938, Schuschnigg grasped, quite accurately, that he had been deserted, but his options were now limited. The domestic situation was collapsing. Although he now accepted the support offered from the disaffected Left (including members of the SDP), which was necessary if he were to challenge the Reich with a war, he remained unwilling to take the measures necessary to take firm control of Austria by decapitating the Nazi party in Austria through ruthless police strikes, followed by military and para-military actions, and placing the *Bundesheer* on a war footing.

Instead, on 4 March Schuschnigg initialized steps for a plebiscite, which became public knowledge on 9 March. In doing so, he surely realized that he would provoke Nazi action against him. Schuschnigg was convinced that a plebiscite would result in a large majority in favor of Austrian independence, and he knew that Hitler's "claims" to Austria abroad had always been based on the premise that the Austrians would overwhelmingly vote to join the Nazi Reich. Moreover, Schuschnigg had contemplated holding a plebiscite for at least ten months, but avoided doing so precisely out of fear of a German invasion. It was self-evident in March 1938 that the risk of a German invasion was far greater. Still, in a desperate gamble, he pressed ahead. When faced with a mobilizing *Wehrmacht* on 10-11 March, accompanied by German demands to cancel the plebiscite, and, finally, an ultimatum for his resignation, Schuschnigg sent out final requests for foreign help. When no aid was proffered, at 3:30 p.m., he submitted again to force and resigned.

Notes

1. Lajos Kerekes, "Wirtschaftliche und soziale Lage Österreichs nach dem Zerfall der Doppelmonarchie," in *Beiträge zur Zeitgeschichte*, ed. Rudolf Neck and Adam Wandruszka (St. Pölten: Niederösterr. Pressehaus, 1976), 87-92; Leo Pasvolsky, *Economic Nationalism of the Danubian States* (New York: Macmillan, 1928), 94-95; Felix Butschek, *Statistische Reihen zur österreichischen Wirtschaftsgeschichte: Die österreichische Wirtschaft seit der industriellen Revolution* (Vienna: Österreichisches Institut für Wirtschaftsforschung, 1996), 20-22; Felix Butschek, *Der österreichische Arbeitsmarkt – von der Industrialisierung bis zur Gegenwart* (Stuttgart: G. Fischer, 1992), 63-65, 72-73; 108-09; Karl Heinz Herner, "Österreichs Industrie und Außenhandelspolitik 1848-1944," in *Hundert Jahre Österreichischer Wirtschaftsentwicklung 1848-1948*, ed. Hans Mayer (Vienna: Springer, 1949), 454, 458-59, 464-67.

2. Other parties at the time included the *Großdeustsche Volkspartei* (Greater German People's Party of Austria, [hereafter GVP] which appeared in September 1920 from the merging of seventeen national and provincial groups), the *Landbund* (an agricultural league of peasants), the Communist Party of Austria (hereafter KDP) and the *Deutsche Nationalsozialistische Arbeiterpartei* (German National Socialist Workers Party, or NSDAP [hereafter Nazi]).

3. G. J. Pulzer, *The Rise of Political Anti-Semitism in Germany and Austria* (New York: Wiley, 246-48; Karl Stadler, *Austria* (New York: Praeger, 129-38; Andrew G. Whiteside, *The Socialism of Fools: Georg von Schöner and Austrian Pan-Germanism* (Berkley, CA: U of Cailfornia P, 1975), 20-70, passim; Radomir Luza, *Austro-German Relations in the Anschluß Era* (Princeton, NJ: Princeton UP, 1975), 3-8, passim.

4. Adam Wandruszka, "Österreichs politische Struktur," in *Geschichte der Republic Österreich*, ed. Heinrich Benedikt (Vienna: Verlag für Geschichte und Politik, 1954), 427- 33; Anton Pelinka, "Political Parties and Ideological Movements in Austria," in *Austria Between Wars: Dream and Reality*, ed. Walter Greinert (Washington D.C.: Smithsonian Institution, 1987), 100-09; Alfred Diament, *Austrian Catholics and the First Austrian Republic: Democracy, Capitalism and the Social Order, 1918-1934* (Princeton, NJ: Princeton UP, 1960), 70-86; Ernst Panzenböck, "Der 'Anschluß' und die Parteien in Österreich," in *Der Weg zum "Anschluß" 1938: Daten und Fakten* (Vienna, 1988), 60, 68, 70-73, 79-80; Klemens von Klemperer, *Ignaz Seipel: Christian Statesman in a time of Crisis* (Princeton, NJ: Princeton UP, 1972), 225-28; Julius Braunthal, ed., *Otto Bauer: Ein Auswahl aus seinem Lebenswerk* (Vienna: Verlag der Wiener Volksbuchhandlung, 1961), 30-35; Alfred D. Low, *The Anschluß Movement, 1931-1938, and the Great Powers* (New York: Columbia UP, 1985), 30-36; Walter Wiltschegg, *Österreich – der "Zweite Deutsche Staat"?: der nationale Gedanke in der Ersten Republik* (Graz: Stocker, 1992), 16, 30, 46-48. See also R. John Rath, "Deterioration of Democracy in Austria, 1927-1932," in *Austrian History Yearbook* 27 (1996), passim; Rainer Nick and Anton Pelinka, *Parlamentarismus in Österreich* (Vienna: Jugend und Volk, 1984), passim; Rainer Nick and Anton Pelinka, *Burgerkrieg – Sozialpartnerschaft: das politische System Österreichs 1. und 2. Republik: ein Vergleich* (Vienna: Jugend und Volk, 1983), passim.

5. I use the term "Nazi" to mean NSDAP members and to refer to the Nazis in Austria *and* in Germany. In the case where one or the other group is specifically meant, the term is preceded by its modifier, for example, German Nazis.

6. Erwin Steinböck, *Die Kämpfe im Raum Voelkermarkt 1918-1919* (Vienna: Österreichischer Bundesverlag, 1969), passim; Stephan Verosta "Die österreichische Außenpolitik 1918-1938 im europäischen Staatensystem 1914-1955" in *Österreich 1918-1938: Geschichte der Ersten Republik*, Vol. 1, ed. Erika Weinzierl and Kurt Skalnik (Graz: Styria, 1983), 130-35; Ludwig Jedlicka, *Ein Heer im Shatten der Parteien: die militärpolitische Lage Österreichs 1918-1938* (Graz: H. Böhlaus Nachf., 1955), 17-31, 56-81; Manfried Rauchensteiner, "Zum 'operativen Denken' in Österreich 1918-1938: Pazifismus statt Kriegstheorien" in *Österreichische Militärische Zeitschrift* Heft 2 (März/April 1978): 153-56; Manfried Rauchensteiner, "Bundesheer und Wehrverbände auf dem Weg zum Bürgerkrieg," *Christliche Demokratie* 2.1 (February 1984): passim; Helge Lerider, "Die operativen Maßnahmen gegen die Nachfolgestaaten der Monarchie von 1918 bis 1938 unter besonderer Berücksichtigung der Ära Jansa," *Militärwissenschaftliche Hausarbeit* (Vienna, 1972), 10-23; Lajos Kerekes, *Abenddämerung einer Demokratie* (Vienna: Europa Verlag, 1966), 11-29; Peter Broucek, "Die militärische Situation Österreichs und die Entstehung der Pläne zur Landesverteidigung," in *Anschluß 1938: Protokoll des Symposiums in Wien am 14. und 15. März 1978* (Vienna: Oldenbourg, 1981), 138-39; Ludwig Jedlicka, "Aufteilungs- und Einmarsch- pläne um Österreich," in *der Festschrift für Franz Loidl*, Vol. 1, (Vienna, 1970), passim; Jürgen Gehl, *Austria, Germany, and the Anschluß, 1931-1938* (London: Oxford UP, 1963), 8; Gerald Stourzh, *Geschichte des Staatsvertrages, 1945-1955: Österreichs Weg zur Neutralität* (Graz: Styria, 1985), 93-98.

7. "Landesleitung Österreichs der NSDAP," *Das Dienstbuch der NSDAP*, preface, March, 1932. See also, Gerhard Botz, *Gewalt in der Politik. Attentate, Zusammenstöße, Putschversuche, Unruhen in Österreich 1918 bis 1934* (Munich: W. Fink, 1976), passim, 172-200; Bruce Pauley, *Hitler and the Forgotten Nazis: A History of Austrian National Socialism* (Chapel Hill, NC: U of North Carolina P, 1981), 70-79; R. John Rath, "The Dollfuss Ministry: The Intensification of Animosities and the Drift toward Authoritarianism," in *Austrian History Yearbook* 30 (1999): 76-77, 81-82, 84-89.

8. ÖStA/AdR, BMfLV/AR, 15- 1933, 15 2/4, 13500, Office of the Bundesminister to the Heeresamt, 12 June 1933; Beitrage zur Vorgeschichte und Geschichte der Julirevolte; Herausgegeben auf Grund Amtliches Quellen (Vienna, 1934), 18-30; Hans Völz, *Daten der Geschichte der NSDAP* (Berlin: A. G. Ploetz,, 1943), 111-12; Ludwig Reichhold, *Kampf um Österreich: Die Vaterländische Front und ihr Wiederstand gegen den Anschluß 1933-1938, Eine Dokumentation* (Vienna: Österreichischer Bundesverlag, 1984), 90-93, 95-96, 101-03; Gehl, Austria, Germany, and the Anschluß, 69; Pauley, *Hitler and the Forgotten Nazis*, 112.

9. Pauley, *Hitler and the Forgotten Nazis*, 104-11.

10. *NARS*, T120/2838/E453708-E453714, "Im Auftrag des Baron von Neurath. . . .," German Embassy London to Bülow, 16 June 1933. See also, *NARS*, T120/2838/E453718, German Foreign Office to London, Paris, Rome, 26 July 1933; *NARS*, T120/2838/E453721, memorandum by German Foreign Office, 2 August 1933; *NARS*, T120/2838/E453770, Reuters's Report, 3 August 1933; *ADAP*, C, I, 383, memorandum Bülow, 31 July 1933; *DBFP*, 2, V, 270, Vansittart to Harvey, 25 July 1933.

11. NARS, T120/2838/E453718, German Foreign Office to London, Paris, Rome, 26 July 1933; *NARS*, T120/2838/E453725, German Foreign Office to [vacationing] Neurath, 1 August 1933.

12. ADAP, C, I, 390, Neurath to Bülow, 4 July 1933; *ADAP*, C, I, 391, memorandum Bülow, 7 August 1933; *DBFP*, 2, VI, 201, Simon to Selby, 23 January 1934. This is not to say that Berlin was not concerned about the effect that Austria's protests were having throughout Europe, protests that the German Foreign Office believed could create real problems. *NARS*, T120/2838/E453743, Aufzeichung [German Foreign Office], 1 August

1933. It is notable that the Austrian Nazis were by no means a unified group subject to the absolute control of either Hitler or Habicht. Nonetheless, it is virtually impossible to imagine that the Nazis could have continued their terror campaign successfully in Austria without the approval and support of Berlin.

13. Ludwig Reichhold, *Kampf um Österreich*, 111-13, 115, 117; Pauley, *Hitler and the Forgotten Nazis*, 106, 109.

14. *DBFP*, 2, VI, Appendix I to 201, [Austrian] *aide-mémoire*, 23 January 1934.

15. *DDF*, 1, V, 275, Corbin to Paul-Boncour, 26 January 1934; *DBFP*, 2, VI, 201, Simon to Selby, 23 January 1934; *DBFP*, 2, VI, Appendix I to 201, [Austrian] *aide-mémoire*, 23 January 1934; *DBFP*, 2, VI, Appendix II to 201, [Austrian] résumé, 23 January 1934; *DBFP*, 2, VI, 202, Selby to Simon, 25 January 1934.

16. *DBFP*, 2, VI, 259, "The German reply to the Austrian Government," 31 January 1934; *NARS*, M1209/2/0622-0630, [German reply to Austria], Kliefoth [U.S. Chargé to Austria] to Hull, 5 February 1934. For Germany's official position on this issue of Austro-German relations, from which they never deviated, see *DBFP*, 2, VI, 259, Phipps to Simon, 7 February 1934.

17. *DDF*, 1, V, 313, François-Poncet to Daladier, 2 February 1934; *NARS*, M1209/2/0634-0639, #73, Kliefoth to Hull, 14 February 1934.

18. *DBFP*, 2, VI, 254, Drummond to Vansittart, 3 February 1934; *DBFP*, 2, VI, 261, Simon to Selby, 8 February 1934. *DBFP*, 2, VI, 273, Drummond to Simon, 13 February 1934.

19. On the Austrian corporate state, in which parties were to be replaced with professional bodies whose mission would be to resolve any class conflict, see Wolfgang Putschek, *Standische Verfassung und autoritare Verfassungspraxis in Österreich 1933-1938 mit Dokumentenanhang: Verfassung und Verfassungswirklichkeit* (Frankfurt: P. Lang, 1993). For the latest scholarship on Dollfuss' turn away from democracy and towards authoritarianism, see R. John Rath, "The Dollfuss Ministry: The Democratic Prelude," passim, 162-66; Rath, "The Dollfuss Ministry: The Intensification of Animosities" passim, 65-66; 100-01. During the socialist revolt, Dollfuss indicated to British ambassador to Vienna Walford Selby that he hoped the government's strong response "would be [a] deterrent to the Nazis as it would prove to them [that] he [Dollfuss] was master in his own house." *DBFP*, 2, VI, 275, Selby to Simon, 13 February 1934.

20. *DDF*, 1, V, 378, Puaux to Barthou, 14 February 1934; *DBFP*, 2, VI, 292, Tyrrell to Simon, 17 February 1934; Gehl, *Austria, Germany, and the Anschluß*, 83. The French and Czechoslovak governments continued to view the Dollfuss regime as a defensive bastion against Germany and deserving of support despite its authoritarian character. *DBFP*, 2, VI, 286, Selby to Simon, 16 February 1934; *DBFP*, 2, VI, 467, Hadow to Simon, 21 June 1934.

21. *DBFP*, 2, VI, 284, Drummond to Simon, 16 February 1934; *DBFP*, 2, VI, 290, Drummond to Simon, 17 February 1934.

22. H. James Burgwyn, "Italy, the Roman Protocols Bloc, and the *Anschluß* Question 1936-1938," *Austrian History Yearbook* 22 (1988): 123-24; Reichhold, *Kampf um Österreich*, 125-126. Dollfuss indicated to Mussolini on 14 March that, he, Dollfuss, could not accept German-Austrian friendship in the future unless it was related to Italian-Austrian friendship. Otherwise, it would lead the takeover of Austria by Germany. *DDI*, 7, XIV, 892, conversation Mussolini and Dollfuss, 14 March 1934. For details of the Roman Protocols, see Reichhold, *Kampf um Österreich*, 138-40.

23. *ADAP*, C, II, 328, Köpke to Rieth, 15 March 1934; *ADAP*, C, II, 389, memorandum by Bülow, 9 April 1934.

24. For an in-depth discussion of the events leading to the murder of Dollfuss and of the role of Hitler and his collaborators see Alexander N. Lassner, "Peace at Hitler's Price: Austria, the Great Powers, and the Anschluß, 1932-1938," Ph.D. diss., Ohio State University, 2002, 25-35. See also, more briefly, Alexander N. Lassner, "The Foreign Policy if the Schuschnigg Government 1934-1938: The Quest for Security," in *Contemporary Austrian Studies, vol. 11, The Dollfuss/Schussnigg Era in Austria,* ed. Günter Bischof, Anton Pelinka and Alexander Lassner (New Brunswick, NJ: Transaction, 2003).

25. Dollfuss' view that Austria "[maintain] with Germany those special relations of common race and culture" was not new. Austria had been pressing for an Anschluß until 1932, and former Chancellor Johannes Schober (chancellor from 1929-1930) had made clear in 1930 that "[*w*]*ir wissen uns in dieser Politik eins mit dem Deutschen Reiche, dem wir in guten wie in bösen Tagen brüderliche Treue halten wollen*" (quoted in Gerald Stourzh, *Geschichte des Staatsvertrages,* 96-97). Italian director general at the ministry of foreign affairs, Gino Buti, told both the French and British ambassadors to Rome that one had to be careful not to offend the Austria's "German sensibilities." DBFP, 2, XII, 47, Murray to Simon, 23 August 1934.

26. *ÖStA/AdR, BMfLV/AR*, 28 4-6 1934, 28-5/19725, "Über die Leitung der Landesverteidigung in Oesterreich," Regel to BMfLV, 15 July 1934.

27. *ADAP*, C, III, 137, report by Erbach, 31 July 1934.

28. ADAP, C, III, 116, German Foreign Ministry to Ministry of Interior, 25 July 1934; ADAP, C, III, 123, Hitler to Papen, 26 July 1934; ADAP, C, III, 149. memorandum by Hüffer, 7 August 1934; ADAP, C, III, 151, Hitler to Hess, Goebbles, Papen, and the office of secret police, 8 August 1934; ADAP, C, III, principles for German policy *vis-à-vis* Austria, 13 August 1934; ADAP, C, III, 167, Guiding Principles for German Policy *vis-à-vis* Austria in the Immediate Future, 19 August 1934; NARS, M1209/3/0654, No. 117, "Further Alleged Attempts to Organize a Movement to Overthrow the Austrian Government," Messersmith to Hull, 30 August 1934; DDI, 7, XV, 757, conversation Mussolini and Galli, 2 September 1934.

29. Contrary to popular myth, Italian troops were already mobilized and on maneuvers at the time of the 25 July 1934 revolt.

30. Article 88 of the Treaty of St. Germain stated that the independence of Austria was inalienable except by consent of the Council of the League of Nations. Articles 10 and 16 of the Covenant of the League of Nations provided for collective defense of states against unprovoked aggression. See The Avalon Project, "The Covenant of the League of Nations," 25 January 2005 <http://www.yale.edu/lawweb/avalon/leagcov.htm> (28 June 2001). The 1922 Geneva Protocol provided for unconditional maintenance of the independence of Austria in agreement with the League of Nations. See League of Nations, *The Restoration of Austria: Agreements Arranged by the League of Nations and Signed at Geneva on 4 October 1922, with Relevant Documents and Statements* (Geneva: 1922).

31. *DDF*, 1, VII, 303, conversation Hornbostel and Massigli, 12 September 1934; *DBFP*, 2, XII, 102, Vansittart to Selby, 20 September 1934.

32. *DDI*, 7, XV, 783, Aloisi to Mussolini, 8 September 1934; *DDI*, 7, XV, 788, Suvich to Mussolini, 9 September 1934.

33. Lassner, "Peace at Hitler's Price," 68-76, 526-27, 631-33.

34. *DBFP*, 2, VI, 288, Simon to Drummond, 17 February 1934; *DBFP*, 2, VI, 290, Drummond to Simon, 17 February 1934; *DBFP*, 2, XII, 124, Phipps to Simon, 28 September 1934.

35. Lassner, "Peace at Hitler's Price," 89-94, 97-99, 101-04, 112, 161-63.

36. Part of the text of this essay (Lassner, "The Foreign Policy of the Schuschnigg Government 1934-1938") is a condensed version of the article that appeared in *Contemporary Austrian Studies*, volume 11.

III: Second Republic Foreign Policy: Turning Points and Continuities

Between East and West: The Origins of Post-World War II Austrian Diplomacy during the Early Occupation Period

Günter Bischof[1]

Austrian postwar diplomacy started in the most treacherous of international environments in the final days of World War II. This essay is more concerned with the institutional efforts of recreating, staffing, and building a foreign office after the war rather than with foreign policy doctrine.[2] It concerns itself more with the launching of Austrian diplomacy, narrowly defined as engaging in a "dialogue between states,"[3] than with discussing more broadly all foreign relations and the options Austria faced in the early Cold War. The Ballhausplatz in Vienna, the site from which Austrian diplomacy is still being conducted, takes pride in a great tradition of conducting foreign affairs ever since Princes Kaunitz and Metternich sent diplomats abroad "to lie for their country." The diplomats on the Ballhausplatz were intent on continuing this great tradition after the war. At all times, however, Austrian diplomacy was conducted in an executive fashion. A small core of professional diplomats and a few cabinet members made foreign policy decisions with minimal input from parliament and little concern for public opinion.[4] In 1945/46 Austrian diplomacy was initially totally isolated from and then severely circumscribed by the occupation powers and the Allied Council. The Ballhausplatz's gradual emancipation from the constrictions of the quadripartite occupation followed a slow and tortuous path. This essay covers these difficult beginnings when Austria's maneuvering space in the international arena was minimal and her initial progress towards regaining sovereignty maddeningly slow and frustrating.[5]

Isolation and Improvisations: Difficult Beginnings (April-August 1945)

The premises of the Foreign Office (to be precise, the State Office for Foreign Affairs in the Federal Chancellery) had been vacated by Baldur von Schirach, the sunny boy of Adolf Hitler's youth movement and *Gauleiter* of Vienna, late in the war. The first diplomats began their work in the final days of April 1945. After the liberation of Vienna in early April, the provisional government of Karl Renner had been formed, and Austria's independence had been declared on 27 April. The biggest challenge for the resumption of Austrian diplomacy was the fact that the Anglo-American powers did not recognize Renner's provisional government. In spite of wartime agreements between the Allies to the contrary, it had been set up unilaterally by Stalin and his Red Army commanders in Eastern Austria. Next to equal numbers of Socialists and People's Party conservatives existed in Renner's cabinet which also had strong Communist representation.[6] The British and Winston Churchill's government above all did not like the fact that they were presented a *fait accompli* in Vienna before their first representatives got there; Whitehall was very concerned about the fact that Communists managed to get the crucial interior and education portfolios. It smacked of Eastern European unilateral Soviet action "all over again" with a puppet being set up in Vienna as had happened previously in Romania, Bulgaria, and Poland. The British would remain the sternest critics of the Renner government, and the Americans had to mediate this early British-Soviet Cold War in Austria until the Allied Control Council began to meet on 9 September and Renner was recognized by all four occupation powers on 20 October.[7]

Before we consider the resumption of diplomatic affairs in the chaotic final days of the war and the equally chaotic early weeks after the war, before the Allied powers moved into their previously assigned occupation zones and sectors, we should also remember a different kind of "foreign affairs" that began to prosper as soon as soldiers liberated the territory of the *Ostmark* (Hitler's *Donau- und Alpengaue*) namely, the encounter between soldiers and the Austrian population with considerable repercussions on Austrian perceptions of the principal powers. As the Allied forces liberated this peripheral terrain of Hitler's crumbled Third Reich, initial encounters ranged between suspicion and hostility; warm welcomes for the liberators were rare.[8] After the brutal battles in Budapest, the regular Red Army soldiers probably did not consciously think that they were entering friendly territory when finally crossing into the hated terrain of the Third Reich beyond the Hungarian border. The resistance of Hitler's forces on the *Ostwall* and the fierce battles for Vienna only confirmed the Red Army soldiers in their hatred of the

Nazis. The raping and looting of the Red Army throughout Eastern Europe and in Austria has to be seen as taking revenge.[9]

Most Allied soldiers probably did not make the fine distinction laid down by wartime "big three" diplomacy that Hitler's "first victim" Austria would be treated as "liberated" territory, while Germany would be considered "defeated" with all its consequences. The Red Army entered the Third Reich when they came across the Hungarian border, and American soldiers ended their campaign against Nazi Germany with their defeat of *Wehrmacht* and SS forces in Austria, when the *Oberbefehlshaber West* Field Marshall Gerd von Rundstedt surrendered in the Salzburg area and was taken prisoner. While the French forces proclaimed in Vorarlberg that they considered Austria a "friendly country," the Americans put up posters in Salzburg that they came as "victors" to Austria since "Austria was a substantial part of the German *Reich* and had been at war against the United Nations." Why? The reason for this unfriendly treatment was that the "wrong" American troops had liberated Austria. Instead of the 5th U.S. Army marching in from Italy, the 3rd Army came from Germany. The military government teams and political advisers for Austria were in the tow of the 5th Army, whereas for Patton's 3rd Army, the defeat of the German forces in the *Ostmark* was simply the completion of their mission to eradicate the German Nazi regime.[10]

The respective behavior of Allied troops shaped Austrians' images of "friends" and "enemies" for the postwar period. This aspect of public opinion also provided straightjackets for Austrian diplomacy. From day one of the occupation, the raping and looting campaign of the Red Army in the Soviet zone destroyed any chance for decent relations with the Austrian population, especially women. Moreover, Austrians harbored long-standing, anti-communist sentiments and cultivated deep-seated fears of bolshevism.[11] While Austrian males eyed the Western soldiers with suspicion, too, much of the female population quickly entered very friendly "foreign relations" with the good looking and well-fed Western troops, especially the American GIs.[12] This came in spite of an official American non-fraternization policy in Austria,[13] which reflected Washington's apprehension that the Nazis would just go underground after the war and continue their resistance against the Allies.[14]

Stephen E. Ambrose's description of the conduct of soldiers from the 101st Airborne division, the "band of brothers" heroized in a ten-part Hollywood film series, gives us a good idea of this other kind of "foreign affairs" and the spectacular failure of American non-fraternization policy:

> "Women, broads, dames, beetles, girls, skirts, frails, molls, babes, frauleins, Madamoiselles [sic!]: That's what the boys wanted,"

> Webster wrote. He went on to describe the results: "The cooks were keeping mistresses; the platoon lovers were patronizing the barn; McCreary had a married woman in town; Reese installed his in a private house; Carson fed an educated, beautiful, sophisticated Polish blond (whom he later married); the platoon staff visited the D.P. Camp nightly; and in Zell am See, home of the most beautiful women in Europe, the lads with the sunburned blondes were fulfilling their dreams—after talking about women for three years, they now had all they could want. It was the complete failure of non-fraternization policy."
>
> For those who had wanted and could afford them, there had been women in London, Paris, along the Ruhr, but, Webster observed, "in Austria, where women were cleaner, fairer, better built, and more willing than in any other part of Europe, the G.I.s had their field day."[15]

Whereas this quotation reveals a treasure trove of evidence for the social and gender historian, it is also a rich mine for the diplomatic historian. Petra Goedde has shown how the GI relationship with German women contributed mightily to a rapid rebuilding of amicable American-German relations, leading to the remarkable integration of West Germany into NATO only ten years after the end of the war. Tens of thousands of American soldiers experiencing the tender side of Germans quickly abandoned their fear of a resurgence of Nazism in Germany. German *Trümmerfrauen* replaced the werewolves in the American imagination. Fraternization transformed Germany's postwar fate. "By 1947, Americans had concluded that Germans no longer posed a threat to their European neighbors but instead required protection and guardianship," notes Goedde and concludes, "[a]nd the United States was eager to prove both."[16]

This rehabilitation of Germany by way of what might be called a myriad of "women ambassadors" was a crucial element in the rebuilding of American relations with (West) Germany. I suspect it was in the case of Austria as well, even though we do not yet have an empirical counterpart for the Austrian case (apart from the marriage of Fritz Molden with Joan Dulles, Allen and Eleanor Dulles' niece) to Goedde's imaginative scholarship. There was "a lot of fraternizing material"[17] in the Western zones in Austria; moreover, unlike "defeated" Germany, Austria presumably was a "liberated" country.

Let's return from this informal level of foreign affairs to the official level of diplomatic interactions and look at the emergence of the Foreign Office[18] in the rubble of Vienna, where the Ballhausplatz presented vistas of broken windows and chickens roaming through the premises.[19]

As if pulled by invisible tethers,[20] the first diplomats began to show up on the Ballhausplatz in the final days of the war once the Renner government began assuming the administration of Vienna and its environs. Most had survived the war in the Vienna area and had served since the final years of the Habsburg Monarchy and during the interwar period. The usual career path for the traditional Austrian diplomat had been a law degree and the course in the venerable old Consular Academy in Vienna (the oldest such institution in the world!). Their political leanings would have been conservative (some sported pan-German bias from their law studies in Vienna). Few had betrayed any discomfitures with the authoritarian Engelbert Dollfuss and Kurt von Schuschnigg governments.[21] Those who had prominently served the anti-Nazi "Christian *Ständestaat*" were sent to Dachau or premature retirement after the Anschluß. Oliver Rathkolb's fine research has demonstrated that twenty-six out of 100 career officials in the Austrian Foreign Service transferred into the Nazi German Foreign Office. Eventually, ten of these *Mitläufer* would return to the Ballhausplatz after the war.[22] Thus we have a complex record of both resistance to and arrangement/maneuvering with (the typical survivalist *lavieren* of bureaucrats) *vis-à-vis* National Socialism a detritus of former Nazi officials making it into the postwar Foreign Office.[23]

Among the first career officials returning to the Ballhausplatz were the brothers Clemens and Heinrich Wildner, Alois Vollgruber, Josef Schöner, the nobleman ("Edler"[24]) Norbert Bischoff, Karl Wildmann, and Ludwig Kleinwaechter; all except Schöner und Kleinwaechter were pre-World War II graduates of the venerable old Consular Academy; about three dozen others joined them. These hard-working officials did more than anyone to rebuild a working Foreign Office and, thus, launched highly successful postwar careers as leading Austrian diplomats. Heinrich Wildner became the fastidious first general secretary of the Foreign Office, the leading position akin to the British permanent undersecretary's job. Theodore Hornbostel, the man who had been in Wildner's job from 1930 to 1938, did not return after the war but stayed in retirement. Considered by many to be the most brilliant Austrian diplomat of his time, Hornbostel had dedicated himself to preventing the Anschluß and to defying Western appeasement before the war.[25] He had failed and had to live with that legacy after the war. Vollgruber and Kleinwaechter similarly had adhered to the anti-Nazi "Austrian ideology" of the Dollfuss and Schuschnigg regimes; both lost their jobs in 1938, and Kleinwaechter ended up spending five years in Dachau.[26]

From late April to early September 1945, the provisional Renner government was in a quasi-exile in its own land; in fact, rarely has a government been so drastically isolated from the rest of the world. Set up unilaterally by the Soviets, it was totally isolated in Vienna due to the refusal of the Western powers to recognize it. "Chinese walls"[27] cordoned off the Soviet zone from the three Western zones of occupation. The very first reports that can be found in the Foreign Office files at the Austrian State Archives are essentially brief reports of domestic reconnaissance missions by Foreign Office personnel into Vienna' surrounding areas. The Renner government initially had no contacts with the Western zones. It sent observers (*Gewährsmänner*) exploring the world beyond the "iron curtain" on the Enns River to gather information on the situation in the Western zones of Austria. Vienna in May/June 1945 was totally blocked off from the rest of the world. No international newspapers reached Vienna in these months. The only contact with the outside world was BBC radio, which was monitored assiduously in the first postwar weeks by Foreign Office officials such as Bischoff; summaries of radio news programs were shared with Renner who was in charge of foreign affairs as well. The Renner government was woefully ignorant of crucial events in Western Austria and in the international arena; it had no idea of vital information that might affect Austria's future. Thus it did not know the exact nature of provisional governments being set up in the Western zones of Austria, or the de-Nazification approaches by the Western powers; it did not know the exact zonal breakdown of Austria or the nature of the control machinery; it had no idea about important decisions being made by the victorious Allied governments in high level gatherings such as the Potsdam Conference on vital issues such as the future of "German assets" in Austria. Such vital information only began slowly to filter in via BBC broadcasts, observers reporting from Western Austria, and the first Western missions coming to Vienna in June and July. Rarely has a government been so uninformed about affairs in its own land and the world at large.[28]

Desperately isolated, Renner faced the first serious foreign policy crisis with the expulsion of "Sudeten Germans" from the newly reconstituted neighboring country of Czechoslovakia—the first country with which he resumed diplomatic relations after the war. Ferdinand Marek looked after Austrian nationals and affairs affecting Austria in Prague even before the war was over. Marek had been Austria's prewar minister to Czechoslovakia and established a fledgling Austrian diplomatic representation even before the Renner government was formed. Throughout the month of May, Marek insisted that Austrians not be treated as Germans and organized transports of Austrian citizens back to Vienna. Sometimes called the "Austrian Wallenberg," Marek suffered the Soviets' accusations of him helping "fascists" flee to Austria. They arrested him on 23 May; sadly, he disappeared into a Moscow prison, where he died before his trial.[29]

A day later, Renner appointed the former concentration camp inmate and, thus, credible "anti-fascist," the experienced diplomat Alois Vollgruber, as accredited "mission chief" in Prague. On 29 May, the Fierlinger government recognized him as "Plenipotentiary Safeguarding the Interests of Austrian Nationals in Czechoslovakia" and promised to protect Austrians to be repatriated (3,000 in Prague alone). This was a first step for Renner in terms of breaking through the ring of international isolation around his government. But Renner and Vollgruber could not stop the newly begun wild expulsions of "Sudeten Germans" (Austrian nationals included) from the Moravian border areas adjoining Austria. "Death to the Germans" became the slogan of enraged Czech nationalists. In June, 20,000 were expelled wildly from Znaim and 30,000 from Brünn. Houses were looted; women were raped. Marauding Czechs crossed the Austrian border for looting expeditions in a desperately poor land. The ugly and inhumane treatment of Sudeten Germans was reminiscent of "wild Aryanization" in Vienna in March 1938. The Czechs were taking cruel revenge on the Germans and their "betrayal" in the prewar period. Contemporary sources spoke of 100,000 refugees pouring across the border into Upper and Lower Austria in June and July of 1945 (later figures are much higher), producing a huge housing and food crisis. Czech officials dismissed protests by the Renner government with the excuse that "certain events could not be prevented in revolutionary times." The wild expulsions ceased in July. But at the Potsdam Conference, Czechosloavkia received permission from the Allied powers to transfer the German population out of the country.[30]

Based on the infamous "Benes laws," almost 2 million Germans were "evacuated" by the end of 1946. Gruber made his first trip abroad to Prague in late September 1945, where he managed to sign a trade treaty and to secure the resumption of Czech coal deliveries to Austria. In 1946, two-thirds of Austrian trade with Eastern Europe was with Czechoslovakia. Gruber had to make a huge concession, namely that the "transfer" of Sudeten Germans was an merely "internal" problem for Prague. While he insisted on minority rights in the case of the Germans in South Tyrol, Gruber noted that the Sudeten Germans had always been troublemakers and that "getting rid of them" was understandable. Rocky Austro-Czech postwar relations thus resumed from day one of this neighborly interaction. The coup in Prague in February 1948 and the Marshall Plan firmed up the "iron curtain" along the Austro-Czech border that came into existence as a result of larger East-West tensions.[31]

Austria's initial resumption of postwar trade relations tells a fascinating narrative of a chaotic postwar world in which individual regions took matters into their own hands in order to barter with their neighbors across borders. While the Renner regime suffered in its isolation and began making contacts with neighboring Czechoslovak regions, provisional governments in the Western zones struck pragmatic deals with their traditional neighbors. Vorarlberg and Tyrol launched a regular trade agreement with Switzerland that lasted into 1947. Raw materials were imported from Switzerland to restart the textile industry on barter terms and/or Swiss credits. Bavaria bartered food with its Austrian border regions. During times when basic survival was at stake, traditional, friendly, neighborly relations between local/regional government entities and people and family networks across borders often made the crucial difference in calories and basic needs. This is also a tale of a *decentered* regional foreign policy approach that indicates that it would take time until the central bureaucracies of Vienna resumed their traditional role of lording it over the provinces in "Josephinian" tutelary fashion.[32]

Cracking the "Chinese Walls": First Contacts with the Western Powers (June-September 1945)

In May 1945, the final agreements on the zonal division of Austria and the Austrian control machinery were held up in the European Advisory Commission (EAC) in London, pending a visit of a British-American military mission to Vienna to reconnoiter the city and its environs. The British never doubted the central importance of Vienna, "Vienna is the key to the Austrian situation, much more than Berlin is in the case of Germany."[33] The Soviets wanted agreement in the EAC on the zonal division of Austria, yet refused to let an Anglo-American military mission into Vienna to ascertain the state of affairs there. Given Stalin's unilateral action in setting up the Renner government, the Anglo-Americans put up a united front, as one high British official noted *vis-à-vis* Churchill: "We and the Americans [. . .] take the line that we should be buying a pig in a poke if we agree to settle anything in the E.A.C. before our Missions have had a chance of making a survey on the spot."[34] Given Soviet intransigence and perceived American naivité, Churchill starkly warned Truman that "we must regard Austria as in the Sovietized half of Europe."[35] Facing this united front, Stalin relented and dropped his objection to their representatives "acquainting themselves on the spot with the condition in the City" to prepare the final proposals for the EAC.[36] The united Anglo-American front seems to have impressed Stalin.

The first Western representatives to see Vienna and the surrounding Soviet zone of occupation stayed from 3 to 13 June. While the joint Anglo-American-French Vienna Mission lifted their veil of ignorance about conditions in Vienna, it kept them in the dark about Renner and his government since they refused to see him. The Soviets had asked for sixty to seventy observers; instead, the West came with 186 representatives, led by three generals. In keeping with the isolation of Renner, no political representatives were included. But the American sent some experienced Office of Strategic Services (OSS) officers to observe the political situation. The Austrian population welcomed these first visitors from the West enthusiastically, obviously hoping for relief from the Soviets and from hunger, and acted as if "there had been something wrong with the earlier Russian liberation."[37] The despondent Viennese population reported the raping and looting by the Red Army during the liberation. With many probably still under the sway of Nazi ideology, they betrayed their stark anti-Slav and anti-Communist prejudice by noting "that they are about to be subjected to a form of domination little different from the tyranny of National Socialism and administered by a race which they consider not only inferior to their recent German masters but even beneath the consideration of civilized people."[38]

The Western representatives worked hard for ten days scouting out the state of destruction, frequently clashing with their Soviet counterparts and Soviet restrictions on their movements, yet with the Americans always seeking compromises and understanding. They witnessed a collapsed city full of rubble, the nervousness of the local population, and the Soviet occupation regime. They talked about food, health, infrastructure, labor, prisoners of war, displaced persons, and vital economic and financial issues. Finding housing for Western occupation forces was a big challenge. However, the biggest divide came over the sectoral breakdown of Vienna. While the West would have liked to maintain the "larger Vienna" the Nazis had created by incorporating many surrounding areas in the *Gau* Vienna, the Soviets insisted on the borders of the much smaller prewar Vienna. The larger Vienna would have given the Western powers access to airfields within the city limits. The Soviets prevailed, and the Western airfields came to be located outside Vienna in the Soviet zone. So the West insisted that access rights from the airfields to the city had to be firmly written into the agreements.[39]

Nothing displayed the total and very awkward isolation of Renner and his fledgling diplomatic efforts like the refusal of Western representatives to see him. Renner had desperately tried to get in touch with the Western missions to present his situation and break through the diplomatic deep freeze. He prepared an "urgent appeal" for the Western governments and tried to get it into the hands of the mission chiefs. It was a *cri de coeur*, signaling all the tremendous problems his government faced in reconstructing the city, as well as meeting the population's basic needs such as food and coal. A currency reform was badly needed to retire the *Reichsmark* currency of the Third Reich and to resume using the Austrian Schilling again; trade had to be started up with the neighbors. Nothing could be achieved in resuming basic governmental responsibilities in Austria as long as the powers could not agree on zones and control machinery. But the missions left Vienna without even contacting Renner. He handed his memorandum, translated into English and French, to the Soviets who killed it by pocket veto. For the West, Renner remained a pariah.[40] Instead of Renner, the Western generals condescended to meet Theodor Körner, the provisional mayor of Vienna. The crusty British general Winterton only relented and shook Körner's hand after being reminded that he was "a perfect gentleman and old general of the Austrian Army."[41] Winterton's iciness was symptomatic of British policy.

Apart from refusing to start official relations with the Renner government, the Vienna Mission was quite successful. On the basis of the information gathered, the EAC in London made its final decisions on the zonal and sectoral breakdown (including access to airfields) on 9 July; the Allied Control Agreement (the First Control Agreement) had been signed on 4 July. The Austrian occupation finally got on track, and the Western powers got ready to move into Vienna.

Renner's appointment of four permanent representatives to begin conducting business with the occupation powers was a major step towards ending the quarantine of his government. He appointed Josef Eckhardt to establish contact with the French (with the Francophile Bischoff looking over his shoulders), Ludwig Kleinwaechter with the Americans, Wilhelm Engerth with the British, and Heinrich Schmid with the Russians. These liaison officials acted as envoys to the Delegations of the Interallied Commission. Their "quasi-legations" were their offices on the Ballhausplatz; their never-received "accreditations" were to the four occupation governments. While the Soviets had set up shop at the glorious Hotel Imperial, the Western powers had not yet established headquarters in Vienna. These Renner envoys hoped to keep the occupation powers informed about the policies of the Renner government, while divining details of their respective occupation policies towards Austria.[42]

Throughout July, they waited for the Western representatives to show up in Vienna. Finally, late in July, the Western advance parties began arriving to prepare for their commanders to move into the Austrian capital. On 27 July, Kleinwaechter joined a meeting between the American advance mission and Vienna city officials to sort out arrangements for headquarters at the National Bank building and for the billeting of U.S. Forces Austria (USFA). Kleinwaechter left with mixed feelings, particularly since Major Martin Herz, an Austrian émigré to the

United States who spoke perfect German, acted "stiff like a Prussian" (not a compliment coming from an Austrian) and behaved "like a victor rather than a friend." Herz, indeed, had grown up in Vienna, but was not "imbued with any particular or emotional hang-ups with respect to Austria."[43] Engerth had a more positive impression in his first meeting with the British advance man Major Prior on 30 July. The British intended to have friendly relations with the Austrians. Engerth also gleaned some information about the set-up of the British occupation element with a "quasi-military government" and a large civilian staff.[44] These meetings were resumed once the Western powers moved into Vienna in early September and *offiziöse* (semi-official) relations were resumed with the four liaisons.[45]

John Erhardt, the American political adviser to Mark W. Clark, the future high commissioner, was the first American official to receive spotty Austrian reports out of Vienna independent of the Vienna Mission. The young Socialist Ernst Lemberger, who had joined the French resistance against the Nazis, managed to slip across the zonal border into Vienna in June. Lemberger's report left Erhardt with the impression that the Renner government was as legitimate as the provisional governments formed in the provinces, and "perhaps more representative than some of them." Erhardt feared that casting Renner aside "might result in deadlock."[46] This fear would contribute to the drive in American policy to establish contacts with Renner in Vienna.

The first Allied representative to meet Renner personally was the OSS officer Edgar N. Johnson on 11 August. The septuagenarian Renner radiated his supreme confidence as a state builder, touting the occupations powers, for "[a]s a careful master of Austrian affairs, he does not believe that the Allies have much to teach him about his management." Renner warned them. "The Allies must not think, he [Renner] said, that they can come to Austria to rule [. . .] It would not be good, he said, to have foreigners representatives of the Austrian people." He insisted that the Soviets had not interfered in the workings of his government after setting it up in late April. Renner felt encouraged by the fact "that he had received from every provincial government in Austria pledges of loyal support." This was probably an exaggeration. He suggested gathering a *Länderkonferenz*, where he could meet representatives of the Western provinces to widen his government (he had already done this in the critical days of 1918 when initiating and building the institutions of the First Republic). He was also not averse to voicing his anti-German prejudice—dumping on the Germans became the first building block of a separate Austrian identity: "Germans were insufferably arrogant, poorly educated, politically naïve, and brutally intolerant people, when compared to the Austrians."[47] This came from the man who in March

1938 had openly advocated the Anschluß. Renner's past pan-German affiliation was another reason the British did not want to recognize his government.[48] While Martin Herz from the U.S. Army began interviewing top officials from the People's Party (Viktor Kienböck, Leopold Figl, Julius Raab), the Socialist (Karl Waldbrunner) and the Communists (Fischer), he apparently refused to see Renner and left him to the OSS.[49]

In August 1945, the Western moves into Vienna were held up by an Anglo-American struggle over who would feed Vienna—with the Americans resolving the impasse. The British insisted that a joint program for feeding Vienna had to be determined before they would set up headquarters in Vienna. London wanted Vienna to be fed from its traditional suppliers of food in Eastern Europe and Lower Austria. According to the Potsdam Agreement, the Soviets were required to feed the city until the establishment of a quadripartite government.[50] General Mark Clark, the commander of USFA and representative on the Allied Council, entered Austria on 7 August in a whirlwind of attention. Clark immediately insisted that the traditional Salzburg music festival be staged—resuming Austria's artistic life, being another building block to foster Austrian identity. He loved to be in the limelight, but he also insisted that the Austrians get their essentials to live and to gain confidence: music and food.[51]

The food situation General Clark resolved in personal meetings with the Allied commanders. He first invited them to Salzburg to the music festival. They met on 20 and 21 August in Salzburg, and he also took them to see Hitler's "Eagle's Nest" in nearby Berchtesgaden. The next day he flew to Tulln and met Marshall Ivan Koniev in the Soviet headquarters in Baden. On 23 August, the Allied commanders met again in Vienna and partially resolved their disagreements on the pooling of food to feed Vienna and agreed on the move into the Austrian capital. Clark's "masterful diplomacy"[52] mediated between the British and the Soviets and made sure that the Soviets did not feel "ganged-up" on. In the words of the British, he was "going whole hog now i.e. setting up control."[53] They did not personally meet Renner yet, but decided to take up quarters in Vienna on 1 September. The logjam was finally broken.[54]

Clark broke the ice between the British and the Soviets and precipitated the move into Vienna and the first meeting of the Allied Council on 9 September. He lifted the pariah Renner out of his isolation at last by meeting him personally on 11 September. The shrewd Renner had already prodigiously praised Clark for his "beautiful words" of benevolence and goodwill spoken at the opening of the Salzburg Festival.[55] Clark returned the favor by praising Renner as a "vigorous" old man. They discussed the food situation, and Renner pushed for the *Länderkonferenz*.[56] This meeting allowed Renner to begin speaking for *all* of Austria. Clark's lead forced General McCreery, the British high commissioner, to see Renner, too; quite predictably, McCreery was not much impressed. However, what came out of the logjam over Renner's status being broken was the *Länderkonferenz*. Renner met with representatives from the Western provinces in Vienna from 24 to 26 September and broadened his government with Western representatives such as Karl Gruber to direct foreign affairs. As a result of this broadened government, the Western powers recognized the Renner government on 20 October and set a date for a general election on 24 November.[57]

Clark's mediation in the Anglo-Soviet Cold War was crucial to normalizing relations with the Renner government, to extending his power to all of Austria, and to preparing for general elections and, thus, for the normalization in the administration of occupied Austria. Lest we forget, Whitehall's obstinacy in resisting unilateral Soviet moves in Austria and preventing another "puppet regime" springing up on the Danube was crucial in containing Soviet power in Central Europe. Churchill had felt after the war that the Americans took a "rosier view" of the Soviets. The British wanted the powerful Communist Minister of the Interior Franz Honner to be replaced in the Renner government and Communist strength reduced. Above all, they wanted an Austrian government in which all the provinces were represented, too. British diplomats who had served in Vienna before the war were afraid of the resumption of traditional Austrian political cleavages; "one of the great weaknesses of pre-war Austria was the cleavage between the urban and the rural populations and the undue predominance of Vienna in relation to the country as a whole."[58] They perceived the Renner government as resuming with this tradition of representing only the narrow territorial base of Vienna and demanded that this defect be remedied quickly. Dennis Mack, the Foreign Office's political representative on the British occupation element, acted as one of the originators of the plan for a *Länderkonferenz* already in June. The Mack Plan averred that once the Western powers moved into Vienna a meeting of provincial delegates should meet to form a provisional Austrian government (as it turned out, provincial representative broadened the Renner government to make it more "Austrian"). The Americans and French supported this plan, and the Foreign Office adopted it as their Austrian policy.[59]

The seminal idea for a *Länderkonferenz*, which broke the Austrian logjam, originated in a parallel fashion in London and Vienna. The conservative and anti-Socialist Mack had served in Austria in the 1930s and knew his Austrian history well. We have heard that Renner (harkening back to a *Länderkonferenz* in late 1918) had suggested such an all-Austrian meeting in mid-August to the OSS's Johnson. Moreover, at a time when Erhardt heard about the scheme from Mack in Verona,

Gruber, the provisional governor of Tyrol, also was floating the idea of a *Länderkornferenz.*[60] In other words, a *Länderkonferenz* was a natural progression for the recognition of the Renner government, steeped in the Austrian historical experience of 1918 to 1920; but the strong British advocacy of it brought the Western powers around to support it.

The British insistence on broadening the Renner government, bringing food supplies to Vienna from Eastern Europe, and tough bargaining over the establishment of the Allied Council in Vienna masked a larger geostrategic concern. They wanted to link these issues and to use the "pawn" Renner to impose conditions "essential to the re-habilitation of not only Austria but of South Eastern Europe." "It is clear that the problem now arising in Austria is only a symptom of the Russian policy in the whole of Eastern and Southern Europe," argued John Troutbeck, who directed Austrian policy in the Foreign Office, and added, "For that reason it would be impossible for a satisfactory solution to be negotiated in the Austrian Control Commission alone." The Western powers had to resist Soviet depredations jointly to make sure Austria was treated as a "political and economic whole." The Soviets, who were taking food and livestock from Austria and redirecting food distribution all over Eastern Europe, now wanted the West to make good on the deficiencies they were creating. The Russians had to be stopped, advocated Troutbeck sternly, "from ruining food production in Europe and impoverishing the world in their own short-term interest."[61] The "politics of food" and economic rehabilitation of Austria and Eastern Europe, of course, quickly aggravated East-West tensions and eventually would produce the Marshall Plan and the division of Europe. In this growing atmosphere of East-West discord, fledgling Austrian diplomacy had to reestablish its contact with the outside world to bring about an eventual end to the occupation and Austrian independence "from the liberators."

Breakout: The Origins of Postwar Austrian Diplomacy with the Outside World (October 1945 - June 1946)

The *Länderkonferenz* was a crucial turning point in the fate of postwar Austria. The inclusion of leaders from the provinces made the provisional government more *representatively Austrian* (rather than Viennese) and brought Renner out of his Viennese exile imposed by the Western powers. It watered down the influence of the Communists and began pulling Eastern Austria out of the exclusive grip of Soviet control. It gave the Western powers more influence over Austrian affairs, moved the entire country towards free elections, and precipitated a turn towards a *Western orientation*. After the November elections, the strict zonal borders ("Chinese walls") were coming down—at least in the West—as the coalition government of conservative Leopold Figl began to pursue his foreign policy agenda. At the top were the continuation of Renner's policies of ending Austria's international isolation, of encouraging economic reconstruction and reactivating foreign trade, and of regaining Austrian sovereignty and political independence, as well as selling the doctrine of "Austria as victim of Nazi Germany" abroad for the reestablishment of an Austrian nation and anti-German identity.[62]

In 1946, the Allies also pursued formal negotiations for peace treaties with Hitler's satellites (Italy, Hungary, Bulgaria, Romania, Finland), as well as initiating the process with Austria and Germany. In the Austrian State Treaty, negotiations securing the "German assets" in Austria and the pre-Anschluß borders quickly emerged as the top issues. The Figl government also invested an enormous amount of its foreign policy (and emotional) capital into regaining the South Tyrol region from Italy—unsuccessfully as it turned out.[63]

In early October 1945, the ambitious and vigorous thirty-six year-old Karl Gruber, World War II resistance fighter and former provisional governor of the Tyrol (May to September 1945), became Undersecretary of State for Foreign Affairs. Gruber's appointment also was linked to winning back the South Tyrol from Italy, which was given high priority in Austria's fledgling diplomacy. Still under the purview of the Federal Chancellery, he was minister without portfolio but enjoyed cabinet rank. With his wartime ties to the OSS, the Americans liked him, while the British kept their distance and the French disliked him intensely.[64] Gruber had a skeleton staff of barely two dozen officials with whom to work in his ministry. He appointed as his personal assistant twenty-one year-old Fritz Molden, another maverick World War II resistance fighter without a diplomatic background; he was disorganized and hung on to his job only until early 1946.[65]

Molden then was replaced by Kurt Waldheim, a graduate of the Consular Academy in 1939 (where he briefly joined the SS student organization) and dutiful soldier in Hitler's Army; as a young lieutenant in Russia and the Balkans, he served as an intelligence officer probably in the know about the worst war crimes committed in Yugoslavia and Greece (brutal retaliation against partisans and deportations of Jews). Never a Nazi party member, he "successfully accommodated himself to the system," as Oliver Ratholb wryly concludes.[66]

Gruber appointed some young talent like the nobleman Heinz Haymerle, Hans Coreth (also an aristocrat and a member of the prewar *Heimwehr*[67]), and Ludwig Steiner to his Foreign Office staff, all to embark on long and distinguished careers in Austrian diplomacy. Due to an ironclad, bipartisan agreement of equal distribution of power between the People's Party (ÖVP) and the Socialist Party (SPÖ) members in the federal bureaucracy (*Proporzabmachung*), Gruber (ÖVP) had to appoint young Socialist party members to his staff as well. Bruno Kreisky, Hans Thalberg, Walter Wodak, and Ernst Lemberger all entered the diplomatic service. Lemberger, as noted above, had fought bravely in the French resistance, while Kreisky, Thalberg, and Wodak were Jews who survived World War II in exile (Kreisky in Sweden, Thalberg in Switzerland, and Wodak in the British Army). All of them turned out to be superb appointments, for they went on to top careers in Austrian diplomacy and politics, Kreisky to become foreign minister (1960-1966) and chancellor (1970-1983).[68]

The maverick Gruber, driven by the emerging postwar bipartisan political culture, thus transformed the Foreign Ministry and quickly embarked on a strictly anti-communist foreign policy of Western orientation.[69] What had been a traditionally *male*, conservative (and formerly aristocratic) preserve became a breeding ground of political and diplomatic talent accessible to Austrians of more modest backgrounds (like Waldheim, Steiner, and Lemberger); women were admitted only slowly, the first three in 1947.[70] In this sense, the Austrian Foreign Office went through a democratization process, no longer being a traditional, elite, aristocratic, and bourgeois bailiwick of yesteryear,[71] similar to what the U.S. State Department had done in the early 1920s. Next to the experienced conservative diplomats who returned to the Ballhausplatz during the first days of Austrian independence—some with an "Austro-fascist" background, Gruber's "young Turks" featured impeccable anti-fascist credentials reflecting Austria's "victimization" during the Anschluß era. Given that Gruber himself had no background in diplomacy, his policies had an aura of improvisation during the early months in office. A former socialist and newcomer to politics, Gruber enjoyed relatively little support within his own party.[72]

The seminal, free elections on 25 November reduced the Communist influence dramatically to one minister in the coalition government formed by Leopold Figl (ÖVP).[73] Austria, with its own legitimate government moving towards partial emancipation from quadripartite control, now had the opportunity to send its first diplomatic representatives abroad. Gruber sent the Francophile Norbert Bischoff to Paris and put Lemberger at his side, well-known as a captain in the French resistance. Gruber dispatched the thirty-nine year-old Socialist Karl Waldbrunner to Moscow. Having worked as an electrical engineer in the Ural Mountains in the 1930s, he knew Russian well, but was totally innocent as a diplomatist. Ludwig Kleinwaechter was dispatched to

Washington with Hans Thalberg at his side. Gruber sent Heinrich Schmidt to London, accompanied by Walter Wodak. All three Austrian diplomatic missions in the capitals of the Western occupation powers thus had the bipartisan mix of experienced conservative "old hands" as mission chiefs with young and enthusiastic Socialist secretaries at their side. Bruno Kreisky was dispatched as the watchdog over conservative Karl Winterstein to Sweden, where young Kreisky had been in exile. What a French observer called the Socialist "*cadre lateral*" may have been quite unique in the annals of diplomacy. These Socialist young Turks, at times, developed their own partisan sideshow of diplomacy, oriented towards the goals of the Socialist Party in Vienna which was jealously watching over the conservative leadership in the Foreign Office, and regularly reported to SPÖ Vice Chancellor Adolf Schärf in Vienna. This SPÖ-driven *Nebenaussenpolitik* persisted through most of the occupation period (1945-1955) until some of these young Socialists moved into ambassadorial appointments and leading positions themselves in the Foreign Ministry—and Kreisky into the top jobs of state secretary (1953-1959) and then foreign minister (1959-1966).[74]

Bischoff with his reputation of masterful diplomatic reporting had a good start in Paris; before the year 1946 was over, he came to replace the inexperienced and frustrated Waldbrunner in Moscow. The Quai d'Orsay wanted to see occupation forces in Austria reduced, intended to support Austria *vis-à-vis* pressures from the Soviet occupation element, and promised to side with Austria in the South Tyrol dispute. The French thought they had superior knowledge of Central European affairs; their friendly policy towards Austria was driven by their principal goal of weakening Germany and preventing a future Anschluß. The French also developed a vigorous cultural diplomacy in their zone, expressing their deep kinship with Austria as a *Kulturnation*.[75]

Austria's mission in Moscow had the most difficult beginning. With the formation of the anti-Communist Figl government, Moscow's policy towards Austria changed. The Soviet occupation element headed towards breakneck economic exploitation of the zonal economy and constant political pressure on the "reactionary" Figl government, which at times resorted to outright blackmail.[76] Within this context, it came as no surprise that Waldbrunner suffered insurmountable difficulties and utter isolation from the beginning (even though he was a Socialist), at a time when all Western missions bitterly complained about being isolated in the Moscow diplomatic ghetto. The Figl government had no foreign currency in its coffers and failed to arrive at a mutually acceptable diplomatic clearing arrangement with the Soviet Union. Waldbrunner was not given a building for housing an Austrian mission; his tiny hotel room thus had to double as his office, where he also received visitors. The Soviet Foreign Ministry was difficult. Molotov was friendly but glum when it came to the rapid return of Austrian POWs held in the Soviet Union. With their new hardline "anti-fascist" policy in Austria, Soviet officials began to stress "the strong roots of fascism in the Austrian people." The Soviets refused to begin negotiations on the Austrian treaty issue at the Council of Foreign Ministers gathering in Paris in the spring of 1946. High Soviet Foreign Ministry officials could also be brutally frank when noting that larger European affairs determined Soviet foreign policy and not what happened in the country itself, "Austria is entirely tied up in the European difficulties." Seven weeks into his inglorious assignment, Waldbrunner came to Vienna "for consultations" in May 1946 and never returned to Moscow. The experienced, forty-six year-old Karl Braunias, who had had entered the Foreign Office in 1946, carried on with business in Moscow. Bischoff assumed duties as mission chief in Moscow in November 1946 and would have an unusually long term as political representative (1946-1953) and then ambassador (1953-1960).[77]

Bischoff assumed his post when the Austro-Soviet Cold War was in full swing and Austria's fate was dangling between East and West. The Soviets kept hammering away at Austria's insufficient de-Nazification efforts, "The little guys are hanged while the heavyweights get off scot-free." Foreign Ministry officials blasted Figl's growing Western orientation which seemed to indicate that "Austria is located on the shores of the Amazon or the Missouri rather than the Danube." Bischoff seemed to agree with Moscow's concerns and penned a secret memorandum for Gruber before his departure to Moscow, suggesting how relations with the Soviet Union could be improved. He noted that the Kremlin did not want Austria to become "an American colony" and the "domain of American banking and industrial capital." Moscow only wanted to secure "some key economic positions in Austria." Bischoff's conclusion was that Austria needed to join the Eastern European economic system where the Kremlin held the keys in its hands. Also, the polemical and hateful statements against Russia in the Austrian press and radio ought to be muffled.[78] Bischoff played gadfly to Gruber's new Westernization course, similar to Henry Wallace in Washington, who suggested Truman continue wartime cooperation with the Soviets. Bischoff was sent to Moscow where he would serve for more than ten years, while Wallace paid for his critique by being fired from his cabinet post.

Gruber simply ignored Bischoff's radical dissent from Austria's Western foreign policy direction that he had personally launched and in which he was invested. Indeed, this advocacy of an *Moscow-oriented Eastern policy* by the former Marxist Bischoff—soon to be considered as a communist "fellow traveler" by Western diplomats in Moscow—probably would have driven Austria towards satellite status. To end the Soviet "blockade" of Austria, Bischoff had already advocated such an orientation of Austria's foreign policy towards Moscow in a rare analytical memorandum (*Denkschrift*) in March 1946, arguing that the United States was not interested in the affairs of Central Europe. In spite of Bischoff's spectacular failure both to divine the U.S.'s role and the nature of the Soviet regime in 1946, Gruber sent him to Moscow and gave him firm instructions that Austria's international position would be one of "*friendships with all the blocs*" (emphasis added). In the growing Cold War, the Figl government pursued a difficult tightrope walk of maintaining equidistance between East and West, one that would ultimately be successful with the neutralization of Austria in 1955.[79]

Austria's representatives in Washington and London struggled to correct the Anglo-American perception of Austria's ambiguous World War II status and Austrians' actions during the war. It was important that both Kleinwaechter and Thalberg sported impeccable anti-fascist credentials because Austria had a "terrible reputation" in the American public mind.[80] When Kleinwaechter presented his credentials to Secretary of State James Byrnes, he at once strongly voiced Austria's foreign policy priorities *vis-à-vis* Washington, namely reduction of occupation forces (which weighed heavily on Austria's budget), American economic aid, and U.S. support to regain the South Tyrol.[81] Kleinwaechter was very successful in securing United Nations Relief and Rehabilitation Aid (UNNRA) and post-UNRRA aid for Austria's economic survival. On Gruber's orders, he rang alarm bells in Washington about Austria's economic crisis as a result of Soviet depredations, which might result in more severe political uncertainties. Gruber did not stop short of veiled blackmail: "Growing unrest and disappointment in the population" might force the Austrian government to seek a *modus vivendi* with the Russians.[82]

But next to securing Washington's crucial economic and political support, Kleinwaechter and Thalberg spent an inordinate amount of their time pushing the official "occupation doctrine" *vis-à-vis* American officials and the public. Their task represented a classical case study of diplomats being sent abroad "to lie for their country." Designing Austria's postwar international legal status was the most important task at hand for the fledgling Foreign Office staff in the spring and summer of 1945. The "occupation doctrine" purported that Austria had been a victim of Nazi aggression in 1938 and that Austrian statehood had lain dormant since the Nazi Anschluß and during subsequent occupation of the country. Austria, therefore, could not be held responsible for any of Hitler's aggression and war crimes and should not have to pay reparations. The Renner government, indeed, could build this doctrine on Allied wartime statements, particularly the Foreign Ministers' Moscow Declaration of 1 November 1943, which proclaimed Austria as "Hitler's first victim." Bischoff and other Foreign Ministry legal experts had designed this doctrine of Austria's international legal status during World War II, and in 1946, Austria's diplomatic representatives began advocating it vigorously in the Allied capitals. [83]

Kleinwaechter, it seems, had to write letters to American newspapers almost daily, disclaiming notions of Austrian responsibility. A letter to the *Washington Post* noted that Austrian were as guilty as Germans and added that Austrians should not "get away with it by just playing innocent, and pleading sympathy all over the world as a victim rather than a perpetrator of aggression." Kleinwaechter had a generic answer to all such attacks that he also shared with the State Department. It built on Allied appeasement in resisting Hitler in the events leading to the Anschluß. It particularly insisted on Austria's "liberated" status *vis-à-vis* Germany status as a "defeated" power and reminded Americans that Austria's separation from Germany was a strategic necessity for the Allies.[84] Frequent charges of the postwar revival of Austria's traditional anti-Semitism were harder to counter. Kleinwaechter and Thalberg conducted a very shrewd campaign in the American media. They organized an invitation from the elite journal *Foreign Affairs* for Gruber to write an article on Austria's international status and foreign policy priorities. Gruber was invited to the United States in October 1946 and gave a talk to the elite New York Herald Tribune Forum. The highlight came in a lunch with President Truman for which the State Department had prepared a basic statement on the U.S. position on Austria, namely that it was "a liberated country comparable in status to other liberated areas and entitled to the same treatment." This signaled a triumphant breakthrough for the international acceptance of the official Austrian "occupation doctrine."[85]

Schmid's and Wodak's job was not easier, for the British government refused to swallow Austria's "victim's status." The British position regarding Austria was ambiguous. In the summer of 1945, the British had not only misread the nature of the Renner regime, but by 1946, they were the originators and chief promoters of a new control agreement that would give the Austrian government more room to maneuver *vis-à-vis* the powers and alleviate the occupation regime (the Second Control Agreement was signed by the end of June 1946). Yet the Foreign Office legal division also insisted that the international legal status of liberated Austria was that of an "ex-enemy state." The British had recognized the Anschluß in 1938 *de facto* and *de jure* (the Americans had never recognized it *de jure*) and, therefore, did not end the "state of war" with

Austria until 1947, once all the peace treaties with Hitler's satellite states had been ratified. In August 1946, the American and French political advisers Erhardt and De Monicault were given full diplomatic status as ministers, while Mack's status was not upgraded to British Minister in Vienna due to Austria's "co-belligerent status." (In the nit-picking world of diplomatic protocol, Mack's status in Austria could not be raised as long as the country was regarded as an "ex-enemy" like Italy; only when the Italian peace treaty was signed and ratified by September 1947 was the British representative in Rome accorded full diplomatic status). Even though the Foreign Office was polite and encouraging to Schmid and Wodak, in their private thoughts, high officials like Troutbeck, who had called Austria a "flabby country" in 1944, made no bones about their true feelings, noting that Austrians ought not to "go on pretending that they never fought against us."[86]

Conclusion

At a time when there was a desperate shortness of paper in Vienna, Nazi stationary with the German *Reichsadler* was still used in government offices until new stationary arrived. Kleinwaechter and Thalberg had to burn such wartime stationary with Nazi insignia in the bathtub of their Washington hotel, where they initially did business.[87] As has been noted above, the Figl government was more successful at convincing Washington and Paris of Austria's "victim's status" than Moscow and London. After all, soldiers hailing from the *Ostmark* had fought bravely at Stalingrad and Kursk and Budapest and Vienna against the Red Army, and "like lions" in the North African desert against the British. Evidence of Austrians' signal contribution as *Vordenker* and in the implementation of the Holocaust kept accumulating in the Nuremberg and Dachau trials. The painful and deep-seated memories of some 140,000 Jewish émigrés dispatched to all four corners of the world could not be erased by facile legal doctrines and historical myth-making in official government publications such as the *Rot-Weiss-Rot Buch* published in the fall of 1946. The notion of Austria being a "lamb fed to the wolves" in 1938 did not square with these memories nor with the historical evidence. Still, for geopolitical reasons due to the emerging Cold War struggle, the Figl government succeeded in having the argument of Austria as "victim" accepted by the Western occupation powers by 1948, which also marked the end of serious de-Nazification in postwar Austria.[88]

The Foreign Office was at the heart of designing the "occupation doctrine" and selling it to the world. But beyond inventing a usable past, they had much more to do in the volatile international arena of 1945/46. They had to launch a full draft and prepare numerous position papers for negotiating an Austrian State Treaty to end the occupation and to gain independence for the country.[89] They fought mightily, but ultimately unsuccessfully, to correct the border with Italy and regain the South Tyrol.[90] They had to counter territorial demands from Yugoslavia and Czechoslovakia and were building up missions with neighbors and numerous other countries.[91] They had to conduct daily diplomacy with the Allied Council in Vienna.[92] They aided in defining as Austria's foreign policy doctrine an Austrian "manifest destiny" of serving as a "*bridge between East and West*"; this ideology would eventually feed into Austria's neutral status once the State Treaty was signed in 1955.[93] All of this occurred in a penurious country choke full of foreign occupation forces and refugees, as well as seriously understaffed and with plenty of neophytes in the world of diplomacy. It speaks to the Figl government's leadership and patience in a geopolitically difficult position, as well as Gruber's wily shrewdness and bold vision, that their principal foreign goals (apart from South Tyrol's return) would be achieved piece by piece.

Austria's patient diplomacy regained the country's independence and achieved the withdrawal of the Red Army—no small accomplishment in the face of fierce East-West tensions at the height of the Cold War, when war scares were more common than negotiated political settlements. David Lloyd George, a strong advocate of the "new diplomacy" during the peace conference in Paris (1919), coined the naughty *bonmot* that "diplomats were invented to waste time."[94] The rocky origins of postwar Austrian diplomacy and the successful conclusion of the Austrian State Treaty proved him wrong, for biding one's time—one of the hallmarks of the "old diplomacy" —still could help to produce results.

Notes

1. Every historian stands on the shoulders of and builds on the work of his fellow scholars in the field. Over the years, I have learned enormously from the fine scholarship on postwar Austrian foreign policy by Reinhold Wagnleitner, Michael Gehler, Oliver Rathkolb, Josef Leidenfrost, Thomas Angerer, Klaus Eisterer, Thomas Albrich, Siegfried Beer, Gerald Stourzh, and Rolf Steininger. I am grateful to them for sharing their ideas and writings with me over the years and for encouraging me in my own pursuit of this topic. I dedicate this article to them. Much of this article contains unpublished portions from my dissertation, "Between Responsibility and Rehabilitation: Austrian in International Politics 1940-1950," Ph.D. diss., Harvard University 1989, of course, updated and refined by recent scholarship.

2. The best analysis of Austria's postwar foreign policy trajectory now is Michael Gehler, *Der lange Weg nach Europa: Östereich vom Ende der Monarchie bis zur EU*, vol. 1, *Darstellung* (Innsbruck: StudienVerlag, 2002).

3. Adam Watson, *Diplomacy: The Dialogue between States* (New York: McGraw Hill, 1983), cited in Frederik Logevall, "A Critique of Containment," *Diplomatic History* 28 (September 2004): 473.

4. Günter Bischof, "Restoration, Not Renewal: From Nazi to Four-Power Occupation—The Difficult Transition to Democracy in Austria after 1945," *Hungarian Studies* 14/2 (2000): 207-31.

5. The only previous scholary studies looking at these challenging institutional beginnings of postwar Austrian diplomacy are Klaus Fieisinger, *Ballhauplatzdiplomatie 1945-1949: Reetablierung der Nachbarschaftsbeziehungen und Reorganisation des Auswärtigen Dienstes als Formen aussenpolitischer Reemanzipation Österreichs* (Munich: tuduv, 1993); Oliver Rathkolb, "Die Wiedererrichtung des Auswärtigen Dienstes nach 1945," unpublished project report, 1988.

6. On Stalin's packing of the Renner government with Communists and his overall intentions for postwar Austria, see the essay by Wolfgang Mueller in this volume.

7. Soviet action and the British response are analyzed in Günter Bischof, *Austria in the First Cold War, 1945-55: The Leverage of the Weak* (Houndmills: Macmillan, 1999), pp. 43-51; the American perspective is dissected in Josef Leidenfrost, "Die amerikanische Besatzungsmacht und der Wiederbeginn des Politischen Lebens in Östereich 1944-1947," Ph.D. diss., University of Vienna, 1986, 148-72.

8. The frosty welcome to the liberators was probably related to the fact that the majority of the population in the *Donau- und Alpengaue* supported the Nazi regime into the final days of the Third Reich; see Evan Burr Bukey, *Hitler's Austria: Popular Sentiment in the Nazi Era, 1938-1945* (Chapel Hill: Univ. of North Carolina Press, 2000).

9. On Soviet raping and looting, see Bischof, *Austria*, 30-42; see also Norman M. Naimark, *The Russians in Germany: A History of the Soviet Zone of Occupation, 1945-1949* (Cambridge, MA: Harvard Univ. Press, 1995), 69-140; Max Hastings, *Armageddon: The Battle for Germany, 1944-1945* (New York: Alfred A. Knopf, 2004).

10. The liberation of Austria by American troops is covered by Kurt Tweraser, *US-Militärregierung in Oberösterreich 1945-1955, vol. 1, Sicherheitspolitische Aspekte der amerikanischen Besatzung in Oberösterreich-Süd 1945-1950* (Linz: Oberösterreichisches Landesarchiv, 1995), 35-88; Franklin L. Gurley, "Der Einmarsch der amerikanischen Armee in Westösterreich, April/Mai 1945," in *Österreich 1945: Ein Ende und viele Anfänge*, ed. Manfried Rauchensteiner and Wolfgang Etschmann (Graz: Styria, 1997), 145-56; on Americans in Salzburg, Leidenfrost, Amerikanische Besatzungsmacht, 252-79; on French and "*pays ami*," see Klaus Eisterer, *Französische Besatzungspolitik: Tirol und Vorarlberg 1945/46* (Innsbrucker Forschungen zur Zeitgeschichte 9) (Innsbruck: Haymon, 1991), 8ff and picture 2 (*vis-à-vis* page 232), and Thomas Angerer, „Frankreich und die Österreichfrage: Historische Grundlagen und Leitlinien 1945-1955," Ph.D. diss, University of Vienna, 183ff.

11. Ingrid Fraberger and Dieter Stiefel, "'Enemy Images': The Meaning of 'Anti-Communism' and Its importance for the Political and Economic Reconstruction in Austria after 1945," in *Contemporary Austrian Studies, vol. 8, The Marshall Plan in Austria* (New Brunswick, NJ: Transaction, 2000), 56-97.

12. Ingrid Bauer has provided a steady stream of insightful scholarship on these issues, see *Welcome Ami Go Home: Die amerikansiche Besatzung in Salzburg 1945-1955. Erinnerungslandschaften aus einem Oral-History-Projekt* (Salzburg: Verlag Anton Pustet, 1998); idem, "'Die Amis, die Ausländer und wir': Zur Erfahrung und Produktion von Eigenem und Fremdem im Jahrzehnt nach dem Zweiten Weltkrieg,' in *Walz—Migration—Besatzung: Historische Szenarien des Eigenen unf Fremden*, ed. Ingrid

Bauer, Josef Ehmer, and Sylvia Hahn (Klagenfurt: Drava, 2002), 197-276.

13. Leidenfrost, Amerikanische Besatzugnsmacht, 263-67.

14. Timothy Naftali, "Creating the Myth of the Alpenfestung: Allied Intelligence and the Collapse of the Nazi Police-State," in *Contemporary Austrian Studies, vol. 5, Austrian Historical Memory and National Identity* (New Brunswick, NJ: Transaction, 1997), 203-46. American GIs had to watch Army movies warning them about the threat of a Nazi underground and "werewolf" guerillas.

15. Stephen E. Ambrose, *Band of Brothers: E Company, 506th Regiment, 101st Airborne From Normandy to Hitlers' Eagle's Nest* (New York: Simon and Schuster, 1992), 286f.

16. Petra Goedde, "From Villains to Victims: Fraternization and the Feminization of Germany, 1945-1947," *Diplomatic History* 23 (Winter 1999): 1-20 (here, 20); see also idem, *GIs and Germans* (New Haven: Yale Univ. Press, 2002); for sensitive personal perspectives of how German women were initiating shy, naïve, and "boyish" GIs into manhood, see Leon C. Standifer, *Binding up the Wounds: An American Soldier in Occupied Germany 1945-1946* (Baton Rouge: Louisiana State Univ. Press, 1997).

17. Eisterer citing an American GI, *Französische Besatzungspolitik*, 22.

18. "Foreign Office" used here as a generic term masks a complex institutional history. From 27 April to 25 September 1945 there existed the *Amt für Auswärtige Angelegenheiten* administered personally by Renner as part of the State Chancellery in his provisional government; after the *Länderkonferenz* of Karl Gruber administered the fledgling *Staatskanzlei—Auswärtige Angelegenheiten*, after the November 1945 elections and the formation of the new Figl government, a minister without portfolio conducted foreign affairs by heading the *Bundeskanzleramt—Auswärtige Angelegenheiten*. Thus foreign affairs remained in the nominal purview of the Federal Chancellery until 1959 when a separate Ministry for Foreign Affairs was instituted. The best institutional summary is given by Gerald Stourzh in *Mitteilungen des Österreichischen Staatsarchivs* 36 (1983): 434-40.

19. The composite picture comes from memoirs and diaries. See the highly informative diary by Josef Schöner, *Wiener Tagebuch 1944/45*, ed. Eva-Marie Csáky, Franz Matscher, and Gerald Stourzh (Veröffentlichungen der Kommission für Neuerer Geschichte 83) (Vienna: Böhlau, 1992); Clemens Wildner, *Von Wien nach Wien: Erinnerungen eines Diplomaten* (Vienna: Herold, 1961); Fritz Molden, *Besetzer, Toren, Biedermänner: Ein Bericht aus Österreich 1945-1962* (Vienna: Molden, 1980); Hans Thalberg, *Von der Kunst Österreicher zu sein: Erinnerungen und Tagebuchnotizen* (Vienna: Böhlau, 1984); see also Michael Derndarsky, "The Foreign Office since 1918," in *The Times Survey of Foreign Ministries of the World*, ed. Zara Steiner (London: Times Books, 1982), 59-74.

20. "Pulled by invisible, magical strings, we gathered on the Ballhausplatz to reconstitute under the leadership of my brother [Heinrich] ... the future Foreign Office, see C. Wildner, *Von Wien*, p. 250.

21. On the student and faculty profiles of the "consular academy" and their ideological predispositions in the interwar years and into the early Nazi period, see the essays by William D. Godsey, Jr., '...nun kaufmännisch zur verfahren bemüssigt ist...': The Consular Academy at Vienna in the First Austrian Republic 1918-1938," and Oliver Rathkolb, "Die Konsularakademie unter dem 'Hakenkreuz' 1938 bis 1941ff," in *250 Jahre: Von der Orientalischen zur Diplomatischen Akademie in Wien*, ed. Oliver Rathkolb (Innsbruck: StudienVerlag, 2004), 141-80.

22. See Oliver Rathkolb's unpublished prosopographic study "The Austrian Foreign Service and the 'Anschluß' 1938"; and his unpublished "Die Wiedererrichtung des Auswärigen Dienstes nach 1945" (1988), Fiesinger, *Ballhausplatz-Diplomatie*, 54-62. See also the essay by R. Agstner in this volume.

23. Lothar Wimmer, Josef Eckardt, and Karl Hudeczek among them.

24. Much of the basic biographical information on the experienced "returnees" to the Ballhausplatz in 1945, who were also graduates of the Consular Academy, can be found in the very rich section by Rudolf Agstner, "Die Direktoren, Hörer und Hörerinnen der Orientalischen Akademie und der Konsularakademie 1754-1941," in *250 Jahre*, ed. Oliver Rathkolb, 405-566, eg., on Bischoff Edler von Klammstein, page. 426, Vollgruber, page 552, the Wildner brothers, page 557.

25. On Hornbostel, see also the essay by Alexander Lassner in this volume.

26. See the informative dispatch "Organisation du Minstère des Affaires Etrangères," EU/30, De Monicault to Leon Blum, 16 January 1947, Vol. 106, p. 13, Autriche 1944-1949, Ministère des Affaires Etrangères [MAE], Archives Diplomatiques, Quai d'Orsay, Paris. On Hornbostel, see Alfred Ableitinger, "Theodor Hornbostel und Friedrich Funder," in *Neue Fakten zu Staatsvertrag und Neutralität*, ed. Alois Mock et al. (Vienna: Politische Akademie, 1980), 125-34.

27. Karl Gruber used this term in a speech to provincial delegates in Salzburg, 29 July 1945 in *Karl Gruber: Reden und Dokumente 1945-1953* (Vienna: Böhlau, 1994), 63.

28. See folder "Radio-Mitteilungen" and various travel reports and Schöner minutes, Box 1, Archiv der Republik [AR], Österreichisches Staatsarchiv, Vienna; see also the very selective volume of documents *Österreich und die Grossmächte: Dokumente zur Österreichischen Aussenpolitik 1945-1955*, ed. Alfons Schilcher (Materialien zur Zeitgeschichte) (Vienna: Edition Geyer, 1980).

29. Martin David, "Österreichisch-tschoslowakische Beziehungen 1945 bis 1974 mit besonderer Berücksichtigung aktueller Themen," Ph.D. diss., University of Vienna, 2002.

30. Bischof, "Responsibility and Rehabilitation," 374-81; Fiesinger, *Ballhausplatz-Diplomatie*, 237-54.

31. *Die Beneš-Dekrete*, ed. Barbara Coudenhove-Kalergie and Oliver Rathkolb (Vienna: Czernin, 2002); Gruber citation in Oliver Rathkolb, "Zentrale Trends in der österreichischen Aussenpolitik nach 1945," in *An der Bruchlinie: Österreich und die Tschechoslowakei nach 1945*, ed. Gernot Heiss et al. (Innsbruck: Studienverlag, 1998), 156; Andrea Komlosy, "The Marshall Plan and the Making of the Iron Curtain in Austria," in *Contemporary Austrian Studies, vol. 8, The Marshall Plan in Austria*, 98-137.

32. Klaus Eisterer, *Die Schweiz als Partner: Zum eigenständigen Aussenhandel der Bundesländer Vorarlberg und Tirol mit der Eidgenossenschaft 1945-1947* (Schriftenreihe des Instituts für Föderalismusforschung 64) (Wien: Braumüller, 1995). See also Stefan Mayer's essay in this volume

33. Letter Grigg (Minister of War) to Eden, 14 February 1945, General Political Correspondence of the Foreign Office [FO 371]/46626/C 1126, Public Record Office [PRO], Kew, London.

34. Sargent to Churchill, 9 May 1945, FO 371/46615/C 2041, PRO.

35. Churchill to Truman, 9 June 1945, in *Foreign Relations of the United States* [FRUS] *1945*, vol. 3, *European Advisory Commission: Austria, Germany* (Washington: GPO, 1968), 132.

36. Stalin to Churchill, 18 May 1945, FO 371/46616/C 2305, PRO.

37. The most flavorful comments on these encounters come from the OSS officer Charles Thayer, see *Hands Across the Caviar* (Philadelphia: J.P. Lippincott, 1952), 175ff; for more general background on the Vienna mission, see Leidenfrost, Amerikanische Besatzungsmacht, pp. 173-95; Donald R. Whitnah and Edgar L. Erickson, *The American Occupation of Austria: Planning and Earl Years* (Westport, CT: Greenwood, 1995), 107-20; James Jay Carafano, *Waltzing into the Cold War: The Struggle for Occupied Austria* (College Station, TX: Texas A & M Univ. Press, 2002), 43-47.

38. Thayer report, "Observations on the Present Political Situation in Vienna," 14 July 1945, repr. in *Gesellschaft und Politik am Beginn der Zweiten Republik: Vertrauliche Berichte der US-Militäradministration aus Österreich 1945 in englischer Orignialfassung*, ed. Oliver Rathkolb (Vienna: Böhlau, 1985), 283-88, here 287.

39. Bischof, *Austria*, 47f; Carafano, *Waltzing*, 45f. See also summary of Flory report, Erhardt to Secretary of State, 17 June 1945, in FRUS, 1945, III, 138-42.

40. See the "Dringliche Eingabe," Renner to Tolbuchin [sic], 14 June 1945, repr. in Schilcher, ed., *Österreich und die Grossmächte*, 2-5.

41. Schöner minute, 11 June 1945, 211-pol/45, Box 1, AR.

42. See the personnel roster of the "Bundeskanzleramt-Auswärtige Angelegenheiten," 73-K/45, Box 1, 1946, Kabinett des Ministers, RA; Engerth minute, 28 July 1945, 641-pol/45, Box 3, RA.

43. Kleinwaechter minute (initialed by Renner), 28 July 1945, 457-pol/45, 706-pol/45, Box 2, RA; see Martin Herz, "Background of the Reports and the Reporting Officer," in *Understanding Austria: The Political Reports and Analyses of Martin F. Herz Political Officer of the U.S. Legation in Vienna, 1945-1948*, ed. Reinhold Wagnleitner (Salzburg: Neugebauer, 1984), 5-8. Herz's political reporting collected in this volume is one of the most insightful sources of Austrian affairs during the early occupation. In his initial report from August 2, for example, he reports that the Red Army was requisitioning much food and "no cooperation at all existed between the government and the Russians, as far as food matters are concerned" and that the population largely had to secure its survival on the black market (24).

44. Engerth minute (initialed by Renner), 30 July 1945, 761-pol/45, 761-pol/45, Box 3, RA.

45. Unsigned minute [probably Bischoff], 6 September 1945, Folder "Staatsvertrag 1945/46," Box 14, Pol-1946, RA.

46. Erhardt (from Verona) to Mathews, 13 July 1945, FRUS, 1945, III, p. 567.

47. This fascinating *tour de force* is recorded in Rathkolb, ed., *Gesellschaft und Politik*, 114-18; Johnson wrote an even more detailed report on "The Renner Government" on 14 September 1945 (Ibid., 174-85).

48. Ibid., 184; see SSU, R & A, 26. September 1945.

49. Wagnleitner, ed., *Understanding Austria*, 27-50 (including his keen "Observations on the Renner Government," 37-40).

50. Erhardt to Secretary of State, 18 August 1945, FRUS 1945, III, 571f.

51. Personal interview with Edwin Kretzman; on Clark, see Günter Bischof, "Mark W. Clark und die Aprilkrise 1946," *Zeitgeschichte* 13 (April 1986): 229-51.

52. Erhardt to Williamson, 19 September 1945, Folder "Erhardt," Box 1, Subject Files Austria 1954-50 (Lot 54 D 331), General Record of the Department of State (RG 59), NA.

53. Winterton to War Office, 22 August 1945, FO 371/46629/C 5222, PRO.

54. For more detail, see Bischof, Between Responsibility and Rehabilitation, 171-75.

55. Renner public statement, 23 August 1945, Folder 2, Box 40, Mark W. Clark Papers, The Citadel, Charleston, SC.

56. Erhardt to Secretary of State, 12 September 1945, FRUS, 1945, III, pp. 589f; Leidenfrost, Amerikanische Besatzungspolitik, 223-27.

57. Ernst Bezemek et al., *Die Länderkonferenz 1945: Dokumente und Materialien* (Vienna: Amt der NÖ Landesregierung, 1945).

58. Harvey memo for Bevin, 16 September 1945, FO 371/46620/C 5876, PRO.

59. The "Mack Plan" first surfaced in a Mack minute on 21 June, and then in the War Office directive to McCreery, 5 July, both in FO 371/46617/C 3456, PRO; "Brief on the Austrian Government for UK Delegation to CFM", September 1945, FO 371/46619/C 5733 (contains French of support). Clark's support is noted in letter Mack to Harvey, 3 August 1945, FO 371/46619/C 4483, PRO.

60. Erhardt to Mathews, 13 July 1945, FRUS, 1945, III, 566, and in more detail in personal letter to Mathews, 13 July 1945 (with a memo from Gruber to Watts [US military government in Tyrol], 24 June 1945, included), Folder "Correspondence 1945, Box 3, Lot 54 D 511, RG 59, NA.

61. Troutbeck memorandum, 15 August 1945, FO 371/46628/C 4749, PRO.

62. Gehler, *Der lange Weg nach Europa*, vol. 1, 119-21.

63. Ibid., 101-16.

64. "Erhardt ... is a great supporter of Gruber and feels that it would be a good thing if there were seven or eight energetic young men like Gruber in the cabinet instead of some of the more elderly and tired ministers." See "Personal and Confidential" letter Mack to Harvey, 31 May 1946, FO 371/55146/C 6592.

65. On Gruber, see Michael Gehler, "Dr. Ing. Karl Gruber – Erster Landeshauptmann von Tirol nach dem Zweiten Weltkrieg," in *Für Österreichs Freiheit: Karl Gruber – Landeshauptmann und Aussenminister 1945-1953*, ed. Lothar Höbelt and Othmar Huber (Innsbrucker Forschungen zur Zeitgeschichte 7) (Innsbruck: Haymon, 1991), 11-70; and *Karl Gruber: Reden und Dokumente 1945-1953*, ed. Michael Gehler (Innsbruck: Böhlau, 1994); and Gruber's memoirs, *Between Liberation and Liberty: Austria in the Postwar World*, trans. Lionel Kochan (London: André Deutsch, 1955). On Molden's brief tenure in the Foreign Office, see his memoirs *Besetzer, Toren, Biedermänner: Ein Bericht aus Östereich* (Vienna: Molden, 1980), 43-63.

66. On Waldheim's World War II trajectory, see Robert Edwin Herzstein, *Waldheim: The Missing Years* (New York: Arbor House, 1988); Waldheim's classical Austrian "*lavieren*" at the consular academy is covered by Rathkolb in *250 Jahre*, 173f.

67. Godsey in Rathkolb, ed., *250 Jahre*, 164-75.

68. On Kreisky, see his abridged, translated memoirs, *The Struggle for Democratic Austria: Bruno Kreisky on Peace and Social Justice*, ed. and trans. Matthew Paul Berg (New York: Berghahn Books, 2000); H. Pierre Secher, *Bruno Kreisky Chancellor of Austria: A Political Biography* (Pittsburgh: Dorrance, 1993); Günter Bischof and Anton Pelinka, eds., *Contemporary Austrian Studies*, vol. 2, *The Kreisky Era in Austria* (New

Brunswick, NJ: Transaction, 1994); on Thalberg, see his highly informative memoirs *Von der Kunst Österreicher zu sein: Erinnerungen und Tagebuchnotizen* (Vienna: Böhlau, 1984); on Wodak see the documentation of his dispatches by Reinhold Wagnleitner, ed., *Diplomatie zwischen Parteiproporz und Weltpolitik: Briefe, Dokumente und Memoranden aus dem Nachlass Walter Wodaks 1945-1950* (Salzburg: Neugebauer, 1980).

69. Josef Leidenfrost, "Karl Gruber und die Westorientierung Östereichs nach 1945," in *Für Österreichs Freiheit*, 101-20; see also Michael Gehler's introduction to *Gruber: Reden*, 20f.

70. In 1931/33 one quarter of the students were women, among them a considerable number of Jewish women. It is remarkable that due to financial pressures, the prewar Consular Academy "paradoxically became a pioneer in the education and preparation of women for foreign service and international work" (Godsey in Rathkolb, ed., *250 Jahre*, 153; see also Rathkolb in ibid., 167f.) The male bias on the Ballhausplatz prevailed after the war, for no women were hired in 1945 on the 3 women hired, see Agstner in this volume, p. 51. Personal stories abound about Gruber having been an archetypical male chauvinist who preferred women in the prone position.

71. The Consular Academy's prewar, elite status as a aristocratic preserve is sociologically analyzed in Gernot Stimmer, "Die Konsularakademie im Spannungsfeld zwischen Leistungs- und Gesinnungselite, in Rathkolb, ed., *250 Jahre*, 105-40, and brilliantly recreated by historian William D. Godsey, Jr., *Aristocratic Redoubt: The Anglo-Hungarian Foreign Office on the Eve of the First World* War (West Lafayette, IN: Purdue Univ. Press, 1999); Godsey also demonstrates how this aristocratic tradition continued into the post-World War I period, albeit in a diminished way, in Rathkolb, ed., *250 Jahre*, 151ff.

72. On "improvisation," see Bischof, Responsibility and Rehabilitation, 393-96; "Proporz" and postwar Austrian foreign policy, see idem, "Spielball der Mächtigen? Österreichs aussenpolitischer Spielraum im beginnenden Kalten Krieg," in *Inventur 45/55*, ed. Wolfgang Kos and Georg Rigele (Vienna: Sonderzahl, 1996), 126-56. See also the valuable edition of Gruber's speeches and the introduction in *Gruber: Reden*.

73. Josef Leidenfrost, "Preventing a Rupture? U.S. Occupational Authorities and Austria's Long and Winding Road to the First Postwar Nation-wide Elections on 25 November 1945," in *Zeitgeschichte* 30/1 (2003): 19-36.

74. EU/30, De Monicault (Vienna) to Leon Blum, 16 January 1947, vol. 106, Autriche 1944-1949, Série Z Europe, MAE. De Monicault in his extensive dispatch on the "organization of the Foreign Ministry" also noted that the Foreign Office had an insufficient number of personnel; well-qualified young people were rare while some of the older generation, who had served the Nazis, were not allowed to return. See also Bischof, "Spielball." Wodak's reports to Schärf are in Wagnleitner, ed., *Diplomatie*; Lemberger's dispatches are in the Schärf Papers, Verein zur Geschichte der Arbeiterbewegung, Vienna.

75. Bischoff's eloquent dispatches from Paris are in –pol-46, Box 6, RA. For more detail, see Bischof, Responsibility and Rehabilitation, 398-401; Angerer, "Frankreich und die Österreichfrage"; Lydia Lettner, "Die französische Österreichpolitik von 1943 bis 1946," Ph.D. diss., University of Salzburg, 1980; Barbara Porpaczy, *Frankreich – Österreich 1945-1960: Kulturpolitik und Identität* (Innsbrucker Forschungen zur Zeitgeschichte 18) (Innsbruck: StudienVerlag, 2002).

76. On Stalin's post-election policy of "discrediting the reactionary character of the Figl government" by means of pro-Soviet and pro-communist propaganda, see the Mueller essay in this volume.

77. Waldbrunner's desperate dispatches are in Box 6, RA. For more details about the Waldbrunner episode, see Bischof, Responsibility and Rehabilitation, 401-5.

78. Smirnov's warning in Braunias to Gruber, 13 November 1946, 111.115-pol/45, 113.427-pol/46, Box 6, RA. Bischoff's remarkable memorandum "Vorschläge zur Bereinigung unseres Verhältnisses zur Sowjet-Union" is dated 27 November, 111.105-pol/46, 113.561-pol/46, Box 6, RA. Gruber may have suppressed a discussion of it, as there are no minutes or comments attached to it.

79. Bischoff's equally pig-headed memorandum of 12 March 1946, penned in Paris, is reprinted in Michael Gehler, *Der lange Weg nach Europa: Österreich von Paneuropa bis zum EU-Beitritt*, vol. 2 *Dokumente* (Innsbruck: StudienVerlag, 2002), 125-28; Gruber's "Instruktionen für Gesandten Bischoff," 29 November 1946, 111.105-pol/46, 113.561-pol/46, Box 6, RA. Top British diplomats such as William Hayter and Harold Caccia considered Bischoff a "fellow traveler," (from personal interviews with the author 26 and 13 March 1986). Kreisky thought he came close of being a "fellow traveler"(Rathkolb interview with Kreisky, 1 February 1984). I am grateful to Dr. Rathkolb for providing me with a copy of this interview's transcript. Waldbrunner had pursued a policy of Austrian "balance between East and West" as he told Frank Roberts, see letter Roberts to Hayter, 26 April 1946, FO 371/55257/C 4790. On Bischoff, see also the informative memoirs of an Austrian junior diplomat in the Moscow Embassy, Otto Eiselsberg, *Erlebte Geschichte 1917-1997* (Vienna: Böhlau, 1997), 200-57.

80. Thalberg, *Von der Kunst*, 163.

81. Memorandum of Conversation, 18 February 1946, FRUS, 1946, I, 308f.

82. Gruber's circular instructions to all mission chiefs from April 1 110.860-pol/46 are more broadly discussed in Bischof, Responsibility and Rehabilitation, 334-39.

83. There is a considerable literature on this issue, which is quite contentious. See Bischof, *Austria*, 52-67; Robert H. Keyserlingk, *Austria in World War II: An Anglo-American Dilemma* (Kingston: McGill-Queens Univ. Press, 1988), and the magisterial Gerald Stourzh, *Um Einheit und Freiheit: Staatsvertrag, Neutralität und das Ende der Ost-West-Besetzung Österreichs 1945-1955* (Vienna: Böhlau, 1998), 11-28.

84. See letter the *Washington Post*, 6 September 1946, attached to Kleinwaechter to Foreign Office, 11 September 1946, 112.221-pol/46, 112.911-pol/46, Folder "Amerika," Box 1, RA. For Kleinwaechter pushing the official "occupation doctrine," see the "letter to the editor" of 26 July attached to the letter to Williamson, Folder "Kleinwaechter," Box 4, Lot 54 D 331, RG 59, NA.

85. Karl Gruber, "Austria Infelix," *Foreign Affairs* 25 (January 1947): 229-38; Kleinwaecher's and Thalberg's subtle behind-the-scenes media strategy is also discussed in Günter Bischof, "Where May Meets Lazarsfeld: American Public Opinion toward Austria in the Early Cold War," in *Rethinking International Relations: Ernest R. May and the Study of World Affairs*, ed. Akira Iriye (Chicago: Imprint, 1998), 309-20.

86. See Troutbeck conversation with Sargent, Sargent minute, 10 April 1946, FO 371/55257/C 4141, PRO. For British policy towards Austria, see Bischof, Responsibility and Rehabilitation, 423-38; and more generally, Robert G. Knight, "British Policy towards Occupied Austria, 1945-1950," Ph.D. diss., London School of Economics, 1986.

87. See the delivery order from the Government Printing Office for Renner's Denkschrift, 216-pol/45, 216-pol/45, Box 1, pol-1945, RA; Thalberg, *Von der Kunst*, 175.

88. Bischof, Responsibility and Rehabilitation, 438-42.

89. Stourzh, *Um Einheit und Freiheit*.

90. Rolf Steininger, *Los Von Rom? Die Südtirolfrage 1945/46 und das Gruber DeGasperi Abkommen* (Innsbrucker Forschungen zur Zeitgeschichte 2) (Innsbruck: Haymon, 1987); Michael Gehler, ed., *Verspielte Selbstbestimmung? Die Südtirolfrage 1945/46 in US-Geheimdienstberichten und österreichischen Akten. Eine Dokumentation* (Innsbruck: Wagner, 1996).

91. Fiesinger, *Ballhausplatz-Diplomatie*, 95-402; Renate Tuma, "Tschechoslowakische Gebietsansprüche gegenüber Österreich 1946/47," in *Für Österreichs Freiheit*, 121-42

92. This crucial area of "domestic diplomacy" is still awaiting a competent historian.

93. Figl stressed the "bridge" theme in his inaugural speech as chancellor on 21 December 1945, reprinted in *Der Weg zu Freiheit und Neutralität: Dokumentation zur österreichischen Aussenpolitiik*, ed. Eva-Marie Csáky (Vienna, 1980), 58-61; Bischof, Responsibility and Rehabilitation, 443f. Gruber, who launched a Westernization of Austrian foreign policy, speaks of Danubian cooperation, but does not address Austria's "bridge" function in his early statements. See his speech before the "Herald Tribune Forum" on 30 October 1946 in Gehler, ed., *Gruber: Reden*, 158

94. Quoted in Margaret Macmillan, *Peacemakers: Six Months that Changed the* World (London: John Murray, 2001), 155.

Neutral Encounters of the Paranoid Kind: Austria's Reactions to the Hungarian Crisis of 1956

Johanna Granville

Hallo, Mr. Bischoff? This is your Chancellor calling from Vienna. How are things in Moscow? Good, good. So . . . have you delivered the protest yet? Excellent! Bye now." Stretching forward with a grunt, Julius Raab put down the receiver, chuckling. How 'bout that? Austria's very own crisis for a change. Let's give the world something to talk about! Pain ripped through his chest, and he gasped. Seventeen years of occupation. No! We can't go back! But those poor kids . . . Can they handle it? They just started training last week. And all that hard work with Nikita Sergeevich. Things were going so well . . .

In contrast to Walter Ulbricht's plight in the German Democratic Republic, the Hungarian revolution and the Soviet crackdown did not threaten Austrian Chancellor Julius Raab's internal political position. On the contrary, it rallied the entire country to face this first challenge to Austria's newly-won neutrality. Austrian workers put in extra hours; chemists donated 600 million units of penicillin.[1] Often a crisis, successfully met, becomes a fond memory in the collective consciousness, despite the humanitarian tragedy it entailed. Austrian historians typically enumerate positive "spillover" effects that the 1956 crisis had upon Austria. They posit that the 1956 crisis provided Austria with its first test of neutrality and that Austria passed it with flying colors. This article will partially debunk that traditional argument; in some ways, Austrian statesmen indeed failed to keep their neutral policy unblemished. A close examination of documents from the Austrian State Archive reminds us both of the difficulties the Raab government faced in steering a neutralist course and of the more repellent spillover effects of the crisis. Archival documents are like personal diaries. Without them, historians would forget the unpleasant obstacles and fall prey to the fallacy of retrogressive determinism. After providing background on

Austria's importance in this period and briefly surveying published literature about the Hungarian crisis's positive forms of spillover, this article will cover in detail three ways in which the crisis "overflowed" onto Austrian territory in disagreeable ways.

First, the crisis hindered Austria's ability to further the cause of Hungarian freedom and, thus, reinforced the *status quo*. Second, despite the generosity and selflessness of the Austrian population, the Raab government had to seek substantial outside help, for it could neither afford the crisis financially, nor provide permanent asylum to the majority of refugees. Third, the crisis worsened Austria's relations with both Hungary and the Soviet Union, undoing the progress made in the months after the State Treaty (*Staatsvertrag*) was signed on 15 May 1955. Needing to justify the invasion and the ousting of Imre Nagy's regime, Soviet and Hungarian propagandists accused Austria of violating neutrality, using the concrete issues of border incidents, espionage, favoritism toward organizations, repatriation of refugees, and hostile propaganda to support their assertions.

The Importance of Austria

Scholars have most often associated the Hungarian revolution with the Polish "October" which occurred just a week earlier and for which one can find a more direct causal link. However, in many ways Austria is an under-researched catalyst of the events. Having persuaded Soviet troops to vacate its territory and achieving neutrality in 1955, Austria set an important precedent that aroused Hungarian desires for a similar Soviet troop withdrawal. While the Raab government's successful negotiation of Soviet troop withdrawal and achievement of neutrality did not directly cause the Hungarian Revolution, it influenced many Hungarians' outlook.[2] Certainly U.S. policymakers like John Foster Dulles hoped that Austria could serve as a magnet to draw the other satellites away from the Soviet Union, showing them that they, too, could "shake off the Soviet presence and Kremlin's iron rule."[3]

Secondly, by its geographical position, Austria was destined to become one of the countries most directly affected by the Hungarian revolution. As the only non-communist country directly bordering Hungary, Austria was bound to receive a flood of refugees, not only from Hungary itself, but also from Yugoslavia.[4] Once part of the Austro-Hungarian Empire, Austria contained a sizeable Hungarian community, especially in its easternmost province, the Burgenland, so along with the influx of refugees came a growing concern about irredentism. (At a cabinet meeting on 20 November 1956, Oskar Helmer, minister of the interior, reported that Burgenland's governor and deputy had visited him, insisting upon the quick transport of refugees away from the area. "Many of them have relatives in Eisenstadt [the capital city of Burgenland]. This has caused an irredentist attitude," Helmer warned his colleagues.)[5] Concern about irredentism further intensified when Hungarian refugees in Austria and other countries began receiving pamphlets entitled "*Út és Cél*" ("Path and Goal") featuring maps of Hungary in 1918, showing the Burgenland as part of Hungary.[6]

Third, viewing the Hungarian crisis through the lens of Austria, a neutral country, allows one to step back from the traditional perspective of U.S.-Soviet power politics. Indeed, the role of the neutral countries in the Cold War has been a relatively neglected research area, at least among non-Europeans.[7] Many have viewed them as bland and uninteresting, as if by being neither friend nor foe, they could not influence political situations. But, in fact, as impartial observers, neutral countries have often been used to mediate in crises, conveying information overtly or covertly between parties, thereby resolving them before they erupt in war. Some have assumed that neutral countries behave like uniform "billiard balls," yet—as one can see in the Hungarian crisis—the response of the neutrals varied widely, with Austria taking the most proactive stance of any neutral country and, indeed, of any Western country.

When the student demonstration turned violent in Budapest on 23 October 1956, Chancellor Raab was on an official visit to Bonn. Circumventing the constitution, Minister of Defense Ferdinand Graf decided the next day to place some sections of the Federal Armed Forces on alert and transferred motorized and armored units from Vienna, Upper Austria, and Styria to the Burgenland. A neutral, off-limits zone (*Sperrzone*) was established close to the border.[8]

Having returned from Germany, Raab convened the Special Ministers' Council (*Sonderministerrat*) in the early afternoon of 28 October, where he and others decided to issue a sharp rebuke and warning to the Soviet Union:

> Having followed with grief and compassion the bloodshed and loss of life which have been going on in our neighboring country of Hungary for no fewer than five days now, the Austrian government earnestly requests the government of the USSR to cooperate in putting an end to the military action and suffering. Based on Austria's freedom and independence which is secured by neutrality, the Austrian Federal Government advocates normalizing the situation in Hungary, with the aim to strengthen and secure peace in Europe through re-establishing freedom and human rights.[9]

The new ambassador of the USSR, Sergei G. Lapin, had just arrived in Vienna to present his credentials, so Raab quickly received him earlier that day, and then delivered the warning to Lapin immediately after the Special Ministers' Council meeting.[10] Ambassador Norbert Bischoff in Moscow was also instructed to deliver the message, as fictionalized in the vignette above.[11] The Federal Army was instructed to shoot any member of the Hungarian or Soviet armed forces who was armed, crossed the Austrian border, and refused to relinquish his weapon.[12] On the same day, Minister of the Interior Oskar Helmer announced asylum for every Hungarian refugee, whatever the cause of his or her arrival.[13] By 28 October, around 3,000 Austrian soldiers in fully motorized units patrolled the border zones.[14] Hence, Austria was the very first Western democracy to officially protest Soviet actions—well before the major Soviet crackdown of 4 November.

Another neutral country, Switzerland, which traditionally exercised strict restraint in military situations, found the Austrian response overly proactive. In a conversation on 1 November between Austrian envoy to Berne, Johannes Coreth, and the Swiss Federal President Max Petitpierre, the latter said Austria's position was admirable, but not worth imitating.[15]

Review of Literature and Positive "Spillover" Effects of the Crisis

As mentioned, most scholars of the Hungarian Revolution have tended to focus on Poland's influence on the revolution. One recent collection of essays (*Das Internationale Krisenjahr 1956*), for example, devotes 700 pages of analysis to the events in Poland, Hungary, and Egypt, but completely omits the situation in Austria.[16] Those scholars who have focused on Austria's reactions to the 1956 crisis have stressed the positive forms of spillover and Austrians' generosity toward Hungarian refugees. Perhaps one of the first, most memorable, accounts of Austria's response to the Hungarian crisis is James Michener's novel, *The Bridge at Andau*. Michener flew to Vienna a few days after the second Soviet invasion and stayed at the border for six weeks, helping the refugees. In an emotional tone, he describes the spirit of the Austrian students:

> Toward midnight a brave team of three Austrian college students decided that something must be done, and they lugged logs into Hungary and repaired the dynamited bridge—not well, but enough for a precarious foothold—and by this means they saved more than two thousand people that night alone. They were just college kids with earmuffs and no caps, but they had abundant courage, for after their

> wet clothes had frozen on them, they crossed their own improvised bridge and combed the Hungarian swamps, dodging communist guards and Russian outposts. They led many refugees to their bridge [. . .] Then came the flood! Hundreds upon hundreds of refugees came across that frail footbridge. [. . .] They would hear the Austrian students cry, "This is Austria!" and they would literally collapse with gladness.[17]

Key works on the refugee situation by Eduard Stanek, Károly Gáal, and Katalin Soós provide useful statistics and illustrate, in a more dispassionate manner, the generosity of the Austrian people toward Hungarians fleeing repression.[18] Valuable research in the Austrian archives conducted in the 1980s by Reiner Eger and Manfried Rauchensteiner indicates that the 1956 crisis drew Austrian political parties—indeed, the whole population—closer together, discredited the Austrian Communist Party, and gave military strategists a useful precedent upon which to base their assessment of the next Soviet invasion of a country on their border twelve years later in Czechoslovakia.[19] Indeed, they point out, the federal army was just forming. Although the federal gendarmerie of the occupation era had been preparing for a year to merge with the regular armed forces, the first 12,500-13,000 young Austrian conscriptees had entered the barracks a mere eight days before the Hungarian students' demonstration on 23 October 1956. They faced severe shortages in equipment and uniforms.[20] Thus the Hungarian crisis tested and boosted Austrian soldiers' courage, enabling them to vindicate the armed forces' past performance in the March 1938 crisis (the Anschluß), which began seventeen years of occupation, first by Nazi Germany and then the Allied Powers. Although the 1938 crisis entailed a failure of political, rather than military, leadership, it nevertheless tainted the army's reputation. These views are also articulated in new research by military historians Hubert Speckner and Erwin Schmidl grounded in texts from the Austrian military archive (*Kriegsarchiv*). As mentioned above, they all conclude that the Austrian armed forces passed their first test with "flying colors" (*mit fliegenden Fahnen*).

The Hungarian crisis benefited Austria in other ways not explicitly stated in the published literature. Austrians experienced a real sense of responsibility for the events in Hungary. As mentioned above, most scholars agree that the 1955 *Staatsvertrag* served as a key psychological stimulus for Hungarians. American scholar Bianca Adair contends that the Austrian State Treaty had a "profound effect" on the events leading to the Hungarian Revolution in October 1956, specifically because it influenced the "policy preferences expressed by dissidents and reformers during the uprising in Hungary."[21] Although Austrian historian Michael

Gehler also sees Austrian neutrality and the exodus of Soviet troops as a psychological stimulus for Hungary, he believes—in contrast to Adair—that "Austria's neutrality was too young and too inexperienced to serve as a well-developed export good."[22] Feeling responsible, in part, for the revolution, Austrians hence found the experience of helping hundreds of thousands of destitute refugees quite gratifying.

Negative Forms of Spillover

Positive aspects aside, however, the Hungarian crisis presented Austria with at least three tangible difficulties or negative forms of spillover. To reiterate, the crisis actually hindered Austria's ability to further the cause of Hungarian freedom, despite Austrian political sympathies. In his 11 November radio speech, Chancellor Raab had said that, while Austria takes seriously "the duties of military neutrality," "such a commitment in no way means a colorless neutralism in political questions." "On the contrary, it is the duty of our Austrian people [. . .] one of the standard-bearers of western Christian culture [. . . .] to bring to the attention of the world [. . .] the misery of the people in those states [. . .] which have been forced to abandon our true European ideals."[23] Yet, in the midst of the Hungarian crisis, Austria actually ended up *reinforcing* the Hungarian *status quo*, its subservience to Moscow. Secondly, very early in the crisis, Austrian authorities had to appeal to the West both for financial and logistical support in providing asylum for the refugees. Thus Austria did not quite serve as the political haven for which it was later credited; it was more of a way station. Thirdly, the Hungarian crisis substantially worsened Austria's relations with both the Soviet Union and Hungary after real improvement had taken place in the months after the signing of the Austrian State Treaty. Each of these problems deserves to be addressed separately.

Restricted Support for a Free Hungary

Thrust into the position of exercising neutrality for the first time and facing constant accusations from the communist bloc, the Raab government soon discovered just how restrictive neutrality could be. By definition, neutrality means immunity from invasion or use by belligerents. The neutral state must adhere to international laws promulgated by the Hague Convention of 1907. It must not participate in a military conflict, support any warring parties with its armed forces, or allow foreign armies to use its territory for military purposes. A neutral state's sovereignty must be respected. While the neutral state may trade with all parties in a conflict, it must not show any favoritism. Since the Cold

War did not involve an actual military conflict between the two superpowers, "neutralism" is a more accurate term, which simply means noninvolvement in the Cold War.[24]

In the heat of the crisis, the Raab administration had to refrain from showing any kind of political support for the Hungarian refugees or for exiled Hungarian movements. Against the chorus of strident Soviet and Hungarian accusations, Austria's need to prove its impartiality seemed to wax paranoiac. As is well-known, former Prime Minister Ferenc Nagy was asked to leave Vienna shortly after his arrival.[25] Archival records are full of additional examples of the Austrians' overcaution. The Austrian Foreign Ministry sent a telegram on 1 November 1956 to the Austrian embassy in Washington requesting that it not issue any more visas to Hungarian émigré organizations. All assistance to Hungary should go exclusively through the International Red Cross.[26]

Minister of Interior Helmer was equally cautious, despite his initial speech on 26 October 1956 encouraging "the liberal movements in Hungary." In the cabinet meeting on 20 November mentioned above, Helmer had also said, "A quick removal of these people [out of the Burgenland] is [. . .] necessary, otherwise we will be permanently burdened by helping Hungary."[27]

On 21 November 1956, an official from the Austrian embassy in Italy requested that the Italian Foreign Office recommend to the Italian Red Cross not to send Hungarian aid workers to Austria.[28] Even Red Cross workers, if they should happen to be of Hungarian descent, were asked not to come to Austria.[29] Hungarian émigrés who had long resettled in Austria and become legal Austrian citizens were forbidden to offer political support to the Hungarians in Austria or in Hungary. But political support and moral support are sometimes indistinguishable. One Hungarian named Karl Vertesy, a former deputy of the Smallholders Party who had fled to Austria after World War II and had become an Austrian citizen, participated actively in a U.S.-supported émigré organization. On 2 November 1957, he gave a speech on Styrian radio encouraging the Hungarians not to give up hope. This was promptly reported to the Austrian Ministry of the Interior, whereby officials curtly stated, "[T]his is unacceptable."[30]

Like individuals, any Hungarian exile nationalist movement or émigré organization that sought support from Vienna usually met with the same rebuff. On 20 May 1957, Austrian Foreign Minister Leopold Figl wrote to Chancellor Raab, asking what to do about a letter from Sándor Kiss, general secretary of the Hungarian National Council in New York. The letter "appealed to the Austrian people to support the efforts of the Council for a Free Hungary within and outside the United Nations." The Council's goals matched those of the Hungarian Revolution of October 1956 (independence and neutrality for Hungary, withdrawal of Soviet troops and withdrawal from the Warsaw Pact, a democratic coalition government until free elections could be held, and a democratic economic system). "In accordance with the directive of fall, 1956, I have not responded to this letter," Figl wrote.[31]

Organizations aiming simply at organizing the Hungarian refugees, helping them to find employment, and providing fellowship during this difficult period of adjustment alarmed Vienna as well. For example, the Culture and Relief Organization of Hungarian Social Democrats appealed to the Foreign Ministry for support. The Foreign Ministry decided on 4 April 1957 to withhold it, writing to the Ministry of the Interior:

> The formation of organizations by Hungarian refugees in Austria gives cause for concern. The fact that these organizations, according to their statutes, only develop cultural or social activities changes nothing about the political dimension of their existence, especially under the current circumstances. The political nature of the organization becomes clear in paragraph 4.2 of the statutes, where it is said that only past members of the Hungarian Social Democratic party may become members of the organization. From the viewpoint of foreign affairs, *one should refrain from everything that could lead to the organization of refugees.*[32]

An official wrote to Foreign Minister Figl on 12 April 1957, "In my opinion, politics are carried out in the camps this way."[33] The Foreign Ministry also recommended that all individual Hungarian émigrés who had entered Austria before 24 October 1956 be warned that "every kind of political or espionage activity in Austria would make their continued stay in the country uncertain, regardless of name or rank."[34]

The Organization of Hungary's Friends also appealed to Vienna for support. This organization wanted to provide moral, spiritual, and material support for Hungarian refugees who were forced to leave their native country for political reasons. It explicitly stated in its bylaws that its activities excluded every form of politics and discrimination. Foreign Ministry official Heinrich Haymerle was still concerned and recommended that the Ministry of the Interior "inform the organization's members that everything that would seem to be political activity should be avoided."[35]

Visits, both of foreigners to Austria and of Austrians to Hungary, were carefully screened, even if the foreigners were non-Hungarians. An American priest, Leopold Braun, for example, wanted to visit Hungary to interview Hungarian refugees as well as the prisoners of war from the Soviet Union (*Russlandheimkehrer*). Austrian authorities gave him excuses: it is too time-consuming to sort through the files, and besides, you can interview the refugees who are already in the United States.[36] Lorenz Karall, president of the Chamber of Commerce for Burgenland in Eisenstadt, planned to visit Budapest on 28 October 1957. The Austrian representative in Hungary, Walter Peinsipp, warned the general secretary for foreign affairs by telephone that such a "friendly visit" (*Freundschaftsbesuch*), given Karall's position and the size of his delegation, would hint at an official visit and would, no doubt, be exploited propagandistically. It would also suggest friendly relations between Vienna and the Kádár regime. The visit was abruptly canceled.[37]

Thus despite Raab's initial vision of spreading "true European ideals" to the miserable people oppressed by communist regimes and of avoiding "colorless neutralism in political questions," the Ballhausplatz (office of the chancellor) actually ended up *reinforcing* the Hungarian *status quo* and subservience to Moscow in an effort to prove its neutrality to the communist bloc.

Financial Support of Refugees

Another negative form of spillover involved the need to finance and to support the refugees. According to the UN Charter, a neutral country should be able to provide asylum to political refugees without discrimination. But given the extenuating circumstances, Austria did have to discriminate and could not accommodate the majority of the refugees.

As early as 27 October 1956, Mr. Puhan in the U.S. Embassy in Vienna assured the Austrians that the United States would provide funds and material assistance "quietly, without propaganda" (*ohne propagandistische Auswertung*).[38] According to the report on 7 November 1956 by the Austrian Ministry of the Interior to the UN Commission for Refugees, the expense for renovating the camps at Traiskirchen and Judenau would be $3,700,000.[39] When Nixon visited Austria in late December 1956 to gather data in order to address Congress, Raab reminded him that Austria had been the first country to declare that it no longer needed European Recovery (Marshall Plan) aid. "At that time Austria had not been confronted with the present refugee problem that clearly exceeds Austria's resources," he explained.[40] Austrian officials told Nixon they estimated the cost of building or rebuilding camps for the temporary refugees to be 40 million shillings, the daily cost of feeding a single refugee to be 1 shilling, and the cost of clothing and transportation to be 150 shillings. The total cost would amount to about eight million shillings for the year 1956.[41] Soviet diplomats followed the financial negotiations avidly, noting that by early September 1957, the overall sum of American aid to Austria amounted to $37 million. "Several times the Austrian government declared that if the United

States and other countries did not provide financial aid, then Austria would not be able to retain the refugees," one wrote.[42]

In a speech to the United Nations on 27 November 1956, Kurt Waldheim (head of the Austrian Mission to the United Nations) explained that Austria had still not fully absorbed the refugees who flooded into the country earlier, in the post-World War II years. Unemployed, these refugees depended entirely on the Austrian system for support.[43] During Nixon's visit, State Secretary in the Interior Ministry Franz Grubhofer also mentioned the earlier postwar refugees. "Of those refugees coming to Austria from Yugoslavia, Czechoslovakia, Hungary, and other countries after 1945, some 128,000 remain on Austrian territory, and 18,700 are living in refugee camps," he explained.[44]

Waldheim dramatized the need for international help in accommodating the refugees, describing the refugees' need to stay in railroad cars because there was no place for them to go.[45] Others stayed in private homes. The Austrian diplomat Peinsipp dramatized the political threat, "Numerous Hungarian students in Austria want to continue the fight from Austrian soil."[46] Back in Washington, psychological warfare expert C.D. Jackson got the message and urged President Dwight Eisenhower to take action, warning, "If the pressure on Austria becomes much greater, it's conceivable that the Austrian border guards will be instructed to turn back the refugees, and if that happens, the cause of freedom will have received a terrible blow. Everything that all of us have said about our side of the Iron Curtain will turn out to be a ghastly lie, and I do not know how we will manage to erase the bitterness."[47]

Furthermore, Austria could not take the credit for providing permanent asylum for the majority of the refugees because Austria was not the final destination for most. Of the 175,369 refugees who crossed the Austro-Hungarian border between 23 October 1956 and 13 September 1957, 145,494 refugees (83 percent) left Austria for other countries. Roughly 12,000 chose to remain in Austria as permanent residents.[48] The top ten countries accepting refugees in this period were the United States (34,119), Canada (24,244), the United Kingdom (20,566), West Germany (11,708), Switzerland (10,357), France (9,594), Australia (8,445), Sweden (5,403), Italy (3,838), and Belgium (3,289).[49]

Moreover, Austria did not get the "best" (that is, most skilled) refugees who could contribute to the economy. According to the *New York Herald Tribune* of 11 August 1957, which was closely monitored by Soviet foreign ministry officials, out of 33,542 refugees who had arrived in the United States during the first half of 1957, "almost three-fourths of them were highly skilled professionals." The *New York Times* on 21 July 1957 stated that American industries were benefiting from "the most successful migration in history."[50]

Deterioration in Austria's Relations with Hungary and the Soviet Union

The sharp deterioration in Austria's relations with both Hungary and the Soviet Union constituted a third form of negative spillover from the crisis. This was especially disappointing to Julius Raab, who had carefully cultivated good relations with the Khrushchev leadership throughout 1954 and 1955, much to Washington's consternation. After signing the Austrian State Treaty and after Raab's visit to Moscow, Austria's relations with both the Soviet Union and Hungary had begun to improve. A Soviet delegation visited Austria for two weeks in July 1956. "We were pleased to meet once again our old friends, the members of the Austrian Parliamentary Delegation which had visited the Soviet Union in 1955," enthused a reporter for *Pravda*. "The members of our delegation had many interesting and substantive discussions with the Austrian political figures. The relations between Austria and the Soviet Union on political, economic and cultural planes—many of the people we met said—must and can be strengthened and expanded."[51] Similarly, Austro-Hungarian relations improved. Hungary was the fifth country to officially acknowledge Austrian neutrality; an Austrian parliamentary delegation was invited to Hungary; and negotiations were resumed on 23 January 1956, after having stalled since the fall of 1953.[52] Hungarian officials had begun to dismantle the barbed wire and to remove the mines near the border, although not completely.[53]

All that changed after the first Soviet invasion of Budapest on 23-24 October 1956. Relations deteriorated rapidly. Seven key issues and accusations prevented good relations and figured prominently in the documents: border incidents, émigré Hungarians and spies in Austria, Austrian sponsorship of organizations, repatriation of Hungarian refugees, and anti-communist propaganda. Communist propagandists used each one to illustrate Austria's violation of neutrality, in spite of the Ballhausplatz's paranoiac efforts to prove otherwise.

Border Incidents

Border incidents were a source of constant irritation, beginning in the summer months of 1956 and continuing well past the Hungarian Revolution. In a discussion with Hungarian Deputy Foreign Minister Sebes on 6 December 1956, Minister Peinsipp estimated that in 1956 alone the incidents had killed or wounded two hundred people and caused "incalculable property damage."[54] While the total number of border incidents cannot be determined from available documents, one might estimate that at least one or two hundred incidents occurred in 1956 and 1957, or a total of at least three hundred incidents in those two years. The following two incidents typify Austrians' experiences.

On 1 June 1957, Farmer Köllner and his wife from the district of Güssing in the Burgenland had arisen early, deciding to start the month off on the right foot, tilling their field. His wife Gisela, an attractive brunette with a delicate, oval-shaped face, was energetically—perhaps a bit too energetically—raking the soil near border marker B/52a/18. Suddenly, at about 11:00 a.m., something exploded beneath one of the rake's tines, leaving Gisela's right foot a mass of bloody gristle and her face a permanent caricature of its former loveliness. Police and customs officials immediately alerted the Mine Removal Service and noted in their report, "We suspect that Hungarian soldiers threw the mines over the border either maliciously or negligently while they were laying new mines in the restricted area along the border."[55] The author included a photograph of Gisela and a detailed map of the incident, "which has caused great concern among the local population." This incident did nothing to endear the communists to the Burgenlanders, who as inhabitants of the former eastern occupation zone had suffered the most from Soviet pillage and rape.[56]

Another incident occurred on 5 June 1957 at 11:00 a.m. in Andau, the border village famous for its tiny bridge described in Michener's novel. First Lieutenant Straka was patrolling the border when he noticed four Hungarian soldiers lying behind border marker A-25 in Hungarian territory but aiming machine guns toward Austrian territory. Straka and his interpreter went over to talk with them about the importance of not crossing the border. While his back was turned, three other armed Hungarian soldiers did just that, walking three meters onto Austrian territory before Straka noticed them. If you do that again, I'll arrest you, Straka fumed. If you do, we'll shoot you, they laughed.

Reporting the above incident, a Foreign Ministry official wrote, "The Hungarian soldiers' behavior shows an attitude of disrespect toward the Austrian border."[57] Certainly, tossing mines over the border, crossing a border physically, and shooting at—many times wounding—a person across a border, all constitute violations of territorial boundaries.[58] The inviolability of state borders is a crucial element of sovereignty. Finally, on 6 November 1957, a high-level meeting took place, attended by Hungarian Foreign Minister Horváth, Austrian representative Peinsipp, and officials such as Pammer from the Ministry of the Interior. They decided to establish a border commission to prevent further incidents by marking the borders more clearly and conducting a thorough mine sweep (*Rückverlegung*) similar to one that had been conducted on the Austro-Czech border.[59]

In his above-mentioned discussion with Peinsipp on 6 December 1956, Hungarian Deputy Foreign Minister Sebes had stressed the positive actions that had been taken thus far to improve Hungary's relations with Austria since the State Treaty had been signed, citing the "elimination of physical barriers" at the border. In addition to reminding Sebes of the injuries and property damage to Austrians since this "elimination" of barriers, Peinsipp pointed out that Austria itself had never erected barriers on its side (such as mines, barbed wire, watchtowers, and the like); Sebes replied defensively that Hungary had been "compelled to erect technical barriers since the Americans had established an army in Burgenland for the invasion of Hungary." Only the State Treaty of 1955, he explained, had "eliminated the danger of intervention." Wittily, Peinsipp shot back that Sebes should not "play around with the lives of Soviet generals, for as soon as Moscow learns that an American army of intervention was stationed in Soviet-occupied Burgenland, surely all the generals of the Soviet Army of Occupation will be shot for treason or dereliction of duty."[60]

The border violations in some cases may simply have reflected the youth and boredom of the Hungarian border guards who did not understand the principle of sovereignty and the larger meaning of their pranks. Whereas the border incidents were used to test Austrian resolve, the following issues were used deliberately to expose Austria's infraction of international law.

Hungarian Émigrés and Spies

Soviet and Hungarian propagandists went for the jugular: Austria was being used as a "springboard" (*Sprungbrett*) for Hungarian émigrés and Horthyist spies, and the Austrians were also equipping Hungarian insurgents with weapons. As mentioned earlier, a neutral country must not permit its territory to be used by foreigners for military (or intelligence) purposes. Accusations to this effect abounded and were lodged against Austria even while Imre Nagy was Hungarian prime minister. On 2 November, Nagy told Peinsipp that he had received reports about armed émigrés who, under the leadership of former Horthyist officers, intended to enter Hungary from Austria. "This makes my situation much more difficult, especially in foreign policy," Nagy complained.[61]

Accusations about espionage by émigrés were annoying enough. To discover—as the Austrian Ministry of the Interior did—numerous cases of real espionage was infinitely worse. When Helmer had promised asylum for all Hungarian refugees, regardless of the reason why they left, he did not intend to invite in spies. "Over and over reports have come in from refugee circles in the past few months that the new Hungarian security agency is sending agents disguised as refugees to stir up trouble in the Hungarian refugee camps or to fulfill other orders," an official from the Ministry wrote despairingly to the Austrian embassy in Budapest.[62]

Take Hungarian refugee Mihály Köteles as an example. Twenty-two years old, unmarried, and poor, he had worked as an iron worker until 1954, when he decided to enlist as a border guard to make more money. Still dissatisfied, he fled illegally to Austria on 3 August 1956 and asked for political asylum. Hearing about Nagy's revolutionary changes, he gullibly returned to Hungary on 1 November, registering at his military unit at St. Gotthard, whereupon he was promptly transferred to the Hungarian counter-intelligence unit at Zalaegerszeg. Threatened with prolonged imprisonment for his desertion, Köteles returned to Austria as a "refugee" to conduct espionage in the Traiskirchen refugee camp. What shall we do with him, officials from the Austrian Ministry of the Interior asked the Foreign Minister. Give him asylum, but "take no official action" was the reply. As we know from the Austrian legation in Budapest, Köteles is "just one of many spies posing as refugees." Use this information against Hungarian authorities "only if the moment seems right," they cagily advised.[63]

The most unsavory refugees usually crossed the border in the first days of the revolution, just after Imre Nagy became prime minister, because they feared retribution. It was enough to make some Ballhausplatz authorities wish the freedom fighters would *not* win. Fewer agents of the security police (ÁVH) and deserting soldiers would then spew forth across the border.[64] "The first refugees were communists," one villager from Nickelsdorf wrote peevishly, "They spoiled the goulash that we prepared for them. That made us mad."[65] On 27 October, a group of about 600 Hungarians, among them soldiers, customs officers, and ÁVH agents, crossed the border at Szentgotthárd, where they presented the Hungarian red, white, and green flag to the gendarmerie and expressed their good will towards the Austrian people. By evening, Austrians had coaxed fifteen of them to return to Hungary.[66] Two days later, as many as 3,000 people from Hungary visited the village of Rattersdorf, this time led by the mayors of Hungarian border communities, bearing more Hungarian flags. Engrossed in jubilant bump-and-grinds at the border, they failed to notice the Rattersdorfers' non-fraternization.[67]

Given Austrian political and military officials' fervent desire to pass this first test of its fledgling neutrality, the fact that communist spies had infiltrated the refugee camps deeply disturbed them. This was negative spillover *par excellence*. Representing interference in Austrian internal affairs and, hence, violating Austrian sovereignty, this plague of espionage also threatened to infect Austria's international reputation. Planners hoped to attract international organizations and to live down the impression of Austria created by *Third Man* (*Dritter-Mann*), a famous film about spies which took place in postwar Vienna. "It matters a lot to Austrian counter-intelligence that everyone knows that no 'Dritter-Mann' atmosphere can emerge in Vienna anymore, as it existed just after World War II," one reporter wrote.[68] As Helmer saw it, "The fierce fight against any form of spy activities is among the responsibilities imposed by Austrian neutrality."[69] It also diverted the energies of personnel in the Austrian embassies in Budapest and Moscow to clip and send home each libelous article in order for the Ministries of Foreign Affairs and the Interior to investigate each alleged case of espionage and to counter all the accusations.[70]

Favoritism toward Organizations

While a neutral state can maintain trade and economic relations with all parties in a conflict, it must not show any partiality. It was especially ironic, then, that the Kádár regime would accuse Austria of favoring the Red Cross organizations that flew supplies only to Vienna's Schwechat airport, rather than directly to Budapest's Ferihegy airport. Communist officials claimed Vienna was using Red Cross and other aid for Austria's own propaganda purposes, and that the Red Cross was really being used to ship in military supplies and weapons —again going for the jugular, since a neutral state is strictly forbidden to permit its territory to be used for military purposes.[71] Minister Peinsipp in Budapest wrote to the Foreign Ministry on 14 November 1956, explaining why stocks of supplies were low, "We had to distribute the provisions quickly, because 1) the Hungarians need them urgently, and 2) they will get stolen otherwise. Some things have already been stolen."[72] In a conversation with Mr. Ripken of the German Red Cross, Peinsipp expressed his reservations about allowing the Hungarian Red Cross to distribute Western aid, saying he "would have to refuse to cooperate with" the organization anyway.[73] The Canadian Red Cross flatly refused to fly to Budapest, wanting to "avoid complications."[74]

Soviet and Hungarian propagandists accused Austrian authorities of showing favoritism toward other organizations, like Socialist International[75] and Radio Free Europe, while discriminating against others, like the World Peace Council and the World Federation of Trade Unions. A Soviet reporter wrote in *Pravda* on 13 February 1957:

> The Austrians who forbid the secretaries of the World Federation of Trade Unions and the World Peace Council to enter Austria justify their actions citing "the fear" of losing neutrality, but do they really fear losing neutrality if they can ignore the demands of the public to shut down the radio station "Free Europe" in Salzburg, Graz, and Vienna, which is a tool of evil propaganda, a weapon of war?[76]

In truth, the ouster of the World Federation of Trade Union Headquarters from Vienna and the refusal of visas to World Peace conference representatives were just two of several actions that U.S. policymakers had listed in a secret report as tactics that would enhance Austria's ties with the West.[77] Similarly, Austrian support of Radio Free Europe (RFE) revealed the country's pro-Western leanings. As one diplomat wrote from the U.S. Embassy in Vienna:

> Radio Free Europe has enjoyed unrestricted access to newly arriving refugees. Despite a continued campaign in the communist press urging the Austrian government to expel RFE, to which was added *genuine Austrian irritation over incidents connected with balloons landing on Austrian territory*, RFE has so far been able without interference to exploit propaganda values among refugees in Austria.[78]

Repatriation of Hungarian Refugees, Including Minors

Bureaucratic bottlenecks concerning the repatriation of Hungarian refugees, especially refugees under age eighteen (*Minderjährige*), also tainted Austria's relations with both Hungary and the Soviet Union. The problem looms large in the memoirs of Frigyes Puja, the Hungarian ambassador to Austria (1955-1959). In his memoirs, published in 1988, a time when no one dared to mention the 1956 *revolution* in Hungary, Puja writes only, "Hungarian dissidents were numerous in Vienna at the time, and the sly old foxes there tried to turn the masses against us."[79] But he gives a detailed chronology of events concerning the repatriation issue and describes his general frustrations, "It was a difficult task to represent Hungary in Vienna in the fall of 1956 and at the beginning of 1957."[80] He felt pressured by the official Austrian bureaucracy and stymied by the almost total lack of direction he received from the Hungarian Ministry of Foreign Affairs. "But we didn't fall into despair. Without any official orders, we delivered a protest to the Austrians and made arrangements for the return of Hungarian property taken during the counterrevolution."[81] Repatriating refugees was harder. On 28 November 1956, the Hungarian Foreign Ministry sent a note to the Austrian Embassy in Budapest regarding the "urgent need for repatriation of children and youth eighteen years of age and younger who are Hungarian citizens and who left the country as a result of the events in Hungary after 23 October 1956."[82] The Austrian Ministry of Foreign Affairs then replied on the same day in an oral note to the Hungarian Embassy in Vienna. We see no reason why the Hungarian refugees (*Rückflüchtlinge*) who wish to cannot return home, the note read. However, at least 5,000 refugees are arriving daily now. We are overloaded with administrative tasks, so it is difficult to deal right now with those wishing to return home.[83]

The next day, 29 November, the Kádár government published an official amnesty to "anyone who crossed the border between 23 October 1956 and 29 November 1956," promising not to "initiate criminal procedures as long as they voluntarily return to Hungary before 31 March 1957."[84] To facilitate the refugees' return, a three-member Repatriating Committee (*Hazatérési Bizottság*) was established, composed of Ferenc Esztergályos, András Börcsök, and Gyula Kelemen.[85]

The stalemate continued nevertheless. Hoping to clarify matters, Hans Reichman, the federal counselor and head of the legal department in the Austrian Federal Chancellery, invited István Beck, the counselor in the Hungarian Embassy in Vienna, for a talk a month later, on 17 December 1956. Beck's detailed account of the conversation—which Puja sent to the Hungarian Ministry of Foreign Affairs—epitomizes the tension between the two countries over the repatriation issue. Beck, perhaps in a bad mood that day, found Reichman overbearing, "lecturing" him about why the refugees could not return to Hungary. Reichman explained that the large number of refugees pouring into Austria each day showed that the Kádár government is consolidating "very slowly."[86] Also, the Austrians needed to discuss the issue with the UN High Commissioner for Refugees who was visiting Vienna soon. Besides, Austria could not permit the members of the Hungarian Repatriating Committee to enter Austria, "because we fear there may be attempts on their lives," Reichman said, adding in a comic understatement, "and this would be rather inconvenient for them." Beck wrote bitterly, "In my reply, I pointed out that his statements only proved that, despite humanitarian phrases," the Austrian government was thwarting "simple Hungarians who just want to go home." The disconsolate Hungarian official added, "The refugee babies will have grown beards by the time our government is consolidated."[87]

One of the bottlenecks stemmed from the fact that the Hungarian memoranda had all been directed to UN High Commissioner Auguste Lindt, awaiting his action. When Lindt did visit Vienna, he told Haymerle that he had reconsidered the whole matter and preferred to see an Austrian commission formed to handle the repatriation issue rather than lead such a commission himself. He discussed this with Minister of the Interior Helmer, who agreed. He planned to raise the issue in New York and Washington and to finalize the matter before the end of the year. As far as the repatriation of minor children, it would "soon be resolved through the International Red Cross."[88] The Austrian Foreign Ministry reported that by December 1956, about 500 Hungarian refugees had expressed the desire to return home, something the Austrian side had, in fact, not hindered. Some ninety internees of the Siezenheim camp in Salzburg chose to return home and left the same day of their decision. By 13 September 1957, approximately 5,343 refugees had voluntarily returned to Hungary.[89]

Meanwhile, in Moscow, reporters exercised their full creative powers, actions only possible in an atmosphere where facts are irrelevant. One reporter for *Komsomolskaia Pravda* compared Austrian camp officials to the *Comprachicos* in Victor Hugo's novel, *L'Homme qui Rit* (*The Man Who Laughs*) in an article published on 16 February 1957. He cited Hugo's description of the "*Comprachicos*" who bought children, disfigured them until they were past recognition, and sold them for entertainment to royal courts. "Out of a normal human being they made a monster. It was a whole science. They stunted the child's growth—twisting his feet, squinting his eyes so his face became a permanent smile. Deformity replaced harmony."[90] Then he wrote:

> The *Comprachicos* of today do not live on some lonely island in the ocean. They live in Vienna, wear smocks, and operate in Austrian camps for Hungarian refugees. In the seventeenth century the *Comprachicos* deformed children's faces. In the twentieth century they deform childrens' souls, force them to forget their mother tongue and homeland. They employ minor girls in whorehouses, turn others into spies.[91]

The article concluded with "quotes" from letters from forlorn parents and siblings, saying, "Please come home; we miss you." Another article by Anatoliev in *Komsomolskaia Pravda* described the young pilot, Dever, who flew off course during the counterrevolution and ended up in Austria, coaxed into working for the American CIA and forbidden to return home.[92]

Propaganda and Graffiti

Propaganda and graffiti constantly aggravated Austrian officials as well. They tried to restrict all propaganda, both communist and anti-communist, and they did their best to reassure Hungarian and Soviet authorities of their efforts. But they had limits, for "Austria is not a police state. As a democracy, it has only democratic capabilities. Where these capabilities can be exercised to prevent hostile propaganda, they will be exercised."[93]

Some propaganda came from foreigners who traveled to Austria. For example, on 3 June 1957, Harry Rudolf Pohl, a West German correspondent of the anti-communist Pissev Publishing House in Frankfurt am Main, was caught at the Austrian border with 6,000 Hungarian flyers appealing to the Hungarian Security Police to stop killing innocent people. Austrian authorities fined Pohl for not declaring his import.[94]

In other cases, propaganda arrived by nonhuman means, as assiduously noted by communist reporters. Ambassador Bischoff clipped an article from *Krasnaia Zvezda* about a visit by Colonels Shegolev and Suslin to an Austrian border station. They reported that the border officer, in their presence, pulled out of the Danube River several sturdy celluloid bags. Cutting one open in their presence, he found thousands of anti-Soviet and anti-Hungarian leaflets in several different Eastern European languages.[95]

Public events, such as the trade fair in Graz on 28 and 29 April 1957, also bred mischief. On that occasion, Hungarian refugees tore down the official Hungarian flag hanging at the main entrance. Incognito, they distributed flyers to the fair's visitors that read:

> Here at this fair you see the Kádár puppet regime's Hall of Propaganda. You know well what the events of October 1956 mean for Hungary and the whole world. Thousands upon thousands have fallen. They wanted nothing other than freedom. Kádár's bloodhounds, Russian bayonettes, bloody terror—this is the way the Hungarian people live behind the Iron Curtain. You have always sympathized with us, so we ask for your continued support. Don't visit those who have betrayed freedom. We thank you. The Hungarian students.[96]

The Hungarian delegation wrote to the Raab government, "We would appreciate any information about the [. . .] punishment of the individuals responsible." The Raab government did, in fact, take the incident seriously. The chancellor had received a separate leaflet from the students that referred to the ongoing executions in Kádár's Hungary, threatening, "If political or diplomatic pressure will not stop the executions, the Hungarian and Soviet diplomats need to be murdered." A Foreign Ministry official wrote, "This is a terrorist threat and must not be underestimated." He sent the file directly to the Ministry of the Interior.[97]

Conclusion

To conclude, the Hungarian revolution and Soviet military crackdown brought many negative spillover effects to Austria which modern historians easily forget, since ultimately the crisis strengthened Austrian political and military self-reliance. It revealed Austria's short-term inability to support the cause of Hungarian freedom and Austria's lack of financial means to provide most of the refugees with permanent asylum, and it unravelled the Austrian rapprochement with Hungary and the USSR of the previous year.

In the Cold War of the 1950s where public image and deterrent ability perhaps counted more than mere military weapons, he who denounced first often appeared right. Harsh accusations could sometimes prevent convincing counter-accusations by the injured. The Khrushchev and Kádár regimes were able to seize upon the issues of border incidents, espionage, discrimination against international organizations, delay in repatriating refugees, and anti-communist propaganda in order to accuse Austria of violating neutrality, thereby putting Austria on the defensive. Such were the difficulties Austria faced in 1956-1957. It was hard enough to remain neutral in the Cold War period in general, let alone during an actual "hot war," especially when Austria was new at exercising neutrality, when the crisis was right on its border, and when the population strongly adhered to Western democratic values of non-violence and freedom of speech. Unlike Ulbricht, who could simply send in the *Kampfgruppen* to muzzle the students at Humboldt University, Raab could not censor the Austrian population (although he was able to punish the Austrian Communist Party organ *Volksstimme* for its treasonous articles). Ideologically pro-West, Austria aspired to integrate itself economically with Western Europe, yet at the same time, to avoid offending the Soviet Union and other communist bloc countries. Indeed, the Raab government found itself between Charybdis and Scylla, a beleaguered umpire between two military giants. As Soviet and Hungarian accusations crescendoed, some Austrian policymakers and the general population alike feared their purpose was to set the stage for "hot pursuit" of the refugees. Although opportunists used this threat to ask for more Western aid, it cannot be denied that, after seventeen years of occupation, Austria could not afford to take chances. The strong conviction of Julius Raab and his colleagues, as expressed in the fictional telephone call above, "not to go back" propelled them forward to manage this first test of their neutrality. While in some respects Austrian leaders did not pass the test with "flying colors," they nevertheless survived it and succeeded in "giving the world something to talk about."

Notes

1. Manfried Rauchensteiner, *Spätherbst 1956: Die Neutralität auf dem Prüfstand* (Vienna: Österreichischer Bundesverlag, 1981), 84.

2. Some historians dispute the view that Austrian neutrality inspired Hungarian intellectuals. See László Borhi, *Hungary in the Cold War, 1945-1956: Between the United States and the Soviet Union* (Budapest: Central European Univ. Press, 2004).

3. Günter Bischof, "The Making of the Austrian Treaty and the Road to Geneva," in *Cold War Respite: the Geneva Summit of 1955*, ed. Günter Bischof and Saki Dockrill (Baton Rouge, LA: Louisiana Univ. Press, 2000), 150.

4. About 200 to 300 refugees arrived from Yugoslavia daily in November 1956, for an approximate total of 5,000 by September 1957. See Österreichisches Staatsarchiv (ÖStA), Archiv der Republik (AdR), Bundeskanzleramt/Auswärtige Angelegenheit (BKA/AA), Abteilung 2, Karton 403, "Situationsbericht über das Flüchtlingswesen in Österreich." During Vice-President Nixon's visit to Austria on 20 December, State Secretary Grubhofer put the figure much higher: 1,000 Yugoslav refugees arriving daily in Austria. ÖstA, AdR, BKA/AA, Zl 792.188 Pol 56, Karton 405, "Besuch des Vizepräsidenten Nixon in Österreich, den 20. Dezember 1956." In Yugoslavia, Tito had ordered numerous people arrested as "Cominformists" in 1956. He called in reserves, sent about 100,000 soldiers to the Yugoslav-Hungarian border, and tried to censor foreign diplomats, demanding, for example, that the British ambassador in Belgrade allow no news about Hungary to be published in the British embassy's bulletin, a demand the British ambassador rejected. See ÖStA, AdR, BKA/AA, "Mitteilung des niederlaendischen Gesandten Star Busmannüber sowjetische Truppenbereitstellungen in Suedosteuropa," Zl 520.445 Pol 56. Karton 402 (UdSSR). Wien. 15 November 1956.

5. Ministerratsprotokoll #16, 20 November 1956. Cited in Wilhelm Svoboda, *Die Partei, die Republik, und der Mann Mit Den Vielen Gesichtern: Oskar Helmer und Österreich II Eine Korrektur* (Vienna: Böhlau Verlag, 1993), 162. As one of Austria's nine provinces, the Burgenland was transferred back and forth between Austria and Hungary in the fifteenth century. It was given to Austria in 1459, but went to Hungary under King Matthias Corvinus in the peace treaty of Ödenburg (1462). Maximilian I won Burgenland back for Austria, while Kaiser Ferdinand II returned it to Hungary without a war. After the demise of the Austrian-Hungarian monarchy in 1918, the inhabitants of Burgenland voted for reunification with Austria. The decision was fixed in the peace treaties of Saint Germain and the Trianon, both signed in 1919.

6. ÖStA, AdR, BKA/AA, Zl. 222.481 Pol 57, Karton 448, "Zeitschrift 'Ut és Cél,' Schädigung der aussenpolitischen Interessen Österreichs durch nationalsozialistische und antisemitisch Schreibweise," 20 July 1957.

7. For a useful historical analysis of several neutral countries in Europe, see Michael Gehler and Rolf Steininger, eds. *Die Neutralen und die europäische Integration, 1945-1995* (Vienna: Böhlau Verlag, 2000).

8. Die Presse, 30 October 1956; *Wochenpresse*, 21-22 May 1968. Also Reiner Eger, *Krisen an Österreichs Grenzen: Das Verhalten Österreichs während des Ungarnaufstandes 1956 und der tschechoslowakischen Krise 1968, Ein Vergleich* (Munich: Verlag Herold Wien, 1981), 65. In an interview, Graf later said, "I could be accused of working too little with the laws. If I had waited for the laws, actions such as the deployment on the Hungarian border would have been impossible. At that time, it was the minister's responsibility alone to decide how many soldiers to send and where" [quoted in *Wochenpresse*, 21-22 May 1968].

9. For the original text, see ÖStA, AdR, Bundesministerium für Unterricht (BmfU), Karton 51. Beschlussprotokoll Nr. 12/A, "Über die ausserordliche Sitzung des Ministerrates am 28. 10. 1956."

10. Erich Wendl, "Der Nachbar Österreich—1956 und danach," in *Ungarn 1956: Reaktionen in Ost und West*, ed. Heiner Timmermann and László Kiss (Berlin: Duncker & Humblot, 2000), 51.

11. "I was congratulated from many sides on the Austrian appeal to the Soviet Union from a political, as well as humanitarian, standpoint," he wrote to the Federal Chancellery on 31 October 1956. ÖStA, AdR, NPA, Zl 791.343, Karton 402, Depeschen: Nr. 28067, 31 October 1956.

12. Erwin Schmidl, "Erste Bewährung Das Österreichische Bundesheer im Einsatz an der ungarischen Grenze 1956," in *Die Ungarnkrise 1956 und Österreich*, ed. Erwin Schmidl (Vienna: Böhlau Verlag, 2003), 258.

13. ÖStA, AdR, BKA/AA, Ministerratsprotokolle Raab II; Verhandlungsschtift Nr. 12a, "Über die Sitzung des a.o. Ministerrates am 28.10.1956."

14. *Wochenpresse*, 21-22 May 1956. See also Eger, *Krisen an Österreichs Grenzen*, 66.

15. Wendl, "Der Nachbar Österreich," 52.

16. Winfried Heinemann and Norbert Wiggershaus, *Das Internationale Krisenjahr 1956: Polen, Ungarn, Suez* (Munich: R. Oldenbourg, 1999).

17. James, Michener. *The Bridge at Andau* (London: Secker & Warburh, 1957), 225.

18. Eduard Stanek, *Verfolgt, Verjagt, Vertrieben. Flüchlinge in Österreich* (Vienna: Europaverlag, 1985); Károly Gáal and Roland Widder, *1956 und das Burgenland: Berichte über die Hilfsaktionen für ungarische Flüchtlinge: eine Dokumentation von Studenten des Fachhochschul-Studienganges Internationale Wirtschaftsbeziehungen* (Eisenstadt: Amt der Burgenländischen Landesregierung, Abt. XII/2, Landesarchiv und Landesbibliothek, 1996); Katalin Soós, *1956 és Ausztria* (Szeged: József Attila Tudományegyetem Bölcsészettudományi Kara, 1999).

19. See Reiner Eger, *Krisen an Österreichs Grenzen: Das Verhalten Österreichs während des Ungarnaufstandes 1956 und der tschechoslowakischen Krise 1968* (Vienna: Verlag Herold, 1981); Manfried Rauchensteiner, *Spätherbst 1956: Die Neutralität auf dem Prüfstand* (Vienna: Österreichischer Bundesverlag, 1981). Interestingly, Schmidl also reveals that Austrian military commanders feared an incursion in 1956 from Czechoslovakia as much, if not more, than one from the Soviet Union via Hungary.

20. Erwin Schmidl, "Erste Bewährung: Das Österreichische Bundesheer im Einsatz an der ungarischen Grenze 1956," in *Die Ungarnkrise 1956 und Österreich*, ed. Erwin Schmidl (Vienna: Böhlau Verlag, 2003), 254.

21. Bianca L. Adair, "The Austrian State Treaty and Austro-Hungarian Relations, 1955-56," in *Die Ungarnkrise 1956 und Österreich*, ed. Erwin A. Schmidl (Vienna: Böhlau Verlag, 2003), 201.

22. Michael Gehler, "The Hungarian Crisis and Austria 1953-1958: A Foiled Model Case?" in *Neutrality in Austria, vol. 9, Contemporary Austrian Studies*, ed. Günter Bischof, Anton Pelinka, and Ruth Wodak (New Brunswick, NJ: Transaction, 2001), 192. "Vienna's political elite still hoped to get a concrete military guarantee of its neutrality from the superpowers, so it did not want to risk exporting its neutrality to Hungary," he writes.

23. "Flammen an Österreichs östlicher Grenze," in *Julius Raab: Ansichten des Staatsvertragskanzlers*, ed. Johannes Kunz (Vienna: Verlag der Österreichische Staatsdruckerei, 1991), 71.

24. Catherine Nielsen, "Neutrality vs. Neutralism: Austrian Neutrality and the 1956 Hungarian Crisis," in *Die Ungarnkrise 1956 und Oesterreich*, ed. Erwin Schmidl (Vienna: Böhlau Verlag, 2003), 217.

25. That did not prevent communist writers from claiming that Nagy "made a tour of Austria to check the combat readiness of units made up of Hungarian emigrants that were formed in Salzburg, Graz and Linz and prepared to be sent to Hungary." "The truth is that Ferenc Nagy was in Vienna for only 3 hours, always accompanied by Austrian officials. He had to leave Austria immediately because the Austrian authorities wanted to avoid complications with our neighboring countries," Ambassador Matsch told the UN General Assembly on 4 December 1956. ÖstA, AdR, BKA/AA, Zl 98 Pol 56, Karton 403a, Österreichische Vertretung bei den Vereinten Nationen, "UN-Generalversammlung-Ungarn-Frage: Österreichische Erklärung," New York, den 6 December 1956.

26. ÖstA, AdR, BKA/AA, Karton 404, "Telegramm in Ziffern an Austroamb., Washington, 1 November 1956 (von Aussenamt)."

27. Ministerratsprotokoll #16, 20 November 1956. Cited in Wilhelm Svoboda, *Die Partei, die Republik, und der Mann Mit Den Vielen Gesichtern: Oskar Helmer und Österreich II Eine Korrektur* (Vienna: Böhlau Verlag, 1993), 162.

28. ÖstA, AdR, BKA/AA, Zl 757-Res 56, Karton 407, "Österreichische Botschaft in Italien, 'Einreise von Ungarn nach Österreich im Zusammenhang mit Hilfsaktionen,' Rom, am 21 November 1956."

29. ÖstA, AdR, BKA/AA, Zl 762 Res 56, Karton 407, "Österreichische Botschaft in Italien, 'Einreise von Ungarn nach Österreich im Zusammenhang mit Hilfsaktionen,' Rom, am 22 November 1956."

30. ÖstA, AdR, BKA/AA, Zl. 215.959 Pol 57, Karton 448, "(Österreich 6-9) Karl Vertesy, ungarischer Emigrant, Rundfunkansprache." 29 January 1957.

31. ÖStA, AdR, BKA/AA, Zl 40 Pol 57, Karton 415, "Österreichische Vertretung bei den Vereinten Nationen, Ungarischer Revolutionsrat; Appell an die österreichische Regierung, New York, den 20 May 1957."

32. ÖstA, AdR, BKA/AA, Zl_218.717 Pol 57, Karton 450, "Verein: Kultur- und Hilfsverein ungarischer Sozialdemokraten in Oesterreich," 4 April 1957. Emphasis added.

33. ÖstA, AdR, BKA/AA, Zl 219.098 Pol 57, Karton 450, "Brief an Figl," 12 April 1957.

34. ÖstA, AdR, BKA/AA, Zl 183.517-2/56, Karton 450, "Politische Betätigung von Ausländern in Oesterreich," 12.6.1957.

35. ÖstA, AdR, BKA/AA, Zl 218.102-Pol 57, Karton 450, "Verein der Freunde Ungarns mit dem Sitz in Wien," 22 May 1957.

36. ÖstA, AdR, BKA/AA, Zl. 221.571-Pol 57, "Pater Leopold L.S. Braun, Amerikaner; Reise nach Österreich zwecks Befragung von Russlandheimkehrern und ungarischen Flüchtlinge." 6 July 1957.

37. ÖstA, AdR, BKA/AA, Zl. 225-797 Pol 57, Karton 458, "Geplanter Besuch des Präsidenten der Burgenländischen Handelskammer," 26 October 1957.

38. ÖstA, AdR, BKA/AA, Zl 519.612 Pol 56, Karton 403a, "Zu erwartender Flüchtlingsstrom aus Ungarn," 27 October 1956.

39. Katalin Soós, "Ausztria és a Magyar Menekültügy 1956-57," *Századok* 5 (1998): 1027.

40. ÖstA, AdR, BKA/AA, Zl 792.188 Pol-56, Karton 405, "Besuch des Vizepräsidenten Nixon in Österreich, den 20. Dezember 1956." *N.B.* Marshall Plan funds were not used to support the Hungarian refugees in 1956.

41. ÖstA, AdR, BKA/AA, Zl 792.188 Pol-56, Karton 405, "Besuch des Vizepräsidenten Nixon in Österreich, den 20 December 1956."

42. *Arkhiv Vneshnei Politiki* (hereafter AVP) RF, F 77, Op 37, Por 36, Papka 53, L. 91. Spravka: "Avstro-Vengerskie Otnosheniia (1956-1957)," ot Stazhera Posol'stva SSSR v Vengrii I. Aleksandrov v MID SSSR, 9 sentybrya 1957.

43. ÖstA, AdR, BKA/AA, Zl 791.756 Pol 56, Karton 403a. "11 UN-Generalversammlung; Dritte Kommission-Behandlung der Flüchtlingsfrage (Erklärung des Gesandten Waldheim in der III. Kommission vom 27.XI.56)."

44. ÖstA, AdR, BKA/AA, Zl 792.188 Pol 56, Karton 405, "Besuch des Vizepräsidenten Nixon in Österreich, den 20. Dezember 1956."

45. ÖstA, AdR, BKA/AA, Zl 791.756 Pol 56, Karton 403a. "11 UN-Generalversammlung; Dritte Kommission-Behandlung der Flüchtlingsfrage (Erklärung des Gesandten Waldheim in der III. Kommission vom 27.XI.56)."

46. ÖstA, AdR, BKA/AA, Karton 403a, "Ungarischer Fluchtlinggstrom nach Osterreich," Wien, am 14 November 1956.

47. Eisenhower Presidential Library, C. D. Jackson Papers, Box 50, Folder "Dwight Eisenhower—Correspondence, 1956." Letter from C. D. Jackson, Time, Inc., New York to Dwight D. Eisenhower, White House, 23 November 1956.

48. AVP RF, F 77, Op 37, Por 36, Papka 53, L. 91. Spravka: "Avstro-Vengerskie Otnosheniia (1956-1957), ot Stazhera Posol'stva SSSR v Vengrii I. Aleksandrov v MID SSSR, 9 sentybrya 1957."

49. ÖstA, AdR, BKA/AA, Zl 8269 - PrM/57, Karton 1 (Flüchtlinge, 1957), "Österreichische Gesellschaft vom Roten Kreuz (bzw. Liga der Rotkreuzgesellschaften); Ausreise ungarischer Flüchtlinge aus Österreich in andere Länder, 20 September 1957, Wien." According to Soviet documents that cited Austrian statistics, 4,752 Hungarian refugees voluntarily returned to Hungary. "In total, according to the data of the Austrian Ministry of Internal Affairs, as of August 1957, 6,634 refugees voluntarily returned to Hungary." [AVP RF, F 77, O 37, Por 36, Papka 53, Ll. 83-97. Spravka: "Avstro-Vengerskie Otnosheniia (1956-1957), ot Stazhera Posol'stva SSSR v Vengrii I. Aleksandrov v MID SSSR, 9 sentybrya 1957."]

50. AVP RF, F 77, O 37, Por 36, Papka 53, L. 66, "Spravka o Polozhenii Vengerskikh Bezhentsev v SShA."

51. ÖstA, AdR, BKA/AA, Karton 402, Sowjetpresse über Österreich, "Sowjetische Abgeordnete in Österreich" *Pravda*, 26 July 1956.

52. ÖstA, AdR, BKA/AA, Zl 511368 Pol 56, Karton 403, "Zur Normalisierung der österreichisch-ungarischen Beziehungen."

53. AVP RF, F 77, Op 37, Por 36, Papka 53, L. 89. Spravka: "Avstro-Vengerskie Otnosheniia (1956-1957), ot Stazhera Posol'stva SSSR v Vengrii I. Aleksandrov v MID SSSR, 9 sentybrya 1957."

54. ÖstA, AdR, BKA/AA, Abteilung 2, II-pol. 1956 (Ungarn 3), Zahl 130-Pol 56, Österreichische Gesandschaft Budapest, "Aussenminister-Stellvertreter Sebes; die Beschuldigungen gegen Österreich am 6. December 1956," p. 2.

55. ÖStA, AdR, BKA/AA, Zl 221792 Pol 57, Karton 461, "Verletzung einer österreichischen Staatsangehörigen durch einen ungarischen Sprengkörper (Minenzünder) im Bereich der Zollwachabteilung Moschendorf," Wien, den 18. June 1957.

56. For an enlightening archival study of Austrians' experience in the Soviet occupation zone, see Klaus-Dieter Mulley, "Befreiung und Besatzung: Aspekte sowjetischer Besatzung in Niederösterreich, 1945-1948," in *Österreich unter Alliierter Besatzung, 1945-1955*, ed. Alfred Ableitinger, Siegfried Beer, and Eduard G. Staudinger (Vienna: Böhlau Verlag, 1998), 361-400.

57. ÖStA, AdR, BKA/AA, Zl 221028, Karton 461, "Zwischenfall an der ungarischen Grenze am 6. Juni 1957."

58. For details on other border incidents, see ÖStA, AdR, BKA/AA, Karton 407, Zl 516.851-Pol/56, 27.7.1956; Karton 403a, 8.11.1956; Karton 461, Zl 223.990, 23.8.1957; Karton 461, Zl 224.960, 23.9.1957; and Karton 461, 12.11.1957.

59. ÖStA, AdR, BKA/AA, Zl 226-762 Pol 57, Karton 458, "Besuch des ungarischen Aussenministers Horváth beim Herrn Bundesminister am 6. November 1957."

60. ÖStA, AdR, BKA/AA, Zahl 130 Pol 56, Österreichische Gesandschaft Budapest, "Aussenminister-Stellvertreter Sebes; die Beschuldigungen gegen Österreich am 6. Dezember 1956. "

61. ÖStA, AdR, BKA/AA, Karton 405, "Angebliche Verletzung der österreichischen Neutralität an der ungarischen Grenze," 2 November 1956.

62. ÖStA, AdR, BKA/AA, "Ungarische Agitation und Spionage in Österreich," Karton 461, Zl 217.836-Pol 57, 15.3.1957.

63. ÖStA, AdR, BKA/AA, "Köteles Mihály, ungarischer Flüchtling, nachrichtendienstliche Tätigkeit," Karton 450, Zl 218405, 30 March 1957.

64. ÁVH stands for Államvédelmi Hatóság, or State Security Authority.

65. Erwin Schmidl, "Erste Bewährung Das Österreichische Bundesheer im Einsatz an der ungarischen Grenze 1956," in *Die Ungarnkrise 1956 und Österreich*, ed. Erwin Schmidl (Vienna: Böhlau Verlag, 2003), 258.

66. Wendl, "Der Nachbar Österreich," 51.

67. Ibid.

68. ÖStA, AdR, BKA/AA, "Spionagekampf um Flüchtlingslisten," Zl 5035A-Pol 57, München, 27.3.1957.

69. Ibid.

70. ÖStA, AdR, BKA/AA, "Sowjetische Presseartikel über Ungarn," Karton 457 (UdSSR 6), Zl 223.904-Pol 57, 11 September 1957. The Austrian Embassy in Moscow sent to the Federal Chancellery an article by P. Baranikov that appeared in *Izvestiia* on 24 August 1957 ("Enemies without Masks, the Activities of Imperialist Spying in Hungary"). The article was then sent to Dr. Pammer in the Ministry of the Interior with the explanation, "This article contains extracts from articles in *Népszabadság* that pertain to Western espionage. In these articles they often claim that Western agents operate from Austrian cities, but refrain from verbal attacks on specific officials. Translations of the passages are enclosed."

71. See Soviet Foreign Minister Shepilov's speech to the UN General Assembly on 19 November 1956. ÖStA, AdR, BKA/AA, "Rede Schepilows vor der Generalversammlung der VN am 19.11.56," Karton 403a. Zl 520769-Pol 56. Also AVP RF, F 77, O 37, Por 36, Papka 53, L. 87. Spravka: "Avstro-Vengerskie Otnosheniia (1956-1957)," ot

Stazhera Posol'stva SSSR v Vengrii I. Aleksandrov v MID SSSR, 9 sentybrya 1957. "On the 25th and 26th of October 1956, 30 to 90 and more airplanes from the Red Cross organization in one day arrived at the Ferihegy airport, carrying medicines and foodstuffs, as well as more than a ton of weapons, military supplies, and leaflets. Thus, this organization played its own black role in addition to other things [. . . .] Cars had slogans painted on their sides, like 'Aid from Austrian Trade Unions' and 'To the Hungarian People from the Austrian Red Cross."

72. ÖStA, AdR, BKA/AA, Karton 403a. Zl 520.419-Pol/56. "Telefongespräch mit der Gesandtschaft Budapest seit der zweiten russischen Intervention."

73. ÖStA, AdR, BKA/AA, Karton 403a, Zl 511190-Pol 56. "Westliche Hilfslieferungen nach Ungarn über das ungarische Rote Kreuz; Gespräch Gesandten Peinsipps mit dem Führer des deutschen Rotkreuzzuges Ripken."

74. Ibid.

75. The Fifth Congress of the Socialist International took place in Vienna from 2-6 July 1957. The Soviet Union viewed Austria's hosting of the congress as an anti-Hungarian act, since it unanimously condemned the "Kádár regime's bloody sentencing" of the Hungarian revolutionaries, as did the conference of the international socialist womens' organization which met on 1 July 1957.

76. ÖStA, AdR, BKA/AA, Karton 457, Zl 216.658 Pol 57, 13 February 1957, "Sowjetpresse über Österreich, Kritik an der österreichischen Politik."

77. National Archives and Records Administration (NARA), RG 59, General Records of the Department of State, Decimal File 1955-1959, Box 2664. Dispatch 777, 15 March 1956, "Survey of Austrian Neutrality." Cited in Nielsen, 218.

78. NARA, RG 84, Records of the Foreign Service Posts, Vienna, Austrian Embassy, Classified General Records, 1956-1958, Box 9. Cited in Nielsen, 227. Emphasis added.

79. Frigyes Puja, *A Szedőszekrénytől a Miniszteri Székig* (Budapest: Népszava, 1988), 187.

80. Ibid., 186-87.

81. Ibid., 187.

82. ÖStA, AdR, BKA/AA, Karton 405, Zl 792.243 Pol 56, "Repatrierung ungarischer Flüchtlinge," 28.11.1956.

83. ÖStA, AdR, BKA/AA, Zl. 628460. Cited in Katalin Soós, "Ausztria és a Magyar Menekültügy,"1039.

84. Magyar Országos Levéltár (hereafter MOL) BKI XIX-J-36-a 305/5/1956.

85. ÖStA, AdR, BKA/AA, Zl 511190 Pol 56. Cited in Soós, "Ausztria és a Magyar Menekültügy," 1040.

86. The situation in Hungary at this time was, indeed, unsettled. On 11 December 1956, the Central Workers' Council of Greater Budapest called a forty-eight hour strike. In response, the Kádár government declared a state of emergency—martial law—and ordered all factory guards to be disarmed. The same day, the Hungarian UN delegation walked out of the General Assembly following attacks on the Kádár government. On 15 December, the very first execution of a revolutionary insurgent was carried out (József Soltész in Miskolc). See Csaba Békés, et al., *The 1956 Hungarian Revolution: A History in Documents* (Washington, D.C.: National Security Archive, 2003), xlvii.

87. The conversation between Reichman and Beck is covered in Soós, "Ausztria és a Magyar Menekültügy," 1040-41.

88. ÖStA, AdR, BKA/AA, Karton 405, Zl 792.243 Pol 56, "Repatriierung ungarisher Fluechtlinge."

89. ÖstA, AdR, BKA/AA, Zl 8269 - PrM/57, Karton 1 (Flüchtlinge, 1957), "Österreichische Geselleschaft vom Roten Kreuz (bzw. Liga der Rotkreuzgesellschaften)"; Ausreise ungarischer Flüchtlinge aus Österreich in andere Länder, 20 September 1957, Wien. According to Soviet documents that cited Austrian statistics, 4,752 Hungarian refugees voluntarily returned to Hungary. "In total, according to the data of the Austrian Ministry of Internal Affairs, as of August 1957, 6,634 refugees voluntarily returned to Hungary. AVP RF, F 77, O 37, Por 36, Papka 53, Ll. 83-97. Spravka: "Avstro-Vengerskie Otnosheniia (1956-1957)," ot Stazhera Posol'stva SSSR v Vengrii I. Aleksandrov v MID SSSR, 9 sentybrya 1957.

90. ÖStA, AdR, BKA/AA, Karton 457, Zl 216.819 Pol 57, "Komsomolskaja Prawda: Artikel über ungarischen jugendlichen Flüchtlinge."

91. Translation is from the Russian article, not from the novel. "*Comprachicos*" (as well as "*comprapequenos*") are compound Spanish words that mean "child-buyers." See Victor Hugo, *Oeuvres Complètes: Roman. XII, I, L'homme Qui Rit* (Paris: Édition Hetzel-Quantin, 1869). In English, see Victor Hugo, *The Man Who Laughs*, trans. Patricia LeChevalier, (Milpitas, CA.: Atlantean, 1991).

92. ÖStA, AdR, BKA/AA, Karton 457, 6.3.1957.

93. ÖStA, AdR, BKA/AA, Zl 226-762 Pol 57, Karton 458, "Besuch des ungarischen Aussenministers Horvath beim Herrn Bundesminister," 6 November 1957.

94. ÖStA, AdR, BKA/AA, Zl 221.348 Pol 57, Karton 461, "Harry Rudolf Pohl, Einfuhr von Flugzetteln aus der BRD," 8 June 1957.

95. ÖStA, AdR, BKA/AA, Karton 458, Zl 225-311-Pol 57, "Angeliche politische Provokation von oesterreichischem Gebiet," 26 September 1957.

96. ÖStA, AdR, BKA/AA, Karton 458, Zl 219-815 Pol 57, "Ungarn feindlich Handlung bei der Grazer Suedostmesse," 30 April 1957.

97. ÖStA, AdR, BKA/AA, Karton 458, Zl 220-271 Pol 57, "Memorandum ungarischer Emigranten betreffend geplanter Terroraktionen," 2 May 1957.

Kreisky – Brandt – Khrushchev: The United States and Austrian Mediation during the Berlin Crisis, 1958-1963

Martin Kofler

Introduction

This article breaks new ground on a neglected aspect of the Cold War: Austrian Mediation in the Berlin Crisis 1958-1963 and U.S. perception of this mediation.[1] It focuses on the Austrian politician Bruno Kreisky[2] of the Socialist Party who became much more well-known as the Austrian chancellor and as a mediator in the Middle East conflict in the 1970s and early 1980s when he met with PLO Chairman Yasir Arafat[3] and Libyan President Muammar al-Qaddafi—but back then during the Berlin Crisis, Kreisky acted as foreign minister of Austria.

Why was Washington interested in Austria's neutrality and foreign policy within its global Cold War strategy in the early 1960s? Why was Austrian neutrality a "special case" for the Kennedy Administration? Compared to the second term of U.S. President Dwight D. Eisenhower with Secretary of State John Foster Dulles' harsh line, the administration of his successor, John F. Kennedy, viewed Austria's *pro-western* neu-trality much more positively. It could even serve as a model for a truly independent and stable Laos. It could be used as an example for Eastern Europe and the non-aligned countries. It could host a summit and present its special neutrality. In contrast, Soviet Chairman Nikita Khrushchev praised Austria's neutrality from his own point of view as an *Eastern* model for the Kremlin's doctrine of peaceful coexistence.

What about Austrian mediation in the Cold War in the late 1950s and early 1960s and Washington's specific perception regarding the Austrian mediators Chancellor Julius Raab from the conservative People's Party and especially Bruno Kreisky? Again, contrary to the late Eisenhower years with its rebuff of Raab's endeavors and skepticism of Kreisky's efforts, Kennedy appreciated the foreign minister's help as an informant and even his status as a secret mediator in the Berlin crisis. Based on his friendship with the mayor of West Berlin, the Socialist Willy Brandt, Kreisky tried his best, learned from his first mistakes in 1959, and kept in closest touch with the U.S. embassy in Vienna.

Kreisky never represented a "mediator" in the truest sense of the word as one who contacted both sides directly and brought them together. First, he constantly tried to push Brandt to make overtures to the Soviet Union; second, he passed on information from the Kremlin to the West that was based on substantial Soviet feelers in his mind. Third, he eagerly pushed for talks between East and West in public or in secret. Kreisky was more than just a passive back-channel!

From late 1961 to mid-1963, Kennedy send out his own feelers to Khrushchev and Austria focused on its European integration for which it deeply needed Bonn's support. Therefore, Vienna remained silent on the West Berlin question during this period. Nevertheless, Kennedy exclusively invited Kreisky to the White House in October 1963 which proved to be the climax of his diplomatic life as Austrian Foreign Minister.

The Kremlin also realized the importance of the Brandt-Kreisky friendship and the eagerness of the young, new Austrian foreign minister to mediate—but there were never direct talks between Brandt and Khrushchev because of internal Western protest or resistance. Moreover, Brandt—who had just become mayor of West Berlin in 1957—did not want to risk too much two or three years later. So, Kreisky was left out in the cold by Brandt and reduced his mediating efforts to merely passing along information to the U.S. ambassador in Vienna, H. Freeman Matthews, and other U.S. officials at the Viennese embassy.

U.S.-Austrian Relations, 1955-1963: An Overview

To explain the U.S. policy shift from Ike to JFK regarding Austria, it is indispensable to go back to 1955—the year of the Austrian State Treaty, the end of the occupation, and the declaration of perpetual neutrality following the Swiss model.[4] Austria had to find its way in the international arena, but now it had lost much of of its importance for the United States. Therefore, the reports of the U.S. ambassadors in Vienna more and more influenced Washington's policy toward Austria.[5]

The first step of Austria's emancipation from Moscow proved to be the 1956 Hungarian Crisis, and its emancipation from Washington was the 1958 Lebanon crisis. During Nikita Khrushchev's visit in Austria in mid-1960—shortly after the U-2 affair and the abortive Paris summit—

the Soviet Chairman used the neutral country as a stage for attacks against Eisenhower and West German Chancellor Konrad Adenauer. Raab remained silent; the Ambassador Matthews and Bonn strongly protested.[6] The National Security Council (NSC) document on Austria from late 1960 (NSC 6020) mostly repeated the position of the preceding document of 1956: Washington's willingness to support a continued *pro-Western*, independent, and stable Austria.[7]

Foreign Minister Bruno Kreisky of the Austrian Socialist Party at the New York Airport, 1963: "Secret" Mediator in the Berlin Crisis (ÖNB, Vienna)

In general, there was a change to accepting a much more positive interpretation of neutrality in the Kennedy years. JFK openly appreciated Austria's neutrality and accepted its special status while John Foster Dulles had called neutrality "immoral" in public—though it could be used or, as Eisenhower stated internally, it could mean a "political commitment to our side." Kennedy expressed great sympathies for Austria's behavior in the Hungarian Crisis of 1956. Secretary of State Dean Rusk told Kreisky at the Khrushchev-Kennedy Summit in Vienna in June 1961 that it was no longer the U.S. government's attitude to call neutrality immoral. There was complete U.S. understanding that the Austrian government took care of its neutral policy. Actually, the Khrushchev-Kennedy Summit in Vienna proved to be the most prestigious event for Austria in the Kennedy years.

In January 1962, the press reported President Kennedy's statement that a policy of neutrality would be the best for certain countries and that such a policy should be supported. Kennedy told the visiting Austrian government's delegation in 1962 that "we had always seen Austria as a special case. Austria was entitled to special consideration, and we were determined to see she got it [. . .] we regarded Austria as having a very special position. We had no wish to see her sucked into the eastern sphere." In spring 1963, Rusk assured the Austrians that the President and he himself knew exactly on which side Austria would stand. The United States respected its neutrality absolutely. Vienna could count on Washington's friendship and help in good times and bad times.[8]

The State Department's new guidelines on Austria of both 1962 and 1964 presented different approaches compared to that of NSC 6020 of 1960. Besides the respect for the country's "special military neutrality," Washington now regarded Austria as a *double model* case. The preser-vation of a stable and independent Austria might serve "(a) for the Sino-Soviet satellites as an example of how neutrality may be successfully maintained in the shadow of Soviet power and (b) for the non-aligned developing nations as an example of how neutrality may be harmonized with a freely expressed, pro-Western, positive national policy."[9]

But at first, when Kennedy took office in January 1961, the most pressing crisis was Laos. Besides plans for intervention, Rusk informed the U.S. Embassy in Laos one month later that Austria "may serve as [a] precedent." U Thant and Khrushchev also pointed at the Austrian solution of 1955. In his press conference on 23 March, JFK stressed that the security of Southeast Asia would be endangered if Laos—"3 times the size of Austria"—lost its neutral independence. At the Vienna Summit, Laos proved to be the only issue of common understanding between Kennedy and Khrushchev. In the end, a coalition government was formed based on the 1962 Geneva Accords. But the solution would be a short-lived one because of the growing importance of the Vietnam issue.[10]

Washington also perceived Austria as a "special case" in the process of European integration because of its geostrategic position, young neutrality following the State Treaty of 1955, and Soviet pressures on Austria's policy of European integration, but felt an Austrian solution should not become a precedent for other applicants to the European Eco-nomic Community (EEC).[11] On the contrary, the Kremlin praised Austria's neutrality as a perfect example for its doctrine of "peaceful coexistence." Khrushchev was proud of his first "great international victory"[12]: the Austrian State Treaty of 1955.

There were no basic problems between the *Ballhausplatz* and the White House in the early 1960s–as long as Austria remained pro-Western! The U.S. ambassadors kept a close eye on Austria's neutral attitude. The Austrian government tried to balance between East and West. Kreisky once summed up that the "main goal" of Austria's foreign policy was "the creation of as much confidence as possible in the West and as little distrust as possible with the East."[13] Austrian politicians also constantly worried that Washington was disinterested in

Viennese affairs.[14] This background sets the stage for the main topic of this article.

Austrian Mediation in the Berlin Crisis and the U.S. Perception of It

Since the late 1950s, Foreign Minister Kreisky kept in close touch with the U.S. embassy in Vienna. Of course, Ambassador Matthews liked his pro-American approach, especially in contrast to the conservative Chancellors Julius Raab (1953-1961) and Alfons Gorbach (1961-1964) who were perceived as more pro-Moscow. When looking at "mediation," two aspects have to be kept in mind.

First, there is a big difference between the U.S. position during the late Eisenhower years and the Kennedy era. After the Austrian State Treaty and Declaration of Neutrality in 1955, Secretary of State John Foster Dulles stressed that the Austrian solution was a unique case and not a model case at all. Dulles also strongly pressed for a summit in 1955 to be held in Geneva, so as not to reward Vienna with a summit. Any Austrian mediation was unwelcome. Everything changed during the Kennedy Administration, in part, because JFK liked secret channels of information himself, such as using the official at the Soviet embassy in Washington, Georgi Bolshakov, as a contact.[15] Kreisky's endeavors were alright; he kept the Americans informed. Kennedy gave his o.k. to hold the summit with Khrushchev in Vienna.[16] Austrian *Western* neutrality could serve as a model for Laos.

Second, one must differentiate between Raab as well as his successor from the People's Party, Chancellor Gorbach, both of whom stressed the importance of Austria as a "bridge" between East and West and the cautious Kreisky who officially refused any mediatory function—but acted secretly and pushed towards informal talks and meetings! Kreisky stuck to this approach—no mediation in public, passing on information in secret—well into the 1960s and 1970s.[17]

But in March 1958, Raab was the first Austrian to make proposals to solve the German and Berlin question. He suggested setting up a four-power commission to prepare elections all over Germany. West German Chancellor Konrad Adenauer—who had proposed an "Austrian solu-tion" for the German Democratic Republic (GDR) to the Soviets at that time[18]—gave his Viennese friend his go-ahead. Raab contacted the Soviet ambassador in Vienna. The Kremlin remained silent. U.S. Ambassador Matthews stated "no one takes Raab's proposal seriously." The Austrian Chancellor's visits in the United States and in the USSR in mid-1958 showed no results at all. The West German ambassador in Vienna, Carl-Hermann Mueller-Graaf, mentioned two motivations for

Raab: first, internal politics to keep his power in the People's Party, and second, an Austrian contribution to German reunification as a first step to free Eastern Europe. But back then, Khrushchev wanted the diplomatic recognition of the GDR, not a unified Germany! A third motivation on Raab's side can be added: the repetition of his diplomatic victory of the State Treaty of 1955. He had shown the West how to negotiate with the Soviets and that it was possible to get the Red Army out of a country—although he strictly opposed an Austrian model case for all of Germany standing in one line with Adenauer. In the fall of 1958, Raab referred to his spring proposal on West German TV stressing in public that he would prefer "secret diplomacy." The aging Raab did not suc-ceed in his attempts as a mediator.[19]

The Soviets took a different approach. Five days before Khrushchev's Berlin ultimatum in November 1958, Foreign Minister Andrei Gromyko sent out feelers to Raab's friend, the Austrian Ambassador Norbert Bischoff, regarding direct West German-Soviet negotiations. Adenauer turned them down.[20]

The situation in 1959/60—with Kreisky and Brandt[21] as new major players—was different. Besides the now-running Berlin ultimatum and the aftermath of the abortive Paris Summit, Khrushchev tried to get in touch with the mayor of West Berlin, Willy Brandt, via Brandt's friend from the exile in Sweden during the Nazi period, Bruno Kreisky, but in the end, Khrushchev never succeeded. Already in mid-1958, the Soviet Embassy in Vienna called Kreisky a clever diplomat—open for talks with the East in private, but officially avoiding making up his mind.[22] The Americans perceived him a year later as the "nation's top expert" in foreign affairs, a stern anti-communist, impressed by the United States, and stressing the necessity for negotiations with Moscow.[23] So, Khrushchev got in touch with the right person.

The first attempt took place in March 1959.[24] According to Kreisky's memoirs, Brandt asked his Viennese friend—back then state secretary in the Foreign Ministry—in late 1958 to check out the chance for a meeting with Khrushchev. In February 1959, Kreisky suggested a special status for all of Berlin in a public speech as well as a newspaper article. The Soviets thought this was Brandt's initiative. The Soviet ambassador in Vienna, Sergej Lapin, got in contact with Kreisky. The Kremlin proposed a meeting between Khrushchev and Brandt via the "Kreisky channel." Adenauer left the decision open for Brandt, but the U.S. official in West Berlin, Bernhard Gufler, spoke out against such a meeting. Brandt agreed—and Kreisky was left out in the cold. In a personal letter to Brandt, Kreisky complained about this affair as one of the "*peinlichsten meiner ganzen bisherigen öffentlichen Tätigkeit.*"[25]

During the visit of Austria's President Adolf Schärf to Moscow in late 1959, Khrushchev took the harsh line and complained that neutral Austria did not recognize the GDR. There were no signs of accommodation, no talks about mediation.[26] Then, in March 1960, Kreisky once again told Brandt that he should check out the Soviets' will to talk, either via the United Nations or Vienna—in coordination with Washing-ton. Brandt only referred to Adenauer and said nothing more.[27]

The Soviet Chairman revived the secret Austrian channel to the Western powers during his visit in Austria in July 1960. Despite Khrushchev's criticism after the U-2 affair and the abortive Paris Summit, in a private talk in Vienna Gromyko asked Kreisky—foreign minister since late 1959—to bring a Berlin memorandum to Brandt's attention because Brandt might be "thinking of the future" and might be "looking for a way out of the blind alley which has come about." The memo basically repeated the Kremlin's position regarding a German peace treaty. Kreisky urged Washington to check out the Soviet feeler. During the NSC discussions on 25 July, Under Secretary of State Douglas Dillon informed Eisenhower about the Soviet initiative and undermined Kreisky by calling him a "friend of Khrushchev."[28] Eisenhower took a firm line, willing to use whatever was necessary for maintaining U.S. security. In the end, Brandt rejected Khrushchev's overtures. The German news magazine *Der Spiegel*[29] publicized the whole incident. Kreisky was snubbed again. Another opportunity was lost.

Kreisky had been more cautious this time, as he told U.S. Ambassador Matthews, after "having been wrapped over knuckles last year in trying at Soviet request to arrange a Brandt-Khrushchev meeting."[30] At the very first, Kreisky had secretly asked for the advice of his new European Free Trade Association (EFTA) partner, British Foreign Minister Selwyn Lloyd, who advised him not to go for Gromyko's request. Internally, Lloyd stressed that there were plenty of other channels the Soviets could have used. In his opinion, they chose Kreisky to drive "a wedge between Adenauer and Brandt."[31] Nevertheless, Kreisky did act and informed Brandt, Adenauer, and Matthews of the "Gromyko memorandum." He told the U.S. ambassador ambiguously that he was unwilling to act as a mediator, but "could not merely sit on the memorandum". It was important to explore every avenue to see whether the Soviet would go for a workable Berlin solution.

Compared to 1959, this time Kreisky had *re*acted to feelers from Moscow, but still wanted to remain a secret player in the East-West conflict. He even falsely informed the Austrian embassies that there was no Gromyko memorandum. The Americans did not want to show any signs of weakness and tried to use Kreisky for their own purpose. Secretary of State Christian Herter instructed Matthews to tell Kreisky that the memo was nothing new, that the Berlin problem could only be solved by overall German elections, and that Kreisky's mediation was unwelcome—it would only be useful if the Foreign Minister could inform the Soviets about the West's ultimate firmness in the Berlin question.[32]

In the fall of 1960, there were no news regarding the Brandt-Kreisky-Khrushchev connection, but Adenauer internally thanked Kreisky for his mediation. Bonn's Chancellor also agreed with Kreisky's opinion that Khrushchev was serious on Berlin.[33] Even a "middle-man" of Adenauer, Klaus Dohrn, got in touch with Kreisky. The Austrian Foreign Minister should deliver a quite far reaching oral message to the Soviets at the U.N. General Assembly. Kreisky demanded a written ver-sion—which he would never get.[34] At that time, Kreisky again suggested privately to his friend Brandt that he should go to Moscow with Adenauer if Washington agreed. Brandt did not move.[35]

Right after the close of the Vienna summit in June 1961 that had ended in a clash over Berlin and another Soviet Berlin ultimatum,[36] Khrushchev reopened the secret "Kreisky channel" to the Western powers. The chairman wrote in his memoirs why, "To tell the truth, I recounted for Kreisky everything I'd told Kennedy. I knew that what I said would get back to Kennedy_and it would also be passed on to Willy Brandt."[37] Indeed, Kreisky promptly briefed Matthews the very next day and repeated the Soviet point of view on the German/Berlin question that the chairman had already told JFK: there had to be a peace treaty with both German states, because reunification was impossible. If the West refused, Khrushchev would have to sign a separate peace treaty with East Germany around the end of the year. Khrushchev had also informed the foreign minister that he was still interested in a solution with the West on Berlin "*etwa nach dem Modell des österreichischen Staatsvertrages*." In the same meeting with Matthews, Kreisky called the summit a huge success for Kennedy; Khrushchev had been impressed by the president's sense of responsibility and his knowledge.[38] The U.S. ambassador rejected an Austrian model for West Berlin right away because this would lead to the removal of the Western troops there.[39]

So, Kreisky had been a secret informant again—despite his denial in public. This time the foreign minister had only acted as a "channel" to the Americans—there is no evidence that he informed Brandt about the new Soviet feeler. The bad consequences of the last approaches might have been too much for the Austrian diplomat![40] Indeed, right after the Vienna Summit, Brandt put the blame on Kreisky when he told the leaving State Secretary of Bonn's Foreign Office, van Scherpenberg, that, in retrospect, the former secret Soviet suggestions via the Austrian Foreign Minister did not seem very trustworthy, "*da man bei Herrn Kreisky nie genau wüsste, wie weit er ihm zugangene Informationen richtig weitergebe oder sich dabei durch Wunschdenken leiten lasse und gar eigene Ideen in die Form einer angeblich von dritter Stelle erhal-tenen Anregung oder Information kleide.*"[41] Egon Bahr quotes a similar-ly skeptical, stern statement of Brandt, "*Um mit Moskau zu sprechen, dürfen wir Kreisky nicht brauchen.*"[42]

Nevertheless, Kreisky kept the U.S. embassy in Vienna informed about his thoughts regarding the Berlin question throughout 1962—although Austrian politics were very much preoccupied with the question of European integration and the national elections. Neutral Austria's strong willingness to seek an arrangement with Brussels caused major Soviet protests—this might have been one reason why there were no more Soviet overtures to Kreisky regarding Brandt. The other reason was the fact of official talks between Secretary of State Dean Rusk and Soviet ambassador to the United States, Anatol Dobrynin. In mid-1962, Kreisky informed the U.S. charge d'affaires in Vienna, Dwight Porter, about his full agreement with this U.S. approach to talk with Moscow based on "numerous examples from postwar Austrian history"[43] of such face-to-face exchanges. The U.S. embassy officials talked to Kreisky extensively after his return from Moscow in the summer, and the Foreign Minister was willing to hand over the full memoranda of conversations in which Khrushchev had talked nicely about JFK.[44]

The position of the GDR on Austrian mediation and the Austrian policy on Berlin was quite similar to the opinion of the Soviet ambassador in Austria, Awilow, around 1962. In general, the Austrian Coalition government of conservatives and socialists had a very, very close relationship to Bonn that should be influenced in the Communist purpose. Awilow even recommended using the Austrian example of 1955 as a solution of the German question.[45] East Berlin knew that Kreisky had stressed in public in April 1962 that there could be no recognition of the GDR because of the extraordinarily useful relations with the Federal Republic of Germany.[46] In fact, the "Hallstein doctrine" made it impossible as well; Vienna did not want to risk any diplomatic clash with Bonn at all. At least the East Germans had a commercial outpost in Vienna.

But in mid-1962, there were internal discussions in the GDR's Ministry of Foreign Affairs to suggest a meeting with Kreisky coming back from Sweden to Austria. The East German official Herbert Plaschke wrote in his memo that there were signs of Austrian interest to talking about the Berlin question. Kreisky might be interested in such a secret get-together,[47] but it never actually took place. There is no evidence for talks with Kreisky having occurred. At least, the GDR's Ministry of Foreign Affairs contacted First Deputy Chairman of the Council of Ministers Willi Stoph and suggested sending out overtures to the Austrians regarding consular relations.[48] In September 1962, Khrushchev used the visiting Austrian Vice Chancellor Bruno Pittermann as a channel to the Americans when he stressed the necessity of a separate peace treaty with the GDR, but no deadlines were mentioned.[49]

In early 1963, another attempt of Khrushchev to meet Brandt did not work out. While staying in East Berlin, he sent out feelers to the West Berlin mayor via West German, Austrian, and Swedish officials. But Brandt's conservative coalition partner blocked a *tête-à-tête*. Adenauer was only willing to give up his worries in case of a go-ahead of the Western powers. The Austrian representative in West Berlin, *Generalkonsul* Peter Müller, had got the green light from Kreisky's Foreign Office to act as mediator.[50] In his meeting with East German officials, the counselor at the Austrian embassy in Moscow, Franz Karasek, bluntly stated, "*Wenn Österreich so wie Brandt gehandelt hätte, würde es heute noch keinen Staatsvertrag besitzen.*"[51]

After de Gaulle's veto of the British accession to the EEC in January 1963, the Austrian government took the "*Alleingang*" (going it alone) approach as the only European neutral engaging in an association with Brussels.[52] The Foreign Ministry in East Berlin might have been right with the following conclusion; in the spring and summer of 1963, the Austrian government said nothing about the German and Berlin question in order to get the support of the EEC member states for the "*Alleingang*," especially Bonn—an Austrian "policy of silence" that had already started in 1962. Bonn's support was crucial for Austria.[53] East Berlin took also notice of Kreisky's *Istwestja* interview in mid-1963 in which the Foreign Minister stressed Austria's willingness to contribute to a period of détente in the Cold War.[54]

The Cuban Missile Crisis

Kreisky had a "comeback" as a minor player in the East-West power struggle during the highly dangerous Cuban Missile Crisis. In October 1962, the NSC's Executive Committee (ExComm) discussed Kreisky's suggestion of a rocket trade during this Cold War crisis that he had made in a public speech in Austria, but it was actually a proposal that U.S. journalist Walter Lippman had made first.[55] In the end, Lippman's article in the *Washington Post* might have influenced Khrushchev to include the Turkish Jupiters in a possible deal.[56] Kreisky's role in the whole affair should not be exaggerated. Only U.S. Ambassador in Moscow Llewellyn Thompson, former ambassador in Austria (!), had mentioned the Kreisky proposal in the ExComm sessions.[57]

Kreisky also told the Americans during the Cuban Missile Crisis that the Soviets had contacted the Austrians regarding another Vienna Summit. But these Soviet diplomats in Vienna might have sent out a singular feeler without instructions from the Kremlin.[58] In the end, as we know, there was no Kennedy-Khruschev summit, but a secret missile exchange deal.

Visiting JFK in October 1963

US President John F. Kennedy exclusively invited Foreign Minister Bruno Kreisky to the White House in October 1963 to talk about the East-West conflict as well as the Berlin Crisis (ÖNB, Vienna).

Kreisky paid a visit to the United States that occurred about one month before Kennedy's assassination in late 1963, and the president exclusively invited the foreign minister to the White House for consultation on Berlin, the Soviet Union, and U.S.-European relations. Why the invitation? Because former U.S. President Harry S. Truman had praised Kreisky's speech in Kansas City as "the best damned talk I have heard in years." Truman might have even called JFK.[59] Advisor Arthur Schlesinger, Jr., briefed the president about the "lively and engaging" Kreisky and called his speech "excellent propaganda for a Democratic foreign policy."[60] During his meeting with Kreisky, Kennedy did not incorporate the State Department's briefing of the American "under-standing of Austria's unique position as a neutral state half-surrounded by communist-controlled countries"; the U.S. president might have been more interested in the paper's statement: "Kreisky considers it Austria's mission to help bridge the gulf between East and West."[61] In their conversation, the foreign minister expressed full agreement with Kenne-dy's policy of communication with the Soviets—an issue *so close to his heart* for years. Kreisky stated that "in this context he had been in favor of Mayor Brandt of Berlin meeting personally with Khrushchev. To make it a question of policy whether to meet with the Soviets or not would always be doomed to failure. It was important to meet."[62]

Notes

1. This article is based on my lecture at the SHAFR Conference in Austin, Texas, in June 2004 where I appeared on the panel, "Mediation in the Cold War, 1958-1963," with Thomas A. Schwartz, James G. Hershberg, Malgorzata Gnoinska, and Timothy J. Naftali. I am deeply grateful to the Austrian Science Foundation in Vienna for providing a travel fund.

The Austrian mediation during the Berlin Crisis is not mentioned in the most recent monumental studies on Kennedy and Khrushchev: Robert Dallek, *An Unfinished Life: John F. Kennedy, 1917-1963* (Boston: Little, Brown, and Company, 2003); William Taubman, *Khrushchev: The Man and His Era* (New York: W. W. Norton & Company, 2003); as well as in the most important studies on the Cold War in the late 1950s and early 1960s: Lawrence Freedman, *Kennedy's Wars: Berlin, Cuba, Laos, and Vietnam* (New York: Oxford UP, 2000), 45-120; John Lewis Gaddis, *We Now Know: Rethinking Cold War History* (Oxford: Clarendon Press, 1997), 113-51; Vladislav Zubok and Constantine Pleshakov, *Inside the Kremlin's Cold War: From Stalin to Khrushchev* (Cambridge, MA: Harvard UP, 1996), 194-209, 236-74.

2. On Kreisky, for instance, see Andreas P. Pittler, *Bruno Kreisky* (Reinbek bei Hamburg: Rowohlt, 1996); at least the Austrian Foreign Minister is mentioned once as a player in the Cuban Missile Crisis in Michael R. Beschloss, *The Crisis Years: Kennedy and Khrushchev 1960-1963* (New York: HarperCollins, 1991), 533; the best introduction to the topic is Hanns Jürgen Küsters, "Konrad Adenauer und Willy Brandt in der Berlin-Krise 1958-1963," in *Vierteljahrshefte für Zeitgeschichte 40* (Oktober 1992): 483-542; see also Martin Kofler, *Kennedy und Österreich: Neutralität im Kalten Krieg* (Innsbruck: StudienVerlag, 2003), 58-68.

3. Most recently on the Kreisky-Arafat friendship is an article in *Profil*, 15 November 2004.

4. For the occupation period above all, see Günter Bischof, *Austria in the First Cold War, 1945-55: The Leverage of the Weak* (Houndmills: Macmillan, 1999); Gerald Stourzh, *Um Einheit und Freiheit: Staatsvertrag, Neutralität und das Ende der Ost-West-Besetzung Österreichs 1945-1955*, 4th rev. and expanded ed. (Vienna: Böhlau, 1998); A. Ableitinger, S. Beer, and E. G. Staudinger, eds., *Österreich unter alliierter Besatzung 1945-1955* (Vienna: Böhlau, 1998); Wolfgang Kos and Georg Rigele, eds.,

Inventur 45/55: Österreich im ersten Jahrzehnt der Zweiten Republik (Vienna: Sonderzahl, 1996).

5. Oliver Rathkolb, *Washington ruft Wien: US-Großmachtpolitik und Österreich 1953-1963* (Vienna: Böhlau, 1997), 93, 278; Günter Bischof and Martin Kofler, "Austria's Postwar Occupation, the Marshall Plan, and Secret Rearmament as 'Westernizing Agents' 1945-1968," in. *Contemporary Austrian Studies, vol. 12, The Americanization/ Westernization of Austria*, ed. Günter Bischof and Anton Pelinka (New Brunswick, NJ: Transaction, 2003), 199-225, here 203-04.

6. Martin Kofler, "Eine 'Art Nabel der Welt': Österreich und der Chruschtschow-Besuch 1960," *Zeitgeschichte 26* (1999): 397-416.

7. NSC 5603, "U.S. Policy Toward Austria," 23 March 1956, Records Relating to State Dept. Participation in the Operations Coordinating Board and the National Security Council 1947-1963, Lot 63 D 351, Box 87, Record Group (RG) 59, General Records of the Department of State, National Archives (NA), College Park, Maryland; NSC 6020, "U.S. Policy toward Austria," 9 December 1960. Ibid., Box 100.

8. See Kofler, *Kennedy*, 14-15, 26-28.

9. State Department's Guidelines for Policy and Operations Austria, March 1962, "Austria General 4/61-5/62" Folder, Countries Files, National Security Files (NSF), Box 9, John F. Kennedy Library, Boston, MA (JFKL); State Department's Guidelines for Policy and Operations Austria, July 1964, Records of the Ambassador at Large, Llewellyn E. Thompson 1961-70, Lot 67 D 2, Box 4, RG 59, NA.

10. Kofler, *Kennedy*, 43-47.

11. Ibid., 77-94.

12. Jerrold L. Schecter and Vyacheslav V. Luchkov, eds., *Khrushchev Remembers: The Glasnost Tapes* (Boston: Little: Brown and Company, 1990), 79-80.

13. Record of Conversation Heath-Kreisky, 14 July 1961, Foreign Office 371, 160815/CU 1052/4, The National Archives, Kew (formerly Public Record Office).

14. Kofler, *Kennedy*, 40-42.

15. For instance: Beschloss, *Crisis Years*, 152-57.

16. See: Martin Kofler, "'Neutral', Host, and 'Mediator': Austria and the Vienna Summit of 1961," in *Contemporary Austrian Studies, vol. 8, The Marshall Plan in Austria*, ed. G. Bischof, A. Pelinka, and D. Stiefel (New Brunswick, NJ: Transaction, 2000), 487-505.

17. Idem, *Kennedy*, 58.

18. Küsters, "Adenauer," 488.

19. Background Paper "Chancellor Raab's Initiative on Germany," 12 May 1958, 763.13/5-1458, Central Decimal File 1955-1959, RG 59, NA; reports Carl-Hermann Mueller-Graaf to Foreign Office/Bonn, 25 February 1958, 27 February 1958, 4 March 1958, and 7 May 1958, Nachlass Mueller-Graaf, Vol. 3, Politisches Archiv/Auswärtiges Amt, Berlin; compare the unconvincing article: Matthias Pape, "Die Deutschland-initiative des österreichischen Bundeskanzlers Julius Raab im Frühjahr 1958," *Viertel-jahrshefte für Zeitgeschichte 48* (April 2000): 281-318; see also: Idem, *Ungleiche Brüder: Österreich und Deutschland 1945-1965* (Cologne: Böhlau, 2000), 481-99.

20. Küsters, "Adenauer," 491-92; see also Erhard Sammer, *Die Berlin-Krise von 1958-1961: Ihre Wahrnehmung durch die österreichische Diplomatie*, Master's thesis, U of Graz 2000, 80-82.

21. For Brandt's early concepts on detente, especially 1956-1958, but overemphasizing the importance of the Berlin ultimatum of 1958, see Wolfgang Schmidt, "Die Wurzeln der Entspannung: Der konzeptionelle Ursprung der Neuen Ostpolitik?" *Vierteljahrshefte für Zeitgeschichte* 51 (Oktober 2003): 521-63, here 549-60.

22. Report Tugarinow (Vienna), 12 June 1958, Folder "Russische Dokumente – Deutsche Übersetzung," Stiftung Bruno Kreisky Archiv (SBKA), Vienna.

23. Fisher (Vienna) to Department of State, 28 August 1959, 763.521/8-2859, Central Decimal File 1955-1959, RG 59, NA.

24. Küsters, "Adenauer," 493-97; Paul Lendvai, "Der Beginner: Mut zum Unvollendeten," in Idem and Karl Heinz Ritschel, *Kreisky: Porträt eines Staatsmannes* (Vienna: Econ/Zsolnay, 1972), 97-143, here 133-34; Sammer, *Berlin-Krise*, 68-74; see also the following memoirs: Willy Brandt, *Erinnerungen* (Frankfurt: Propyläen, 1989), 51-53; idem, *People and Politics: The Years 1960-1975* (Boston: Little, Brown and Company, 1976), 99-103; Bruno Kreisky, *Im Strom der Politik: Erfahrungen eines Europäers* (Berlin: Siedler, 1988), 9-22; Hans J. Thalberg, *Von der Kunst, Österreicher zu sein: Erinnerungen und Tagebuchnotizen* (Vienna: Böhlau, 1984), 253-6; Egon Bahr, *Zu meiner Zeit* (Munich: Karl Blessing Verlag, 1996), 127-9 (which downplays Kreisky's role); a text critical of Kreisky who might have overestimated his status as a mediator, Hella Pick, *Und welche Rolle spielt Österreich? Vom besetzten Grenzland zum offenen EU-Staat: Die Alpenrepublik im internationalen Blickfeld* (Vienna: Kremayr & Scheriau, 1999), 104-05.

25. Note Brandt, 10 March 1959, quote in Kreisky to Brandt, 11 March 1959, Beruflicher Werdegang und politisches Wirken in Berlin 1947-1966, 66, Willy-Brandt-Archiv, Archiv der Sozialen Demokratie der Friedrich-Ebert-Stiftung (ADF), Bonn; Kreisky, *Strom*, 8-20.

26. See the documents in: GZ. 73982-4(pol)/60, Österreich 1, II-pol, Bundesministerium für Auswärtige Angelegenheiten, Österreichisches Staatsarchiv/Archiv der Republik (BMfAA, ÖStA/AdR).

27. Memorandum of Conversation Kreisky-Brandt, 6 March 1960, Beruflicher Werdegang und politisches Wirken in Berlin 1947-1966, 69, Willy-Brandt-Archiv, ADF.

28. 453rd Meeting of National Security Council, 25 July 1960, NSC Series, Box 12, Papers of Dwight D. Eisenhower as President, 1953-61 (Ann Whitman File), Dwight D. Eisenhower Library, Abilene, Kansas.

29. *Der Spiegel*, 27 July 1960.

30. Matthews (Vienna) to Secretary of State, 18 July 1960, 762.00/7-1860, Central Deci-mal File 1960-1963, RG 59, NA.

31. Bowker (Vienna) to Foreign Office, 6 July 1960, Selwyn Lloyd to Bowker, 8 July 1960, Foreign Office 371/153983, The National Archives, Kew (formerly Public Record Office).

32. Martin Kofler, "Österreich und der Chruschtschow-Besuch 1960," 409; Kofler, *Kennedy*, 60-61.

33. See: Ibid.; Adenauer: ". . . um den Frieden zu gewinnen": Die Protokolle des CDU-Bundesvorstands 1957-1961 (Düsseldorf: Droste, 1994), 809; Küsters, "Adenauer," 520.

34. Bruno Kreisky, *Zwischen den Zeiten: Erinnerungen aus fünf Jahrzehnten* (Berlin: Siedler, 1986), 451; K. Gotto, H. Maier, R. Morsey, and H.-P. Schwarz, *Konrad Adenauer: Seine Deutschland- und Außenpolitik 1945-1963* (Munich: dtv, 1975), 239.

35. Note Brandt, 10 November 1960, Beruflicher Werdegang und politisches Wirken in Berlin 1947-1966, 70, Willy-Brandt-Archiv, ADF.

36. The memoranda of the conversations are in Folder "USSR Khrushchev Talks (President)," Countries Files, NSF, Box 187, JFKL; the best account of the Soviet position is: Petr Luòák, "Khrushchev and the Berlin Crisis: Soviet Brinkmanship Seen from the Inside," *Cold War History* 3.2 (January 2003): 53-82; see also: Hope M. Harrison, *Driving the Soviets up the Wall: Soviet-East German Relations, 1953-1961* (Princeton, NJ: Princeton UP, 2003); Beschloss, *Crisis Years*, 174-78; on the big picture, see Martin Kofler, "Juni 1961: Das 'Wiener Gipfeltreffen' Chruschtschow-Kennedy," in *Die Augen der Welt auf Wien gerichtet: Gipfel 1961 Chruschtschow-Kennedy*, ed. Monika Sommer and Michaela Lindinger (Innsbruck: StudienVerlag, 2005), 14-31.

37. Strobe Talbott, ed., *Khrushchev Remembers: The Last Testament* (Boston: Little, Brown and Company, 1974), 501.

38. Note Fuchs on Meeting Kreisky-Matthews, 6 June 1961, Zl. 25916-4(pol)/61 (GZl. 23618-4/61), USA 1, II-pol, BMfAA, ÖStA/AdR.

39. Matthews (Vienna) to Secretary of State, 6 June 1961, 661.63/6-661, Central Decimal File 1960-1963, RG 59, NA.

40. Kofler, *Kennedy*, 62.

41. Scherpenberg to Brentano, 9 June 1961, 83.20/94.29, Ref. 704, PA/AA.

42. Bahr, *Zu meiner Zeit*, 129.

43. Porter (Vienna) to Secretary of State, 15 June 1962, "Austria General 6/62-10/63 and undated" Folder, Countries Files, NSF, Box 9, JFKL.

44. Kofler, *Kennedy*, 64.

45. Awilow (Vienna) to Iljitschew, late 1961/early 1962, Folder "Russische Dokumente – Deutsche Übersetzung," SBKA.

46. Bernatek (Vienna) to Peuker (Berlin), 28 April 1962, Microfiche A 12886, Ministerium für Auswärtige Angelegenheiten der DDR, PA/AA; also: Information 5. Europäische Abteilung/Sektion III, 9 May 1962, A 12857, ibid.

47. Plaschke to Wandel, 10 June 1962, Microfiche A 12863, ibid.

48. Winzer to Stoph, 26 June 1962, Abteilung Internationale Verbindungen DY 30/IV 2/20, 266, SED-ZK, Stiftung Archiv der Parteien und Massenorganisationen der DDR im Bundesarchiv (SAPMO), Berlin.

49. Kofler, *Kennedy*, 64.

50. Küsters, "Adenauer," 540-42; Erich Böhme and Klaus Wirtgen, eds., *Willy Brandt: Die SPIEGEL-Gespräche 1959-1992* (Stuttgart: Deutsche Verlags-Anstalt, 1993), 77-88; also: Note Eberlein, 18 January 1963, Büro Walter Ulbricht DY 30, 3512, SAPMO; for Adenauer's opposition: *Akten zur Auswärtigen Politik der Bundesrepublik Deutschland 1963* (Munich: R. Oldenbourg Verlag, 1994), 90; in retrospect, Brandt thought it had been "foolish" to decline a meeting with Khrushchev. Brandt, *People and Politics*, 103.

51. Abraham (Moscow), Note on Dinner with Karasek, 30 January 1963, Microfiche A 12863, Ministerium für Auswärtige Angelegenheiten der DDR, PA/AA.

52. The best account is: Michael Gehler, *Der lange Weg nach Europa: Österreich vom Ende der Monarchie bis zur EU*, 2 vols. (Innsbruck: StudienVerlag, 2002).

53. Information 5. Europäische Abteilung/Sektion III, 19 April 1963, 19 June 1963, Microfiche A 15795, Ministerium für Auswärtige Angelegenheiten der DDR, PA/AA.

54. Analysis Knoblauch (Vienna), 29 June 1963, A 12863, ibid.

55. Kofler, *Kennedy*, 74.

56. Aleksandr Fursenko and Timothy Naftali, *"One Hell of a Gamble": Khrushchev, Castro, and Kennedy, 1958-1964* (New York: W. W. Norton & Company, 1997), 275.

57. Ernest R. May and Philip D. Zelikow, eds., *The Kennedy Tapes: Inside the White House during the Cuban Missile Crisis* (Cambridge, MA: Belknap Press of Harvard UP, 1997), 513, 534, 593, 600.

58. Kofler, *Kennedy*, 72-74.

59. Ibid., 65.

60. Schlesinger to JFK, 11 October 1963, "Austria 1962-1963" Folder, Countries Files, President's Office File, Box 111, JFKL.

61. State Department Briefing Paper, 11 October 1963, ibid.

62. Memorandum of Conversation Kennedy-Kreisky, 11 October 1963, *Foreign Relations of the United States, Vol. XVI, 1961-1963* (Washington, D.C.: U.S. GPO, 1994), 388-92; Talking Paper, 9 October 1963, "Austrian Foreign Minister Kreisky's Visit to NY (US) September - Washington October 1963" folder, Bureau of European Affairs, Records Relating to Austria, Lot 68 D 123, RG 59, NA; this attitude is not to be mixed or confused with Kreisky's improvement of relations with Austria's Communist neighbors in the East that has been strangely called Austrian *Ostpolitik* as a forerunner of the events of the late 1960s. Compare: Oliver Rathkolb, "Austria's 'Ostpolitik' in the 1950s and 1960s: Honest Broker or Double Agent?," *Austrian History Yearbook* XXVI (1995): 129-45; idem, "Bruno Kreisky's Perceptions of the United States," in *From World War to Waldheim: Culture and Politics in Austria and the United States*, ed. David F. Good and Ruth Wodak (New York: Berghahn Books, 1999), 36-50, here 43-44.

From Cooperation to Integration: The Foreign Policy/ies of the Austrian *Länder*

Stefan Mayer

Introduction

Austria is a federal state. It is composed of nine states, the *Länder*. The Federation (*Bund*) as well as the *Länder* have their own fields of competence, sometimes on concurring matters. Embedded in the context of Central Europe with its short distances and shared—though multi-faceted—history, Austria has an orientation towards its neighbors and further European partners that has proven to be indispensable for this small nation.

"The nation-state is becoming too small for the big problems of life, and too big for the small problems of life," the sociologist Daniel Bell writes.[1] So who is it, then, that takes the lead in solving problems that span national borders and that achieves regional interests in the solutions? In a federal setup such as that found in Austria, the answer is quite clear: if there are sub-national units with sufficient competence, they will come up with a form of foreign relations on their own, thus creating another level of foreign policy. Given the state's monopoly on foreign politics and representation, is the behavior of these sub-national units a form of *Nebenaußenpolitik* (states' parallel foreign policy)? This question, in turn, leads to more questions: who are the partners, what areas and issues are at stake, who are the prime actors, and what does the institutional and historic framework look like? Answering these questions is key to understanding foreign policy and the Austrian *Länder*; therefore, this article focuses on the time of Austria's Second Republic, beginning in 1945 and continuing to the present. However, the prerequisites of modern, regional, foreign policy are rooted in a wider historical context that needs to be mentioned as well.

Austria's Federal System

Following the tracks of federalism in Austria, one has to go back in time as far as to the Habsburg Empire when, as a result of the 1848 revolution, free and autonomous local self-government based on tax communities was acknowledged.[2] The federal tradition, composed of historically-developed entities and a multi-ethnic populace during the Austro-Hungarian Empire, mainly influenced the design of the new republic after World War I. Therefore, the federal (*bundesstaatlich*) principle was incorporated explicitly into the federal Constitution. However, the Austrian federal system was characterized by a reversed decentralization of traditionally unitary structures rather than by a union of historically sovereign states.[3] Nevertheless, after the collapse of the Habsburg Empire, the nine *Länder* established provisional assemblies on their own, parallel to the central government in Vienna.[4]

The federal Constitution of 1920 represents a compromise between the two diverging views, between the advocates of a federal state with strong subunits—linked to the ÖVP, the conservative Austrian People's Party—and those of a decentralized unitary state which is generally associated with the SPÖ, the Social Democratic Party of Austria. The tension between these two basic views still affects the constitutional and political discussion today.[5] The unifying effect among all relevant democratic parties of the political spectrum after the end of World War II reaffirmed the previously existing federal structure.

Institutions and Processes

Austria's Federal Constitution shapes the system as a federal state with centralist features.[6] The regulation of competence distribution is delineated in the Constitution. Being a constituent part of the federal system, the nine regional legislatures (*Landtage*) are entitled to enact laws and elect the members of the *Landesregierung*, the government of a *Land*. They further supervise the *Land* executive, the *Landesregierung* (usually six to eight members), which is headed by a governor (the *Landeshauptmann*).

Besides informal cooperation structures, the Federal Council (*Bundesrat*) as the constitutional counterpart to the National Council (*Nationalrat*) should secure the participation of the *Länder* in national legislation. Therefore, it has to be asked for approval of any constitutional laws that reduce the legislative and/or executive power of the *Länder*. However, its competence and, hence, its political influence are weak, since vetoing it can only delay bills passed by the *Nationalrat*. Law enforcement in Austria takes place on various levels. The concept of indirect federal administration regulates the devolution of power and the separation of competence in the *Bund-Land* dimension. Legislative power is transferred down as far as to the *Landtage* and to the *Landeshauptleute* that are, on the one hand, bound to directives of the federal government or ministers, while on the other, they can, in turn, issue directives to the *Land* institutions.

Development in the Second Republic

Apart from constitutional provisions, the *Länder* are "a conglomerate of political, economic, socio-cultural, and bureaucratic interests."[7] Hence, the various networks of "corporate federalism" are primarily based on informal cooperation. In 1951, a liaison office for the Austrian *Länder* (*Verbindungsbüro der Bundesländer*) was established in Vienna in order to coordinate and to integrate the various interests. The Conference of the Governors (*Landeshauptleutekonferenz*) convenes twice a year in order to coordinate positions, thereby promoting *Länder* demands. Although not institutionalized by law, it is considered to have a decisive impact on Austrian federalism.

Prior to the early 1970s, the Austrian *Länder* had not engaged in significant cross-border cooperation.[8] The years after World War II were characterized by endeavors within each *Land* to reconstruct the economy and to re-establish a political structure for addressing domestic policy issues. External relations of a *Land* were seen as an asset "nice to have," but they mainly resulted in cooperation agreements and symbolic bilateral declarations of keeping on good terms with a neighboring region. If there were exceptions to this rule, they were rooted in unresolved border and ethnic conflicts left over by the St. Germain treaty and were most significantly found in Tyrol and, to a lesser degree, in Carinthia.

In addition to participating in applicant and member activities in the European Union, starting from 1972 Austrian *Länder* have been involved in other various interregional associations, such as the Alpen-Adria working community, the Arge Alp, or the Assembly of European Regions.[9] In addition to the *Länder* governments, parliamentary and administrative delegations strengthened bilateral and multilateral relations with neighboring regions. *Ad hoc* working contacts with participation of experts as well as officials have become routine over the past decades as well.[10]

The right to sign state treaties individually with neighboring states has been a demand since the mid 1970s, clearly with the realistic self-restraint that such acts needed approval of the federal government.[11] In 1974, Austria provided its *Länder* with the competence to sign inter-federal treaties between themselves as well as with the *Bund* being the second partner. In the late 1980s, Austrian federalism reached a stage of autonomy that entitled the *Länder* to act equally to the state with regard to competence on signing international treaties. The *Länder* were also granted the right to bring an action to the Austrian Constitutional Court if their rights are infringed by state treaties that are unlawful. However, no *Land* has ever taken advantage of this provision in the past.

The autonomous competence on completion of state treaties has partially rendered the *Länder* entities of international law; nevertheless, a number of restrictions remain. Politically, their competence is mainly preparatory, after negotiating and wording a treaty, the *Land* must seek final approval from the federal president. A 1988 constitutional amendment entitles *Länder* to sign state treaties with states or their subnational units neighboring Austria on issues that have an impact on their autonomous competence. This competence, on the one hand, formally strengthened *Länder* power with regard to foreign policy; on the other, it reflected and sanctioned an existing *status quo* of interregional cooperation activities. In fact, no such treaty has been signed yet (although there were concrete preparations to do so), emphasizing that the *Länder* prefer informal channels through which to pursue their interests.

Starting in 1995, Austria's EU membership brought about a significant shift both in the allocation of foreign policy expertise and resources within the *Länder* themselves and in terms of the *Bund-Länder* relations. At an early stage, the *Länder* prepared themselves for the forthcoming negotiations on Austria's accession to the European Union. In 1990, the Austrian *Landeshauptleute* formally demanded participation and co-decision rights since the Austrian federal Constitution only provided for a right to deliver a consultative opinion lacking binding effects even if a decision was unanimous. Article 15a of the Constitution entitles both *Bund* and *Länder* to enter agreements among themselves according to their respective sphere of competence. Following a three year phase of preparation, the federal chancellor, the minister for federalism, and the nine *Landeshauptleute* signed an agreement on participatory rights of *Länder* and municipalities on matters of European integration on 12 March 1992. It enables the *Länder* to represent their vital interests concerning issues of integration policy via four core elements:

1. The *Bund* is obliged to include the *Länder* position in relevant negotiations.
2. The *Länder* are to be informed on projects regarding European integration.
3. The *Länder* are entitled to participate in national negotiation delegations, and they can send permanent representatives to the Permanent Representation of Austria in the European Union in Brussels.

4. The *Bund* is obliged to institute proceedings against EU institutions in case of unlawful or default actions if the autonomous sphere of competence of the *Länder* is affected.

Although providing its subnational divisions with extensive rights of autonomous self-government, the Austrian federal constitution does not explicitly concede competence of foreign representation to the *Länder*. However, on the informal level, *Länder* representatives are increasingly playing an important role in influencing the European decision-making process, sometimes concurrently to the state. Three main channels of interest promotion can be detected:

1. participation of *Länder* representatives in consultative bodies of the European Union, primarily in the Committee of the Regions;
2. binding mandates for members of the federal government in the Council of Ministers. Furthermore, EU law after the Maastricht Treaty theoretically opened the door for a *Landeshauptmann* or a *Landesrat* (minister of a *Land* government) to participate in the Council with full voting competence on matters that directly affect the *Länder*. Besides informal participation, this right has not yet been exercised; and
3. the informal lobbying networks of the *Länder* for EU institutions via liaison bureaus in Brussels, coordinated by a joint *Länder* representative.

Characteristics of Regional Foreign Policy

Before analyzing the Austrian situation empirically, a definition of what is understood by regional foreign relations has to be made. It is the sum of activities, policies, discussions, and relations set or carried out by regional actors that are aimed at institutions and processes beyond national borders. This can be done directly (actor to actor) or indirectly via, for example, national governments. The actors mainly are governments (especially the *Landeshauptmann* in Austria), the legislatures, administrative specialists, and further institutions of the regional political life.

Low Level vs. Big Politics

From a perspective of international relations studies, regional foreign policy typically is "too small" to be considered. It is not nation states that set actions; the channels of influence and the arena of politics are more informal. Scholars of international relations, therefore, often speak of paradiplomacy—ranging from minimal (*ad hoc*, technical cooperation) activity to maximal cooperation if competing with national foreign policy or protodiplomacy (preparing a secession) when addressing and categorizing these phenomena.[12] Quite often, this form of small diplomacy and symbolic foreign policy is ceremonial rather than substantive, lacking direct impact on the substance of national foreign policy; however, the political atmosphere is influenced.[13]

Concreteness vs. Ideology

Quite different from national foreign politics, regional foreign relations take place on a highly depoliticized level. The goals and the means are rarely debated in the political arena, so media scrutiny and coverage is low. Apart from symbolic gestures, policies are carried out by specialists behind closed doors. Differing ideologies usually can not be detected; it is, rather, a question of individual style how a ruling party shapes the foreign relations of a subnational unit. The typical topics and issues of cooperation and discussion are concrete problems of everyday life.

Nine *Länder* Observed

Burgenland

Burgenland became the youngest of the nine Austrian *Länder* in 1921. Previously, it had been part of the Kingdom of Hungary in the Austro-Hungarian Empire. Even today, Hungarian and Croatian minorities in Burgenland are a reminder of this historical past. Unlike in Tyrol or Carinthia, the new border did not create long-lasting disputes among the ethnic groups.[14] Burgenland was the welcoming gate for thousands of Hungarian refugees after the abortive uprising in Hungary against Communist rule. After World War I, Burgenland had shifted from being in the center of the former Empire to the easternmost edge of the Austrian Republic. This situation worsened in the Cold War era and limited foreign relations substantially. It is, therefore, understandable that expectations were optimistic after the Iron Curtain was torn down in 1989.[15] Institutional interregional participation had been established two years earlier when Burgenland joined the Arge Alpen-Adria.[16] Concerning Hungary, Burgenland already shared ties with the administrative regions of Györ-Sporon and Vas. Common efforts mainly dealt with cooperation in education and culture as well as projects concerning rivers in border regions. This collaboration was further strengthened in 1993 by the founding of a cross-border regional council. In 1999, the Euregio West[17]/Nyugat Pannonia was founded, creating a new level of cooperation between Burgenland and the Hungarian administrative re-

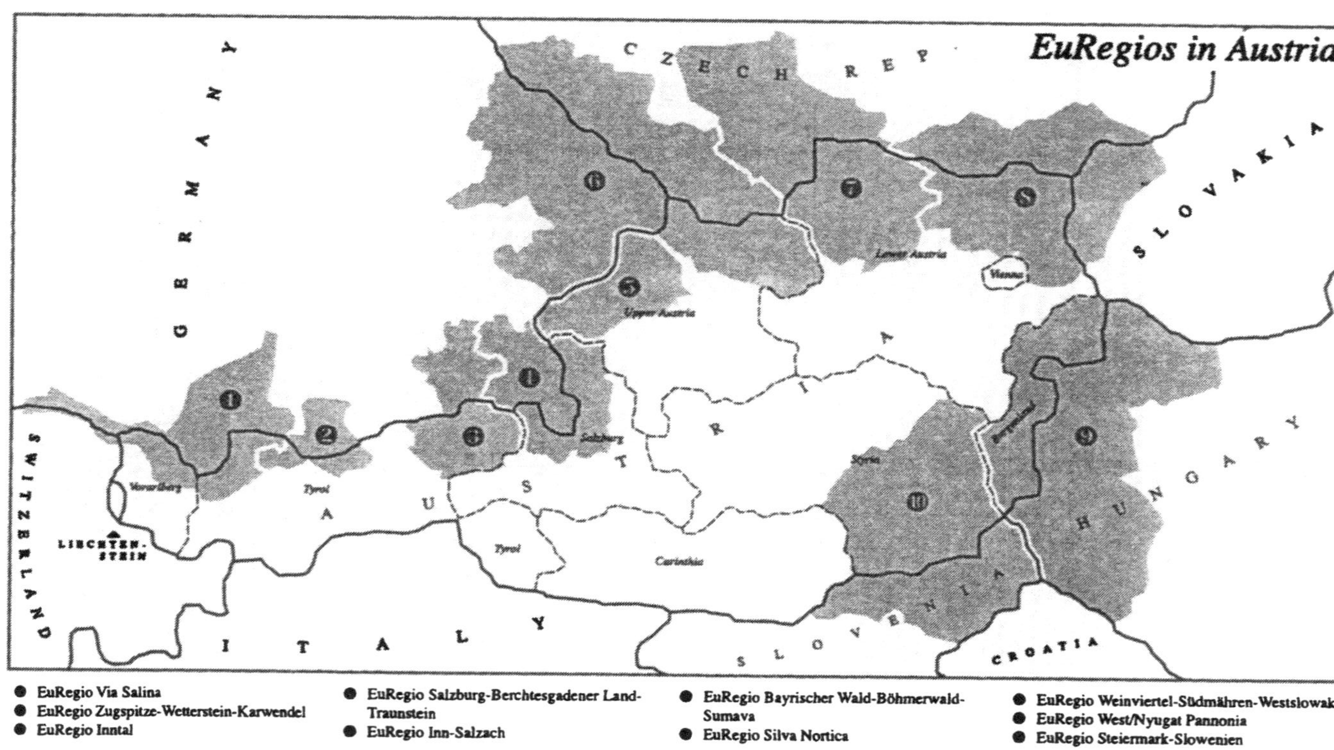
EuRegios in Austria
CZECH REP.
SLOVAKIA
HUNGARY
CROATIA
SLOVENIA
ITALY
AUSTRIA
GERMANY
SWITZERLAND
LIECHTEN-STEIN
Vorarlberg
Tyrol
Salzburg
Upper Austria
Lower Austria
Vienna
Styria
Carinthia
EuRegio Via Salina
EuRegio Zugspitze-Wetterstein-Karwendel
EuRegio Inntal
EuRegio Salzburg-Berchtesgadener Land-Traunstein
EuRegio Inn-Salzach
EuRegio Bayrischer Wald-Böhmerwald-Sumava
EuRegio Silva Nortica
EuRegio Weinviertel-Südmähren-Westslowakei
EuRegio West/Nyugat Pannonia
EuRegio Steiermark-Slowenien

gions of Györ-Moson-Sopron, Vas, and Zala focusing on transportation, economy, tourism, environmental protection, public health, education, and culture.

Beyond the neighboring regions, Burgenland established ties with the former Soviet Republic of Moldavia and with Czechoslovakia. It developed further institutional activities with the Arge Donauländer[18] and the Assembly of European Regions.[19] Burgenland was the only Austrian *Land* between 1945 and 1991 to experience a change of the leading party in government (from ÖVP to SPÖ in 1964). This did not affect the traditionally modest foreign relations of the Burgenland regional government.

After Austria's accession to the European Union, Burgenland clearly aimed at maximizing the benefits of the EU's regional policy for itself. Being classified as a most favorable funding area, more than € 830 million were provided until the year 2000; the second funding period will continue until 2006. Because interregional cooperation is a major concern of EU regional policy, a variety of cross-border activities with Hungary as well as with Slovakia have been established. In a rather pragmatic way, Burgenland since 1995 has made good use of the chances offered by European integration bringing the region from isolation to modernization. A political profile on external relations was neither aimed at nor necessary.

Carinthia

Austria's southernmost *Land* has traditionally been inhabited by German and Slovenian ethnic groups. After World War I, the newly emerged south Slavic state tried to integrate parts of Austrian Carinthia, and after 1941, the National Socialist regime in turn annexed the Upper Kranj region as part of the German Reich. An expatriation of Carinthian Slovenes followed, and after World War II, Yugoslavia again raised territorial claims, creating a boiling cauldron of mutual distrust. The Austrian State Treaty of 1955, assuring full sovereignty and independence for Austria, also brought about the obligation that ethnic minorities be granted cultural autonomy. In Carinthia, this refers to the Slovene minority and has not fully been accomplished yet.[20]

In the early 1970s, a discussion arose concerning bilingual Carinthian place-name signs in German and Slovenian (*Ortstafelstreit*) which evoked historic prejudices that were thought to have been overcome. A national law asserted that official signposts in areas with large numbers of Slovenes had to be bilingual. The Carinthian government enforced this law in areas predominantly inhabited by Slovenes only. This was too much of a concession for right-wing pressure groups to accept and led to the resignation of the former Carinthian Socialist *Landeshauptmann* Hans Sima "because he was viewed as too obliging towards the Slovenes."[21] Although primarily a problem of domestic politics, the controversy is one of the few examples of a regional policy counteracting national foreign policy. The national legislation was changed in favor of the Carinthian demands and, consequently, led to serious tensions between Vienna and Belgrade.

Alpen Adria has become a motto in the 1960s signifying cooperation between Carinthia and the neighboring regions of Slovenia (at that time a federal subdivision of Yugoslavia) and Friuli Venezia Giulia (Italy) where three European cultures (German, Slavic, and Romance) intersect. In 1965, *Landeshauptmann* Sima started to intensify bilateral contacts with his adjacent counterparts in Ljubljana and in Trieste and Udine, which consequently facilitated cross-border trade with Yugoslavia.[22] A closer cooperation of the three partners in the fields of culture, transportation connections, and sports followed the predominantly economic cooperation that had previously taken place. Following the *Ortstafelstreit*, a change in the official regional government towards foreign policy took place. Sima's successor, Leopold Wagner, assessed foreign policy activities of smaller regions as "inexpedient."[23] Nevertheless, in 1977 Carinthia invited its neighbors to cooperate in a working community. Slovenia rejected this invitation at first, but one year later, the Arge Alpen-Adria was founded.[24] The impetus, however, came from Styria, even though Carinthia had a long-standing tradition of bilateral cooperation. Carinthia's involvement peaked in 1987/88 when the *Land* presided over the community, signaling to the Yugoslav Federal Republics and to the Hungarian administrative regions a closer cooperation by the Millstatt Declaration.[25] In 1989, the heads of the governments of Carinthia, Friuli Venezia Giulia, and Slovenia signed an agreement for a joint bid for the 1998 Olympic Winter Games according to the motto *senza confini* (without borders) which—after failing—was postponed twice and then abandoned.

In October 1991, the depiction of the Carinthian *Fürstenstein* (a stone relic of the Slavic tribal state of the seventh or eighth century CE) on a provisional banknote of the newly established Republic of Slovenia caused irritation among Carinthians. Politicians of all parties protested, and the *Landtag* sent an official complaint to the Republic of Slovenia against the "abuse" of a solely Carinthian symbol. However, the argument was quickly settled, and the stone became a symbol of Carinthian-Slovene friendship just a few years later.[26]

Beyond cross-border activities—such as a trilateral meeting of Carinthian, Slovene, and Friulian parliamentary delegations in 1995—a cooperation treaty with the Chernihiv area in Ukraine fostered fledgling relations with this new partner and revealed this *Land*'s interest in broadening its contacts to regional and not just neighboring entities.

Lower Austria

Like Burgenland, Lower Austria—the largest *Land* of Austria—borders countries that formerly belonged to the Eastern bloc. Its late active involvement in foreign relations and its membership in the Arge Donauländer constitute another similarity.[27] Former *Landeshauptmann* Siegfried Ludwig (ÖVP) came up with the idea in 1982, and the headquarters of the working community are located in Lower Austria. Main areas of cooperation are the economy, spatial planning, transportation, environmental protection, tourism, culture, and science. Regarding bilateral, regional cooperation, Lower Austria has agreements with the Flemish Region in Belgium, Zala in Hungary, and the Southern Moravian region. Cooperation with the Polish *Skierniewice* voivodship proved to be inefficient due to the distance between the two regions.

Since Austria's EU membership, Lower Austria has focused its activities on cross-border cooperation promoted by EU funding programs in order to anticipate the EU enlargement which took place on 1 May 2004. By taking advantage of the EU's Interreg program,[28] border areas in Lower Austria extending to Slovakia and the Czech Republic were prepared for their new role in the enlarged Union. On the communal level, a Euregio with partners in Lower Austria, Southern Moravia, and Western Slovakia was formally founded in 1997, so far mainly as a means to carry out and to promote cross-border projects. In terms of its relationship to the federal government, the traditionally ÖVP-dominated regional government of Lower Austria repeatedly stressed its special position as a buffer zone to new member states in the East, sometimes risking a differing position from that of other *Länder* and the common position within the ÖVP.[29]

Salzburg

One of the smaller *Länder,* Salzburg largely owes its economic success to international tourism and to foreign trade relations, predominantly with southern Germany. Consequently, interregional contacts developed primarily with Bavaria. There are further cooperation agreements with Lithuania (since 1970), the Trento region (since 1981), and Slovenia (since 1992). Participation in interregional organizations is comparable to western Austrian *Länder*. Salzburg was a founding member of the Arge Alp working community in 1972.[30] The *Land* declared its status as an active observer in the Arge Alpen-Adria finished in 1999 after a gradual withdrawal. In the transregional arena, Salzburg participated in the "Europe of the Regions" conference[31] and joined the Assembly of European Regions in 1990.

Since 1995, the "EuRegio Salzburg – Berchtesgadener Land – Traunstein" has stimulated communal, cross-border cooperation, for it's an efficient structure for executing projects funded by the EU's Interreg program. By interest and by political performance, Salzburg is typically located in the middle between the eastern *Länder* oriented towards former Eastern bloc countries and the western *Länder* sharing traffic problems due to the alpine landscape (*Transitverkehr*) and united in a critical position against anti-federalist tendencies. Networking and finding political alliances on the institutional level, especially after Austria's accession to the European Union, can be named as the trademarks of Salzburg's foreign relations policy. Be it an (although not quite sustainable) initiative of alpine regions within the Committee of the Regions in the European Union to push forward their specific interests in 2001 or master minding REG LEG, the conference of EU regions with legislative powers since 2002, Salzburg has been a driving diplomatic regional force behind the scenes.

Styria

Another traditional border region, Styria in southeastern Austria actively participated in cross-border relations with its neighboring regions since the 1950s. Regional foreign policy was understood as a means of overcoming the *Lands*'s location at the geopolitical edge.[32] After World War I, the *Untersteiermark* representing one third of the former total area was lost.

The year 1960 saw the establishment of regulations facilitating regular border traffic between Yugoslavia and Styria (*Kleiner Grenzverkehr*). The level of institutionalization grew over the years backed by government resolutions on both sides. Styria's role in the Arge Alpen-Adria in the beginning sought integration with the western Hungarian administrative regions. Slovenia's nation building process in the late 1980s and early 1990s—which was vehemently supported by Austria—rendered Styria's bilateral cross-border activities less significant since the Slovenian government then treated the Austrian federal government as its primary counterpart.[33] On the other hand, competition for EU funding arose in the light of Slovenia's EU accession intentions. As early as 1996, the Styrian *Landtag* demanded that the federal government should counter a potential disadvantageous treatment of Styria compared to the Slovenian border region concerning negotiations on EU regional policy and should advocate Styria's funding so as not to neglect the regional transport infrastructure.

This helps explain why Styria's foreign relations focus shifted to interregional contacts during the 1990s, such as partnerships with the French *département de la Vienne*, the Hungarian administrative region of Baranya, the Polish voivodship Piotrokóv-Trybunalski, or the Lviv region in Ukraine.

Tyrol

Split after World War II into a northern Austrian and a southern Italian part (leaving an eastern Austrian part without geographical connection to the northern Tyrolean section), Tyrol tried during the Second Republic to overcome this separation through its foreign diplomacy. Since the 1990s, the traffic crossing the *Land* via the Inn Valley and the Brenner Pass became the second major issue in this respect.

The 1946 Gruber-De Gaspari Agreement[34] provided equality between the German-speaking inhabitants of Bolzano and the Italian inhabitants. However, in 1948 the two provinces of Bolzano and Trentino were combined into one region, thus reversing the majority of the population from German-speaking in South Tyrol to Italian in the new and larger administrative Trentino-Alto Adige region. The policy of North (Austrian) Tyrol towards South Tyrol has a constant characteristic: from 1945 on, it was exclusively carried out by the *Landeshauptleute*, all of whom were from the ÖVP.[35] The momentum of reunifying the two parts faded among the population after 1950 and became the domain of a small group of intellectuals and politicians.[36] Since the Italian interpretation of the 1946 agreement was not shared by Austria and since repeated attempts to make Rome change its policy failed, Austria referred the matter to the United Nations in 1960. Tyroleans were in the joint delegation of Austria that started direct negotiations with Italy. Although complicated by terrorist acts carried out by nationalist extremists, a new compromise called the *Paket* was achieved in 1969. On both sides, the national governments followed the goals of the German speaking Tyroleans. In order to "help foster an appropriate transborder political atmosphere"[37] the two neighboring regions also established joint sessions of the Tyrolean and South Tyrolean parliaments and settled the *Accordino* agreement[38] substantiating specific needs, predominantly economic in nature. On 19 June 1992, Austria and Italy formally resolved their dispute about South Tyrol before the United Nations. The same year marks the beginning of political efforts for a *Europaregion* Tyrol as a modern compensation for the historic separation enriched by the aspect of a common European spirit. Given the new dynamics of European integration, a basic agreement drafted by international law specialists was signed by the two Tyrolean governments. The agreement was soon caught up in the old, ethnic cleavages, resulting in a political standstill. A new strategy was implemented in 1998 by orienting the instruments of cooperation at the Euregio with less political and administrative goals rather than pragmatic cross-border solutions on a communal level.

The only remarkable diplomatic irritation in foreign relations connected to a *Land* in the past twenty years also has its roots in the Tyrol question. As did eight of the nine Austrian *Länder*, Tyrol opened an EU liaison office in Brussels in 1995.[39] Unlike the others, it was a joint office with South Tyrol and the Trentino region, a fact that elicited skeptical reactions from the Italian government. Above all, Italian regions lacked the legal authority to open representations on their own, a shortcoming that was corrected the following year by the Italian Parliament.[40]

Apart from the Tyrol question, the *Land* focused its interregional activities through its status as a founding member of the Arge Alp working community; currently, it is hosting the headquarters of the organization in Innsbruck. On the interregional level, cooperation agreements with Brabant (Belgium) and the French regions of Provence-Alpes-Côtes d'Azur and Rhône-Alpes were signed. A tradition of parliamentary cross-border conventions dates back to 1970 when the assemblies of North and South Tyrol held their first joint session. Including Vorarlberg and the Trentino region, it became a *Viererlandtag* in 1991. The two Tyrol governments officially held their first joint session in 1994.

Upper Austria

A center of Austrian industry as an armament production site between 1938 and 1945 and as a site of reindustrialization after World War II with U.S. support and a locus of a large and historically grown agricultural sector, Upper Austria has seen its internal and external politics closely tied to these two conditions of its existence. Until 1955, the Enns and Danube Rivers constituted the demarcation line between the Soviet and U.S. occupying forces, cutting apart the *Land*. Consequently, foreign relations developed with western as well as eastern neighbors. Practically, it meant long-lasting, bilateral cooperation with the Free State of Bavaria as well as with the Southern Moravian region in Czechoslovakia and later in the Czech Republic. Beyond the neighborhood contacts, an agreement with the—at that time still—Soviet Republic of Ukraine was signed in the late 1980s. Upper Austria is ac-

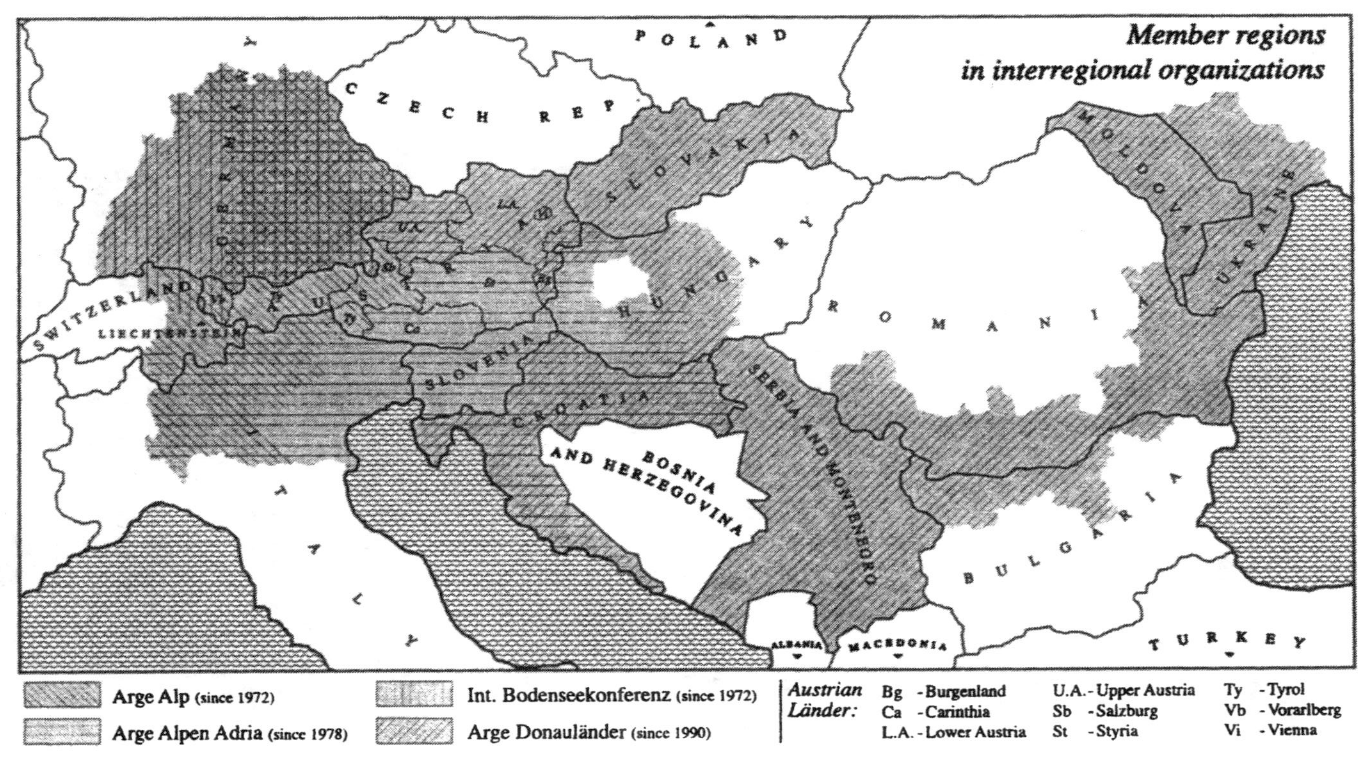
Member regions in interregional organizations
POLAND
CZECH REP.
GERMANY
SLOVAKIA
HUNGARY
ROMANIA
MOLDOVA
UKRAINE
SWITZERLAND
LIECHTENSTEIN
AUSTRIA
SLOVENIA
CROATIA
BOSNIA AND HERZEGOVINA
SERBIA AND MONTENEGRO
BULGARIA
ITALY
ALBANIA
MACEDONIA
TURKEY
U.A.
L.A.
Arge Alp (since 1972)
Arge Alpen Adria (since 1978)
Int. Bodenseekonferenz (since 1972)
Arge Donauländer (since 1990)
Austrian Länder:
Bg - Burgenland
Ca - Carinthia
L.A. - Lower Austria
U.A. - Upper Austria
Sb - Salzburg
St - Styria
Ty - Tyrol
Vb - Vorarlberg
Vi - Vienna

tive in nearly all interregional working communities. More than other Austrian *Länder*, the Upper Austrian government got involved in the "Europe of the Regions" conference in the early 1990s. This loose union of regions was installed in 1989 as a consequence of a temporary political weakness of the Assembly of European Regions due to vacancies of important positions there. The Conference differs from the Assembly of European Regions in that it exclusively aims at implementing the regional idea into the institutional framework of the European Union and, therefore, only addresses EU institutions because it considers itself to be the political spearhead for regional concerns. This conceit may be somewhat justified; the thirty-six founding member regions represented the most highly developed regions, both legally and economically.

Two Euregios were instituted. In 1994, as a premiere in Austria, the Euregio Bayerischer Wald-Böhmerwald with partners from Upper Austria, Southern Moravia, and Bavaria was founded. The Austrian-Bavarian Inn-Salzach Euregio was founded one year later, but activities there lagged, and after 2000, Upper Austrian involvement shifted towards regional development within the domestic areas. Causes of this shift can be seen in the prevailing economic and structural disparity as well as the general problem of public perception.[41] On the other hand, it seems that the Upper Austrian government restructured resources and money from EU funds for the benefit of its own regions rather than for the support of cross-border activities. Via the federal government but also by joining forces with neighboring *Länder*, Upper Austria lobbied against nuclear power plants in Temelin (Czech Republic) and Mochovce (Slovakia) between 1995 and the accession of the two countries to the European Union. A compromise, however, was achieved on the national level, resulting in the operators accepting higher security standards.

Vienna

The only enclave among Austrian *Länder* and a hybrid of *Land* and city at the same time, Vienna focused its foreign relations on cities with comparable problems and interests. In 1987, it signed the charter of European cities together with Hamburg, Munich, and Zurich; the charter stressed the cultural asset of urban living. With the former Eastern bloc countries returning to democracy in the early 1990s, Vienna once again acted as a bridge between the West and the East as it had before World War II. It enjoys close ties to Budapest, Bratislava, Brno, and Prague. On migration matters in connection with Eastern Europe opening up towards the West, the mayors of Vienna, Prague, and Budapest signed a joint declaration in 1990. Bilateral agreements followed five years later with Ljubljana and Zagreb. In the same year, Vienna also joined

EUROCITIES and the Union of European Capitals, two lobbying institutions and interest groups, and in 1998, it joined the Airport Regions Conference. These organizations are mainly debating practical urban issues; larger summits and gatherings predominantly lead to declamatory statements and declarations of intent.

Apart from engaging in communal cooperation, Vienna also signed an agreement with the Slovak Republic in 1990 dealing with upgrading the Slovakian bank system and spas as well as with cultural exchange. The city of Vienna also participates in interregional organizations, mainly in the Arge Donauländer and the Assembly of European Regions.

In sum, Vienna's foreign relations during the past thirty years are aimed at solving practical problems of a big city rather than acting as a regional authority in the institutional and political arena.

Vorarlberg

Vorarlberg shares 80 percent of its borders with Germany, Liechtenstein, and Switzerland, making cross-border relations a prerequisite for joint solutions and a thriving economy. Hence, Vorarlberg's economy is clearly oriented towards its neighbors; in the mid-1990s, more than half of the regional production was exported. In addition, the export ratio *per capita* amounted to 70 percent beyond the Austrian average in the beginning of the 1990s. On the other hand—although being at the top of critics against any form of centralist tendencies on the federal level—the Vorarlberg governments used domestic politics and participation as the primary means for advancing its interests concerning foreign relations.[42]

In the early 1950s, a couple of disagreements over the exact border definition with its neighboring countries of Switzerland, Liechtenstein, and Germany, as well as Tyrol to the east needed clarification that was achieved successively through the mid-1970s by bilateral treaties.[43] In order to overcome the disastrous economic situation after World War II, a cooperative economic authority was established to administrate the economic relations with Switzerland (*Wirtschaftsstelle Vorarlberg-Schweiz*). Although Vorarlberg's relations with its foreign neighbors were numerous, they were clearly not based on sovereign action, but on "business to business" terms and did not go beyond the fields of economic cooperation, transportation, and the environment.[44] The latter became a hot issue between Vorarlberg and Switzerland in the 1960s.

Swiss authorities planned to build energy plants next to the Austrian border. On this issue, the *Land* experienced itself as "passively affected."[45] The vigorous rejection of the plants by Vorarlberg's populace also emphasized the fact that in this, Austria's westernmost *Land*, an early and well-founded green movement had developed. In 1974, parliamentary cooperation started with Baden-Württemberg (Germany); similar relations with the autonomous Trento region (Italy) followed in 1989. Cross-border discussion groups on an administrative level have been established in all neighboring countries. Vorarlberg is a founding member of the Arge Alp working community, and it joined the Association of European Regions in 1987. Another environmental emphasis is set within the international conference of regions bordering Lake Constance (*Internationale Bodenseekonferenz*).[46] The *Alpenrhein* international governmental commission comprising the Swiss canton of St. Gallen, the state of Liechtenstein, and Vorarlberg deals with cross-border issues concerning the alpine part of the Rhine River. This cooperation was the basis for an Interreg program starting in 1995. The first Euregio in western Austria was established in 1997 in Vorarlberg's border region with Germany and Tyrol, but the initiatives' origin could be traced outside Vorarlberg.[47]

The Tyrol question also affected Vorarlberg; however, after 1993 the *Land* gradually withdrew its involvement in the four region parliamentary conventions, the result of a closer orientation towards the Lake Constance region and the fact that Vorarlberg, unlike Tyrol, was never separated.[48]

Conclusion

In brief, the answer to whether the Austrian *Länder* perform(ed) foreign policy in Austria's Second Republic is formally, yes; informally, yes; and practically, not really. Formally, this occurred via constitutional provisions, mainly fostered by the right that entitles the *Länder* to independently sign state treaties. However, no *Land* has yet made use of this formal right. Informally, they created policy by the various cooperative and lobbying activities of the *Länder* on the cross-border, transregional, and European levels. Practically, the formal rights are not applied—even after they were expanded—since the interests of the *Länder* can and could be pursued sufficiently on informal terms and within existing structures. The conflict potential with the federal government is small as long as a silent agreement is accepted by both sides: the *Länder* acknowledge the prerogative of the federal government in the field of international relations and diplomacy and the *Länder* see themselves as complementary actors on low-level cross-border relations mainly focused on the close neighborhood areas. This system is characterized by stabilizing rather than controversial effects. The Europeanization process that took place since the 1990s did not alter this existing *modus vivendi* although it brought about new arenas of transregional decision making, structurally with the Committee of the Regions on the EU level or by the establishment of Euregios on the communal crossborder level. European affairs were integrated into the regional policy agenda. On the other hand, existing transregional working communities such as Arge Alp or Arge Alpen Adria have decreased in importance since the Europeanization process offered further options and structures for interest coordination and decision making for the *Länder*.

Notes

1. Quoted in Reinhard Rack, "Europäische Integrationspolitik—eine neue Querschnittsmaterie und ihr innerstaatliches 'handling,'" in *Außenpolitik der Gliedstaaten und Regionen*, ed. Peter Pernthaler, (Vienna: Braumüller, 1991), 33-52, here 33.

2. See Doris Wastl-Walter, "Decentralising Federal States: The Experience of Austria," in *Local government in the New Europe*, ed. Robert J. Bennett (New York: Halsted Press, 1993), 155-66.

3. See Werner Pressien, *Föderalistische Strukturverschiebungen. Zur stillen Aufwertung der Länder im Kontext des österreichischen EU-Beitritts* (Vienna: Institut für Höhere Studien, 1996), 14.

4. It has to be kept in mind that after the collapse of the Habsburg Empire, the identification with Austria as a nation was far from the level that it has reached after World War II. There was open support for an Anschluss to Germany. The 1919 Peace Treaty of St. Germain clearly restricted such intentions, although spontaneous—and eventually ineffective—separatist plebiscites in Tyrol, Salzburg (in favor of joining Germany), and Vorarlberg (in favor of joining Switzerland) afterwards showed that, especially in the Western parts of Austria, there was no confidence among the population towards an Austrian nation. See also Anton Pelinka, "Austria," in *Federalism and International Relations: The Role of Subnational Units*, ed. Hans J. Michelmann and Panayotis Soldatos (Oxford: Clarendon Press, 1990), 124-41, here 127.

5. See Herbert Dachs, "The Politics of Regional Subdivisions," in *Contemporary Austrian Politics*, ed. Volkmar Lauber (Boulder: Westview Press, 1996), 235-52.

6. It seems helpful to provide an explanation of the basic concepts and institutions in connection with the federal setup of Austria. The German terminology is preferable since it denotes the political and legal concept more precisely than an English translation.

7. Dachs, "The Politics of Regional Subdivisions," 244.

8. *Regionalism and Foreign Policy: How the Länder participate in Austria's European Policy* (Salzburg: Amt der Salzburger Landesregierung, 1996), 11.

9. See notes 16, 19, and 300 for a description of these interregional and transregional organizations.

10. For an in-depth analysis of the institutional framework of *Land* participation in foreign relations and on European level, refer to Stefan Mayer, *Regionale Europapolitik. Die österreichischen Bundesländer und die europäische Integration: Institutionen, Interessendurchsetzung und Diskurs bis 1998* (Vienna: Braumüller, 2002), 158-83.

11. See Pelinka, "Austria," 125-26

12. See Klaus Faupel, "Philosophie und System der gliedstaatlichen Außenpolitik," in *Die regionale Außenpolitik des Landes Salzburg*, ed. Roland Floimair (Salzburg: Amt der Salzburger Landesregierung, 1993), 27-47; Eric Philippart, "Le Comité des régions confronté à la 'paradiplomatie' des régions de l'Union Européenne," in *Le Comité des Régions de l'Union Européenne*, ed. Jacques Bourrinet (Paris: Economica, 1997), 147-80.

13. See Pelinka, "Austria," 138

14. Initially, Hungarian *franctireurs* offered resistance to Burgenland's joining of Austria and the city region of Sopron (*Ödenburg*) was integrated in the new Hungarian state after a controversial referendum.

15. Quite literally, Alois Mock and Gyula Horn, then foreign ministers of Austria and Hungary, cut through the barbwire at Klingenbach on 27 June, opening the border for a massive influx of citizens of the German Democratic Republic into Western Europe via Hungary.

16. Founded in 1978, this interregional working community comprised member regions from Austria, Italy, and (former) Yugoslavia. The number of members grew to fifteen by the mid-1990s.

17. Euregio has become a standard concept of interregional cooperation forms on communal level according to a German-Dutch prototype of the mid 1960s.

18. In this further interregional working community, twenty-four member regions along the Danube River cooperate on a rather informal basis since 1990.

19. This most comprehensive transregional European representation of interests was founded in 1985 and comprises more than 300 regions in thirty-five European countries.

20. Pelinka, "Austria," 136.

21. Ibid., 137.

22. See Hellwig Valentin, "Kärnten und die Alpen-Adria-Idee," in *Geschichte der österreichischen Bundesländer seit 1945. Kärnten*, ed. Helmut Rumpler (Vienna: Böhlau, 1998), 172-215, here 173.

23. Ibid., 178.

24. The Alps-Adria Working Community started on 20 November 1978 with members from Austria, two former Yugoslav Federal Republics, and two Italian regions.

25. See Peter Pernthaler, "Die auswärtigen Beziehungen von Ländern und Regionen als neue Dynamik der wirtschaftlichen Integration," in *Europäischer Regionalismus am Wendepunkt: Bilanz und Ausblick*, ed. Fried Esterbauer and Peter Pernthaler (Vienna: Braumüller, 1991), 129-43, here 137.

26. See Claudia Fräss-Ehrfeld, "Das Kärntner Landesbewusstsein," in *Geschichte der österreichischen Bundesländer seit 1945. Kärnten*, ed. Helmut Rumpler (Vienna: Böhlau 2000), 777-801, esp. 794-96.

27. See note 18.

28. The Interreg program can be considered the most pre-eminent EU program to mobilize regional actors. Interreg was launched in 1990 to counteract the expected changes on peripheral regions due to the final implementation of the EU's Single Market. For the first time, a system of "double partnership" in the conceptualization and implementation of the program was achieved. Besides the vertical dealing from Community institutions via national authorities down to regional and local bodies, cooperation of similar partners beyond borders was possible.

29. See Mayer, *Regionale Europapolitik*, 265-67.

30. German and Austrian *Länder* and Italian regions as well as Swiss cantons are dealing with traffic, environmental protection, spatial planning and agriculture, culture, public health, and family policy as well as economic issues in five commissions.

31. This conference is discussed in the section on Upper Austria located later in the article.

32. See Mayer, *Regionale Europapolitik*, 293.

33. See Maria Ranacher, "Die Außenpolitik der Steiermark—rechtliche Bestandsaufnahme und Bewertung," Master's thesis, Graz, 1996, 64.

34. Karl Gruber and Alcide de Gaspari were Foreign Secretaries of Austria and Italy respectively.

35. See Michael Gehler, "Selbstbestimmung, geistig-kulturelle Landeseinheit, Europaregion? Die Tiroler Südtirolpolitik 1945-1998," in *Geschichte der österreichischen Bundesländer seit 1945. Tirol*, ed. Michael Gehler (Vienna: Böhlau, 1999), 569-728, here 571.

36. Ibid., 696.

37. Pelinka, "Austria," 134.

38. The Accordino was signed in 1949 and also includes Vorarlberg and the Italian region of Trentino.

39. See note 42.

40. See Mayer, *Regionale Europapolitik*, 298-99. Nevertheless, the Constitutional Court in Rome ruled in 1997 that the opening of the liaison office was an offence against the foreign representation monopoly of the Italian Republic.

41. See Gerhard Kagerer, *Die Inn-Salzach-Euregio. Voraussetzungen und Möglichkeiten einer Form der grenzüberschreitenden Zusammenarbeit zwischen Bayern und Österreich* (Regensburg: Roderer, 1997), 76.

42. As the only Austrian *Land*, Vorarlberg has not opened a liaison office to the EU in Brussels.

43. See Gerhard Wanner, "Die landespolitischen Beziehungen zum Ausland und zu Ausländern," in *Geschichte der österreichischen Bundesländer seit 1945. Vorarlberg*, ed. Franz Mathis and Wolfgang Weber (Vienna: Böhlau, 2000), 522-48, here 522-23. The village of Mitterberg in the Kleinwalser valley can only be reached by car from Germany, making it an area with exclusive custom regulations and the German Mark as currency until Austria's accession to the European Union in 1995 and the introduction of the euro in 2002 gradually rendered them obsolete.

44. Ibid., 544.

45. Johannes Müller, "Die auswärtigen Beziehungen des Landes Vorarlberg im Wandel," in *Das Länderbeteiligungsverfahren an der europäischen Integration*, ed. Peter Pernthaler (Vienna: Braumüller, 1992), 103-15, here 105.

46. Founded in 1972 as a reaction to the worsening water quality of Lake Constance, the conference was reorganized in 1979 and brings together regions from Germany, Switzerland, and Liechtenstein as well as Vorarlberg on the Austrian side. Tasks have widened towards conserving the Lake Constance region as an attractive area of living, nature, culture, and economy.

47. See Karl Weber, "Der Föderalismus," in *EU Mitglied Österreich. Gegenwart und Perspektiven. Eine Zwischenbilanz*, ed. Emmerich Tálos and Gerda Falkner (Vienna: Manz, 1996), 67-82, here 59.

48. See Mayer, *Regionale Europapolitik*, 313.

ESDP and Austria: Security Policy between Engagement and Neutrality

Gunther Hauser

Introduction

When the European Union Treaty entered into force on 1 November 1993, the creation of a Common Foreign and Security Policy (CFSP) became one of the main objectives of all member states of the European Union (EU), including the so-called neutral and non-aligned states of Austria, Finland, Ireland, and Sweden. In CFSP, security policy is a part of foreign policy, not separate from it. Upon achieving CFSP, Europe should finally be able to speak with one voice. Achieving this goal shall also include the creation of a common defense policy, if the European Council so decides. The concept of a European Security and Defense Policy (ESDP) was launched during the Austrian EU presidency in the second half of 1998. French President Jacques Chirac and British Prime Minister Tony Blair decided in Saint Malo (3-4 December 1998) to strengthen the European defense pillar. In Saint Malo, both political leaders accepted the French position that the "union must have the capability for autonomous action" on defense matters, whereas the United Kingdom was keen to stress the organic link between the European Union and the North Atlantic Treaty Organization (NATO).[1] Before, at the informal European Council meeting in the Austrian town of Pörtschach, 24-25 October 1998, the United Kingdom for the first time publicly referred to its altered position on European defense cooperation. Prime Minister Tony Blair stated that Europe's policies relating to Bosnia-Herzegovina and Kosovo were "unacceptable" and marked by "weakness and confusion."[2] In the spring of 1999, the NATO air attacks against the Federal Republic of Yugoslavia to stop "ethnic cleansings" in Kosovo made it clear that Europe depends on U.S. military capabilities. Pörtschach, therefore, symbolized the first explicit step by EU member states toward establishing a European crisis management capability backed by a more effective military infrastructure.[3] At the Cologne and Helsinki European Council Summits in 1999, heads of state decided that the European Rapid Reaction Forces (EU RRF)—about 60,000 troops—should have the capacity to undertake autonomous actions until 2003 so the European Union "can take decisions and approve military action where the Alliance as a whole is not engaged."[4] Therefore, the EU RRF should strengthen the European NATO pillar. To fulfill the whole spectrum of Petersberg tasks—from peacekeeping to peace enforcement actions—the European Union will need advanced military capabilities to close capability gaps between the United States and the European allies. The primary task for the European Union is now to increase and coordinate capabilities both for its own security and for the stabilization of the European area. Austria as a member of the European Union should strengthen the EU's chances of reaching this goal. By declaring permanent neutrality, Austria is not able to participate fully in deepening and effecting EU security and defense. This article intends to show the main steps and challenges of Austria's role in developing CFSP and ESDP processes by analyzing the paths of Austrian politics towards a comprehensive European security system.

The Concept of Neutrality and Cooperative Security

Neutrality is a concept for avoiding involvement in wars with other states. Non-involvement in war-fighting was interpreted differently by neutral states and other states that were interested in becoming neutral themselves. The permanently neutral state must credibly arrange its peacetime foreign policy in order to avoid involvement in future conflicts. On 18 October 1907, the essential rights and duties of neutral states in wartime were codified for the first time in the Fifth and Thirteenth Hague Conventions. A neutral power is obliged to prevent by force any attempts to violate its neutrality. Further obligations are non-participation in war and military coalitions, impartiality toward belligerents, and agreement not to provide mercenaries for belligerents. Neutral states' foreign policy has to be arranged in such a way as to minimize the possibility of becoming entangled in any war. In order to avoid becoming a security risk to its neighbors, a neutral state must provide for an adequate internal defense. Neutrality can only be declared voluntarily, not by force.

This concept was qualified and restricted in 1945 after creating the United Nations (UN) to maintain international peace and security, and to that end to take effective collective measures for the prevention and removal of threats to the peace, and for the suppression of acts of aggression or other breaches of the peace; and to bring about by peaceful means, and in conformity with the principles of justice and international law, adjustment or settlement of international disputes or situations which might lead to a breach of the peace (*Charter of the United Nations*, Chapter I, Article 1). Therefore, "all members shall give the United Nations every assistance in any action it takes in accordance with the present Charter, and shall refrain from giving assistance to any state against which the United Nations is taking preventive or enforcement action." This Article 2(5) of the UN Charter forbids impartiality when peace and security are endangered. The system of classical war parties of the Hague conventions was replaced by a system of collective security that shall guarantee peace and stability.

During the Cold War, the UN system was not able to prevent wars, as the United States and the Soviet Union fought for global influence. At the beginning of the Cold War, many European states decided to become neutral—as did Austria, Finland, and Sweden—due to their geopolitical situation between East and West. The neutral status of Austria—declared by the Austrian Parliament through the Federal Constitutional Law on Austria's neutrality on 26 October 1955—was a condition for the withdrawal of post-war Soviet and allied occupation forces. This Constitutional Law assumed that Austrian neutrality would be modelled on that of Switzerland. But quite soon, Austria's neutrality differed from that of Switzerland; as early as December 1955, Austria joined the United Nations. Ireland proclaimed its military neutrality while struggling for independence from Great Britain. All of these neutral countries became members of the United Nations. The opinion in these states was that UN membership would cause no damage to their neutrality. For Austria, Finland, Ireland, and Sweden, neutrality also included an active, positive foreign policy in pursuit of international peace and justice, in order to make contributions to peace and stability. As Austrian President Heinz Fischer explained during a presidential election campaign, "only neutrality combined with international solidarity, only that kind of neutrality policy Austria is focusing on, can be the fundament for a new peace policy today the world needs particularly urgent."[5]

In 1995, Austria joined the NATO Partnership for Peace (PfP) together with Ireland, Finland, and Sweden; in 1996 Switzerland—since 10 September 2002 a UN member—decided as a "neutral" country to join this comprehensive security coordination system. The PfP goals focus on command and control, the development of interoperability with NATO, host nation support, and enhancement of capabilities of units made available for NATO-led PfP operations while also responding to the risks arising from the proliferation of weapons of mass destruction. In 1996, Austria and Sweden were founding members of the UN Multinational Standby High Readiness Brigade for United Nations Operations (SHIRBRIG), which was also founded by NATO members

Canada, Denmark, the Netherlands, Norway, and Poland. SHIRBRIG counts fourteen member states including *non-aligned* Finland, *neutral* Ireland, and the NATO members Italy, Lithuania, Romania, Slovenia, and Spain. Austria took the SHIRBRIG presidency in 2004, coordinating UN operations. Austria's contingent to SHIRBRIG consists of a transportation company.

Neutrality is best defined in contrast to military alliances, which involve an obligation for collective defense. In 1991, the Warsaw Pact vanished, and NATO partly rewrote its doctrine. During the 1990s, European *neutrals* started to commit to the growing system of security and politico-military cooperation within the European Union and to supporting the tasks of NATO's Partnership for Peace, including humanitarian and rescue tasks, peacekeeping tasks, and tasks of combat forces in crisis management, including peace enforcement. On 12 March 1999, three former parts of Warsaw Pact system—the Czech Republic, Hungary, and Poland—became members of NATO. On 29 March 2004, seven former communist countries—Bulgaria, Romania, Slovakia, the former Soviet republics of Estonia, Latvia, Lithuania, and the former Yugoslav republic of Slovenia—joined NATO.

Since the fall of the Iron Curtain and Austria's accession to the European Union on 1 January 1995 and to the NATO-Partnership for Peace on 10 February 1995, the Austrian security and political situation has changed significantly and today is directly linked with developments in the European Union and NATO. Austrian chancellor Wolfgang Schüssel therefore declared, "classical all-round neutrality must give way to common solidarity within the European family"[6] and called for mutual assistance under the umbrella of EU membership. During a visit to Austria on 8 February 2001, Russian president Vladimir Putin reiterated the lasting international importance of Austrian neutrality, despite the fact that opposing blocs no longer existed. Putin said Austrian neutrality was "a question that the Austrian people themselves must decide."[7] Russia has always been regarding Austrian neutrality as a stabilizing factor in Central Europe.

On 12 December 2001, the National Council (First House of the Austrian Parliament) adopted the new Security and Defense Doctrine. Drafted by an expert commission appointed in May 2000, it replaces the Austrian National Defense Plan that, in part, dates back to 1975 and that was adopted on 22 November 1983. The 1983 Defense Plan became obsolete in the light of both the new security situation in Europe after the fall of Berlin Wall in 1989, and of Austria's EU membership starting on 1 January 1995. Austria joined the European Union without a reservation regarding its neutrality. EU membership was accepted by a majority of the people who supported permanent neutrality due to a government promise that EU membership was compatible with Austrian neutrality. A special provision (Article 23f) was added to the Austrian Federal Constitution to ensure that participation in the CFSP would not be restricted by the 1955 Neutrality Act, although providing the possibility in 1998 to participate in combat missions in the context of crisis management outside the European Union including peacemaking missions—within the framework of Petersberg tasks that became part of the EU Treaty in 1999. The Austrian Security and Defense Doctrine was adopted and supported by the political parties forming Austria's government at this time, the *Österreichische Volkspartei* (ÖVP, Austrian People's Party) and the *Freiheitliche Partei* (Freedom Party). The new doctrine was rejected by the opposition parties, the *Sozialdemokratische Partei Österreichs* (SPÖ, Social Democrats) and the Green Party.

The new doctrine is based on a comprehensive security concept. In it, the principle of international solidarity is embraced instead of the concept of an autonomous neutral security policy:

> The concept of permanent neutrality in Europe has been eroded not only due to the end of the Cold War but mainly due to increasing political and economic dependencies, to new forms of political cooperation and integration and strengthened supranational EU structures. Instead of a policy of "deliberate non-commitment," the new situation requires a policy of solidarity.[8]

Austria's security is indivisibly bound up with the security of the European Union. The current threats to Austria's security cannot be countered by any single country, but only through international cooperation within an international (reliable) security partnership. The analysis section of the document states that, since Austria's unconditional participation in the EU Common Foreign and Security Policy (CFSP), its status of permanent neutrality under international law has changed fundamentally. Therefore, Austria's status no longer corresponds to that of a neutral state, but to that of an alliance-free state. The doctrine advocates Austrian solidarity and active participation in the European Security and Defense Policy (ESDP), the aim of which is currently to equip the European Union with the necessary capacities for civilian and military crisis management. As the Austrian government under chancellor Wolfgang Schüssel emphasized, Austria supports all future endeavors to realize the possibility of a collective European mutual defense.

Austria also assessed the value of NATO membership. The option of joining NATO was kept open by the ÖVP until October 2004,[9] but it never seemed to be a realistic possibility. In 1998, the two governmental parties, the ÖVP and the SPÖ, clashed on the issue of NATO when it came time to elaborate a new doctrine on security policy—the Option Report. This option was rejected by the SPÖ. In the SPÖ's view, there was no need for Austria to enter into a collective security and defense organization with the United States, for Austria would lose its sovereignty and neutrality if it did so. Neutrality is, in the SPÖ's view, an anchor of stability. In 2004, the majority of the Austrian population (about 70 percent) also preferred to maintain neutrality, although opinion polls indicate that more than 70 percent of the Austrians approve the creation of a European army. For a time, politicians of all political parties could imagine reasons for Austria to join NATO. However, the SPÖ and the Greens opposed—with few exceptions—NATO accession due to the huge influence of the United States within the alliance. From the early 1990s until 2004, some politicians of the conservative ÖVP and the nationalist *Freiheitliche Partei Österreichs* (FPÖ) envisioned Austria joining NATO, but refused to talk about it in public. At the moment, NATO is no real option for Austria. This option can only be used if there is the necessary two-thirds majority in Parliament for the passing of a constitutional act. If one third of the Parliament so decides, a referendum on the future of neutrality could be held. Austria, as a member of the NATO PfP, uses the NATO Planning and Review Process (PARP) and the Political-Military Framework (PMF) for NATO-led PfP operations as a planning mechanism for contributions to the ESDP Headline Goal within the framework of the "tailored cooperation program." The NATO CMX 01 crisis management exercise in February 2001, with participation by the PfP countries, including Austria, provided an opportunity to test the functioning of the PMF in a simulated peace support operation. Another exercise, the Cooperative Best Effort 2001, was held in Styria on 10-21 September, hitherto the largest PfP manoeuvre to have been held in Austria. Some 1,500 personnel from twenty countries, with the use of sixteen helicopters and more than 400 land vehicles, trained core aspects of peace supporting operations like the set up and operation of checkpoints. Although NATO accession is not really an option for Austria, Austrian security policy is directly linked to the NATO PfP and—as member state—to the European Union.

Defining European Security and Defense Policy

With the entry into force of the Treaty on the European Union on 1 November 1993, the CFSP became an essential part of the EU Treaty as an intergovernmental pillar in Title V (Articles 11 to 28 of the EU Treaty). Article 11 sets out its five main principles of CFSP:

> The Union shall define and implement a common foreign and security policy covering all areas of foreign and security policy, the objectives of which shall be:
>
> - to safeguard the common values, fundamental interests, independence and integrity of the Union in conformity with the principles of the United Nations Charter;
> - to strengthen the security of the Union in all ways;
> - to preserve peace and strengthen international security, in accordance with the principles of the United Nations Charter, as well as the principles of the Helsinki Final Act and the objectives of the Paris Char-ter, including those on external borders;
> - to promote international cooperation;
> - to develop and consolidate democracy and the rule of law, and respect for human rights and fundamental freedoms.

These principles were extended by the European Convention in the European Constitution (Article III-292) as follows: to safeguard security; to prevent conflicts; to foster the sustainable economic, social, and environmental development of developing countries, with the primary aim of eradicating poverty; to encourage the integration of all countries into the world economy, including through the progressive abolition of restrictions on international trade; to develop international measures to preserve and to improve the quality of the environment and the sustainable management of global natural resources in order to ensure sustainable development; to assist populations, countries, and regions confronting man-made or natural disasters; and to promote an international system based on stronger multilateral cooperation and good global governance. These objectives emphasize the European security model of comprehensive multilateral cooperation. This is evidenced by Paragraph 2 of Article 11 in the EU Treaty which states that "the Member States shall work together to enhance and develop their mutual political solidarity. They shall refrain from any action which is contrary to the interests of the Union or likely to impair its effectiveness as a cohesive force in international relations."

The CFSP is also mentioned in Article 2 of the common provisions of the EU Treaty, which stipulates that one of the Union's objectives is "to assert its identity on the international scene, in particular through the implementation of a common foreign and security policy including the progressive framing of a common defense policy, which might lead to a common defense [. . .]."

Title V constitutes a separate pillar of the European Union, since the way it operates and its intergovernmental nature distinguish it from the traditional pillars of the Community, such as the single market and trade policy. This difference is most striking in the decision-making procedures, which require member state consensus, whereas in traditional Community areas, a majority vote suffices. Article 301 of the EC Treaty combines the first and second pillar by allowing the Council to apply economic sanctions on behalf of the Union.

NATO obligations of EU member states are not in contradiction with engagement in EU security and defense issues:

> The policy of the Union [. . .] shall not prejudice the specific character of the security and defense policy of certain Member States and shall respect the obligations of certain Member States, which see their common defense realized in the North Atlantic Treaty Organization (NATO), under the North Atlantic Treaty and be compatible with the common security and defense policy established within that framework.

Furthermore, "The progressive framing of a common defense policy will be supported, as Member States consider appropriate, by cooperation between them in the field of armaments" according to Article 17 (1) of the EU Treaty. Within the CFSP, it is possible to adopt measures by a qualified majority vote, with the dual safeguards of "constructive abstention" in Article 23 (1)[10] and the possibility of referring a decision to the European Council if a member state resorts to a veto. This is known as the "emergency brake."

The Military Integration of the Western European Union into the European Union

Specifically, Article 17 (1) of the Treaty of Amsterdam stated that the CFSP covers "all questions relating to the security of the Union, including the progressive framing of a common defense policy, [. . .] which might lead to a common defense, should the European Council so decide." In this article, the Western European Union (WEU) was "an integral part of the development of the Union providing the Union with access to an operational capability [. . .]" for Petersberg crisis management operations. Article 17 (1) introduced a "possibility of integration" for the WEU to join the EU, "should the European Council so decide." In Article 17 (3), the European Union "will avail itself of the WEU to elaborate and implement decisions and actions of the Union which have defense implications." In case of Petersberg tasks, Article 17 (3) states that

> [. . .] all Member States of the Union shall be entitled to participate fully in the tasks in question. The Council, in agreement with the institutions of the WEU, shall adopt the necessary practical arran-

gements to allow all Member States contributing to the tasks in question to participate fully and on an equal footing in planning and decision-taking in the WEU.

With the Amsterdam Treaty, all of the Petersberg tasks have been incorporated into new structures of the Union, as have subsidiary bodies of the Western European Union such as the Satellite Center in Torrejón, Spain, and the Institute for Security Studies in Paris, which have been operational within the European Union since January 2002.

The role of the WEU has not developed further since the majority of its powers have been transferred to other international institutions, notably NATO and the European Union. The WEU's main responsibility relates to Article V (taken together with Article IV) of the modified Brussels Treaty, collective defense with all military assets,[11] and its transfer to the European Union seems to have been postponed. In fact, Article V embodies the only binding European mutual defense commitment. Nevertheless, the Western European Union played an important role in implementing the initial Petersberg tasks, such as the sending of police to Mostar, Bosnia-Herzegovina, and cooperation with the police in Albania. The Cologne Summit Declaration of 4 June 1999 confirmed that the European Union will eventually take over the crisis management and conflict prevention function of the WEU to strengthen the European Defense and Security Identity (ESDI). The Helsinki Summit of December 1999 launched the European Security and Defense Policy and proposed the later creation of an EU Rapid Reaction Force. In the Marseilles Declaration of 13 November 2000, the WEU Ministerial Council decided to formally disband all of its organizational structures and hand them over to the European Union as of 30 June 2001. Therefore, a decision was endorsed by the European Union at the Nice Council.[12]

Austria still has observer status in the WEU, and also participates in arms cooperation. Since November 2000, Austria has been a full member of the Western European Armaments Group (WEAG).

Towards a European Security and Defense Policy

The Franco-British meeting in Saint Malo, and subsequently the Cologne European Council summit (3-4 June 1999), gave the political impetus to and set out the guidelines required for the strengthening of the European Security and Defense Policy. In Cologne, European governments declared that "the Union must have the capability for autonomous action, backed up by credible military forces, the means to decide to use them, and a readiness to do so, in order to respond to international crisis without prejudice to actions by NATO."[13] EU leaders saw the need to strengthen European capabilities in the fields of intelligence, strategic transport, and command and control, which implies efforts to adapt, exercise, and bring together national and multinational European forces. The capacities and structure of the ESDP, which have developed significantly since 1999, are divided into three components. The first two, military crisis management and civilian crisis management, are known as the Petersberg tasks. Conflict prevention, dealing with pre-conflict preventive diplomacy,[14] is the third component of the main aims of EU external policy. The Petersberg tasks have been incorporated into Title V of the Treaty of Amsterdam. This was a crucial step forward at a time when there had been a resurgence of local conflicts posing a real threat to European security, even though the risk of large-scale conflicts had fallen significantly compared to that of the Cold War period. The Petersberg tasks represent a very fitting response by the Union, enshrined in Article 17 (2) of the EU Treaty and embodying the member states' shared determination to safeguard security through operations such as humanitarian and rescue tasks; peacekeeping tasks;[15] tasks of combat forces in crisis management, including peacemaking;[16] and peace enforcement.[17]

The incorporation of the Petersberg tasks in the Treaty of Amsterdam was based on a Swedish and Finnish initiative put forth by the so-called non-aligned countries. Peacekeeping forces should be deployed to regions where crises may escalate into conflicts, but before acute crises arise. Therefore, the European Union will be able to define its leadership role by preventing conflicts and will be empowered to use all instruments, "from conflict prevention measures of various kinds to armed peacekeeping actions,"[18] to do so. In 1997, Italy obtained a UN Security Council mandate[19] and implemented a stabilization program, Operation Alba, though this was supported by a joint force of some 7,000 soldiers drawn from Austria, Denmark, France, Greece, Italy, Romania, Spain, and Turkey. This was the first crisis management conducted in Europe by a multinational military force comprised of units from exclusively European countries. In June 1999, the Cologne European Council placed crisis management at the core of the process of strengthening the CFSP. This action led to priority being given to conflict prevention two years later at the Gothenburg Summit. Conflict prevention does not only mean preventing the initial outbreak of violence, but also its escalation and later recurrence.[20] Major efforts were underway to assess and improve the EU's capability to act, as evidenced, for example, by the joint report on conflict prevention presented to the Nice European Council in December 2000 by the Secretary-General (who is also the High Representative) and Commission, and the endorsement at the Gothenburg European Council in June 2001.

This report outlined the EU program for the prevention of violent conflicts. Yet, conflict management also deals with how to respond to a crisis that has crossed the threshold into armed conflict, to prevent it from escalating and to bring it to a conclusion.[21]

NATO intervened in Kosovo in 1999, launching air-strikes against Yugoslavia. On 12 June 1999, NATO deployed the 40,000-strong Kosovo Force (KFOR). In June 2003, the North Atlantic Council confirmed that NATO would maintain an adequate level of forces to ensure a safe and secure environment in Kosovo. Austria has been deploying troops to Kosovo since fall 1999; in 2004, these troops numbered 600 soldiers.

On the basis of the declaration at the NATO summit held in Washington in April 1999, the Union should be able to conduct operations with recourse to NATO resources and capabilities. To implement this category of operations, specific arrangements were agreed upon with the Alliance. At the Helsinki European Council meeting of 10-11 December 1999, the heads of state and government confirmed that they intended to give the European Union autonomous capacity[22] to make decisions and made clear their intention, where NATO as a whole was not engaged, to launch and conduct EU-led military operations in response to international crises worldwide.

Military Component

The military component was introduced by the Helsinki (10-11 December 1999) and Nice (7-9 December 2000) European Councils. First, Helsinki established the *headline goal* for the EU Rapid Reaction Force to be deployable within sixty days and to sustain for at least one year, up to fifteen brigades (or 50,000 to 60,000 persons). However, the member states should also be able to deploy smaller rapid response elements with very high readiness. These forces must be self-sustaining, with the necessary command, control, and intelligence capabilities; logistics; other combat support services; and, additionally as appropriate, air and naval elements. A provision taking effect in 2004 requires a 5,000-strong military force to be kept in a state of permanent readiness for humanitarian operations and for actions to rescue populations under immediate threat. The EU RRF does not intend to establish a European army. The commitment and deployment of national troops are based on sovereign decisions taken by member states.

Since 20 November 2000 when member states took part in a Capabilities Commitment Conference (CCC) and one year later participated in a Capabilities Improvement Conference (CIC), the member states committed themselves, in the framework of their national reforms, to continue to strengthen their capabilities to implement multinational solutions, including better ways to pool resources. The CCC confirmed the creation of the EU RRF to deploy peacekeeping and enforcement operations by 2003. At the Laeken Summit of December 2001, EU member states launched the European Capabilities Action Plan (ECAP) in order to close the shortfalls in military capabilities; this plan was based on the Helsinki Headline Goal Catalogue (HHG) which is regularly adapted to new security challenges.

This development was accompanied by new military structures introduced in Nice, the most important being the Political and Security Committee (PSC). Replacing the Political Committee, the PSC keeps track of international developments, helps define foreign policies, and monitors implementation of agreed upon policies. It exercises, under the responsibility of the Council, political control and strategic direction of all EU-led crisis management operations. The PSC is authorized by the European Council to take appropriate actions exercising political control and strategic direction of crisis management operations carried out in the context of ESDP. Composed principally of national representatives with the rank of Ambassador, it is the linchpin of crisis management activities that has a central role in the definition and follow-up of EU response to a crisis. Relating to Article III-307 of the EU Constitution:

> [. . .], a Political and Security Committee shall monitor the international situation in the areas covered by the common foreign and security policy and contribute to the definition of policies by delivering opinions to the Council at the request of the latter, or of the Union Minister for Foreign Affairs, or on its own initiative. It shall also monitor the implementation of agreed policies, without prejudice to the powers of the Union Minister for Foreign Affairs.

The PSC shall exercise, under the responsibility of the Council and of the Union Minister for Foreign Affairs, political control and strategic direction of crisis management operations, further clarification of which is found in Article III-309 (ex 17). Compared to Article 25 of the EU Treaty, in the last sentence, "the Presidency" and "the Commission" have been replaced by "the Union Minister of Foreign Affairs."

The PSC is assisted by a politico-military working group, a committee for civilian aspects of crisis management, as well as the European Union Military Committee (EUMC) and the European Union Military Staff (EUMS). The EUMC provides military advice to the PSC and the High Representative and exercises military command over all military activities. On 22 January 2001, the EUMC, a body of military representatives comprised of member states' Chiefs of Defense, was established as a Council group to give military advice to the PSC and to direct the work of the EUMS. The EUMC is the forum for military consultation and cooperation between EU member states in the field of conflict prevention and crisis management. It is not legally subordinate to the PSC, but advises it on the Concept of [Military] Operations (CONOPS) developed by the Operation Commander and the associated Operation Plan (OPLAN). It is the Operation Commander, especially appointed for a new crisis management operation, who supervises the actual military planning. The planning for the actual military operations will be a decision of the Committee of Contributors, an ad hoc group to be formed from countries contributing military units to an EU force. The EUMS, which is part of the Secretariat of the Council, is responsible for early warning, strategic planning, and situation assessment. It supplies military expertise. The EUMS consists of 132 military and sixteen civil experts from EU member states. The task of EUMS is to provide early warning, situation assessment, and strategic planning for crisis management operations, including the identification of national and multinational European forces, and to implement policies and decisions as directed by the EUMC. The EUMS works under the military direction of the EUMC, but it is a "Council Secretariat Department directly attached to the SG/HR."[23] The structure of the military staff includes five divisions: Policy and Plans, Intelligence, Operations and Exercises, Logistics and Resources, and Communications and Information Systems.

The member states of the European Union have also established common capability goals in command and control, reconnaissance, and strategic transport. For those member states which are also members of NATO, their military capabilities must allow them to play their full role in NATO operations, as well.

At the EU Foreign Ministers meeting at Kastelorizo, Greece, in early May 2003, ministers ordered *Mr. CFSP*, Javier Solana, to work on a statement of purpose for the EU security doctrine to be presented at the Porto Carras/Thessaloniki, Greece summit on 19 June 2003. The EU's first global security strategy brought its security concerns broadly in line with those of United States. As in the U.S. security strategy, European Union force could only be used as a *last resort*, in contrast to U.S. strategy, EU enforcement actions should be authorized by the UN Security Council. The Union intends to strengthen the role of multilateral organizations ("effective multilateralism with the UN at its core")[24] and the role of international law. Effective multilateralism is a key aspect of EU foreign policy. As former NATO General Secretary Lord Robertson emphasized, the security strategies of the United States and Europe remain compatible and reinforcing. NATO is putting these strategies into practice by taking on new missions in Afghanistan and the Mediterranean, by developing new capabilities, and by transforming its military structure.[25] The EU's strategy paper, "A Secure Europe in a Better World"—prepared by EU High Representative for Common Foreign and Security Policy (CFSP) Javier Solana and adopted during the European Council on 12 December 2003—identifies terrorism, the proliferation of weapons of mass destruction, failed states, and organized crime as key threats for EU security. As part of the implementation of the European Security Strategy, the Council also adopted an EU Strategy against the Proliferation of Weapons of Mass Destruction (WMD) to prevent the proliferation of WMD and their means of delivery by promoting the universalization and reinforcement of multilateral agreements, by reinforcing export controls, and by enhancing physical protection of nuclear materials and facilities.

In the aftermath of the Madrid terror attacks of 11 March 2004 in which 191 people died and about 1,500 were injured by attacks on city trains, the European Council adopted the declaration on terrorism guiding anti-terrorism activities and created the office of a European anti-terrorism coordinator. On 25 March 2004, Mr. Gijs de Vries from the Netherlands was appointed counter-terrorism coordinator to improve coordination and visibility of the EU's actions in this field. The United States is leading the global fight against terrorism. Key issues of counter-terrorism are improved cooperation between intelligence and security services and between these services and the police, timely implementation of existing instruments, and implementation of improvements based on the results of member state evaluations in the field of terrorism and the fight against chemical, biological, radiological, and nuclear (CBRN) terrorism. The fight against international terrorism has become an important task of the ESDP since 11 September 2001.

The EU Council agreed on 12 December 2003 to move forward work on the establishment of a civilian/military cell within EU Military Staff (EUMS) and further agreed that the cell should begin its work by the end of 2004 at the latest. At NATO Supreme Headquarters Allied Powers Europe (SHAPE), a small EU cell was established—heading also the NATO liaison arrangements with the EUMS. The European Council agreed to move forward work on establishing an operations center—available by 1 January 2006 at the latest. There will not be a standing headquarters; the main option for autonomous military operations remains national headquarters.

Civilian Component

The civilian component, developed at the Feira European Council (June 2000) and Gothenburg European Council (June 2001) with extensive contributions by the Commission, aimed to improve actions in a field where the international community has shown itself to be lacking. In order to provide added value, the European Union intended to establish, before 2003, four main instruments that are mutually dependent:

- police cooperation which would provide up to 5,000 policemen, including 1,000 within thirty days, for tasks ranging from restoring order in cooperation with a military force to the training of local police (candidate countries and NATO members Iceland and Norway participate in this cooperation by providing police capacities);
- strengthening the rule of law by providing up to 200 judges, prosecutors, and other experts in the field;
- civilian administration which would provide a team to establish or guarantee elections, taxation, education, water provision, and perform similar functions; and
- civil protection which would assist humanitarian efforts in emergency and other operations and would require the European Union be capable, within three to seven hours, of providing two to three assessment teams consisting of ten experts as well as intervention teams consisting of 2,000 people.

Therefore, the Feira European Council resolved to set up the Civilian Crisis Management Committee (CIVCOM), which was formally established by a Council decision on 22 May 2000 and met for the first time on 16 June 2000. CIVCOM provides expert advice on civilian crisis management. It reports formally to the Committee of Permanent Representatives (COREPER),[26] but receives guidance from and provides information to the PSC. Since then, conferences on the improvement of civil capabilities have been organized and a plan of action adopted for police capabilities. On 10 May 2001, "Mr. CFSP," Solana, confirmed that a unit for police operations would be established in the External Action Division of the External Relations Directory General of the Council Secretariat. In June 2001, the Gothenburg Council approved more specific requirements for the planning and execution of police operations. These included a planned police ministers' summit for resolution of strategic planning issues, for development of draft status of forces agreements to provide legal cover for deployment, for development of command and control procedures, for enhancement of interoperability, and for financing arrangements.

On 19 November 2002, the conference on civilian crisis management capabilities noted that voluntary commitments by the member states had outstripped the specific goals set for 2003 by the European Council for priority areas (police, rule of law, civil protection, and civil administration). With the goal of promoting peace and stability, the four main objectives are:

- to make more systematic and co-ordinated use of the Community's instruments,
- to identify and combat causes of conflict,
- to improve the capacity to react to nascent conflicts, and
- to promote international cooperation in this area.[27]

A rapid reaction mechanism, developed by the Commission, was created in February 2001. Used to provide rapid financing for crisis management, the mechanism may be implemented where there is a threat to public order or public safety, or in other similar circumstances that might destabilize a country. This aid is provided in the short term, takes the form of grants, and encompasses all of the activities not covered by the European Commission Humanitarian Aid Office (ECHO). In this way, the European Union was able to launch the political, economic, and social rebuilding of Afghanistan. Moreover, the Union does not intend, in most cases, to use its crisis response assets independently, choosing instead to recognize the lead role of the United Nations in orchestrating the international community's response to security crises in which the European Union is most likely to be a player.

The European Union Monitoring Mission (EUMM) was established by the European Community Monitor Mission (ECMM) in 1991 to report on political, economic, and humanitarian developments in the former Yugoslavia (including Bosnia-Herzegovina, Croatia, and the Former Yugoslav Republic of Macedonia[28]) and Albania. The mission, led by an ambassador from a member state and appointed by the Council, has over 100 monitors who work in the Balkan countries and who are organized into mobile teams for easy deployment. The EUMM's purpose is to give special attention to border monitoring, inter-ethnic issues, and refugee return. Norway and Slovakia, two non-EU member countries at this time,[29] also participate in the EUMM. The headquarters of EUMM are based in Sarajevo. On 25 April 2001, the European Union agreed with the Yugoslav government on the opening of mission offices in Belgrade and elsewhere for the deployment of a team of monitors from EUMM. Monitors are unarmed and have full diplomatic status. In 1999, the ECMM worked with the Kosovo Verification Mission of the Organization of Security and Cooperation in Europe (OSCE).

The operational capability that the European Union acquires under the ESDP may prove to be an important element in conflict prevention and crisis management operations conducted by the United Nations. The establishment of the European Union Police Mission (EUPM) in Bosnia-

Herzegovina provided an opportunity for practical cooperation with the United Nations to effect the transition between the two operations. The EUPM followed the UN International Police Task Force (IPTF) which had been in place since December 1995. In accordance with the objectives of the Paris-Dayton Agreement of 1995, EUPM monitors, in cooperation with Bosnian police units, combat organized crime and corruption and prosecute terrorists. Thus 530 police officers from thirty-tree countries—about 80 percent from EU member states and 20 percent from third states—perform monitoring, mentoring, and inspection activities. The EU Council decided on 11 March 2002 to take over this mission from the UN; subsequently, the UN's Peace Implementation Council Steering Board agreed that the European Union take over this mission, which is evidenced in UN Security Council Resolution 1396. The EUPM should last three years (until 31 December 2005); the costs will be about € 38 million, with € 20 million being financed by the European Community budget. Launched on 1 January 2003, EUPM represents the EU's first-ever civilian crisis management operation under the ESDP.

Austria's security interests are mainly focused on stabilizing neighboring southeast Europe. Therefore, Austria supports joining international security operations in the Balkans and shares these goals with Greece, as pronounced at the meeting of Austrian Minister of Defense Günther Platter with Greek colleague Spilios Spiliotopoulos in Athens on 20 August 2004.

EU Relations and Cooperation with NATO

NATO formed a strategic partnership with the European Union so that both could bring their combined assets to bear in enhancing peace and stability. From 26 September 2001 to 31 March 2003, this partnership has successfully demonstrated its capabilities in the former Yugoslav Republic of Macedonia (FYROM).[30] The European Union and NATO combined to prevent civil war, and in Kosovo, their intervention helped to defuse conflict. Both the European Union and NATO created forums for enhanced comprehensive cooperation with Russia, the Ukraine, and within the Mediterranean Dialogue.

The ESDP cannot be defined without making reference to NATO. Since 1 May 2004, nineteen European Union member states are members of NATO and are bound by a collective defense clause by virtue of Article 5 of the Washington Treaty. Those states, with the exception of Denmark, are also members of the WEU and have, therefore, entered into a similar, if not wider, commitment under Article 5 of the Brussels Treaty. Six EU member states (Austria, Cyprus, Finland, Ireland, Malta, and Sweden) define their security policies as neutral or non-aligned. Austria, Finland, Ireland, and Sweden cooperate with NATO under the PfP Program and take part in the Euro-Atlantic Partnership Council (EAPC). They also have observer status in the WEU.

Denmark enjoys special arrangements in the EU framework by virtue of a Protocol annexed to the EU Treaty. Pursuant to that Protocol, Denmark does not participate in the elaboration and the implementation of decisions and actions of the Union which have defense implications and does not prevent the development of closer cooperation between member states in this area.

Article 17.1 of the EU Treaty makes explicit reference to the obligations arising from the North Atlantic Treaty for those member states which are members of NATO:

> The policy of the Union in accordance with this Article shall not prejudice the specific character of the security and defense policy of certain Member States and shall respect the obligations of certain Member States, which see their common defense realized in the North Atlantic Treaty Organization (NATO), under the North Atlantic Treaty and be compatible with the common security and policy established within that framework.

That means that under no circumstances, nor in any crisis, will the ESDP be used against any ally and that NATO military crisis management will not undertake any action against the European Union or its member states.[31] At the EU Council Nice summit (7-9 December 2000), it was agreed to create permanent consultations with European non-EU members in security, defense, and crisis management issues. The principle should be fifteen plus six, that is, fifteen EU member states and the six concerned NATO members and associated WEU members: Iceland, Norway, Turkey, the Czech Republic, Hungary, and Poland. Therefore, a Committee of Contributors should be created to play a key role in preparing EU operations.

Relating to the EU RRF, arguments between Greece and Turkey over the use of NATO assets and possible deployments in the Aegean Sea and Cyprus threatened the existence of the EU Rapid Reaction Force. At the European Council of Brussels (24-25 October 2002), Greece gave up its resistance. The "Berlin plus" agreement,[32] which would guarantee access to NATO capabilities for the European Union, was concluded by the signing of the EU-NATO agreements on 14 March 2003. Arrangements were adopted at the Brussels European Council of 24-25 October 2002 for the involvement of non-EU European allies in EU-led operations when using NATO assets and capabilities.

On 23 September 2002, four European headquarters were designated as NATO international rapidly deployable headquarters at NATO's European strategic command, Supreme Headquarters Allied Power Europe (SHAPE), in Mons, Belgium. These rapidly deployable command elements can be quickly dispatched to lead troops sent to a crisis area. Each corps-size headquarters can command up to 60,000 troops. The four land-based headquarters are the Rapid Deployable German/Netherlands Corps in Münster, Germany; the Rapid Deployable Italian Corps in Milan, Italy; the Rapid Deployable Spanish Corps in Valencia, Spain; and the Rapid Deployable Turkish Corps in Istanbul, Turkey. More than one billion euro had already been invested by European NATO members in creating such capabilities. The Allied Rapid Reaction Corps (ARRC)[33] was the first deployable headquarters, based in Rheindahlen, Germany, since 1992. Including the ARRC, there are five deployable headquarters. The sixth command was formed with the Eurocorps in Strasbourg consisting of Belgian, French, German, Luxembourg, and Spanish units. The Eurocorps has signed a technical agreement with NATO; therefore, it also can be under NATO command.

At the NATO Summit in Prague on 21-22 November 2002, the transformation of NATO was concluded to respond to new threats. A NATO Response Force (NRF) comprised of 21,000 troops, exhibiting high readiness, and planned to be deployable within five days has been partially operational since 13 October 2004 and will reach full operability by October 2006.[34] The NRF consists of a technologically advanced, flexible, deployable, interoperable, and sustainable force, including land, sea, and air elements ready to move quickly to wherever needed, and it will be complementary to the EU RRF.

While the EU RRF is a low-tech, small peacekeeping force which would only be capable of handling low-level peacekeeping operations in a crisis with no prospect of escalation, the NRF will be able to deal with crises where the possibility of escalation is great. The NRF is, therefore, more of a deterrent force. With a three-pronged approach to improving alliance defense capabilities—a new capabilities initiative (the Prague Capabilities Commitment[35]), the creation of the NRF, and a streamlining of its military command structure—NATO should be equipped to respond to the full spectrum of modern military missions. Recognizing that the traditional, more static forces of the Cold War are no longer valid, NATO is creating forces that are able to be moved faster and further afield, to apply military force more effectively, and to sustain themselves in combat. Moreover, the Prague Capabilities Commitment and the European Union's efforts to develop military capabilities are intended to be mutually reinforcing. All this should help to close the capabilities gap that has opened between the United States and its allies.

The EU member states decided to reinforce military capabilities by developing the Union's new military capabilities objective, the "Headline Goal 2010,"[36] to set new requirements for rapid deployment, sustainability, and interoperability by developing criteria and standards for measuring improvements in this field. On 17 May 2004, during the Irish EU presidency, EU defense ministers also approved proposals by "Mr. CFSP" Javier Solana concerning the concept for rapidly deployable battlegroups. From 2007 onwards, these forces—thirteen military units each comprising 1,500 troops—should be available for deployment to crisis areas outside Europe. The battlegroups are planned to be deployed to crisis theaters as far as 6,000 kilometers away from Brussels. The Initial Operational Capability of these forces is planned to be reached in 2005. Strong contingents would be deployable within ten days and able to stay on the ground for a few months in response to a UN request. At the informal meeting of EU defense ministers in Noordwijk, the Netherlands, on 17 September 2004, the member states agreed to establish EU battlegroups and to harmonize EU battlegroups and the NRF. EU defense ministers also agreed to consider the possi-bility of third countries participating in EU battlegroups. Austria sup-ports this concept, although the Austrian governmental members to the European Convention proposed to establish by the end of 2003 "a permanently available, immediately deployable special unit equipped with the highly modern equipment" comprising 3,000 to 5,000 troops and recruted from special forces.[37] Austria will create a battlegroup together with Germany (950 soldiers) and the Czech Republic (350 soldiers). 200 soldiers from the Austrian army (*Bundesheer*) are planned to take part.

In Noordwijk, the ministers of defense of France, Italy, Spain, Portugal, and the Netherlands signed a Declaration of Intent concerning the establishment of a European Gendarmerie Force (EGF). The EGF will be a police force with military status, deployable within one month, and suited to deployment during or immediately after a military operation for maintaining public order and safety and in situations where local police forces are not (sufficiently) deployable. It will also be possible for the rapidly-deployable EGF to conduct operations in support of the fight against organized crime and the protection of participants in civil missions. The EGF is a multinational unit that is not only allocated to the European Union, but also to the UN, the OSCE, and NATO. The initiative for establishing EGF was taken in 2003 by the French minister of defense, Michèle Alliot-Marie. The force headquarters in Vicenza, Italy, is planned to be established in 2005; the EGF itself will become operational at the end of 2005.[38] By 2007, the EGF should consist of 3,000 troops.

The Globalization of EU and NATO Missions

EU-NATO arrangements initiated on 16 December 2002[39] permitted the EU[40] to take over NATO's Task Force Fox/Allied Harmony[41] mission in Macedonia—the first EU military operation (31 March-15 December 2003). This was the first concrete implementation of the Berlin Plus arrangements in support of EUFOR's Concordia, a small peacekeeping operation mounted using NATO assets and with NATO's Deputy Supreme Allied Commander in command. This operation was requested by Macedonia and backed by UN Security Council Resolution 1371. EUFOR Concordia was composed of 350 troops from thirteen EU countries and fourteen non-EU states. At first, EUFOR had a six-month mandate to oversee the political reforms stated in the Ohrid Peace Agreement and to monitor the security situation. It was also responsible for the protection of international monitors from the European Union and the OSCE. The operational commander was Admiral Reiner Feist (Germany) while the EUFOR commander was Brigadier-General Pierre Maral. Finally, Concordia was succeeded by a police operation, EUPOL, also run by EU Proxima (as the 200-strong EUPOL is called), and it was launched on 15 December 2003 on the basis of a Joint Action adopted by the General Affairs and External Relations Council held on 29 September 2003. It followed an invitation from Macedonian Prime Minister Branko Crvenkovski to the European Union through SG/HR Javier Solana. This operation helps Macedonian authorities develop their police forces to European and international standards and also focus on supporting the government's efforts to fight organized crime. The total cost of the mission amounts to € 15 million for the first year, including start up costs of € 7.5 million, all funded through the EU budget.

The first EU police operation started on 1 January 2003 in Bosnia-Herzegovina; the European Union took over this mission from the United Nations' policing operation. The EU-NATO arrangements allow the organizations to work closely together to manage crises in Europe and beyond. The development of this partnership is important for the further stabilization of the Balkans. The first NATO-EU joint crisis management operation started in 2003 when the European Union took over NATO's Allied Harmony operation in Macedonia. In 2003, the European Union also expressed its intention to take on the SFOR command in Bosnia-Herzegovina. NATO has been running this peacekeeping operation in the country since 1995 in accordance with the UN Security Council Resolution 1031. As decided at the NATO Istanbul

Summit at the end of June 2004, NATO handed over command of the former SFOR mission to the European Union on 2 December 2004, the first major EU-led military crisis management operation called EUFOR Althea. EUFOR is commanded by a British Army two-star general and stays under the oversight of NATO's Deputy SACEUR in the *Terms of Reference for Strategic EU Command*, as defined in the Berlin Plus Agreement. NATO continues to maintain a presence through a Military Liaison and Advisory Mission (NATO HQ Sarajevo) and assists with specific competencies such as defense reform and preparations for the country's potential future membership in the NATO PfP program.

On 25 June 2004, Austria started to deploy 135 troops to Bosnia-Herzegovina to be followed by 100 more in December 2004. Since 1996, Austria was engaged in IFOR/SFOR missions in the framework of the NATO Partnership for Peace. From 1995 to 2001, Austria has participated as PfP partner in IFOR and SFOR missions. In March 2001, Austrian troops were redeployed in order to fulfill the criteria to participate in the EU RRF with 2,000 soldiers. On 28 February 2003, the government Wolfgang Schüssel II has reduced the number of participating troops to 1,500. During the last six months on SFOR, Austrian soldiers participated as a multinational specialized unit (MSU) together with Slovenian troops by Italian command to support restoring the rule of law on the basis of UN Security Council Resolution 1491 (11 July 2003). UN Security Council Resolution 1551 still identifies the situation in Bosnia-Herzegovina as a threat to peace and stability in the region.

On 12 June 2003, the Council adopted a decision on the launching of the EU military operation (Operation Artemis) in the Democratic Republic of Congo. This decision followed the Council's 5 June 2003 adoption of a joint action on this operation in accordance with the provisions of Article 14 of the EU Treaty. France acted as the framework nation for the operation. Major General Bruno Neveux was appointed EU operation commander; force commander was Brigadier-General Jean-Paul Thonier. The operational headquarters were located in Paris and included staff members from the General Secretariat of the EU Council, as well as officers from several participating member states. Under the authority of the Council, the Political and Security Committee (PSC) exercised the political control and strategic direction of the operation. A total of 1,800 troops, most of them French, were sent to the north-eastern Congolese region of Ituri to stop fighting and atrocities, to contribute to the stabilization of security conditions and of the humanitarian situation in and around the city of Bunia, to ensure the protection of the airport and the internally displaced persons in the camps in Bunia, and, if required, to contribute to the safety of the civilian population, UN personnel, and the humanitarian presence in the town. Artemis was an

EU-led military operation which was conducted in accordance with the mandate set out in United Nations Security Council Resolution 1484 of 30 May 2003. This resolution authorized the deployment of an Interim Emergency Multinational Force in Bunia in close coordination with the United Nations Organization Mission in the Democratic Republic of Congo (MONUC) until 1 September 2003. Now MONUC is provided with a wider mandate, more robust rules of enga-gement, and an 18,000-strong multinational force.

On 11 August 2003 and at the request of Germany, the Netherlands, and Canada, NATO took the leading role in the International Security Assistance Force (ISAF) in Kabul, Afghanistan,[42] under its existing UN mandate, by assuming strategic coordination, command, and control (C3). This was NATO's first direct involvement in peace or support missions beyond Europe, although individual NATO member countries—originally the United Kingdom and Turkey—had provided the backbone of the ISAF since it was established. Before NATO took over the ISAF III and following missions, Germany and the Netherlands shared lead nation responsibilities and commanded a multinational force of approximately 4,600 troops drawn from twenty-nine nations. In 2002, Austria provided about 75 personnel in support of ISAF; two years later, ten staff officers were deployed to Kabul. The goal of NATO's mission was to continue to assist the Afghan Transitional Authority (ATA) headed by Hamid Karzai in maintaining security in Kabul and the surrounding area so that the authority and United Nations personnel can carry out their work in a secure environment.

On 9 August 2004, Europe's five-nation military force, Eurocorps, took command of the ISAF VI—the NATO-run peacekeeping force—for six months. French General Jean-Luis Py, assisted by German General Wolf-Dieter Loeser, commanded Eurocorps to help safeguard the presidential elections on 9 October 2004, the first since the radical Islamic Taliban regime was forced from power. Eurocorps is made up of detachments from Belgium, France, Germany, Luxembourg, and Spain. This multinational 60,000-man force was created in 1992 by France and Germany (*La Rochelle Report*) and later put at the service of the European Union and has been certified since 2002 by NATO as a rapid deployable corps. Starting in 2002, those NATO and/or EU member states that so desired could also contribute to the Eurocorps staff at Strasbourg headquarters. Therefore, officers from Austria, Canada, Finland, Greece, Poland, and Turkey have been integrated into the Eurocorps staff. Italy, the Netherlands, and the United Kingdom have liaison officers with the headquarters, but they are not integrated into its structure. The Afghanistan operation was its first outside Europe. Eurocorps troops took part in the NATO-led Stabilization Force (SFOR) in Bosnia-Herzegovina between 1998 and 2000. The Eurocorps mission in Afghanistan remained under the political and military authority of NATO in Kabul. ISAF comprises 7,000 troops from thirty countries and was set up by the United Nations in December 2001 weeks after U.S.-led forces ousted the Taliban.

The Crisis over Iraq

The crisis and war in Iraq in 2002/2003 caused rifts within the European Union and NATO member states in relation to crucial foreign policy matters that had serious consequences for the CFSP. Deep divisions among EU governments over the war against Iraq were apparent, ranging from Britain's firm support of the U.S. line to firmly anti-war France and Germany. In the view of the U.S. and British governments, the Saddam regime became a threat to world security planning to produce weapons of mass destruction. The U.S. administration regarded the Iraqi Baath regime as a threat in the aftermath of 9/11. Eight European leaders called on France and Germany to stand united with America in the battle to disarm Iraq, while warning the United Nations that its credibility was on the line.[43] On 30 January 2003, the leaders of Britain, the Czech Republic, Denmark, Hungary, Italy, Poland, Portugal, Spain, and, one day later, Lithuania combined to make an unprecedented plea for unity and cohesion. This joint appeal was suggested by former Spanish Prime Minister José María Aznar.[44] U.S. Defense Secretary Donald Rumsfeld denounced France and Germany as "old Europe," for he thought that the center of gravity was shifting to Eastern Europe (new Europe) whose states supported U.S. policy towards Saddam Hussein.

The European Union officially had no union-wide position dealing with war on Iraq, and member states were split. Austria declared itself neutral, because the UN Security Council had not mandated the U.S.-led war against the Saddam Hussein regime. The Presidency's Statement on Iraq, given in Athens on 16 April 2003, implored the United Nations to "play a central role including in the process leading towards self-government for the Iraqi people, utilizing its unique capacity and experience in post-conflict nation building." The United States had a different standpoint, believing the United States and United Kingdom should play a central role. A compromise was found in UN Security Council Resolution 1483:[45] UN agencies would coordinate humanitarian and reconstruction assistance with the support of non-governmental organizations. The United Nations recognized the specific authorities, responsibilities, and obligations under applicable international law of the United States and the United Kingdom as occupying powers under unified command. UN Security Council Resolution 1511 calls for enhanced cooperation within the international community to restore peace and stability to a sovereign, democratic and independent Iraq as soon as possible.

During the EU-U.S. Summit, which took place in Dromoland Castle, County Clare, Ireland, on 25-26 June 2004, President Bush declared an end to differences between the United States and Europe over the Iraq war and secured an EU promise to assist the incoming Iraqi government. The Dromoland Castle Summit pledged a common commitment to Iraq's future and a continued and expensive engagement of the UN in Iraq after the transfer of sovereignty, including support for "the training and equipping of professional Iraqi security forces"[46] as requested by the interim Iraqi prime minister Ilyad Allawi in a letter to NATO Secretary General Jaap de Hoop Scheffer from 22 June 2004. The Alliance, in accordance with UN Security Council Resolution 1546, responded positively to this request. On 30 July 2004, two days after the United States handed over sovereignty to the interim Iraqi government, the North Atlantic Council (NAC) reached agreement on the establishment of a NATO Training Implementation Mission (NTIM) in Iraq. NTIM was a distinct mission under the political control of the NAC, led by Major General Carel Hilderink of the Netherlands and initially comprised approximately fifty officers and non-commissioned officers from several NATO nations. NTIM tasks included working closely with the Iraqi authorities to support them develop their organizational infrastructure, in particular in the Ministry of Defense and Military Headquarters. For this purpose, the NTIM started training personnel for selected Iraqi headquarters and training Iraqi security personnel. These decisions reflected NATO's commitment to implement as quickly as possible the decisions taken in Istanbul on 28 June 2004 which was the first NATO summit after the 2003 rift over Iraq. Through the NTIM, NATO started to contribute substantially to the goal shared by the entire international community: to help Iraq provide for its own peace and security in order to arrive at the day when international forces are no longer required in Iraq.

The Changes of the CFSP in the European Constitution

The Creation of an EU Minister of Foreign Affairs

At the end of 2002, Working Group VII on external action recommended that greater coherence of EU action and clarity in EU representation could be found by creating a position that combines the functions of the High Representative, who acts as the Union's external face in the framework of CFSP and ESDP, and those of the Commissioner for External Relations. Draft articles on external action in the Constitutional Treaty of 23 April 2003[47] had already foreseen the need to create the position of Minister of Foreign Affairs, appointed by the European Council with the agreement of the president of the Commission. This new minister should exercise tasks previously assigned to the High Representative, the Presidency, and the Commission. The Minister of Foreign Affairs will have the right of proposal for CFSP matters (former first pillar issues) and an explicit role in the formulation and implementation of policy decisions. According to Article I-40 (4), the CFSP will "be put into effect by the Union Minister for Foreign Affairs and by the Member Sates, using national and Union resources." The CFSP will be implemented by the Union's Minister for Foreign Affairs. The Minister may be granted a mandate by the Council of Ministers and the European Council to act on behalf of the Union on the international scene. He will defend the Union's positions and conduct a dialogue with third countries and international organizations. The right of initiative is shared by the Minister for Foreign Affairs—alone or together with the Commission—and the member states. Article I-40 (2) defines the role of the European Council in this field as being to "identify the Union's strategic interests and determine the objectives of its common foreign and security policy. The Council shall frame this policy within the framework of the strategic guidelines established by the European Council [. . .]." This text partly reproduces Article 13 (2) of the EU Treaty on common strategies, with the change in name relating to decisions on strategic interests and objectives. Article III-305 underscores that "Member States shall coordinate their action in international organisations and at international conferences. They shall uphold the Union's positions in such fora. The Union Minister for Foreign Affairs shall organize this coordination."

The ESDP As Integral Part of the CFSP

The Constitution clearly states in Article I-41 (1) that the ESDP is an integral part of the CFSP, "It shall provide the Union with an operational capacity drawing on civil and military assets. The Union may use them on missions outside the Union for peace-keeping, conflict prevention and strengthening international security in accordance with the principles of the United Nations Charter." For that purpose, the Petersberg missions have been updated, and the provisions for crisis management provide for a more coherent use of civilian and military instruments.

Article I-41 (2) states that

> the common security and defense policy shall include the progressive framing of a common Union defense policy. This will lead to a common defense, when the European Council, acting un-

animously, so decides. It shall in that case recommend to the Member States the adoption of such a decision in accordance with their respective constitutional requirements.

As stated in Article 17 of EU Treaty, the policy of the Union does not prejudice the specific character of the security and defense policy of certain Member States and shall respect the obligations of certain Member States, which see their common defense realized in the North Atlantic Treaty Organization (NATO), under the North Atlantic Treaty, and be compatible with the common security and defense policy established within that framework.

Extending Petersberg Tasks

The European Convention decided in its draft constitution in Article III-309 to adapt the Petersberg tasks to the new challenges and threats in security policy. The tasks in the performance of which the Union may use civilian and military means include joint disarmament operations,[48] humanitarian and rescue tasks, military advice and assistance tasks,[49] conflict prevention and peace-keeping tasks, and tasks of combat forces in crisis management, including peacemaking and post-conflict stabilization. All these tasks contribute to the fight against terrorism, including actions to support third countries in combating terrorism in their territories. The European Convention Working Group VIII on Defense recommended this new definition of Petersberg tasks.

Improvement of Capabilities

The EU Constitution states:

Member States shall undertake progressively to improve their military capabilities. An Agency in the field of defense capabilities development, research, acquisition and armaments (European Defense Agency) shall be established to identify operational requirements, to promote measures to satisfy those requirements, to contribute to identifying and, where appropriate, implementing any measure needed to strengthen the industrial and technological base of the defense sector, to participate in defining a European capabilities and armaments policy, and to assist the Council in evaluating the improvement of military capabilities (Art. I-41 (3) in accordance with Art. III-311). Those Member States which together establish multinational forces may also make those forces available to the CFSP (Art. I-41 (3)). This agency shall be open to all Member States wishing to be part of it. Military and civilian capabilities should be made

> available to the CFSP. These are the multinational military units which have already been created by Member States, and which have headquarters or general staff. This is the case with Eurocorps (land forces: Belgium, France, Germany, Luxembourg, Spain); Eurofor (land forces: France, Italy, Portugal, Spain); Euromarfor (maritime forces: France, Italy, Portugal, Spain); European Air Group (Belgium, France, Germany, Italy, Spain, United Kingdom); Multinational Division (Centre) (Belgium, Germany, Netherlands, United Kingdom); and the General Staff of the German-Netherlands First Corps (Germany, Netherlands and the United Kingdom). There are also other multinational forces established between Member States, but which do not have joint headquarters—for example the British-Netherlands Landing Force and the Spanish-Italian Amphibious Force) and multinational military units (like the Scandinavian NORDCAPS, with the participation of three Member States—Denmark, Finland and Sweden—and also of Norway).

The European Defense Agency (EDA) was established on 12 July 2004; it evaluates, for example, the pledged military contributions of the EU member states. The EDA also promotes further multinational cooperation and prevents the fragmentation of European defense efforts. The steering board of the EDA met for the first time on 17 September 2004 in Noordwijk, the Netherlands, under the chairmanship of the High Representative of the EU, Javier Solana.

Austria is not playing a decisive role in the field of armaments either as a market or as a producer, but in the view of Austrian Convention members, "it can only benefit from any form of closer cooperation in the armaments sector."[50] In November 2000, Austria became member of the Western European Armaments Group (WEAG), but cooperation within WEAG has "declined in importance."[51] Mainly EU states cooperate within the framework of OCCAR (France, Great Britain, Germany, Italy) and in the "Letter of Intent (LoI) Group" (France, Great Britain, Germany, Italy, Spain, and Sweden). There is no interest by LoI countries in including EU states that have less clout in terms of their armaments industry. Therefore, Austria proposed that the LoI Group "be open to EU States that are willing and able to cooperate" and propo-sed to develop LoI into a European Armaments Agency[52] so that "effective cooperation with the armaments industry in the EU area would lead to standardisation of the equipment of the EU armed forces and to reductions in the cost of the acquisition of armaments."[53]

"Mutual Assistance" and "Structured" Cooperation

In their contribution to the European Convention, Austrian governmental members supported in conformity with the Austrian Security and Defense Doctrine (Resolution of 12 December 2001) future efforts to realize the possibility of a common defense including a mutual security guarantee in the Treaty on European Union.[54] Both members were convinced in November 2002 that "from today's perspective, it appears likely that fundamental aspects of a comprehensive common defense will also in the foreseeable future remain within the framework of NATO. It would therefore be advisable to work towards a harmonization of EU and NATO membership in the long term."[55] When British Prime Minister Tony Blair began to support the introduction of mutual assistance in the EU Constitution in October 2003 after negotiating an agreement with U.S. President Bush for this path, Austria changed its opinion and proposed, together with the neutral and non-aligned states Finland, Ireland, and Sweden, to introduce a limited mutual assistance. Therefore in the Union framework, limited mutual assistance is given in case of armed aggression:

> If a Member State is the victim of armed aggression on its territory, the other Member States shall have towards it an obligation of aid and assistance by all the means in their power, in accordance with Article 51 of the United Nations Charter. This shall not prejudice the specific character of the security and defense policy of certain Member States" (Art. I-41 (7))

The second part of this sentence continued to be effective due to the role of Austria, Finland, Ireland, and Sweden to be neutral or non-aligned states. Austria proposed in 2000 to introduce a mutual assistance defense clause into the EU Treaty; this proposal was rejected by all EU states—during a time when fourteen EU member states supported political sanc-tions against the Austrian government.

The reason for the sanctions was the participation of the nationalist *Freiheitliche Partei Österreichs* (FPÖ) in the coalition government with the conservative *Österreichische Volkspartei* (ÖVP). The sanctions started on 4 February 2000 and ended on 12 September 2000. Only France could entertain the idea of introducing a mutual assistance clause in the EU Treaty during this time. After British political leadership started to support the idea of introducing mutual assistance in the EU Constitution in October 2003 together with France and Germany, the Italian EU presidency submitted a proposal for mutual military assistance to be included in the EU Constitution during the EU summit in Naples on 28 November 2003—along with the idea of replacing the WEU Treaty's policy of robust mutual military commitment. Suddenly, the Austrian government began to oppose this project by emphasizing Austria's neutral status. Former Foreign Minister Benita Ferrero-Waldner underscored the necessity of coordination with the governments of the other neutral and non-aligned countries: Finland, Ireland, and Sweden. The compromise of the EU Summit on 12 December 2003 was to agree to mutual assistance, but with consideration given to "the specific character of the security and defense policy of certain Member States." That's why Austrian Chancellor Wolfgang Schüssel, former Foreign Minister Benita Ferrero-Waldner, and Minister of Defense Günther Platter emphasized compatibility of neutral status and mutual military commitment. As Austrian President Heinz Fischer declared, EU security policy has to take into account the specific constitutional characters of Austria, Finland, Sweden, and Ireland.[56] In Article I-41 (7), military means are no longer explicitly mentioned as an element of that aid and assistance. Minister of Defense Platter leads Austria in its desire to be involved "in the assistance clause in the framework of legal possibilities."[57] There is again uncertainty about the manner in which the security of the six EU member states which are not NATO members—Austria, Cyprus, Finland, Ireland, Malta, and Sweden—is to be guaranteed, since the "Constitutional Treaty is silent on the way in which the European Union should take military responsibility for the defense of its members."[58] A robust mutual assistance commitment as originally proposed by the Austrian government did not become reality.

In 2005, ten of the EU's member states were members of the WEU and were, therefore, bound by a robust mutual defense commitment under Article 5 of the Brussels Treaty. That is undoubtedly a form of cooperation outside the framework of the Union; hence there is a need to introduce closer cooperation enabling those wishing to do so to *repeat* the commitment already entered into under Article 5 of the Brussels Treaty in the Union framework. Member states who wish to engage in closer cooperation with others could take up in the Union framework the mutual assistance commitment made by Article 5 of the Brussels Treaty.

Relating to Article I-41 (6), "those Member States whose military capabilities fulfil higher criteria and which have made more binding commitments to one another in this area with a view to the most demanding missions shall establish permanent structured cooperation within the Union framework. Such cooperation shall be governed by Article III-312." The concerned states should notify their intention to the Council and to the Union Minister for Foreign Affairs. The Council acts by a qualified majority after consulting the Union Minister for Foreign Affairs (Article III-312 (3)), but only members of the Council representing the participating member states take part in the vote. This qualified majority is defined as at least 55 percent of the members of the

Council representing the participating member states, comprising at least 65 percent of the population of these states. A blocking minority must include at least the minimum number of Council members representing more than 35 percent of the population of the participating member states, plus one member, failing which the qualified majority shall be deemed attained (Article III-312 (4)). Participating member states could also make use of Union structures such as the PSC and the Military Committee. However, operations undertaken by that group of member states would not be Union operations.

The New "Solidarity Clause"

A "solidarity clause" will enable member states to mobilize all the necessary military and civilian instruments within the Union to prevent terrorist threats. Article III-294 (2) reads, "The Member States shall support the common foreign and security policy actively and unreservedly in a spirit of loyalty and mutual solidarity." Furthermore, "they shall refrain from any action which is contrary to the interests of the Union or likely to impair its effectiveness as a cohesive force in international relations." This formulation exists also in Article 11 (2) of the EU Treaty. Article I-40 (1) reads, "The European Union shall conduct a common foreign and security policy, based on the development of mutual political solidarity among Member States [. . .]." The requirement to consult and cooperate is stronger than in the EU Treaty, which reads as follows in Article 16, "Member States shall inform and consult one another within the Council on any matter of foreign and security policy of general interest in order to ensure that the Union's influence is exerted as effectively as possible by means of concerted and convergent action." Article I-43 (1), in accordance with Article III-329 of the Constitution, contains the "solidarity clause" which reads:

> The Union and its Member States shall act jointly in a spirit of solidarity if a Member State is the object of a terrorist attack or the victim of a natural or man-made disaster. The Union shall mobilise all the instruments at its disposal, including the military resources made available by the Member States, to:
>
> - prevent the terrorist threat in the territory of the Member States;
> - protect democratic institutions and the civilian population from any terrorist attack;
> - assist a Member State in its territory at the request of its political authorities in the event of a terrorist attack;
> - assist a Member State in its territory, at the request of its political authorities, in the event of a natural or man-made disaster.

Articles I-43 and III-329 follow directly from the EU Convention Working Group VIII on Defense Issues' recommendations for the inclusion of a solidarity clause in the Constitution. As regards assistance to a member state following a terrorist attack, states need to take action immediately after the event. Accordingly, the second paragraph provides that assistance should be triggered automatically at the request of the member state in question. The affected member state will need to specify its requirements, and the other states, meeting in Council, will coordinate the action and resources needed to remedy the situation.

The Austrian government agreed to invoke this security clause. In its contribution to the European Convention, the Austrian proposal reads:

> In the event of a future terrorist attack against an EU State which does not result in the application of Art. 5 of the NATO Treaty, Art. 17 para. 2 could nevertheless also allow military action by the EU against the origin of the terrorist attack and against eventual further threats. Such action would not fall under the "common defense" clause Art. 17 para. 1 which requires an appropriate decision by the European Council.[59]

The Austrian delegation clarified the meaning of the solidarity clause and attempted to "formalize a mutual military assistance guarantee in the event of a serious terrorist attack."[60]

Conclusions

The European Union and NATO coordinate action in comprehensive security issues, from policies towards enlargement to crisis management operations. NATO and the EU also share common interests in assisting the countries of the Balkans with their future integration into Euro-Atlantic political structures. Austria also has pivotal interests in integrating Central, Eastern, and South Eastern European states into Euro-Atlantic policy, economic, and security structures. Both the European Union and NATO have developed a framework for an enhanced dialogue on and a concerted approach to security and stability in the Balkans. In June 2003, the Greek EU presidency launched at the Porto Carras/Thessaloniki Summit a new political forum creating a Balkans European Integration Process that should increase the visibility of the Stabilization and Association Process (SAP) with five Western Balkan countries: Albania, Bosnia-Herzegovina, Croatia, the Former Yugoslav Republic of Macedonia, and Serbia-Montenegro. The first steps were initiated in November 2000 at the EU Zagreb Western Balkan summit promoting regional political and security cooperation and free trade. On

22 May 2003, five Western Balkan countries subscribed in Ohrid to a Common Platform for improving border security in the region to combat organized crime, which was creating ideal conditions for drug smuggling, gun-running, human trafficking, terrorism, and political violence. The Platform was developed by the European Union, NATO, the OSCE, and the Stability Pact. In June 2004, Croatia has already been granted candidate status at the European Council in Brussels. This development "should be an encouragement to the countries of the Western Balkans to pursue their reforms. It reaffirms its commitment to the full implementation of the Thessaloniki agenda, which makes clear that the future of the Western Balkans rests within the European Union."[61]

The European Union and NATO also share common interests in integrating Russia, the Ukraine, Central Asia and the Mediterranean countries in North Africa and in the Middle East into a Euro-Atlantic stabilization process exporting stability in these regions. In this context, both the European Union and NATO are mutually reinforcing. In spring 2004, the European Union established the European Neighborhood Policy (ENP) with neighbor countries both east and south, including the Caucasian states of Armenia, Azerbaijan, and Georgia. The former Austrian Foreign Minister Benita Ferrero-Waldner was nominated EU Commissioner for external relations including ENP issues. Since 22 November 2004, Ferrero-Waldner oversees strengthening cooperation with European neighbors on the basis of partnership building on values of democracy and respect of human rights. The ENP should accelerate democratic reform process in these countries.[62]

Relating to this EU-NATO security cooperation, neutrality as an EU member is not the way to strengthen comprehensive trans-Atlantic and common EU security initiatives. Nevertheless, all neutral states in the world have pledged to support the goals and resolutions of the United Nations, up to and including military actions. Austria's goal is to increase its participation in peace-keeping operations in the framework of NATO, EU, and UN missions. Therefore, coordinated force planning in the EU and trans-Atlantic contexts are based on the Headline Goal Catalogue 2010, the EU Framework Nation Concept, and the criteria of force planning within the NATO Partnership for Peace. International crisis management now contains the following scenarios: Conflict Prevention (CP), Separation of Parties by Force (SOPF), and Steady State (SS). The European Union defined the length of CP and SOPF scenarios as lasting eight to twelve months.

Austria intends to improve its rapid reaction capability to meet national needs and to support international crisis management and humanitarian operations. Therefore, the defense budget was planned to be increased from 0.78 percent of GDP in 2003 (about € 1.7 million,

U.S. $1.5 million) to 1 percent of GDP in the future. In 2003, only six EU member states spent more than 2 percent of GDP: Great Britain, France, Portugal, Greece, Sweden, and Finland. The percentage of the remaining EU states was around or over 1 percent. Austrian Convention members agreed "that those EU Member States whose percentage is below the EU average will progressively raise their percentage to the EU average of 1.8 percent within a period yet to be determined."[63] In this context, Austria plans to be able to provide a brigade-sized force for EU-led operations by 2005. Austria continues to provide personnel in support of other forces, including observers and specialists to UN, OSCE, and EU missions, for "[s]olidarity is the key to security."[64]

Presently, Austria concentrates on the elements that are mainly covered by the formula "Petersberg plus PfP." In 2004, about 1,200 troops were active in twelve peacekeeping operations, mostly in southeast Europe (about 800) and on the Golan Heights between Israel and Syria (370). Since 1960, about 60,000 Austrian troops participated in sixty international peacekeeping operations. Since 1995, Austria has been a host nation for multinational troops crossing the country for peace support operations in southeast Europe. Austria was crossed by approximately 160,000 international troops in about 70,000 transports and more than 200,000 international military aircraft. About 50,000 international troops were hosted in Austrian camps.[65] These facts demonstrate that Austria, while maintaining a form of neutrality, is not taking a free ride. The Euro-Atlantic Partnership Council (EAPC) provides the opportunity for Austria, as a non-NATO member, to take part in NATO's consultative and decision-making process. Austria takes an observer status in the WEU. Within the common European security cooperation and coordination, the *Bundesheer* must build capacity as to contribute to a common defense effort. In order to achieve these aims, interoperability of the Austrian Airforce is a key requirement. The purchase of eighteen *Eurofighter* aircraft must be seen in this context. These aircraft will represent the backbone of a future European Airforce. As Austrian EU Convention members urged, EU states should provide a progressive harmonization of their interests in foreign and security policy issues, "A true Union can only be achieved with a single foreign and security policy and a common defense."[66] The main objective for Austria is, therefore, to strengthen the coordination of EU forces for international peace operations and to enhance effective cooperation within CFSP. The *Bundesheer Reform Commission Report* from June 2004 guides the process of adapting Austrian forces to international operation standards from the territorial defense strategy as anchored in the former Austrian Defense Plan of 1983. The mobilized establishment—as proposed by the *Reform Commission*—should be lowered from approximately 110,000 to 50,000 troops, including about 3,000 ready for international peace operations. Austria's security policy continues along the lines of pragmatic neutrality by participating in EU, Petersberg, and NATO-PfP tasks.

Notes

1. Peter van Ham, "Europe's New Defense Ambitions: Implications for NATO, the U.S., and Russia," *The Marshall Center Papers* No. 1: 6.

2. Ibid., 5.

3. Ibid.

4. Washington Summit Communiqué, issued by the heads of state and government participating in the meeting of the North Atlantic Council, Paragraph 9a., Press Release NAC-S(99)64, 24 April 1999.

5. Heinz Fischer, "Neutralität bewahren," *SPÖ Steiermark*, 22 April 2004, <http://www.stmk.spoe.at/index.php/land/content/view/full/30781/> (11 Nov. 2004).

6. "Putin 'rates' Austrian Neutrality," *CNN.com./WORLD*, 8 Feb. 2001 <http://www.cnn.com/2001/WORLD/europe/02/08/moscow.austria/> (11 Nov. 2004).

7. Jolyon Naegele, "Russia: Austria's Neutral Status Resurfaces With Putin Visit," *Radio Free Europe/Radio Liberty*, n.d. <http://www.rferl.org/nca/features/2001/02/08022001111948.asp> (11 Nov. 2004).

8. Austrian Security and Defense Doctrine, Analysis, Draft Expert report as of 23 January 2001, Chapter "Neutrality versus Solidarity," 6.

9. During Alpbach Party convention on 15 October 2004, the ÖVP declared that the option of Austria's NATO accession became an obsolete. The ÖVP, therefore, proposed to anchor neutrality in Austria's new constitution.

10. "Decisions under this Title shall be taken by the Council acting unanimously. Abstentions by members present in person or represented shall not prevent the adoption of such decisions. [. . .]."

11. In contrast, Article 5 of NATO's Washington Treaty (4 April 1949) states that member states take collective defense measures only "as it deems necessary" to them.

12. Presidency Conclusions Nice European Council, Annex VI, "Presidency Report on the European Security and Defense Policy."

13. Cologne EU Presidency Conclusions, 3-4 June 1999.

14. Preventive diplomacy refers to the full range of methods described in Article 33 of the United Nations Charter—"negotiation, enquiry, mediation, conciliation, arbitration, judicial settlement, resort to regional agencies or arrangements, or other peaceful means"—when applied before a dispute has crossed the threshold into armed conflict. ("EU Crisis Response Capability. Institutions and Processes for Conflict Prevention and Management," International Crisis Group (ICG), ICG Issues Report No. 2, Brussels, 26 June 2001).

15. Peacekeeping involves the deployment of military or police, and frequently civilian personnel, to assist in the implementation of agreements reached between governments or parties who have been engaged in conflict. Peacekeeping presumes cooperation, and its methods are inherently peaceful. The use of military force, other than in self-defense, is incompatible with this concept (ICG Issues Report No. 2, 2001, p. 5).

16. Peacemaking is a close relative of preventive diplomacy, involving the same range of methods described in Article 33 of the UN Charter, but applied after a dispute has crossed the threshold into armed conflict (Ibid.). One example is the activity by the European Union in the Balkans, notably the role of Finnish President Martti Ahtisaari as an EU intermediary in the resolution of the Kosovo conflict in 1999.

17. Peace enforcement is the threat or use of military force, in pursuit of peaceful objectives, in response to conflicts or other major security crisis (Ibid.).

18. This is from "Swedish-Finnish Initiative to Strengthen Conflict Management Capability," an article by Minister for Foreign Affairs Lena Hjalm-Wallén and Tarja Halonen on a Swedish-Finnish initiative designed to strengthen the EU's conflict management capability. It was published in Finland (Helsingin Sanomat) and Sweden (Dagens Nyheter) on 21 April 1996.

19. UNSC Resolution 1101 (1997), 28 March 1997, "to establish a temporary and limited multinational protection force to facilitate the safe and prompt delivery of humanitarian assistance, and to help create a secure environment for the missions of international organizations in Albania, including those providing humanitarian assistance."

20. "EU Crisis Response Capability: Institutions and Processes for Conflict Prevention and Management," International Crisis Group (ICG), ICG Issues Report No. 2, Brussels, 26 June 2001, p. 2.

21. Ibid., 3.

22. "Autonomous" means in accordance with NATO. See Washington Summit Communiqué, issued by the heads of state and government participating in the meeting of the North Atlantic Council in Washington D.C. on 24 April 1999, paragraph 10, Press Release NAC-S(99)64.

23. SG/HR stands for Secretary General/High Representative. See Council Decision on the Establishment of the Military Staff of the European Union, 22 January 2001, Official Journal, L 027, 30/01/2001, p. 4.

24. Presidency Conclusions, Brussels European Council 17 and 18 June 2004, para. 50.

25. "Lord Robertson visits Germany," *North Atlantic Treaty Organization Home Page*, 24 June 2003 <http://www.nato.int/docu/update/2003/06-june/e0624a.htm> (11 Nov. 2004).

26. Comité des représentants permanents.

27. "The Common Foreign and Security Policy: Introduction." *The European Union Online* <http://www.europa.eu.int> (11 Nov. 2004).

28. Turkey recognizes the Republic of Macedonia with its constitutional name.

29. Slovakia together with nine candidate countries joined the European Union on 1 May 2004.

30. NATO Operation Amber Fox and the operation following it, Allied Harmony, had the specific mandate to contribute to the protection of international monitors who oversaw the implementation of the peace plan. Before 26 September 2001, Operation Essential Harvest, the thirty-day mandate to collect small arms, had ended.

31. European Council Presidency Conclusions, Brussels, 24 and 25 October 2002, Annex II, ESDP: Implementation of the Nice Provisions on the Involvement of the Non-EU European Allies, paragraph 2.

32. The "Berlin Plus" arrangements (Paragraph 10 of the 1999 NATO Washington Summit Declaration) contain four elements: assured EU access to NATO operational planning, presumption of availability of NATO capabilities and common assets to the EU, NATO European command options for EU-led operations including the European role of Deputy Supreme Allied Commander Europe (SACEUR), and adaptation of the NATO defense planning system to assess the availability of forces for EU operations.

33. The ARRC framework nation is the United Kingdom; its first operation was leading forces to Bosnia-Herzegovina (IFOR/SFOR) following the Dayton Peace Accord (Operation Joint Endeavor) in 1995/1996 and to Kosovo in 1999 (KFOR, Operation Joint Guardian). These are examples of NATO's non-Article 5 missions. The ARRC was concluded at NATO's Rome Summit in 1991 in the framework of the strategic concept. In peacetime, the ARRC consists of 5,000 troops from seventeen nations, including Belgium, Denmark, Canada, the Czech Republic, Germany, Greece, Hungary, Italy, Luxembourg, the Netherlands, Norway, Poland, Portugal, Spain, Turkey, the United Kingdom, and the United States (*North Atlantic Treaty Organization Home Page* <http://www.nato.int>).

34. U.S. Defense Secretary Donald Rumsfeld proposed the creation of a rapid-reaction NRF at the NATO Defense Ministers meeting in Warsaw on 24-25 September 2002.

35. The Prague Capabilities Commitment (PCC) differs from its predecessor, the Defense Capabilities Initiative (DCI). Individual allies have now made firm political commitments to improve capabilities in more than 400 specific areas, an initiative endorsed at the Washington Summit in 1999. These capabilities include chemical, biological, radiological, and nuclear defense; intelligence; surveillance and target acquisition; air-to-ground surveillance; command, control, and communications; combat effectiveness, including precision-guided munitions and suppression of enemy air defenses; strategic air and sea lift; air-to-air refueling; and deployable combat support and combat service support units. Once implemented, the PCC will at least quadruple the number of large transport aircraft in Europe, from four to sixteen, or possibly more. It will also significantly increase air-to-air refueling capacity by establishing a pool of ten to fifteen refuelling aircraft. Moreover, it will increase NATO's stock of non-U.S., air-delivered, precision-guided munitions by 40 percent by 2007. (*NATO after Prague: New Members, New Capabilities, New Relations*. NATO Office of Information and Press, 2002).

36. Document 6309/6/04.

37. Contribution by Messrs. Hannes Farnleitner and Reinhard E. Bösch, members of the Convention: "A New Impetus to the European Security and Defense Policy," CONV 437/02, Brussels, 28 November 2002, 4.

38. Signature of Declaration of Intent for a European Gendarmerie Force, Noordwijk, 17 September 2004, Press Release, The Dutch EU Presidency, Ministerie van Buitenlandse Zaken.

39. A joint declaration adopted by the European Union and NATO on 16 December 2002 has opened the way for closer political and military cooperation between these two organizations. The landmark Declaration on the European Security and Defense Policy provides a formal basis for cooperation between the European Union and NATO in the areas of crisis management and conflict resolution. It outlines the political principles for EU-NATO cooperation and gives the European Union assured access to NATO's planning and logistics capabilities for its own military operations. NATO and the European Union have collaborated in crisis management before, most notably in the former Yugoslav Republic of Macedonia, but the formal framework for cooperation did not previously exist. The Agreement on the Security of Information between the European Union and NATO was signed in Athens on 14 March 2003.

40. In this arrangement with NATO, the European Union agrees to ensure "the fullest possible involvement of non-EU European members of NATO within ESDP, implementing the relevant Nice arrangements, as set out in the letter from the EU High Representative on 13 December 2002. NATO is supporting ESDP in accordance with the relevant Washington Summit decisions, and is giving the EU . . . assured access to NATO's planning capabilities, as set out in the North Atlantic Council decisions on 13 December 2002." ("EU-NATO Declaration on ESDP," NATO Press Release 142, 16 Dec. 2002.) "The North Atlantic Council agreed to adopt a series of decisions with a view to maintaining a close and transparent relationship with the European Union and supporting EU-led operations in which the Alliance as a whole is not engaged militarily in accordance with the decisions taken at the Washington Summit." ("Statement by the Secretary General," NATO Press Release 140, 13 Dec. 2002.)

41. The decision to end the operation was taken by the North Atlantic Council on 17 March 2003.

42. NATO decided on 16 April 2003 to enhance its support of ISAF by taking on the command, coordination, and planning of the operation.

43. Philip Webster, "Eight Leaders Rally 'New' Europe to America's Side," *The Times* 30 January 2003.

44. Ibid.

45. Adopted by the Security Council at its 4761st meeting on 22 May 2003.

46. EU-U.S. Declaration of Support for the People of Iraq, Dromoland Castle, 26 June 2004.

47. The European Convention, Brussels, 23 April 2003, CONV 685/03, Chapter 1.A.

48. Weapons destruction and arms control programs.

49. "Defense outreach" is defined as "cooperation with the military forces of a third country or of a regional/subregional organization on developing democratically accountable armed forces, by the exchange of good practices, e.g. training measures" (Working Group VIII, Defense, paragraph 51).

50. Contribution by Messrs. Hannes Farnleitner and Reinhard E. Bösch, members of the Convention: "A new Impetus to the European Security and Defense Policy," CONV 437/02, Brussels, 28 November 2002, 10.

51. Ibid.

52. Ibid.

53. Ibid.

54. Ibid., 4.

55. Ibid.

56. Interview with *Bundespräsident* Heinz Fischer, *Wiener Zeitung*, 4 September 2004.

57. Minister Platter beim Forum Alpbach, "EU-Verteidigungspolitik mitgestalten," Speech at the European Forum of Alpbach/Tyrol, 1 September 2004. Source: Austrian Ministry of Defense.

58. Assembly of Western European Union/The Interparliamentary European Security and Defense Assembly, The European Security and Defense Policy following EU and NATO enlargement—reply to the annual report of the Council, Report submitted on behalf of the Political Committee by Mr. van Winsen, Rapporteur (Netherlands, Federated Group), Document A/1860, 4 June 2004, 17.

59. Contribution by Messrs. Hannes Farnleitner and Reinhard E. Bösch, members of the Convention: "A new Impetus to the European Security and Denfense Policy," CONV 437/02, Brussels, 28 November 2002, 3.

60. Ibid, 4.

61. Presidency Conclusions, Brussels European Council 17 and 18 June 2004, para. 39.

62. Ibid, para. 65.

63. Contribution by Messrs. Hannes Farnleitner and Reinhard E. Bösch, 2002, 6.

64. Austrian Minister of Defense Günther Platter, "EU-Verteidigungspolitik mitgestalten," Speech at the European Forum of Alpbach/Tyrol, 1 September 2004.

65. Source: Austrian Ministry of Defense.

66. Contribution by Messrs. Hannes Farnleitner and Reinhard E. Bösch, 2002, 10.

Foreign Policy in the Age of Globalization: Does Globalization Constrain Nation States' Sovereignty in Conceiving and Maintaining their Foreign Policy?

Romain Kirt

Introduction

"*Panta rhei* – everything is in a state of flux." There is no formula that captures the ongoing changes in the international system over the last two decades better than Heraclitus' concise, two and half thousand-year-old observation. If one asks about the exact cause of this universal and sweeping mutation and transformation process, the often standardized and simplistic answer provided by either political scientists or politicians is always the same: globalization. This term is surely today's most fashionable catchword.

So far, disciplines such as the humanities or social sciences have fallen short in delivering a commonly accepted definition of the phenomenon called globalization. In part, this shortcoming might be due to the widespread assumption that globalization is not only the major trigger and catalyst for those transformation processes set in motion in the 1980s, but globalization is also considered as being responsible for the emergence of a general feeling of *uncertainty* prevalent in many societies at the beginning of the twenty-first century. As a consequence, this widespread feeling of uncertainty has increased pressure on national political elites to step up efforts to develop alternative forms of governance and political leadership. Those among us observing these ongoing radical socio-political changes from the angle of a neutral, non-professional observer may come to the conclusion that globalization is a process affecting our lives in a way we cannot escape nor influence as individuals. It impacts our lives with the intensity of a natural disaster and leaves many people disoriented and without the sheltering feeling of certainty and security. Metaphorically speaking, globalization turns many people into orphans in their hearts and minds.

The British journalist Paul Kingsnorth finds that today:

> [. . .] our world is subject to rapid and far-reaching changes in the economical, social, political and technical sphere. These changes sweep away traditional political structures, familiar economic models, social safety, and differences between nation states. Nothing remains unchanged. With the dissolution of the Eastern bloc the big conflict between the two competing ideologies ceased to exist. Capitalism had finally won the Cold War. It celebrates its victory and shows its flag on every political fortress around the globe. Everything is exposed to its grip. [. . .] No more is there a place in the world where one could escape it. We [. . .] have reached the end of history. [1]

The developments gloomily described by Kingsnorth are, as I mentioned earlier, usually summarized under the label "globalization." The over-use of the "g-word" has eventually turned it into a popular everyday catchword, which cannot, of course, be missed in any respectable political debate. However, the word's ubiquity has by no means been conducive to agreeing on a precise and commonly accepted definition about its content. Or, as Paul Kingsnorth puts it, "The frequency of its use is in proportion to the uncertainty of its meaning."[2]

The majority of people still think of globalization as a phenomenon affecting first and foremost the economic realm. They believe it owes its existence to the emergence and dominance of neoliberalism, an ideology declared as the dominant economic paradigm by a group of obscure hard-core capitalists in the post-confrontative era. Now, let us bear in mind right at the start of this article: there can be no doubt that globalization is not solely an economic phenomenon. Every attempt to define globalization within these confines is doomed to remain insufficient. What is more, the simplistic definition usually provided by political scientists who reduce globalization to a qualitative and quantitative expansion of activities that transcend national boundaries does not do justice the phenomenon's multidimensionality. Political scientists hold that these activities undermine the foundations of the traditional nation state and shrink the political and regulatory room in which its political leaders must maneuver. Clearly, this approach to globalization does not live up to the phenomenon's numerous facets and dimensions, not to speak of those approaches which one-sidedly depict globalization as a purely cultural phenomenon resulting in the Americanization or in the even more coarse "McDonaldization" of the world.[3]

Overall, the academic debate about globalization, especially the one led by sociologists and political scientists, has not yet contributed to a more precise and satisfying understanding of globalization. If we put aside those broad definitions that can be found in dictionaries and encyclopaedias, we will see that there is still no such thing as a commonly accepted, clear-cut, and succinct definition of the word "globalization." This lack of a definition has obviously caused the word "globalization" to become the showpiece of a variety of different academic concepts. As such, globalization is sharing the destiny of the majority of neologisms, which is to develop into an arbitrarily usable word.

Supporters of globalization use the word to point at the inevitability of globalization (or to justify not having tried to ease or to divert its negative effects). They view globalization as a heaven-sent force that disseminated the successful model of western capitalism into the global economy after the failure of the Soviet experiment of the planned economy. They believe it even triggered an increase in global wealth. For them, globalization is a magic formula, comparable to the political maxim of former German Chancellor Ludwig Erhard who proclaimed "welfare for everyone." They firmly believe in globalization's strong problem-solving capacity in regard to economic, social, and world affairs. What is more, they also see globalization as a tried and proven method of overcoming what they consider anachronistic and old-fashioned social and political norms and local customs and traditions. Furthermore, globalization is, in their eyes, the perfect means to introduce democracy into non-democratic states, a means to establish global human rights, and a way to slowly build knowledge-based societies around the world.

Globalization's detractors who are notorious for being adversaries of globalization naturally draw our attention to its dark side.[4] Currently, their arguments are met with a more positive public response than those of globalization's optimistic supporters. When talking about globalization, those critics demonize everything it allegedly implies. To them, globalization is nothing but a nightmare. They associate the word with, among other things, the exporting of manufacturing and production sites, the dislocation of domestic jobs to low-wage economies, the exploitation of developing countries, the undermining of the welfare state, environmental degradation, cultural homogenization, and the disempowerment of the political classes. Adversaries of globalization, dismissively called "pop-economists" by Paul Krugman, and like-minded academics use the word "globalization" almost like a political *kampfbegriff*. Their gloomy warnings about the "globalization trap" and globalization's negative consequences in general do sometimes carry an even slightly fanatic overtone.[5] They use the "g-word" like a whip which they crack in order to scourge the phenomena embedded in globalization such as deregulation, liberalization, increasing flexibility, and rationalization. They dismiss the greed for profit of those who allegedly advocate unbridled "turbo-capitalism" and "the tyranny of the market," for they gradually bring about the loss of jobs, the deterioration of our welfare system to the level of that of developing states, and the disempowerment of politics. Those processes set off the era of the "end of the nation state" which follows the era of the "end of employment" and the era of the "farewell to the welfare state."

Revival of the Nation State

Parallel to the numerous prophecies circulated about the coming end of the nation state, efforts to strengthen the nation state and its socially beneficial institutions can be observed as well. Thomas Hanke und Norbert Walter write, "Since a few years, the nation state has received a fresh impetus," adding, "For many people, the nation state is now the ultimate aim again."[6] Although the causes for this revival may be very complex in detail, we can identify two major reasons for the new embracing of the nation state. These reasons are paradigmatic: the re-implementation of formerly abandoned national sovereignty rights and the strong integrative power of the nation state.

Until the end of World War II, nation states were not necessarily the sole, but clearly the most important, actors in the global economy and the international system. Our history of the past two centuries has been shaped by nation states in an unprecedented way. In Europe, however, the nation states used to bring about more pain than relief. "In recent European history nation states were the sources of growing rivalries finally leading to hostility rather than islands of peace and stability," Lothar Späth finds, "Two devastating wars have shown us at a dreadful price where the overemphasizing of national interests can take us."[7]

Against the backdrop of the extremely shattering experiences of World War II, international cooperation intensified to an unparalleled degree by the end of the 1940s and the beginning of the 1950s. Ever since, many governments have transcended the confining boundaries of the nation state by concluding agreements and contracts with like-minded governments on economic and cultural cooperation, security cooperation, common defense, and foreign policy. Although those governments are bound to respect the principle of national sovereignty, they partly transferred national sovereignty to supranational institutions, which in turn matured into important political and economic actors. Nation states lost more of their predominance as major actors in the international system with the rise of the transnational and multinational enterprises in the 1980s that increasingly widened their sphere of influence on the international stage.[8]

It is this development of the seemingly continual transfer of sovereignty laws and the resultant loss of formerly exclusive sovereignty rights that led some political forces to reconsider the nature of the nation state. Those political forces have their ideological roots in the traditional thinking of the nineteenth century, and they tend to operate within the confines of the nation state only. Even though their attempt to reverse the ongoing process of creating binding international and supranational laws may appear absurd, those forces are reclaiming national sovereignty. If the nation state could re-implement some of its already abandoned sovereignty, so the argument by proponents of the strong nation state goes, then national decision-making would be strengthened. However, the fact that nation states are integrated in a dense web of supranational structures does not by itself pose a threat to the nation state since the former created and legitimize international and supranational institutions. A real danger for a nation state is political isolation, as can be seen in the example of Switzerland. It has repeatedly suffered from political isolation in the past. It would also be a threat to the nation state if a country decided to revive obsolete, even archaic principles of statehood such as national autonomy, which in modern times has never existed in a pure form anyway.

Times marked by change and uncertainty are often stylized as times of severe crisis. It is in those times that people seek security by turning towards institutions and authorities that have repeatedly proven to be the unshakable foundations of civilization in the past and to which most people do not have a close relationship in normal times. One of those "good old" institutions is the nation state. In good times, the nation state, and the way power is handled within it, is usually eyed suspiciously. But in times when the economic or general political state of affairs makes people apprehensive, the nation state's popularity suddenly rises.

The second possible reason for the nation state's comeback, which can be observed throughout Europe, is less political than psychological and socio-cultural in character. Since Aristotle, Western thought has understood man as a *zoon politikon,* a sociable being that prefers to live in communities. Human beings need a social environment in which they feel happy and safe. This social environment needs to have manageable size. The family, clan, tribe, and *volksgemeinschaft* are social entities of a manageable size. Compared to the dimensions of a whole continent, the nation state is a manageably sized entity as well. This applies even more to geographically and demographically small states such as Lichtenstein or Andorra who come close to being provinces rather than states.

In the age of globalization, even large nation states such as Germany or France are probably the last bastions with which the individual can identify aside from familiar entities such as the family, village, town, or region. In a borderless world that is growing closer together every day, the nation state is advancing as the last reliable unit. Although it may seem paradoxical, in a world without boundaries, individuals find it difficult to orient themselves. The nation state serves as a point of orientation and a framework for identification in this increasingly incomprehensible global environment. The recourse to citizenship serves the individual as a focal point of identification. Being identified by the nation state is the precondition for an individual's identification with the nation state. Consequently, the nation states regains its former capacity, namely that of integrating society. The Swiss professor of international law Peter Saladin thinks, "As a positive and legal fact, the state is to a certain extended the result of integration. And its purpose is to secure the continuous renewal of integration. [. . .] By way of its overall structure, its whole behaviour and with all its basic goals and principles the state is supposed to guarantee continuous integration."[9]

Globalization, Economization, and Multilateralization

The revival/comeback of the state as just described is not only a typical feature or even a consequence of the current volatility of the world system in the post-Cold War era, a system which is fragile and susceptible to the upsurge of violent conflicts. The comeback/revival of the nation state exists also in sharp contradiction to two other major characteristics of the current international system, namely economization and multilateralization.

"Volatility" is a technical term by which economists understand the "frequency in variations of a curve,"[10] or more precisely, the variations in share prices, exchange, and interest rates caused under the conditions of globalization and by the use of modern technologies.[11] The international system is volatile and thereby exposed to variations because no stable regime of governance has been erected since the beginning of the 1990s. The new world order some political scientists announced against the backdrop of Soviet-American cooperation during the First Gulf War has proved to be but wishful thinking. Multipolarity did, indeed, replace the bipolar structure of the international system during the Cold War. The result of this sudden disappearance of the bipolar structures and the disciplining and sorting power of this former antagonism is the rise of local liberation movements. The rousing new sentiments of national pride created an arena for actors with regional, hegemonic ambitions leading, as a result, to the upsurge of a variety of small, local, or regional crises and conflicts.

The problems of global scope (refugees, migration, terrorism, employment) that result in the evolution of the international system towards multilateralization are responsible for the growing importance of multilateral approaches to problem solving. There are many problems with which the nation state is overtaxed and which are best tackled through supra- and international organizations and institutions such as the European Union, the United Nations, NATO, the International Monetary Fund (IMF), and the World Trade Organization (WTO). Globalization is asymmetric, for it has created strong interdependent relationships among the Organization of Cooperation and Development (OECD) countries and some emerging economies in Asia and Latin America, thus marginalizing most parts of the developing world. Because globalization has put economic interests at the top of its global agenda, the international system has been "economized." As a consequence of this economization, state actors are more (inter-)dependent on one another than ever before.

Globalization and its accompanying phenomena such as liberalization, rationalization, deregulation, and increasing flexibility create more demands on the state. One could also say that the state has to steadily expand its problem-solving capacities. Not surprisingly, this sometimes leads to its partial collapse, which might appear rather paradoxical in the face of the widespread formula of the "end of the nation state." The state loses much of its autonomous problem-solving capacity due to globalization; its capacity to act becomes noticeably limited, leading some observers to the conclusion that the nation state is currently in crisis. The state will only pull itself out of this crisis if it is prepared to adapt to the changing environment. In short, the state will have to evolve. The German political scientist Hans W. Maull differentiates between two basic models of adaptation: "the construction of the postmodern state within existing national boundaries and the reconfiguration of the state beyond the boundaries of the nation state."[12]

According to Hans W. Maull, the first type of adaptation includes "reform of the state within the framework of traditional territorial boundaries."[13] This would basically mean the reform of national institutions and rules in accordance with external changes in the prevailing conditions in the international system. This adaptation could create what Richard Rosecrance has called the "virtual state," or what Philip Cerny coined the "post-modern competition state." According to Maull such a reform project could be accomplished by "streamlining and privatising (e.g. of employment agencies), by outsourcing state functions (by handing them over to independent central banks), by creating a business friendly environment and targeting investors with incentives, by reducing national debt and keeping inflation rate low, and by taking replenishing measures such as investments into higher education, vocational training and infrastructure."[14]

The second type of adaptation aims at increasing a state's ability to act by introducing public-private partnerships as well as by improving its channels of cooperation on the regional and the supra-national level. These two measures require state actors to accept the partial transfer of sovereignty to supranational institutions and to share competences with other actors in regard to affairs that were formerly handled by the nation state exclusively. According to Maull, classical state functions will be taken out of the traditional national framework and resurrected within a larger geographical context. Such a reform process would enable the nation state to either regain its ability to act or to win new competences, as well as new fields of engagement.

Globalization does not only cast a new light on the question of statehood. As it contributes to a more and more *boundary-less world*, it strengthens regional political institutions in places such as the European Union, North America, and Southeast Asia. Aside from leading to the construction of post-modern statehood within traditional national boundaries, globalization invigorates an opposite trend, too, that of regionalization. Examples of this are the European Union, which is the most developed case, the free trade zone of the NAFTA member states, and the comparatively loose alliance of the ASEAN states. According to Joachim Rau, "whether these trade blocs will exist in isolation from one another or whether they will melt together and by so doing come close to the WTO's ideal of world economy freed from all trade barriers, something it views as the ultimate, one and only market, remains to be seen."[15]

With regard to the "end of the nation state," the nation state's ability to autonomously pursue external relations gains new importance. The repeatedly raised question in this context is as follows: Is an independent and sovereign foreign policy feasible in the era of globalization? Or have nation states lost much of their room to maneuver when charting and pursuing their foreign policy?

Foreign Policy in the Era of Globalization: Its Scope and Limitations in a Globalized World

It bears repeating that no other political catchphrase has been used as excessively to characterize the end of the bipolar age as the term "globalization"; no other word has been quoted/cited so many times to explain the technological developments that affect every corner of our lives and to describe the internationalization of foreign policy and economic and domestic affairs. Globalization is the cipher of the turn of the millennium. However, the reality of world politics is still marked by the contradiction between economic, cultural, and political globalization, in other words, by radical segmentation. It seems as if Emile Durkheim's concept of *anomalie* is almost being confirmed. Shortly before the turn of the century, we again became witnesses of war on the European continent.

The rise of nationalism and of ethnic, religious, and social conflicts appears to be a tragic anachronisms seen against the background of the ongoing internationalization. These anachronisms disrupt the peaceful co-existence of the different people (*Völker*) and, as in the case of Yugoslavia, sometimes lead to war. Where political blocs disintegrate, suddenly creating a power vacuum, often irrational and thus unpredictable forces try to fill the void. The Carnegie Endowment for International Peace states in one of its reports that "war is still booming." This logic applies even more at places where national identity used to be oppressed by the state and where people try to reclaim their identity by subscribing to chauvinistic and sometimes fundamentalist policies. Although John Herz announced the downfall of the nation state as early as 1957, even nowadays one can still not seriously allege the end of the dominance of the state (*staatenwelt*). This, notwithstanding the influence of the *gesellschaftswelt*, is steadily becoming more apparent. *Gesellschaft* is constituted by tradition, culture, and religion – in short, by its members' identity. Sometimes *gesellschaft* is not formed in a peaceful way; in recent times, violent processes have been more likely to usher it in. For this reason, it has become of utmost importance that international organizations and institutions act unanimously and with firm determination. Those international bodies, be they the United Nations together with the IMF and the World Bank, the (OSCE), the European Union, the West European Union (WEU), the Atlantic alliance (NATO), or the Organization of Cooperation and Development (OECD), are all defined as the union of sovereign nation states. The governments of nation states that are acting on behalf of their domestic interests, more precisely on behalf of the interests of the *gesellschaft* they are representing, remain the major players of the game. In this game, the way nation states deal with their external relations is primarily driven by self-interest; it is, therefore, classical foreign policy.

The constraints of modern political life complicate our traditional understanding of the historical and institutional settings of foreign policy. As globalization causes formerly independent policy fields to be more intertwined with one another and as it blurs the boundaries between areas of different responsibilities, foreign policy understood as *realpolitik* is hardly feasible in the age of globalization. On the one hand, foreign policy has developed into a complex endeavor encompassing economic, security, and cultural affairs to a degree beyond its traditional scope. International institutions, on the other hand, and their influence on domestic affairs are turning foreign policy into domestic policy. For these reasons, it is no longer a secret that the question as to whether domestic policies have to be prioritized over foreign policy is a false one. However, foreign policy still finds itself in a "privileged" position compared to other policy fields simply because the latter are less affected by international politics. In practice, foreign policy is exposed to the influence of a large number of non-governmental and international actors by which its transnational nature is further underlined.

At first sight, the task of devising transnational policies seems less leashed to strict rules and regulations compared to purely domestic policy fields that are more prone to public scrutiny and accountability. Overall, everyday foreign policy is taking place without vast media attention which is why it reminds us of what used to be called Bismarck's *geheimdiplomatie*. This should come as no surprise to us since the pattern of standard behavior tells us that the electorate usually rewards political decisions that noticeably better their lives. Citizens are not directly affected by foreign policy decisions; furthermore, foreign policy is not subject to intense parliamentary control unless it involves decisions on crisis intervention or war. The state handles its external relations by keeping its citizens outside.

The most important thing to bear in mind is, *foreign policy operates on the international level, but its agenda is grounded in the realm of domestic interests*. As simplistic as this formula may sound, to actually put it into practice is a whole other issue. Theoretical concepts for the analysis of foreign policy decisions are not yet comprehensive and systematic enough. However, they make clear that foreign policy is a highly complex process in which a variety of determinants and factors intervene.

Foreign policy is about taking charge. Those authorized and in charge of dealing with a state's external affairs—be it the head of government or the foreign minister—collect information, evaluate it against the background of their domestic interests, weigh different replies or courses of action against each other, eventually make a decision, and implement this decision in a second step. It goes without saying that there are numerous actors involved in this process of decision-making and final implementation. This rather basic portrayal illustrates how close the field of decision-making in foreign policy and the discipline of psychology are. It is not without reason that in the United States, the discipline "political psychology" with its focus on analyzing actors' motives, behavior, and actions from a rational-choice perspective has its roots in the disciplines of psychology and political science.

But a whole range of other disciplines is necessary to make for good foreign policy: public administration management which seeks to make administrative processes more effective and efficient, political theory which is about moral and ethical dimensions of statehood, and peace research as well as integration theories, which both place analytical emphasis on international cooperation. The phase of decision-making and that of action in foreign policy is characterized by the intermingling of various levels of government and the consequent interplay of the various variables attached to the different levels, leading to the question, how many actors are in charge?

Are the decision makers independent, or do they rely on political coalitions and other forms of alliances? Do other states, international institutions, or multinational companies have a say? Are we talking about foreign policy decisions of everyday character that have to be made routinely, or are we talking about the exception of a crisis situation? Which psychological, strategic, or rational factors influence a foreign policy decision? How are decisions reflected upon by decision-makers once they have been implemented, and how do their repercussions, in turn, affect future decisions? Which theoretical concept is best suited to account for the complex mechanisms of foreign policy decision-making? Is it the behaviorist concept with its emphasis on action and re-action as just described? Is it rational-choice theories, which stress the meaning of interests and preferences of actors, or is it realism with its emphasis on the power and capabilities and its belief in zero-sum games? Or should we instead consider structural theories, which tend to stress the structural and systemic limitations of every foreign policy?

We could easily broaden this array of questions. However, it is obvious that the explanatory power of old school realism as conceived by Hans J. Morgenthau does not sufficiently address the complexity of a globalized world.[16] Idealizing foreign policy as an act of leadership and decision-making based on rational calculations is an approach that has fallen short. In fact, realism could only claim to be true by pointing to a few outstanding politicians who in extraordinary times acted wisely. Yet, the central analytical variables in Morgenthau's theory, "power" and "interest," remain the central motives in today's foreign policy. Today's actual degree of interdependence and the general level of interaction in foreign policy go beyond realism's analytical framework. Above all, interdependence and interaction have become transnational.

This comprehensive framework of cooperation within which foreign policy is designed and implemented and which ultimately is embedded in and restricted by the political culture of a nation needs to be taken into consideration. So in order to embark on a comparative analysis of foreign policy, we need to gather more empirical evidence and overhaul our available theoretical tools. It is true that factors such as a political leader's personality, political socialization, and experience may complicate such a project. However, to discuss foreign policy in an appropriate manner it will be more promising to fathom how central political terms are interpreted and translated into practical policies. These central terms need to be looked at more closely.

Central to foreign policy analysis is a society's understanding of the nation state and its legitimate and illegitimate interests. The end of the Cold War, the revolution in Eastern Europe, the fall of the Berlin Wall, the opening of the frontiers in Eastern Europe are responsible for both the demise of the traditional west-versus-east antagonism and the questioning of the sovereign nation state's predominance as a major actor in the international system. More than ever, we need to ask about the new structure of the international order and the nation state's role within it. In so doing, we will ask about the scope and limitations of national foreign policy. Put differently, where do we have to allocate foreign policy in the coordinate system of the new international order? Is traditional foreign policy concentrating on the nation state still possible?

First of all, it is remarkable that ever since the demise of the Warsaw Pact, European states have not significantly changed their maxim of foreign policy even though the structuring circumstances under which international coalitions and relations had been forged vanished abruptly. One country that had been involved in the epoch-making changes at the beginning of the 1990s, as probably no other country was, is Germany. In order to pre-empt any nationalistic movements, the German government has always emphasized that German reunification was part of creating and deepening the European Union and a crucial element to Western Europe's integration. In other words, European integration and German foreign policy were seen as two sides of the same coin.

Overall, for the historically significant developments of the past decade, the EU member states' foreign policy is marked by continuity. To assert that a fundamental turn in foreign policy has taken place would, therefore, be wrong. However, the future may show that Europeans will not be able to follow their internationalist approach of harmonious multilateralism without becoming trapped in conflicts. This applies even more in cases in which areas of responsibility overlap between international institutions or in cases in which those areas have to be defined in the first place. The blurring boundaries of responsibility and competence among organizations such as the WEU, NATO, the OSCE, and the UN serve as an example of this, raising the question, how compatible is the widening of the WEU with that of NATO? In the future, the quality of international cooperation as well as the way in which nation states will participate in international coalitions will depend on the nation states' ability both to define and to enunciate their interests. This process of defining national interests does not necessarily lead to tensions between national and international interests. For some nation states such as Germany, explicitly defined national interests are not considered to be a natural part of their foreign policy agenda. Other countries, such as France or Denmark, however, do not find it difficult to reconcile both dimensions.

Sometimes, it can have a facilitating effect on international cooperation when actors restrain themselves from pronouncing their national interests in an overly self-confident manner. Being a member of an alliance or of an integration process can provide relief from the duty to clearly identify one's position. On no account can national interests be identified from a purely national perspective. This is why in the future the degree to which foreign policy is embedded in international coalitions and integrated into multilateral cooperation will be crucial. It is indispensable that states identify their own interests and position in the international system. The yardsticks for this self-identification are easily found: the general ability to cooperate in a multilateral framework, the ability to form alliances, and the ability to build constructive partnerships in the European Union and the European and Atlantic chambers. The latest developments in Europe show that the demarcation of self-interests within the confines of cooperative multilateral frameworks is necessary because member states have to convey their opinions to third parties.

Nation states naturally try to take advantage of multilateral institutions. In order to strike a supranational agreement successfully, all the parties involved must be assured that each will employ the same means to reach the joint aim. Such a mission would be successful as long as every member regards the joint aims and principles as being conducive to its national interests and as being in accordance with the political, security, financial, and economic priorities of its foreign policy agenda.

It is incumbent on any nation state to examine the advantages and downsides of being integrated into alliances by taking into account their national interests independently from their weight within the multilateral framework. This logic will apply to future multilateralism as well, despite all binding agreements, *de facto* dependence, and moral commitment to which a state might be exposed. The EU member states are developing their Common Foreign and Security Policy (CFSP) with the purpose of avoiding the prevalent impression that multilateral policies are running the danger of "over-running" the member states' national foreign policy agenda. The overarching aim is to bring closer together national points of view and to develop a shared basic agenda at the same time. This is how the complicated, but feasible, balancing act can be reached. However, according to Henry Kissinger, such a shared agenda will not be implemented automatically; instead, the shared agenda needs to be re-negotiated constantly. Integration is no automatic process. It can only be reached through negotiation and hard work.

In practice, the CFSP, although often criticized as ineffective, is of symbolic importance in reassuring small member states that larger member states will not overrun their national interests. The core function of the CFSP, against the background of globalization and interdependence, is to make sure that each member's national interests are protected with the help of the group. This is to be achieved in two ways. First, the CFSP serves as a forum for the exchange of views and information. Second, it serves as a platform where diverging national positions can be reconciled and shared principles and positions developed.[17]

The Treaty on the European Union calls for the political solidarity of all twenty-five member states. One exception is the so-called "Luxembourg Compromise," which allows a member state in exceptional cases and for well-founded domestic reasons to block a decision for which a qualified majority is required. Aside from the Luxembourg Compromise, the principle of solidarity is seen as a primary way to protect member states' interests, especially those of the small states. By introducing this principle, the Intergovernmental Conference, which had gathered in Amsterdam to revise the treaty on the European Union, responded to the shortcomings of the CFSP, which had been discovered as another important field of cooperation rather late. However, the CFSP remains untested. It could prove disadvantageous that the CFSP was meant to take place as an informal consultation and dialogue process. The sheer number of twenty-five EU members today (and more in the future) may require restrictions on informality, leading to a more rigid process. In addition, transparency could suffer from the sheer number of members, too.

If this scenario becomes true, what will happen is exactly what was initially meant to be avoided. Small member states will be left outside. The bigger members could create and position themselves right at the center of informal and, thus, more flexible circles within the EU. By so doing, they would isolate smaller members and undermine community solidarity from within. The original purpose of the CFSP would be entirely undermined. Therefore, political leaders in the European Union will face the task of reintegrating the smaller member states. Sovereign and autonomous foreign policy is limited by the necessity to reconcile a state's own national interests with the international system, its structures, and the interests of other nation states. These limits should be respected by each nation state. It is only under this precondition that small EU members will accept coalition-building and the search for compromise on global issues as a natural and necessary element of their foreign policy agenda.

A foreign policy that carries a cooperative and constructive spirit reconciles international responsibility and national interests, *weltbürgertum* and revitalized national identity. In order to achieve this equality, foreign policy needs an unmistakable and clear-cut agenda. If foreign policy is domestic politics through different means, as Ralf Dahrendorf contends, how do we describe foreign policy? How do we find the right balance between values and interests? Foreign policy is meant to serve the well-being of the citizens, which means welfare and security in the first place. However, it also includes political and societal participation. Both aspects are codependent. If foreign policy is not supposed to be exclusively driven by domestic interests and, thus, by power politics and the drive for hegemony, then foreign policy has to show that it is mutually beneficial.

Consequently, there will be no escaping asking the allegedly antiquated "*wertfrage*" which used to be associated with members of the neorealist school that was felt to be committed to the Charter of the United Nations. *Wertfrage* means to ask the question of how foreign policy can be both ethical and harmonized with national politics of self-interest. Reimund Seidelmann has pointed out correctly that the democratization of foreign policy does not only concern the question of participation, but is also a matter of agreeing on and describing its political agenda. When—as explained above—the Treaty on the European Union demands the political solidarity of each of the twenty-five member states, then this principle corresponds to a process that Hans W. Maull has called "civilizing world politics," an idea that ultimately draws upon the concept of the *zivilgesellschaft*, according to Norbert Elias.

The idealistic concept of civilian power in international politics lies at the heart of the questions about whether there is a new global order and what is the impact of interconnectedness in the age of globalization. In this context, we can neglect the difference between foreign policy understood as monocentrically structured policy and international politics seen as a polycentrically organized system of interaction. It is important to bear in mind that foreign policy and international politics do not follow a self-referential logic, but that foreign policy is part of a homogeneous policy field.

This is why the same issues are at the center of both domestic politics and foreign policy. These are topics such as freedom, peace, democracy, rule of law, human rights, comprehensive security and welfare, justice, and solidarity. According to the former German President Roman Herzog, these issues are the cornerstones of a shared ethical agenda upon which international actors should act. There can be no doubt that only liberal democracies can seriously exert civilian power on the basis of their core values and principles. Only they have the legitimacy, will power, and ability to pursue ethical foreign policies and to choose the appropriate aims and means. However, against the backdrop of increasing international interdependence, politicians will be exposed to growing domestic pressure to justify their actions on the international stage. The basis for legitimizing foreign policy has to be transparency and accountability. Seen from this perspective, we cannot underestimate national foreign policy's valuable contribution to the international system.

Conclusion

The principal mechanism of the interplay between the nation state and supranational organizations is clear: the fact that foreign policy has in essence adopted a more cooperative and integrative approach is the nation state's reply to a globalized world characterized by fewer military threats and more social violence. The nation state has to understand and to communicate to its electorate that international organizations are best suited to protect and to assert their national interests. This does not exclusively apply to the field of trade and the battle for international markets. Multilateralism itself has become a principal aim of national foreign policy. The historian Arnold Toynbee knew that, in the long term, only those civilizations and people prevail which are capable of finding viable solutions to new challenges. Today, this can only happen within the multilateral framework. The European Union offers a perfect platform for the assertion of essential national interests.

Notes

1. Paul Kingsnorth, *Global Attack! Der neue Widerstand gegen die Diktatur der Konzerne* (Bergisch Gladbach: Lübbe, 2003), 87. The author of this article has freely translated Paul Kingsnorth's words from German to English. The quotation may, therefore, not be identical with Paul Kingsnorth's original English words.

2. Ibid., 88.

3. On the Austrian context of this phenomenon, see Günter Bischof and Anton Pelinka, eds., *The Americanization/Westernization of Austria, vol. 12, Contemporary Austrian Studies* (New Brunswick, NJ: Transaction, 2004).

4. See, e.g., Joseph E. Stiglitz, *Globalization and Its Discontents* (New York: W. W. Norton, 2002).

5. Hans Peter Martin and Harald Schumann, *Die Globalisierungsfalle. Der Angriff auf Demokratie und Wohlstand*, 8th ed. (Reinbek: Rowohlt, 1996).

6. Thomas Hanke and Norbert Walter, *Der Euro – Kurs auf die Zukunft. Die Konsequenzen der Währungsunion für Unternehmen und Anleger* (Frankfurt: Campus, 1997), 163.

7. Lothar Späth, "Relativierung des Nationalstaatsmodells. Regionalismus als dritte Kraft," in *Keine Angst vor Europa. Föderalismus als Chance*, ed. Andreas Doepfner (Zürich: NZZ-Verlag, 1992), 42.

8. Karl Kaiser, "Zwischen neuer Interdependenz und altem Nationalstaat. Vorschläge zur Redemokratisierung," in *Demokratie am Wendepunkt. Die demokratische Frage als Projekt des 21. Jahrhunderts*, ed. Werner Weidenfeld (Berlin: Siedler, 1996), 312: "Nations between societal actors whose interactions transcended national borders began to emerge parallel to the realm of international politics which was marked by relations between nation states acting like closed entities. In addition, non-state actors such as international organisations became increasingly important."

9. Peter Saladin, *Wozu noch Staaten? Zu den Funktionen eines modernen demokratischen Rechtsstaats in einer zunehmend überstaatlichen Welt* (Bern: C.H. Beck, 1994), 15 f.

10. Rainer Hank, *Das Ende der Gleichheit oder: Warum der Kapitalismus mehr Wettbewerb braucht* (Frankfurt: S. Fischer, 2000), 273.

11. See Jakob Wolf, *Lexikon Betriebswirtschaft* (München: Heyne, 1995), 302.

12. Vgl. Hans W. Maull, "Der Kleinstaat in den Zeiten der Globalisierung: Nutznießer, Opfer oder Akteur?," in *Der Kleinstaat – Plädoyers gegen Vorurteile*, ed. Romain Kirt (Esch-sur-Alzette: Editions Le Phare, 2003), 75-90, here 79.

13. Ibid., 80.

14. Ibid., 79.

15. Joachim Rau, *Märkte, Mächte, Monopole. Was die Wirtschaft im Innersten zusammenhält* (Zürich: Oesch, 2001), 52.

16. Hans J. Morgenthau's theory is summarized in his classic study *Politics Among Nations: The Struggle for Power and Peace*, first published in 1948.

17. See also the chapter by Günter Hauser in this volume.

References

Egon Bahr, *Der Nationalstaat: überlebt und unentbehrlich* (Göttingen: Seidl, 1998)

Guenter Bischof, Anton Pelinka, eds., *The Americanization/Westernization of Austria.* (Contemporary Austrian Studies vol. 12) (New Brunswick, London: Transaction, 2004).

Henri Bourguignat, *La tyrannie des marchés. Essai sur l'économie virtuelle* (Paris: Economica, 1995).

Richard Cooper, *The Post Modern State and the World Order* (London: Demos, 1996).

John Gray, *Die falsche Verheißung. Der globale Kapitalismus und seine Folgen* (Berlin: Alexander Fest, 1999).

Jean-Marie Guehenno, *La fin de la démocratie* (Paris: Flammarion, 1993).

Rainer Hank, *Das Ende der Gleichheit oder: Warum der Kapitalismus mehr Wettbewerb braucht* (Frankfurt/Main: S. Fischer, 2000).

Thomas Hanke, Norbert Walter, *Der Euro - Kurs auf die Zukunft. Die Konsequenzen der*

Währungsunion für Unternehmen und Anleger (Frankfurt/M., New York: Campus, 1997).

Karl Kaiser, „Zwischen neuer Interdependenz und altem Nationalstaat. Vorschläge zur Redemokratisierung", in *Demokratie am Wendepunkt. Die demokratische Frage als Projekt des 21. Jahrhunderts*, ed. Weidenfeld, Werner (Berlin: Siedler, 1996): 311-328.

Paul Kingsnorth, *Global Attack! Der neue Widerstand gegen die Diktatur der Konzerne*, (Bergisch Gladbach: Lübbe, 2003).

Peter Köpf, *Stichwort Globalisierung* (München: Heyne, 1998).

Paul Krugmann, *Der Mythos vom globalen Wirtschaftskrieg. Eine Abrechnung mit den Pop-Ökonomen* (Frankfurt a. M. - New York: Campus, 1999).

Hans-Peter Martin, Harald Schumann, *Die Globalisierungsfalle. Der Angriff auf Demokratie und Wohlstand*, 8th ed (Reinbek: Rowohlt, 1996).

Hans W. Maull, „Der Kleinstaat in den Zeiten der Globalisierung: Nutznießer, Opfer oder Akteur?", in *Der Kleinstaat - Plädoyers gegen Vorurteile*, ed. Kirt, Romain (Esch-sur-Alzette: Editions Le Phare, 2003): 75-90.

Hans J. Morgenthau, *Politics Among Nations. The Struggle for Power and Peace*, 6th ed. (New York: Knopf, 1985).

Thomas Nowotny, *Strawberries in Winter. On Global Trends and Global Governance* (Frankfurt/M., Berlin, Bern et al.: Peter Lang, 2004).

Joachim Rau, *Märkte, Mächte, Monopole. Was die Wirtschaft im Innersten zusammenhält* (Zürich: Oesch, 2001).

Jeremy Rifkin, *The End of Work. The Decline of the Global Labor Force and the Dawn of the Post-Market Era* (New York: Warner Books, 1995).

Peter Saladin, *Wozu noch Staaten? Zu den Funktionen eines modernen demokratischen Rechtsstaats in einer zunehmend überstaatlichen Welt* (Bern, 1994).

Lothar Späth, „Relativierung des Nationalstaatsmodells. Regionalismus als dritte Kraft", in *Keine Angst vor Europa. Föderalismus als Chance*, ed. Doepfner, Andreas (Zürich: NZZ-Verlag, 1992): 42-50.

Joseph E. Stiglitz, *Globalization and Its Discontents* (New York: W. W. Norton & Company, 2002).

Jakob Wolf, *Lexikon Betriebswirtschaft* (München: Heyne, 1995).

Recent Balkans Diplomacy from an Austrian Perspective

Wolfgang Petritsch

Introduction

The years 2005 and 2006 are arguably a decisive period for the resolution of the last big military conflict on European soil in the twentieth century. What you are about to read is not a scholarly account, a treatise, about Balkans diplomacy. Rather, it is an essay about how international politics reacted—and failed—in dealing with the wars on the territory of the former Yugoslavia. This is an issue which is characterized by fundamental disagreements on the part of the international community about its root causes and, consequently, about the ways and means to bring the conflict to an early end. How should the international community deal with a failing state when the doctrine of "state sovereignty"—standard practice in international law and enshrined in the United Nations (UN) Charter—severely restricts, if not excludes, any meaningful outside intervention? What then about the egregious violations of human rights, what about the humanitarian casualties of civil strife, of "asymmetric" internal conflicts, where the government dispatches the military against its own citizens? (Only in 2001 did an international panel establish the "responsibility" of governments or—in their absence—the international community "to protect" its citizens. But even today—after Bosnia and Rwanda—in Sudan and Chechnya, the basic notion of state sovereignty is largely uncontested.)

Regarding the Yugoslav drama of the 1990s, there are other, more vexing questions to be answered. Was it "ethnicity" in conflict, in which Southern Slavs fought against their fellow Southern Slavs? Was it a "religious" conflict, pitting Christian Orthodox Serbs against Roman Catholic Croats—and both against Muslim Slavs, called Bosniacs? Or was it simply about the preservation of raw political power, status, and privileges by a few former communist leaders turned "ethno-nationalists"? Was it—more generally—a "crisis of modernity," the "collapse of transformation by implosion," a meltdown of historical proportions, caused by what some Balkans scholars refer to as the "Serbian revitalization movement"?

Certainly, there are no clear-cut and easy answers, one of the reasons why peace and reconciliation still eludes the peoples of the former Yugoslavia. But there are conclusions to be drawn. Failure or success in tackling complex security challenges hinges in equal measure on sound analysis and timely action, both diplomatic and otherwise. But before exploring further conclusions that can be drawn, it is important to discuss a few points up front.

Regarding the term "Balkans," there are many who believe one should not use this expression considered to be derogatory; they prefer the less charged "Southeastern Europe." Personally, I am neutral when it comes to geographic names. I am, moreover, convinced that negative stereotypes can only be altered by an overall positive change of circumstances. Once the region will have recovered from its past tribulations (and I am confident it can), then "Balkans" will become just another term for Southeastern Europe, maybe one considered more colorful. The European Union obviously shares this opinion, since in its parlance "Western Balkans" refers to Albania, Bosnia and Herzegovina (BiH), Croatia, the Former Yugoslav Republic of Macedonia, and Serbia and Montenegro. This text, however, deals mainly with the EU's post-conflict management in BiH and Kosovo.

Regarding Austria, its policy—both domestic and foreign—needs to be increasingly conceived as part and parcel of wider EU policy. "With the EU and through the EU," that seems to me to be the best way to secure Austria's "national interest," its specific position in what again has become the center of a once deeply divided Europe. This specifically applies to Austria's Balkans policy, now primarily driven by economic opportunities for its small and medium size industry, in particular its banking sector. Austria is the prime investor in many of those countries. The once tense and historically fraught relations between Austria and the states of the region are mostly a thing of the past. Political and ideological strife has been replaced by economic competition. Consequently, the focus of this article is on the evolving political framework, that is the policy of the European Union in the Balkans.

Finally, I am not presenting the official Austrian view on the region. Instead, it is a rather personal assessment from the perspective of a practitioner who has spent a considerable part of his professional life in this alleged "powder keg" called the Balkans.

"The Hour of Europe Has Come" —Has It?

There is arguably no other event that puzzled post-Cold War Europe as much as the violent break-up of Yugoslavia. When, in June 1991, Jacques Poos, the then-foreign minister of Luxemburg and acting head of the European Community (EC) emphatically pronounced the "hour of Europe" in the Balkans, a hitherto unknown "can-do mentality" seemed to have seized the hearts and minds of the leadership of the Old Continent. Indeed, there was cause for optimism in these early summer days of 1991. An improvised European crisis management had just helped to end the stand-off between the Yugoslav Army and independent-minded Slovenia. The Brioni Agreement of 7 July 1991 ended the first war on the territory of the imploding Socialist Federative Republic of Yugoslavia (SFRY).

These early successes of European diplomacy came to a screeching halt when the crisis in Croatia erupted. By then, the international community's balancing act between the preservation of the territorial integrity of Yugoslavia and the right to self-determination by individual republics had long failed. Despite increased efforts by the Europeans to activate the regional mechanisms of the Conference for Security and Cooperation in Europe (CSCE; since 1994, the OSCE) and the collective security mechanisms of the United Nations, the Yugoslav crisis had dramatically escalated in the course of 1991 and 1992, both in scope and in depth. This was definitely not the finest "hour of Europe." On the contrary, Europe and its Euro-Atlantic security partners singularly failed to comprehensively address what was to become the bloodiest conflict on its territory since 1945.

Neither the hectic and, at times, uncoordinated activities of the European Community, nor the "Conference on Yugoslavia," which had taken up its "mission impossible" in September 1991 in The Hague, nor the countless resolutions passed by the UN Security Council, nor an arms embargo, nor economic sanctions were able to stop the carnage.

The crisis slipped out of the hands of the international community when the war had moved on to Croatia and Bosnia-Herzegovina, the latter being in many ways a "small Yugoslavia" in itself. The 1992-1995 war in Bosnia—a deadly mix of Serb aggression and civil war between the three ethnic communities, the Bosniacs (Muslims), Croats and Serbs—ended in almost total destruction of this traditionally multi-ethnic Balkans society. The terrible consequences are now known to be over 200,000 civilians killed, many more maimed, and more than half of the population of four million either internally displaced or living as refugees in Europe and beyond due to a brutal campaign of "ethnic cleansing" masterminded by Serbia's strongman Slobodan Milosevic and emulated by his Croat counterpart, President Franjo Tudjman.

Vukovar and Sarajevo, Dubrovnik and Mostar, the Krajina and, above all, Srebrenica became symbols for a *Kulturbruch*, a cultural "rupture," incomprehensible at the end of this terribly bloody European century.

Why took it so long to put an end to this carnage? What happened to the principle of human rights, enshrined in European covenants and the UN Charter? What of the "never again" of post-Holocaust Europe? These questions still haunt the political class of Europe.

In the end, it was the United States—and not Europe—that concluded the war in the Balkans.

The Self-Marginalization of Europe

Throughout the first half of the 1990s, European leaders were too divided in their interpretations of and approaches to the Yugoslav conflict to be successful. Old European divisions re-emerged, and historic alliances seemed to be more relevant than present dangers. The ugly melange of withering communist power and the "pervasive criminal instincts" characteristic of fratricidal conflicts prompted the creation of a leadership in Belgrade, which threw this onetime champion of the "Third Way"—Tito's Yugoslavia—into chaos and destruction. Europe, in the words of Stefan Lehne, "lacked the cohesion, determination and instruments to bring the crisis under control."[1]

So it was the United States, the "reluctant superpower" of the time, that belatedly entered the Balkans conundrum. It is a truism that at the height of the carnage in Bosnia, President Bill Clinton was duly impressed by Robert Kaplan's book *Balkan Ghosts* (1993) and its "ancient hatreds" thesis, which, according to the author, best explains the conflict in the Balkans and, consequently, renders it unsolvable.[2] Some commentators even detected a "clash of civilizations" in the Yugoslav conflict, thus rendering continued coexistence in the same state practically unfeasible, even undesirable. A partition of Yugoslavia seemed unavoidable.

The term "Balkanization"—first used by *The New York Times* in 1919—was the old cipher for state fragmentation and ethnic conflict that had gained renewed usage in the early 1990s. "No outside solution is feasible" was the prevailing credo, both in Washington and in some Western-European capitals. International involvement was, consequently, limited to a policy of containment, effectively restricted to humanitarian aid. Regrettably, the UN's role was a mere bystander of the ensuing Bosnian tragedy.

It was worldwide public outrage, triggered by the "CNN effect," that eventually convinced the Clinton Administration of the political necessity to intervene militarily and through diplomatic mediation efforts, led by Richard Holbrooke, in order to bring an end to the forty-four month Bosnian war. The Dayton Accords of November 1995, named after the U.S. Air Force base in Ohio where the negotiations took place, created a highly complex and, in many ways, ungovernable state of Bosnia and Herzegovina under the tutelage of the international community. Because of the questionable role the United Nations had played in this conflict, Dayton created an US-led "coalition of the willing" of fifty-five governments and international agencies in support of an independent and multi-ethnic Bosnia.

The European role in ending this conflict can at best be described as marginal. Consequently, in the course of the second half of the 1990s nothing much changed in the "division of labor" between the United States and Europe. Europe assumed the role of major payer, while the United States maintained, even expanded, its position as the lead political player. Roughly speaking, Europe to a substantial degree provided funds, expertise, and manpower for the crisis region in the Balkans; in turn, the United States provided political and military leadership.

Slow Changes: The Kosovo Crisis of 1999

After the collapse of Albania in 1997, the European Union again missed an opportunity to take a stronger political and security role in the Balkans when proposals for a Western European Union (WEU) stabilization were blocked in the EU Council. It was up to the OSCE, which turned to former Austrian Chancellor Franz Vranitzky to mediate and to the Italians to provide military cover in an operation appropriately dubbed "Alba" to bring Albania, one of the poorest countries in Europe, back from the brink of civil war.

The Kosovo crisis of 1998-1999 commenced roughly along the same lines. When the conflict in this Serb province escalated and the resistance against the Milosevic regime, which had abolished the province's autonomy status in 1989, turned violent, the United States swiftly named Chris Hill, its ambassador to neighboring Macedonia (FYROM), as Special Envoy for Kosovo. It took the European Union half a year and much public embarrassment to follow suit. In October 1999, I was appointed EU Special Envoy to deal with the conflict alongside Hill. Against the backdrop of an ever-increasing wave of persecution of ethnic Albanians by Serb security forces, we managed to produce a rough proposal for a peace treaty that got the support of the so-called Contact Group (made up of the United States, Russia, France, Germany, Italy, and the United Kingdom), which by then was the main actor in the Serb-Albanian conflict.

Our "shuttle diplomacy" between Belgrade and Pristina was eventually overtaken by events when, in mid-January 1999, a massacre committed on civilians in the Kosovo-Albanian village of Racak forced the international community to act. The two warring parties were summoned to Rambouillet near Paris for peace talks. The Contact Group, co-chaired by the French and British Foreign Ministers, appointed Hill, Boris Mayorski of Russia, and me as mediators. Despite the fact that the deal was, in the end, broken by Milosevic, for the first time in a decade the European role in the Balkans had become distinctly visible and substantive. While, understandably, in the ensuing NATO intervention the United States resumed its leading role, the end of the conflict and its aftermath carried a considerably enhanced European imprint.

Turning Point 2000

The year 2000—roughly a decade into the Yugoslav conflict—can be considered a turning point. I agree with Stefan Lehne, Javier Solana's point man for the Balkans, who states, "As the EU's Balkan policy became more coherent and proactive, the US-European relationship in the Balkans shifted towards greater equality."[3] As the top civil administrator for Bosnia and Herzegovina between 1999 and 2002, I could personally witness these shifts across the region. With the danger of renewed strife subsiding over time, the civilian aspects of the international rescue mission became increasingly more important. State and institution building, economic reform, matters of justice and home affairs took precedence over mere military peace-keeping. Thus, in the transformation of Southeastern Europe in general and in the war-torn regions of ex-Yugoslavia in particular, European "soft power" gained currency and strength. There are two key underlying reasons for this shift in Europe's role.

The first addresses the historic changes in the region. With the death of President Tudjman of Croatia in late 1999 and the democratic "October revolt" of 2000 in Serbia that brought down President Milosevic, the two main culprits for the Yugoslav tragedy had left the political scene. For the first time ever, all countries of the Balkans had democratically elected governments. That, in turn, helped the European idea take root in these otherwise still deeply divided societies. Now, as then, there is one wish that unites all citizens, and that is to become "European," to be part of the historic project of European integration, to join the European Union.

Today, five years after this historic turn, enormous problems remain; think of Kosovo. However, while the double-transition from war to peace and from communism to western-style democracy remains a challenge for the "double-name states" Serbia and Montenegro, Bosnia and Herzegovina, the risk of the return of "war as the continuation of politics" has arguably been banned from the region. These radically changed political circumstances allow for the European Union to take a long-term and proactive approach in the region.

The second reason is the shift from failed intervention to policy coherence and operational capacity. It took the member states of the European Union too many years to arrive at a basic consensus on the nature of the Balkan conflict. However, it was not just the reflex of past alliances or sheer ignorance regarding a seemingly ancient feud—a conflict, more "personal" than political, as many in Europe thought—that prevented the Europeans from getting their act together. It took the human suffering of hundreds of thousands of refugees, temporarily displaced into our own communities, the suffering brought to our own footsteps, to eventually forge a common European policy. The shared interest in the stabilization of the region was equally fostered by a humanitarian impetus and the political spill-over effects of the conflict.

But it took another reform of the European Union to move from a mere reactive pose to political management. The creation of the high representative for Europe's Common Foreign and Security Policy (CFSP) in 2001 greatly enhanced the European Union's ability to provide a swifter and more coordinated response. It was in the Balkans where the European Union and Javier Solana, the *de facto* EU foreign minister, had to pass their first credibility test. Thanks to the proactive role played by Solana and his competent team, Macedonia, the small former Yugoslav republic with the imposed name FYROM and which for the longest time had escaped internal unrest, was brought back from the brink of civil war between the Slavic majority and the rebellious Albanian minority in 2001 as witnessed by the Ohrid Agreement.

In the same fashion, the new constitutional arrangement between Serbia and Montenegro, which in 2003 brought to a peaceful end the last of the Yugoslavias, was brokered by the strong hand of the EU high representative and enshrined in the Belgrade Agreement of 2002.

As an expression of the Union's commitment to the region, over the past several years three out of the total seven EU Special Representatives have dealt with the Balkans. In Bosnia and Herzegovina, all four high representatives—Carl Bildt of Sweden, Carlos Westendorp of Spain, me, and my successor Paddy Ashdown of the United Kingdom—were proposed by the European Union.

During my tenure as the international community's top civil administrator in Bosnia from 1999 through 2002, a robust "Europeanization" process was put into effect. European funds—roughly two-thirds of the bill is covered by the European Union—and European know-how are key to Bosnia's difficult state-building efforts. The U.S. notion of an "exit strategy" for the international community was step by step replaced by an "entry strategy" for Bosnia into European structures. As a result of this enhanced European strategy Bosnia and Herzegovina was accepted as a full member of the Council of Europe in April 2002.

Charged with streamlining the international presence in Bosnia and Herzegovina, I proposed, among other things, the termination of the UN mission (UNMIBH) and the transfer of responsibility to local authorities and to European institutions respectively. *Samoodgovornost,* local ownership and responsibility, became the keyword in the public discourse about the future of Bosnia as a "stable, viable, peaceful and multiethnic Balkans country, cooperating peacefully with its neighbors and irreversibly on track towards EU membership," as the international community's Mission Implementation Plan reads.

At the same time, the European Union increased its operational capacity in civilian and military crisis management. It was, thus, no coincidence that these new instruments were first deployed in Bosnia and Herzegovina. In early 2003, the European Union took charge of the police operation, and by the end of 2004, NATO-led SFOR was replaced by EUFOR. Europe continues to enhance its role in Macedonia where, since mid-2003, it has replaced NATO's military presence. Now the European Union is in charge of the police mission there.

While less visible in Kosovo, the European Union as part of the wider UN mission (UNMIK) is in charge of, among other things, economic reconstruction and reform such as privatization and other pertinent institution-building efforts.

It needs to be stated that European policies in the Balkans were in no small measure shaped by the parallel enlargement process. The accession of eight Eastern European countries in May 2004—the Ex-Yugoslav republic of Slovenia being one of them—undoubtedly helped to sharpen the EU's approach in stabilizing the Balkans. Despite the remarkable difference in dealing with the transformation crises in their respective countries, the countries of Eastern and Southeastern Europe historically share many structural deficiencies. Their societies and economies, as well as their political systems, were all burdened with the communist legacy. It was, thus, clear that the EU's evolving Balkans strategy would be considerably informed by its enlargement experience.

A Comprehensive Strategy for the Balkans

The West's military intervention against Milosevic's Yugoslavia to stop the humanitarian disaster in the rebellious province of Kosovo in 1999 was a clear indication that the piecemeal approach to solving the

Balkans crisis had run its course. A comprehensive new policy approach, the departure from past reactive modes, was overdue. The European Union thus decided on a two-pronged approach of continued stabilization efforts combined with the promise of association and the gradual integration of the countries of the Western Balkans into European structures. While the European Commission, the EU's executive branch, negotiated bilateral treaties with each of these countries and deployed important policy instruments in areas such as trade and assistance, the Stability Pact for Southeastern Europe was charged with promoting intra-regional cooperation.

Most importantly, the Thessaloniki Summit, which brought together the European Union and the Western Balkans countries in this northern Greek city in mid-2003, officially granted these countries the possibility of future EU membership. "The future of the Balkans is within the European Union," reads the Thessaloniki Declaration of 21 June 2003.

The Stabilization and Association Process (SAP) for the first time establishes a road map for EU accession. The conditions and requirements are roughly the same as those that applied to the Eastern European candidate states, including neighboring Bulgaria and Romania. Moreover, Thessaloniki stipulated to put several instruments of the enlargement process—like the availability of Community and administrative twinning programs—at the disposal of those Balkans countries. These measures effectively narrow the gap between the SAP and the pre-accession process, which for many of the affected countries still seems too far away.

Thessaloniki has brought forward a new quality to European Balkans policy. The prospect of Union membership, preceded by SAP implementation, has, thus, become the major "pull-factor" for the countries of the region, albeit still too abstract for the average citizen. Nevertheless, "Europe" has by now become the unifying idea in these post-conflict societies of the Balkans.

A note of caution is warranted: In spite of the remarkable progress achieved in guiding this underdeveloped region towards calmer waters, the Stabilization and Association Process is essentially one-sided. It is the European Union that defines the terms of reference; the affected countries have little say, with the exception of the Stability Pact, where, under the persistent leadership of Austria's Erhard Busek, regional cooperation can serve as a means to promote individual country interests. Equally important for the donor countries of the Pact is the fact that, unless issues like organized crime and trafficking in human beings are tackled in the region, they will invariably result in even greater problems in many member states of the European Union; the same applies to the ever-increasing challenge of migration.

Towards Stabilization, Association, and Integration of the Balkans

While in the early phase of the Yugoslav conflict Europe's role was rendered inefficient by policy divisions, strategic incoherence, and operational challenges, it took the Kosovo crisis of 1998/99 and the political changes in Serbia and Croatia—following the death of Tudjman and the transfer of Milosevic to The Hague—to reach a common European understanding on a comprehensive strategy for the Balkans. The changes in European political attitudes regarding this troubled part of the continent were already visible in the ensuing crises in southern Serbia and in Macedonia starting in 2000, when in parts of both of these countries an ethnic Albanian insurgency took advantage of the volatile regional situation. The Union, supported by NATO and the United States, took the lead in managing these crises and was instrumental in the successful post-conflict stabilization efforts.

The following years of 2002 and 2003 were periods of relative calm, contributing to a substantive reduction of foreign troop deployment in the Balkans. International troop levels came down, both in Bosnia and Herzegovina and in Kosovo, from close to 70,000 in 2000 to roughly 30,000 in mid-2004.

Conversely, the EU engagement—civil and, increasingly, military—experienced a robust upturn. European "soft power" was reinforced by the gradual deployment of European military "hard power."

The reasons for these changes are the swift evolution and subsequent deployment of the European Security and Defense Policy (ESDP), which only took off after the end of the Balkans wars. Guidelines for strengthening operational coordination and communication of EU action in the Western Balkans, adopted in late 2002, reinforced greater cooperation in the field of external assistance and translated the Union's financial contribution into political visibility, leverage, and influence.

This new and improved approach was also reflected in the "European Security Strategy" of December 2003. Upon the initiative of Javier Solana and in response to a similar American exercise (the National Security Strategy of September 2002), member states for the first time ever formally adopted a broad and comprehensive European Security Strategy. It came as no surprise that the Balkans figured high on the list. Already in Chapter Two, entitled "Strategic Objectives," the doctrine, which adopted a "broad" definition of security, stresses the task of promoting a ring of well-governed countries to the east of the European Union and on the borders of the Mediterranean with whom close and cooperative relations are desirable. Then it continues:

„The importance of this is best illustrated in the Balkans. Through our concerted efforts with the US, Russia, NATO and other international partners, the stability of the region is no longer threatened by the outbreak of major conflict. The credibility of our foreign policy depends on the consolidation of our achievements. The European perspective offers both a strategic objective and an incentive to reform.“[4]

As a consequence, a new division of labor emerged between Europe and the United States that had formerly taken the lead in the Balkans crisis, but after 9/11 had to shift its political attention and military power to other theaters and topics.

With the departure of wartime leadership in virtually all the successor states, the era of conventional wars in the Balkans has been successfully brought to an end. This, however, does not mean that the overall security situation is satisfactory. Now, instead of an overpowering military presence, policing and other civilian matters such as the creation of strong democratic institutions and the fight against organized crime and corruption take center stage. In these matters, considered to be long-term endeavors, the European Union with its wealth of resources and soft-power experience is well suited to contribute in a decisive manner.

Kosovo: A Gordian Knot?

While this is particularly true for Bosnia and Herzegovina, where, although still weak and not yet self-sustaining, a real breakthrough was achieved in returning a million displaced persons to their original homes, the same cannot be said of Kosovo. The tragic events of March 2004, when an Albanian mob killed more than a dozen ethnic Serbs and ransacked minority villages and orthodox holy sites, have reminded an increasingly complacent international community that peace, security, and prosperity still evade this part of former Yugoslavia. Clearly, Kosovo has wider, regional ramifications. Unless the UN Security Council and the Contact Group find a satisfactory solution to the status of Kosovo soon, stabilization and, consequently, the integration of the whole Balkans region into the European Union will remain elusive.

I am aware that tackling the status question holds potential risk and temporary heightened instability. It is, thus, of the utmost importance to be well-prepared for the highly complex and undoubtedly cumbersome negotiations between the Kosovo-Albanian leadership, representing approximately 90 percent of the province's population, and the Serb side. To be sure, the positions are mutually exclusive. While Belgrade insists on Kosovo remaining an integral part of Serbia, albeit with an enhanced autonomy, Albanians are fiercely united in their quest for independence. Since the turmoil of March 2004, the international community is aware that waiting longer is no solution. It might, on the contrary, exacerbate the long-standing economic and social crisis and lead to renewed confrontation, this time even with the UN "protectors."

Consequently, soon after the March events, a comprehensive *Standards Implementation Plan* was adopted, which follows the *Standards before Status* strategy, introduced by then-SRSG Michael Steiner in 2002. Steiner's structured approach tries to bridge the vast gap between the diametrically opposed aspirations of the two sides. It puts progress in building democratic institutions, ensuring the rule of law, and protecting the rights of the minorities and their freedom of movement in relation to the resolution of the status issue. Mid-2005 was identified by the Contact Group as the review date for these democratic standards in Kosovo, which, in turn, will lead to the envisioned status negotiations mediated by the United Nations.

The "Halo-Effect" of Europe

It is safe to say that 2005 will be crucial in bringing a modicum of self-sustainable stability to the region; even though the search for an equitable solution for Kosovo will temporarily rock the Balkans boat. Thus, for the foreseeable future, bold European leadership in the Balkans is called for.

It is not just the central issue of Kosovo that needs close scrutiny. Neighboring Macedonia, too, will need continued attention. This third post-conflict area, BiH and Kosovo being the other two, where Europe remains strongly engaged, is slowly recovering and making progress in building ethnically mixed institutions and state structures.

Developments in Macedonia, uneven yet pointing in the right direction, are in many ways emblematic of the overall transition process in the Balkans. Tangible progress has been achieved in improving "human security." The times of outright war are arguably over; focus has shifted to economic and social issues and to the generally weak institutional architecture of the states of the region. Post-conflict Bosnia and Herzegovina, Serbia and Montenegro, Macedonia as well as Albania and UN-run Kosovo continue to be hampered by the "weak state syndrome," providing fertile ground for criminal networks involved in trafficking in humans, drugs, and weapons. In some of these states, there are still too many links between former power structures, war criminals, and organized crime.

Ten years after the massacre of close to 8,000 Bosnian Muslims in Srebrenica, the main culprits—Radovan Karadzic and Ratko Mladic—are still at large. The murder of Serbian Prime Minister Zoran Djindjic in 2003 exemplifies the existing links between politics and crime. Bringing war criminals to justice, combating organized crime, and establishing the rule of law is the necessary corollary to the frustratingly slow process of democratization and economic reform in this part of the Balkans.

Although the European Union is by now operationally up to speed and the undisputed leader in reconstruction efforts, it still has not overcome its inertia in taking the necessary bold political decisions. It is, therefore, of the utmost urgency that Europe's Balkans strategy takes one big leap forward.

The momentous changes since the year 2000 constitute a real breakthrough; success is tangible. However, in order to "finish the job," more needs to be done. Granted, the new European Commission, which took up its work in November 2004, has set an important marker by moving the five countries of the Western Balkans from the External Relations portfolio to "Enlargement" Commissioner Olli Rehn. This is undoubtedly a welcome and timely move, which must now be reflected in tangible improvements of the accession perspective. The mere status of "associate country," or the so-called pre-accession status, has so far not produced the desired results. On the contrary, this approach is perceived by the affected populace as utterly bureaucratic and does, according to widespread opinion, not take into account the specific needs and challenges of the respective countries.

But there is ample reason to be optimistic. For the wider region of Southeastern Europe, the year 2004 has ended with decisions by the European Council (consisting of the twenty-five heads of state and government), that will have a tremendous impact on the future of the European project. I limit myself to the consequences for the Balkans and shall not delve into the highly sensitive issue of Turkey's possible membership, which has already at this stage irreversibly altered the traditional concept of "Europe." The EU's "Halo Effect" seems to work even beyond the perceived borders of the continent.

Apart from Croatia, which has commenced membership negotiations in March 2005, the remaining four Western Balkans countries are by all accounts at least ten years away from negotiating full membership with the European Union. Clearly, this time frame is no incentive for the governments to reform and for the citizens to accept the resulting painful changes. Consequently, the lure of EU membership is in danger of losing its lustre.

European Balkans policy is, thus, today faced with the twin challenge of forging an early UN-sponsored solution to the problem of Kosovo's status (together with the United States and Russia) and simultaneously offering a vastly improved EU perspective for the whole region. Both issues—the Kosovo status and the EU membership perspective—are, of course, interrelated. Unless the European Union comes up with a "compensation offer" for Belgrade that it cannot refuse, a peaceful untangling of the "Gordian knot", Kosovo, seems rather elusive. Europe has yet to demonstrate that it can pre-empt crises such as the one with which it would be confronted in Kosovo if the status talks go awry.

Proposals such as "structured membership" or the formation of a group of "Junior Members," in short, a kind of phasing-in strategy for these "problem candidates," seem headed in the right direction.[5] What needs to be avoided under any circumstances is the creation of a kind of "Balkans Ghetto" comprising most of the region's Serbs, Albanians, and Bosnia's Muslims, concentrated behind ever-growing visa hurdles, preventing them from migrating to the western member states of the European Union. Unless the European Union moves more resolutely towards the gradual and time-bound integration of the Western Balkans into the New Europe, we will see the already worrisome development gap grow ever wider in this part of Europe. That, in turn, would seriously impair Europe's stated ambition to become a viable global partner.

Suggested Further Reading

Batt, Judy, ed. *The Western Balkans: Moving On*. Paris: Institute for Security Studies, 2004.

Banac, Ivo. *The National Question in Yugoslavia: Origins, History, Politics*. Ithaca, NY: Cornell Univ. Press, 1984.

Bildt, Carl. *Peace Journey: The Struggle for Peace in Bosnia*. London: Weidenfeld and Nicolson, 1998.

Buckley, William Joseph, ed. *Kosovo: Contending Voices on Balkan Interventions*. Grand Rapids, MI: William B. Erdmans, 2000.

Cohen, Lenard J. *Serpent in the Bosom: The Rise and Fall of Slobodan Miloševic*. Boulder, CO: Westview, 2001.

Cooper, Robert. *The Breaking of Nations: Order and Chaos in the Twenty-First Century*. New York: Atlantic Monthly Press, 2003.

Dobbins, James, et al. *America's Role in Nation-Building: From Germany to Iraq*. Santa Monica, CA: Rand, 2003.

Drakulic, Slavenka. *Café Europa: Life after Communism*. 1st American ed. New York: Norton, 1997.

Fukuyama, Francis. *State-Building: Governance and World Order in the Twenty-First Century*. Ithaca, NY: Cornell Univ. Press, 2004.

Glenny, Misha. *The Balkans: Nationalism, War, and the Great Powers, 1804-1999*. 1st American ed. New York: Viking, 2000.
Kaser Karl, Dagmar Gramshammer-Hohl, Robert Pichler: *Europa und die Grenzen im Kopf – Enzyklopädie des Europäischen Ostens*, Band 11. Klagenfurt: Wieser, 2003.
Habermas, Jürgen. *Der gespaltene Westen*. Frankfurt: Suhrkamp, 2004.
Holbrooke, Richard. *To End a War*. New York: Random House, 1998.
Jelavich, Barbara. *History of the Balkans: Eighteenth and Nineteenth Centuries*. Cambridge: Cambridge Univ. Press, 1983.
———. *History of the Balkans: Twentieth Century*. Cambridge: Cambridge Univ. Press, 1983.
Kurspahic, Kemal. *Prime Time Crime: Balkan Media in War and Peace*. Washington, D.C.: Institute of Peace Press, 2003.
Papić, Žarko, et al. *International Support Policies to South-East European Countries: Lessons (Not) Learned in Bosnia-Herzegovina*. Sarajevo, 2001.
Petritsch, Wolfgang. *Bosnien und Herzegowina fünf Jahre nach Dayton—Hat der Friede eine Chance?* Klagenfurt: Wieser, 2001.
———. *Bosnia i Hercegovina od Daytona do Evrope*. Bosnian and Serb/Cyrillic ed. Sarajevo, 2002.
———, and Robert Pichler. *Dugi put u rat. Kosovo i medunarodna zajednica 1989-1999*. Belgrade, 2002.
———. *Kosovo-Kosova. Der lange Weg zum Frieden*. Klagenfurt: Wieser, 2004.
———. *Rruga e gjatë në luftë. Kosova dhe Bashkësia Ndërkombëtare 1989-1999*. Pristina, 2002.
———, Karl Kaser, and Robert Pichler. *Kosovo/Kosova. Mythen, Daten, Fakten*. Klagenfurt: Wieser, 1999.
Power, Samantha. *"A Problem from Hell": America and the Age of Genocide*. New York: Basic Books, 2002.
Report of the International Commission on Intervention and State Sovereignty. *The Responsibility to Protect*. Ottawa, 2001.
Ramet, Sabrina. *Balkan Babel: The Disintegration of Yugoslavia from the Death of Tito to Ethnic War*. Boulder, CO: Westview, 1996.
Schöpflin, George. *Nations, Identity, Power: The New Politics of Europe*. New York: New York Univ. Press, 2000.
Sells, Michael A. *The Bridge Betrayed: Religion and Genocide in Bosnia*. Berkeley, CA: Univ. of California Press, 1996.
Shatzmiller, Maya, ed. *Islam and Bosnia: Conflict Resolution and Foreign Policy in Multi-Ethnic States*. Montreal: McGill-Queen's Univ. Press, 2002.
Solioz, Christophe and Svebor Dizdarevic, eds. *Ownership Process in Bosnia and Herzegovina: Contribution on the International Dimensions of Democratization in the Balkans*. Baden Baden: Nomos, 2003.
Solioz, Christophe and Tobias K. Vogel, eds. *Dayton and Beyond: Perspectives on the Future of Bosnia and Herzegovina*. Baden Baden: Nomos, 2004.
Todorov, Tzvetan. *Hope and Memory: Lessons from the Twentieth Century*. Princeton, NJ: Princeton Univ. Press, 2000.
Todorova, Maria. *Imagining the Balkans*. New York: Oxford UP, 1997.

Wachtel, Andrew Baruch. *Making a Nation, Breaking a Nation: Literature and Cultural Politics in Yugoslavia.* Stanford, CA: Stanford Univ. Press, 1998.

Notes

1. Stefan Lehne, "Has the Hour of Europe Come at Last?" in *The Western Balkans: Moving On*, ed. Judy Batt (Paris: Institute for Security Studies, 2004), 111.

2. Robert D. Kaplan, *Balkan Ghosts: A Journey through History* (New York: Vintage/Random House, 1993).

3. Lehne, "Hour of Europe," 114.

4. European Security Strategy, *A Secure Europe in a Better World* (Brussels, 2003), 10.

5. Franz-Lothar Altmann, *EU und Westlicher Balkan. Von Dayton nach Brüssel: Ein allzu langer Weg?* (Berlin: Stiftung Wissenschaft und Politik, 2005), 6.

NON-TOPICAL ESSAY

The Institutionalization of American Studies at Austrian Universities: The Innsbruck Model

*Susanne Mettauer**

American Studies as "the efforts to build up a systematic knowledge and understanding of America and its civilization as a connected whole"[1] is a relatively recent scholarly activity at European universities and can be observed in considerable intensity only after World War II. Before that, the study of American civilization was not at all conducted in a systematic manner. Research in the field of American Studies usually took place in connection to or at least closely associated with English Studies departments. This observation would make it seem probable that the institutionalization of American Studies within European academia in general, and at Austrian universities in particular, is related to the increased intervention by the United States in European cultural life in the post-World War II period, when in a huge propagandistic and "psychological offensive"[2] the United States put its distinctive stamp on the field of public diplomacy, as it would come to be called in the 1970s.

The attempt to influence and to shape the Austrian educational system was certainly an important component of the U.S. cultural mission because it was here that the general goal of reeducating (or, more mildly, reorientating) those Europeans who had been brainwashed by totalitarian, antidemocratic regimes could truly take effect. This essay examines how American Studies as an academic subject came to be established and institutionalized at universities, "the natural centers of intellectual life, where research is organized and knowledge accumulated and passed on."[3] The focus is on the American Studies department

---

* I am grateful to Dr. Günter Bischof, Dr. Arno Heller, and Dr. Sonja Bahn for their valuable comments and suggestions.

at the University of Innsbruck. For one, it was the first of its kind in Austria (and has remained independent to this day); moreover, the university and departmental archives in Innsbruck made source materials comparatively readily accessible. In addition, there is a second focus on the development within the first two decades, up to the mid-1970s. This restriction will serve to illustrate the relationship between U.S. and Austrian forces and interests at work in the founding and establishing of this institution.

The Study of America at Austrian Universities

The United States of America had been a topic of interest at European institutions of higher education since the end of the eighteenth century,[4] though on a far from systematic level. In their study of the degree of this interest in regard to research and teaching at Austrian universities, Margarete Grandner and Birgitta Bader-Zaar point out that up to 1955, it was only in the field of geography that the North American continent was "canonized" to some extent and, thus, became part of the standard university curriculum.[5] Concerning the field of history, North America was dealt with in survey lectures, but not too extensively. Considerable progress for the cause of American Studies could be seen when events from the history of the United States were chosen as watershed dates, that is, to mark the beginning or end of an epoch.[6] Such a choice can certainly be seen as an acknowledgement of and concession to the growing importance of the United States on the world stage.

Yet the recognition of American political and historical importance does not necessarily mean that the same status was granted in the realms of literature and culture. Quite the contrary, here the prejudice that Europeans were confronted with an uncultured, degenerate nation still persisted, particularly among the educated classes.[7] American literature was frequently regarded as a provincial appendix to English literature, and other cultural products (art, music, film, and so forth) as not worth studying in an academic context. The study of the United States was frequently associated with the study of English (meaning British) language and literature, and a widespread Anglo-centric bias (in Austria as well as in Germany) led to favoring the "pure" Anglo-Saxon original over the decadent offshoot from overseas.[8] Therefore, it is not surprising that an investigation of the status of American Studies within English Studies reveals a rather strained relationship. A point worth mentioning in this respect is that the field of English Philology as such consolidated itself at a rather late point as well. Even though English language courses had been taught since the 1840s, English departments at Austrian universities were not institutionalized until the end of the nineteenth century.[9] Discussing the situation in Germany, Hans Galinsky notes that it lasted until 1914 for all German universities to have chairs in English Philology. The discipline of *Anglistik* apparently competed with the fields of Romance and Germanic languages before it finally gained its unquestioned place at German universities.[10] Therefore, it would seem to be a mere repetition of history that English Philology, too, resisted ceding ground to the up-and-coming "sister" discipline. This unequal relation-ship is mirrored very graphically in such phrases as American Studies standing "in the shadow of big brother Anglistik,"[11] or when Karl Pivec, the second director of the Innsbruck *Amerika-Institut*, stated that the new discipline, more or less inevitably, had to encounter "the psychological obstacles of the old queen, English studies."[12]

This common perception of American Studies as an appendix to English Philology resulted, first of all, in frequent connections in terms of administration, resources, and personnel. Galinsky ventures the thought that perhaps these entanglements were created "in the hope of containing such a dynamic thing as Americana within the fold of English language and literature."[13] Whether that is true or not, later attempts by American Studies to emancipate itself from English Philology were undoubtedly made more difficult by these organic interrelations.[14] Another feature that American Studies inherited from this close connection was the (classically philological) emphasis on language and literature. As a result, history or cultural studies were often strongly neglected (and sometimes continue to be so to this day).[15] An issue that was discussed at the University of Innsbruck in 1976 may serve to illustrate this point. In its comment on the new curriculum, the curriculum committee of the English department did not agree with the suggestion that *Landes- und Kulturkunde* (cultural studies) should become a separate subject of examination. The committee pointed out that a *Kunde* can never be a *Wissenschaft.* The *Kunde* in question here should only be afforded scholarly attention insofar as it contributed to a deeper understanding of literary and linguistic topics, implying that, taken by itself, it was not of academic value.[16] This opinion indicates that, at least in 1976, the perception of American Studies was still very much in sync with the traditional areas of inquiry of English Philology, that is, literature and language.

Yet by this time, the most contemporary definitions of American Studies had already tremendously broadened the concept, so that this discussion about the legitimacy of a *Landes- und Kulturkunde* seems somewhat backward-looking. American Studies as it is mostly understood today means a truly comprehensive, interdisciplinary enterprise that holistically encompasses numerous aspects of the United States such as history, literature, society, politics, geography, economics, and so forth (a breadth of scope that has led to the pejorative description, "six or more subjects in search of a discipline"[17]). This interdisciplinary approach to the study of North America was also a rather late development in the United States itself, starting only after World War II. The University of Minnesota was an early center of the movement that was programmatically outlined in the book *American Studies*, published in 1948 by the Minnesota professor Tremaine McDowell. For the European scene, Arno Heller mentions the John F. Kennedy Institute at the Berlin Free University, founded in 1945, which served as the model of an integrated, interdisciplinary American Studies program.[18]

The U.S. Interest in Promoting American Studies

The U.S. Cultural Mission after World War II

The role of the United States in institutionalizing American Studies in Austria has to be seen in the wider context of the U.S. cultural mission in Austria after World War II. Up to 1938, U.S. foreign relations in matters of culture had consisted of informal, private contacts. Business people, tourists, philanthropists, missionaries, and other professional elites as well as various foundations served as unofficial cultural ambassadors who, apart from their own agendas, always had American values and ideas in their baggage when traveling abroad. Instead of centralized and orchestrated efforts, such voluntary initiatives seemed more in line with the liberal, individualistic, progressive creed that was to be spread and, thus, to modernize the rest of the world.[19] Yet, if terms like isolationism, non-intervention, and indifference had long become inadequate with respect to characterizing U.S. foreign policy,[20] they have certainly never been applicable to the realm of U.S. culture. The missionary fervor and earnestness that seem to accompany the spreading of their presumably morally superior ideology (linked to a materialistically advanced society) are an indispensable constituent of American exceptionalism, a constituent which in the eyes of many Americans may easily blur the line between self-interest and altruism.

However, this cultural mission only became a definitive and outspoken agenda at the dawn of World War II, when U.S. policymakers realized that the informal channels employed until then were insufficient, especially when compared to the ideological influence of the Axis powers, and most crucially in the context of protecting U.S. interests in Latin America. This new "world of power diplomacy"[21] demanded a different approach to cultural policy. As a consequence, agencies were created with the aim of conducting and coordinating a "cultural offensive" which, before long, had assumed a strong anticommunist component. Since the beginning of the 1950s, the United States Information Agency (USIA) has been the central bureau in charge of U.S. cultural exchange and information programs.[22]

Furthermore, it became quite clear that "certain foreign policy objectives can be pursued by dealing directly with the people of the foreign countries, rather than with their governments."[23] But this strategy was at least as difficult as the one along "official" channels if the (formal or informal) ambassadors of U.S. culture met with negative prejudices. Anti-American feelings were not deeply rooted in the Austrian mind; they had only recently been indoctrinated by Nazi propaganda, but had often already consolidated into persistent stereotypes.[24] To be sure, actual contacts with Americans, usually GIs, sometimes worked toward eroding these prejudices, especially so among the younger generation of Austrians. On the other hand, these encounters also frequently corroborated the negative image when time and again Europeans experienced American soldiers as arrogant and uncultured. The persistence of these prejudices, particularly among the elites proved to be a major obstacle to pursuing American interests abroad, which is why it was pivotal to counter them and replace them with more positive and favorable images.

The spreading of a desirable and positive image of the United States is inseparable from the second objective of the U.S. cultural mission in occupied countries, namely dispelling the fascist, authoritarian, and antidemocratic patterns that the conquered regimes had implanted in the people. The reeducation and reorientation of the people in order to securely place them within the Western value system was believed to be best achieved by putting the American model in front of their eyes.

The U.S. Educational Mission

These efforts to reeducate the former citizens of the Nazi regime naturally also made use of the formal levels of institutionalized education, although this is not at all typical of the U.S. postwar cultural mission. Usually this large-scale project proceeded by way of the "fast" mass media and "Madison Avenue techniques" (that is, in the realm of popular culture), rather than the "slow" channels such as books, art, education, and scholarship.[25] Yet the inclusion of education in the planned exportation of American ideas and ideals perfectly served the twofold objective of the overall cultural mission. First, it would help enhance the perceptions about the United States by conveying a more favorable picture than the traditional one, and this to recipients who were at a rather impressionable stage in their lives so that the effects would be comparatively long-term. Furthermore, academics, scholars, and teachers count among the opinion leaders of a nation, which is why a positive U.S. image in their eyes could be hoped to have a strongly resounding, if not multiplying, effect. Above all, stepping away from self-interest as the sole guiding motive, the U.S. influence would help liberalize a system of education that seemed no longer up-to-date in its emphasis on idealism and subjectivity, a focus that completely disregarded the rationalistic and empiricist turn that state-of-the-art pedagogy had taken.[26]

On the primary and secondary levels of education, U.S. agencies wanted to achieve an improvement and strengthening of English language teaching as well as of U.S. related topics as an integral part of the curriculum. Through the exchange program "American Field Service" (AFS) that was initiated in 1950/51, high school students were given the opportunity to experience the United States, with the organizers trusting in the potential and durable snowball effect of first-hand impressions. What Günter Bischof says about Fulbrighters must certainly be true about a lot of AFS participants as well, "Not only were these young Austrians internationalized in their outlook but they tended to return from the United States with a positive image of the country."[27]

The attention given to universities in these reorientation/reeducation efforts was, to a large extent, due to the fact that secondary school teachers were educated at universities. What they heard at university comprised a big part of what they themselves would be teaching. As can be seen from the study by Grandner and Bader-Zaar, before 1955, American culture and civilization were not at all a significant part of the teaching done at Austrian universities, so it is no surprise that teachers who obtained their accreditation during this time often simply did not have the knowledge to include U.S. related topics in their own teaching units. Distinctive experts in American Studies were rare; the fact that the first explicitly *Americanist* dissertation in Innsbruck was completed in 1948[28] may suffice as evidence. The situation was equally bleak in terms of resources for research and study. Primary and secondary sources on American literature and culture were hardly available. For example, even as late as 1949, the English library at the University of Innsbruck did not have the collected works of such pivotal authors as Walt Whitman, Ralph Waldo Emerson, or Edgar Allan Poe.[29] In all these respects, the U.S. agencies and initiatives that were concerned with fostering American Studies in Austria in the postwar period provided considerable relief.

U.S. Agencies and Initiatives Involved in the Cultural Mission

Information Services Branch (ISB)

The Information Services Branch (ISB) was in charge of organizing the multiple U.S. efforts to reeducate Austrians of all ages and social levels. The thirteen sections of the ISB covered "Press Scrutiny," "Theater and Music," "Films" and other mass media, "Youth Clubs," "Exchange of Persons" (including the newly established visitor and exchange programs), and the "Education Division" which was responsible for the de-Nazification and reformation of institutionalized education on all levels. The section that was most relevant for the initial foundation of American Studies in Austria is "Graphic Display," which was responsible for the United States Information Centers (USICs), also called "*Amerika-Häuser.*" Between 1945 and 1955, USICs were set up in twelve Austrian cities; the branch in Innsbruck was opened in 1949. At first, the center was located in the former "*Café München*" on Erlerstraße. In 1953, it was moved to the first floor of the building at Anichstraße 2.[30] The goals of the *Amerika-Häuser* were in line with the general objective of reeducating Austrians along the lines of Western ideals: They aimed at "projecting democratic ideals and the American way of life."[31] In order to achieve this, the information centers engaged in various activities. Primarily, they served as libraries, and soon they became even more popular than Austrian libraries. One reason for this popularity was that an *Amerika-Haus* charged no fees for the borrowing of books. Their holdings also comprised scholarly journals, which is why they came to play an important role in bringing Austrian scholars and scientists into contact with the state-of-the-art scholarship in the United States. Apart from their library function, the USIC locations served as reading rooms, concert halls, galleries, movie theaters, lecture halls, or simply a warm place where people could be comfortable for a little while. The opportunities and activities offered by the USICs, among them a variety of courses, met with tremendous interest. In the year 1950, more than 1.9 million Austrians visited the *Amerika-Häuser*; in only nine months of the same year, 254,332 people stopped by the branch in Innsbruck.[32]

In 1956, the *Amerika-Haus* on Anichstraße closed down for financial reasons and was taken over by the Austro-American Society.[33] The society also received fiction titles from USIC book holdings, which by 1955 had expanded to 20,000 volumes.[34] But the well-stocked reference section, which consisted of 4,500 titles, was handed over to the University's new *Amerika-Institut*, and this collection literally became the foundation of that department.[35]

Austrian-American Educational Commission/Fulbright Commission

The Fulbright program goes back to an initiative by Senator J. William Fulbright, who had the idea to finance an exchange program from the sale of army surplus goods after World War II. He eventually initiated a bill "authorizing the use of credits established abroad for the promotion of international good will through the exchange of students in the fields of education, culture, and science."[36] The initial exchange agreement with Austria was signed on 6 June 1950 in Washington, D.C. Until 1963, the Fulbright program was solely funded by the Americans; the organizational work was done by the United States Educational Commission. An agreement in 1963 provided for the establishment of the bi-national Austrian-American Educational Commission (or "Fulbright Commission") consisting of five American and five Austrian members. Executive secretary of the Fulbright Commission from 1955 to 1983 was the Austrian professor Anton Porhansl, whose farsightedness as well as commitment tremendously furthered the cause of American Studies. The 1963 agreement also concluded that Austria would henceforth cover two-thirds of the program costs with revenues from the *ERP Fonds* which had been established from counterpart funds resulting from Marshall Plan aid.[37]

Senator Fulbright's idea made possible a large-scale exchange of students, professors, researchers, and teachers and facilitated "bringing the wartorn countries back into the mainstream of international educational and scientific life."[38] The presence of Fulbright guest professors at Austrian universities since 1951 was vital in making up for the lack of true experts in the field of American Studies. Even though these professors usually only stayed for one year (which caused a certain amount of discontinuity, on the one hand, as well as broad variety, on the other) and were not allowed to supervise theses, for example (which, if they could have done so, might have resulted in more students specializing in American Studies), they contributed tremendously to the institutionalization process. The content as well as didactic style of their lectures and seminars attracted and impressed many students. Some critics saw them merely as a part of U.S. propaganda during the Cold War, a view that Heller vehemently opposes, "They surely were messengers of the best the American way of life could offer, but on the other hand they never hesitated to point out its negative sides as well."[39] Often the Fulbright professors helped to integrate Austrian scholars into an international network. In other instances, they developed closer ties to Austria: Tyrus Hillway, for example, who was appointed to the first chair in American Studies at the University of Salzburg in 1974, had been a Fulbright visiting lecturer in 1970/71. Certainly, the Fulbright exchange was truly inspirational the other way round as well, when Austrians received the opportunity to study or to do research at American institutions.

Furthermore, the Fulbright Commission played an indispensable role in consolidating American Studies from a financial point of view. Their funding helped the departments to considerably increase their book holdings which often were very poor, whether due to lack of money for purchases or lack of interest in or knowledge of American Studies as an academic subject. Yet serious scholarly work in all the humanities is virtually impossible without the standard canon titles in a research field. Therefore, the building of comprehensive, well-stocked libraries was a high priority in the establishment of American Studies at Austrian universities and was acknowledged as such by the authorities involved. For example, until 1976, the Fulbright Commission granted the American Studies department in Innsbruck an annual sum of money (in the mid-1970s, 40,000 Austrian *Schilling*) for book purchases. Taking into consideration all these various forms of support, Wagnleitner conclusively states that it is "certainly no exaggerated claim that only [the Fulbright program] created the prerequisites for modern American Studies."[40]

The ERP Counterpart Funds

When the ERP counterpart funds (that is, the *Schilling* funds that had accumulated from the sale of U.S. sponsored goods on the Austrian market[41]) were turned over to the Austrian government in 1962, the accompanying regulation (BGBl. no. 206/1962) between the Austrian republic and the U.S. government stated that a certain amount of this money (up to 7.5 million *Schilling*) was to be earmarked for a five-year program to facilitate American Studies on the university level. It was decided that three chairs in American Studies (or with the alternative designations *Amerikanische Sprache und Literatur* or *Amerikakunde*) should be established in Vienna, Graz, and Innsbruck.[42] The Austrian-American Educational Commission (Fulbright Commission), which was in charge of administrating the counterpart funds, would cover the expenses for the chair, an assistant's post, and book orders for five years.[43] After these five years, the Austrian federal government would be responsible for maintaining the chair. One important concern of the Austrian educational officials in this preparatory phase was that the universities not concede the right to nominate the candidates, which is why it had to be ensured that these chairs were systematized within the federal financial act (*Bundesfinanzgesetz*).

There was a big question mark as to potential candidates for the chairs that were to be established. The U.S. side suggested nominating American professors, and members of the Innsbruck Faculty of Philosophy readily admitted that there were no native assistant professors qualified for this position at that point in time. However, they emphasized that, if there was to be an American candidate, it would be highly desirable that he stayed for at least three years in order to be able to "train a true generation of students."[44] If American citizens were actually selected for professorship, there was the issue of what status they could be granted since foreigners could not be appointed *Ordinarius*.[45] Therefore, the two most likely designations for U.S. citizens on an Austrian chair seemed to be honorary professor or guest professor.

In Vienna in 1950/51, the respective department was renamed *Seminar für englische und amerikanische Literatur und Sprache*,[46] thereby clearly showing that the American Studies aspect was supposed to play an important role in their research and teaching. In March 1962, there were plans to name the field in which the ERP-funded chair would be established "*Studien über Amerika*," or "*Wirtschafts- und Gesellschaftskunde der USA*." The same document states that the holder of the American Studies chair in Vienna should be required to be able to give lectures in German.[47] However, in spite of all these favorable signs, the Minister of Education writes in a letter from 9 April 1970 that the Viennese Faculty of Philosophy "from the start renounced the establishment of a chair and rather applied for L1 [that is, lecturer] positions for the Department of Translation."[48]

Disregarding the fact that the chairs in Graz and Innsbruck were still or again vacant in 1970, the *Hochschule für Welthandel* (academy of international trade) wished to establish an *Amerika-Institut* as well. This led to a discussion about the legal possibility of such an endeavor. The counterpart regulation preceding the establishment of American Studies chairs had had to pass parliament. For that reason, the clear mission of the ERP funds could not be disregarded. One restriction in the agreement clearly stated that these chairs were to be set up only at "universities," not at "*Hochschulen*," so technically the *Hochschule für Welthandel* did not qualify.

In Graz, the firm establishment of American Studies courses was initiated by Professor Franz Karl Stanzel.[49] In 1962, Stanzel was appointed to the chair in *Anglistik*. Upon accepting his appointment, he was assured two more chairs, and apparently it was thanks to his initiative that, with U.S. help, an independent American Studies department was established in 1965.[50] In Salzburg a chair in American Studies was finally established in 1974, and arguably it was "founded on the basis that had been laid by American Fulbrighters since 1967."[51] This is most obvious in the fact that the first professor of American Studies in Salzburg, Tyrus Hillway, was a former Fulbright professor.

Networking

One general form of support that scholars of American culture and civilization received from U.S. agencies were various ways of facilitating contacts with U.S. scholars. In October 1975, for example, the *Institut für Amerikanistik* in Innsbruck received an offer from the U.S. Embassy in Vienna that they would like to forward the papers from a recent meeting of the Modern Language Association (MLA), which was and remains probably the most significant professional association in the field of American and English Studies. These papers were circulated by the U.S. Information Agency in Washington, D.C. "with a view that they might stimulate direct dialogue between the papers and the foreign scholars receiving them."[52]

The Cultural Affairs Office (CAO) of the Embassy in Vienna was in regular contact with and consistently supported the consolidation and intensification of American Studies by offering lecturers, funding, contacts, and all sorts of valuable information.[53] The CAO played a particular role in the founding of the most important network for Americanists in Austria. In April 1973, Cultural Attaché Norris D. Garnett announced that, from 9 to 11 November of the same year, a national American Studies conference would take place at Schloss Leopoldskron in Salzburg.[54] One of the explicit aims of this conference was to discuss ways of linking Austria with the European Association of American Studies (EAAS). The EAAS had been founded in 1953, also at Leopoldskron,[55] and was to hold its 1974 conference in Vienna. This would be a perfect opportunity for Austrian American Studies research to reach out in order to engage in an exchange with European (and, eventually, American) scholars working in the same field. This national conference announced by Garnett actually predated the origin of a national American Studies association, for the Austrian Association for American Studies (AAAS) was founded one year later, in 1974. Its main purposes include fostering the institutionalization of American Studies at universities, supporting American Studies research, increasing the exchange of ideas, and establishing international contacts. The first general meeting took place—not surprisingly—at Schloss Leopoldskron, and the AAAS continued to hold its annual conferences there for the next fifteen years. After 1989, the conference took place in the city of the university that presided over the association during the respective year. The chairmanship annually rotates between Salzburg, Vienna, Graz, Klagenfurt, and Innsbruck. The Fulbright Commission in the person of its long-time executive secretary Professor Porhansl was considerably involved in the evolution of the AAAS since it sponsored the meetings during its consolidating period and provided consistent financial backing.

American Studies at the University of Innsbruck

Foundations

The original incentive for the establishment of the *Amerika-Institut* in Innsbruck was to ensure that the contact, the "*lebendige Draht zur amerikanischen Wissenschaft*," on the university level would be maintained, thereby continuing the networking function of the *Amerika-Haus*. The Innsbruck side (expressly Rector Arnold Herdlitczka and Vice-Rector Richard Strohal) as well as U.S. agencies in Vienna supported this plan. As already mentioned, the reference section of the former USIC in Innsbruck formed the basis of the newly established *Amerika-Institut*. Within the first few months, 850 fiction titles from the holdings of the U.S. Embassy in Vienna were added to this stock. With the financial help of the Embassy's Cultural Affairs Office, the book acquisitions continued for a while, usually by way of book lists that were sent to Vienna.[56] Apart from the book holdings, an objective of at least equal importance was the maintenance of journal subscriptions, which amounted to up to 120 titles. The Ministry of Education decreed that the department was to provide specialist literature and teaching material for the disciplines of medicine, the social sciences, political science, social psychology, physics, and chemistry.[57] For these disciplines, it was particularly important to have access to up-to-date contributions in scholarly journals.

The previous ministry decree indicates that, at first, the department was not assigned to a single faculty, but designed as a supra-faculty institution. This structure was meant to ensure that all interests were considered and provided for. Accordingly, the department was headed by a board of four professors from different faculties. The board's first chairman and, thus, director of the department was Karl Brunner, the head of the English department. In 1957, the medievalist Karl Pivec succeeded the retired Brunner. Although he did not seem to have been concerned with the United States up to that point, Professor Pivec served very ably in this position. He soon received an appointment as the Innsbruck representative to the Fulbright Commission board. In 1966, Professor Pivec initiated the process of integrating the *Amerika-Institut* into the Faculty of Philosophy.[58]

The *Amerika-Institut* was formally opened on 20 February 1956, on which occasion it was handed over to the University of Innsbruck by the

U.S. Embassy.[59] Its very beginnings are also spatially connected to the former *Amerika-Haus* because during the first years it was located in the same rooms. It was only in 1960/61 that the department moved to the university building. There was yet another continuation related to the former USICs. The new departmental rooms were equipped with furniture that became available after the *Amerika-Häuser* were closed after 1955 (with the exception of the center in Vienna). Technically and legally, the department was not a gift but a long-term loan, which is why, on its ten-year anniversary in 1966, Professor Pivec could write that it was still owned by the Cultural Affairs Office of the U.S. Embassy.[60]

The Functions of the Amerika-Institut

One crucial function of the department was to enable and, hopefully, to intensify contacts with the academic world in the United States. Apart from the library, this was mainly achieved through lecture courses by American professors that came through the Fulbright program. Out of a total of five annual Fulbright positions in Austria, before 1961, the Fulbright Commission assigned two American Studies professorships (one in the field of language and literature, one in history) to the department in Innsbruck. This was a huge advantage due to these professors' expertise, as well as in regard to the variety of new topics and approaches that were introduced to the students. Yet the problem of discontinuity hindered the department since the visiting professors usually only stayed for one academic year. Furthermore, they did not have the authority to supervise dissertations or to hold doctoral exams.[61] The lack of a "local" professor in American Studies was a serious disadvantage that was finally remedied after the ERP counterpart regulation had been signed by both the United States and Austria.

The department was officially in charge of the Innsbruck Fulbright program, a responsibility which definitely heightened its visibility, for the Fulbright program was rapidly growing in scope as well as popularity. As a result of that function, the *Amerika-Institut* attempted to provide a connection between American and Austrian Fulbrighters in Tyrol. Moreover, according to Professor Pivec, the department felt responsible for American students attending the University of Innsbruck—a gesture that was extended more or less in return for the material support received from U.S. authorities.[62] Apart from that, the department was interested in and aimed at initiating other "Overseas Programs."[63] Hand in hand with that went the advising of students who were interested in studying abroad. A very new opportunity for doing so was the "Notre

Dame Sophomore Year" in cooperation with Notre Dame University in Indiana, which has been in effect since the winter semester of 1964/65.[64]

Filling the Chair in American Studies

After the ERP funds had been handed over to Austria, the respective universities did preliminary work on the details of the future American Studies chairs. The position of the University of Innsbruck was formulated by the dean of the Faculty of Philosophy after consulting Harro H. Kühnelt, professor in the English Studies Department.[65] From the very beginning, it was pointed out (very likely upon Professor Kühnelt's insistence) that the American Studies chair should not affect the petition that had been submitted for a second English Studies chair, "*Englische Philologie II*." Not surprisingly, the intensification of American Studies should not and did not come at the expense of the traditional "mother discipline," English Studies.

An important point of debate revolved around the exact naming of this chair. The faculty suggested the designation "*Amerikakunde unter besonderer Berücksichtigung der Sprache und Literatur der Vereinigten Staaten*."[66] According to Professor Pivec, this would have been completely in line with "the clear research focus on American Studies, which the Amerika-Institut received upon my suggestion by the unanimous decision of the board in the meeting of 15 November 1957"[67]—definitely another proof of the far-sightedness and capability that Pivec exhibited as director of the *Amerika-Institut*. As might have been expected, his wish not to restrict the young institution and the accompanying chair to the boundaries of the "common" European university disciplines, but to introduce the rather modern interdisciplinary American Studies approach (in the sense of *Amerikakunde*) was not too well received by the *Anglistik* department. This competition has already been discussed above; Pivec described the conflict as follows: "scholars rarely like to give away a province."[68] When outlining the department's "mission statement" in 1966, Pivec emphasized once more that the discipline should not be limited to literary studies, but should offer a "comprehensive view on cultural-historical phenomena," a synthesis of various disciplines, and here again we have a vision of American Studies in the most contemporary sense of the term.[69]

Yet when the dean of the Faculty of Philosophy formulated his letter to the Ministry of Education in 1962, he expressed being in favor of leaving the issue of the designation of the chair open until definitive negotiations were taken up. The name would then be chosen in accordance with the research focus of the future appointee (this was apparently common at other universities in the German-speaking area as well).

But there was a clear emphasis on the fact that until then no *venia docendi* had been extended in Austria solely for the fields of *Amerikanistik* or *Amerikakunde.* Therefore, it was important to avoid this designation due to its inherent danger of superficiality, which might even result in accusations of pro-American propaganda. This remark was supported by a list of several comparable institutions in Germany in order to prove that there were indeed no separate American Studies without a link to English Studies.[70] Even at the University of Minnesota, the "birthplace" of American Studies, the professor in question was a "professor of English," and not American Studies. This led up to the following demand, "In particular, it should be demanded that the discipline will be strongly anchored within the philologies, especially within English Studies," a statement which very likely reflects Professor Kühnelt's involvement in the drafting. Apparently it was Kühnelt who objected to "*Amerikakunde*" as being "much too vague and unphilological."[71]

In July 1962, the shortlist of the candidates selected for the American Studies chair was passed on to the Ministry of Education. The list presented the following order: 1. ao. Prof. Dr. Bernhard Fabian (Univ. Münster), 2. Prof. Dr. John Hinz MA (New York City College), 3. Doz. Dr. Ulrich Suerbaum (Univ. Münster).[72] The statements by the committee as to who would be selected, and why, and who would not be considered for the shortlist are very enlightening in regard to university policies of the time. For example, Fabian's reviewer, Professor Edgar Mertner, who was department head at the University of Münster, added the following comment:

> make sure that an appointment will happen within this year; otherwise your list might no longer be realizable. There is a large number of vacant chairs, and their filling causes considerable difficulties. [. . .] Also, don't forget that very soon appointments will be made to chairs at newly founded universities.[73]

In the light of these considerations and looking at how long the selection and appointment procedure eventually took, it is not really surprising that the first-ranked candidate rejected the call to Innsbruck. About the candidate on the third place, Suerbaum, the commission remarked that so far he had produced no research on American literature, "yet emphasized that he would very much like to . . . deal with American literature."[74] The number of explicitly qualified people, that is, those with first-hand experience in American Studies, must have been very small if such a declaration of intent was enough to be ranked third for a position of this kind.[75] Two other applicants (professors Virgil Heltzel and Karl Hammerle) had the same kind of "handicap," namely not having done anything in the field of American Studies until then. Yet what differentiated them from Suerbaum was that, apparently, they were too old to adapt to something so new so that most definitely "activities in the fields of American language or literature are not to be expected from both gentlemen."[76]

As was already mentioned, Professor Fabian rejected the call to Innsbruck in February 1962. He had also been accepted in Münster and Mainz, and the Ministry of Education was apparently very slow in making their offer during the negotiations. It was at this point that the dean of the Innsbruck Faculty of Philosophy stated in a letter to the Ministry in Vienna that he had heard rumors about Hinz's (the second-ranked candidate) high demands, and that Suerbaum had been appointed to a chair in Cologne.[77] Yet, due to the latter surmise, the first rumor was disregarded, and negotiations with John Hinz ensued.

John Hinz had spent the academic year 1961/62 as Fulbright Professor at the University of Graz. He had been recommended by Professor Stanzel, the English Studies department head in Graz. An interesting footnote is the fact that in this statement it was explicitly mentioned that Hinz was able to give lectures in German.[78] The prediction that the negotiations with Hinz would be very complicated became a reality. In fact, it must have been so bad that Professor Karl Ilg, then dean of the Faculty of Philosophy, asked the Ministry of Education for permission to prepare a new shortlist, especially since "as against the time around 1963, today there are junior Austrian scholars available."[79]

Or maybe Ilg was merely concerned with keeping the damage to a minimum because he sensed trouble. In any case, Hinz was formally appointed to the chair in American Studies in Innsbruck by Minister of Education Drimmel in November 1965. He was categorized in salary bracket five, which led to a lengthy correspondence. Hinz was not at all satisfied with the salary he was assigned. Moreover, he wanted to be compensated for the cost of his move. Both wishes were not granted; nevertheless, Professor Kühnelt wrote a number of letters on behalf of Hinz, supporting his cause.

Yet, in spite of all these difficulties, Hinz apparently took up teaching in the summer semester of 1966. It is certainly safe to say that there was hardly any satisfaction with the way he did his job. Even worse, after the summer break in 1967, he did not return to fulfill his teaching obligations. When his salary for October 1967 had already been transferred but could not be retrieved again, his checking account was frozen by the university. Letters to Hinz were not answered; there were rumors that his father had died. On 26 November, a telegram from Hinz arrived: "Hinz lives though buried in problems letters follow."[80] One month later, the university teachers' association took up disciplinary proceedings against Hinz on the grounds that he failed to fulfill his official duties.[81]

After that, the official sources remain silent about John Hinz. It seems that the chair remained vacant for a longer period after that. It was still not filled in April 1970 (neither was the American Studies chair in Graz, apparently). However, the discipline had to be taught at both universities, so it became a kind of habit that Fulbright professors informally and temporarily filled the vacant American Studies chairs in Innsbruck and Graz. One consequence of this arrangement was that other universities, or departments other than those related to the literature/language/history complex, hardly ever got Fulbright professors assigned to them, while at the same time the American Studies teaching activities in Innsbruck and Graz were paid from the Fulbright endowment and not from the money originally earmarked for this purpose. Therefore, speedy appointments at both universities were urgently needed from the perspective of the Fulbright Commission.

In July 1968, Professor Kühnelt had become substitute American Studies chair and acting director of the *Amerika-Institut.*[82] The two departments plus the Department of Translation, of which Kühnelt was also in charge, became interlinked in a rather complicated way as far as personnel was concerned. One assistantship was temporarily delegated to the Department of Translation. This set-up definitely made American Studies a mere appendix to English Studies and created an accumulation of resources that was unlikely to be given up voluntarily. In the academic years of 1969/70 and 1970/71, Professor William R. Manierre from Rutgers University was Fulbright professor of American Literature at the *Amerika-Institut*, and after these two years he was appointed to the vacant chair. However, he eventually, much to the regret of the American Studies faculty, declined the offer due to lack of support from Professor Kühnelt, with whose department he would have had to cooperate.[83]

When Professor Brigitte Scheer, at that point assistant professor at the Department of English Language and Literature in Salzburg, was eventually appointed to the American Studies chair in February 1974, the clear separation between her own and the English Department was one of her major concerns. She wanted to have the faculty members work in only one department instead of having divided loyalties. According to Tyrus Hillway, Professor Scheer was "[t]he first Austrian fully trained for a position in American Studies."[84] With her appointment, the American Studies chair in Innsbruck was eventually permanently filled, after having been virtually vacant for twelve years after its establishment in 1962. Shortly after this appointment, in June 1974, the designation of the department was changed from *Amerika-Institut* to *Institut für*

Amerikanistik. It was argued that this was more in line with the common practice at German-speaking universities. Furthermore, the new name emphasized the academic character of the department.[85] Together with Professor Scheer's insistence on having the faculty members working at only one department, this may be interpreted as an attempt on her part to give the institution a clear image and structure and, thus, a heightened visibility. One of the most urgent concerns on the part of the department was to have adequate premises. The location at Fischnalerstraße 4 became much too small, especially since Professor Scheer was able to enlarge the faculty as a result of her negotiations with the Ministry previous to her appointment. Yet these problems were resolved only in 1981/82 when the department eventually moved to the new building at Innrain 52.

In a personal interview, Professor Scheer commented that after few inevitable complications in her first years in Innsbruck, she found that things settled down and the department got established. Especially after she had been elected dean of the humanities in 1976, she felt that she as well as her department had finally gained their due respect and no longer needed to justify their very existence. Asked about concrete developments that in her opinion had jeopardized her department, she could not think of any serious ones up to that point in 1999/2000 when, without previous notice, the Faculty of the Humanities wanted to fuse the American Studies Department with the English Department. In view of the departmental proportions, this might well have meant a serious reduction of American Studies as they had been practiced until then at the University of Innsbruck. However, the merger was avoided, and the department maintained its independence.[86] This occurrence is strikingly echoed in a letter to the Ministry of Education from April 1977, in which Professors Scheer and Jürgen Peper, the American Studies department head in Graz, listed "arguments and counterarguments concerning the continued existence of the American Studies departments in Graz and Innsbruck."[87] The points they mentioned, for example the tendency toward the reabsorption of American Studies professorships by English Studies as well as the risk of becoming dependent on American Studies abroad, are still perfectly valid today and were certainly enumerated in 1999/2000 as well. However, one of the most important arguments brought forth on the latter occasion was that the department's predecessor, the *Amerika-Institut*, had been founded jointly by Austria and the United States and was based on a mutual agreement that could not be cancelled unilaterally by technically closing down the department. Thus, though unwittingly, the American participation in institutionalizing American Studies in Austria has literally saved the department in Innsbruck as the earliest visible sign of those efforts.

Conclusion

The previous discussion showed how the Austrian as well as the American side were involved in the process of institutionalizing American Studies in Austria after World War II, what their aims and concerns were, and how they managed to realize them. By means of taking a closer look at the first two decades of the development of the American Studies department at the University of Innsbruck, many of the initially outlined considerations were illustrated during a phase of initiation and consolidation.

The resulting picture is, at least for the Innsbruck model, a successful one. The study of American culture and civilization was conducted and intensified through those and many following years up to the present time, even though one can never be sure how new players in the academic game will change the rules and, therefore, potentially upset or even destroy well-established structures and patterns. These concerns have gained new relevance in view of contemporary academic developments in Austria, when departmental libraries are being closed, chairs remain vacant for years due to lack of resources, future fillings are more than uncertain, and the reabsorption of American Studies by English departments becomes once again a real possibility. Currently, a "systematic knowledge and understanding" of the United States seems to have low priority, and the efforts of the founding generation of American Studies are highly threatened with destruction.

One question that is certainly relevant in regard to the institutionalization of American Studies in all of Europe is whether the promotional enthusiasm on the American part was only another, well-disguised form of cultural imperialism that, in the words of Marcus Cunliffe, "was drumming home the ideology of the frontier thesis and demanding room in the curriculum for a purportedly brilliant national culture."[88] Yet, at least the Innsbruck model does not reveal any form of cultural imperialism related to the way in which the study of America became institutionalized. In their post-World War II cultural mission in Austria, the United States may have taken recourse to propagandistic means more often than not; they may have cleansed the book shelves of the *Amerika-Häuser* of un-American books during the McCarthy craze, and with unnecessary zeal; and they may have intervened to an almost unbelievable degree with the Salzburg Seminar.[89] Thus Wagnleitner is certainly right in his suggestion that the rise of organized American Studies in Austria was to a certain degree and among other things "a continuation of the Cold War by different means."[90] Yet at least in Innsbruck, the relevant authorities seem to have supported the process of institutionalization as much as possible, but interfered in the methods and products of scholarly activity as little as necessary.

According to the development plan proposed by the Rector of the University of Innsbruck in July 2005, the American Studies Department will be merged with the English Studies Department. Therefore it seems very unlikely that the department will go into its 50th year of existence as an independent institution.

Notes

1. Sigmund Skard, *The American Myth and the European Mind: American Studies in Europe 1776-1960* (Philadelphia: Univ. of Pennsylvania P, 1961), 7.

2. Official U.S. Department of State directive in September 1950, cf. Reinhold Wagnleitner, *Coca-Colonisation und Kalter Krieg: Die Kulturmission der USA in Österreich nach dem Zweiten Weltkrieg* (Vienna: Verlag für Gesellschaftskritik, 1991), 94.

3. Skard, *The American Myth*, 8. Skard also lists primary and secondary schools as the other important loci of American Studies, which in spite of its granted significance cannot be dealt with here in detail. Factors to be taken into consideration for such an analysis would be the design of school curricula as well as textbooks in regard to their inclusion of U.S. specific topics, or the existence of exchange programs for the secondary level. Such an investigation would be partly overlapping with the area of higher education, e.g., as far as the training of secondary school teachers is concerned. For further remarks on the U.S. influence on primary and secondary schooling, see, e.g., Reinhold Wagnleitner, *Coca-Colonisation und Kalter Krieg: die Kulturmission der USA in Österreich nach dem Zweiten Weltkrieg* (Wien: Verlag für Gesellschaftskritik, 1991), Chapter Six.

4. Skard, *The American Myth*, 18.

5. Margarete Grandner and Birgitta Bader-Zaar, "Lehre und Forschung über Nordamerika an Österreichs Universitäten vom Beginn des 19. Jahrhunderts bis 1955," in *Nordamerikastudien: Historische und literaturwissenschaftliche Forschungen aus österreichischen Universitäten zu den Vereinigten Staaten und Kanada*, ed. Thomas Fröschl, Margarete Grandner, and Birgitta Bader-Zaar (Vienna: Verlag für Geschichte und Politik, 2000), 108-73, here 171.

6. For example, the lecture General History from the Separation of the English Colonies in North America to the July Revolution (*Allgemeine Geschichte vom Abfall der englischen Colonien in Nordamerika bis zur Juli Revolution*) by Professor Karl Johann Vietz at the University of Prague in 1857 (when Prague still belonged to the Habsburg Empire); Grandner and Bader-Zaar, "Lehre und Forschung," 113.

7. For a survey of anti-American images in Austria cf. Günter Bischof, "Two Sides of the Medal: The Americanization of Austria and Austrian Anti-Americanism," in *American Culture in Europe: Americanization and Anti-Americanism since 1945*, ed. Alexander Stephan (New York: Berghahn, 2005) [forthcoming].

8. As a U.S. official noted in a 1946 memorandum, "there exists a decided bias toward British accent and CULTURE [sic] among Austrian English teachers," and certainly not teachers alone; qtd. in Wagnleitner, *Coca-Colonisation*, 198. For a similar judgment as to the situation in German cf. Philipp Gassert, "Between Political Reconnaisance [sic] Work and Democratizing Science: American Studies in Germany 1917–1953," *Bulletin of the German Historical Institute* [Washington D.C.] 32 (2003) <http://www.ghi-dc.org/bulletinS03/32.30-47.pdf> (accessed 19 Mar. 2004), 33-50, here 41.

9. Grandner and Bader-Zaar, "Forschung und Lehre," 123.

10. Hans Galinsky, "American Studies in Germany: Their Growth, Variety and Prospects," *American Studies: An International Newsletter* 13.2 (1974): 3-9, here 4. Furthermore, Galinsky suggests an interesting analogy: just as it took Germany two "shocks of recognition" in the eighteenth century (the Treaty of Utrecht 1713 and the Treaty of Paris 1763) before it came to fully realize the implications of Britain's political ascendancy, it needed two reminders in the twentieth century (1918 and 1945) before it learned the "American lesson" and became truly aware of the U.S. role and impact (ibid., 3-4).

11. Prof. Brigitte Scheer to Cultural Attaché Peter H. Jacoby, October 1976, Departmental Archive American Studies, University of Innsbruck [= DA], Box "Studien-Kommission, AAAS, -1976, A.A.E.C., Embassy."

12. "*den psychologischen Hindernissen der alten Königin, der Anglistik*"; Karl Pivec, "Das Amerika-Institut der Universität Innsbruck," in *Americana-Austriaca: Festschrift des Amerika-Instituts der Universität Innsbruck anläßlich seines zehnjährigen Bestehens*, ed. Klaus Lanzinger (Vienna: Braumüller, 1966), 1-16, here 12.

13. Galinsky, "American Studies," 5.

14. Cf. the respective comments on the situation in Innsbruck below.

15. Yet on the whole there is a gradual development toward comprehensive American Studies, cf. Roberta Maierhofer, "American Studies in Austria," in *Austria – USA, Austria – Canada* (Kooperationen: Higher Education), ed. Österreichischer Austauschdienst (Vienna: Österreichischer Austauschdienst, 2002), 39-40, here 39.

16. Studienkommission des Instituts für Englische Sprache und Literatur to Bundesministerium für Unterricht, 21 May 1976, DA, Box "BMfWF 1974-76."

17. Qtd. in Arno Heller, "Cultural Studies im Wandel: Zur Modellfunktion der American Studies," in *Grundlagen der Kulturwissenschaften*, ed. Elisabeth List and Erwin Fiala (Tübingen: Francke, 2003), 39-54, here 41.

18. Arno Heller, "American Studies in Europe," Innsbruck ca. 1977 (unpubl. lecture notes), 1.

19. On the origins of U.S. cultural policy cf. Frank A. Ninkovich, *The Diplomacy of Ideas: U.S. Foreign Policy and Cultural Relations, 1938-1950* (Cambridge: Cambridge Univ. P, 1981), and Emily S. Rosenberg, *Spreading the American Dream: American Economic and Cultural Expansion, 1890-1945* (New York: Hill and Wang, 1982).

20. Wagnleitner, *Coca-Colonisation*, 58.

21. Ninkovich, *Diplomacy of Ideas*, 23.

22. Rosenberg, *Spreading the American Dream*, 202-18; Wagnleitner, *Coca-Colonisation*, 62-80.

23. "Winning the Cold War: The U.S. Ideological Offensive," Congressional Committee on Foreign Affairs, 27 April 1964, qtd. in Wagnleitner, *Coca-Colonisation*, 76.

24. Thomas Albrich, "Fremde," *Historicum* 48 (1996): 22-28, here 25.

25. Ninkovich, *Diplomacy of Ideas*, 116-19, here 118.

26. Wagnleitner, *Coca-Colonisation*, 189.

27. Bischof, "Two Sides," n.p. (manuscript).

28. By Harro H. Kühnelt, the later professor of English Studies in Innsbruck as well as head of the same department; Grandner and Bader-Zaar, "Forschung und Lehre," 126.

29. Wagnleitner, *Coca-Colonisation*, 197.

30. "ERP-Fonds war 'Baustein' für den Tourismus in Tirol," *Innsbruck informiert* July 2000: 10; Wagnleitner, *Coca-Colonisation*, 161.

31. Qtd. in Wagnleitner, *Coca-Colonisation*, 160.

32. Ibid., 164-65.

33. "ERP-Fonds," 10. The Austro-American Society had been founded in 1950. It served as a meeting point for American citizens in Tyrol and additionally organized courses and lectures. According to departmental reports, there were a number of guest lectures hosted together with the American Studies department, which took place in the rooms of the Austro-American Society.

34. Wagnleitner, *Coca-Colonisation*, 164.

35. Klaus Lanzinger, "Tätigkeit des Amerika-Instituts der Universität Innsbruck 1956–1966," in *Americana-Austriaca: Festschrift des Amerika-Instituts der Universität Innsbruck anläßlich seines zehnjährigen Bestehens*, ed. Klaus Lanzinger (Vienna: Braumüller, 1966), 17-31, here 19.

36. Qtd. in Walter Grünzweig, "Seeing the World as Others See It: J. William Fulbright, International Exchange, and the Quest for Peace," in *Fulbright at Fifty: Austrian-American Educational Exchange 1950–2000*, ed. Lonnie Johnson, Karin Riegler, Austrian-American Educational Commission, 2000 <http://www.fulbright.at/fb/festschrift.pdf> (accessed 2 Apr. 2004), 4-13, here 8.

37. Lonnie R. Johnson, "Fulbright at Fifty: Austrian American Educational Exchange 1950-2000," in *Fulbright at Fifty: Austrian-American Educational Exchange 1950–2000*, ed. Lonnie Johnson, Karin Riegler, Austrian-American Educational Commission, 2000 <http://www.fulbright.at/fb/festschrift.pdf> (accessed 2 Apr. 2004), 14-18, here 15; Wagnleitner, *Coca-Colonisation*, 196.

38. Henry J. Kellermann, *Cultural Relations as an Instrument of U.S. Foreign Policy: The Educational Exchange Program between the United States and Germany, 1945-1954* (Washington, D.C.: U.S. Government Printing Office, 1978), 173.

39. Arno Heller, "I will never forget the lecture he gave on...," in *Fulbright at Fifty: Austrian-American Educational Exchange 1950–2000*, ed. Lonnie Johnson, Karin Riegler, Austrian-American Educational Commission, 2000 <http://www.fulbright.at/fb/festschrift.pdf> (accessed 2 Apr. 2004), 28-29, here 29.

40. "*sicherlich nicht übertrieben zu behaupten, daß [das Fulbright-Programm] überhaupt erst die Voraussetzungen für eine moderne Amerikanistik schuf*"; Wagnleitner, *Coca-Colonisation*, 197.

41. Hans Seidel, "Austria's Economic Policy and the Marshall Plan," in *The Marshall Plan in Austria, vol. 8, Contemporary Austria Studies*, ed. Günter Bischof, Anton Pelinka, and Dieter Stiefel (New Brunswick, NJ: Transaction, 2000), 247-89, here 262.

42. Bundesminister Sickinger (Bundesministerium für Unterricht) to the Dekanat der Phil. Fakultät der Univ. Innsbruck, Zl. 120.012-VII/3/69, 9 April 1970, University Archive Innsbruck, files of the Faculty of Philosophy, "Amerika-Institut 1956-74" [= UA].

43. Dekan Werner Heissel (Phil. Fakultät der Univ. Innsbruck) to Bundesministerium für Unterricht, Zl. 881/62, 14 March 1962, UA.

44. "*eine wirkliche Schülergeneration heranzubilden*"; Dekan der Phil. Fakultät der Univ. Innsbruck to Bundesministerium für Unterricht, Zl. 213/61, 11 May 1961, UA.

45. Bundesminister Drimmel (Bundesministerium für Unterricht) to Dekanat der Phil. Fakultät der Univ. Wien, Zl. 106.095-1/61, 15 February 1962, UA.

46. Grandner and Bader-Zaar, "Forschung und Lehre," 130.

47. Dekan der Phil. Fakultät der Univ. Wien to Werner Heissel (Dekan der Phil. Fakultät der Univ. Innsbruck), Zl. 113/4 aus 1960/61, 12 April 1962, UA.

48. "*von vorneherein auf die Errichtung einer Lehrkanzel verzichtete und vielmehr Ll Posten am Institut für Dolmetscherausbildung beantragte*"; Bundesminister Sickinger (Bundesministerium für Unterricht) to the Dekanat der Phil. Fakultät der Univ. Innsbruck, Zl. 120.012-VII/3/69, 9 April 1970, UA.

49. Grandner and Bader-Zaar, "Forschung und Lehre," 135.

50. Alwin Fill and Alois Kernbauer, *100 Jahre Anglistik an der Universität Graz* (Graz: Akademische Druck- und Verlagsanstalt, 1993), 17.

51. The University of Salzburg as an institution was not restored until 1964; Reinhold Wagnleitner, "A Long Lasting Affair," in *Fulbright at Fifty: Austrian-American Educational Exchange 1950–2000*, ed. Lonnie Johnson, Karin Riegler, Austrian-American Educational Commission, 2000 <http://www.fulbright.at/fb/festschrift.pdf> (accessed 2 Apr. 2004), 33-35, here 33.

52. Cultural Attaché Norris D. Garnett/U.S. Embassy to Amerikanistik-Institut Innsbruck, 15 October 1975, DA, Box "Studien-Kommission, AAAS, -1976, A.A.E.C., Embassy."

53. Personal interview with Prof. Brigitte Scheer, 16 June 2004.

54. U.S. Embassy/Norris D. Garnett to Brigitte Scheer (Institut für Englische Sprache und Literatur, Salzburg), August 1973, DA, Box "Studien-Kommission, AAAS, -1976, A.A.E.C., Embassy."

55. Schloss Leopoldskron is also the birthplace of another important project in regard to American Studies in the whole of Europe, which by now has evolved to a globally oriented institution. The Salzburg Seminar in American Studies was founded in 1947 by Clemens Heller, an Austrian emigré and Harvard graduate who wanted to create a place of open intellectual discourse in spite of the surrounding destruction caused by World War II. For a more detailed account of the Salzburg Seminar, cf. Oliver Schmidt, "No Innocents Abroad: The Salzburg Impetus and American Studies in Europe," in *"Here, There and Everywhere": The Foreign Politics of American Popular Culture*, ed. Reinhold Wagnleitner and Elaine Tyler May (Hannover: Univ. Press of New England, 2000), 64-79.

56. Lanzinger, "Tätigkeit," 19-20.

57. Bundesminister Drimmel (Bundesministerium für Unterricht) to Rektorat der Univ. Innsbruck, Zl. 25.849/I-1/56, 16 January 1956, UA.

58. Franz Huter, "Karl Pivec (Nachruf)," *Mitteilungen des Instituts für Österreichische Geschichtsforschung* 83 (1975): 557-64, here 562.

59. Lanzinger, "Tätigkeit," 17.

60. Pivec, "Amerika-Institut," 10.

61. Dekan der Phil. Fakultät der Univ. Innsbruck to Bundesministerium für Unterricht, Zl. 213/61, 11 May 1961, UA.

62. Pivec, "Amerika-Institut," 2.

63. Ibid., 14.

64. Lanzinger, "Tätigkeit," 18, 30-31. The friendship agreement between the University of Innsbruck and the University of Notre Dame continues to this day.

65. Dekan Werner Heissel (Phil. Fakultät der Univ. Innsbruck) to Bundesministerium für Unterricht, Zl. 881/62, 14 March 1962, UA.

66. Dekan der Phil. Fakultät der Univ. Innsbruck to Bundesministerium für Unterricht, Zl. 213/61, 11 May 1961, UA.

67. "*der klaren Forschungsrichtung auf American Studies, die das Amerika-Institut auf meinen Vorschlag durch einstimmigen Beschluß des Vorstandes in der Sitzung am 15. November 1957 erhalten hatte*"; Pivec, "Amerika-Institut," 6.

68. "*Gelehrte geben selten eine Provinz gerne ab*"; ibid., 11.

69. "*Gesamtschau kulturgeschichtlicher Phänomene*"; ibid.

70. The decided orientation toward Germany becomes obvious time and again. The departmental archive, for example, contains numerous descriptions of the set-up of similar departments in Germany.

71. "*Zu fordern wäre also vor allem die feste Verankerung des Faches im Rahmen der Philologien, besonders in der Anglistik*"; "*viel zu vage und unphilologisch*"; Dekan der Phil. Fakultät der Univ. Innsbruck to Bundesministerium für Unterricht, Zl. 881/62, 14 March 1962, UA.

72. As well as the following quotations: Dekan der Phil. Fakultät der Univ. Innsbruck to Bundesministerium für Unterricht, Zl. 1221/62, 17 July 1962, UA.

73. "*sehen Sie zu, daß eine Berufung noch in diesem Jahr erfolgt; anderenfalls könnte es sein, daß Ihre Liste nicht mehr realisierbar ist. Die Zahl der vakanten Professuren ist groß, und ihre Besetzung macht erhebliche Schwierigkeiten.* [. . .] *Vergessen Sie auch nicht, daß demnächst schon Berufungen auf Lehrstühle an neugegründeten Universitäten ausgesprochen werden*"; ibid.

74. "*betonte aber, er würde sich sehr gerne . . . mit der amerikanischen Literatur beschäftigen*"; ibid.

75. Judging from a statement by Galinsky, the selection criteria for similar appointments in Germany were equally questionable: "Being an English professor of American nationality apparently qualified one for a full professorship of American literature in Germany"; Galinsky, "American Studies," 6.

76. "*mit einer Tätigkeit auf dem Gebiet der Sprache oder der Literatur der Vereinigten Staaten ist bei beiden Herren nicht zu rechnen*"; Dekan der Phil. Fakultät der Univ. Innsbruck to Bundesministerium für Unterricht, Zl. 1221/62, 17 July 1962, UA.

77. Dekan der Phil. Fakultät der Univ. Innsbruck to Bundesministerium für Unterricht, Zl. 55/63, 13 February 1963, UA.

78. As already mentioned, the University of Vienna stated as a requirement the knowledge of German for an American Studies professor.

79. "*gegenüber der Zeit um 1963 heute österreichische Nachwuchskräfte zur Verfügung stehen*"; Karl Ilg (Dekan der Phil. Fakultät der Univ. Innsbruck) to Bundesministerium für Unterricht, Zl. 321/65, 18 May 1965, UA.

80. Dekan der Phil. Fakultät der Univ. Innsbruck to Anton Porhansl (Austrian American Education Commission), Zl. 907/67, 8 January 1968, UA.

81. Bundesministerium für Unterricht to John Hinz, Zl. 46.242-I/4/1968, 8 February 1968, UA.

82. Bundesminister Piffl (Bundesministerium für Unterricht) to Dekanat der Phil. Fakultät der Univ. Innsbruck, Zl. 65.315-I74/68, 31 July 1968, UA.

83. Personal e-mail Arno Heller to author, 16 December 2004. Dr. Heller also emphasizes that Professor Manierre's encouragement was greatly responsible for his own decision to write a *Habilitation* (the first of this kind in Innsbruck) in American Studies.

84. Tyrus Hillway, "American Studies in Austria," in *American Studies Abroad*, ed. Robert H. Walker (Westport: Greenwood, 1975), 89-94, here 91.

85. Dekan Franz Fliri (Dekanat der Phil. Fakultät der Univ. Innsbruck) to Bundesministerium für Wissenschaft und Forschung, Zl. 656/74, 11 June 1974, UA.

86. Personal interview with Prof. Brigitte Scheer, 16 June 2004.

87. "*Argumente und Gegenargumente zum Weiterbestand der Institute für Amerikanistik in Graz und Innsbruck*"; Scheer and Peper to Bundesministerium für Wissenschaft und Forschung, April 1977, DA, Box "Studien-Kommission, AAAS, -1976, A.A.E.C., Embassy."

88. Qtd. in Wagnleitner, *Coca-Colonisation*, 204.

89. Wagnleitner, *Coca-Colonisation*, 169-72; Bischof, "Two Sides," n.p. (manuscript).

90. "*eine Fortsetzung des Kalten Krieges mit anderen Mitteln*"; Wagnleitner, *Coca-Colonisation*, 204.

ROUNDTABLE[1]

The Historiography and Memory of the Austrian Occupation (1945-1955)

The Allied Occupation of Austria in Recent International and Austrian Historiography

Günter Bischof

Fotocredit: APA/BARBARA/GINDL/ERICH LESSING
State Treaty Belvedere Balcony Scene 1955-2005
The public presentation of the Austrian State Treaty, just signed inside the Schloss by the four Foreign Ministers and Foreign Minister Figl, from the balcony of Castle Belevedere to a cheering crowd has become iconic in terms of Austrian memory. During State Treaty commemorations in 1965 and 1980, the "balcony" scene" was re-enacted by the visiting Foreign Ministers of the former occupation powers; it was re-enacted again before a much smaller crowd of Austrians on May 15, 2005, with only the Russian and French Foreign Ministers in attendance.

This short essay briefly assesses the historiography on the post-World War II quadripartite occupation of Austria. I first speculate why in recent analyses of historical case studies of the United States as an occupation power, as well as in U.S. "nation building" efforts, the successful American occupation regime in postwar Austria is entirely ignored. Secondly, I run through the cycles of scholarly preoccupation with the Austrian occupation and note that the highpoint came with the works of the Austrian "baby boomer" generation in the 1980s. Occupation studies have largely fallen by the wayside as a priority in recent Austrian contemporary history research.

The Neglect of the Postwar Austrian Occupation as a Historical Case Study in Comparative Occupation Research

When preparing for post-conflict operations in Iraq, the U.S. Army was scrambling for viable historical models of successful operations of U.S. military government in occupied territories. James Carafano asserts that the U.S. Army has a long "tradition of forgetting" when it comes "to dealing with battlefields after battle." In the "fog of peace" the U.S. military have always been reluctant occupiers and averse to thinking "deeply about the place of peace operations in military affairs," just as Carl von Clausewitz worried about the "fog of war," but failed to mention peace operations in his classic *On War*.[2]

But once the occupation of Iraq began to deteriorate into another quagmire like Vietnam, the comparative study of American occupations throughout history experienced a sudden renaissance. In the recent think tank and academic literature of comparative postwar American occupations and nation-building efforts, a strange thing has happened: the four-power post-World War II occupation of Austria has dropped out of sight. In the major Rand study by James Dobbins and associates, *America's Role in Nation-Building,* seven historical case studies are analyzed (Germany, Japan, and more recently Somalia, Haiti, Bosnia, Kosovo, and Afghanistan) from which to draw lessons for Iraq. The Austrian occupation is ignored.[3]

Similarly, in Minxin Pei's and Sara Kasper's Carnegie Endowment for International Peace study, *Lessons from the Past,* fifteen case studies are analyzed (Afghanistan, Haiti, Panama, Grenada, Cambodia, South Vietnam, Dominican Republic (1916-24, 1965-66), Japan, West Germany, Haiti, Nicaragua, Cuba (1906-09, 1917-22), and Panama). The postwar occupation(s) of Austria (along with Korea and Italy) are conspicuously absent.[4]

Niall Ferguson's ambitious *Colossus* features an appendix with a list of nineteen "Major American Occupations of Foreign Territory, 1893-

2003": Hawaii, Puerto Rico, Guam, The Philippines, American Samoa, Panama (Canal Zone), Virgin Islands, Dominican Republic, Haiti, West Germany, Japan, Northern Mariana Islands, Palau Micronesia, Marshall Islands, South Korea, South Vietnam, Afghanistan, and Iraq. In this odd list of American "major occupations," the postwar occupations of Japan, Korea, and West Germany are listed, but Austria is off Ferguson's radar. Presumably, the thirty-nine year American presence in Micronesia and the Marshall Islands (1957-1986) was "major" in terms of understanding U.S. occupation and state-building behavior, while the ten-year Austrian postwar occupation can safely be ignored.[5]

Moreover, in the extensive electronic debates by specialists in various Internet fora such as H-Diplo and History News Network (HNN), as well as high-brow journals such as *Foreign Affairs* and *Boston Review*, historical comparisons of American occupations experienced a renaissance.[6] Every possible analogy to the current American occupation of Iraq has been mined and analyzed, yet there's a curious absence of the Austrian occupation as a successful American state-building effort.

What might be the reasons for such benign neglect of the Austrian occupation by scholars and American think-tank experts in general and in recent literature on "nation-building" in particular? After all, was the quadripartite occupation of Austria—next to the postwar occupations of (West) Germany and Japan—not one of the few highly successful American nation-building efforts in the modern era? Austria's quadripartite occupation evidenced a complex interaction of four occupation powers within the larger East-West divide, but so did Germany's. The Austrian occupation has always been overshadowed by the German one, where more was at stake and for which scholars were more likely to receive generous research grants. The complexity of making sense of the ten-year four-power occupation of Austria cannot be the reason for ignoring it, but being second rank to Germany is. Considering Ferguson's list, was the American nation-building effort in Austria not more successful in reintegrating Austria into the stable democratic family of Western nations than those in the notoriously unstable Haiti and Panama, or in South Vietnam, where the Communists have ruled for thirty years? Has the American contribution to Austria's economic reconstruction through the Marshall Plan not shown more impressive results than similar efforts in Samoa and the Dominican Republic, especially when taking into account that Austria, considered economically non-viable after World War I and in dire straits after World War II, has been listed as the fifth wealthiest nation in the world in per capita income in a recent survey of the Organization for Economic Cooperation and Development? What, then, might be the reasons for the scholarly shunning of the Austrian occupation?

First, after the signing of the Austrian State Treaty in 1955, Austria ceased to be a "*Sorgenkind*" of the international community in the East-West conflict. The Austrian Treaty and the withdrawal of the occupation forces by the four powers (actually few Western troops were left by 1955), Austria took off as a *politically "stabilized"* (that is, democratized) and *economically reconstructed* society.[7] The ÖVP/SPÖ "grand coalition," so carefully monitored and nurtured by the Western occupation powers, survived for another decade after the end of the occupation, and the economy injected with an overabundance of European Recovery Program funds, produced "miracle" growth figures that matched and at times surpassed the German ones.[8] Maybe for the Rand and Carnegie Endowment "think tankers" Austria is too small, unimportant, and quaint to provide lessons for Iraq. When it comes to small country occupations, maybe the recent short-lived occupation in Grenada and the disastrous one in Somalia provide better lessons for Iraq than the successful Austrian one.

Second, Austrian neutrality was considered a paragon of probity during the Cold War and increasingly morphed into an oddity in the post-Cold War era. While most of Austria's neighbors are now safely ensconced in that North Atlantic Treaty Organization (NATO) and are part of the Western defense community, Austria has maintained its neutral status in a dramatically changing European and global security environment. While the conservative parties would like to move the country into NATO, the Socialists and Greens (regularly backed by up to 70 percent of the public) stubbornly resist Austrian NATO membership.[9] Yet in spite of this stubborn embrace of "permanent neutrality," membership in the European Union has further "thinned out" (*Ausdünnung*) Austria's neutrality.[10] Securing the survival of neutrality in the post-Cold War world may have been one of the reasons behind the election of Socialist Heinz Fischer to the Austrian presidency in late April 2004. Fischer has long been one of the strongest advocates of preserving Austrian neutrality, even though he softened his stance during the campaign.[11] "Being neutral" has become part of Austria's post-World War II identity.

I venture to guess that Americans and most of Austria's neighbors consider Austrian neutrality as political "fence-sitting" and security "free-riding" and as a lack of international commitment to participating in the maintenance of world order (Austrian diplomatic activism in the Balkans and United Nations (UN) "peace-keeping" contingents notwithstanding). In Donald Rumsfeld's divisive rhetoric, Austria would be a member of "old Europe." In this view, then, one of the legacies of the Austrian occupation and the 1955 "neutral solution" was the shutting down of Austrian air space after the Lebanon crisis of 1958 for NATO aircraft; this continued in the post-Cold War world during NATO's air campaign against Yugoslavia in the Kosovo conflict. Moreover, Austria prohibited the shipment of military hardware from American bases in Germany to the Near East through its borders during the current Iraq conflict. From the perspective of the current residents of the Pentagon and the White House, Austrian neutrality, then, might seem as "quaint" as the Geneva Convention. The utilitarian great power interest in neutral Austria as a principal site of diplomatic mediation, namely Austria as a respected venue in East-West conflict resolution and Vienna as a premier site for great power summitry and nuclear arms limitation/reduction negotiations, experienced a precipitous demise when the Cold War ended in 1989/90.

Could it be that the current American neglect of the lessons of the Austrian postwar occupation reflects the Bush administration's disrespect for Austrian neutrality and the perceived lack of Austrian solidarity in the nation-building efforts in Iraq? In an age of East-West bloc consolidation, the Eisenhower administration was never very pleased with the "neutralization" of Austria in 1955. But Austrian neutrality was the price to pay to get the Soviets out of Austria, to bring the interminable occupation of a "liberated" country to an end, and to reestablish an independent Austria. "Fence-sitting" neutral regimes were never much respected in Cold War Washington and seem to be even more out of favor in the post-Cold War international arena.[12] In the age of fighting terrorism, neutrals and neutralism may again be considered "free riders" in Washington.

Third, Austria was never *militarized* during the Cold War like the other "occupied enemies," Germany and Korea (and to a lesser degree Japan with the massive U.S. military bases in Okinawa and elsewhere). Divided Germany and Korea, of course, became principal allies of the two respective superpowers and were inundated with American military bases. The global American base system has correctly been identified as constituting one of the principal assets in the postwar "American empire."[13] Initially, bases guaranteed the presence of often overwhelming American forces in these countries along with the growing ties of friendship and intimacy and "foreign relations" between GI's and German, Japanese, and Korean civilians.[14] The continued presence of these troops also fortified bilateral relations on the state level and led to regular military cooperation.[15] While West Germany kept supplying "GI brides" to American soldiers for more than forty years during the Cold War, Austrians stayed at home in their neutral haven and remained absent from such intensifying security cooperation with Washington. Austrians, it stands to reason, were not "Americanized" and "Atlanticized" to the degree the West Germans were.

During the recent debates about the Iraq conflict, Americans were aggrieved and hurt by the opposition of their most reliable ally in continental Europe. Germany refused to join the "coalition of the willing." Few people in the American public seem to even have noticed that Austria also was safely ensconced in the "coalition of the unwilling." The Austrians experienced none of the depth in personnel (for example, through military exchange programs) and mutual emotional infatuation that developed between West Germans and Americans during the Cold War.[16] Americans, of course, see this close and often intimate relationship with the West Germans as the result of the highly successfully political democratization and economic stabilization of West Germany during the American occupation (as the late Stephen Ambrose doggedly repeated, "America's young men had gone to Europe not to conquer, not to enslave, not to destroy, but to liberate,"[17] or as George W. Bush has said, "[W]e did not leave behind occupying armies, we left constitutions and parliaments"). So while the German (and South Korean and Japanese) occupations are seen as great success stories from the perspective of "nation-building" and strong post-occupation alliance partnerships, the success of the Austrian occupation can be safely ignored by today's American "defense intellectuals" since it never led to such intimate bilateral ties and strategic partnerships.

Fourth, Austria, particularly as part of the American occupation presence, was culturally and mentally *Americanized* (or in Reinhold Wagnleitner's words "coca-colonized") like the rest of Western Europe and the world.[18] Niall Ferguson sees this cultural Americanization as part of informal, American postwar empire-building, positing "that foreigners will Americanize themselves without the need for formal rule"[19] (what Geir Lundestad has called "empire by invitation"[20]). This is juxtaposed to traditional European formal empire-building by territorial expansion overseas. While the American occupations after World War II pushed and accelerated Americanization trends launched before the war, the process continued into the post-occupation period. The Austrian occupation is no exception here and can be safely ignored by scholars such as Ferguson as a possible model of American nation-building via consumerism and mass culture infusion since it is not unique in any way. Ferguson, by training a historian of British and European economic history, is less conversant with the fine points of American history and American Studies literature; he ignores Wagnleitner's trend-setting study as one of the early, path-breaking scholarly contributions to the Americanization discourse. In other words, Anglo-American scholars such as Ferguson are not familiar with the Austrian occupation because they are conversant with the larger literature on "empire," but less so with the specificity of Cold War scholarship, of which the Austrian occupation is a part. With their inclination to generalize, scholars such as Ferguson simply turn a blind eye to the specificity of case studies such as Austria. The mirror image of this would be narrow-minded Austrian scholars who ignore the larger trends of Cold War scholarship and/or comparative occupation studies.

The Austrian Occupation and the Cycles of its Historiography

Scholarly contemporary history research is driven by archival access. Western archives usually begin opening most archival records twenty-five to thirty years after the event. These archival access practices directed scholarly attention in the 1970s and 1980s increasingly to the Austrian occupation period. As British and American archives began opening their post-World War II records on the Austrian occupation regime and their Cold War policies in Central Europe in the 1970s, scholarship on the Austrian occupation began to pick up and prosper. Apart from "lone wolf" efforts such as Manfried Rauchensteiner,[21] the most valuable work came largely out of the dissertations originating from the seminars of Gerald Stourzh in Vienna[22] and Fritz Fellner in Salzburg,[23] complemented by Rolf Steininger's new Contemporary History Institute established at the University of Innsbruck in 1982.[24] Siegfried Beer, Oliver Rathkolb, and Reinhold Wagnleitner's seminars in Graz, Vienna, and Salzburg in the 1990s continued this tradition in Austrian occupation studies.[25] Only some of these valuable dissertations on the Austrian occupation have appeared in book form. Probably the most useful summaries of—for want of a better term—this "baby boomer" generation of Austrian occupation scholarship is conveniently provided in their respective articles in the collections *Die Bevormundete Nation* (1988), and *Österreich unter allierter Besatzung 1945-1955* (1998).[26]

Even though valuable dissertations like Thomas Angerer's study of the French occupation policies continued to be written in the 1990s, it seems to me that there was no longer a group of young scholars pushing Austrian occupation studies forward and inspiring and reinforcing each other's work through a community of scholars as had the 1970s/1980s "baby boomers." Maybe the retirement of Professors Stourzh and Fellner in the late 1990s took the momentum out of occupation studies. I suspect that the demise of political and international history in Austrian *Zeitgeschichte* scholarship is also related to the "cultural studies" and "gender studies" booms at Austrian institutions of higher learning and in the Federal Ministry of Science itself. In the 1990s/2000s, the third and fourth postwar generations engaged World War II, Holocaust, and memory studies. Political, diplomatic, and military studies on the occupation or other periods of contemporary history, simply put, are no longer fashionable or *de rigeur* in the trendy historical profession. Political and diplomatic history are no longer at the forefront of historical studies in Austria (and in the United States as well), particularly in the field of contemporary history.[27]

Whereas research into the German occupation—especially the Soviet zone—continued unabated due to the opening of formerly East German, Eastern bloc, and Russian archives, a similar delayed interest in the Soviet zone of occupation in Austria has not produced many results yet, even though historical editing projects are on the way in Vienna and Graz. To date, the young Viennese historian Wolfgang Müller seems to operate largely in a void.[28] Lately, Stefan Karner's *Boltzmann Institut für Kriegsfolgenforschung* in Graz got into the business of vigorously studying the newly opened Russian sources on the Soviet zone of occupation, when lucrative contracts beckoned for the 2005 commemoration cycle of the fiftieth anniversary of the *Staatsvertrag*. Apart from Müller's work, I have seen few studies, even of article length, on Soviet occupation policies in Austria based on the new sources. There is nothing comparable to stream of publications from the IfZ in Potsdam and German universities,[29] let alone a *magnum opus* such as Norman Naimark's path-breaking *The Russians in Germany*.[30] Similarly, no major study of the Austrian occupation as a whole has been written of the caliber of John Dower's magisterial analysis of the Japanese occupation, *Embracing Defeat*.[31] Of course, Gerald Stourzh's latest version of his "*Staatsvertragsgeschichte*" is magisterial, but it is not on the occupation regimes *per se*, but on how to get rid of them by way of an Austrian state treaty, which, in fact, was the Allied "peace treaty" with postwar Austria.[32] The reason may be lack of funding sources in Austria, but just as likely, it is the usual nasty infighting and envious bickering within the Austrian scholarly community and "*Neidgenossenschaft*" when it comes to pooling resources for a large project that would redefine the field.

A peculiar Austrian malady is the scarcity of large historical sources editing projects in contemporary history.[33] Austrians still have to rely largely on *Foreign Relations of the United States*, *Documents of British Policy Overseas*, and *Documents Diplomatiques Francais* along with many published German, Italian, and Swiss sources for the reconstruction of the international politics of the occupation period. The publication of the minutes and discussions of the Austrian Council of Ministers (cabinet records) is the only significant document publication project of Austrian sources for the occupation period but it crawls along at a snail's pace. The project is still in 1945, only at the end of Renner's provisional government, with one volume published in 1995 and two more last year.[34] At this pace, we will not see any volumes on Julius Raab's government in our lifetime. Anybody who has perused these volumes knows how valuable a primary source is in reconstructing the Austrian perspective in dealing with the Allied occupation and the occupation governments. Given that access to these cabinet records has been handled very restrictively in the past by the Austrian State Archives in Vienna, a more rapid pace in this editing project would be highly desirable.

Contributions by foreign scholars to the scholarship of the Austrian occupation have been steady and significant ever since the studies by the two "Bills" in the 1960s—namely William "Bill" Lloyd Stearman and William "Bill" B. Bader.[35] It does strike me as very odd, though, that Bader's Stanford dissertation, *Austria between East and West 1945-1955*, valuable when it was published in 1966 and still a classic when I wrote my dissertation in the 1980s, would be published in a German translation thirty-six years later (2002). The translation of the original volume was published without any updating of the sources or interpretation, as if archives never opened in the 1970s and the scholarly advances in Austrian occupation studies by the "baby boomer" generation mentioned above were negligible and unworthy of Bader's attention. Gordon Craig, whose work on Germany I much admire (and Bader's *Doktorvater*), wrote a preface for the German translation. In it he concluded with the sentence, "*Vielleicht aber ist die junge Generation in Österreich selbstkritischer und weniger selbstzufrieden als ihre Vorfahren.*"[36] The "*vielleicht*" I find quite superfluous, if not offensive, to the past two generations of Austrian scholars on World War II and the occupation period. During the past twenty years, this very critical younger generation of historians seems to have done little else—especially from the perspective of Austrian officialdom—but debunk the "victims' myth" constructed by their father's/grandfather's generation.[37] Their work is entirely ignored by Bader (and Craig).

One is left wondering who paid for the translation for Bader's book, whose hidebound, traditionalist, Cold War interpretation may have been fitting in the 1960s but is totally out of date in 2004. Why translate Bader but not, say, Robert Keyserlingk's groundbreaking, revisionist account of Allied planning on Austria during World War II?[38] Similarly, Joan Hill's 1975 King's College dissertation, *Britain and the Occupation of Austria*, was published twenty-five years later in 2000 by Macmillan, again without any updating of sources and scholarly interpretation.[39] Meanwhile Robert Knight's valuable 1986 LSE dissertation, "British Policy towards Occupied Austria, 1945-1950," was never published.[40]

Yet older works such as Manfried Rauchensteiner's 1979 classic *Der Sonderfall* are republished in Austria, too, without serious updating of recent scholarship. Republished in the 2005 anniversary year as *Stalingplatz 4* (referring to the seat of the Allied Council), Rauchensteiner has added some new translated sources from Soviet archives and a very small number of new publications and secondary works that have appeared in the past twenty-six years.[41] He willfully ignores almost the entire Anglo-American scholarly production of the past quarter-century and many recent dissertations and publications from younger Austrian colleagues. The interpretative results are stuck in both traditionalist ruts of Cold War scholarship and the Austrian "victim's doctrine." Like in a time warp, it reads as if the various "revisionisms" of the 1980s and 1990s never occurred.[42]

I was a "lone wolf" writing on the Austrian occupation while living in the United States in the 1980s, yet was spirited on by—and a member of—the "baby boomer" generation in the 1980s.[43] Ralph Brown was working alone on Austria at the University of Tennessee, just like James Carafano at Georgetown.[44] Yet both Brown writing in the 1990s and Carafano in the 2000s, no longer could rely on a well-defined generational community of Austrian colleagues as I did in the 1980s.[45] It seems to me that, apart from Stourzh's updated history of the Austrian state treaty, Carafano's *Waltzing into the Cold War* on American military policies during the Austrian occupation is the only significant monograph on the Austrian occupation published in the past five years.[46] This would indicate that the scholarly study of the Austrian occupation is no longer as thriving a scholarly field as it was in the 1980s. In the end, that may well be the principal reason why scholars investigating historical case studies of previous American occupations and nation-building efforts in a larger comparative context may ignore the complex quadripartite Austrian occupation these days.

Notes

1. In June 2004 the Stanford Institute for International Studies invited a number of scholars to reflect on the Austrian occupation in a comparative Cold War context. The papers published in this Roundtable present a selection of this workshop. We are grateful to Prof. Norman Naimark and the Stanford Institute for International Studies for permitting us to publish these essays.

2. James Jay Carafano, "Post-Conflict Operations from Europe to Iraq," unpublished paper in the possession of the author. The best account of the U.S. military's failure to plan for the post-conflict occupation of Iraq is James Fallows, "Blind Into Baghdad," *Atlantic Monthly*, January/February 2004, pp. 52-74.

3. James Dobbins et al., *America's Role in Nation-Building: From Germany to Iraq* (Santa Monica: Rand, 2003).

4. Minxin Pei and Sara Kasper, *Lessons from the Past: The American Record in Nation-Building* (Washington, D.C.: Carnegie Endowment for International Peace, 2003).

5. Niall Ferguson, *Colossus: The Price of America's Empire* (New York: Penguin Press, 2004), 303 (Table 1); the best review of Fergusson's *Colossus* is Paul Kennedy, "Mission Impossible?," *New York Review of Books*, 10 June 2004, pp. 16-19.

6. David Greenberg, "Why Vietnam Haunts the Debate Over Iraq," HNN, <http:// hnn.us.articles/4779.html>; Leslie S. Lebl "Fixing Germany Wasn't Easy Either," HNN, <http://hnn.us/articles/1649.html>; Gil Troy, "Germany Wasn't Rebuilt in a Year, Nor Shall Iraq," HNN, <http://hnn.us/roundup/entries/4552.html>; see also the discussion thread in H-DIPLO on "Behavior of Allied Troops in Post-War Germany" in July/August 2004; John W. Dower, "A Warning from History: Don't expect democracy in Iraq," *Boston Review* February/March 2003 <http://bostonreview.mit.edu/BR28.1/dower.html> (accessed 31 March 2004); see also "That Was Then: Allen W. Dulles on the Occupation of Germany," *Foreign Affairs* (November/December 2003): 2-8.

7. Günter Bischof, *Austria in the First Cold War, 1945-55: The Leverage of the Weak* (Basingstoke: Macmillan, 1999).

8. Manfried Rauchensteiner, *Die Zwei: Die Grosse Koalition in Österreich 1945-1966* (Vienna: Bundesverlag, 1987); Günter Bischof, Anton Pelinka, and Dieter Stiefel, eds., *The Marshall Plan in Austria, vol. 8, Contemporary Austrian Studies* (New Brunswick, NJ: Transaction, 2000).

9. Erich Reiter, *Neutralität oder NATO. Die sicherheitspolitischen Konsequenzen aus der europäischen Aufgabe Österreichs, vol. 1, Forschungen zur Sicherheitspolitik* (Graz: Styria, 1996); Erich Reiter, ed., *Österreich und die NATO. Die sicherheitspolitische Situation Österreichs nach der NATO-Erweiterung. Vol. 2, Forschungen zur Sicherheitspolitik* (Graz: Styria, 1998).

10. See the hard-hitting polemical critique by Karl Zemanek, "Wie lange währt 'immer'?" *Die Presse-Spectrum*, 13 November 2004; for a more scholarly analysis of Austria's neutral status within EU common foreign policy and security efforts, see the essay by Gunther Hauser in this volume.

11. "Neutralität 'nicht immerwährend'," *Die Presse*, 7 January 2004, <http:/ www.diepresse.at/Artikel.aspx?channel=p&ressort=i&id=397458> (accessed 3 March 2005).

12. H.W. Brands, Jr., *The Specter of Neutralism: The United States and the Emergence of the Third World, 1947-1960* (New York: Columbia Univ. Press, 1989); Michael Ruddy, "European Integration, the Neutrals, and U.S. Security Interests: From the Marshall Plan to the Rome Treaties," in *Die Neutralen und die europäische Integration 1945-1995*, ed. Michael Gehler and Rolf Steininger (Vienna: Böhlau, 2000), 13-28.

13. Andrew J. Bacevich, *American Empire: The Realities & Consequences of U.S. Diplomacy* (Cambridge, MA: Harvard Univ. Press, 2002); Ferguson, *Colossus*; Dana Priest, *The Mission: Waging War and Keeping Peace with America's Military* (New York: W.W. Norton, 2004).

14. Petra Goedde, *GIs and Germans: Culture, Gender, and Foreign Relations, 1945-1949* (New Haven, CT: Yale Univ. Press, 2003).

15. Dewey A. Browder, *Americans in Post-World War II Germany* (Lewiston: Edwin Mellen Press, 1998); Thomas Leuerer, *Die Stationierung amerikanischer Streitkräfte in Deutschland: Militärgemeinden der U.S. Army in Deutschland seit 1945 als ziviles Element der Stationierungpolitik der Vereinigten Staaten* (Würzburg: Ergon, 1997); Saki Dockrill, ed., *Controversy and Compromise: Alliance Politics between Great Britain, the Federal Republic of Germany, and the United States of America, 1945-1967* (Bodenheim: Philo, 1998).

16. Heinz Bude and Berndt Greiner, eds., *Westbindungen: Amerika in der Bundesrepublik* (Hamburg: Hamburger Edition, 1999).

17. Stephen E. Ambrose, *To America: Personal Reflections of an Historian* (New York: Simon and Schuster 2002), 120.

18. Reinhold Wagnleitner, *Coca-Colonization and the Cold War: The Cultural Mission of the United States after the Second World War*, 2nd ed., trans. Diana Wolf (Chapel Hill, NC: Univ. of North Carolina Press, 2001).

19. Ferguson, *Colossus*, 13.

20. Geir Lundestad, *The American "Empire" and Other Studies of U.S. Foreign Policy in a Comparative Perspective* (London: Oxford Univ. Press, 1990).

21. Manfried Rauchensteiner, *Der Sonderfall: Besatzungszeit in Österreich 1945 bis 1955* (Graz: Styria, 1979).

22. Josef Leidenfrost, "Die Amerikanische Besatzungsmacht und der Wiederbeginn des Politischen Lebens in Österreich, 1944-1947," Ph.D. diss., University of Vienna, 1985; Wilfried Mähr, "Von der UNRRA zum Marshall-Plan: Die amerikanische Finanz- und Wirtschaftshilfe an Österreich, 1944-1947," Ph.D. diss., University of Vienna, 1985.

23. Reinhold Wagnleitner, "Grossbritannien und die Wiedererrichtung der Republik Österreich," Phil. diss. University of Salzburg 1975; Lydia Lettner, "Die französische Österreichpolitik von 1943 bis 1946," Phil. diss. University of Salzburg 1980.

24. Klaus Eisterer, *Französiche Besatzungspolitik: Tirol und Vorarlberg 1945/46, vol. 9, Innsbrucker Forschungen zur Zeitgeschichte* (Innsbruck: Haymon, 1991); on the foci of the Innsbruck Institute, see Günter Bischof and Ingrid Böhler, "Forschung und Lehre am Innsbrucker Institut für Zeitgeschichte (1983-2003). 'Die Innsbrucker Schule' in der österreichischen Zeitgeschichteforschung," *Zeitgeschichte* 30 (November/December 2003): 387-98.

25. A more extensive treatment of the cycles of Cold War scholarship and its repercussions in Austrian academe is Günter Bischof, "Eine historiographsiche Einführung: Die Ära des Kalten Krieges und Österreich," in *Östereich im frühen Kalten Krieg 1945-1958: Spione, Partisanen, Kriegspläne*, ed. Erwin A. Schmidl (Vienna: Böhlau, 2000), 19-54.

26. Günter Bischof and Josef Leidenfrost, eds., *Die Bevormundete Nation: Österreich und die Allierten 1945-1949, vol. 4, Innsbrucker Forschugnen zur Zeitgeschichte* (Innsbruck: Haymon, 1988); Alfred Ableitinger, Siegfried Beer, and Eduard G. Staudinger, eds., *Österreich unter allierter Besatzung 1945-1955* (Vienna: Böhlau, 1998); see also Anton Pelinka and Rolf Steininger, eds., *Österreich und die Sieger* (Vienna: Braumüller, 1986).

27. For a generational model of cycles of Austrian historical interpretations, see Ernst Hanisch, "Der forschende Blick. Österreich im 20. Jahrhundert: Interpretationen und Kontroversen," *Carinthia* 189 (1999): 579-82; idem, "Die Dominanz des Staates: Österreichs Zeitgeschichte im Drehkreuz von Politik und Wissenschaft," in *Zeitgeschichte als Problem: Nationale Traditionen und Perspektiven der Forschung in Europa*, ed. Alexander Nütznadel and Theodor Schieder (Göttingen: Vandenhoeck & Ruprecht, 2004), 54-77. For a critique of Austrian *Zeitgeschichte*, see Thomas Angerer, "An Incomplete Discipline: Austrian Zeitgeschichte and Recent History," in *Austria in the Nineteen Fifties, vol. 3, Contemporary Austrian Studies* (New Brunswick, NJ: Transaction, 1995); see also Günter Bischof, "Östereichs Scheu vor Machtpolitik," *Die Presse*, 7 February 1996, 2. In a recent survey among Austrian historians of contemporary history, approximately 17 percent were researchers in cultural history, whereas only 5

percent researched political history, and less than 1 percent (only one person!) had interests in international relations (Heinz Niederleitner, "Näher an der Gegenwart: Die Beziehungen von östereichischen Zeithistoriker/innen zu aktuellen Medien im Vergleich mit anderen Historiker/innen," unpublished manuscript in possession of the author).

28. Wolfgang Müller, "Die sowjetische Besatzungsmacht in Östereich 1945-1955. Forschungsstand, Quellenlage und Fragestellungen," *Zeitgeschichte* 28 (March/April 2001): 114-29; idem, "Sowjetbesatzung, Nationale Front und der 'Friedliche Übergang zum Sozialismus': Fragmente sowjetischer Österreich-Planung 1945-1955," *Mitteilungen des Österreichischen Staatsarchivs* 50 (2003): 133-56; see also his essay in this volume.

29. See, for example, Hartmut Mehringer, ed., *Von der SBZ zur DDR: Studien zum Herrschaftssytem in der Sowjetischen Besatzungszone und in der Deutschen Demokratischen Republik* (Munich: R. Oldenbourg, 1995), or the ongoing controversy over the "Stalin Notes" of 1952, Wilfried Loth, *Stalin's Unwanted Child: The Soviet Union, the German Question and the Founding of the GDR* (Basingstoke: Macmillan, 1998), and idem "The Origins of Stalin's Note of 10 March 1952," *Cold War History* 4 (January 2004): 66-88.

30. Norman M. Naimark, *The Russians in Germany: A History of the Soviet Zone of Occupation 1945-1949* (Cambridge, MA: Belknap, 1995).

31. John W. Dower, *Embracing Defeat: Japan in the Wake of World War II* (New York: W.W. Norton, 1999).

32. Gerald Stourzh, *Um Einheit und Freiheit: Staatsvertrag, Neutralität und das Ende der Ost-West-Besetzung Österreichs 1945-1955* (Vienna: Böhlau, 1998); for the larger international context, Bischof's *Austria in the First Cold War* compliments Stourzh.

33. On historical editing in contemporary history and the lack thereof, see the analysis by Michael Gehler in this volume.

34. See citations in Gehler's essay of this volume, p. 15-22.

35. William Lloyd Stearman, *The Soviet Union and the Occupation of Austria: An Analysis of Soviet Policy in Austria, 1945-1955* (Bonn: Siegler, 1962); William B. Bader, *Austria between East and West, 1945-1955* (Stanford: Stanford Univ. Press, 1966).

36. William B. Bader, *Österreich im Spannungsfeld zwischen Ost und West 1945 bis 1955*, trans. Alexandra Stibor-Milovcic (Vienna: Braumüller, 2002), viii (Craig quotation).

37. A summary of sorts is provided by Günter Bischof, "Victims? Perpetrators? 'Punching Bags' of European Historical Memory? The Austrians and Their World War II Legacies," *German Studies Review* 27 (February 2004): 17-32. The work of the "Austrian Historians Commission" on World War II appearing in fifty-two volumes is the most eloquent testimony of Austrians no longer shunning their World War II past.

38. Robert H. Keyserlingk, *Austria in World War II: An Anglo-American Dilemma* (Kingston-Montreal: McGill-Queens Univ. Press, 1988).

39. Alice Hills, *Britain and the Occupation of Austria, 1943-1945* (Basingstoke: Macmillan, 2000).

40. Robert Graham Knight, "British Policy towards Occupied Austria, 1945-1950," Ph.D. diss., London School of Economics, 1986.

41. Manfried Rauchensteiner, *Stalinplatz 4: Österreich unter alliierter Besatzung* (Vienna: Edition Steinbauer, 2005).

42. This literature, as it were, was conveniently summarized for the Austrian scholarly community writing on the Cold War by Günter Bischof, "Ein historiographische Einführung: Die Ära des Kalten Krieges und Österreich," in *Österreich im frühen Kalten*

Krieg 1945-1958. Spione, Partisanen, Kriegspläne, ed. Erwin A. Schmidl (Vienna: Böhlau, 2000), 19-54. Both Rauchensteiner and Schmidl are leading Viennese military historians, so presumably they know of each other's work. Moreover, any scholarly writing on the Cold War ought to regularly peruse the leading journals *Journal of Cold War Studies* (U.S.) and *Cold War History* (U.K.), as well as *Diplomatic History* (U.S.) and *Diplomacy & Statecraft* (U.K.). Rauchensteiner does not cite a single article from these scholarly journals of record.

43. Günter Bischof, "Between Responsibility and Rehabilitation: Austrian in International Politics, 1940-1950," Ph.D. diss., Harvard University, 1989. Earlier in the decade came Patricia Blythe Eggleston, "The Marshall Plan in Austria, 1945-1950," Ph.D. diss., University of Alabama, 1980.

44. Ralph W. Brown, III, "A Cold War Army of Occupation: The U.S. Army in Vienna, 1945-1948," PhD. diss., University of Tennessee, 1995.

45. On the importance of generations in history, see David Kaiser, "Ernest R. May and the Silent Generation," in *Rethinking International Relations: Ernest R. May and the Study of World Affairs*, ed. Akira Iriye (Chicago: Imprint, 1998), 241-47.

46. James Jay Carafano, *Waltzing into the Cold War: The Struggle for Occupied Austria* (College Station, TX: Texas A & M Press, 2002), see also K. Tweraser's review in this volume.

The "Allied Occupation" and the Collective Memory of Austrians after 1945: "Ending a 17 year-long path of bondage full of thorns"

(Leopold Figl, 15 May 1955)

Oliver Rathkolb

Focusing on ways in which the Allied liberation of Austria has been represented in the Austrian public sphere and on political narratives of the Allied liberation as compared with those of the "Allied occupation," I have to exclude the historiographical debates about Austria being a "trusteeship" (1945-1955 and afterwards), or Austria defined as a "*Bevormundete Nation*," a patronized nation, in the volume with the same title edited by Günter Bischof and Josef Leidenfrost,[1] a definition later turned on its head by Thomas Angerer who referred to the French occupiers being patronized by the Austrians.[2]

I shall concentrate on high points of the debate, from 1945 to 1955, and conclude with a recent debate from 2002 in an effort to describe briefly the main perceptions in the collective public memory. A public opinion poll of October 1995 asked the question, "Since when has Austria been free?"[3] It produced an amazing result: 87 percent of the public said "since 1955," not 1945, the year of the Allied liberation. This 87 percent split into 52 percent in favor of May 1955, the signing of the Austrian State Treaty and 35 percent in favor of October 1955, the month when the neutrality law passed the Austrian Parliament. It would seem, then, that the ten years of Allied administration, the Marshall Plan, and the reestablishment of democratic structures and bureaucratic procedures are widely considered as "occupation."

The concepts of "liberation" of Austrians and of the integration of innocent "little Nazis" into the new society without major purges came out of Soviet political language at the time. From the first moment of public debate, the declaration of the Provisional Government of Austria on 27 April 1945, this language was transformed into the key national doctrine of Austria: the "victim only" doctrine. The propaganda proclamation of the Moscow Conference in October 1943 (the Moscow Declaration, describing Austria as the first country to fall victim to Hitler's aggression) was integrated into the 1945 declaration. The responsibility clause was omitted in the 1945 version, as were references to taking account of Austrian resistance before a final judgment was made.[4]

HOTEL
AUFBAU
ALLIIERTE BESATZUNG
1947
FÜR ÖSTERREICH
"... so, ich dank euch schön, jetzt werd' ich mich schon weiterwursteln"
Aus einer Zeitung, 1947

In this newspaper cartoon Austria, symbolized by the child, gratefully acknowledges American aid. The four occupation powers represented by the "four in the jeep" and Austrian Chancellor Leopold Figl are looking on. The caption in German reads: "Thank you very much, now I'll muddle through."

Despite the fact that Austria would not have been liberated from the Nazi regime without the military capabilities and the human losses of the Soviet Red Army and U.S., British, and French Armed Forces, and despite the fact that large areas of Austria would not have survived without Allied food aid (primarily, but not exclusively, the western provinces), Austrian politicians immediately began to attack the Allied presence (including Allied occupation costs paid by the Austrian taxpayer) during and after the November 1945 election campaign.

A significant statement from State Chancellor Karl Renner's report to Parliament on 19 December 1945, after eight months of postwar government reads, "The die has been cast. Our country is being occupied at once by the four great powers and our people are caught up in the sphere of influence agreements of these four victorious powers [. . .] this four-power administration will only be ended after a peace treaty is signed and only then will we truly be free."[5]

The Austrians were described purely as victims of the Nazi regime even when commemorating Allied losses during the liberation of Austria. Leopold Figl, for example, then governor of Lower Austria, later to be chancellor, referred to them as such at the opening ceremony of the Soviet soldier's monument on the Stalin-Platz (today Schwarzenbergplatz) on 19 August 1945.[6]

The sense of having been liberated should have been strengthened by the perception that, apart from a small group of ardent, largely pre-1938 Nazis, the Austrian population had been totally suppressed.[7] The perception of liberation, however, was overruled by the psychological fact that many decision makers were well aware of the collaboration of Austrians with the Nazi regime and of their active participation in suppression, exploitation, and terror acts against Jews, POWs, forced laborers, and others.[8] In fact, Renner, who drafted the Declaration of 27 April 1945, had not only pleaded in favor of the Anschluß in 1938, but had even defended in writing the destruction of democratic Czechoslovakia and, in 1939, had praised German nationalism during the Nazi period.[9]

My first thesis, then, is that the collective Austrian memory had to exclude very early on the facts of liberation since it was suppressing the "Nazi past." By constructing a totally innocent political and social entity, the main political campaign very early on discounted the perpetrators as well as the bystanders during the Nazi regime and took aim at the occupiers.[10]

The first and main target was the Soviet Union, an easy target since the looting, plundering, and raping during the first weeks after the liberation destroyed any positive images of the Russians. The Communist Party of Austria did not dare to protest the looting and raping and, therefore, had no chance to gain broader voter support. One of the reasons for the relative success of the People's Party lay in their use of anti-Russian codes in the election campaign. Compared with the 1949 campaign, however, the debate was channeled outside the public campaigning by posters and similar measures.[11]

In 1946, President of the National Assembly Karl Seitz, a Social Democrat and survivor of Nazi prisons, attacked the Allies because they maintained the option to veto and to block Austrian laws passed by parliament.[12] Even in a newsreel after his death in 1950, one of Seitz's speeches was cited in which he remembered how the British, French, Russian, and especially American people had fought for their independence and closed with a plea in favor of keeping little Austria's dignity. One year later, the Allied (including U.S.) opposition and amendments demanded by the Allied Council to the Austrian new de-Nazification law were criticized and interpreted as being imposed on the Austrian people.[13] The People's Party and the Socialists had already agreed upon a rather loose de-Nazification policy mainly aimed at large-scale integration of former Nazi Party members.

Public opinion polls as early as March 1947 show that 43 percent of Austrians in the U.S. zones of Austria (Upper Austria, Salzburg, and parts of Vienna) regarded the Allied presence as "hindering the reconstruction of Austria" while only 23 percent took the opposite view, and 17 percent answered that the Allies were both helping and obstructing.[14] The Socialist Vice-Chancellor Adolf Schärf made special use of the anti-Western propaganda of the Communists to plead for relaxation of the burdens of the occupation, such as occupation costs, censorship, and inter-zonal traffic control. In general, however, he moved completely into the pro-American camp by asking for a strong U.S. presence in the context of the Cold War. This is one of the examples of double speak: due to the fear of becoming part of the Communist block, the Austrian Socialists and the People's Party leaders asked for close U.S. cooperation and the presence of U.S. and British forces in Austria.[15] At the same time in 1948, both the Socialists and the People's Party demonstrated against the occupation in the 1 May demonstrations throughout Austria.[16] The general political target was the Soviet occupation. But public opinion in the short term did not follow the political splitting of perception into good Western occupation and bad Soviet occupation. That was more a feature of the long term, since one sees that today only the Soviet occupation is considered to be a "real occupation" and is integrated into the whole period of suppression from 1938 to 1955. Memories of the British, U.S., and French occupation are marginalized, or surface in historical projects such as the Salzburg one.[17]

"Liberated from the Occupiers. . .": this is a fragmentary citation from the official 1955 speech of Foreign Minister Leopold Figl who is considered in Austrian public opinion today to be the most important politician of the Second Republic (the Social Democratic legend Bruno Kreisky ranking second in the public opinion poll for the Austrian *lieux de mémoire* project).[18] In the collective memory, Figl is still held to be the father of the Austrian State Treaty who used the traditional image of the nice and cozy (*gemütlichen*) Austrian to persuade the Soviets and others during endless nights at the *Heurigen* (wine restaurants) to leave the country finally in 1955. His famous sentence "*Österreich ist frei*" ("Austria is free") is still so strong that it will be used for an exhibition at the Schallaburg (Lower Austria) by Stefan Karner to run from 15 April through 1 November 2005, despite its showing an outdated inclination to revive the postwar "victim only" narrative.[19]

In this 1955 speech, Foreign Minister Figl erased the last distinctions between the Nazi terror period (1938-1945) and the period of Allied occupation tutelage, even though such tutelage had been considerably reduced after 1946/47. After 1950, it had become a rather loose administration with few areas of conflict. In many cases, the Austrian decision makers played a skillful game in pitting the former Allies against each other, and the "tutors" became an object of Austrian tutelage. As early as May 1948, U.S. political analysts referred to the psychological problem of the occupation image when discussing the reduction of concrete occupation policies and turning over military government functions to the Austrians, "Austrians think there is so much to turn over and because in actuality there is so little, we have nothing to lose by an announcement that all Military Government functions will be turned over forthwith."[20]

Figl said in 1955, "The thorny path of not being free is finally over after 17 years! The sacrifices that the Austrian people have been making and their unshakable faith in the future are finally bearing late fruit. For ten years we have longing for this day when the foreign ministers of the four powers would come to Vienna [. . .]."[21] Forty-seven years later, in 2002, this speech was taken up during a heated debate about a speech of the FPÖ politician Ewald Stadler:

> Death has been a grim master among our people during this past century. And our people during this past century have not always experienced liberation, as those merciless do-gooders are trying to tell us these days with their *Wehrmachts*-events and their *Wehrmachts*-exhibits. In 1918 we were supposedly liberated from the tyranny of monarchy, and in 1934 apparently from the chaos of democracy. In 1938, so we are told, we were liberated from clerical fascism. And in 1945, so the established state ideology pretends to tell us, we were allegedly liberated from fascism and tyranny again, only to fall subject to another tyranny on the very soil we inhabit today. Lastly, in 1994 we were liberated from our independence, when our country decided to join the European Union on January 1, 1995.[22]

Here for the first time a broader public debate concerning the perception of 1945 as liberation and/or occupation started after Stadler described the political and military transformations since 1918 as "tyranny," referring primarily, but not exclusively, to the Soviet presence in Lower Austria, the Burgenland, Mühlviertel, and Vienna. The relatively "narrow discourse" about liberation in 1945 was much broader in 2002 since the "victims only" theory was losing ground in the media, with the elites, and within a younger and better educated generation.

My second thesis is that with the decline of the "victim only" doctrine Austrian public opinion is gradually accepting the liberation perception as part of the collective memory of 1945. (The perception of liberation was, of course, always present from the beginning in connection with the liberation of the concentration camps.)[23]

The third thesis is connected with one of the completely neglected facets of the "Allied presence" during 1945-1955. In a rather young nation with a still very weak national identity, Austrian political elites and public opinion continued throughout this decade to use the Allies as targets and scapegoats. But they overemphasized the perception of the strength and role of the Austrians in the rebuilding of the Austrian economy, political structures, and the like. This is obvious when we analyze early postwar national identity icons like the power plant in Kaprun (excluding forced labor pre-1944 or U.S. Marshall Plan investment), the rebuilding of the Vienna State Opera (destroyed by "Allied bombing" and the rebuilt initially with Soviet aid and assistance), and—above all—the Austrian State Treaty.

This 1948 poster suggests ten years of Austrian imprisonment, thus telescoping both the Hitlerite and Allied postwar occupations into one historical continuum.

The treaty is still generally viewed—as has been mentioned before—as a result of Leopold Figl's social skills including his drinking prowess (leaving aside the evening during the decisive negotiations in Moscow in April 1955 when he had to be carried away because he was so drunk). The actual facts—that the geopolitical framework was perfect for the treaty solution and that Chancellor Raab had established a perfect communication channel to the Soviets—are not remembered. The Allies, even though they may come to be perceived as the liberators of 1945, remain the occupiers of 1955, eventually pushed out by the clever and kindly Austrians. The Allies remain the "others," the "foreigners" who occupied the country (after the liberation of 1945). Their influence upon Austria's society, economy, and political structure seems to me to have been completely erased from the public understanding of history. They still remain the scapegoats to some extent. While the Russians are seen in a somewhat better light now, the American image is declining as a result of growing anti-Americanism. The British and French presence has been largely reduced to local and regional fragmentary memories and has become merely the province of historians.

In conclusion, I have to add that the Austrians—as a people with a rather young identity which has grown considerably—rank in the public opinion polls on national pride within the top four worldwide.[24] Meanwhile, they have found a successor for the "Allied occupation" as a scapegoat, namely the European Union. In 1995, we welcomed integration into Europe as if it was "liberation" from the exclusion by the "West." Since then, the public mood has shifted considerably, and Austrians have become rather skeptical about and negative towards the European Union and EU enlargement. For me, history seems to repeat itself, but at the same time, there is no real opting out clause in the European Union and no second State Treaty in sight! After the EU sanctions against the People's Party/Freedom Party government in 2000, the national front tendencies (*Österreich über alles*) have grown considerably and were used as propaganda patterns in the recent campaigns for the European Parliament by all parties.

Notes

1. For a general overview, see the introduction to Günter Bischof and Josef Leidenfrost, eds., *Die bevormundete Nation. Österreich und die Alliierten 1945-1949* (Innsbruck: Haymon, 1988), 21.

2. Thomas Angerer, "Der 'bevormundete Vormund': Die französische Besatzungsmacht in Österreich," in *Österreich unter alliierter Besatzung 1945-1955*, ed. Alfred Ableitinger, Siegfried Beer, and Eduard G. Staudinger (Vienna: Böhlau, 1998), 159-204.

3. Sozialwissenschaftliche Studiengesellschaft, panel discussion *Österreich ist Frei* (Vienna: unpublished paper, 26 October 1995).

4. The governments of the United Kingdom, the Soviet Union, and the United States of America are agreed that Austria, the first free country to fall a victim to Hitler's aggression, shall be liberated from German domination. They regard the annexation imposed on Austria by Germany on 15 March 1938 as null and void. They consider themselves as in no way bound by any charges effected in Austria since that date. They declare that they wish to see a free and independent Austria reestablished, thereby opening the way for the Austrian people themselves, as well as those neighboring states which will be faced with similar problems, to find that political and economic security which is the only basis for lasting peace. Austria is reminded, however, that she has a responsibility, which she cannot evade, for participation in the war on the side of Hitler's Germany, and that in the final settlement an account will inevitably be taken of her own contribution to her liberation. For the text, see Csáky, *Freiheit und Neutralität*, 33. The proclamation of 27 April 1945 is published in ibid., 36-37. The text of the declaration of the provisional government on 27 April 1945 is published in ibid., 33. On the instrumentalization of the Moscow Declaration by the Austrians and on its original purpose, see Günter Bischof, *Austria in the First Cold War, 1945-55: The Leverage of the Weak* (Basingstoke: MacMillan/St. Martin's, 1999), 25-29 and 52-67.

5. "*Die Würfel sind gefallen, daß unser Land von vier Großmächten zugleich besetzt und unser Volk in die Einflußsphäre der vier siegreichen großen Nationen geraten sind* [...] *nach vollzogenem Friedensschluß diese vierfache Verwaltung ganz abzulösen und dann erst in Wahrheit frei zu sein.*" [Österreichische Bundesregierung, ed., *Für Recht und Frieden. Eine Auswahl der Reden des Bundespräsidenten Dr. Karl Renner* (Vienna: Österreichische Staatsdruckerei, 1950), 20.]

6. Heidemarie Uhl, "Transformations of Austrian Memory: Politics of History and Monument Culture in the Second Republic," *Austrian History Yearbook 32* (2001): 153.

7. Evan Burr Bukey, *Hitler's Austria: Popular Sentiment in the Nazi Era, 1938-1945* (Chapel Hill, NC: Univ. of North Carolina Press, 2002), 3.

8. Gerhard Botz, "Janus Headed Austria: Transition from Nazism and Restoration, Continuity and Learning Process," in *Modern Europe after Facism 1943-1980s*, ed. Stein Ugelvik (New York: Columbia Univ. Press, 1998) 3.

9. Gerhard Oberkofler and Eduard Rabofsky, *Pflichterfüllung für oder gegen Österreich* (Vienna: Globus, 1988), and Heinz Fischer, "Karl Renner und sein Manuskript über den Anschluß und die Sudetendeutschen," in *Zwischen Austromarxismus und Katholizismus. Festschrift für Norbert Leser*, ed. Anton Pelinka et al. (Vienna: Braumüller, 1993).

10. Peter Thaler, *The Ambivalence of Identity: The Austrian Experience of Nation-Building in a Modern Society* (Purdue, IN: Purdue Univ. Press, 2001), 81-109.

11. Manfried Rauchensteiner, *Der Sonderfall. Die Besatzungszeit in Österreich 1945-1955* (Graz: Styria, 1979).

12. Bischof and Leidenfrost, *Bevormundete Nation*, 19-20.

13. Oliver Rathkolb, "NS.-Problem und politische Restauration: Vorgeschichte und Etablierung des VdU," in *Verdrängte Schuld – Verfehlte Sühne. Entnazifizierung in Österreich 1945-1955*, ed. Sebastian Meissl, Klaus-Dieter Mulley, and Oliver Rathkolb (Vienna: Verlag für Geschichte und Politik, 1986), 73-99; Dieter Stiefel, *Entnazifizierung in Österreich* (Vienna: Europa Verlag, 1981).

14. Reinhold Wagnleitner, ed., *Understanding Austria: The Political Reports and Analyses of Martin F. Herz, Political Officer of the U.S. Legation in Vienna, 1945-1948* (Salzburg: Wolfgang Neugebauer Verlag, 1984), 129.

15. Bischof and Leidenfrost, *Bevormundete Nation*, 21.

16. See *Arbeiter-Zeitung*, 1 May 1948.

17. Ingrid Bauer, *Welcome Ami Go Home: Die amerikanische Besatzung in Salzburg 1945-1955* (Salzburg: Verlag Anton Pustet, 1998), 169. For additional information and images see: *"Liberators and the Liberated," "Occupiers and the Occupied"* <http://www.image.co.at/image/salzburg/> (accessed 1 Feb. 2005).

18. Emil Brix et. al., eds., *Memoria Austriae I. Menschen, Mythen, Zeiten* (Vienna: Verlag für Geschichte und Politik, 2004). In a letter to the author dated 8 March 2004, Ernst Bruckmüller wrote that 21 percent chose Mozart as a person of whom the Austrians are proud, while 14 percent chose Figl, 12 percent Kreisky, and 10 percent Raab, the State Treaty chancellor of 1955.

19. Landesausstellung Niederösterreich, *"Österreich ist frei": 50 Jahre Staatsvertrag*, 2005 <http://www.oesterreichistfrei.at/> (accessed 1 Feb. 2005).

20. Wagnleitner, *Understanding Austria*, 389.

21. "*Ein 17 Jahre lang dauernder, dornenvoller Weg der Unfreiheit ist beendet! Die Opfer, die Österreichs Volk in dem Glauben an seine Zukunft gebracht hat, haben nun ihre Früchte getragen: Wir haben zehn Jahre auf diesen Tag gewartet, an dem die Außenminister der vier Mächte nach Wien kommen sollten* [...]" [Csáky, *Dokumentation*, 409.]

22. The text to Stadler's speech can be found at <http://www.a-e-m-gmbh.com/wessely/fstadl.htm> (accessed 1 Feb. 2005): *Reiche Ernte hat der Tod im vergangenen Jahrhundert unter unserem Volk gehalten. Und es war nicht immer eine Befreiung, wie es uns die gnadenlosen Gutmenschen, die heute Wehrmachtsveran-*

staltungen und Wehrmachtsaaustellungen gestalten, einreden wollen, die unser Volk im vergangenen Jahrhundert erfahren hat. 1918 sind wir angeblich von der Tyrannei der Monarchie befreit worden. 1934 wurden wir angeblich vom Chaos der Demokratie befreit. 1938 wurden wir angeblich vom Kleriko-Faschismus befreit. Und 1945 – und das ist zur Staatsideologie geworden—sind wir angeblich vom Faschismus und von der Tyrannei befreit worden, und in die nächste Tyrannei geraten, insbesondere hier auf diesem Boden, auf dem wir uns heute befinden. Und letztlich, 1994, sind wir von der Selbstständigkeit befreit worden, als unser Land entschieden hat, in die Europäische Union mit 1.1.1995 einzutreten.

23. The memory policies concerning the concentration camp Mauthausen near Linz are analyzed by Bertrand Perz, "'*Selbst die Sonne schien damals ganz anders* [...].' *Die Entstehung der KZ-Gedenkstätte Mauthausen 1945 bis 1970*," in *Steinernes Bewußtsein. Die öffentliche Repräsentation staatlicher und nationaler Identität Österreichs in seinen Denkmälern*. vol. 2, ed. Heidemarie Uhl (Vienna: Böhlau, 2003).

24. In 1998, one study by the National Opinion Center at the University of Chicago, based on opinion polls from 1995, even ranked Austria second following the United States, but surpassing Bulgaria, Hungary, and Canada. [Tony W. Smith and Lars Jarkko, "National Pride: A Cross-national Analysis." May 1998. General Social Survey Project Cross-National Report 19. National Organization for Research at the University of Chigaco. <http://www.norc.uchicago.edu/new/part1.pdf> (accessed 1 Feb. 2005).

Still "Occupied" by Germany 1945-1955? Arguments, Concepts, and Strategies in the Austrian Struggle against a Crucial Dependence

Michael Gehler

Austria's statehood after 1945 was burdened with a quadruple trauma: one arising from the myth of the "economic non-viability" of the First Republic, another from the dependence on foreign countries, a third from the civil war, and, finally, one from the end of national independence as a result of the 1938 Anschluß. Thus considerable difficulties existed with the strengthening of the underdeveloped idea of an Austrian *nation* which was required for the reconstruction and consolidation of the state after 1945. In spite of all the positive Austrian-specific nostalgia for the Habsburgs, the centuries-long tradition of a cosmopolitan and transnational alignment of the monarchy did not prove beneficial.

This paper concentrates on the developments before 1955, the often-cited "*annus mirabilis*."[1] In 1955, the occupying powers were removed, but beyond that, national independence from Germany was secured by a treaty. I present an overview here of political arguments, demands, concepts, strategies, patterns of behavior, and actions which the Austrian government employed to try to uncouple itself from the Nazi problem Germany had in order to find its own path in the European community of nations.

Tactics of the Austrian Government for Securing Independence

First, Austria's taking on a *historical role as a victim of Nazism* was more than just a tactic, it was actually a strategy, one that was not wholly unwarranted. Laying claim to victim status arose from the carefully thought-out deliberation that victims can be entitled at all times to the advantages of always being right and being able to place blame on others. This strategy targeted two groups. First, it found application in hindsight to Austria's role in the Nazi period and, thus, with a view toward Germany. Second, it was applied to the Allied powers and, thus, also with a view toward the primarily Western community of nations, which had compelled Austria to its unwanted independence in 1919[2] and from whose same protection it was expelled in 1938. For both points of view, there were good reasons, even though historical reality turned out to be more complicated than the wishful thinking of Austrian politicians.

The avowedly radical separation from Germany and the renunciation of everything German to the point of defamation, dispossession, and expulsion of the "Reich Germans" in 1945, which matched a sort of "clean slate" policy was another important point. The hatred of everything German went so far that in 1946 Chancellor Leopold Figl declared that German tourists were "unwelcome." Germans became scapegoats for Austrians' own misdeeds and failures. Was this an expression of self-hatred?[3]

Another goal was the demand to give up the Greater German concept in Austria's foreign policy. This attitude was to influence Austria's dealings with Germany and to be expressed in the policy of unequivocal repudiation of the Greater German concept in the domestic field. This aim served to build faith with the Four Powers, to illustrate acceptance of their occupation system, and to once and for all repudiate the temptation for Anschluß.

Second, a political stance which created effective guarantees against any sort of Anschluß policies on the part of Germany went hand in hand with the *politics of the gradual normalization of bilateral relations*. This was based on the recognition of the territorial *status quo* and the quadripartite occupation system excluding territorial claims and minor adjustments of borders.

To prevent it from becoming a Western state in the manner of Bonn, Austria had to achieve political unity, for the danger of division always meant a renewed hazard of Anschluß. The repudiation of any alternative policy in favor of one which maintained the concept of a single integral state was the best guarantee against a partial or complete Anschluß.

The *policy of an inner balance* both among the major Austrian political parties and between the Western and Soviet occupation forces became condition *sine qua non* to the avoidance of German political dominance. Because of the obstructions ensuing from the unsettled German Peace Treaty, only by stalling tactics was success to be reached in Austrian foreign relations. For Austria, this also involved maintaining the Four Power Occupation of the country which served as a protection guarantee against new German aspirations *vis-à-vis* Austria.

Third, the Austrian *public appeal* in German policy was to be "European," "responsible," and "rational." The purpose was to bring about respect for the independent existence of the southern neighbor and an immunization from any Anschluß tendencies. There was also a simultaneous consciousness raising about the necessity of normalizing relations beyond the economic field. The occupation system could also appeal as an European solution of the Austrian question as well as an answer to the German Question.

Fourth, the *recommendation of the solution of the Austrian question* as a minor Allied priority in comparison with Germany and as an essential precondition to peaceful conflict resolution in Europe, a prelude and contribution to the reduction of tensions on the continent, was an ambivalent idea. These display-window politics had two functions, one direct and one indirect. First, it was supposed to have served to make the Soviet Union more willing to withdraw its troops from Austrian soil. Second, it could have been understood as a contribution toward defusing the tensions regarding the German question.[4]

Out of this came the recommendation of the Austrian model for a successful solution of the German problem. However, and this difference is decisive, the method of negotiating on a Four Power level was crucial. Yet the Austrian model could not be applied. In 1955, when the Austrian solution was in the offing, the dissimilarity of the situations in Austria and Germany was emphasized by the simultaneous implication of possibly equal or similar roads to solution. All of this required the approval of all of the Four Powers. This policy excluded a recommendation of the "Austrian Solution" for Germany ("incomparability"). The Austrian goal of the restoration of national sovereignty was not to be jeopardized, however.[5]

Fifth, a *(mutual) policy of the principle of non-interference*, above all with regards to Germany, based upon reciprocity and the respect of the different choices of foreign policy options (in the case of Austria, Western orientation, full national sovereignty, neutrality, and unity; in the case of Germany, total integration with the West, NATO alliance, partial national sovereignty, and two-states status) played a crucial role. Austria officially respected Bonn's Germany-centered political option and the so-called "Hallstein Doctrine," which precluded relations with any third countries that recognized the GDR. Bonn, on its part, more or less accepted Vienna's neutrality option.

Now we should deepen and underline these five points.

Tactic One: Austria's Status as Victim

Regarding point number one above, the Moscow Declaration of 1943[6] by the Anti-Hitler Coalition on the Reestablishment of Austrian Independence, for whatever reasons it was proclaimed, offered both in letter and spirit various political opportunities Austria was willing to take.

The "victim status" and "occupation theory" offered—not exactly to the joy of the Germans[7]—the possibility of maneuvering the country away from the wake of the Third Reich. This would exempt Austria from demands for reparations and claims for compensation by victims of persecution after the Anschluß and by relatives of victims and exiles. A policy of rectification in the international arena in the manner of the Federal Republic of Germany never came into question for Vienna, and this was not met by Allied objections. Given these facts, Austria was confronted only with an occupation "lite." Demands for restitution by representatives of Jewish interests were only partially fulfilled, and these were the only individuals to whom payments were made. With regards to restitution to Israel, Austria was able to get away with not paying, under the countenance of the West and with the far-reaching help of the ready and able to pay Federal Republic of Germany behind it.

The "shadow of the German question,"[8] however, still hung over Austria in the form of contentious "German property" in Austria, on which the victorious powers had claims according to the resolutions of the Potsdam Conference (1945). This question of German assets stalled the State Treaty negotiations (1947-1949) for almost a decade and resulted in tensions and conflicts not only between the Allies, but on a broader international stage as well.

From the Moscow Declaration forward, Austria's national destiny could be defined only as a type of antithesis to Germany. After the Second World War, Austria's politicians saw in this "defensive stance" the only chance for "national liberation" from the "Reich" and the point of departure for the national process of emancipation from Germany which they considered necessary. Thus harsh measures ensued under the protection and consent of the politicians in the newly liberated country against those German citizens who remained in the country (totaling 346,000 in 1945 and 18,600 in 1955) who were treated thoughtlessly, had their property expropriated, and were disciplined, expelled, or deported.[9] This was "clean slate" politics, which left no room for criticism of Austria's own conduct in the Nazi era.

Point Two: Avoiding Anschluß, Ensuring Sovereignty

From the point of view of the victors, the Austrian case was associated with the German question on the basis of the "Anschluß" trauma in a still narrower connection than before 1938. Because of that, Austria became in many ways not only an instrument of the Allied policy toward Germany, but also an aim of itself. Austro-German relations after 1945 were fully under the control of the occupation powers. Only in 1953 could the first signs of emancipation be witnessed.

The Ballhausplatz was well-informed about conditions in Germany, even though any regular diplomatic representation in the German zones did not yet exist. For the time being, the so-called "liaison offices" in Germany were put in charge of consular officials. The first Austrian representatives took up official duties in Bonn in the beginning of the 1950s.

With the beginning of negotiations for a state treaty, Vienna stressed the desire "to guarantee a clear and lasting separation from Germany, not only politically, but economically and financially as well." This made necessary a clear distancing from any thought of Anschluß. It was emphasized that Austria had "much more pressing problems to solve than to get lost in obsolete ideologies." In order to stress national self-determination and to prevent Allied interference, it was emphasized that "under no circumstances were international measures required" in order to refuse a reunification with Germany. Nevertheless, the victorious powers reserved the right to subject bilateral relations to their control, to impose an Anschluß ban on Austria, and to oblige Germany to recognize the independence of the Alpine republic.[10]

While Austria with regard to the Second Control Agreement of 1946 possessed a meaningful "lead toward statehood" over Germany,[11] the occupying powers treated it as a mere appendage of the German question.[12] Austria had to complain regularly about being relegated to the lower rungs of the international ladder. From 1947 to 1949, it became the victim of Germany once again. This time, it was the victim of inter-Ally disagreements in the handling of the German question. That this fact stood in contradiction to the liberation postulate of the Moscow Declaration did not escape public scrutiny, but public criticism regarding this breach had little effect. Austria's politicians could not have known in 1947 that this 1943 Allied document was a product of wartime psychological propaganda interests.[13]

As long as this had a negative influence on the policy of self-interest and a conflict of goals could grow out of it, Bonn was neither able nor willing to help Vienna out of this dilemma. For West Germany, a rapid signing of a state treaty coupled with troop withdrawal and obliging Austrian freedom from alliance were not desirable. Just such an international status would have endangered West Germany's realization of Western integration, especially in terms of public opinion. Though Vienna absolutely had to avoid implementing the "German solution" in its own country, Bonn categorically rejected an "Austrian solution" to the German question. Chancellor Konrad Adenauer saw "having wrung the neck of the dragon of neutrality" as "his greatest achievement."[14]

The Western powers would hardly have been prepared in 1955 to give their assent to the "Austria solution" if Adenauer had wanted to adopt it as a model for the solution to the German question. Vienna could, therefore, be happy over the German chancellor's position, and it was reassuring to see that for Adenauer an Anschluß never came into question. He considered the Greater German solution a closed matter, in spite of a certain nostalgia in the German Foreign Ministry.

In the estimation of the Austrian foreign minister, the formation of the German "Bizone" in 1947 had "led to a deterioration of the cooperation in the Allied Control Council of Berlin." That "lack of coordination of views, which disturbed international relations" was looked upon as one of the primary reasons for the delay in concluding the State Treaty. Because of this, the clearing-up of the German question was in Austria's best interests. Once the German question was resolved, the Austrian solution would inevitably have to follow.

While Vienna increasingly made the conclusion of a state treaty the centerpiece of its diplomatic initiatives from 1947 to 1949, the term "peace treaty" disappeared more and more from the vocabulary and the political agenda of West German politicians. In Austria, the occupation forces continued to have a certain common interest in maintaining state unity and a working relationship in the Allied Council, which acted as an important platform for Four Power discussions, what the French called "*le quadripartisme*."[15] In Germany, the conflicts of interest among the Occupation Powers quickened, culminating in the Berlin Blockade of 1948-1949, where the framework for partition was already laid. The Allied Control Council in Berlin failed.[16] In this tense situation, the Ballhausplatz officially put forth the thesis that the German and Austrian situations could not be compared. Between Vienna and Berlin a "huge difference" existed. Austria had, first of all, a single currency and, secondly, a recognized government, "so that a partition of Austria could only succeed if the government were eliminated by force." With the Western Powers, the Austrian foreign minister saw their focus on eliminating the Berlin crisis. He perceived no inclination on their side "to give up the rehabilitation of West Germany." For Austria, the solution would be "to push forward with the policy of stalling for time in the long term" which made sense for two reasons. First, the more distant the war was, the better the treaties would be; second, if the world's political situation were not to change, Foreign Minister Gruber argued, Austria would always remain in a dangerous position. The more time that passed, the more likely it was that change would occur in the international arena. Despite all public reassurances, the Ballhausplatz was in crisis. The Western Allies took into consideration as well the possibility of a Berlin-style airlift in case of a possible blockade of Vienna.[17]

An essential precondition for the *annus mirabilis* of 1955 was the astounding cooperation between former enemies in the civil war of the 1920s and 1930s, namely the Socialists and the Christian Socials (the modern day SPÖ and ÖVP). The Austrian government judged that maintaining the inner balance, that is, maintaining the Grand Coalition and the presence of *all* of the occupying powers, was a political necessity for the preservation of its integrity. The Four Power control, "*quadripartisme*,"[18] was only supposed to have been an interim solution until the final withdrawal of all troops and the achievement of national sovereignty.

Tactic Three: Normalizing Austro-German Relations

The founding of the Federal Republic of Germany did not simplify the linkage of the Austrian and German questions in regards to the policies of occupation and sovereignty. In 1949, Austria's foreign minister did not fail to point out that the present situation was "degrading" to the Austrian people. "What is even more disturbing" was that the Allied policy in Germany pointed out to Austrian youth

> to observe events in Germany with even greater mindfulness than those in Austria, because it is repeatedly hammered home to them by the Allies that what is occurring in Germany will also determine their destiny. This perhaps undesirable result is diametrically opposed to the principal idea of the Moscow Declaration.

Both problems remained interwoven not only because of past developments, but also because of present interdependencies. As long as the German Question was not resolved in favor of a definitive alliance with the Western Allies, Austria had to remain patient. "Germany first" in accordance with "to keep the Russians out, the Germans down, and the Americans in" confessed by Lord Ismay,[19] remained valid. Thus the consequence of this element of "triple containment" was "Austria second."

The French Foreign Ministry repeatedly expressed anxiety over a premature troop removal from Austria, which would bring into question the entire occupation, control, and integration of (West) Germany. A premature withdrawal and the resulting neutrality of the Alpine Republic would be interpreted as a "negative example" and an undesirable precedent for Germany. In 1955, even though the die was cast, these fears played no small role.

An increasing bilateralization of trade relations took place within the framework of the Organization for European Economic Cooperation. West Germany became a member one year after Austria, and a gradual normalization of economic relations and the return to the trade structure of the prewar era ensued. After an agreement on the exchange of goods had been concluded between Austria and the Bizone in August of 1948, a trade treaty with the Trizone was signed in the same month of the following year and went into effect on 1 October 1949. Before these agreements, Austria's trade minister, Ernst Kolb, had declared that, in view of the great need for goods, Austria had "the firm will to resume serious trade relations with Germany." The new quota list provided that Austria would export primarily timber, magnesite, textiles, and finished steel to West Germany, while coal, machinery, chemicals, raw steel, scrap metal, and electrical equipment would be exported to Austria.

Tactic Four: Distinguishing Austria from Germany in Resolving its Political Status

Basically, the question is whether Vienna considered the partition of Germany to be fact and, thus, irreversible, or whether room was left for the possibility of a reunification. The material that is available today yields no precise answer. However, it appears that in 1947-1948, the Ballhausplatz already recognized that events were proceeding toward a partition of Germany, meaning Germany would remain an "occupied ally" (*ein besetzter Verbündeter*), as Hermann-Josef Rupieper pointed out, while Austria should be restored as a liberated and secret ally of the West.[20]

In the beginning of the 1950s, Vienna included in its deliberations increasing certainty of the German partition being a *fait accompli*, thus emphasizing even more explicitly the lack of a basis for comparison between Austria and Germany. This seemed to happen with the intention of excluding deliberations on the applicability of the "German model," which would have meant the end of existence as a state and nation for the Alpine republic.

Neues Österreich, the publication of the Austrian democratic parties, warned in September 1951 against those who erringly "hold up Germany as an example and want to make us believe that Germany is already further along the road to freedom than we are." It called to mind three dangers: "the continuation of the division and the split," the perpetuation of the occupation "with its gigantic burden and restrictions on sovereignty," and this overall situation resulting in "the obligation to armament."

The Germany policy of the Soviet Union was also seen as instructive for Austria. Joseph Stalin's first note of 10 March 1952 is worthy of mention here. In it, the Soviet dictator had proposed a block-free, quasi-neutral (a seemingly neutralized) and unified Germany, which in the West was hardly welcomed with open arms.[21] Stephan Verosta of the Office for International Law of the Austrian Foreign Ministry asked himself whether the Soviet proposal on Germany might not also be valid for Austria.

Only a few nonconformist West German historians, such as Rolf Steininger or Wilfried Loth, persuasively argue for the serious intent of the March 1952 note, while the determined opponents insist (for, among others, reasons of loyalty to the policy of West Germany, political fears, and public expediency) that Stalin's offer was unacceptable for both the West and Adenauer. That is beyond argument. It alters neither the gravity of the note, nor the fact that if attention had been given to Stalin's offers and they would have been accepted, then Germany's formation as a Western state and the integration of Western Europe would have been foiled. That, however, was precisely in the interest of the Red Dictator. It remains to be discussed, however, whether in the case of Germany "Austrian solutions" would have been applicable. The fact remains that Moscow opposed the Western integration of the German Federal Republic and instead offered a bloc-free status along with the institution of national armed forces. All this did not prevent Austria's foreign policy from seriously taking into consideration just such a solution for Austria in 1952/53.

During his state visit to Bonn in May 1953, Austria's Foreign Minister Gruber argued that his country still under occupation should not pursue any policy which would initiate a process of partition. Adenauer seemed to have understood Austria's position on a rational level[22], but he had few sympathies for four-power controlled Austria. He was basically displeased by the "Allied cooperation" there in the form of the Allied Council. By itself, this "Austrian model" filled him with dread, let alone the troop withdrawal that had occurred and the permanent neutrality that had been declared in 1955. For Austria, this was the *annus mirabilis*, for Adenauer, absolute horror. Two years before, a basic arrangement had been worked out in Bonn.

Mutual agreement was achieved over "the different nature" of the two countries and the "incomparability" of the two situations. Vienna counted on the existence of a system which was stable and allowed Austria to defend itself militarily and to which Germany ought to belong also. This excluded any suggestion of a German policy of neutrality. Austria once again supported the normalization of relations and the intensification of economic cooperation with West Germany as a means to national consolidation and to the strengthening of territorial integrity, for which a political Anschluß would clearly be harmful. After his return from Bonn, Austria's foreign minister had the impression "that the German government would not go through with an Anschluß" (!), while he was of the opinion that there should be "no Anschluß, but also no Chinese wall." Because of growing negative experiences of the Austrian people from 1938 to 1945, a resurrection of Anschluß was seen by the Ballhausplatz as "an efficient and lasting guarantee against any experiments in that area."[23]

There were two things that lay in Austria's interest: first, both a definitive decision in the German question, which became apparent for West Germany in 1954-1955, and second, a broad-based reduction of tensions on the international level in order to revive the stalled state treaty negotiations. Vienna desired to eliminate the occupation of Austria, which by this time was seen as no longer necessary.

Vienna would have been a suitable venue for an international conference in the 1950s, but the bloodily suppressed uprising in the GDR on 17 June 1953 brought the shadow of the German question back over Austria, even if the Russian occupation element had tried to begin a liberalization in its zone in Austria. How the events of 17 June originated and proceeded was precisely analyzed by the Ballhausplatz with respect to any change of the Soviet attitude towards Austria. The Austrian foreign minister pointed out that, at this point, it became apparent that the advantage of Austria's position was clearly an advantage for the Great Powers as well, "They could liquidate their position without there being the danger of an explosion and without having to deal with a loss of their prestige."[24] The official Austrian foreign policy was one of restraint and "not barging in." It was emphasized that West Germany's alliance policy was "exclusively the affair of the Bonn government and that it had no influence upon Austria's foreign policy."

Austrian Chancellor Julius Raab and German Chancellor Konrad Adenauer held opposing points of view regarding foreign policy, and both consistently stuck to their line.[25] Neither had much room in which to maneuver. In October 1953, Karl Gruber came to the conclusion that if there were anything left that could be changed regarding the German question, it would take place *in Austria,* which was serving as a display window. While still in office, Gruber was convinced "that the greatest chance existed to improve the domestic position" because the Soviet Union sought a reduction in tensions and had a need "to better arrange its display window, in order to influence public opinion partly in Germany and partly in all of Europe." The more this happened, the more the new line in Russian policy could "be favorably used by us."[26] With this assessment, Gruber was wrong concerning 1954, but correct for 1955. A ray of hope, for the moment, was that in February 1954, Austria was admitted to the Foreign Ministers' Conference in Berlin with the new Foreign Minister Leopold Figl and Undersecretary for Foreign Affairs Bruno Kreisky as negotiating partners with equal rights, while West

Germany had to wait for this status until the Foreign Ministers' Conference in Geneva in the autumn of 1955.

Tactic Five: Mutual Non-Interference

In the mutual refutation of the other country's model lay the solution of respective policies of national interest: in 1955, Adenauer's Germany was freed from its neutralization trauma—in part because Vienna did not officially recommend an "Austrian solution"—and the existence of the West German state was solidified. Raab's Austria was free of both occupation and partition trauma; with its neutrality, it had bought unity and freedom. The acceptance of the "Stalin note of 1955 for Austria"[27] did not result in Sovietization, but made possible a further Western orientation of the country, while Germany remained divided. With the cementing of this state of affairs in 1955, Austria also became formally free from Germany. The definitive Western orientation of the German Federal Republic fostered the process of detachment from "Big Brother." Adenauer's policy sacrificed reunification for Western European integration. It also contributed indirectly to Austria's becoming independent and its formation as a sovereign state.

Apart from external factors, Austria's own policy was an essential precondition for the *annus mirabilis.* Vienna in this phase of semi-détente gained political capital for its own interests. It was a strategy of winning time for foreign policy and maintaining balance in domestic policy. Thus it was a considerable political achievement. So the *annus mirabilis* had preconditions specific to Austria.

What seems to be certain is this: in 1955, Germany was still an important issue to the Soviet Union. Above all, Moscow aimed at preventing or delaying the ratification of the Paris Treaties and, thus, the rearmament of West Germany and its NATO membership. In contrast to Bonn, Vienna reacted to the new signals from Moscow and began a process of sounding out the Kremlin with a seasoned representative there.

Chancellor Raab approved of German rearmament for reasons of European security. However, because of information coming from the foreign ministry, he feared that after the ratification of the Paris Treaties by the German parliament,

> a reunification of Germany would be prevented for a long time, the outcome of which could be a stiffening of both sides of the front in the East-West conflict and finally the tearing apart of Austria if the American and Soviet general staff became doggedly fixed on their strategic positions in Austria.[28]

Raab could not help but officially note that Adenauer's policy was "successful" for West Germany. It increased Austria's security, yet for a long time, it also hindered and endangered Austria's independence. According to Raab, the real source of Soviet fears was the impending dominance of the Germans on the continent, not an Anschluß of Austria as in Hitler's times. The reason why Raab had his reservations concerning the neutrality option was that he was afraid that it would create difficulties for Adenauer. For him, "difficult questions [arise] if we begin a neutralization, especially because of Germany." He worried about who would stop the Russians if they were to march to the Atlantic. On the other hand, Raab intimated that a willingness to negotiate should not be rejected. In spite of possible negative repercussions toward the Federal Republic of Germany, Raab pleaded for bilateral Austrian negotiations with the Soviets, although he wanted "no Austrian independence as a Russian protectorate." He was of the opinion that the Soviets would "naturally withdraw from Germany as well as Austria if the Americans would also retreat and Germany would declare itself neutral." For Raab, there was no doubt that the Soviets would have an offer ready for Adenauer which was similar to the Austrian solution. He understood, however, that for Adenauer, this would be "not only an unbearable submission, but an unwise one as well." It was a bitter

> but politically unmistakable fact that Germany could not afford such an "Austrian escapade." It would be just too big and strong. Bonn had a "particular responsibility" which limited its freedom of motion. Austria's relative lack of size and importance were its strengths. Underlining Austria's significance "suited Soviet interests."[29]

The maneuvering room for Austrian diplomacy was severely restricted by the Soviet linkage of the German and Austrian questions. Before 1955, Moscow maintained its point of view that the Austrian State Treaty would only be concluded after the German question was solved. However, limiting the agenda to purely Austrian issues might lead to a conclusion of the State Treaty. That is why Vienna gave no recommendations regarding the "model case" since a renewed coupling of the two questions would once again put the Austrian solution on the back burner. Neutrality ought to have given a definite answer to the Anschluß danger, to the German Question and—most importantly—to the question of how to end the Allied occupation of Austria. A neutral Germany was not in the offing. This difference made any new Anschluß impossible. Therefore, as with Switzerland, Raab considered the "climate of neutrality" best for the solidification of Austrian patriotism.

In spite of these considerations, Raab viewed a partitioned Germany in the long run as a flashpoint, a potential source of danger to peace and, thus, an endangerment to Austria's independence as well. The "nightmare of Austrian policy" was the application of the German solution to the Austrian question, which was easily imaginable! With skill and luck, this horror scenario was averted by Vienna.

It could not at all be foreseen that the interplay between Vienna and Bonn on an official level would function so compatibly in preventing the raising of arguments regarding precedent-setting and the rejection of applying one country's "model case" solution to the question of the other. Since this could not be anticipated, it is not surprising that the Western powers in 1955 viewed Austria's readiness and agreement to negotiate with Moscow with great reservations.

The Austrian delegation was fully aware of the fact that Western agreement to neutrality could only be achieved if such neutrality would not set a precedent for Germany. Kreisky's statements, which explicitly excluded the possibility that Austria could be an example for solving the German question, demonstrated this. Certain circles in the Austrian Social-Democratic Party supported him through their statements, according to which the USSR wished to maintain Germany's division and only made proposals for Germany's reunification in the hope that they would be rejected.

Conclusion

The reattainment of Austrian independence in 1955 during the very days when the Paris Treaties were ratified meant emancipation from Germany not only on official and national levels, but also a far-reaching emancipation of Austrian foreign policy. Despite Austria and Germany's respective national independence, relations in the areas of economic and monetary policy became closer than before.

For Austria, the time of occupation only signified an interim solution, but it had an important long-term impact. Getting the foreign troops out of the country was the starting point for postwar Austrian nation building and part of a bigger success story of the Second Republic. No Russians remained in Austria after 1955, but Russians stayed in Germany until the 1990s.

Notes

1. Gerald Stourzh, *Um Einheit und Freiheit. Staatsvertrag, Neutralität und das Ende der Ost-West-Besetzung Österreichs 1945-1955*, 4th ed. (Vienna: Böhlau, 1998).

2. Thomas Angerer, "Frankreich und die Österreichfrage. Historische Grundlagen und Leitlinien 1945-1955," Ph. D. diss., University of Vienna, 1996.

3. Ernst Hanisch, "'Selbsthaß' als Teil der österreichischen Identität," *Zeitgeschichte* 23.5/6 (Mai/Juni 1996): 136-45.

4. Reiner Bollmus, "Die Bundesrepublik und die Republik Österreich 1950-1958. Stationen einer skeptischen Freundschaft," *Christliche Demokratie* 1.3 (1983): 9-23.
5. Michael Gehler, "Vom Sonderfall zum Modellfall? Österreich im Spannungsfeld von Kaltem Krieg, 'Tauwetter,' Semi-Détente und sowjetischer Deutschlandpolitik 1945-1955: Ein Literaturbericht mit zeitgeschichtlichen Kontroversen," in *Historische Debatten und Kontroversen im 19. und 20. Jahrhundert. Jubiläumstagung der Ranke-Gesellschaft in Essen*, ed. Jürgen Elvert and Susanne Krauß (Stuttgart: Steiner, 2003), 175-205.
6. Robert H. Keyserlingk, *Austria in World War II: An Anglo-American Dilemma* (Kingston: McGill-Queen's Univ. Press, 1988).
7. Matthias Pape, *Ungleiche Brüder. Österreich und Deutschland 1945-1965* (Cologne: Böhlau, 2000).
8. Michael Gehler, "'Kein Anschluß, aber auch keine chinesische Mauer.' Österreichs außenpolitische Emanzipation und die deutsche Frage 1945-1955," in *Österreich unter alliierter Besatzung 1945-1955* (Studien zu Politik und Verwaltung 63), ed. Alfred Ableitinger, Siegfried Beer, and Eduard G. Staudinger (Vienna: Böhlau, 1998), 205-68.
9. Matthias Pape, "Die deutsch-österreichischen Beziehungen zwischen 1945 und 1955. Ein Aufriß," in *Historisch-Politische Mitteilungen. Archiv für Christlich-Demokratische Politik* 2 (1995): 149-72.
10. Kurt Fiesinger, *Ballhausplatz-Diplomatie 1945-1949. Reetablierung der Nachbarschaftsbeziehungen und Reorganisation des Auswärtigen Dienstes als Formen außenpolitischer Reemanzipation Österreichs* (tuduv-Studien, Reihe Politikwissenschaft 60) (Munich: tuduv, 1993).
11. Manfried Rauchensteiner, *Der Sonderfall. Die Besatzungszeit in Österreich 1945 bis 1955* (Graz: Styria, 1979).
12. Gehler, "Kein Anschluß."
13. Keyserlingk, *Austria in World War II*; Günter Bischof, "Die Instrumentalisierung der Moskauer Erklärung nach dem 2. Weltkrieg," *Zeitgeschichte* 20.11/12 (November/December 1993): 345-66.
14. Matthias Pape, "Die deutsch-österreichischen Beziehungen."
15. Thomas Angerer, "Integrität vor Integration. Österreich und ‚Europa' aus französischer Sicht 1949-1960," in *Österreich und die europäische Integration 1945-1993* (Institut für Zeitgeschichte der Universität Innsbruck, Arbeitskreis Europäische Integration, Historische Forschungen, Veröffentlichungen 1), ed. Michael Gehler and Rolf Steininger (Vienna: Böhlau, 1993), 178-200.
16. Gunther Mai, "Der Alliierte Kontrollrat in Deutschland 1945-1948. Von der geteilten Kontrolle zur kontrollierten Teilung, " in *Aus Politik und Zeitgeschichte* B 23/88 3.6. (1988): 3-14.
17. Erwin A. Schmidl, "'Rosinenbomber' über Wien? Alliierte Pläne zur Luftversorgung Wiens im Falle einer sowjetischen Blockade 1948-1953," in *Österreichische Militärische Zeitschrift* 36.4 (1998): 411-18; idem, "The Airlift that Never Was: Allied Plans to Supply Vienna by Air, 1948-1950," *Army History* 43 (Fall 1997/Winter 1998): 12-23.
18. Thomas Angerer, "Integrität vor Integration."
19. Geir Lundestad, *"Empire" by Integration: The United States and European Integration, 1945-1997* (Oxford: Oxford Univ. Press, 1998).
20. Stourzh, *Um Einheit und Freiheit*; Günter Bischof, "Österreich—ein geheimer 'Verbündeter' des Westens? Wirtschafts- und sicherheitspolitische Fragen der Integration aus der Sicht der USA," in *Österreich und die europäische Integration. Aspekte einer wechselvollen Entwicklung* (Institut für Zeitgeschichte der Universität Innsbruck, Arbeitskreis Europäische Integration, Historische Forschungen, Veröffentlichungen 1), ed. Michael Gehler and Rolf Steininger (Vienna: Böhlau, 1993), 425-50; Oliver Rath-

kolb, "Historische Bewährungsproben des Neutralitätsgesetzes. Am Beispiel der US-Amerikanischen Österreich-Politik 1955 bis 1959," in *Verfassung. Juristisch-politische und sozialwissenschaftliche Beiträge anläßlich des 70. Jahr-Jubiläums des Bundesverfassungsgesetzes*, ed. Nikolaus Dimmel and Alfred-Johannes Noll (Vienna: Verlag der Österreichischen Staatsdruckerei, 1990), 122-41.

21. Andrej A. Gromyko, *Erinnerungen* (Düsseldorf: Econ, 1989).

22. Karl Gruber, *Zwischen Befreiung und Freiheit. Der Sonderfall Österreich* (Vienna: Ullstein, 1953).

23. Gehler, "Kein Anschluß."

24. Michael Gehler, *Karl Gruber: Reden und Dockumenten, 1945-1953: eine Auswahl* (Vienna: Böhlau, 1994).

25. Oliver Rathkolb, "Austria's 'Ostpolitik' in the 1950s and 1960s: Honest Broker or Double Agent?", in *Austrian History Yearbook* 26 (1995): 129-45; Josef Foschepoth, ed., *Adenauer und die Deutsche Frage* (Göttingen: Vandenhoeck & Ruprecht, 1988).

26. Gehler, *Karl Gruber*.

27. Michael Gehler, "Österreich, die Bundesrepublik und die deutsche Frage 1945/49-1955. Zur Geschichte der gegenseitigen Wahrnehmungen zwischen Abhängigkeit und gemeinsamen Interessen," in *Ungleiche Partner? Österreich und Deutschland in ihrer gegenseitigen Wahrnehmung. Historische Analysen und Vergleiche aus dem 19. und 20. Jahrhundert*, ed. Michael Gehler, Rainer F. Schmidt, Harm-Hinrich Brandt, and Rolf Steininger (Stuttgart: Steiner, 1996), 535-80.

28. "Bericht der Studiengruppe Südost "Neuorientierung der österr. Außenpolitik?", B/Arb/142/54, 15. 3. 1955, Valjavec an AA, 18. 3. 1955. PA/AA, Abt. 3, Referat 304, Österreich 94.19, Bd. 46 (38), 83.00, Zl. Zl. 403/55.

29. Confidential Report, "Wiener Widerhall der außenpolitischen Stellungnahme des deutschen Bundeskanzlers," a letter by Prof. Fritz Valjavec, 25 April 1955 to K. Döring/Auswärtiges Amt. PA/AA, Abt. 3, Referat 304, Österreich 94.19, Bd. 40 (32), 82.50-82.80.

Soviet Plans and Policies for Austria's Transition to Socialism, 1945-1955

Wolfgang Mueller

Soviet Planning, 1943-1945

In the Moscow Declaration of 1 November 1943, the Soviet Union and the Western Allies had agreed to liberate Austria from Nazi influence and to restore it as an independent democratic state.[1] On 29 March 1945, Red Army troops on their way to the full destruction of Nazi Germany entered Austria. A special proclamation of the Soviet government, issued on this occasion, stated that "the Soviet government does not intend to annex any part of the Austrian territory or to change the Austrian social system. The Soviet government adheres to the Moscow Declaration of the Allied Powers on Austrian independence. It will fulfill this Declaration."[2]

While it is certainly true that the highest ranking Soviet aims concerning postwar Austria were to create a democratic and de-Nazified, "Soviet-friendly" independent state, further Soviet intentions, for a long time, remained, in Winston Churchill's memorable phrase, "a riddle wrapped in a mystery inside an enigma."[3] Given the non-accessibility of Russian archives, the long-term goals of the USSR in Austria had to be decoded from public declarations and other low-level sources. The first Austrian monograph dealing with the issue, Wilfried Aichinger's doctoral thesis, "Sowjetische Österreichpolitik 1943-1945,"[4] relied heavily on Soviet official and printed sources and could not draw on internal Soviet documents. In his conclusion, Aichinger denied that the Soviet Union in 1945 had any other political intention than to restore Austria to its independent, democratic status. In particular, he stated that the USSR did not want to transform Austria politically into a people's democracy. Until recently, Aichinger's interpretation remained unquestioned among Austrian historians dealing with the question.[5]

However, newly accessible Soviet documents reveal a different picture and suggest that 1) the USSR expected the political transformation of the country into a people's democracy and 2) the means for this political transformation envisioned by the USSR was a national front regime which the USSR planned to establish (and actually did establish) in Austria. In his famous memorandum dated 11 January 1944, Ivan Maiskii, then head of a Special Planning Commission of the Foreign Ministry, suggested that the political regimes in European countries liberated from Nazi rule should be formed as national front governments consisting of all democratic parties including communists.[6] Maiskii did not mention Austria explicitly, but it appears to have been considered as one of those countries where a national front government should be formed. In particular, the wartime planning of Austrian communist émigrés in Moscow reveals the intention to create such a government in Austria after the war.[7] Although it was never called a national or people's front, the Austrian communists' program which was discussed and agreed upon with Georgii Dimitrov[8] had all its ingredients: a bloc of all "anti-fascist democratic" parties, a non-communist prime minister with a communist deputy and communist ministers of interior, education, and economy.[9]

As recent publications emphasize,[10] the Soviet national front strategy was closely linked with the political goal of establishing socialism. Concerning further political developments, Maiskii was convinced that after the war all of Europe or "at least its continental part becomes socialistic." [11] This was not understood to be the result of an outright revolution, but as a long-term process lasting thirty to fifty years. These expectations were confirmed by Communist Party of the Soviet Union (CPSU) Foreign policy curator Andrei Zhdanov who, in June 1944, wrote in a draft about "the peaceful transition of Germany, Austria and Hungary to socialism."[12] Therefore, the communist and Soviet plans to form a national front government in Austria (as was the case with Soviet support for national front governments in Poland, Rumania, Bulgaria, and Hungary) have to be seen as the first step in the Soviet strategy to transform the country politically into a people's democracy.

Soviet Occupation Policy in Austria, 1945-1955

This thesis is even further underscored by the directives and actions of the Soviet occupation authorities in Austria. In April 1945, Stalin ordered Dimitrov to form an *Initiativgruppe* consisting of Moscow-trained Austrian communists in order to build political power bases for the Communist Party in Austria (CPA) right after the end of fighting and before the formation of the national front.[13] While the *Initiativgruppe* would be active, the Soviet authorities in Austria were instructed to prohibit all other political activities except communist ones among the Austrian population.[14] Only after the arrival of the Western Allies and the formation of an Allied Commission in Austria was it planned to give other democratic parties freedom of action and to let them join the communists in forming a national front government. This Soviet concept looks very much like the Soviet policy in Germany.[15] In Austria, the plan was frustrated by the sudden appearance of the social democrat and former Austrian chancellor Karl Renner who, in April 1945, contacted the Soviet occupation authorities and offered to form a provisional government. Stalin decided to accept this offer, to drop the *Initiativgruppe*, and to move on to the second stage in his plan, the formation of the national front. The Soviet authorities made Renner understand that they would support him if he, while forming the government, fulfilled the communist demands.[16]

Renner's government consisted, initially and in equal numbers, of social democrats, conservatives, and communists. Despite the communists having received all the cabinet posts they had wanted (the post of a vice-chancellor, the ministries of interior and education, and approximately one-third of all seats), they soon came under pressure from Renner himself who, after the approval of the government by the Russians, obviously did not care very much about what his communist ministers wanted, and also from the social democrats who resisted the communist invitations to form an *Aktionseinheit* (joint action program).[17] Neither in the decision-making in the cabinet, the discussion of a new constitution, the establishment of communists in the administrative apparatus, nor in the formation of three-party mass organizations (for example, the *Freie österreichische Jugend*) were the communists able to achieve their goal. The Soviet authorities in Austria were to learn that Renner's and the other parties' policy in several cases was directed outright against the communists' interests.[18] Due to their preoccupation with plundering the country, the problems posed by the disastrous discipline of Soviet troops, the redeployment of the occupation forces, and the change in the high command, the Soviets were not ready to intervene until two months later.[19] By then, Soviet action had to be very cautious in order not to spread rumors about having created another "puppet government" and, thus, run the risk that the other Allies might refuse to approve the Renner government.

One of the Western Allies' preconditions for approval the Renner government was to hold general elections in 1945. At the 25 November elections, the Austrian Communist Party received only 5.4 percent of the vote and subsequently lost all but one cabinet seat. This was a major setback for the Soviet strategy. Nevertheless, the political aim to strengthen communist influence and to prepare Austria's political transition to socialism remained unchanged. Due to the presence of the Western Allies in Austria and the limitation of the Allied responsibilities set down in the 2nd Control Treaty of June 1946, the Russians had little direct influence on the political situation in Austria. In order to implement its political aims, the Soviet element of the Allied Commission for Austria relied mainly on the following policies: 1) strong control over the Austrian government, the non-communist parties, and the media "according to the present occupation regime;" 2) "discrediting the reactionary character of the Figl government" by the means of pro-Soviet and pro-communist propaganda; 3) and "unleashing the initiative of the democratic forces by helping the Communists" with financial, political, and propagandistic support.[20]

In the following years, these policies became major elements of Soviet strategy. The official statement of the Soviet mission in Austria declared:

> "The Soviet element of the Allied Commission in Austria is responsible for: 1) the control upon the activity of the Austrian government [. . .] in their fulfilling of the decisions of the four powers concerning the democratization, denazification and demilitarization of Austria [. . .]. 2) the organization of the political work and propaganda among the Austrian population about the Soviet Union and the people's democracies by the means of press, radio, cinema and other means. 3) the support of Austria's democratic [that is, communist. WM] organizations by consolidating their influence in the Soviet zone and the Soviet companies and by raising their role in the country's social and political life. [. . .]"[21]

The central role of these tasks is illustrated by the fact that the Soviet Propaganda Department in Austria, which was mainly responsible for these tasks, was the biggest of all twenty-eight functional units of the Soviet apparatus. It was twice as big as the second-ranking Economic Department, by itself making up almost 25 percent of the whole staff.

While it is certainly true that the Soviet Union did not fulfill every wish of its foreign "friends" (that is, the communists), the Austrian Communist Party remained the one and only important political partner of the USSR in Austria. It was supported by the USSR financially and politically, as well as in the Soviet propaganda. In 1946, the Soviet Politburo granted the CPA a first major subsidy of two million schilling, in the following years the subsidies reached the sum of more than öS 65 million ($2.5 million).[22] Politically, the communists' "reactionary" opponents, that is, the non-communist parties, were considered to be enemies by the Russians, too. The hostile Soviet attitude towards the Austrian government after the defeat of the communists, the growing Soviet pressure on government officials, and their ambition to frustrate Austrian attempts to reduce communist influence in the administrative apparatus and police are all examples of how the Soviets tried to fulfil their political mission to gain support for communism.[23] Furthermore, the Soviet authorities in Austria kept on calling for a new constitution, further de-Nazification, and "democratic reforms," thus trying to "unmask" the "reactionary" policy of the non-communist parties. In its propaganda, the Soviet Union also underscored its sympathy for the communists.

In order to weaken the non-communist parties and to find new coalition partners for the CPA, the Soviet element and the communists supported pro-Soviet and pro-communist groups in Austria. In 1946, the Soviet element established contacts to the social democrat dissident Erwin Scharf who, after expulsion from his party, founded the Socialist Workers' Party and, on the eve of the general elections of 1949, formed the *Linksblock* together with the communists. This merger was, as Deputy High Commissioner Aleksei Zheltov wrote, inspired and funded by the Soviet element which tried to influence the elections in a pro-communist way.[24] The *Linksblock* was designed to serve as a nucleus for a new pro-Soviet Austrian "unity front of the democratic and patriotic forces."[25] After the national front of 1945 had died a sudden death in the same year, the new bloc led by the communists was primed to take power in one of the following elections. Despite these efforts, the communist share of the vote stagnated at 5.08 percent.

Four years later, the pro-Soviet Democratic Union, also by invitation of the Soviets, joined this bloc with the communists and the leftist socialists, thus making it a new "national front."[26] The so-called *Volksopposition* was supposed to serve as a multi-party bloc after the model of the people's democracies.[27] The ambitious Soviet plans with the *Volksopposition* were frustrated by the third defeat of the communists in the general elections of 1953 who received only 5.28 percent of the vote. Nevertheless, the constant Soviet support for the Communist Party and for the Soviet-sponsored formation of the *Linksblock* in 1949 and the *Volksopposition* in 1952-1953 reveal the Soviets' intentions to strengthen communist influence in Austria and the fact that, by these means, the Soviet element hoped at least until 1953 to secure the creation of a communist-led, national front government and Austria's transformation into a people's democracy.

Inner Limitations and Contradictions of the Soviet Plans and Policies

Among many other reasons (for example, deeply rooted Austrian anti-communism, the unpopular Soviet behavior, the presence and the efforts of the Western Allies), this strategy failed for internal reasons.

Soviet political aims were limited by other goals and considerations of Soviet policy. In 1945, the Soviet attempt to gain support for the communists and to create a Soviet-friendly atmosphere clashed with Soviet economic aims in Austria, namely, the massive dismantling and removal of factories in the Soviet zone in order to support the economy of the USSR.[28] Nevertheless, the Soviet Union was not willing to reduce its economic demands. After the elections of 1945, the Soviet element was even less prepared for a compromise, and it went on with the sequestration of former "German property."

A second point that hindered Soviet political aims was that the USSR considered the occupation of Austria a temporary, even a short-term, phenomenon and that it was not willing to keep troops in Austria in order to make the country a people's democracy.[29] From the Soviet perspective, political goals had to be implemented either by the communists with the help of the Soviet element during its presence in Austria or by the communists alone after Soviet withdrawal. Although the Soviets used their military presence in Austria as a means to keep Hungary and Romania in line,[30] there is no indication that the Soviet leadership or the Soviet element considered it appropriate to extend the Soviet military presence in Austria in order to secure Austria's transformation into a people's democracy.

Furthermore, the USSR did not want to risk a military confrontation with the West over Austria. Indeed, the Soviets never took any political steps themselves to prepare a communist *putsch*, for any open political involvement of the Soviet occupation authorities in Austrian inner affairs would have provoked complications with the Western Allies. The political transition to socialism was planned to be peaceful. This became obvious on many occasions, most notably during the widespread strikes of October 1950. Technically, the Soviet element supported the communist strike movement by lending the strikers trucks, by hindering the Austrian police in its actions against the rioting communists, and by granting them propagandistic support on the Soviet element's radio program. But Soviet troops did not get involved into the riots—for the obvious reason that such an involvement could have provoked a similar Western military intervention. The historian William B. Bader states:

> "The Soviet Union was simply not prepared to go the limit. Confronted with the dilemma of either allowing the Communist Party to suffer a crushing defeat or committing the Soviet troops necessary to stave off such a setback, the Russians backed off. The Russians had done everything possible to indirectly aid the Communists. But [. . .] when the non-strikers successfully defended themselves and broke the Communist strike, the Russians refused to intervene directly. Soviet troops had never been used directly in creation of "people's demo-

cracies" throughout Eastern Europe, and the Soviet Union did not break this pattern in Austria. [. . .] Force [. . .] was a weapon the Soviet Union was apparently not prepared to use."[31]

Last but not least, the Soviet Union did not want to risk a split of the country. Soviet documents reveal as early as 1946 that the Soviets very much feared this possibility. On 16 September 1946, the Deputy Political Advisor of the Soviet element, Mikhail Koptelov, asked the leaders of the CPA if "the rumours about the attempts to split Austria in a Western and a Eastern zone are true."[32] The communists accused the other Austrian political parties—especially the conservative People's Party and the United States—of having such plans in mind. On the other hand, the Austrian communists themselves, in the following year, developed a strategy aiming for the secession of the Soviet zone under communist leadership. In 1948, the party leaders Johann Koplenig and Friedl Fürnberg were even summoned to Moscow where Andrei Zhdanov told them that he had learned that the Austrian communists felt that "a division of Austria would be better than any other alternative." [33] However, the Soviet Union would not agree to a scenario that entailed a partition of the country. Zhdanov clearly stated that this was not acceptable to the Soviet leadership. The CPA leaders had to recant their strategy. As long as the Western powers occupied the western provinces of Austria, a division of Austria would have provided them with the strategically more important part of the country. Regardless of the Soviet goal to create a communist-led government in Austria and to transform the country into a people's democracy, the solution of a partition of Austria seems to have been unacceptable to the Kremlin.

Nevertheless, the Soviet attitude toward Austria's inner political affairs, the clandestine involvement in the party system, especially the support of the communists, the strong pro-communist propaganda efforts, and the hostile and intransigent attitude to all non-communist political forces are signs of how the Soviet Union tried to fulfill its mission to assist Austria's peaceful transition to people's democracy and socialism. Obviously, the idea of "democratizing" Austria was not given up, at least not until 1953. Many years later, after the signing of the Austrian State Treaty and the Soviet withdrawal, Viacheslav Molotov still deplored that the Soviets had left Austria "without making it democratic."[34]

In his article "Rethinking the Role of Ideology in the International Politics during the Cold War,"[35] the historian Nigel Gould-Davies asserts that Soviet leaders did take the communist ideology as seriously as the security interests of their country. The "dual" nature of Soviet foreign policy made it possible to pursue *Realpolitik* and ideology at the same time (with uncertain success as it turned out). The Austrian example shows that Soviet foreign policy was neither as irrational and obsessed with world revolution as Cold War historiography tried to make us think, nor as apolitical as many revisionists believed.

Notes

1. On the Soviet planning and policies on Austria see: Wolfgang Mueller, "Die politische Mission der sowjetischen Besatzungsmacht in Österreich 1945-1955," PhD. diss., Vienna University, 2004; and *Russische Dokumente zur sowjetischen Besatzungspolitik in Österreich*, ed. Gennadii Bordiugov, et al. (Vienna: Verlag der Österreichischen Akademie der Wissenschaften, 2005). The author expresses his gratitude to Gennadii Bordiugov, Aleksandr Chubar'ian, Barry McLoughlin, Norman Naimark, Larisa Rogovaia, Arnold Suppan, the Russian and the Austrian Academies of Sciences, and the Fond zur Förderung der wissenschaftlichen Forschung.

2. Declaration of the Soviet government, 9 April 1945, *UdSSR – Österreich 1938-1979: Dokumente und Materialien* (Moscow: Novosti, 1980), 22.

3. Quoted in Donal O'Sullivan, *Stalins "Cordon Sanitaire": Die sowjetische Osteuropapolitik und die Reaktionen des Westens 1939-1949* (Paderborn: Schöningh, 2003), 107.

4. Wilfried Aichinger, "Sowjetische Österreichpolitik 1943-1945," PhD. diss., Vienna University, 1977.

5. Manfried Rauchensteiner, *Der Sonderfall: Die Besatzungszeit in Österreich 1945 bis 1955* (Graz: Styria, 1979); Oliver Rathkolb, "Historische Fragmente und die „unendliche Geschichte" von den sowjetischen Absichten in Österreich 1945," in *Österreich unter alliierter Besatzung 1945-1955*, ed. Alfred Ableitinger et al. (Vienna: Böhlau, 1998), 137-58.

6. Maiskii to Molotov, 11 January 1944, *SSSR i Germanskii vopros 1941-1949: Dokumenty iz Arkhiva vneshnei politiki Rossiiskoi Federatsii*, vol. 1, ed. Georgii Kynin and Jochen Laufer (Moscow: Mezhdunarodnye otnosheniia, 1996-2003), 333-60, here 348. Cf. Aleksei M. Filitov, "V komissiiach Narkomindela...," in *Vtoraia mirovaia voina*, ed. Oleg A. Rzheshevskii, et al. (Moskau: Nauka, 1995), 54-71; Vladimir O. Pechatnov, "The Big Three After World War II: New Documents on Soviet Thinking about Post-War Relations with the United States and Great Britain," *Cold War International History Project Working Paper* 13 (1995).

7. Karl Vogelmann, "Die Propaganda der österreichischen Emigration in der Sowjetunion für einen selbstständigen österreichischen Nationalstaat 1938-1945," PhD. diss., Vienna University, 1973; Oliver Rathkolb, "Wie homogen war Österreich 1945? Innenpolitische Optionen," in *Inventur 45/55: Österreich im ersten Jahrzehnt der Zweiten Republik*, ed. Wolfgang Kos and Georg Rigele (Vienna: Sonderzahl, 1996), 157-80; Manfred Mugrauer, "Die Politik der Kommunistischen Partei Österreichs in der Provisorischen Regierung Renner, " Master's thesis, Vienna University, 2004.

8. Entry, 4 April 1945, *The Diary of Georgi Dimitrov, 1933-1949*, ed. Ivo Banac (New Haven, CT: Yale UP, 2003), 366. Cf. Ernst Fischer, *Erinnerungen und Reflexionen* (Reinbek: Rowohlt, 1969), 467-69.

9. Political Platform of the Austrian Communist Party, [April 1945], Rossiiskii gosudarstvennyi arkhiv sotsial'no-politicheskoi istorii, Moscow, (RGASPI) 17/128/781/22-27. Text in *Russische Dokumente zur sowjetischen Besatzungspolitik in Österreich 1945-1955*.

10. Edward Mark, "Revolution by Degrees: Stalin's National-Front Strategy 1941-1947," *Cold War International History Project Working Paper* 31 (2001); O'Sullivan, *Stalins "Cordon Sanitaire."*

11. Maiskii to Molotov, 11 January 1944, *SSSR i Germanskii vopros*, vol. 1, 333-60, here 335.

12. Tatiana Volokitina, "Stalin i smena strategicheskogo kursa Kremlia v kontse 40-kh godov: ot kompromissov k konfrontatsii," in *Stalinskoe desiatiletie kholodnoi voiny*, ed. Aleksandr Chubar'ian, et al. (Moscow: Nauka, 1999), 10-22, here 13.

13. Entry, 2 April 1945, *The Diary of Georgi Dimitrov*, 365-66; Dimitrov to Stalin, 3 April 1945, *Komintern i vtoraia mirovaia voina*, vol. 2, ed. Nataliia Lebedeva and Mikhail Narinskii (Moscow: Pamiatniki istoricheskoi mysli, 1994/98), 486-87.

14. Draft Directive on the Duties of the Political Group for Austrian Affairs, [April 1945], Arkhiv vneshnei politiki Rossiiskoi Federatsii, Moscow, (AVPRF) 06/7/26/325/4-9. Cf. Wolfgang Mueller, "Sowjetbesatzung, Nationale Front der friedliche Übergang zum Sozialismus: Fragmente sowjetischer Österreich-Planung 1945-1955," *Mitteilungen des österreichischen Staatsarchivs* 50 (2003): 133-56.

15. Norman M. Naimark, *The Russians in Germany: A History of the Soviet Zone of Occupation, 1945-1949* (Cambridge, MA: Harvard UP, 1995), 252-60.

16. Ernst Fischer, *Das Ende einer Illusion: Erinnerungen 1945-1955* (Vienna: Molden, 1973), 65-68; Adolf Schärf, *Österreichs Erneuerung 1945-1955: Das erste Jahrzehnt der zweiten Republik* (Vienna: Volksbuchhandlung, 1955), 35; OSS Interview with Leopold Kunschak, 21 August 1945, *Gesellschaft und Politik am Beginn der Zweiten Republik: Vertrauliche Berichte der US-Militäradministration aus Österreich 1945 in englischer Originalfassung*, ed. Oliver Rathkolb (Vienna: Böhlau, 1985), 136-37.

17. *Protokolle des Kabinettsrates der Provisorischen Regierung Karl Renner 1945, vol. 1: „...im eigenen Haus Ordnung schaffen": Protokolle des Kabinettsrates 29. April bis 10. Juli 1945*, ed. Gertrude Enderle-Burcel, et al. (Horn: Berger, 1995). Cf. Anton Pelinka, "Auseinandersetzung mit dem Kommunismus," in *Österreich: Die Zweite Republik*, vol. 1, ed. Erika Weinzierl and Kurt Skalnik (Graz: Styria, 1972), 169-201, here 174-79.

18. Report of acting political advisor in Austria, Koptelov, about the meeting with communist government members, 16 May 1945, *Velikaia Otechestvennaia, vol. 14/3-2: Krasnaia Armija v stranakh Tsentral'noi, Severnoi Evropy i na Balkanakh: Dokumenty i materialy 1944-45*, ed. Institut voennoi istorii (Moscow: Terra, 2000), 661-64.

19. Cabinet Protocol 23, 7 August 1945, *Protokolle des Kabinettsrates der Provisorischen Regierung Karl Renner 1945, vol. 2: „Right or wrong—my country!" Protokolle des Kabinettsrates 17. Juli 1945 bis 5. September 1945*, ed. Gertrude Enderle-Burcel, et al. (Vienna: Verlag Österreich, 1999), 211-13. Cf. Robert Knight, "The Renner State Government and Austrian Sovereignty," in *Austria 1945-95: Fifty Years of the Second Republic*, ed. Kurt Richard Luther and Peter Pulzer (Aldershot: Ashgate, 1998), 29-46, here 32-33.

20. Head of Propaganda Dept. of Soviet Army Burtsev to CPSU Suslov, 23 May 1946, RGASPI 17/128/112/112-115.

21. Decree of the Council of Ministers of the USSR on the Mission of the Soviet element of the Allied Commission for Austria, [February 1952], Gosudarstvennyi arkhiv Rossiiskoi Federatsii, Moscow, (GARF).

22. Politburo Protocols, Rossiiskii gosudarstvennyi arkhiv noveishei istorii, Moscow, (RGANI) 89/38/16/1-5, 89/38/24/1-2, 89/38/26/1-2, 89/38/28/1-5, 89/38/33/2-3.

23. For further details, see Mueller, "Die politische Mission der sowjetischen Besatzungsmacht."

24. Soviet Deputy High Commissioner in Austria Zheltov to CPSU Grigor'ian, [18 August 1949?], RGASPI 17/137/112/21-32.

25. Head of Soviet Propaganda Dept. in Austria Dubrovitskii on the elections in Austria, 27 October 1949, RGASPI 17/137/117/2-35.

26. Soviet High Commissioner in Austria Sviridov to CPSU Smirnov, 21 March 1953, RGANI 5/28/70/1-56.

27. Kurt Skalnik, "Parteien," in *Österreich: Die Zweite Republik*, vol. 2, ed. Erika Weinzierl and Kurt Skalnik (Graz: Styria, 1972), 197-228, here 225.

28. Rathkolb, "Historische Fragmente," 147-52; Günter Bischof, *Austria in the First Cold War, 1945-1955: The Leverage of the Weak* (Basingstoke: Palgrave, 1999), 36-43.

29. Conversation of Zhdanov with Koplenig and Fürnberg, 12 February 1948, RGASPI 77/3/100/9-16. Text in *Russische Dokumente zur sowjetischen Besatzungspolitik in Österreich 1945-1955.*

30. Wolfgang Mueller, "Anstelle des Staatsvertrages: Die UdSSR und das Zweite Kontrollabkommen 1946," in *Die Gunst des Augenblicks: Neuere Forschungen zu Staatsvertrag und Neutralität*, ed. Manfried Rauchensteiner and Robert Kriechbaumer (Vienna: Böhlau, 2005).

31. William Banks Bader, *Austria between East and West* (Palo Alto, CA: Stanford UP, 1966), 181, 197.

32. Conversation of Soviet High Commissioner Kurasov with the leaders of the CPA, 16 September 1946, RGASPI 17/128/910/195-210. Text in *Russische Dokumente zur sowjetischen Besatzungspolitik in Österreich.*

33. Conversation of Zhdanov with Koplenig and Fürnberg, 12 February 1948, RGASPI 77/3/100/9-16. Ibid.

34. *Molotov Remembers: Conversation with Felix Chuev*, ed. Albert Resis (Chicago: Ivan R. Dee, 1993), 10.

35. Nigel Gould-Davis, "Rethinking the Role of Ideology in International Politics during the Cold War," *Journal of Cold War Studies* 1 (Winter 1999): 90-109, here 105.

Stalin and the Austrian Question[1]

Norman M. Naimark

Joseph Stalin remains something of an enigma for historians studying his policies in Europe after World War II. To be sure, the opening of the Russian archives after the fall of communism and the publication of memoirs, like those of his chief deputies Viacheslav Molotov and Lazar Kaganovich, have made possible interesting insights into his objectives and actions. But the sources for reconstructing his foreign policy remain only partial.[2] First of all, we have no firm understanding of how much material remains classified in the Russian Presidential Archives. Of those documents which were turned over to the Party Archives in Moscow (RGASPI), approximately a quarter have not yet been declassified. Second, the archives of the Russian Foreign Ministry (AVPRF) remain among the most difficult to use in Moscow. Despite the increasing amount of material that has become available to historians, either for research in the archives or in published document collections, the inability of scholars to use the archival guides of the Foreign Ministry papers makes it impossible to undertake systematic research on Soviet foreign policy. Finally, there is the problem of Stalin himself, who, as far as we know, left no diaries or intimate reflections on his policies and, when engaging his lieutenants, foreign guests, and communist and non-communist interlocutors, was consistent only in his dissimulation and in his propensity to adopt a persona that met his and their needs at the moment. Even the best of the many new biographies of Stalin—those of Simon Sebag-Montefiore, Donald Rayfeld, Yoram Gorlizki and Oleg Khlevniuk, and, most recently, Robert Service—are disappointing when it comes to helping us come to terms with Stalin's intentions in Europe after the war.

Despite these limitations, one can identify a number of general principles of postwar planning in foreign policy to which Stalin most probably subscribed. First of all, Stalin held a healthy respect for the power of nationalism and, therefore, for the principle of national sovereignty. This derived both from his experiences as Commissar of Nationalities in the early 1920s and from his understanding of the fearsome potential of revanchist nationalism in Europe during the 1930s. Thus those East European communists who hoped to turn their countries into republics of the Soviet Union met with Stalin's strict disapproval. The countries of Eastern and Central Europe would be reconstituted on a national basis. Not only that, Stalin shared the postwar proclivities of national majorities in these newly constituted countries to expel their minorities. He raised no objections to Polish and Czechoslovak attempts to engage in the ethnic cleansing of Germans and Ukrainians in the former case, or Germans and Hungarians in the latter. There is also no reason to doubt Stalin's repeated injunctions that Germany should be independent and united, though early on in the war Stalin was perfectly willing to go along with Winston Churchill and Theodore Roosevelt's ruminations about carving up Germany into various territorial units. Even in the immediate postwar period, Stalin feared, as did the Americans and British, that a divided Germany would provoke German nationalism and revanchism and cause another war. In Stalin's scheme of things, Austria would be independent, in part as a way to deny her to a potentially greater Germany, in part because he thought that a small and weak Austria would be easier to influence and to dominate.

The second principle of Soviet foreign policy under Stalin in this period had to do with the eventual transformation of European nations into socialist entities. This would be a long-term process, which would see each country take its own peaceful road to socialism. Repeatedly, Stalin told communist leaders from both Eastern and Western Europe that there was no reason they needed to endure the Soviet trauma of civil war and dictatorship of the proletariat. Through the formation of multi-party national fronts, modeled on the "Popular Fronts" of the 1930s, all the countries of Europe, including Germany and Austria, would evolve in the direction of People's Democracies. Everywhere there would be parliamentary institutions and coalition governments of the left and center. Communist parties were instructed by Stalin to reign in or to expel radicals and revolutionaries, so-called "sectarians," who were considered extremely dangerous opponents of Soviet aims in Europe. Stalin even told members of the British Labor Party that they should ignore the monarchy and work for the peaceful construction of a People's Democracy in Great Britain.

The third principle of Stalin's foreign policy in this period was that of spheres of influence, one shared by Churchill and Great Britain, but undermined, rhetorically at least, by Roosevelt and the United States. The most consistent demand for Soviet influence during the war involved those territories conceded to the Soviet Union by the Nazi-Soviet Pact, including its secret annexes. This meant that the Baltics, Moldova (Bessarabia), and Eastern Poland (Western Belorussia and

Western Ukraine) would be incorporated into the Soviet Union. In addition, Germany would lose East Prussia, and Czechoslovakia would cede Carpatho-Ukraine. According to an 11 January 1945 memorandum by Deputy Foreign Minister Maxim Litvinov, in addition to territorial gains in the west, the Soviets sought a sphere of influence in Poland, Hungary, Czechoslovakia, Romania, Yugoslavia, Bulgaria, Turkey, and Finland. Interestingly, Albania was not mentioned, perhaps because it would be "swallowed," as Stalin later mentioned in discussions with Milovan Djilas, by Yugoslavia. Litvinov also noted that the Soviets would seek a sphere of influence in Sweden and Norway. The British sphere of influence would include Greece and Western Europe: Holland, Belgium, France, Spain, and Portugal. Between the Soviet and British spheres of influence, wrote Litvinov, was the "neutral zone," Denmark, Germany, Switzerland, Italy, and Austria, "[. . .] in which both sides could cooperate on an equal basis with ongoing consultations between themselves." Litvinov added that the British would not be happy at all about having Sweden, Norway, Turkey, and Yugoslavia in the Soviet zone. They would also try to include Sweden and Norway, as well as Denmark and Italy (from the neutral zone) in their sphere of influence. In such a case, Litvinov assumed, there would be room for "trade and compromise."[3]

The fourth principle of Stalin's foreign policy at the end of the war and beginning of the peace related to the eventual disposition of Red Army forces. "Whoever occupies a territory also imposes on it his own social system," so Stalin famously proclaimed to Milovan Djilas during World War II, "Everyone imposes his own system as far as his army can reach. It cannot be otherwise."[4] This statement is often used by historians to demonstrate that Stalin understood both that the Soviet system would be spread as far as the Red Army was able to march and that the Anglo-Americans would impose their bourgeois form of democracy on the territories that they liberated from the Nazis. The presence of Red Army forces in every area, however, did not assure the development of a Soviet-style system. The Soviets fully occupied the Danish island of Bornholm in the Baltic Sea from 9 May 1945 to 5 April 1946 when, with the quiet urging of the Danes (but little pressure from the Allies), they withdrew all of their troops and returned Bornholm to the Danish government. Similarly, the Soviets withdrew from Austria, though it took until the State Treaty in 1955 to do so. In neither case, one should add, was a Soviet-style government constructed. One could also point to those countries, on the other hand, like Czechoslovakia and Finland, where the immediate withdrawal of Soviet forces in 1945 did not obviate the development of governments "friendly" to Moscow.

The question of why the Soviets left Austria and signed the State Treaty when they did is discussed in considerable detail in the historiography, though without, in general, the benefit of using internal Soviet archives.[5] Equally interesting, but much less discussed, is the question of why the Soviets stayed as long as they did, given the fact that the occupation of Austria was costly both financially and politically, and was unnecessary from a long-term strategic standpoint. Scholars have argued that the Soviets could justify the presence of their troops in Hungary with reference to the need to support their occupation of Austria.[6] The initial justification for the maintenance of troops in Poland was to sustain lines of military communications from eastern Germany to the Soviet Union. Some historians have also suggested that the Austrian State Treaty was held hostage to the successful resolution of the German question from the Soviet point of view.[7] Thus Austrian independence was a bargaining chip in the Soviet struggle, initially to prevent the division of Germany and, later, to forestall the joining of West Germany with the North Atlantic Alliance. However one judges the strategic context of the Austrian occupation, already by the end of its first year it was clear to everyone, including the Soviet authorities in Vienna and in Moscow, that the ongoing presence of Red Army troops in Austria undermined positive Austrian-Soviet relations and made the Austrian Communist Party even more unpopular than it already was. Initial Soviet concerns about the joining of Austria to Germany (a "new Anschluß") or about an Austrian-centered and British-dominated Danubian federation quickly dissipated. Once the Soviets had seized and exploited oil reserves in the eastern part of the country and removed those industries they deemed necessary to rebuilding back at home, there was no more reason to be there, especially if they could be compensated for the relatively unproductive and uncompetitive industries directed by the so-called USIA (Administration for Soviet Property in Austria) and the Soviets' other economic institutions in their zone. Over time, it became increasingly difficult for these industries to sell their products, acquire raw materials, and pay their workers.

According to the Moscow Declaration on Austria of 1 November 1943, the Great Powers declared that Austria was a victim of Nazi aggression and deserved to be returned to a state of independence as it was prior to 1938.[8] There was no talk of a long-term occupation of Austria and no intent to remain beyond the time necessary to ensure the final defeat of the Third Reich. In preparation for the occupation, Stalin stated clearly to Dimitrov, "We want Austria restored to its status quo as of 1938."[9] Similar statements by Molotov and his deputies in the Foreign Ministry corroborated Litvinov's conception, cited above, that Austria would belong to a group of non-aligned countries in the middle of Europe. When the Soviets marched into Vienna in April of 1945, their proclamation "To the Austrian People" reiterated that Austria fell "as the first victim of German aggression" and that the Red Army would liberate the Austrians from "German-Prussian domination."[10] Immediately, the Soviet authorities sought out Karl Renner, head of the Austrian Social Democratic Party—"that old fox," as Stalin called him—to run the new Austrian administration.[11] The Western Allies were initially very hesitant about Renner and his administration, fearing that he was too much of a leftist and would be too compliant with Soviet wishes. But Renner proved to be strikingly adept at keeping the trust of the Soviets and allowing the communists of the KPÖ to join his administration in a trilateral arrangement with the Social Democrats and the People's Party, while following his own "Austrian" national path. That the Austrians themselves approved of this path was demonstrated in the election of December 1945, which was, from the Soviet and KPÖ point of view, a catastrophic defeat. The communists received only 5.4 percent of the vote, in comparison to almost 45 percent for the Social Democrats, and, most surprisingly, 50 percent for the Austrian People's Party.

Although it is unlikely that Stalin and the Soviets had any interest in occupying Austria longer than was necessary to ensure their claims to German assets and to veto Austria's potential integration with Germany, the elections made crystal clear that they could not count on support from the Austrian population for their presence. Between December 1945 and June 1946 when the Austrian government was recognized by the four-power occupation as having control over its own laws, the attitude of the West towards the Renner government changed radically. Now the British and the Americans were much more supportive of extending Austrian governmental sovereignty than were the Soviets, who were frustrated and annoyed by Renner's growing power and independence.[12] Still, there was considerable hope in western diplomatic circles and in Austria that a state treaty could be signed and occupation forces withdrawn. But two obstacles stood in the way. One was Soviet claims on German assets in Austria, as initially defined at Potsdam, and eventually involved compensation for the USIA-run industries; the second was the Soviets' backing in 1946 and 1947 of Yugoslav border demands on Austrian Carinthia.[13]

Nikita Khrushchev claimed in his memoirs published during the Mikhail Gorbachev period that Stalin's desire to support Yugoslav demands in Trieste was critical to the Austrian negotiations.[14] After the Soviet-Yugoslav split became public in June 1948 and Josip Tito proved more resistant to Soviet pressure than Stalin had anticipated, it was no longer necessary or desirable to back Yugoslav claims. Khrushchev reports, "I remember Stalin saying, 'We didn't sign any peace treaty [with Austria]. Why did we have to refuse to sign? That was a mistake, all because of Trieste. Now that issue doesn't even exist anymore.'"[15] In the documents of the Soviet Element of the Allied Control Commission in Austria during 1948 and 1949, there are repeated references to the imminent withdrawal of all Allied occupation forces in Austria.[16] The question was not whether the withdrawal would occur, but what would happen when it did. Audrey Kurth Cronin believes that the Soviets were ready to sign the State Treaty during the June 1949 Paris Foreign Ministers Conference. The Yugoslav border issues were no longer important, and the Soviets and the West had come to an understanding about compensation for Moscow's economic assets in Austria. In her view, disagreements among the Western powers and within the U.S. government between the Departments of State and Defense delayed the signing. By the time the West had its negotiating house in order and returned to the Soviets with a firm proposal in hand in November 1949, the Soviets were no longer willing to come to the table.[17]

Khrushchev's portrait of Stalin repeatedly returning to the issue of signing the State Treaty is backed up by internal Soviet documents that show Stalin's interest in getting out of Austria even before problems with the Yugoslavs were beyond remedy. Andrei Zhdanov, in his discussions with visiting Austrian communist leaders Johann Koplenig and Friedl Fürnberg (13 February 1948), represented the Central Committee of the CPSU(b) and, no doubt, Stalin. Zhdanov berated the Austrians for being satisfied with the occupation of their country and for looking to the division of Austria between east and west to solve their problems, "The TsK of the KPÖ builds its tactics on the proposition that Soviet troops should stay for an extended period on Austrian territory. The TsK of the CPSU(b) does not agree." Moreover, the Austrian communists should not be depressed by the "perspective of the liquidation of the occupation regime." Instead, they should seize the moment for defending the full national sovereignty of Austria, which is the wish of true Austrian democrats and patriots. The presence of Soviet occupation troops in Austria is a "necessary evil," but an "evil" nonetheless, one that needed to be removed in order for Austria to develop in a democratic fashion. Zhdanov concluded by advising the KPÖ chiefs to seize the issues of independence, sovereignty, and the removal of occupation troops from the right and center of the political spectrum and staunchly to defend the Austrian national cause. "We believe in your strength," stated Zhdanov disingenuously, "You don't. That's the main difference between us."[18]

We still have no firm understanding of why Stalin allowed the Austrian situation to stagnate after the initiatives of 1948-1949 came to naught. There was every reason to pull out. The number of occupation troops in the west and east had dwindled to nominal numbers, and the Austrian government almost completely controlled the internal policies of the country. Soviet troops continued to embarrass the political authorities with periodic sprees of violence, rape, and lawlessness, as well as desertion. The KPÖ remained weak and divided; the party was a constant source of worry for and criticism from Soviet bosses. Meanwhile, Moscow repeatedly berated the leaders of the political and propaganda apparatus of the Soviet Element for their passivity, for their inability to make any headway in the Austrian countryside, for their poor relations with the communists, and for any number of other sins. We know from Khrushchev that Stalin episodically returned to the subject of Austria before his death. Clearly, there were those in Austria, pro-Soviet communists and pro-Western democrats, who saw it in their interests to prolong the occupation. But the Austrian government and the vast majority of the Austrian people longed for an end to the four-power presence. Only Khrushchev's determination to act on the State Treaty after Stalin's death ended the anomaly of the unwanted and counterproductive occupation.

Notes

1. This essay derives in part from my article, "Stalin and Europe in the Postwar Period, 1945-53: Issues and Problems," *Journal of Modern European History* 2.1 (2004): 38-41.

2. See Norman M. Naimark, "Cold War Studies and New Archival Materials on Stalin," *The Russian Review* 61 (January 2002): 1-15.

3. G.P. Kynin and I. Laufer, eds., *SSSR i Germanskoi Vopros 1941-1949*, vol. 1 (Moscow: Mezhdunar. Otnoshenie, 1996), 596.

4. Milovan Djilas, *Conversations with Stalin*, trans. Michael Petrovich (New York: Harcourt, Brace, Jovanovich, 1962), 114.

5. See especially Gerald Stourzh, *Geschichte der Staatsvertrages 1945-1955: Österreichs Weg zur Neutralität*, 4th ed. (Wien: Böhlau, 1998).

6. Hungarian communist party leader Matyas Rakosi worried about the withdrawal of Soviet troops if a peace treaty were signed. In April 1947, Molotov told him that he need not be concerned for the time being, for "[a] treaty with Austria will certainly not be signed this year." (Constantine Pleshakov and Vladislav. Zubok, *Inside the Kremlin's Cold War: From Stalin to Khrushchev* [Cambridge, MA: Harvard Univ. Press, 1996], 99.)

7. See, for example, Michael Gehler, "'Kein Anschluß, aber auch keine chinesische Mauer,' Österreichs außenpolitische Emanzipation und die deutsche Frage 1945-1955," in *Österreich unter Alliierter Besatzung 1945-1955*, ed. Alfred Ableitinger, Siegfried Beer, and Eduard G. Staudinger (Wien: Böhlau, 1998), 205-30.

8. Günter Bischof, *Austria in the First Cold War, 1945-1955* (New York: St. Martin's, 1999), 25-26.

9. Dimitrov, Georgi, *The Diary of Georgi Dimitrov*, ed. Ivo Banac (New Haven, CT: Yale Univ. Press, 2003), 365.

10. Arkhiv Vneshnei Politiki Rossiiskoi Federatsii (AVPRF), "K Avtriiskomu Narodu!", in "Ob Avstrii, no. 3797-g.

11. For Renner and the Soviets, see Robert Knight, "The Renner State Government and Austrian Sovereignty," in *Austria 1945-1995: Fifty Years of the Second Republic*, ed. Kurt Richard Luther and Peter Pulzer (Aldershot: Ashgate, 1998), 30-36, and Wilfried Aichinger, "The Sowjetunion und Österreich 1945-1949," in *Die bevormundete Nation: Österreich und die Alliierten 1945-1949*, ed. Günter Bischof and Josef Leidenfrost (Innsbruck: Haymon, 1988), 275-79.

12. Foreign Relations of the United States (FRUS), vol. 5, 1946, p. 364.

13. AVPRF, "Ob Avstrii," no. 3797-g.

14. Khrushchev, Nikita. *Khrushchev Remembers: The Glasnost Tapes* (Boston: Little, Brown, 1990), 72. See the somewhat fuller Russian version of the Austrian story, "Memuary Nikity Sergeevicha Khrushcheva," *Voprosy istorii*, 8 (1993): 73-88.

15. Khrushchev, *Khrushchev Remembers*, 72. Apparently, there were differences between the Yugoslavs and the Soviets on the Austrian issue. Tito urged the Austrian Communists to seek a division of Austria.

16. Gennadii Bordiugov, Wolfgang Müller, Norman M. Naimark, and Arnold Suppan, eds., *Russische Quellen zur Sowjetbesatzung in Österreich, 1945-1955* (forthcoming).

17. See Audrey Kurth Cronin, "Eine verpasste Chance? Die Großmächte und die Verhandlungen über den Staatsvertrag im Jahre 1949," in *Die bevormundete Nation*, ed. Bischof and Leidenfrost, 347. See also Cronin's *Great Power Politics and the Struggle Over Austria, 1945-1955* (Ithaca, NY: Cornell Univ. Press, 1986).

18. Discussion between Zhdanov, Koplenig, and Fürnberg, 13 February 1948, in Rossiiskii Gosudarstvennyi Arkhiv Sotsial'no-politicheskoi Istorii (RGASPI), fond 77, opis 3s, delo 100, listy 9-16.

REVIEW ESSAYS

Borders in Recent Austrian Historiography

Andrea Komlosy, *Grenze und ungleiche regionale Entwicklung: Binnenmarkt und Migration in der Habsburgermonarchie* (Vienna: Promedia Verlag, 2003).

Joachim Becker and Andrea Komlosy, eds., *Grenzen Weltweit, Zonen, Linien, Mauern im historischen Vergleich*, Historische Sozialkunde/Internationale Entwicklungen 23 (Vienna: Promedia Verlag & Südwind, 2004).

Josef Köstlbauer

Borders, boundaries, and frontiers have been a recurrent theme of scholarly studies. At least until the 1980s, the territorial and political aspects of borders clearly dominated research.[1] Since then new views on borders have flowered, mainly because of changing methodological and topical approaches imparted by the social sciences on historiography. Borders became crucial in understanding cultural transactions and change as well as the construction of national, regional, or ethnic identities. Moving beyond the relationship of border and territory, the dynamic boundaries between social, cultural, or economic spheres have become major topics of research.[2]

The 1990s have brought about a new awareness of borders in Europe. The fall of the Iron Curtain as well as the ongoing integration of the European Union have led to the disappearance of strict border regimes within a considerable part of Europe and have, thus, brought greater permeability of borders. At the same time, the European Union's external borders became increasingly well protected and immigration even more restricted.[3] The disappearance of a once menacing borderline cutting through the whole of Europe from north to south, bristling with minefields, watchtowers, and heavily guarded border posts, was an event which left its mark in the public consciousness, especially in those Central European countries that bordered the Iron Curtain on both sides (Germany, the Czech Republic, Slovakia, Hungary, and Austria).

All member states of the European Union or candidates aspiring to membership now share the experience of a gradual abolition of the Union's internal borders, an experience that has been massively reinforced by the introduction of the common European currency, the Euro.[4] This is significant by any standard; after all, monetary currency is one of oldest signs of territorial, administrative, and economic unity. Today, Europeans may travel over the whole of the EU, from Portugal to Finland, from Ireland to Greece, using the same currency, knowing they are moving within a politically and economically integrated space. Of course, this integration is by no means complete, and it is not even certain if this is desired by the various peoples of the Union or achievable politically. After all, EU enlargement has also been characterized by worries about the economic impact of the Union's expansion. The integration of national economies with lower wage- and price-levels is perceived by many in the Union's older member countries as a threat to economic security while the looming specter of mass immigration from countries with high jobless rates and few hopes for the young has fuelled outright xenophobia. This demonstrates the ambivalence of borders, be they rigid, impermeable delineations or easy to cross. Additionally, it shows the importance of borders for identity, for our sense who we are and where we "end," of who is "in" and who is "out."

The changed perceptions and new awareness of borders has spilled over into the world of historiography. This should not be a big surprise since historians are contemporaries, too. Who amongst us does not dream, at least secretly, of the chance to explain something that is of undeniable and acute relevance to society, a chance to demonstrate our discipline's relevance? Andrea Komlosy, professor of social and economic history at the University of Vienna, has obviously grasped such a chance. In 2003, she published her habilitation[5], *Grenze und ungleiche regionale Entwicklung* (*Borders and Disparate Economic Development*), on internal borders, migration, and regional diversity in the Habsburg Empire.[6] Komlosy herself points out in her preface (9) that she could not have written this book before 1989. Moreover, she repeatedly compares her findings concerning the diversity within the Habsburg Empire to the contemporary problems of European integration.

Adopting the methodological framework of the World System Theory,[7] Komlosy treats the Habsburg Empire as a kind of world economy of its own, with its own centers and peripheries (23-26). Combining this approach with a focus on borders both as objects and instruments of research, she examines economic and political changes in the

Western part of the Habsburg Empire in the eighteenth and nineteenth centuries. Her findings break with established perceptions. At the core of her work lies the assertion that the Habsburg Empire by the late nineteenth century was a modern state. It did not collapse because of large economic and regional disparities; quite the contrary, the integrative management of these imbalances was key to the Empire's economic success (Komlosy 18f.). The economic and political diversity provided the dynamics necessary for modernization instead of hindering it. She points out that the industrialized western provinces, including the internal peripheries that were interconnected through migration, kept pace with Western European industrialized states. The vast peripheries in the East provided agricultural products and raw materials and served largely as military buffer zones and staging areas. Migration from these areas in the nineteenth century was to Germany and the United States, their labor force being lost for the Empire. So the eastern territories were more or less excluded from the periphery-center relationships that fueled the modernization of the western parts of the empire. The Empire's economic success within the framework of the industrializing Western world was based on this tension between integration and disintegration. Komlosy regards borders as key to understanding social reality. She presents borders as multi-faceted, as boundaries as well as gateways or "membranes" between different social groups, orbits of power, and economic spheres. Borders are also a form of discourse used to legitimize mechanisms of social, cultural, or economic inclusion and exclusion (Komlosy 11). In the context of modernization, Komlosy examines two important ways in which borders changed. Starting in the late eighteenth century, internal tariff barriers were gradually abolished to create larger homogenous markets within the empire. This process at the same time fostered growing economic disparities between the regions and created regional division of labor. An assertion of state control and the creation of an increasingly centralized bureaucracy occurred simultaneously. Passports and a population census were introduced; taxation and conscription districts were consolidated into single territorial units. Central to these changes was the concept of *Heimatrecht* (right of origin), tying citizens to one place of origin in order to exert control over population movements, especially labor migration, and to enforce conscription. Essentially, this meant that people could be denied residence elsewhere and could (even by force) be deported to their communities of origin, thus protecting local markets and jobs. While economic barriers were abolished, the administrative streamlining and increasing control of migration created new regions and new borders within the empire. It also changed the way people looked at their environs and created their own identities.

The success of such a multi-national, regionally varied state and the importance of internal borders provides parallels to the process of European integration, "While the Habsburg Empire and the European Union are not the same, the Habsburg Empire, unlike any other European state, is an example to draw lessons from history about the integration of highly diverse regions."[8] Komlosy suggests that the gradual disappearance of economic and other barriers within the EU (for example, in higher education) may not have the effect of eliminating economic and political inequalities, but may reinforce or create new ones (Komlosy 392).

One of the weak points of her work is the almost exclusive focus on Austria and Bohemia (*Cisleithania*), virtually ignoring all other parts of the Habsburg Empire. While these territories indeed formed the historical core of the Habsburg territories, this fact alone does not automatically recommend them as focal areas for such a study. In addition, the resulting assumption that these areas represented the part of the empire with the highest intensity of interregional linkages (Komlosy 37) is made without further comment or evidence. The author notes that the kingdom of Hungary (*Transleithania*) was virtually an autonomous state. But the *transleithanian* part of the Empire did not exist in an isolated sphere, especially economically. What about the Habsburg possessions in northern Italy or Belgium? It might have been interesting to explore the economic integration of regions like Tyrol and Styria and the Adriatic Littoral within both the Habsburg Empire and a larger European sphere. One wonders whether the territories of Austria and Bohemia really constitute a viable base of research.

A rather astounding statement is made regarding the economic disparities between the regions of the Habsburg Empire: Komlosy likens them to the relationship between motherland and colonies! "The Habsburg Empire was characterized by large internal regional disparities, which in many respects resembled the relationship between imperial core and colonies."[9] This thought is not very clear, and the author gives neither proof nor source. Without doubt, there was an imperial center: the court at Vienna. But where is the motherland and where are the colonies in this empire? I am highly skeptical about attempts to apply the concept of postcolonial studies everywhere and especially to the Habsburg Empire.[10] Neither was this dynastic state a colonizing power in the classical sense, nor did it differentiate between its subjects as colonial powers did. Although it may be tempting to apply useful (and fashionable) concepts like postcolonialism in new and yet untested circumstances, such an application always holds the danger of distortion. To designate every form of *dependence* as colonialism ultimately deprives this concept of its intended meaning. Nevertheless, Andrea Komlosy's study of internal borders in the Habsburg Empire is a most interesting work. While the sheer complexity of the topic may be in part responsible for some shortcomings, this is without doubt a major contribution to border studies in Europe. One can only hope that the author keeps following the numerous threads and ideas contained in this book in her future research.

Komlosy's writings about the significance of internal borders can also be read in a comparative collection of essays titled *Grenzen Weltweit: Zonen, Linien, Mauern im historischen Vergleich* (*Borders throughout the World: A Historical Comparison of Zones, Delineations, Walls*). This volume was edited by Komlosy together with Joachim Becker, professor at the Vienna University of Economics and Business Administration. Her interest in the significance of the internal borders of the Habsburg Empire and the peculiar conditions of its modernization combines nicely with Becker's background in the theory of regulation and his studies of globalization and its repercussions.[11]

In the introduction, the editors stress the multi-faceted character of borders: territorial state borders, internal borders, regional borders, and economic borders delineating regional markets as well as borders created by imbalances in economic development and social, cultural, ethnic, and religious borders. They emphasize again the ambivalence of changing borders, and the topic's relevancy for modern discussions about European integration or globalization of markets is obvious.

With these ten essays, the editors hope to give the reader insights on five aspects of borders:

- formality and informality of borders
- character of borders, border conflicts
- border markings, fortified borders, border regimes
- permeability of borders: for whom or what and in which direction
- experiencing borders (Becker and Komlosy 9).

Combined, the assembled essays span the whole globe in their study of borders, which was the professed and rather ambitious goal of the editors. This open-mindedness is countered by a caution that every region's or state's position within the international division of labor has to be taken into account. This suggests an outlook that is profoundly shaped by economic theory, more specifically World System and Dependence Theory. While this certainly is valid, it is a rather narrow point of view which runs counter to the all-encompassing thrust of this compilation avowed by the editors. The editors proceed to introduce three different categories to examine borders from yet another angle: border and state (*Grenze und Staat*), state borders and ethnic minorities (*Staatsgrenze und Minderheiten*), and nation-state and supra-national integration (*Nationalstaat und supranationale Integration*). While this plurality is laudable, it creates an impression of inconsistency. The editors seem to be unable to present a clear mission statement contained in one short paragraph. Instead, the whole introduction seems to be pasted together from several different articles. A more focused introduction would have been useful, especially since this is a comparative work whose quality depends on clear guiding questions.

In a confusing move, the editors have decided to follow up the introduction with a first essay, co-written by themselves, that is meant as a theoretical introduction and presents different types of borders, from medieval town walls to the Iron Curtain. The result is a redundancy that reinforces the impression of a hastily assembled volume. With a fair bit of editorial streamlining, this could have been easily avoided, and the book would have profited enormously. This is especially true since this first essay stands out because of the way the five aspects of borders defined in the introduction are followed through and are moulded into a sweeping and engaging overview.

In the second essay, Hans Heinrich Nolte presents a very short and superficial comparison of the German medieval *Ostgrenze*, the southern frontier of early modern Russia, and the American West. The following three essays investigate how the character and organization of states and empires shape and form borders. Joachim Becker and Asli E. Odman compare the organization and specific characteristics of the disintegration of the Habsburg and Ottoman Empires. Andrea Komlosy herself contributes a comparative analysis of the relationships between interior and external borders within the Habsburg Empire and the European Union. Henning Melber presents an overview over the development of borders in Namibia and problems posed by the creation of postcolonial states within colonial borders.

The last five essays are concerned with economic, social, and cultural borders. Viktoria Waltz follows the labyrinthine problems of creating boundary lines between Israeli and Palestinian territories. She describes how different legal systems and their various forms of land ownership have been instrumentalized in the conflict between Palestinian communities and Israeli settlers. Helga Schulz studies so called "twin cities," like, for example, Èesky Tìšín and Cieszyn (Teschen), Frankfurt and Slubice, or Goricia (Görz) and Nova Gorica. These cities separated by borders out of necessity created crossborder relationships, and Schulz argues that they have become pathfinders for European integration. Hannes Hofbauer writes about the disintegration of the former Yugoslavia and the historical, national, ethnic, and economic aspects borders assumed in the secession conflicts. The Argentine monetary crisis of 2001/2002 is discussed by Joachim Becker and Paola Visca. They show

how Argentina's monetary system disintegrated and practically ceased to exist and how "Dollarization" and the use of various parallel currencies at that time led to new delineations within Argentine society or magnified existing ones. Karen Imhof looks at the U.S.-Mexican border and examines how the dissolution of economic barriers prescribed by the North American Free Trade Agreement (NAFTA) has led to increasing immigration from Mexico to the north. This movement has, in turn, resulted in new efforts by American authorities to control this immigration. She also shows how mass migration changed communities within Mexico, both culturally and economically, effectively making them peripheries of the U.S. market, supplying the north with a cheap workforce while at the same time the North American market integration destroys jobs in those areas.

While some articles are very concise and add new ideas to the study of borders, others lack both depth and scholarly exactitude. Especially where the early modern period is concerned, some authors commit to paper troubling superficialities. Problems also arise from the complications inherent in comparative research. After all, structural comparisons are probably one of the most difficult forms of historical research. The most striking negative example is Hans-Heinrich Nolte's comparative essay on the medieval German *Ostgrenze*, the southern frontier of Russia, and the American frontier. He refrains from providing a reason for the selection of these three examples, other than the fact that there are some obvious parallels: all three borders were moving frontier zones of expansionist powers. While this is certainly true, it does not in itself add up to a theory of explanatory value. Nolte comes up with a pretty vague conclusion, stating a "radicalization of the border." Of course, frontiers of expanding empires are radical. This hardly is a revelation—conquest is a pretty radical business most of the time. Nolte continues in very general terms; he attributes European expansion to a religious radicalization emanating from the Latin West and the Church's lack of tolerance towards non-Christians, which served to legitimize wars against other people (Komlosy and Becker 69f.). European expansion, the way Nolte understands it, seems to be a continuous process stretching from medieval crusades to the nineteenth century!

I have grave doubts concerning both the validity of the selected examples and the conclusions drawn by the author. After all, these three borders are separated in time by several centuries and were shaped by very different societies and historical processes. To declare some undefined aggression inherent in Western societies responsible for historical events as varied as the crusades or early modern European expansion is about as valuable an explanation as *homo hominem lupus est*. Such banalities explain everything as long as one does not aim at actually understanding things. Do not historians have the duty to reveal the complexity of the past instead of producing texts which basically say that a bunch of land-hungry religious fanatics conquered other peoples' territories?

Especially troubling is how Nolte explains the history of the North American frontiers. He presents a strictly linear view, without even mentioning the various processes of negotiation and intercultural contact that shaped American history and which have been the subject of a wealth of studies over the last two decades. This is even more puzzling as Nolte cites Richard White's seminal work *The Middle Ground* (Komlosy and Becker 65), which runs counter to Nolte's teleological interpretation of history. Nolte is almost more "Turnerian" than Frederick Jackson Turner himself, originator of the eminently influential frontier thesis.[12] Nolte unhesitatingly presents the Frontier as the root of American democracy, almost as if the American Constitution and the British common law tradition had not existed at all: "*Hier wurde jeder Waffen tragende Mann für grundsätzlich gleich angesehen. Die 'Frontierstaaten' bildeten deshalb die politische Grundlage für die Durchsetzung des Prinzips, ein Mann, eine Stimme' in den USA. Hier wurde aus dem in den Kolonien tradierten Ständwesen die Demokratie eine Stufe weiterentwickelt* [...]."[13] Generalization is a necessary and difficult undertaking, but it must not end in teleological narratives, unfit to be included even into the most basic history textbook.

Also implicitly tying the Teutonic Order's crusades against the Slavs to the battle between the Habsburgs and Bohemians at the White Mountain in 1620 is mildly absurd (Becker and Komlosy 70). Even more troubling is the author's attempt to imply a connection between these historic events and the Nazis' war against the "Slavic *Untermenschen*" and the various expulsions of ethnic Germans from Eastern countries immediately after 1945 (Becker and Komlosy 60).

Bringing historical depth to matters of contemporary or recent experience does not mean that one can jump over several centuries and suggest continuities and causalities that are strained at best. The case of Bohemia in 1620 was a matter of saving and asserting dynastic power, not of race or nation! Such linear constructs neglect the different frames of mind (different from us, that is), the different worldviews prevalent in the past and barely imaginable today—ideas and concepts that ultimately shaped the actions and possibilities of those living before us. Is it not the historian's duty to show the complexity of the past, the ways in which people shaped their lives according to their world and the way they experienced it? History as an open process is characterized by constant change and adaptation and—more often than not—surprise.

Henning Melber, a renowned specialist on modern Africa, especially Namibia, also makes some extremely perfunctory remarks on the period of European expansion and colonialism. He identifies an "internal colonization of Europe" (*innere Kolonisierung*), meaning both the emergence of the nation-state and the "drilling" (*Abrichtung*) of the respective subjects (Becker and Komlosy 126f.). Since when is colonization the same as state formation? What is the "*Abrichtung der Untertanen*" given the human capacity to subvert even the most radical attempts at total state control in the long run? Used in this way, the term "colonization" becomes meaningless! While such subjective statements are fine to sum up one's personal views, they are not exactly persuasive historical analysis. Melber's essay on the problems posed by colonial borders for postcolonial African states would be as enlightening and interesting to read without them.

Likewise, the introduction co-written by Becker and Komlosy contains some irritating statements in this vein:

> The USA, like Canada, could develop as a melting pot of settlers only because the indigenous population had been killed, expelled, or marginalized. At the same time the young nation did not accept existing colonial borders, but aimed at colonial expansion. Historical points of reference were the borderlands of the medieval *Ostexpansion*, the Spanish Reconquista and Russia's expansion into Central Asia.[14]

Is there really somebody out there who thinks that colonial and later American settlers, businessmen, cowboys, and railroad workers, got inspired by the medieval German *Ostexpansion*? I doubt it—so why imply historical causalities that are flat out wrong? I guess that more careful editing and cross-reading could have eliminated many of the sweeping generalizations that characterize some of the essays in this book. Even more disturbing are statements like the one that the EU's "core states" act like colonial powers towards the "peripheral" member states (Becker and Komlosy 17). Not only is no example and no source given to substantiate this surprising statement, there is also no explanation provided for the seemingly all-encompassing meaning of colonialism as used by the authors/editors. I'm afraid such remarks would seem frivolous from the perspective of those who did experience colonial life.

Browsing through this compilation caused some mixed feelings. It certainly is an ambitious enterprise to tackle such a broad theme on a global scale; still the overall impression is one of remarkable inconsistency. There are articles contained in this volume that would have needed serious reworking, while a few others are outstanding, like, for example, Helga Schultz's examination of twin cities or Joachim Becker and Paola Visca's essay on the Argentine monetary system. The very good and the very bad seem to coexist unhappily in this volume. Rather than two introductory essays, such a diverse set of texts might have merited a final essay to present a kind of unifying argument.

In the introduction to an often cited compilation of essays on borders in the early modern period, *Menschen und Grenzen in der Frühen Neuzeit*, the German historians Wolfgang Schmale and Reinhard Stauber have pointed out the fundamental problem of border studies: "border" has acquired a rather too expansive spectrum of meaning, making it an unwieldy category of research.[15] In this respect, Andrea Komlosy's monograph on internal borders and regional disparities within the Habsburg Empire represents a very valuable addition to the field of border studies. She introduces a very concise concept of borders, and her innovative take on borders as objects of historical research yields definitive new insights on integration processes in the context of modernization, breaking with longstanding assumptions about the causes of this Empire's demise.

The compilation Komlosy co-edited with Joachim Becker is a more controversial product. It suffers from a weakness common amongst such compilations: while the editors' approach is very ambitious, there is little tying the various essays together. In the end, there are just a couple of articles of unequal quality, and even those of high merit achieve little in the way of adding to or broadening the concept of borders as both instrument and object of historical research. Especially troubling are the obvious lacunae in the treatment of European expansion and the emergence of the nation-state in the early modern and modern period. After all, the early modern period was of crucial importance for the construction of Western ideas of borders and delineation and all their multifaceted aspects.[16] Unfortunately, some of the authors apparently have a penchant for wild generalization and produce teleological views of a linear, seemingly unstoppable process of European expansion and conquest. Their essays seem to be driven by the dogmatic new left agenda of world system analysis.[17] But nowadays, it is not exactly a revelation that American natives were killed or expelled, and Africans enslaved and transported to the New World. There are pretty few historians around who still write tales of heroic national accomplishments. So I wonder if some of the authors here are rising to challenge a way of writing history that has been discarded long ago. As the American historian Amy Turner Bushnell has pointed out, the paradigm of the victim in historiography is nothing more than a history of the powerful reversed.[18] It doesn't give credit to the "victims" if their actions and their successful strategies to adapt to radically changed conditions go unrecognized.

Notes

1. See, for example, Lucien Febvre, *Der Rhein und seine Geschichte* (Frankfurt a.M.: Campus Verlag et al., 1994); Idem, "'Frontière' – Wort und Bedeutung," in Febvre, *Das Gewissen des Historikers*, ed. and trans. Ulrich Raulff (Berlin: Wagenbach, 1988), 27-38.

2. See, for example, Wolfgang Schmale and Reinhard Stauber, eds., *Menschen und Grenzen in der Frühen Neuzeit* (Berlin: Berlin Verlag, 1998); Richard Faber and Barbara Neumann, eds., *Literatur der Grenze – Theorie der Grenze* (Würzburg: Königshausen & Neumann, 1995); Etienne François, *Die unsichtbare Grenze. Protestanten und Katholiken in Augsburg 1648-1806* (Sigmaringen: Thorbecke, 1991).

3. In 1985, the Schengen Agreement was signed by Germany, France, Belgium, Luxembourg, and the Netherlands to coordinate the removal of border controls. The Schengen Convention of 1990 (effective in 1995) abolished all border controls within "Schengenland" and regulated immigration into Schengen countries. The Amsterdam treaty of 1997 (effective since 1999) transferred the Schengen Convention into the EU legal framework. For further information see: *Europa, Gateway to the European Union: Schengen Convention European Commission* <http://europa.eu.int/comm/ justice_home/ fsj/freetravel/frontiers/fsj_freetravel_schengen_en.htm> (accessed 19 March 2005).

4. So far, the Euro has been introduced in twelve of the twenty-five EU member states.

5. The habilitation is a postdoctoral thesis which in some European countries is required for attaining professorship.

6. Andrea Komlosy recently made a summary of her research available to the English-speaking world in an essay published in the Review of the Fernand Braudel Center: "State, Regions, and Borders: Single Market Formation and Labor Migration in the Habsburg Monarchy, 1750-1918," *Review Fernand Braudel Center* 27.2 (2004): 135-77.

7. Immanuel Wallerstein, *The Modern World System*, vol.1-3 (New York: Academic, 1974-1989).

8. Komlosy, *Grenze und ungleiche regionale Entwicklung*, 392. "*Ohne Habsburgermonarchie und Europäische Union [. . .] gleichzusetzen, eignet sich die Monarchie wohl wie kein anderes europäisches Staatengebilde, um aus der Geschichte Lehren für die Integration höchst ungleicher Teilräume zu ziehen.*"

9. Komlosy, *Grenze und ungleiche regionale Entwicklung*, 15. "*Die Habsburgermonarchie war durch starke innere Gefälle zwischen den Regionen geprägt, die in vieler Hinsicht dem Verhältnis zwischen Mutterland und Kolonien ähnelten.*"

10. A recent example of postcolonial approaches to the history of the Habsburg Empire is Johannes Feichtinger, Ursula Prutsch, and Moritz Casaky, eds., *Habsburg postcolonial. Machtstrukturen und kollektives Gedächtnis* (Innsbruck: Studienverlag, 2003).

11. See, for example, Joachim Becker, *Akkumulation, Regulation, Territorium. Zur kritischen Rekonstruktion der französischen Regulationstheorie* (Marburg: Metropolis Verlag, 2002); Joachim Becker, et al., eds., *Finanzmärkte und neoliberale Herrschaft* (Wien: Promedia/Südwind, 2003).

12. Frederick Jackson Turner, *The Significance of the Frontier in American History* (New York: 1920). For a critique of the Turner thesis, see Patricia Nelson Limerick, "Turnerians All: The Dream of a Helpful History in an Intelligible World," *The American Historical Review* 100.3 (June 1995): 697-716.

13. Becker and Komlosy, Grenzen Weltweit, 15. "*Hier wurde jeder Waffen tragende Mann für grundsätzlich gleich angesehen. Die 'Frontierstaaten' bildeten deshalb die politische Grundlage für die Durchsetzung des Prinzips ,ein Mann, eine Stimme' in den USA. Hier wurde aus dem in den Kolonien tradierten Ständwesen die Demokratie eine*

Stufe weiterentwickelt [. . .]."

14. "Die *USA—wie auch Kanada—als melting pot von Siedlern konnte freilich nur entstehen, weil die indianische Urbevölkerung ausgerottet, vertrieben bzw. aus der Gesellschaft ausgegrenzt wurde. Gleichzeitig begnügte sich der junge Staat nicht mit den Kolonialgrenzen, sondern setzte auf koloniale Expansion. Er orientierte sich dabei an den strategischen Grenzsäumen, die die mittelalterliche Ostexpansion, die spanische Reconquista und den Vormarsch Russlands nach Zentralasien geprägt hatten.*"

15. Schmale and Stauber, Menschen und Grenzen, 16: "*Die Gefahr terminologischer Überdehnung wird dabei sicher im Auge behalten werden müssen.*"

16. Ibid., 7: "*Für die Entwicklung von Grenze-Vorstellungen jedweder Art bedeutet die Frühe Neuzeit eine Schlüsselepoche, die auf diese Weise bis in die Gegenwart fortwirkt.*"

17. A fresh and decidedly non-dogmatic approach to World System Theory is offered by Thomas J. McCormick. See: McCormick, "World Systems," in *Explaining the History of American Foreign Relations*, ed. Michael J. Hogan and Thomas G. Paterson (Cambridge: Cambridge Univ. Press, 1991), 89-98.

18. Amy Turner Bushnell, "Gates, Patterns and Peripheries: The Field of Frontier Latin America," in *Negotiated Empires: Centers and Peripheries in the Americas, 1500-1820*, ed. Christine Daniels and Michael V. Kennedy (London: Routledge, 2002), 16f.

Provenance Research as History: Reconstructed Collections and National Socialist Art Looting

Sophie Lillie, *Was Einmal War: Handbuch der enteigneten Kunstsammlungen Wien* (Vienna: Czernin Verlag, 2003)

Birgit Schwarz, *Hitler's Museum: Die Fotoalben Gemäldegalerie Linz Dokumente zum "Führermuseum"* (Vienna: Böhlau, 2004)

Ilse von zur Mühlen, *Die Kunstsammlungen Hermann Görings: ein Provenienzbericht der Bayerischen Staatsgemäldesammlungen* (Munich: Bayerische Staatsgemäldesammlungen, 2004)

Jonathan Petropoulos

In the mid-1990s, after a hiatus of some forty years, the topic of Holocaust-era cultural property re-emerged in the public consciousness. The reasons for this are complex and not entirely understood, but among the factors one would count generational change, the path-breaking scholarship of certain historians, the collapse of the Soviet empire (which precipitated a discussion of "trophy art" in Russia and temporarily opened archives), the re-unification of Germany (prompting property claims in the East), and the revelations about the comportment of Swiss banks during and after the Holocaust. It became clear to observers that there was, in Stuart Eizenstat's words, a great deal of "unfinished business of World War II."[1]

The renewed interest in Holocaust victims' assets found expression in myriad ways: international conferences with high level government officials were convened (in London, Washington, Stockholm, and Vilnius); national commissions featuring prominent historians were formed in twenty-four countries; lawsuits for allegedly unrestituted property were filed; and provenance researchers went to work, examining museum collections and vetting artworks offered for sale at auction houses and galleries. The process that began (or was rekindled) in the mid-1990s is now yielding results: lawsuits have now advanced past the preliminary stages and are heading to trial (for example, Altmann v. Austria, where the jurisdictional issues were adjudicated by the U.S. Supreme Court), and the provenance research that had been commissioned is now appearing in the form of books and elaborate websites.[2] Three outstanding exercises in provenance research have been published in the past year by Sophie Lillie, Birgit Schwarz, and Ilse von zur Mühlen. These exhaustively researched books tell us much about the field, both past and future. We understand why it has taken so long to produce this research, for this kind of scholarship requires enormous work: one must plough through voluminous record groups (one archivist from the National Archives and Records Administration testified before the Presidential Commission on Holocaust Assets in the United States that the College Park facility contained over 15 million pages related to Holocaust era assets). Furthermore, provenance research requires the difficult task of making connections between collectors, dealers, museums, and government agencies. But only this kind of detailed work can convey the scope of the Nazis' depredations and lead to appropriate measures to rectify past injustices.

In *Was einmal War*, Sophie Lillie has reconstructed the collections of 148 Viennese Jewish families. This accomplishment will undoubtedly prove useful to survivors, heirs, and their attorneys who seek to reclaim lost property (Lillie herself spent six years helping track works while employed at the *Israelitische Kultusgemeinde* in Vienna). In this regard, Lillie's efforts have been recognized with the Bruno Kreisky Prize from the Renner Institute. Even though her study is subtitled a "*Handbuch*" and has qualities that make it a reference book, it is a stunningly vivid work of history. Lillie creates a portrait of a Jewish community that was culturally vibrant and central to the city's identity. Numbering approximately 220,000 in 1938, Vienna's Jewish community featured members with diverse socio-economic status; clearly, not all individuals were prosperous or well educated.[3] But the city was home to a number of dazzling collections, perhaps most notably those of the Rothschilds, Bondys, Wittgensteins, Gomperz, Lederers, and Bloch-Bauers. These collections typically featured "blue-chip" artworks, including Old Masters, nineteenth-century paintings by German and Austrian painters, and works that we would today label classic modernism (by Gustav Klimt and Egon Schiele, among others). While some Viennese Jews collected Judaica, their holdings in general attest to the high degree of assimilation. Indeed, Sophie Lillie rejects the suggestion that these collections were specifically "Jewish" and notes that this was a fabrication used by the Nazis to help justify the expropriations (20). In reading *Was einmal War*—a book in excess of 1,400 pages—one gains the impression of a community that once flourished and was central to the city's cultural life. One now understands Hugo Bettauer's 1922 dystopic novel, *Die Stadt ohne Juden*, where Vienna without its Jewish population has been reduced to a dull, provincial, Tyrolian town.[4] Because Lillie also provides nuanced and insightful biographical sketches, her book is not merely a compendium of lost property. Indeed, her organizational schema shows why artworks had such personal meanings for the owners: they were part of people's lives, and in many cases, part of their familial traditions, passed down from one generation to the next.

Lillie's book is also a testament to the greatest plundering operation in history. Of course, Vienna was in many ways a kind of starting point in the Nazis' expropriations (historians are wellversed in Adolf Eichmann's "*Modell-Wien*" which paradigmatically denuded victims of their property before emigration, ghettoization, or worse). The spree of "wild Aryanizations"—that is, spontaneous and usually non-sanctioned acts of dispossession— that accompanied the *Anschluß* in March 1938 is also generally understood, even if many details of specific acts have now been lost. Lillie, however, shows how quickly the plundering machine went into operation once the initial flare of "wild Ayanizations" was dampened by government authorities who themselves assumed control of the expropriation process. In June and July of 1938 alone, the *Oberfinanzdirektionen* for Vienna and the surrounding areas in Lower Austria and Burgenland processed over 50,000 coerced declarations of property worth some 2 billion Reichsmarks (13). A small army of employees helped execute the expropriations: bureaucrats who made the appraisals and filed the paper-work, workers at moving companies who packed and transported the property to warehouses, experts at auction houses such as the state-owned Dorotheum that liquidated the works, and so on. Beyond the swelling-ranks of the "*Handlanger*," one sees the energetic and direct involvement of the Nazi leaders: starting with Adolf Hitler, Hermann Göring, and Heinrich Himmler, continuing on through to the local powers (initially Arthur Seyss-Inquart and Josef Bürckel, and later Baldur von Schirach), and down to less exalted officials with an array of positions in the Nazi Party, the state, and the municipal government. Again, the scale of Sophie Lillie's book helps convey the scope of the crimes or, more specifically, how theft preceded mass murder, how depriving victims of their property was part of the dehumanization process, and how making individuals complicit in the expropriations was part of the radicalization process that culminated in murder.

The focus of Sophie Lillie's book, however, is not on the perpetrators but on the victims. Despite the powerful message communicated by the scale of the study, it is most moving when one becomes engrossed in the lives of specific individuals. Her treatment of the Gomperz family offers one example. Philipp Gomperz and his siblings were the children of Max Ritter von Gomperz, the president of the Rothschild-founded Creditanstalt. Lillie notes that they were not only "*Geldarisotraktie,*[. . .] *sondern vor allem in ihren Salons der Mittel- und Treffpunkt von Politik, Wissenschaft, Kunst und Literatur*" in Vienna (417). The siblings were forced to flee Austria in 1938, and the Nazi authorities set to seizing and dividing up their property. The Gestapo, headed in Vienna by Dr. Karl Ebner, led the way in confiscating objects, but they did not keep collections intact. Göring acquired some of their tapestries, ten works were directed to the *Führermuseum* planned for Linz, and *Reichsstatthalter* Baldur von Schirach commandeered Cranach the Elder's *Madonna with Child.* Lillie traces the plundering with creative and wide-ranging research; she utilizes the Gestapo (or VUGESTA) files, which are finally available to scholars after decades of inaccessibility. She found the reports from restitution efforts, including documents from the *Bundesdenkmalamt* and U.S. Federal Bureau of Investigation (the former becoming accessible after the 1998 Austrian "*Kunstrückgabe Gesetz*"). Her reconstruction of the Gomperz collections also reflects tips from other researchers (what she calls "*freundliche Hinweise*"). She even includes press statements from New York Governor George Pataki with regard to the resolution of the above-mentioned Cranach *Madonna with Child,* which was discovered in the North Carolina Museum of Art in 1999 (and restituted the following year to the Gomperz heirs, who then sold it back to the museum at a favorable price in much praised act of alternative dispute resolution). The point of this wealth of materials is to discount theories that there continues to be a systematic effort to thwart research. Lillie herself suggests that the greatest challenge is not files closed due to *Datenschutz* and concealed by archives, but the enormous quantity of materials that makes provenance research seem like looking for needles in haystacks (19). Lillie concludes her reconstruction of the Gomperz collection with a list, a partial reconstruction of the holdings of family members (in this case based on a 1943 evaluation that was found in the papers belonging to *Führermuseum* founding-director Hans Posse and now housed in the *Bundesdenkmalamt*). These lists, which appear frequently in Lillie's book, summarize the tremendous losses of Viennese Jews. The list for the collection of Alphonse and Clarice Rothschild, which runs to 106 pages (1004-1010) and encompasses 3,444 objects, is especially notable as a testament to their wealth and their losses, but also to Lillie's precise and indefatigable scholarship.

Birgit Schwarz has also reconstructed a mammoth collection— this one, of course, belonging to Hitler. Her study of the planned *Führermuseum* is based on sources long overlooked by scholars. She has located nineteen of thirty-one photo albums documenting the *Führer-museum* that were created and stored at Hans Posse's home institution, the Dresden *Gemäldegalerie* (today they are housed in the Berlin *Oberfinanzdirektion*). The gap created by the missing albums is largely filled by a 1943 index (only the contents of volume 29 are completely lost). Schwarz, like Lillie, has produced a study that will be of tremendous use to provenance researchers and to those attempting to assist victims and heirs in the recovery of artworks. The Dresden albums contain photos of the individual works; while previously there were often only titles and artists' names to identify works in Hitler's collection (and the titles were often hopelessly vague, such as "Portrait of a Young Girl"), there are now high quality images that facilitate identification. Hopefully, the catalogues will soon be put on the Internet with a searchable database of not only artists, but also previous owners, dealers, and other significant keywords.

The main thrust of Schwarz's book, however, is a reconception of the *Führermuseum*. The path-breaking report written by art historian S. Lane Faison, Jr.—one of a series of reports on Nazi art plundering written by the Office of Strategic Service's Art Looting Investigation Unit right after the war—placed the number of paintings acquired for the Linz museum at around 5,000 (the primary reason for the high estimate was the belief that all the works in the Altaussee salt mine were intended for Linz, when in fact many were placed there by other agencies, notably the *Institut für Denkmalpflege* in Vienna).[5] Subsequently, some scholars calculated that Hitler and his agents amassed a collection of over 8,000 paintings.[6] Schwarz argues, based on the Dresden catalogue and complementary documentation, that the number intended for the *Führermuseum* was much smaller—on the order of 1,000 to 1,200 paintings and sculptures. Schwarz holds the reader in suspense about her tally. It would have been nice to deliver the news up front rather than take the reader through all the other estimates, but when she delivers her calculations on page sixty-eight, her arguments are persuasive.

A question that arises from Schwarz's study is: does the reduced number of paintings actually intended for the *Führermuseum* really matter? The answer is both no and yes. In that Hitler and his agents acquired at least 4,000 paintings (not to mention books, coins, armor, and other kinds of cultural property), the *Sonderauftrag* Linz still represented the most ambitious collecting initiative in history—surpassing even Napoleon and his experts. Regardless of what works were destined for the walls of the *Führermuseum* itself, the fact remains that his agents snapped up works at an unrivalled rate by both purchase and plunder. One might add that Posse himself commandeered hundreds of paintings from the Viennese Jewish collections chronicled by Lillie. In short, the distinction would matter little to victims of Nazi spoliation and their heirs. But Schwarz does provide the most nuanced treatment to date of the work of the *Sonderauftrag* Linz staff; she exhibits a mastery of the secondary source literature, pointing out where previous authors (including this reviewer) have made errors, and elucidating the way that the organization was in many ways a clearinghouse coordinating a program to send lesser works to Austrian provincial museums.

While the "*museologischer Blick*" of Birgit Schwarz explodes the myth that the *Führermuseum* was "*das grösste Museum der Welt*" (8), she also shows that there was a specific design schema. The selection of paintings constituted a polemical intervention regarding the history of art. Hitler played a hands-on role in this respect and worked with Posse (and his successor Hermann Voss) to create a revisionist chronological narrative about the history of art. According to Hitler's conception, the genius of the Italian Renaissance gave way to the Dutch Masters, who in turn were followed by eighteenth-century French artists such as François Boucher and Jean-Honoré Fragonard. Thereafter, the German accomplishment was emphasized (and that of the French ignored); the nineteenth-century galleries of the *Führermuseum* featured German Romantics (Caspar David Friedrich and Otto Runge), as well as exponents of the Austro-Bavarian school (Carl Spitzweg, Thoma, Hans Makart). These latter artists, Hitler believed, had not been given the respect they deserved. The Linz Museum would help rectify this. Birgit Schwarz's careful study, therefore, helps us understand more precisely the art historical argument made by Hitler, as well as the aesthetic judgments made about specific works.[7] With lesser works going to Austrian provincial museums, she concludes that the *Führermuseum* would not have been a monstrosity, that Posse and Voss planned a high-quality gallery that they hoped would endure. It would have been interesting to have a more extended analysis of the artworks that were collected by Hitler's representatives and not intended for the *Führermuseum*, for the excluded works might tell us much about their worldview and taste. But considering space limitations (Schwarz's book is over 500 pages in length), the more narrow focus is understandable.

Ilse von zur Mühlen has also focused on one collection, that of Hermann Göring, the second most powerful man in Germany for much of the Third Reich who had the second most significant art collection. The OSS Art Looting Investigation Unit Report from 1945 estimated that the *Reichsmarschall* had some 1,375 paintings (although a new, forthcoming *catalogue raisonné* by Nancy Yeide, a curator at the National Gallery of Art in Washington, D.C., will offer a significant upward revision of that number).[8] While von zur Mühlen provides a lucid overview of Göring's collecting efforts, she focuses on those works now in the possession of the *Bayerischen Staatsgemäldesammlungen* (BSGS)[9]. In accordance with postwar Allied and West German statutes, the art that Göring acquired with state funds became the property of the Federal Republic of Germany (which in turned loaned it to museums throughout the country, including the BSGS); those works that Göring acquired with private funds went to the province (*Land*) in which they were located at war's end. In that most of Göring's art was stored on trains that were near Berchtesgaden in May 1945, the province of Bavaria made out well in this respect.

In the wake of the Washington Conference on Holocaust Era Property that took place in December 1998, the BSGS, in accord with key resolutions from the conference, undertook a systematic study of the artworks in its collections. Art historian Ilse von zur Mühlen was engaged, and this volume is one of the fruits of her labor. It is, quite simply, a dazzling exercise in provenance research. Von zur Mühlen combed the BSGS's extensive archives for clues and made especially fine use of old auction catalogues. She traveled to archives in Europe and the United States. She also networked with other provenance researchers who, at the time, were conducting similar work at other German museums. Her book is like a guidebook for provenance research (noting that such a guide is already in existence).[10] *Die Kunstsammlung Hermann Görings* contains excellent photographs including images of the backs of paintings featuring evidence such as customs stamps, inventory numbers from Nazi plundering agencies, and notations from Allied restitution authorities.

As with Sophie Lillie's book, it is the detailed analysis in von zur Mühlen's study that is so breath-taking. She traces the provenance of 126 artworks not only to Göring and the preceding owners, but in most cases back centuries to earlier collectors. To take one example, Lucas Cranach the Elder's *The Faithful Captain under the Cross of Christ* from 1539 was in the collection of a confraternity in Hildesheim until 1822; it then went to the Princes of Lippe and was housed at their castle as Bückeberg where it remained until 1929 when the Frankfurter dealer J. Rosenbaum acquired it. The painting then made its way to Paris in 1941, where it was confiscated by the Nazi plundering agency, the ERR, and traded to Swiss dealer Theodor Fischer with an exchange value of Sfr. 18,000. Göring purchased it, and it had an inventory number of 849 in his collection. At the Allies' restitution center, the Munich Central

Collecting Point, it was given the number 5,756. It was subsequently taken over by the Federal Republic's *Treuhandverwaltung*, which, in turn, transferred it to the BSGS in 1961 (113). Even with this combination of creative detective work and careful scholarship, significant questions remain. In the case of the Cranach just discussed, what happened to the work once it was in the possession of J. Rosenbaum (the "gap" between 1929 and 1941)? What happened to Rosenbaum himself? Is there a rightful heir who has not been discovered? Was it correct for the Federal Republic to assume ownership of this work?

During her tenure at the BSGS, Ilse von zur Mühlen conducted research that is paradigmatic for provenance researchers. As noted above, this book, like the volumes produced by Sophie Lillie and Birgit Schwarz, shows the potential of provenance research as a genre of history (and art history). But no researcher can answer all the questions. In the case of Ilse von zur Mühlen's work at the BSGS, the question remains, "What about the other works in the collection?" During the Third Reich, the BSGS, under Nazi Director Ernst Buchner, acquired thousands of artworks. Buchner was complicit in various aspects of the Nazi art plundering program, for example, by personally escorting a commando to France to seize the Van Eyck brothers' altarpiece, *The Mystic Lamb*. What von zur Mühlen did with the Göring paintings should be done for the rest of the works in the Bavarian State collections.

Provenance research is time consuming, which means that it is also expensive. The BSGS, like many other institutions in Europe and the United States, felt the financial pressures of this research, and von zur Mühlen, like many researchers hired in the late-1990s, did not see her contract extended. It should be stressed that the BSGS is not alone in this regard; many institutions that engaged experts in the wake of the Washington Conference have now let them go. This is certainly not the preference of most museum directors and curators, who would have liked to see the research continue. But it is difficult to argue with budgets. Still, despite a commitment made in December 1998 by the German government and museum community at the Washington Conference on Holocaust Era Assets, where they committed to undertake a thorough review of art collections, the results have been mixed. According to Anne Webber at the European Commission for Looted Art, only twenty-three (out of hundreds of) German museums have published information about the works in their collections.

The three exercises in provenance research conducted by Sophie Lillie, Birgit Schwarz, and Ilse von zur Mühlen are powerful works of history. They document the extraordinary richness of prewar European collections, the monumental scale of the theft, and the complex issues that remain unresolved. These three scholars have led the way, but others must still follow—and do so quickly, before the last survivors are gone.

Notes

1. Stuart Eizenstat, *Imperfect Justice: Looted Assets, Slave Labor, and the Unfinished Business of World War II* (New York: Public Affairs, 2003).

2. See the website of the Central Registry of Information on Looted Cultural Property, 1933-1945 at <http://www.lootedart.com>, as well as the website of the American Association of Museums at <http://www.nepip.org>. Other useful websites for provenance research can be found and include <http://www.nationalmuseums.org.uk>; <http://www.beutekunst.com>; <http://www.lootedart.de; <http://www.museum-security.org/ww2/>; and <http://www.ushmm.org>.

3. Bruce Pauley, *A History of Austrian Anti-Semitism* (Chapel Hill: U of North Carolina P, 1992), 275.

4. Hugo Bettauer, *Die Stadt ohne Juden: ein Roman von Übermorgen* (Hamburg: Achilla Presse, 1996).

5. S. Lane Faison, Jr., *Consolidated Interrogation Report No 4. Linz: Hitler's Museum and Library* (Washington, D.C.: Strategic Services Unit, 1945).

6. Lynn Nicholas, *The Rape of Europa: The Fate of Europe's Treasures in the Third Reich and the Second World War* (New York: Knopf, 1994), 49.

7. More generally, see the recent book by Frederick Spotts, *Hitler and the Power of Aesthetics* (London: Hutchinson, 2002).

8. Theodore Rousseau, *Consolidated Interrogation Report No. 2: The Goering Collection* (Washington, D.C.: Strategic Services Unit, 1945).

9. Bavarian State Painting Collections

10. Nancy Yeide, Konstantin Akinsha, and Amy Walsh, *The AAM Guide to Provenance Research* (Washington, D.C.: Association of American Museums, 2001).

The Cold War and 1956 in Hungary

László Borhi, *Hungary in the Cold War* (Budapest: CEU Press, 2004)

Johanna Granville, *The First Domino: International Decision Making during the Hungarian Crisis of 1956* (College Station: TX: Texas A&M Univ. Press, 2004)

Holly Case

Two recent historical studies of the early Cold War years in Hungary—László Borhi's *Hungary in the Cold War, 1945-1956*, and Johanna Granville's *The First Domino: International Decision Making during the Hungarian Crisis of 1956*—lend nuance to our understanding of the macro-political maneuverings behind Hungary's integration into the Soviet Bloc and the awkward period of de-Stalinization leading up to the 1956 uprising.

Borhi's work, which attempts to determine how and when Hungary's fate as a Soviet satellite was sealed, traces the origins of independent, democratic Hungary's demise to the final years of World War II. Drawing on a variety of archival and other sources, he argues that the Allies cynically encouraged Hungary to jump out of the Axis war camp so that Germany would occupy Hungary and be less prepared for the Allied invasion of Normandy. Borhi insists that the nations of East-Central Europe "were not the masters of their own fate" and that the "Allies hoped to prosper from Hungary's desperate situation."[1] The outcome of Hungary's defection from the Axis was, indeed, German occupation and the annihilation of a large part of Hungary's Jewish population, who—if they had survived—could have provided critical support to the Allies in their drive to establish a democratic government in postwar Hungary. Borhi argues that the short-sighted interest President Roosevelt and Prime Minister Churchill had in ending the war as quickly as possible, coupled with Roosevelt's relative indifference toward the fate of Axis-camp members like Hungary, facilitated Hungary's integration into the Soviet Bloc after the war.

Based primarily on the correspondence and writings of the Hungarian Stalinist leader Mátyás Rákosi, Borhi also argues—counter to earlier historiography on Cold War politics of the immediate postwar years—that Stalin intended to fully integrate Hungary into the Soviet Bloc from the very beginning. It was thus not the United States' unsubtle pedaling of the Marshall Plan to East-Central Europe that precipitated a "shift" in Soviet policy *vis-à-vis* Hungary and other would-be satellites from 1945 to 1947. Instead, Borhi concludes, Soviet policy remained consistent in everything but the level of restraint with which the Soviets and their Hungarian sympathizers pursued set policy goals. Already in 1946, for example, Rákosi announced the "liberation of the proletariat," after which "parliament was a fig leaf that concealed the true scope of Communist influence."[2]

Perhaps Borhi's most interesting and novel contribution, however, is his assessment of the Soviets' economic penetration of Hungary. In a fascinating fourth chapter based mainly on Hungarian and American sources, Borhi describes the intensity with which the Soviets sought to take control of Hungary's economy by becoming its "predominant investor and trading partner."[3] Nonetheless, the monetary benefits the USSR derived from the economic exploitation of Hungary were, it seems, overshadowed and in many cases undercut by the Soviets' political interest in increasing their control over the East-Central European satellites and in preventing U.S. investments from becoming ideological bribes. Yet although economic penetration was the means to a political more than to an economic end, the economic benefits derived from exploiting Hungary's economy—in combination with other "imperial services" Hungary offered the USSR—were significant enough, in Borhi's view, to affect the Soviets' decision to invade Hungary during the 1956 uprising. The exploitation model also partially explains why the Soviets chose not to intervene in 1989. "In 1956, despite its many problems Hungary was still an asset; in 1989 it was probably a liability," Borhi concludes.[4]

Despite the relative wealth of Hungarian, Soviet, and U.S. sources now available to researchers, there is still disagreement as to what factors were decisive in provoking the second Soviet invasion of Hungary on 4 November 1956. Borhi concludes that it was the bombing of Egypt and the decline of communist influence, coupled with the rise in anti-communist violence, that provoked the invasion. Whereas Borhi insists that the Kremlin's decision was not influenced by American actions, Granville—while she acknowledges that "Khrushchev's determination to keep Hungary in the Warsaw Pact probably arose primarily from post-World War II strategic and ideological imperatives"—believes that Radio Free Europe's propaganda initiatives "influenced the Soviet officials' assessment of the Hungarian situation somewhat and increased their determination to retain the satellite as a Warsaw Pact member."[5]

Granville's book revises a number of commonly held beliefs about 1956 by looking at a variety of sources across state contexts. Her analysis of the responses of Yugoslavia and Poland—and Tito and Władysław Gomułka respectively—to the 1956 events shows how other communist states' fear that anticommunist ideas emanating from Hungary could spill over "across their own borders" contributed to the de-legitimization and removal of Imre Nagy.[6] Although both Tito and Gomułka shared with Nagy the belief that each country should take its own road to socialism, their stances on the significance of the Hungarian uprising were informed by domestic concerns. Tito was inclined to go along with Nikita Khrushchev's hard line against the Hungarians, but dissident voices within the Yugoslav polity (Edvard Kardelj, Emil Soldatić, Milovan Đilas), and Tito's own *Realpolitik* interest in not alienating the West limited the extent to which he could denounce Nagy. Yugoslavia thus did not condemn the Soviet invasion, but later offered asylum to the Nagy group in the Yugoslav Embassy in Budapest. Meanwhile, in Poland, Gomułka feared that if the Polish leadership were to fully endorse the initiatives of the Nagy government, "Polish citizens would probably pressure him to have Soviet troops withdrawn from Poland."[7] A Soviet withdrawal would have had the effect of destabilizing Poland's relations with both the USSR and the GDR, and given the new and fragile nature of the borders with both countries, particularly the GDR, Gomułka was not willing to risk such a move.

Finally, Granville shows that there was disagreement within the Soviet camp, as well, regarding the most appropriate course of action to take with the Hungarians. Whereas Khrushchev and Vyachslav Molotov were the "hawks" behind the use of force, Georgy Zhukov and Anastas Mikoyan were "doves" who apparently opposed military intervention. But even Khrushchev "acknowledged the existence of nonviolent options" and wavered in his decision to initiate an invasion.[8] Once the Soviets had resolved to go through with Operation *Vikhr* (whirlwind), they expected an easy victory. Yet despite the fact that they were able to crush the uprising and force Nagy off the scene by 12 November, Granville believes that "the November events were only the prelude to a long, arduous process of normalization in Hungary."[9] Because the 1956 uprising instilled in the Hungarian people a proclivity toward "passive resistance," Granville argues that it effectively "prepared the way for Kádár's relatively tolerant domestic policies," and was really "the first 'domino' in a process that resulted ultimately in the Soviet Union's loss of hegemony over Eastern Europe in 1989."[10]

There is no doubt that these two books provide very apt and intriguing scholarly analyses. Nevertheless, their arguments are sometimes overshadowed by presentation styles or analytical frameworks that seem, at times, awkward or misleading. Borhi's insistence on the absolute helplessness of Hungarian politicians and diplomats to achieve and to maintain Hungarian independence, for example, serves to downplay the moments when their initiatives and decisions *did* affect the fate of the country (with their enthusiastic acceptance of territorial compensation from the Axis with the First and Second Vienna Awards, for example). Furthermore, although his chapter on Soviet economic penetration is fascinating, the fact that Borhi relies mainly on U.S. and Hungarian sources limits his ability to conclusively determine Soviet motivations behind these policies. The same holds for his dependence on the writings and correspondence of Rákosi to assert that the Soviets planned to take control of Hungary all along. In Granville's case, her concluding emphasis on the "psychological" underpinnings of decision making (*à la* Robert Jervis) has the effect of obscuring some of her own, in this reviewer's opinion, more interesting conclusions and observations on the timing and motivations behind key decisions. Her treatment of the role of ideology in the Soviet reaction to the Hungarian uprising is also somewhat unsatisfying. She writes that ideology, in the form of "the communist version of the 'domino theory'", helped tip the scales in favor of military intervention.[11] It is questionable, however, that the "domino theory"—as understood by either the Soviet Union or the United States—was more informed by ideology than it was by Cold War *Realpolitik*. Still, the meticulous research, skillful organization, and insightful analysis offered by both books far outweigh any shortcomings they may have.

On the whole, these two works add sharpness and clarity to our picture of the early Cold War years in Hungary and, by extension, East-Central Europe. Still, much work remains to be done, and buried in the pages of both books are details that point to a variety of unexplored aspects of Cold War, regional, and Hungarian history. One is the question of how "nationalist" the uprising and its participants were. There can be no doubt that Tito, the pro-Soviet Hungarian communists, and Khrushchev came to see the Nagy government and its supporters as dangerously "reactionary,"[12] but a more careful study of the participants in Nagy's would-be coalition and the various groups fighting the Soviets would help readers to determine the extent to which Nagy—a devoted communist and "nationalist" only in the Stalinist sense[13]—was a party of one.

It would also be interesting to know how the relative temporal proximity of the Second World War affected both the decisions of the East-Central European and Soviet leaderships during this time period. Both authors hint that unstable borders and lingering territorial and minority concerns colored the ways in which Tito, Gomułka, and even Rákosi and Romania's Gheorghiu-Dej interpreted the events in and decisions of neighboring or other East-Bloc states and their leaders.[14] Furthermore, recent research by Soviet historian Amir Weiner shows that the Soviets themselves struggled with the legacy of World War II during the fallout of 1956, especially as Ukrainian Gulag returnees absorbed the "spillover" from the Hungarian uprising.[15] Borhi is to be commended for starting his narrative of early Cold War Hungary during World War II, but the fact remains that much work has yet to be done on the effects the war had on policymakers and dissidents alike.

Historians of Hungary in particular, and scholars interested in the uses of national meta-narratives in general would also do well to consider how the Hungarian rebels understood phrases linking the revolution of 1848 to the uprising of 1956, particularly given that the legacy of 1848 contained such a wide variety hermeneutic strains (democratic, nationalist, socialist, and so forth).[16] These ambiguities were highlighted by the twenty-six year-old Viktor Orbán on 16 June 1989, when he spoke at Imre Nagy's reburial, "Hungary has only once had the chance, only once had the strength and the courage to attain her ambitions of 1848; we will not renounce any of the goals of 1848, as we cannot renounce 1956, either."[17] The fact that the fall of communism in 1989 was fashioned after these two rather heterogeneous events in Hungarian history (1848 and 1956) means that the Hungarian state of today is in some sense built on a contested legacy, as was revealed in 2003, during which the ruling socialist coalition and Orbán's conservative opposition held separate ceremonies to commemorate 1956.[18]

Last but not least, a critical dissection of characterizations of U.S. and Soviet behavior *vis-à-vis* the states of East-Central Europe as "imperial" or "colonial" seems long overdue. Borhi, for example, observes that from the economic standpoint, "the Soviet Union behaved as a traditional imperial power."[19] This sentiment was shared by U.S. Mission Chief Arthur Schoenfeld who observed in 1945 that "one time economically independent Hungary has in the space of little more than a year gone far towards becoming a Soviet economic colony."[20] Yet at the same time that Radio Free Europe was condemning the Soviet "colonial empire" for trying "to crush the peoples' longing for freedom with their tanks," Gomułka "opined publicly that 'the Western aggression in Suez' was much worse than the Soviet intervention in Hungary, because in the latter case, the Soviet Union was not trying to transform Hungary into a colony."[21] It is clear that colonialism—real or imagined—was fresh in the minds of Cold War politicians and diplomats at the time. Determining the extent to which these accusations accurately described the reality of superpower-satellite relationships would help historians to discern the limits and usefulness of the colonial model for the Cold War case, as well as for other contexts.[22]

Clearly, the works of Borhi and Granville are indicators that Cold War studies are experiencing a renaissance and that there are still new ways to combine and interpret old documents while uncovering new ones. More importantly, however, these two books also contain the seeds of future work that will enrich historians' understanding of how the Cold War narrative of this region fits into more localized and universal historiography of an expanding range of periods, places, and ideologies.

Notes

1. Borhi, *Hungary*, 17, 21.

2. Ibid., 81.

3. Ibid., 153.

4. Ibid., 333.

5. Granville, *The First Domino*, 200.

6. Ibid., 124.

7. Ibid., 119.

8. Ibid., 74.

9. Ibid., 123.

10. Ibid., 157, xv.

11. Ibid., 213.

12. Ibid., 104.

13. The words "nationalism" and "nationalist" are very slippery in the Cold War context. While Tito was considered a nationalist by Stalin, by 1956, Khrushchev distinguished between "Tito's way" and the "reactionary" behavior of the Hungarian insurgents of 1956, who used Tito's "third path" rhetoric to "camouflage their own nationalistic designs" (Granville, *The First Domino*, 104). Furthermore, in the eyes of pro-Soviet communists, both Nagy and Gomułka were noted for their "nationalist convictions" (Granville, *The First Domino*, 51). As such, a study of the use of the "nationalist" label and how it was understood and used by contemporaries would add a new dimension to a reader's understanding of "nationalism" in a broader sense.

14. See Granville, *The First Domino*, 102, 119, 131-32, 185; Borhi, *Hungary*, 86-87. It should also be noted that Granville plans to write another book detailing the roles of the Czechoslovak, East-German, Bulgarian, Romanian, and Austrian leaderships in the 1956 crisis (Granville, *The First Domino*, 38).

15. Amir Weiner, "The Empires Pay a Visit: When Gulag Returnees Encountered East European Rebellions on the Soviet Western Frontier" (a paper presented at the Berkeley

Workshop on Political Violence in Eurasia, May 2004). Cited with permission of the author.

16. See Granville, *The First Domino*, 55.

17. "Viktor Orbán's Speech at the Reburial of Imre Nagy," *Uncaptive Minds* 2.4 (8 Aug.-Sept.-Oct.): 26.

18. "Óvatos gesztusok a forradalom ünnepén" *Népszabadság Online*, 2003. okt. 24. <http://www.nepszabadsag.hu>.

19. Borhi, *Hungary*, 326.

20. Borhi, *Hungary*, 153. In his memoirs, Sándor Kopacsi, Chief of the Budapest Police and a Nagy supporter himself, described Serov's "blunt tone a colonial master uses to describe how he makes and unmakes his provincial masters." Sándor Kopacsi, *In the Name of the Working Class* (London: Fontana/Collins, 1989), 240.

21. Granville, *The First Domino*, 176, 120.

22. Borhi's conclusion that Hungary was an asset to the USSR in 1956 and a liability in 1989 is all the more interesting if viewed from a "colonial" perspective. His comparison calls to mind the work of David Good on the economy of the Habsburg Empire and the relationship between the Austrian center and Hungarian economic development. See David Good, *The Economic Rise of the Habsburg Empire, 1750-1914* (Berkeley, CA: Univ. of California Press, 1984).

BOOK REVIEWS

Georg Rigele, *Zwischen Monopol und Markt. EVN das Energie- und Infrastrukturunternehmen* (Maria Enzersdorf: Selbstverlag der EVN AG, 2004)

Franz Mathis

EVN stands for *Energie-Versorgung Niederösterreich* and is the name of one of the largest Austrian enterprises that produces and provides electricity and natural gas. Its beginnings date back to 1907 when a company was founded in the province of Lower Austria in order to electrify the already very popular, so-called Mariazeller railway. After World War I, it became the nucleus of the NEWAG (*Niederösterreichische Elektrizitätswirtschafts-AG*), which was to promote the electrification of the province by building power stations and establishing a network of power lines. In 1954, the NEWAG and the provincial government founded a natural gas company, which in the mid-1980s merged with NEWAG to form EVN. From the very beginning, the company was a public firm with the province of Lower Austria and the city of Vienna as its main shareholders. After World War II, Lower Austria remained the single owner of the company until 1989 when 49 percent of its share capital was sold to private investors. Since the 1990s, additional utilities have been taken up such as waste utilization, water supply, waste water disposal, telecommunication, and communal services. In 2001, when the utilities market was liberalized in Austria, EVN lost its former monopolistic position.

Thus, given the fact that market oriented structures have but recently been introduced into Austria's utility sector and that this part of EVN's history is treated only in the final and relatively short chapter of the book, its main title seems somewhat misleading. In the light of the long-time public character of the company, it might have been more appropriate to choose a title like *Zwischen Gemeinnutz und Eigennutz* focusing on the question of whether common interests or self-interest prevailed in its businesses, a question which is repeatedly alluded to, but not discussed in an explicit way. Although the company's responsibility for the various stakeholders such as its owners, customers, employees, or society in general is referred to in some detail, no attempt has been made to engage in a more profound discussion of its long- and short-term priorities including the company's price policy or other benefits for the customers or the tax-payers as its real owners.

Instead, the book offers a lot of valuable information on various aspects of the company's activities from its founding up to the present day. Whereas the first of the four main chapters highlights some of the most important features of its recent history, the following two provide a chronological survey of the company's development since 1907 and of its achievements since World War II. Many of the sub-chapters begin with a general depiction of international trends such as the oil crises of the 1970s, the problem of nuclear power stations, environmental protection, Austria's membership in the European Union, and so forth, followed by an analysis of the impact they had on EVN. Contrary to what might be expected from a company history written by its archivist, Rigele has not shrunk back from treating in detail the firm's main crisis in the 1960s when its top executive almost ruined the company by his dubious practices. Besides the rich information provided by the author himself, the book contains a number of short observations by people involved in the company as well as numerous pictures compiled by Alexander Rendi, which have been conceived as a photo documentary of its own.

Rupert Pichler, ed., *Innovationsmuster in der österreichischen Wirtschaftsgeschichte. Wirtschaftliche Entwicklung, Unternehmen, Politik und Innovationsverhalten im 19. und 20. Jahrhundert* (Innsbruck: Studienverlag, 2003)

Franz Mathis

Given the fact that, today, Austria ranks among the top ten of the world's richest economies, it seems timely to ask whether the traditional picture of Austria as a technologically backward nation is still valid or—as a matter of fact—has ever been valid at all. Although several authors of articles contained in the volume, which comprises the papers given at a conference at the University of Vienna in 2002, refer to this view, only some of them provide studies that might help verification or falsification of it in the light of recent research.

The difference between the so-called *Technologielücke* (technological gap) and the good performance of the Austrian economy causes Michael Peneder from the *Österreichischen Institut für Wirtschaftsforschung* to talk of a structure-performance paradox. He tries to explain the paradox by referring to the "natural" catching up effects of the 1970s followed by years of relatively lower growth rates and to other aspects that are harder to measure. Since the notion of a technologically backward Austria dates back to the nineteenth century, Juliane Mikoletzky has looked at the rich sources generated in the course of applying for patents or monopolistic concessions (*Privilegien*) in the first half of that century. They give evidence of a considerable innovative potential, which, however, is characterized by incremental improvements rather than spectacular inventions. More detailed information is provided in the articles of Hubert Weitensfelder, Günter Dinhobel, Peter Eigner, and Karl-Heinz Leitner. After some critical remarks about the way Austrian inventors have been treated in Austrian historiography, Weitensfelder presents two case studies on Karl Auer von Welsbach and Viktor Kaplan, two of the most prominent inventors of the nineteenth century. Günter Dinhobel shows how much the assessment of an innovation depends on the point of view from which it is observed. Compared with traditional railway construction, the railway across the Semmering Mountain was revolutionary insofar as it was laid out in serpentines instead of straight lines in order to overcome the mountains, but less revolutionary when compared with traditional road building in the mountains that had already utilized the technique of serpentines before. In an elaborate study, Peter Eigner investigates why the world famous game of Scrabble invented by an American in the 1940s has become so much more popular than the similar game of Typ Dom invented by a Viennese in the 1930s, and concludes that besides mere accidents, it must have been the huge U.S. market that made the difference. A much broader sample has been chosen by Karl-Heinz Leitner, who has analyzed fifty of about 500 successful innovations made by Austrian companies during the last quarter of the twentieth century. They amply prove the rich innovative potential and strength within the Austrian economy, in particular with regard to new technologies geared towards niche markets, which may be a promising path for small countries in particular.

Other authors, such as Andreas Resch and Michael Pammer, take a more general look at nineteenth century innovations in Austria's economy. Resch is particularly interested in industrial cartels and shows that the theoretical assumption that they can encourage as well as discourage innovations holds true when tested—as he does—by means of an empirical analysis of the glue, the machine building, and the electric bulb industries. Traditional and new financial markets as well as traditional and new forms of investing personal savings are dealt with by Michael Pammer. Besides a number of different aspects influencing the financial activities of nineteenth century Austrians, he can distinguish groups of both traditional and innovative investors. Only a few remarks on innovations may be found in Wolfgang Meixner's article on two Tyrolean companies during the Nazi period; he includes much more, however, on the histories of the metal processing works in Jenbach and Reutte (Plansee) in general.

The same holds true for most of the other articles published in the volume. They deal with subjects that either refer to innovations in a more general way or are only marginally linked to the question of technological innovation. Although Rupert Pichler presents a broad and detailed study of the trade and tariff policies of the Habsburg governments in the nineteenth century, only little is said about their influence on innovations. Wolfgang Neurath wants to know how strongly Austrian researchers and research institutions are already interconnected with each other, and pleads for the creation of a national innovative network. Whether national research policies have been better administered in

Austria or in the Netherlands is the subject of Erich Grießler's contribution to the volume, and Michael Stampfer is interested in the language and the verbal pictures used in and reflected on during the parliamentary debate over the 1967 law on the promotion of research in Austria. Reinhold Hofer considers the methods of evolutionary economics particularly well suited for analyzing historical patterns of innovation. The famous Austrian economist Erich Schumpeter, who strongly emphasized the innovative role of entrepreneurs, is at the center of two different studies, one by Hardy Hanappi, the other by Irene Bandhauer-Schöffmann. Hanappi looks at Schumpeter as part of the Austrian School of Economics, whereas Bandhauer-Schöffmann deplores the prevailing masculinity and the complete lack of women in his concepts. Helmut Gassler and Wolfgang Polt stress the importance of regional aspects of economic development and, by doing so, could at least to some degree explain why between 1870 and 1910 the German economy grew so much faster than the Austrian economy, a question posed by Max-Stephan Schulze at the very beginning of the book. The relative unimportance of little productive agriculture versus the more productive manufacturing industries is strongly related to the various regions and their different levels of development within each country, a topic which has little to do with innovation, but could well be discussed at another conference.

Matti Bunzl, *Symptoms of Modernity: Jews and Queers in Late Twentieth-Century Vienna* (Berkeley: Univ. of California Press, 2004)

Dagmar Herzog

This lucid and scrupulously thoughtful book provides a historically situated ethnographic account of the evolving conditions and experiences of Viennese Jews and queers over the last one hundred years, with particular emphasis on the six post-Nazi decades, and concluding with the unusually dramatic turns of the past ten years. For nigh to a half-century *after* the Holocaust, Jews and queers in Austria continued to be subjected to varieties of visceral hostility from the general populace, government, and media, and, with a few exceptions, they reacted by retreating into a private realm and carefully avoiding public visibility. Within the last decade, however, Jews and queers alike have become singled out as celebrated citizens whose presence on the public stage guarantees Austria's—and especially Vienna's—new image of cosmopolitan sophistication. Matti Bunzl deftly analyzes the paradigmatic events marking the stages in this remarkable trajectory and captures the complex emotions they evoked in diverse participants.

Yet even as the book provides a model for historically informed anthropological analysis, it also does more. Its broadest relevance, I would argue, lies in two (interrelated) contributions, one explicitly foregrounded, the other implicit, but no less important. The first has to do with Bunzl's pathbreaking conceptualization of the self-definition of the Central European nation-state specifically in the modern age—and the crucial constitutive function for the modern nation-state of the exclusion of those minorities designated as impure—coupled with his corollary insights into the extraordinary disintegration of this exclusionary impetus in the transition to a postmodern era shaped more by supranational than national dynamics. The second contribution, less overtly thematized but particularly pertinent for historians, involves the challenging puzzles that Bunzl's work raises about the whole phenomenon of historical causation and the difficulty we have identifying the determinative factors and motors of historical change.

Far from seeing them as incommensurate objects of investigation—even as he remains acutely alert to the obvious differences—Bunzl persuasively makes the case for the value of sustained comparison between the situations of Jews on the one hand and gays and lesbians on the other. The late nineteenth century, after all, did not just see the rise of newly intensified racialized understandings of Jewishness as no longer amenable to erasure through religious conversion. It also saw the emergence of "the homosexual" as a professionally as well as popularly recognizable category (or, as Michel Foucault famously put it, a "species"). In both cases, these reconfigurations were part of broader epistemological transformations: societies were increasingly viewed in biologistic terms, while sexual orientations were being reimagined as something rooted in and suffusing individual identities. Taking a strongly constructionist approach, Bunzl sees both minority groups as "symptoms of modernity" as he argues for "the emergence of Jews and homosexuals as a quintessentially modern phenonemon" whose "very creation," indeed, "underpinned the rise of nationalism and the nation-state": "Codified as an ethnically homogeneous and intrinsically masculinist entity, the German nation presupposed the presence of constitutive outsiders for its operative narration" (p.16). Jews' and homosexuals' abjection and their fantasized roles as the bearers of racial and sexual impurity buttressed and gave (an otherwise elusive) "coherence to the fiction of German nationness" (p.16).

For Austria, with its delayed nationhood and ambivalent relationship both to German nationalism and to the multiethnic Habsburg Empire out of which it was carved, the stunningly positive popular reception of Nazism in Austria could not be acknowledged after 1945. Nor could the intensified persecution—and, soon thereafter, organized murder—of Jews and (although of course in fewer numbers) also of homosexuals be acknowledged after 1945. In a gambit with which most observers and scholars of European history are generally familiar but whose pernicious consequences have rarely been so fully or as well articulated as in Bunzl's book, the Austrian government and populace managed for approximately four decades to present the Austrian nation as Nazism's first victim, rather than its ready collaborator. Bunzl both offers close and compelling readings of the sequence of foundational government declarations—and ensuing elaborations by politicians and the mass media—which secured the durability of the myth of Austrian victimhood and charts the effect of the myth on Jewish and queer lives.

Austria was one of the few Western European nations which criminalized lesbian as well as male homosexual activity and Bunzl's chapters on post-1945 queer lives—the near-complete invisibility of lesbianism and the clandestine and vulnerable networks and spaces available to men who sought same-sex encounters—are informative and well argued. These chapters provide important information on the extent of postwar prosecutions of homosexuals and the multi-year prison sentences that were standard until the liberalization of the law in 1971 (over 13,000 convictions since 1945), as well as on the ongoing systemic homophobia and the new legal strictures which continued to limit queer visibility and self-organization until well into the 1990s (a twenty-year delay in gay and lesbian liberation compared, for instance, to the United States, France, or West Germany). The pressures to perform heterosexuality by entering into (often unhappy) marriages are noted. Moreover, the role played by the Catholic Church in maintaining criminalization and abjection of homosexuality is explicated, as is the disturbing truth that the Socialist party was hardly committed to providing much of a contrasting legal agenda.

Bunzl's argument about the intensity of postwar homophobia could have been strengthened further if he had incorporated more of the most recent research on the unevenness and ambiguities in National Socialism's antihomosexual project. It might also have been helpful if Bunzl had placed his discussion of postwar persecution of homosexuality into a broader framework of postwar sexual politics that explained attitudes and practices with regard to premarital heterosexual activity as well. But these are minor quibbles.

Nowhere is Bunzl more revelatory than in his discussion of postwar Jewry. His book provides an especially powerful synthetic interpretation of the persistence of aggressive anti-Semitism in post-Holocaust Austria, which should be required reading for students in modern European history and for anyone seeking to understand the profound differences in Germany's and Austria's strategies of post-Nazi memory management. Ten thousand Jews lived in Vienna in the post-Holocaust decades. But if Jewish suffering in Nazi Austria and Austrian gentiles' participation in both systematic disenfranchisement and genocide had been admitted, the so strenuously maintained fiction of Austria's victimhood would have collapsed.

Austrian gentiles warded off the reality of what had transpired between 1938 and 1945 by going on the offense. Jews were portrayed, and understood, not as individuals whose livelihoods and lives had been destroyed—as people, in short, with thoroughly legitimate claims both to financial restitution and to public apologies and formal recognition of the immense hurts they had sustained—but rather as vengeful predators who endangered innocent Austrians and deserved their abjection. Indeed, the immediate postwar years were marked by a pogrom-like atmosphere of violence and virulent anti-Semitic commentary. Return and restitution were the key issues. A survey conducted in 1946 found

46 percent of Austrians opposed to the return of Jewish emigres and survivors. In addition, Jews' attempts to repossess the property that had been stolen from them was treated as a threat to Austria's economic viability and was even met in 1948 by an organized campaign which lobbied on behalf of the rights of "Aryanizers." But subsequent decades did not bring much improvement. As late as 1974, the widely read *Neue Kronen Zeitung* (two million readers in a nation of seven million) published a series on "The Jews in Austria" which repeatedly argued that "one of the major reasons for antisemitism can be found in the Jew himself" (p. 43). Into the early 1980s, surveys showed that 80 percent of Austrians not only rejected Jewish claims for restitution, but also deemed Jews to be at least partially responsible for their own repeated persecution. Over and over again, the categories of victim and perpetrator were simply reversed.

Bunzl details the coping strategies developed by Jews in the face of persistent aggression. His informants describe anti-Semitic encounters in daily life and the strict compartmentalization of private and public worlds as well as a strong emotional identification not with Austria but with Israel that were common and logical responses. But some of the most wrenching material in the book concerns Jews with public roles. There are especially powerful passages on Bruno Kreisky— Socialist chancellor from 1970 to 1983—and the ways he actively downplayed his own Jewishness even as it simultaneously was symbolically significant. In Bunzl's careful analysis, Kreisky's own "persistent refusal of public Jewish identification" was certainly sincere, yet at the same time also contributed to the "collective exoneration" of Austrian guilt and "abetted the structural exclusion of Jewish experience from postwar Austria's political field" (pp. 39-40). Later, in 1986, in the midst of the international scandal surrounding presidential candidate Kurt Waldheim's former Nazi affiliations and his knowledge of deportations and interrogations, the *Israelitische Kultusgemeinde* (IKG), the official governing body for Austrian Jewry, was so fearful of exacerbated anti-Semitic fallout if it were to publicize the reality of postwar Austrian anti-Semitism that it actually "found it prudent to defend the country against 'foreign' accusations of antisemitism" (p. 56). The real victims, in short, were obliged to participate in the national charade.

Yet Bunzl also sees the Waldheim affair as a turning point in intergenerational relations within the Jewish community, and the moment at which younger Jews began to develop a more "resistive" and assertive style. It would not be until 2000, however, that—in response to the entry of right-wing and openly Nazi-sympathizing politician Jörg Haider and his Freedom Party into the nation's governing coalition—Viennese Jews "took to the streets to demonstrate against postwar Austria's political hegemonies" (p. 90). What happened between 1986 and 2000 was complicated.

Increasingly, the younger generation accused its elders of complicity with the tormentors, challenging the elders to stop being the "alibi Jews of Austria's national lie [*Lebenslüge*]" and declaring that the time for being "well-behaved" was over (pp. 95-96). Members of this younger generation gradually acquired the reins of Jewish communal leadership as they developed a theretofore unknown critical public style; the formerly so diffident IKG, of all things, became one of central loci of progressive politics in Austria, speaking up in defense of immigrants and asylum seekers and involving itself in a range of antiracist initiatives. (The point here is crucial, and bears emphasis: precisely this moment of heightened Jewish self-assertion and attention to Jewish particularity coincided with, rather than conflicted with, broader universalist democratic and human rights commitments.) Meanwhile, another signal development was that the Waldheim affair also spurred a number of non-Jewish scholars to begin undertaking revisionist history and to establish both the extent of Austrian complicity with Nazi crimes and the mechanisms by which that complicity had been systematically hidden in the postwar era. Third, and no less significant, the international spotlight trained on Austria with the Waldheim debacle reconfigured the calculus by which Austrian politicians had long operated.

Bunzl again finds parallels between Jewish and queer developments from the 1980s to the early twenty-first century. Just as the Jewish community had in the course of the later 1980s and early 1990s become gradually more publicly visible and critical, so, too, did those years see a transition from what had been in the early 1980s only a tiny handful of homosexual rights activists and one openly queer collective house (called the Rosa Lila Villa) to, by 1996, a massive Rainbow Parade (ten thousand marchers and twenty thousand spectators) on the city's historic Ringstrasse. As Bunzl notes, for years queer activists had been operating in utter isolation from the vast majority of Vienna's gays and lesbians, who had absolutely no desire to leave the closet behind. The 1996 parade "transformed Vienna's lesbians and gay men into a socially visible mass, recognizable both to itself and to the cultural field at large" (p. 141). Bunzl elucidates both the precursor steps that made possible this remarkable event as well as its effects, documenting the incremental expansion in the early 1990s of openly queer space (a bookstore, a café) and the advent of queer periodicals which highlighted a wider gay social scene, and also explicating the 1996 Rainbow Parade as a "constitutive moment of collective subjectification" with "enormous ramifications for the queer individuals who came to recognize themselves as part of the community [that the event] made manifest" (p. 141). But although Bunzl gives all due credit to the courageous activists who pioneered a more visible queerness despite their own constituencies' resistance, the ultimate riddle of historical causation remains. As Bunzl notes, the dramatic success of the Rainbow Parade was due not just to its deliberately depoliticized joyous party atmosphere, but also very much to a transformed political situation in which, internationally, events like it "had become a sign of the cosmopolitan character of their host cities" (p. 143). The spectacle appealed to 1990s Viennese politicians' desires to see Vienna as being in the cultural vanguard, that is, "no longer [. . .] the little sister of Europe's capitals" (p. 144).

The final chapters detail the abrupt turnaround in Jews' and queers' public roles since the mid-1990s. Bunzl identifies Austria's entry into the European Union in 1995 as a key moment forcing Austria to rewrite its relationship to Jewishness. The European Union deliberately conceived itself in opposition to exclusionary nationalisms and "treated Nazism as a baseline of negative identification"—as "Europe's most painful historical lesson" (p. 160). From being feared and reviled outsiders, Austria's Jews suddenly became the best means to demonstrate Austria's commitment to the "European values of tolerance and pluralism" (p. 160) Visible representations of the reconfigured relationship were such phenomena as the founding and (theretofore unheard of) lavish state funding of the Jewish Museum in Vienna or the newly *de rigueur* presence of the non-Jewish Austrian political elite at Jewish communal functions. Fascinatingly, a main effect of the state's newly affirmative relationship to Austrian Jews was a precipitous decline in popular anti-Semitism as well. Entry into the European Union also created opportunities for undoing homosexuals' legal subordination. The legal autonomy of individual states was simply waning. In a terrific conclusion, Bunzl charts Jews' and queers' "epochal" transformation from "symptoms of modernity" into "symptoms of postmodernity"—of which the city of Vienna's official web page's proud foregrounding, in 2000, of the city's now exuberantly pro-queer attitude and wide range of resources for queer individuals was only the most dramatic instance. "Gay chic" had now become desirable for heteros as well, and—as with Jews—the municipal government's turnaround was accompanied by radical shifts in media and popular sensibilities as well. Bunzl brilliantly points out that the result is not without its ironic problems: the postmodern regime's tendency to affirm rather than to reject alterity "fortifies rather than deconstructs Jewishness and queerness as categories of subjectification" (p. 218), congealing and creating a seeming clarity of identities when the lived reality of both ethnicity and sexual desire could actually be far more fluid and complex. Additionally, in a thoughtful reading of Haider's own recent about-faces and new self-styling as a supporter of Jews and queers, Bunzl notes that the most pressing exclusionary danger is facing a new set of "Others": Eastern and Southeastern Europeans, Africans, and Muslims.

Ultimately, then, this book is not only, though certainly also, about the experiences of Jews and homosexuals. It is centrally concerned with the vagaries and fate of the phenomenon of the European nation-state. It not only demonstrates beyond a doubt what enormously important symbolic functions quite small minorities can serve for national identities—with painfully real consequences on those minorities—but also suggests that the unraveling of the nation-state as a central locus of power is accompanied by far-reaching configurations in the relationships between majorities and minorities. As Bunzl puts it, "by the late twentieth century [. . .] the exclusionary project had outlived its usefulness" (p. 216). On the one hand, *Symptoms of Modernity* tells a specifically Central European story, a tale of Austrian exceptionalism. This exceptionalism is perhaps most evident in the overtness and intensity of postwar anti-Semitism. On the other hand, it is not least because of Bunzl's unflinching attention to the history of the present and his interest in the breathtakingly rapid normalization of homosexuality in our current political juncture in the West—a normalization so long fought for, so long resisted, so much to be celebrated, and, of course, not yet fully secure—and his assessment that the origins of this normalization remain perplexing, only inadequately explainable by reference to organized activism, that the book should be read by scholars interested in a broad range of other national contexts as well.

Margareth Lun, *NS-Herrschaft in Südtirol. Die Operationszone Alpenvorland 1943-1945* (Innsbrucker Forschungen zur Zeitgeschichte 15) (Innsbruck: Studienverlag, 2004)

Gerald Steinacher[*]

South Tyrol, a small alpine region on the Austrian-Italian border with approximately 450,000 inhabitants of German and Italian language, appears on the European map as being negligible in size. Nevertheless "South Tyrol brings into sharp focus an important part of twentieth-century Central European history," as the historian Hans Heiss puts it.[1] U.S. historians often are confronted with this region only in connection with Benito Mussolini and Adolf Hitler's foreign policy and the planned resettlement of the South Tyroleans in 1939.[2] Tyrol, a province with its own strong identity, had been part of Austria for over 500 years and was mainly German-speaking. The Tyrol was split after World War I and the southern part was awarded to Italy as "spoils of war." The border area South Tyrol played an important role in German, Austrian, and Italian foreign policy ever since. After the rise of Italian fascism in 1922, a policy of Italianization was implemented ruthlessly. All places, up to the tiniest hamlet, were given Italian names, and even the family names were translated.

The process intensified in the 1930s when Mussolini's government encouraged thousands of Italians to relocate to the region. It is puzzling that Hitler did not do anything about it. He incorporated the Saarland region, marched into the Sudetenland, and later invaded Poland. But in South Tyrol, where the German speaking population really was treated badly, he did not bother, because he courted his friend Mussolini as an ally. This shows that Hitler was less moved by the condition of the German minorities outside Germany than the opportunities they provided to justify the expansion of the Third Reich. In 1939, South

---

* I am grateful to Dr. Günter Bischof and Mag. Josef Köstlbauer for their comments and suggestions.

Tyroleans were sacrificed to the alliance of the two dictators, Hitler and Mussolini. The Tyroleans were confronted by the choice of either opting for German citizenship, which was connected with being resettled out of their homeland, or deciding to retain Italian citizenship, which came with the threat of total Italianization or even deportation to Sicily. The majority of the South Tyroleans (approximately 86 percent) chose German citizenship and resettlement to the Third Reich or to a territory that Germany conquered in the East. The so called "Option", no doubt, was the most painful chapter in South Tyrol's history. During the war, the emigration quickly came to a halt.

With the overthrow of Mussolini, Italy's switch to the side of the Allies, and the occupation of South Tyrol and northern Italy by German troops on 9 September 1943, the overwhelming majority of South Tyroleans felt themselves to have been freed from the Italian yoke. After twenty years of Italian fascist rule, the long-awaited day of national liberation seemed to have arrived. Hopes were flying high that South Tyrol would return "*heim ins Reich.*" Nevertheless, the hoped-for official annexation of the South Tyrol to the German Reich and, thus, the reunification of the Tyrol did not materialize. A sort of de facto annexation did take place. The northern Italian, former Austrian territories of Trento, Bolzano and Belluno were to become Hitler's "Operational Zone Alpine Forelands," which played a crucial role in the Third Reich's strategic policies towards the Austrian/northern Italian borderlands. The Operational Zone/South Tyrol region has emerged as a crucial case study for understanding Nazi Germany in general and its Italian policies in particular. On top of that, Allied fears that Hitler might build an "Alpine Fortress" (*Alpenfestung*) as the last retreat of his regime worried the military planners to no end and influenced General Dwight Eisenhower's strategy in the final months of the war considerably.

The history of the occupied, Italian northern provinces was studied for the first time in 1969 by the Austrian Historian Karl Stuhlpfarrer.[3] For many years, his book remained the only case study about this important topic. Only in the last years has a more open and critical dealing with the past in regional contemporary history emerged. Accordingly, the number of the publications and the diversity of topics and research have increased strongly.[4] Margareth Lun has written an extensive and in some aspects excellent text about South Tyrol in "the Operational Zone Alpine Forelands" from 1943 to 1945. Lun demonstrates clearly the importance and long-lasting heritage of the twenty months of German civil administration of the "Operational Zone Alpine Forelands." Important pre-conditions were created for the postwar period: the emigration of the South Tyroleans was stopped and the majority of the people stayed in the country. The South Tyroleans were not forced to leave after

1945; they were lucky not to share the fate of millions of Germans in Eastern Europe.

As Lun points out, the Tyrolean Nazi *Gauleiter* Franz Hofer developed a policy whose goal was the actual fusion of the Operational Zone with his own Gau Tyrol. Hofer and his Tyrolean Nazis—with some supporters in Berlin—wanted to achieve the reunification of the Tyrol within its traditional borders under the swastika. From the outset, this group pushed Hitler and the leaders of the Reich toward the annexation of this area. Hofer's strategy was not accepted because Hitler gave consideration to Mussolini and did not want to expose his weak ally. Hitler forbade all measures that might give the impression of an official annexation. South Tyrol remained officially a part of Italy, even if Mussolini's influence was virtually nil.

The strength of Margareth Lun's book lies in the chapters about the military and police administration. Lun bases her research largely on sources from German archives in Koblenz and Freiburg and the State Archives in Rome and evaluates these very exactly and with a love for detail, providing many new insights. For example, an order dated 6 November 1943, mandated universal conscription throughout the entire operational zone. Whoever sought to avoid enlistment could expect to receive the death penalty. In the process of conscription, there was, in principle, no differentiation between those who had opted for Germany and those who had chosen Italian citizenship. In fact, the minority of the South Tyroleans with Italian passports were the first to be sent to the front. This meant that Italian citizens were forced into German units, a clear contravention of international law. In South Tyrol, police regiments were formed. One company of the police regiment "Bozen" had been transferred to Rome, and this unit was the target of a bomb attack carried out by Communist partisans that claimed the lives of thirty-three South Tyroleans while marching trough the Via Rasella in Rome. In reprisal, SS men under the command of Herbert Kappler and Erich Priebke murdered 335 Italian hostages in the Ardeatine Caves. In the 1990s, these reprisal executions were again subject of an investigation by the Italian military judiciary.

The phenomenon of permanently arising competence conflicts between military and civilian administration, typical of the entire National Socialist bureaucracy, manifested itself in that Operational Zone Alpine Forelands very clearly. Thus the military powers of the high commissioner *Gauleiter* Hofer had been already specified with a letter by field marshal Erwin Rommel in September 1943. But Hofer's position had to be confirmed again and again because of frequent authority disputes between civil and military offices. The military powers of the high commissioner Hofer in the Operational Zone went partially beyond those of the respective military commanders. Franz Hofer was subordinated directly to Hitler; between Hofer and the *Führer*, there was no other instance of authority. All correspondence of the authorities from Mussolini's *Repubblica Sociale Italiana* to the Operational Zone had to run through Hofer's office. The psychological influence of Hofer cannot, therefore, be underestimated. Lun's final chapters in the book concerning the Resistance, the Allies, and the end of the war are merely a summary of the secondary literature. The index of the persons in the book provides short biographies of the individuals involved and is helpful. However, the page numbers are missing in the index, and in a book of 611 pages, this is quite unpractical.

The prominent South Tyrolean journalist Hans Karl Peterlini labeled Lun's book the "chronicle of a time gap—a carefully researched, dispassionate work about a horror period" (*Chronik einer Zeitlücke - Eine sorgfältige, distanzierte Arbeit zu einer Gräuelzeit*)."[5] For a book concerning a period of terror, Lun writes with considerable calm. She tends to hold back her own position or opinion and reports "neutrally," often without valuation. This basic stance is like a red thread in the book, which is no problem in chapters about the military structure of the *Wehrmacht*, for this can be presented in a "neutral" style and without taking sides. However, in some other instances, such a distanced position may be questionable. National Socialism in South Tyrol repeatedly appears in the book as a mere import product. In the paragraph on the leader of the South Tyrolean "*Volksgruppe*," Peter Hofer (111), she never uses the term "Nazi" or "National Socialism." Part of the job description of the historian is to make judgments and to evaluate the sources. Lun writes about the highest civil official in South Tyrol during the Operational Zone, "*Hofer wird von seinen Zeitgenossen, die bis heute Sympathie für diesen ‚Mann aus dem Volk' durchklingen lassen, als einfacher Mann charakterisiert. Er galt als ausgezeichneter Organisator und Propagandist, der ‚mit größter Überzeugung, sein Ziel verfolgte.*"

Peter Hofer died in an air raid on Bozen in December 1943. Hitler sent a wreath to his funeral; the other seventy-one wreaths came from German generals, the fascist Hungarian government, and the Japanese emperor in recognition of the South Tyrolean *Nibelungentreue*.

About Peter Hofer's successor as the highest civil authority, Karl Tinzl, she quotes local historians without comment, "*Der christlich-soziale Tinzl übte sein Amt als Präfekt der Provinz Bozen, in jeder Beziehung korrekt' aus besorgte seine Amtsführung in einer Weise, dass auch nach 1945 keine italienische oder alliierte Behörde, kein Staatsanwalt und kein Sondergericht ihm etwas anhaben konnte.*" Governor Tinzl was certainly not a Nazi, and he tried to work as a moderate and to prevent the outbreak of violence in his province. Yet the high office alone compromised him to a certain degree—he was installed by the German authorities and exercised this function in their name. He was involved in the system of recruiting men for the military service. The fact that Tinzl and many others like him managed to continue their political careers after 1945 can be attributed to the missing de-Nazification and de-fascization in South Tyrol.

The national question was crucial in the disputed borderland and was used by Fascists and Nazis for their cause. Hitler's dictatorship at least spoke the South Tyroleans' own language and fostered their own traditions. Traditions had to conform to Hitler's ideology or they were infiltrated by it; for example, the Christmas tree was supposed to become the Germanic tree of life, while "*Tirolertum*" was supposed to be seen as a preliminary stage of the *grossdeutscher* spirit. The author embellishes nothing. Sometimes, however, one might get the impression that the description of fascist Italian injustices is easier for her than the injustices committed by her South Tyrolean compatriots in the name of the swastika. She describes it in a pragmatic, precise, and distanced manner. Yet distancing oneself as a historian seems questionable when the events are as outrageous as the following: the transition camp in Bolzano, from which many were taken to Dachau or Mauthausen to face death; the extinction of the Jewish community in Merano; the killing of people with disabilities; the arrest of priests; and the Nazi terror in the villages. Lun controls herself, qualifies, and points out the exact circumstances; precision is an effective weapon. No revisionist can question the facts Lun unearths about the Third Reich. Still, sentences like the following appear unreflected, "Deserters and conscientious objectors, who were put to death, could be seen as victims of National Socialism in the broadest sense [...]."

The National Socialist seizure of power in South Tyrol was possible only with the eager cooperation of the Tyrolean *Gauleiter* and the leading South Tyrolean National Socialists, many of whom later became Nazi functionaries in the Operational Zone. In interaction with German authorities, the guidance of the leading South Tyrolean "optionists" for Germany made possible the immediate seizure of power from the inside and, thus, the immediate introduction of the Nazi regime in the province of Bolzano, South Tyrol. For this successful and smooth usurpation of power, the personnel and the structural and ideological continuities of the South Tyrolean National Socialists were decisive. Local functionaries took the sceptre into their hands immediately after the military occupation of South Tyrol, for the time being as provisionally appointed office-holders. After the appointment of the Austrian *Gauleiter* Franz Hofer as the highest commissioner of the Alpine Zone, all offices and authorities, as well as the functions of mayor, were put into the hands of the "*Deutsche Volksgruppe.*" Against this background of the development of a South Tyrolean mechanism parallel to that of the Nazi party, the historian Michael Wedekind calls the official prohibition of the National Socialist Party (NSDAP) in the Operational Zone a "pure farce." The Tyrolean *Gauleiter* Hofer prevented the readmission of Mussolini's fascist party in South Tyrol by this same farce. This "prohibition of the NSDAP" has led to this day to an often heard position ignoring the existence of a South Tyrolean Nazi group. This transparent argument is simple: since there was no party with the name "NSDAP" in South Tyrol, there were no National Socialists in the South Tyrol. The "Operational Zone Alpine Foreland," however, was subject to the strong influence of Nazi ideology.

The impact of Nazi rule and its heritage still needs to be scrutinized, and this can best be done on a regional basis. What is still missing are more studies on South Tyrol, now underway thanks to the initiative of historians like Wedekind and Lun and research centers like the University of Innsbruck's Institute for Contemporary History, the South Tyrolean State Archive (*Südtiroler Landesarchiv*) and others. Not only did the experience of the "Operational Zone Alpine Forelands" between 1943 and 1945 affect life in the South Tyrol profoundly, but it also gave birth to many powerful mythological topoi in the South Tyrolese collective memory. The most important and long lasting topos seems to be the idea of National Socialism as an imported phenomenon. Studies about the Nazi rule with many different points of view have to be done. In the meantime, Lun's book about "Nazi rule in South Tyrol" serves as a point of departure for anyone interested in this small, but historically rich, region in the heart of Europe.

Notes

1. Hans Heiss, "Fortschritt und Grenzen des Regionalismus. Südtirol nach dem Zweiten Weltkrieg," in *Die Nationalisierung von Grenzen. Zur Konstruktion nationaler Identität in sprachlich gemischten Grenzregionen*, ed. Michael G. Müller and Rolf Petri (Marburg: Verlag Herder, 2002), 229-35.

2. Only recently Rolf Steininger, professor at the University of Innsbruck, published an excellent overview about South Tyrol's History: Rolf Steininger, *South Tyrol: A Minority Conflict of the Twentieth Century* (New Brunswick, NJ: Transaction, 2003).

3. Karl Stuhlpfarrer, *Die Operationszonen "Alpenvorland" und "Adriatisches Küstenland"* 1943-1945 (Vienna: Hollinek, 1969).

4. Michael Wedekind, *Nationalsozialistische Besatzungs- und Annexionspolitik in Norditalien 1943 bis 1945. Die Operationszonen "Alpenvorland" und "Adriatisches Küstenland"* (Militärgeschichtliche Studien 38) (Munich: Oldenbourg, 2003). See also Gerald Steinacher, ed., *Südtirol im Dritten Reich/ L'Alto Adige nel Terzo Reich. NS-Herrschaft im Norden Italiens/L'occupazione nazista nell'Italia settentrionale 1943-1945*

(Veröffentlichungen des Südtiroler Landesarchivs 18) (Innnsbruck: Studienverlag, 2003) and Gerald Steinacher, *Südtirol und die Geheimdienste 1943-1945* (Innsbrucker Forschungen zur Zeitgeschichte 15) (Innsbruck: Studienverlag, 2000).

5.Hans Karl Peterlini, "Chronik einer Zeitlücke," *FF-Südtiroler Illustrierte* 27 May 2004: 50f.

James Jay Carafano, *Waltzing into the Cold War. The Struggle of Occupied Austria* (College Station: Texas A&M University Press, 2002)

Kurt Tweraser

Occupations are attempts to sustain military victory and to manage its wider aspects. They require detailed planning involving multiple agencies, special types of military forces, a multi-year military commitment, and an exit strategy. Given the present American difficulties in transforming military victory into winning the peace, a closer look at one of the supposedly more successful past occupations may give us valuable insights into post-conflict requirements. James Jay Carafano, a military historian, uses the occupation of Austria from 1945 to 1955 as an example of how not to conduct post-conflict operations. He asks how well the American military were prepared for their occupational tasks; he touches on measures taken to master the chaos of the first months; he discusses the relationship between the tactical and military government units. Since the occupation of Austria was quadripartite, he also deals with the manner in which all four powers became enmeshed in the conflict over the future of Austria. He endeavors to determine the degree of deliberate calculation with which the Western powers decided to oppose the Soviet Union in Austria. He asks, further, what the changes were in international relations during the occupation and how these changes affected occupation mission and policies.

Carafano's narrative is based on the major thesis that "security concerns, as interpreted and expressed by professional military officers, played an inordinately significant role in determining the course of affairs. This militarization represented a shift in the role of the occupation force from rehabilitating and reconstructing Austria to enlisting the state as a partner in NATO's defense" (p. 8). There was a "reverse course," a decreased emphasis on certain occupation programs and increased emphasis on others. Methodologically, the author maintains that he adheres neither to an orthodox Cold War narrative, nor to a revisionist interpretation, nor to a post-revisionist critique since he finds these paradigms unsatisfying. Rather, he adheres to an interpretation that stresses the central role of national security as the most effective concept with which to understand the United States' foreign policy during the Cold War.[1]

In his narrative, the author sets the stage by inquiring into what he calls the Army's "rhythm of habits." The most powerful force of habit shaping U.S. occupations was a "tradition of forgetting" (p. 11). Although the American Army had experiences in overseas post-conflict operations, these experiences were not incorporated into Army tradition, organization, and training. For each overseas engagement, the wheel had to be reinvented. Even after the outbreak of World War II, the necessity of special training for occupational tasks was a matter of debate. Not before 1942 was a military government school established, not before 1943 a Civil Affairs Division created and the general staffs expanded to include a civil affairs G-5 section. The low priority of Civil Affairs and Military Government was succinctly summarized by the Assistant Secretary for Civil Affairs, responsible for planning and supervising post-conflict preparations, attempting to straighten out the Department of State: "The Army is not a welfare organization. It is a military machine whose mission it is to defeat the enemy on the field of battle. Its interests and activities in military government and civil affairs administration are incidental to the accomplishment of the military mission" (p. 12). Given this limited perspective indicating the inadequate institutional weight which "winning the peace" had, it is no wonder that the American Army was ill-prepared for post-conflict operations. The personnel and material resources for occupations were much too little to correct the short memory of the Army, the insufficient training in cooperating with other organizations, and the superficial training of military government officers.

Still inadequate, but somewhat more promising, were the planning endeavors of the Supreme Headquarters Allied Expeditionary Forces in London (SHAEF) and Allied Forces Headquarters of Supreme Command Mediterranean Theater (AFHQM), although the small planning group for Austria faced a bureaucratic obstacle course and, above all, the clear priority of planning for Germany. Several changes of the planning forum, caused by the shifting fortunes of war, intensified the confusion. The only clearly identifiable mission for the planners was the destruction of Germany and its war-making capacity. Occupational tasks were conceived as an ancillary part of the combat mission, not a mission *sui generis*. The handbooks, late in coming, that were to guide the occupation were, likewise, infused with the idea that the destruction of the enemy had to override all other considerations. One of the root causes hampering military planning was the lack of timely top political decision-making for Austria, which considerably delayed the establishment of a properly designed military government and invited numerous jurisdictional squabbles and policy errors. Given the tradition of forgetting, lack of experience, inadequate skills in interagency operations, unimaginative doctrine, poor training, and shallow professional education, it seems almost a miracle that the occupation of Austria was not a disaster.

In imposing order on the chaotic conditions in their occupation zone, the military government detachments were guided by common sense and the ability to improvise rather than by the not very helpful instructions in the handbook, the standard operating procedures, and the checklists. In establishing civil government, demobilizing enemy soldiers, cleansing the civil service, and taking care of Displaced Persons, the occupation performed relatively well, primarily because the occupiers encountered a pliable population. What Carafano does not sufficiently stress is the fact that, in performing the admittedly difficult tasks of establishing order, the inherently pragmatic military government officers failed to consider the political ambitions of the pre-National Socialism elites and relied instead on the traditionally conservative and obedient bureaucratic apparatus, for military government had to be "unpolitical." The best way to keep the military government out of party disputes was to outlaw all political activity and to rely on bureaucrats. But by doing thusly, the military government made a political choice, since the administrators almost always represented social and economic conservative interests. The American authorities were *nolens volens* involved in indigenous politics. The creation of a situation free of politics was an American illusion which had to be dispelled. In the fall of 1945, the top American authorities in Vienna began to realize that the concept of an "unpolitical" military government based on "military necessity" was inadequate to bring about a functioning political system. By the end of the year, writes Carafano, the Army had convinced itself that the occupation was a success. They had succeeded in implementing the disease and unrest formula before the first postwar winter set in. "Helped in large part by the docile nature of the Austrian people and the passivity of the defeated forces, the army quickly and effectively performed what it believed to be its only appropriate post-conflict tasks: demobilizing the enemy and eliminating the physical remnants of Nazi influence" (p. 76).

According to Carafano, this optimism was, however, shortlived, and the concerns over disease and unrest would be overtaken by the dark fears of communist aggression. In six meaty chapters, he discusses the measures taken by the Americans to counter the perceived threat. Throughout these chapters, Carafano provides the reader with succinct biographical portraits of the military leaders who had put their stamp on the occupation policy. Extremely valuable also are his descriptions of the bureaucratic politics involving the various departments in Washington, the Allies, and the Austrian government in Vienna. He deals first with the intelligence establishment, the "largest single industry" of the occupation. It was in large part the influence of military intelligence which prompted the occupation force to undergo a gradual transition from liberators and occupiers to cold warriors. "An endless stream of classified reports reshaped perceptions, providing evidence to compel jettisoning constabulary duties in favor of more traditional warrior tasks" (p. 80). Now the purpose of the United States Forces in Austria (USFA) could be re-thought and the unloved occupation duties transformed into a real military mission. The real mission turned out to be the rearmament of Austria.

In the next chapter, Carafano raises the "on-the-job" training of the American military leaders. His special focus is General Geoffrey Keyes, successor to General Mark Clark as high commissioner and commanding general of USFA. While the first generation of leaders, personified by Mark Clark, had been chosen for the prestige they brought to the task, Keyes belonged to a second generation of occupation leaders who had neither the prestige nor the training in political-military affairs to master an assignment that turned out to be unexpectedly difficult. Keyes was an excellent warrior who had distinguished himself in the Mediterranean theater and had gained the complete trust of his superiors, Generals George C. Marshall, George Patton, Omar Bradley, Dwight D. Eisenhower, and Clark. Keyes held the central belief that Austria was a key piece in an emerging geostrategic confrontation between East and West. Austria would be the linchpin for holding back communism. Even before the communist coup in Prague in February 1948, Keyes had bombarded Washington with dire assessments of the conditions in Austria that required a determined response to the Soviet threat. Austria's occupation had to be continued "not only as an extension of the defense of Germany, but also for its own positional advantages" (p. 103). The Joint Chiefs of Staff approved of Keyes' position. Since Keyes's views ran counter to the State Department's endeavors to bring about a state treaty for Austria, clashes between Keyes and the representatives of State proved unavoidable. Carafano is highly critical of Keyes' single-minded pursuit of a confrontational policy. He believes that it was the policy vacuum of the early Cold War years, when national security policy was in transition, which allowed a determined field commander to push successfully for radical changes in Austrian policy, "Keyes's conviction that the occupation merited commitments and strategies on a par with . . . those applied to the German question was an example of how a field commander's perspective could yield a skewed and totally unrealistic assessment of national priorities" (pp. 116-17).

In the next two chapters, the author analyzes the transformation of occupiers back into warriors and the incorporation of the Austrian territory into various Western European defense plans. Although Keyes had been sent home in October 1950 and replaced by a civilian high commissioner, the confrontational policy was set, and successive military commanders built upon the foundation laid by Keyes. An amazing number of military schemes to protect "the southern flank" of the North Atlantic Treaty Organization were developed by the military planning staffs: Pincher, Totality, Broiler, Crankshaft, Halfmoon, Offtackle, Dropshot, Flatiron, Ironback, and Pilgrim Dog. The various plans ranged from outright retreat from Austria in case of a Soviet attack to a forward defense of Austria. Even though there was no credible evidence that during the occupation period the Soviet Union intended an assault on Austria, "the dynamics of Cold War national security concerns," says the author, not without a sense of irony, "convinced Washington to take a stake in defending a country that could add little real security to the West's defenses" (p. 153).

The final substantive chapters deal with the politics of secretly arming Austria. Plans for making use of Austria's defensive potential in time of war had already begun in 1947, helped along by both Americans and Austrians. After 1948, "alarm formations" were established as part of the Gendarmerie in the Western occupation zones. These were reformed in 1951-1952 with the designation "B-Gendarmerie." The CIA had already stocked a number of arms caches, intended for use by the Austrians in conducting guerilla warfare. The problem that USFA faced in the militarization of Austria was twofold. One was the lack of American manpower. The solution was to recruit Austrian manpower. In February 1952, a willing Austrian government agreed to begin the secret registration of qualified personnel. The B-Gendarmerie was designed to be the core of the future Austrian Armed Forces that were to be set up after the conclusion of a state treaty. The other problem to be resolved was to provide the necessary material assistance not only for the B-Gendarmerie, but also for the entire future Austrian army. It took frequent and aggressive lobbying of USFA in Washington since Austria was not on the Pentagon's priority list for military assistance. Furthermore, Congress did not give the Executive branch a blank check in dispensing military aid freely, and it took some convincing by the administration before Congress would adopt language which would allow the furnishing of military assistance to Austria. In the end, in a twist of supreme irony, it was the buildup of the B-Gendarmerie and the stockpiling of military supplies for Austria's self-defense force, pushed by a military establishment hostile to an Austrian state treaty, which gave the president and state the necessary security argument to sign the state treaty and conclude the occupation.

What puzzles this reviewer about the well-written and well-researched book are the author's expressions of doubt about the usefulness of the "revisionist" paradigm. A comparison of his work with the best revisionist treatment of the same topic reveals, however, essential agreement in the details of the story, so much so that Carafano's work confirms rather than challenges the revisionist author who did not have access to primary sources in the American military archives.[2] This reviewer shares Carafano's doubts. He would have found it useful, though, if the author had enlarged his meager methodological discussion with an explanation of why and in what ways he differs from revisionist and post-revisionist treatments of the topic.

What can we learn from the occupation of Austria? In a skeptical epilogue, which he appropriately titles "Flawed Triumph," Carafano points out that military forces designed for war are necessary, but are inadequate and insufficient tools for winning the peace. The military is an improper instrument of a postwar foreign policy since its habits, practices, and traditions are adequate only for fighting battles. He is especially critical of the military attempts to save Austria from Soviet aggression without having any firm evidence. He also sees the Austrians as perfectly capable to cope with communist-inspired unrest short of a Soviet invasion, which the Allies could not have prevented anyway. His final thought is appropriate for today, too: "Peace and stability operations cannot be conducted like military maneuvers, they must assume a character appropriate to the task at hand. Leaders who are serious about ending conflicts on the most advantageous terms possible must be willing to invest the commensurate intellectual and material resources in their armed forces so that they are ready when called" (p. 198).

Notes

1. Melvyn P. Leffler, *A Preponderance of Power: National Security, the Truman Administration, and the Cold War* (Stanford: Stanford Univ. Press, 1992).

2. Christian Stifter, *Die Wiederaufrüstung Österreichs. Die geheime Remilitarisierung der westlichen Besatzungszonen 1945-1955* (Innsbruck: Studien Verlag, 1997).

Heinz P. Wassermann, *Verfälschte Geschichte im Unterricht. Nationalsozialismus und Österreich nach 1945* (Vienna: StudienVerlag, 2004)

Peter Utgaard

It is difficult to live up to a bold title, but authors can be forgiven for attracting attention to their years of hard work. Employing quantitative and qualitative analysis, Heinz P. Wassermann examines official lesson plans *(Lehrpläne)* and textbooks from the 1950s through the late 1990s with an emphasis on their treatment of the Second World War, fascism, and the Holocaust. Does he demonstrate that Austrian textbook authors and the education ministry falsified history? Not really.

Verfälschte Geschichte im Unterricht runs into problems near the beginning. When discussing the state of research on textbook studies, Wassermann states that there are few textbook studies beyond article length, but my own *Remembering and Forgetting Nazism* (Berghahn, 2003), which Wassermann does not cite, is a study that incorporates nearly every relevant history textbook (as well as reading books) from the late 1940s through the mid-1990s. While this work may not have been available to the author as publication approached, it points to the larger problem of Wassermann's weak bibliography. Indeed, the bibliography does not include any of the English language works on postwar Austria relevant to his study, yet Robert Knight is briefly quoted in English (p. 15). Even Evan Bukey's *Hitler's Austria*, which has been translated into German, is absent from the bibliography. In the end, Wassermann's textbook analysis exists largely outside the larger context of postwar Austrian historiography

The heart of the book is a qualitative and quantitative analysis of Austrian textbooks. Wassermann counts the pages of the books that are devoted to fascism and National Socialism and measures the total of these pages as a percentage of the book. For example, Franz Heilsberg and Friedrich Korger's 1953 *Allgemeine Geschichte der Neuzeit von der Mitte des 19. Jahrhunderts bis zur Gegenwart* includes 163 pages of which seventeen are devoted to fascism and National Socialism. One page is dedicated to Austro-fascism (pp. 76-77). He is then able to trace the space dedicated to key content in the textbooks and make comparisons between books published over the years in absolute and relative terms. Wassermann's qualitative analysis focuses upon key categories that are subdivided. For example, there are three categories of fascism: Austro-fascism, National Socialism, and "other" fascisms. National Socialism is then subdivided by time: the period up to 1933, 1933-1939, and 1939-1945. Finally, there is a sub-group analysis of Austria in the Third Reich (not including the Anschluß, but including resistance and victims of the war), the Holocaust (including Austrian Jews), and "other" victims (resistance and other persecution and annihilation) (pp. 74-75). The result of this methodology is a thorough book-by-book analysis of the themes of Nazism, the war, the Holocaust, and the role of Austrians in them as portrayed in the textbooks. These analyses could very useful to anyone wanting a summary of particular postwar Austrian textbooks, especially Austrian high school teachers who want an overview of postwar textbooks and how they have changed from the 1950s to the 1990s.

However, Wassermann's methodology yields too little fruit for the amount of research he completed. The summaries can make for tedious reading, and Wassermann has a tendency to overuse exclamation points, apparently to demonstrate dismay at what he has read. The quantitative/qualitative approach ultimately falters because too much context is missing. This stems, in part, from the weak bibliography (as mentioned above), but is also due to the incomplete analysis of key questions. For example, how, when, and why did Austrian textbooks change? Another key question is how do the textbooks compare to the historiography of the time? Wassermann ultimately sees a great continuity in the postwar books, arguing that "through decades the textbooks embraced the totalitarian theory along with the intentionalist theory of fascism," whereby the ideologies of fascism and National Socialism were identified mainly with the figures of Benito Mussolini and Adolph Hitler (p. 203). There is much to the continuity argument, but Wassermann gives short shrift to real and meaningful changes that came about in Austrian textbooks beginning in the mid 1980s—not coincidentally at the same time as the Kurt Waldheim scandal and affair. Wassermann also accurately points to the textbooks' tendency to embrace collective victimization, which takes the voluntary support for Nazism and "sweeps it completely under the rug" (p. 205). Again, this is an accurate observation, but why was collective victimization so important? Finally, who is responsible for all of this falsified and adulterated history? Throughout the book, Wassermann points to the Ministry of Education as the responsible party. Of course, there is a textbook commission which approves textbooks, so the Education Ministry *is* responsible, but one sometimes has the feeling that "the ministry" is hiding the truth in a vault somewhere on Minoritenplatz, all the while doling out lies to Austrian youth. What is missing from the analysis is a discussion of the Education Ministry as a product of the Austrian political system, especially *Proporz*. The threads of continuity that Wassermann demonstrates are examples of what has been called "coalition history," which was a kind of intellectual *Proporz*. While Wassermann mentions this briefly (p. 73), his study would have benefited from more contextual analysis throughout.

ANNUAL REVIEW

Austria 2004

Reinhold Gärtner

Presidential Elections (2004)
EU Parliamentary Elections (2004)
Elections in Vorarlberg
New Faces in the Government
FPÖ: Business Unusual
Economic Data

Presidential Elections

On 25 April, the new president was elected. President Thomas Klestil had served for two terms (1992-2004), for the Austrian president is elected for a six year term and can run for a second one, as well. Thus Foreign Minister Benita Ferrero-Waldner and longtime President of the State Diet Heinz Fischer competed to become Klestil's successor. Because there were no other viable candidates, it was clear that one of them would win in the first round. Ultimately, it was Heinz Fischer who prevailed with 52.4 percent of the votes cast.

Fischer, born in 1938, had been first president of the State Diet from 1990-2002. He was the first SPÖ candidate since 1980 who could win this election. The voter turnout was relatively low (70 percent).

Sadly, former President Thomas Klestil died on 6 July—just two days before Heinz Fischer was installed as president.

Figure 1:
Austrian Presidents of the Second Republic, 1945-2004

Candidate	Party	Years in Office
Karl Renner	SPÖ	1945-1950
Theodor Körner	SPÖ	1951-1957
Adolf Schärf	SPÖ	1957-1965
Franz Jonas	SPÖ	1965-1974
Rudolf Kirchschläger	SPÖ	1974-1986
Kurt Waldheim	ÖVP	1986-1992
Thomas Klestil	ÖVP	1992-2004
Heinz Fischer	SPÖ	since 2004

EU Parliamentary Elections

The elections for the European Parliament were held on 13 June 2004, and there were a few astonishing results. First, Hans Peter Martin, former SPÖ Member of Parliament (MP) in the European Parliament, ran with the "Liste Hans Peter Martin" and gained 14 percent of the vote. This was surprising, for Hans Peter Martin had only one issue: the alleged privileges of EU MPs. Second, Martin's success was partly possible because of the dramatic losses of the FPÖ. In 1999, the FPÖ had received more than 23 percent of the vote; now they fell back to 6.3 percent. In addition, right-winger Andreas Mölzer could win the seat because of votes of preference from the moderate Hans Kronberger.

Overall, the SPÖ finished first with 33.3 percent of votes cast, the ÖVP second with 32.7 percent, and the Greens got 12.9 percent. The voter turnout was remarkably low at only 42.4 percent.

Elections in Vorarlberg

The elections in Vorarlberg were held on 9 September 2004. Again, the FPÖ was the loser of this election. The FPÖ lost as much as 14.5 percent, thus more than half of the 27.5 percent they had in 1999. The ÖVP again relied on its traditional stronghold of Vorarlberg (54.9 percent), and both the SPÖ and the Greens would win as well. For a long time, the SPÖ had been third in Vorarlberg, but they managed again to finish second. The Greens were as strong as in the early years in Vorarlberg, winning four seats as in 1984. But the voter turnout in Vorarlberg (for the first time without electoral duty) was only 60 percent.

Figure 2:
Election Results, Vorarlberg 2004

Party	Change in Percentage of Votes (+/-)	Change of Number of Seats (+/-)
ÖVP	54.9 (+9.2)	21 (+3)
SPÖ	16.9 (+3.9)	6 (+1)
FPÖ	13.0 (-14.5)	5 (-6)
Grüne	10.1 (+4.1)	4 (+2)

Source: Interior Ministry, Official Election Results.

New Faces in the Government

In 2004, some members of the government were replaced. First, Minister of Justice Dieter Böhmdorfer resigned and was follow by Karin Miklautsch in June 2004. From 1991 until 2004, Miklautsch had been in the office of the Carinthian government. In October, Ursula Plassnik followed Betina Ferrero Waldner as Minister of Foreign Affairs. This change had become necessary when Ferrero-Waldner became the Austrian member of the EU Commission of Barroso. Finally, in December, Liese Prokop succeeded Ernst Strasser as Minister of the Interior. Strasser had resigned for personal reasons.

New state secretaries included Eduard Mainoni (FPÖ), who in June headed the Federal Ministry for Transport, Innovation, and Technology, and Sigisbert Dolinschek (FPÖ), who in January 2005 took over the reins at the Federal Ministry for Social Security, Generations, and Consumer Protection).

FPÖ: Business Unusual

The decline of the FPÖ continued beyond the EU Parliamentary elections and the elections in Vorarlberg. Early in 2005, community elections were held in Lower Austria and Styria; in both cases, the result for the FPÖ was dramatic. In many communities, the FPÖ found it impossible to compete for votes because no party candidates ran for election.

Figure 3:
Results of Community Elections in Lower Austria and Styria, 2003-2004

	Lower Austria 6 March 2004	**Styria 13 March 2003**
Party	**Change in Percentage of Votes (+/-)**	**Change in Percentage of Votes (+/-)**
ÖVP	48.9 (+0.5)	43.4 (+0.3)
SPÖ	38.9 (+3.6)	43.3 (+4.5)
FPÖ	3.3 (-4.6)	6.1 (-5.3)
Grüne	3.8 (+1.3)	2.3 (+0.2)

Source: Interior Ministry, Official Election Results.

But the situation became even worse. The gap between Jörg Haider, his sister Ursula Haubner (Minister of Social Security, Generations, and Consumer Protection), the other FPÖ members of government, and many of the FPÖ MPs on the one hand and the right-wingers Andreas Mölzer (European Parliament), Ewald Stadler (Lower Austria), and Heinz Christian Strache (Vienna) on the other serve became more and more. On 4 April, Haider and his supporters declared both their withdrawal from the (old) FPÖ and their founding of a new party: the *Bündnis Zukunft Österreich* (BZÖ). At the moment, it is not clear if both the FPÖ and the BZÖ will survive politically and if other FPÖ members and politicians will or will not leave their party to join the BZÖ. In the FPÖ's party convention on 23 April Heinz Christian Strache (Vienna) was elected new chairman of FPÖ.

Economic Data

In 2004, on average 3,199,000 people were employed, and 244,000 were unemployed (compared to 240,000 in 2003). The rate of unemployment was 4.5 percent (International Labor Organization criteria + 0.2 percent and 7.1 percent respectively, + 0.1 percent).

The GDP was at € 235 billion; inflation was at 2.1 percent (1.3 percent in 2003). According to Maastricht criteria, the public deficit was 1.3 percent of GDP (remaining steady with 1.3 percent in 2003) and the public debt was lower at 64.7 percent of GDP, or € 150.9 billion (compared to 65.8 percent in 2003).

List of Authors

Rudolf Agstner, minister plenipotentiary, Head, Bonn office, Austrian embassy Berlin

Günter Bischof, professor of history and director, Center for Austrian Culture and Commerce and interim director of the Eisenhower Center for American Studies, University of New Orleans

Reinhold Gärtner, associate professor of political science, University of Innsbruck

Holly Case, assistant professor of history, Cornell University, Ithaca, NY

Michael Gehler, professor of contemporary history, University of Innsbruck

Johanna Granville, Fulbright scholar at the University of Yekaterinburg

Gunther Hauser, Institute for Strategy and Security Policy at the National Defense Academy, Vienna

Dagmar Herzog, professor of history at the Graduate Center, City University of New York

Romain Kirt, political scientist and policy advisor for the government of Luxembourg

Josef Köstlbauer, 2004/5 Ministry of Science Fellow at Center Austria, University of New Orleans, and doctoral candidate at the department of history, University of Vienna

Martin Kofler, historian and deputy director Studienverlag, Innsbruck

Günther Kronenbitter, *Privatdozent*, modern and contemporary history, University of Augsburg, guest professor, University of Bern, Switzerland

Alexander Lassner, assistant professor of history, U.S. Air Force Air Command and Staff College, Montgomery, AL

Franz Mathis, professor of history and chair of the department of economic and social history, University of Innsbruck

Stefan Mayer, press officer, Land Salzburg government, and lecturer for the Austrian political system, Salzburg College

Susanne Mettauer, 2004/5 Nick Mueller Fellow at the University of New Orleans and lecturer in American Studies, University of Innsbruck

Wolfgang Mueller, historian and researcher in the Austrian Academy of Sciences, Vienna

Norman Naimark, Robert and Florence McDonnel Professor of Eastern European Studies, Stanford Institute for International Studies, Stanford University, Palo Alto, CA

Eva Nowotny, Austrian Ambassador to the United States of America

Anton Pelinka, professor of political science and dean of the school of political science and sociology, University of Innsbruck, and director of the Institute of Conflict Research, Vienna

Wolfgang Petritsch, Austrian Permanent Representative to the UN, WTO and the Conference on Disarmament in Geneva, Switzerland

Jonathan Petropoulos, John V. Croul Professor of European History, Claremont McKenna College, and visiting fellow at Cambridge University, England

Oliver Rathkolb, professor of contemporary history, University of Vienna, and director Ludwig Boltzmann Institute for European History and Public Sphere

Gerald Steinacher, historian and archivist for modern history at the South Tyrolean State Archive in Bozen/Bolzano, 2005/6 research fellow at the Holocaust Museum, Washington D.C.

Kurt Tweraser, professor emeritus of political science, University of Arkansas, Fayetteville

Peter Utgaard, chair of history and social sciences, Cuyamaca College, El Cajon, CA

Contemporary Austrian Studies

Günter Bischof and Anton Pelinka, Editors

Transaction Publishers, New Brunswick (N.J.) and London (U.K)

Volume 1 (1993)
Austria in the New Europe

Volume 2 (1994)
The Kreisky Era in Austria
Oliver Rathkolb, Guest Editor

Volume 3 (1995)
Austria in the Nineteen Fifties
Rolf Steininger, Guest Editor

Volume 4 (1996)
Austro-Corporatism: Past – Present – Future

Volume 5 (1997)
Austrian Historical Memory & National Identity

Volume 6 (1998)
Women in Austria
Erika Thurner, Guest Editor

Volume 7 (1999)
The Vranitzky Era in Austria
Ferdinand Karlhofer, Guest Editor

Volume 8 (2000)
The Marshal Plan in Austria
Dieter Stiefel, Guest Editor

Volume 9 (2001)
Neutrality in Austria
Ruth Wodak, Guest Editor

Volume 10 (2002)
Austria and the EU
Michael Gehler, Guest Editor

Volume 11 (2003)
The Dollfuss/Schuschnigg Era in Austria. A Reassessment
Alexander Lassner, Guest Editor

Volume 12 (2004)
The Americanization/ Westernization of Austria

Volume 13 (2005)
Religion in Austria
Hermann Denz, Guest Editor

For Product Safety Concerns and Information please contact our EU representative GPSR@taylorandfrancis.com
Taylor & Francis Verlag GmbH, Kaufingerstraße 24, 80331 München, Germany

www.ingramcontent.com/pod-product-compliance
Lightning Source LLC
Chambersburg PA
CBHW050558270326
41926CB00012B/2100

* 9 7 8 1 4 1 2 8 0 5 2 1 6 *